Praise for
The Savage Wars of Peace

"A great story and a compelling read. Boot combines wide-angle perspective with an eye for detail. . . . **[An] important and timely contribution**. . . . By reviewing the nation's past, he shows its future."

　　—*Foreign Affairs*

"[A] nuanced and lively contribution. . . [A] fascinating history. . . Admirably evenhanded."

　　—*Christian Science Monitor*

"An analytical treatment of low-intensity conflict [and] **a fascinating set of case studies worth reading for the stories alone**. . . . Americans like to think of war as an anomaly, at least in their own history. . . . Boot explodes the myth and shows it to be as pernicious as it is wrong."

　　—*Washington Post Book World*

"**Rollicking**. . . . At heart, Boot is that rare creature: a do–gooding conservative. Throwing down the gauntlet to isolationists, Boot provocatively says we must carry out the vital work of 'state building' in countries that, ravaged by disorder, are unable to govern themselves. . . . **Boot's narrative bustles with engaging personalities and forgotten heroes**."

　　—*Chicago Tribune*

"Anyone who wants to understand why America has permanently entered a new era in international relations must read [this book]. . . . Vividly written and thoroughly researched. . . [Boot] **explodes a number of myths about the military.**"

   —*Los Angeles Times*

"[An] **excellent yet concise history**. . . Boot combines meticulous scholarship with great storytelling and provocative opinions. He draws from his research direct lessons for a nation confronting the threat of global terrorism."

   — *Philadelphia Inquirer*

"**Excellent**. . . There are some cracking good stories here—the exploits of Marine Corps legend Smedley Butler in China, the Phillipines, Nicaragua, and Haiti—but also some important lessons."

   —*U.S. News & World Report*

"In his high-spirited early chapters, Max Boot's *The Savage Wars of Peace* recalls Patrick O'Brian's Aubrey and Maturin saga. . . . In his concluding comments, Boot sets out a thoughtful list of lessons that should have been learned."

   —*New York Review of Books*

"Boot's well–written narrative is not only fascinating reading, but didactic as well, as we learn that **most of our current orthodoxy is neither historically nor logically sound**. . . . The events after September 11 give *The Savage Wars of Peace* an uncanny timeliness and sadly confirm all of Boot's dispassionate warnings. . . . [Boot's] message is. . . a moral one—and never more timely than now."

   —*The Weekly Standard*

"**Excellent**."

   —*The Washington Monthly*

"He tells the story with clarity and verve, rediscovering on the way some lesser-known American heroes. . . Enjoyable. . . Informative."

   —*The Economist*

"Entertaining, provocative, and often insightful history. . . **Boot elucidates very nicely the devil our country knows best** and helps to establish what should have been obvious to students of our nation's history: Small wars are not going away."

—*Policy Review*

"Mr. Boot's analysis is very **compelling and sensible. . . . An important book**, which teaches a real and essential lesson about American foreign policy makers and army generals. May we heed its lessons in the years to come."

—*The New Criterion*

"This book is not only an **eminently readable and entertaining** narrative history of America's small wars, but also a **serious analysis of current strategic challenges**. . . . Boot is an exceptional writer and his engaging style is tailor-made for this type of narrative."

—*National Review*

"Max Boot's book on America's small wars comes at a particularly good time. . . . [Boot's] narrative is crisp and exciting. . . . It is **a great read with some very solid conclusions**. . . an outstanding addition to this body of literature."

—*Washington Times*

"What a pleasure to read a crisp preface that promises a fun read, and to have the rest of the book deliver. *The Savage Wars of Peace* is an entertaining jaunt through many of the expeditions, counterinsurgencies and (insert your preferred term of art here) that the United States armed forces have undertaken since the beginning of the Republic. Along the way the author offers political analysis that hits its mark time and again."

—*Journal of Military History*

"Boot has written a readable and thought-provoking book—one that might well influence the behind-the-scenes debates over the future of military policy."

—*Library Journal*

"A book that is as readable as it is timely."

—*First Things*

"Few books published this decade will be timelier than Max Boot's *The Savage Wars of Peace*. . . [A] fine book."

—*Commentary*

"A timely manual on the post-Cold War challenges. . . Max Boot understands. Read this book; you will too."

—*New York Post*

"The book of the season. . . 9/11 and its aftermath brought Boot's message—from which the adjective 'timely' might have been invented—into eye-opening focus."

—*National Journal*

"By collecting the best exploits from some of the most significant small wars between two covers, [Boot has] done **a real public and strategic service.**"

—*Slate*

"A book that has become—very much like [Paul] Kennedy's, [Francis] Fukuyama's and [Samuel] Huntington's—**'must' reading in Congress,** the Pentagon and among Washington's columnists and think-tankers."

—*Business Times*

"Boot gets the central issue right. Americans like to think of war as an anomaly, at least in their own history. Boot explodes the myth and shows it to be as pernicious as it is wrong."

—*Chicago Sun-Times*

MAX BOOT

THE
SAVAGE WARS
OF PEACE

*Small Wars and the
Rise of American Power*

BASIC
BOOKS
A Member of the
Perseus Books Group

To my in-laws,

THE BAILEYS AND McCARTYS,

who have fought our nation's wars, big and small

Copyright © 2002 by Max Boot

First Published by Basic Books, A Member of the Perseus Books Group, in 2002.
First paperback edition published by Basic Books in 2003.

Text design by Jeff Williams
Set in 10.5-point Adobe Caslon by the Perseus Books Group

A CIP catalog record for this book is available from the Library of Congress.
ISBN 0-465-00720-1 (hc); ISBN 0-465-00721-X (pbk.)

03 04 05 / 10 9 8 7 6 5 4 3

OTHER BOOKS BY MAX BOOT

*Out of Order: Arrogance, Corruption and
Incompetence on the Bench*

CONTENTS

PART THREE: SUPERPOWER

LIST OF MAPS

The history of the United States shows that in spite of the varying trend of the foreign policy of succeeding administrations, this Government has interposed or intervened in the affairs of other states with remarkable regularity, and it may be anticipated that the same general procedure will be followed in the future. It is well that the United States may be prepared for any emergency which may occur. . . .

—U.S. MARINE CORPS,
Small Wars Manual (1940)

The conduct of small wars is in fact in certain respects an art by itself, diverging widely from what is adapted to the conditions of regular warfare, but not so widely that there are not in all its branches points which permit comparisons to be established.

—C. E. CALWELL,
Small Wars: Their Principles and Practice (1906)

Reservists and citizen-soldiers stand ready, in every free nation, to stand to the colors and die in holocaust, the big war. Reservists and citizen-soldiers remain utterly reluctant to stand and die in anything less. . . . The man who will go where his colors go, without asking, who will fight a phantom foe in jungle and mountain range, without counting, and who will suffer and die in the midst of incredible hardship, without complaint, is still what he has always been, from Imperial Rome to sceptered Britain to democratic America. He is the stuff of which legions are made.

—T. R. FEHRENBACH,
This Kind of War (1963)

PREFACE

Another American Way of War

The first airliner slammed into the World Trade Center at precisely 8:46 A.M., the second 15 minutes later. I was on my way to work, to an office opposite the Twin Towers, when it happened. I emerged from the bowels of the subway tunnel a few blocks from ground zero and was confronted by a scene of devastation that could have come straight from the London Blitz six decades before: refugees streaming away from the disaster, sirens blaring, police and emergency workers rushing around, and, enveloping all in a dark haze, clouds of ash and soot and smoke. The first of the World Trade Center towers had already collapsed. Before long I would watch the second one falling as easily as a Lego toy under a child's fist. The bile rising in my throat, saddened, disgusted, dazed, I walked away from this scene of horror, looking back only occasionally, in wonderment, at a Manhattan skyline that in one terrifying moment had been transformed forever.

In the hours and days that followed many compared the events of September 11, 2001, to those of December 7, 1941—another day of infamy. Just as Franklin D. Roosevelt declared war following the attack on Pearl Harbor, so George W. Bush declared war following the attack on the World Trade Center and the Pentagon. But what kind of war would it be? It soon became clear that the "war on terrorism" would bear little resemblance to World War II. After December 7, 1941, America mobilized as never before. Millions of men traded civilian clothes for military uniforms, millions of women left home to take jobs left vacant, whole factories were retooled from making cars and tractors to manufacturing tanks and artillery shells. After four years of supreme exertion, America's sacrifices were rewarded with the unconditional surrender of its foes—Imperial Japan, Nazi Germany, Fascist Italy.

No such triumph would be likely over the forces of terrorism—any more than total victory could be declared in the war on crime, or the war on drugs, or the war on poverty. Just as this was not a conflict that would result in total victory, so it would not call for the total mobilization of the home front. No draft was instituted after the attack, nor was industry put on alert. This war would be fought by a relatively small number of professional soldiers, sailors, airmen, marines. They would be pitted against the men of the shadows, holy warriors who wore no uniform, who shirked open battle, who took refuge among civilians and emerged to strike when least expected at the infidel's most vulnerable outposts. Traditional weapons systems, designed to pulverize enemy armies, would have a role to play in this conflict, but often only a marginal one. The greatest challenge in fighting terrorism was not to kill the enemy; it was to identify the enemy. Spies, police officers, covert operators, even diplomats would be on the front lines; and civilians would suffer more heavily than the uniformed military.

This "long twilight struggle," to borrow John F. Kennedy's phrase, must seem utterly alien to those schooled in the history of America's big wars—which is to say virtually anyone interested in American military history. The big wars, especially the Civil War and World War II, are celebrated in countless books, movies, and documentaries. As it happens, these were America's only experiences with total war in which the nation staked all of its blood and treasure to achieve the relatively quick and unconditional surrender of the enemy. Yet somehow many of us have come to think of Gettysburg and D-Day—conventional, set-piece engagements—as the norm, not the aberration. Some historians even speak of an "American way of war": war that annihilates the enemy; war that relies on advanced technology and massive firepower to minimize casualties among U.S. forces; war that calls on legions of citizen soldiers; war that results in total victory.

But this is only one way of American war. There is another, less celebrated tradition in U.S. military history—a tradition of fighting small wars. Between 1800 and 1934, U.S. Marines staged 180 landings abroad. The army and navy added a few small-scale engagements of their own. Some of these excursions resulted in heavy casualties; others involved almost no fighting. Some were concluded in a day or two; others dragged on for decades. Some were successful, others not. But most of these campaigns were fought by a relatively small number of professional soldiers pursuing limited objectives with limited means. These are the nonwars that Kipling called "the savage wars of peace" and that a modern author, Bob Shacochis, has evocatively described as "a foggy, swamp-bottomed no-man's land . . . an empty space in an army's traditional reality, where there are no friends and no enemies, no front or rear, no victories and, likewise, no defeat, and no true endings."

When I started researching this book, most of these actions were terra incognita to me. And yet there was something strangely familiar about these long-ago events. American troops hunting a warlord? Could be the pursuit of Pancho Villa in 1916—or Muhammed Farah Aidid in 1993 or Osama bin Laden in 2001. The U.S. Navy protecting merchant shipping in the Middle East? Could be the war against the Barbary pirates in 1801–1805—or the "tanker war" against Iran in the Persian Gulf in 1987–1988. U.S. Marines invading a Caribbean island? Could be Haiti in 1915—or 1994; the Dominican Republic in 1916—or 1965; or perhaps Grenada in 1983.

Intrigued by these parallels, I was drawn deeper into this subject when I stumbled across fascinating stories—tales of blunders and bravery, low cunning and high strategy, nobility and savagery—involving forgotten heroes of American history. Men such as David Porter, a leading captain of the early navy who tried to adopt into the "great American family" a cannibal kingdom in the South Pacific and was later court-martialed for infringing Spanish sovereignty while pursuing pirates. "Fighting Fred" Funston, an army officer who helped end the Philippine War by leading a daring commando raid to capture the leader of the *insurrectos*. And Smedley Butler, American's foremost colonial soldier in the early years of the twentieth century, who, on retiring from the Marine Corps, turned into a leading anti-imperialist and pacifist.

What lessons might these small wars of the past teach us about small wars in the future? In the late 1990s—the decade of Somalia, Haiti, Bosnia, and Kosovo—I was intrigued by these recurring conflicts and hoped to read a book to answer that question. Not finding one, I decided to write it myself. So here it is: a concise history of America's small wars abroad that tries to relate the past to the problems confronting the United States today.

This book focuses on what was known around the turn of the twentieth century as "small wars." These days social scientists and soldiers usually call them either "low intensity conflicts" or—a related category—"military operations other than war." Whatever you call them, most still fit the classic definition offered by a British officer at the end of the nineteenth century: "campaigns undertaken to suppress rebellions and guerrilla warfare in all parts of the world where organized armies are struggling against opponents who will not meet them in the open field." There are at least four distinct types of small wars that will be covered here: punitive (to punish attacks on American citizens or property), protective (to safeguard American citizens or property), pacification (to occupy foreign territory), and profiteering (to grab trade or territorial concessions). Some operations serve more than one purpose. The term "small war"—a literal translation of the Spanish word *guerrilla*—refers to the tactics employed, not the scale of combat. Even Vietnam was in many respects a small war, which explains why it is treated at length in this book.

These conflicts might as well be called "imperial wars"—a term that, American sensitivities notwithstanding, seems apt to describe many U.S. adventures abroad. Indeed, having set out to write a purely military history, I found myself of necessity also chronicling the political course of American empire. Along the way, I offer a number of interpretations that diverge from the conventional wisdom, especially about the "Banana Wars" in Central America and the Caribbean, which too often have been caricatured as interventions undertaken to install dictators friendly to the interests of big business.

Small war is necessarily an elastic, inexact term. Perhaps the best way to define these conflicts is to say what they are not: They are not America's major conventional conflicts, the War of Independence, War of 1812, Mexican War, Civil War, Spanish-American War, World War I, World War II, the Korean War, or the Gulf War. Nor, at the other end of the spectrum, is this book concerned with pure shows of force, such as Theodore Roosevelt's dispatch of the fleet to Morocco in 1904 after a wealthy American expatriate was kidnapped by a bandit chief called Raisuli. ("This government wants either Perdicaris alive, or Raisuli dead!") Generally, for an action to qualify as a small war, some shooting is required.

For purposes of brevity and focus, I have made no attempt to mention, let alone describe, every American small war. There is nothing here on small wars in colonial America; this book starts after the birth of the federal government in 1789. Nothing on the quasi-war with France (1798–1800), a series of purely naval battles against a Great Power; this book focuses on confrontations between American forces and those of less-developed countries. Nothing on the many wars against Native Americans, the primary occupation of the U.S. Army until 1890; this book focuses strictly on American small wars abroad.

The bulk of this book consists of a narrative that tries to tell the history of America's small wars in all their rich, fascinating, sometimes gory detail. The final two chapters are more analytical, trying to tease out the lessons of small wars past for small wars present and future.

The conflicts discussed in this book can be divided into three distinct periods of U.S. history:

(1) Commercial power (late 1700s to the 1890s). The United States grew rapidly economically during this period but not militarily, because the country lacked a central government strong enough to mobilize much military power except in extraordinary circumstances such as the Civil War. Yet even during periods of "peace," American sailors and marines were often killing and being killed far from home. No matter how small the navy, its hot-blooded captains always stood ready to avenge even the slightest insult, real or perceived, against American people and property. And thanks to the enterprise of Yankee merchants, who sent their speedy clipper ships and whaling ships all over the globe, there was never a shortage of "incidents" to send cannonballs flying. The longest and most important small war to result was waged against the Barbary States of North Africa, the subject of Chapter 1. Chapters 2–3 chronicle many minor landings abroad throughout the nineteenth century in locales ranging from Sumatra to Samoa, each typically lasting only a few days. These forays— which I describe, borrowing a bit of slang from British India, as "butcher and bolt"—served much the same function as World Trade Organization negotiations do today: to open up more of the world to Western commerce. For most of the nineteenth century, American merchants benefited from the protection of the Royal Navy. But if Britain was the world's policeman, the United States was a junior constable, often working hand in glove with the British to defend freedom of the seas and open markets in China, Japan, and elsewhere. The U.S. Navy even joined from time to time in the Royal Navy's most idealistic mission, to stamp out the slave trade.

(2) Great power (1898–1941). The United States heralded its arrival as a force to reckon with by humiliating an old, decrepit power, Spain, and snatching some of its colonies in 1898. Thereafter interventions would become longer and more ambitious, none more so than the costly and controversial campaign (described in Chapter 5) to put down resistance from Filipinos who did not want to trade one colonial master for another. Wars of territorial conquest— mostly fought against the Indians—were common in U.S. history, but the Philippine War was an aberration, a war of annexation waged overseas. A better harbinger of the future was the campaign that resulted from the Boxer uprising in China in 1900. America joined in a multinational expedition to rescue the besieged legations in Peking (Chapter 4). While the European and Japanese participants were determined to carve out their own spheres of influence in China, the United States pointedly committed itself to maintaining free trade for all—the Open Door.

America was only one of many powers active in the Far East, but closer to home it established itself as a hegemon. Under Theodore Roosevelt's corollary to the Monroe Doctrine, the U.S. announced that, in order to forestall European intervention, it would police the Caribbean itself. Chapter 6 suggests that this policy was motivated by a variety of considerations: strategic (the security of the Panama Canal), economic (American-owned plantations, railroads, banks, and other businesses), and idealistic ("the white man's burden"). Whatever his motives, Uncle Sam brought virtually every Central American and Caribbean nation under his sway. Most were not annexed outright (the exceptions being Puerto Rico, the Panama Canal Zone, and the Virgin Islands) but, like Cuba, turned into Yanqui protectorates. The United States preferred to exercise power through diplomatic and economic means—Dollar Diplomacy. But having made a commitment to dominate the Caribbean, it sometimes found itself drawn into small wars against its will. To take one example from Chapter 6, Teddy Roosevelt had no desire to intervene militarily in Cuba when a revolt flared in 1906, but the government forced his hand by resigning. Rather than risk a loss of prestige, he reluctantly undertook a three-year occupation.

This policy, inaugurated by Theodore Roosevelt and William Howard Taft, was expanded by Woodrow Wilson, who emphasized the moral (critics would say moralistic) dimension of U.S. foreign policy. His goal was "to teach the South American republics to elect good men." In 1914 the United States briefly occupied Veracruz, Mexico's principal port, in order to force from power a brutal dictator (Chapter 6). In 1915 and 1916, Wilson ordered the occupation of Haiti and the Dominican Republic in an attempt to create stability on the island of Hispaniola. America wound up running Haiti for 19 years, the Dominican Republic for eight years (Chapter 7). Along with the occupation of the Philippines, this provided the armed forces with their most extensive experience in running a foreign country, what today would be called nation building.

Wilson was drawn once again into Mexico because of its continuing turmoil. When the rebel chief Francisco "Pancho" Villa raided a New Mexico town in 1916, the president dispatched General John J. Pershing with more than 10,000 men south of the border to crush the Villistas (Chapter 8). A couple of years later the United States found itself drawn into another major revolution, the Bolshevik takeover of Russia. Woodrow Wilson committed 15,000 soldiers to Siberia and northern Russia in 1918 in response to entreaties from France and Britain (Chapter 9).

The Republican administrations of the 1920s tried to curtail American commitments overseas, but a brief pullout of marines from Nicaragua backfired. Another civil war broke out at once, and back came the marines. They would spend six years, 1927–1933, chasing the rebel leader Augusto Sandino around the jungles of Nicaragua (Chapter 10). In the early 1930s, in the midst of the

Great Depression, the United States finally eschewed military intervention in the Caribbean and Central America as part of FDR's Good Neighbor policy. Still, America in the '30s was not completely isolationist. U.S. troops remained on peacekeeping duty in China, trying with some success to protect American missionaries and businesses from revolutionary unrest and, with considerably less success, to protect China from the creeping menace of imperial Japan (Chapter 11).

(3) Superpower (1941–present). The attack on Pearl Harbor signaled the end of the U.S. peacekeeping mission in China, and with it the end of an era of small wars. Most professional soldiers disdain such conflicts against irregular foes as unsporting and unpleasant, preferring to prepare for combat against other large, well-organized armies. The Marines alone embraced these missions as part of their raison d'être, and in the decade leading up to World War II they compiled the lessons of their hard-won experience in the *Small Wars Manual* (Chapter 12). This incisive handbook was all but forgotten, however, by the time America became embroiled in Vietnam. General William Westmoreland and the army high command chose to fight a conventional big-unit war—with tragic consequences. Chapter 13 reinterprets the Vietnam War through the prism of small wars, suggesting the United States might have had better luck had it tried to implement a pacification strategy of the sort that had worked well in the past.

Chapter 14 looks at how the U.S. armed services have struggled with the bitter legacy of Vietnam. Their dominant reaction was summed up in the Powell Doctrine, which holds that America should unsheath its sword only when its vital interests are threatened, and then only if it is prepared to use overwhelming force with total public support to achieve a fast victory and then go home. This mindset proved a poor fit with the actual missions the Pentagon was forced to undertake in the post–Cold War era. It was almost as if a great mathematician were called upon to fill out tax forms—and found himself flummoxed by this quotidian challenge. Chapter 15 looks at the lessons of past small wars and suggests how they might prove a better guide to the future than the big-war mindset embodied in the Powell Doctrine.

If there is one theme that emerges from this book it is that, though the reasons have changed over the years, the United States has always found itself being drawn into the "the savage wars of peace." America's strategic situation today presents more opportunities than ever before for such entanglements. Since the fall of the Berlin Wall, America has stood head and shoulders (and also probably torso) above all other nations, possessor of the world's richest economy and its most potent military. In many ways the chaotic post–Cold War environment resembles that of the post-Napoleonic world, with the United States thrust willy-nilly into Britain's old role as globocop. Unlike nineteenth-century Britain, twenty-first century America does not preside over a formal empire. Its "empire" consists not of far-flung territorial possessions but of a family of democratic, capitalist nations that eagerly seek shelter under Uncle Sam's umbrella. The inner core of the American empire—North America, Western Europe, Northeast Asia—remains for the most part stable and prosperous, but violence and unrest lap at the periphery—in Africa, the Middle East, Central Asia, the Balkans, and other regions teeming with failed states, criminal states, or simply a state of nature. This is where America has found itself getting involved in its recent small wars, and no doubt will again in the future.

Why wars? The United States has many other tools—diplomatic, economic, cultural—to shape the international environment to its liking, but when all else fails the use of force cannot be ruled out. As *New York Times* columnist Thomas Friedman writes: "The hidden hand of the market will never work without a hidden fist. McDonald's cannot flourish without McDonnell Douglas, the designer of the U.S. Air Force F-15." Why small wars? To begin with, because big ones are unlikely. Knock on wood, there are few major powers willing or able to challenge the big kid on the block. North Korea, Iraq, and perhaps Iran are B-level threats; with the demise of the Soviet bloc, there are no remaining A-level threats, though one may emerge in the future (perhaps from a rising China or a resurgent Russia).

But that does not mean there are no threats. As America discovered on September 11, 2001, terrorists using primitive means can inflict terrifying casualties in what strategists call "asymmetric warfare." In the 1990s America had the luxury of undertaking small wars to help shape the international environment in ways conducive to its ideals—Somalia, Haiti, Bosnia, Kosovo, and all the rest. Following the attacks on the World Trade Center and the Pentagon, it would wage these conflicts for the more direct protection of its citizenry.

Whatever the specific causes of each war, we should not lose sight of a larger truth. Economists call it a yield curve: When cost is low, demand is high. America has long been more powerful than all but a handful of countries, so the cost of intervention in small states has always been low. Or so it appeared before virtually every conflict; it did not always work out that way. The perceived cost grew dramatically during the Cold War, when every use of American force risked provoking a clash of superpowers. But in the post–Cold War world, the price of exercising power appears low once again. If you want to see what lies in store for the armed forces in the future, you could do worse than to cast your gaze back to the past.

Part One

COMMERCIAL POWER

1

"To Conquer Upon the Sea"

Barbary Wars, 1801–1805, 1815

It was 7:00 P.M., and the African night was turning blue-gray beneath the faint light of a crescent moon when the small ship entered the harbor of Tripoli. The two-masted ketch, driven by a light breeze, made a slow, two-and-a-half-hour journey through the cavernous harbor. Visible on deck were half a dozen men in Maltese costume; above them fluttered a British flag. In the distance, at the end of their journey, lay a forbidding stone castle, its ramparts several feet thick and bristling with 115 heavy cannons like needles on a porcupine.

It was February 16, 1804.

By 9:30 P.M. the ketch had reached a strangely stunted vessel, lacking a foremast or sails, anchored directly beneath the castle's guns. This was the U.S. frigate *Philadelphia*, which had been captured the previous fall when it had run aground outside the harbor. Most of its crew now languished in Tripolitan prisons, working as slaves breaking rocks while surviving on black bread. The *Philadelphia* had been part of a flotilla dispatched from America to the distant waters of the Mediterranean to wage war on Tripoli, whose warships preyed on American merchantmen. Losing the *Philadelphia* had been a cruel blow to America's hopes—and a big boost to the pasha of Tripoli, whose puny fleet had gained a powerful punch by salvaging the U.S. frigate with its 36 cannons.

Now the *Philadelphia* was manned by the Pasha's men. When they saw the small vessel drawing close they shouted out a challenge. As they did so, the

Tripolitan crew double-shotted their guns and made ready to fire. The men on board the smaller ship knew that if they gave the wrong answer they would literally be blown out of the water. The pilot declared in Arabic that this was a Maltese trading boat that had lost both its anchors in a recent storm. He asked for permission to tie up for the night next to the *Philadelphia*.

As he spoke, the small craft edged closer and closer. About 20 feet from the *Philadelphia*, it coasted to a stop . . . becalmed in the still night air . . . helpless before the guns of the man-of-war. Even across the expanse of two centuries one can almost hear the crew's intake of breath, their hearts thumping in their chests, but the sailors calmly lowered a small rowboat to tie the two vessels together. The small ship's crew then grunted and heaved on the rope to draw the two ships side-by-side. As the smaller ship approached the bigger one, the *Philadelphia's* Tripolitan sailors finally realized what was going on. A voice screamed, "Americans!"

The pilot of the smaller vessel, a Sicilian named Salvatore Catalano, yelled in panic: "Board, captain, board!" If the crew had taken his advice many would have fallen into the water. But another voice calmly boomed out, "No order to be obeyed but that of the commanding officer!" Lieutenant Stephen Decatur Jr., standing on deck dressed in Maltese costume, waited a few seconds that must have seemed an eternity until his ketch had kissed alongside the *Philadelphia*. Then he gave his own command: "Board!"

"The effect was truly electric," recalled a surgeon's mate under Decatur's command. "Not a man had been seen or heard to breathe a moment before"—some 70 of them had been hiding in the stifling hold—"at the very next, the boarders hung on the ship's side like cluster bees; and, in another instant, every man was on board the frigate."

The ketch had been captured by Decatur from the Tripolitans the previous December, and was now dubbed the *Intrepid*. She had made a wearying voyage to reach this point, spending a week at sea being tossed and pounded by a heavy storm. Rats and vermin infested the ship and many of the improperly packed provisions had gone bad. But the sailors and marines, volunteers all, had refused to abandon their mission. Now they swarmed aboard their target, careful not to fire a shot that would alert the pasha's castle. Wielding knives and pikes and cutlasses, the Americans overwhelmed the Tripolitan crew in about 10 minutes. "Poor fellows! About 20 of them were cut to pieces & the rest jumped overboard," Midshipman Ralph Izard Jr. wrote.

The Americans could perhaps have tried piloting the *Philadelphia* out of the harbor, but since it did not have any foremast—it had been cut down just before the ship was captured—it would have been tough going. At any rate their orders were to destroy the ship. So the boarders split up into several parties and placed combustibles around the ship. As the wooden hull began to crackle and hiss with the spread of the flames, the Americans jumped back onto the *Intrepid* in a dense cloud of smoke. The last man aboard was Lieutenant Decatur, who barely managed to outrun the flames roaring out of the hatchways to grab the *Intrepid*'s rigging at the last second. "It is a miracle that our little vessel escaped the flames, lying within two feet of them & to leeward also!" Izard marveled.

But the *Intrepid* was hardly home safe. Seeing the tiny ship illuminated by the burning *Philadelphia*, the Tripolitan gunners in the pasha's castle and the nearby ships blazed away. Luckily for the *Intrepid*, their aim was poor and the little vessel was unscathed save for one shot through her topgallant sail. As the *Intrepid* negotiated its way out of the harbor, the hardy Jack Tars (as sailors were then known) laughed and cheered, admiring the "bonfire" in the southern sky. A midshipman captured the spectacle of the *Philadelphia* burning: "The flames in the interior illuminated her ports and, ascending her rigging and masts, formed columns of fire, which, meeting the tops, were reflected into beautiful capitals; whilst the occasional discharge of her guns gave an idea of some directing spirit within her." In its death throes the man-of-war discharged a broadside straight into Tripoli, before breaking loose of its moorings and drifting closer to the castle, where it exploded with a terrifying roar that further shook the nearby city.

The tale of this astonishing feat—burning a captured ship while under the guns of the enemy, and not losing a man in the process—reverberated from one corner of the globe to another, gaining newfound respect for the nascent American navy. Lord Nelson of the Royal Navy called it "the most bold and daring act of the age." In reward, the *Intrepid*'s crew received an extra two months' pay from Congress, and Decatur, just 25 years old, became the youngest person ever promoted to captain, then the navy's highest rank.

Decatur seems to have stepped out of a storybook. One of the handsomest officers in the navy, he had broad shoulders, a slim waist, curly chestnut hair, and dancing dark brown eyes that ladies found irresistible. His future wife, the daughter of a Virginia merchant, was said to have fallen in love with him merely from seeing a miniature portrait of him. She was not the only one enamored of him. A fellow officer wrote, upon first meeting him, "I had often pictured to myself the form and look of a hero, such as my favorite Homer had delineated; here I saw it embodied." A marine private testified: "Not a tar, who ever sailed with Decatur, but would almost sacrifice his life for him."

Decatur was born with salt spray in his veins: His father, Stephen Decatur Sr., had been a famous naval captain of the Revolutionary War and the quasi-war against France. Indeed the elder Decatur had at one time commanded the *Philadelphia*, the very vessel that his son now burned. The Decaturs were a prominent Philadelphia family, but Stephen was born on January 5, 1779, on the Eastern Shore of Maryland, where his mother had fled after the British had occupied their hometown during the War of Independence. His mother, Ann, wanted him to be a bishop but an ecclesiastical life was at odds with his nature; contemporaries recalled him "in every scheme of boyish mischief or perilous adventure taking the lead."

He went to sea late by the standards of the age: He was commissioned a midshipman in 1798, when he was almost 20 years old, after briefly attending the University of Pennsylvania. His decision to leave the university is cloaked in some mystery. Rumor has it that he wanted to leave the country in a hurry after being acquitted of having struck "a woman of doubtful integrity" who subsequently died. Whatever the truth of this charge, we do know that in 1801 he sailed for the Mediterranean, seeking glory and adventure as a 22-year-old first lieutenant aboard the frigate *Essex* at the start of the Barbary Wars. Needless to say, he found plenty of both.

By the time he had returned home from North Africa, Decatur was being fêted and celebrated across the land, making him "America's first nineteenth-century military hero." It is no exaggeration to say that his exploits, by helping to kindle the flames of patriotism, helped forge a new nation out of 13 former colonies not long united under one flag.

Today Decatur is remembered, if at all, for coining the phrase, "My country, right or wrong." (What he actually said, in a toast, was: "Our country! In her intercourse with foreign nations, may she always be in the right; but right or wrong, our country!") The Barbary Wars in which he made his name are all but forgotten, save as the subject of children's stories about pirates and the first line of the Marine Corps anthem ("to the shores of Tripoli"). Yet they deserve to be disinterred from the grave of history, for it was because of these wars that the United States gained a navy and a marine corps and a role on the world stage.

Barbary Coast

At the turn of the nineteenth century, there were four states—Morocco, Algiers, Tripoli, and Tunis—situated on the northern edge of Africa along what Europeans called the Barbary Coast (from the Greek word for foreigners) and Arabs knew as al-Maghrib (the West). Morocco was and is an independent country ruled by the Alawite dynasty. The sovereigns of the other Barbary states were variously styled as bey or dey or pasha, all Turkish honorifics, and since the sixteenth century they had professed nominal loyalty to the sultan in Constantinople, but in practice, given the weakness of the Ottoman Empire by the eighteenth century, they were largely masters of their own fate.

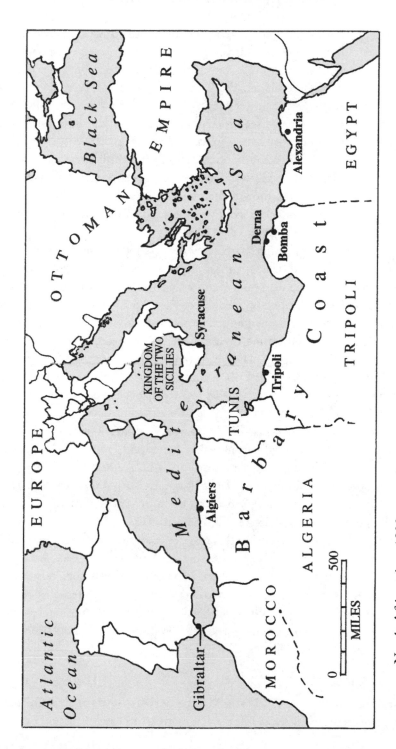

MAP 1.1 North Africa, circa 1800

To finance their governments they would routinely declare war on a European state and set either naval vessels or privateers to seize enemy shipping. This was a lucrative business: Captured cargoes and captives were auctioned off to the highest bidder, the latter being sent to flourishing slave markets unless they were wealthy enough to ransom their release. Although piracy had declined by the eighteenth century from its heyday in the sixteenth and seventeenth centuries—when Algiers alone held 30,000 Christian captives—it was still the foundation upon which the Maghrib states built flourishing and sophisticated civilizations. Many European states too had held Muslim slaves in years past, though this practice was dying out by the eighteenth century; America of course continued to hold many African slaves of its own, a few Muslims among them.

It is tempting to compare the Barbary States to modern Islamist states that preach and practice jihad against infidel unbelievers. It is a temptation best resisted. The rulers of the Ottoman Empire and its North African tributaries were not particularly xenophobic nor especially fundamentalist. By the standards of the day, they were uncommonly cosmopolitan and tolerant in many respects, offering more protection than did many European states to flourishing Jewish communities that played a prominent role in their commercial affairs. Ali Karamanli, pasha of Tripoli from 1754 to 1795, was even said to have been much influenced by his Jewish mistress, a corpulent woman known as "Queen Esther."

It is also tempting to speak of the Barbary "pirates," as contemporary Europeans and Americans did, but in reality the corsairs of North Africa were no more—and no less—piratical than Sir Francis Drake or Sir John Hawkins, two of the more illustrious figures in English naval history, both of whom operated as privateers, using the authority given them by letters of marque to seize enemy shipping. Americans also resorted to privateers to harass their foes; the U.S. government was so attached to this practice that it refused to sign the 1856 Declaration of Paris outlawing privateering as a weapon of war. As in the American and British navies, the Barbary rulers gave captains and crews a portion of the "prize money" captured by their ships. The difference is that in Europe and America the legally sanctioned capture of enemy merchantmen typically served some larger state purpose; it was not an end unto itself, as it became for the Ottoman regencies.

The European states occasionally attacked the Barbary States but usually found it more convenient to buy them off. Starting with Cromwell's England in 1646, the Europeans chose to ransom their hostages and buy "passports" to allow their ships free passage in the Mediterranean. The British, French, and Dutch also encouraged the Barbary corsairs to target ships belonging to their enemies. Until 1776, American ships were protected by English tribute and the Royal Navy. As many as 100 American merchantmen made annual voyages to the Mediterranean, carrying salted fish, flour, lumber, sugar, and other goods, which they traded for lemons, oranges, figs, olive oil, and opium, among other valuable items. After the Revolution, the enterprising merchants of New England tried to reestablish this lucrative trade but found it dangerous going.

Morocco captured and then released the U.S merchantman *Betsey* in 1784. The following year Algerian corsairs swooped down on the *Maria* and the *Dauphin*. Eleven more American ships were seized by the Algerians in the summer of 1793 after Portugal ended its war on Algiers, which had kept Barbary ships from slipping past the Straits of Gibraltar. More than 100 Americans became captives of the dey of Algiers—triggering a debate in the newly established Congress about whether it was time to build a navy. John D. Foss, a young sailor captured aboard the brig *Polly* in 1793, described a hard life in Algerian prisons. His captivity began when 100 Algerians swarmed his ship, stripped the crew down to their underwear and took the nine Americans back to the city of Algiers, where they were paraded before jeering crowds and presented to Dey Hassan Pasha, who crowed, "Now I have got you, you Christian dogs, you shall eat stones."

They did not literally eat rocks but they did have to work as slaves, breaking and hauling rocks while clanging around in 40 pounds of chains. Along with 600 other prisoners, they were housed in a dingy fortress, made to sleep on the stone floor, and fed nothing but vinegar and bread that, Foss complained, "was so sour that a person must be almost starving before he can eat it." Slaves who were found guilty of malingering could expect up to 200 *bastinadoes*—whacks on the feet with a five-foot cane. A slave who spoke disrespectfully to a Muslim could be roasted alive, crucified, or impaled (a stake was driven through the anus until it came out at the back of the neck). A special agony was reserved for a slave who killed a Muslim—he would be cast over the city walls and left to dangle on giant iron hooks for days before expiring of his wounds.

Other captives were better treated. James Leander Cathcart, captured at age 17 on the *Maria* in 1785, spent 11 years in Algerian captivity. He progressed from palace gardener to *coffeegie* (coffee brewer) to various clerical positions and finally became chief Christian secretary to the dey. Although he was bastinadoed on occasion, his situation "was very tolerable." Indeed he bought several taverns and made so much money that he was able to purchase a ship to take him back to the United States, before returning to North Africa as an American diplomat.

But it was not Cathcart's story (never published in his lifetime) that captured popular imagination in the U.S. Rather American public opinion was inflamed by the books and letters produced by Foss and other captives, chronicling what Foss vividly described as "the many hellish tortures and punishments these piratical sea-rovers invent and inflict on the unfortunate Christian who may by chance unhappily fall into their hands."

Drifting Toward War

Opinion was divided in the U.S. about how to handle the Barbary hostage crisis. Thomas Jefferson, when he was minister to Paris in 1785, thought it would be "best to effect a peace through the medium of war." But John Adams, minister to London, argued that paying ransom would be cheaper: "We ought not to fight them at all unless we determine to fight them forever." Soaring maritime insurance rates due to Algiers's seizure of 11 American merchantmen in 1793 finally inclined President George Washington toward the martial approach.

But the young Republic had nothing to fight with. All of the Continental Navy's 35 warships had been destroyed or captured during the Revolution, and the new federal government had refused to maintain a standing military force in peacetime, viewing it as a threat to the people's liberties and billfolds. A bitter debate now raged in Congress over whether to create a navy. Ironically, considering their leaders' views on how to deal with the Barbary pirates, Jefferson's Republican Party opposed the proposal, while Adams's Federalists supported it. It was only by the narrowest of margins that parsimonious lawmakers authorized the construction of six ships at a cost of $688,888.82. President George Washington signed the bill on March 27, 1794, the birthday of the United States Navy, which was called into being—we should remember—to fight a small, undeclared war halfway around the world.

Joshua Humphreys, a well-known shipbuilder, and Josiah Fox, an equally prominent maritime architect, were commissioned to design the six frigates. The work of building the ships was carefully allocated to shipyards in many different states in order to maximize political support for the project—a strategy that supporters of arms programs follow to this day. The resulting ships would eventually be hailed as marvels of marine design. Though smaller than ships-of-the-line—the U.S. had none of these behemoths, deploying 60 to 100 guns or more, until 1815—the frigates Humphreys designed were faster and more powerful than comparable vessels in other navies. Three would field 44 guns, the others 36 guns.

But before any of the frigates could be completed, peace broke out. American envoys agreed to pay the dey of Algiers $642,000 along with an annual tribute of arms. The total value of the tribute to Algiers eventually came to more than $1 million, one-sixth of the federal budget. As part of America's first "arms for hostages" deal, the dey released his Yankee slaves on July 12, 1796—or at least the 88 out of 119 who had survived the ordeal. Similar deals were concluded with the pasha of Tripoli in 1796 (the U.S. paid him $56,486) and the bey of Tunis in 1797 (for $107,000). Congress stopped the building of three frigates and allowed the other three to go forward mainly as a jobs program; the navy's pork-barrel strategy had paid off. The Washington administration dispatched envoys to the Barbary States. Alas, this policy of appeasement, far from sating the demands of the North African rulers, only whetted their appetite for more.

On September 17, 1800, after a 40-day crossing from Philadelphia, the *George Washington*, a 24-gun vessel, anchored in Algiers harbor to deliver America's tribute to the dey. Captain William Bainbridge—one of the unluckiest, or most maladroit, officers in the U.S. fleet—made the mistake of tying up his ship directly underneath the guns of the dey's castle. He was then summoned to an audience with Dey Bobba Mustapha, who delivered a startling ultimatum: The *George Washington* must sail under Algiers's flag to deliver the dey's embassy and tribute to his nominal master, Sultan Selim III, in Constantinople—or else, the *George Washington* would be smashed by the dey's guns and its crew sent into slavery. The dey in essence told Bainbridge: You pay me tribute, by that you become my slaves.

The hapless Bainbridge had no choice but to comply. He even had to hoist the Algerian flag on his masthead. Not only did he take on board $800,000 in coins and jewelry and the dey's ambassador to Constantinople, but also the ambassador's suite of 100 black slaves and 60 harem women and a veritable menagerie consisting of "20 Lions 3 Tigers 5 Antelopes 2 Ostriches & 20 Parrots." This whole noisy, smelly collection was stuffed into the *George Washington*'s quarters, already cramped with 220 crew members. The only mild revenge Bainbridge exacted during the journey—other than hauling down the Algerian flag—was to tack his ship sharply, forcing all the Muslims to constantly shift directions so that they could address their prayers toward Mecca. But not even the warm reception that the Americans received in Constantinople—where it turned out that nobody had heard of this upstart New World republic before—could make up for the indignity of becoming a messenger service for a foreign potentate. After making a quick return trip to Algiers, Bainbridge sailed for home, arriving in Philadelphia on April 19, 1801.

Even before the *George Washington* reached home, the new president, Thomas Jefferson, had determined to act on his long-standing desire to take a tough line against the Barbary States. "I know," he wrote, "that nothing will stop the eternal increase of demands from these pirates but the presence of an armed force, and it will be more economical & more honorable to use the same means at once for suppressing their insolencies." The humiliation of the *George Washington* was the final straw; according to Secretary of State James Madison, it "deeply affected the sensibility, not only of the President but of the people of the United States."

But the Jefferson administration found itself hobbled by its own penny-pinching ways—and by the president's many contradictions. Like many great men, the red-haired master of Monticello was a bundle of paradoxes. The most obvious, and most widely noted, is that he penned the Declaration of Independence, with its immortal proclamation that "all men are created equal," at the same time that he held more than 100 blacks in bondage. There were other inconsistencies. He was a critic of a strong federal government and a champion of states' rights, but as president he would take a sweeping view of his own authority in foreign affairs, even going so far as to purchase the Louisiana Territory from France in 1803—an action he admitted was not strictly authorized by the Constitution. And, though a longstanding advocate of vigorous military action against the Barbary pirates, Jefferson was at the same time an opponent of a large ocean-going navy required for such a task, preferring to rely on a fleet of small gunboats best suited for coastal defense.

It was the last of these paradoxes that now caught up with him. The U.S. Navy had briefly swelled in size during the quasi-war against France from 1798 to 1800, but Jefferson and his penny-pinching Treasury secretary, the Swiss-born Albert Gallatin, had insisted on trimming it severely in order to pay off the debt and cut taxes. The navy was left with only six frigates. The entire officer corps was reduced to nine captains, 36 lieutenants, and 150 midshipmen.

Even mobilizing this small force was not easy. When Jefferson convened his cabinet to discuss the Barbary situation in May 1801, Attorney General Levi Lincoln objected that only Congress could declare war—and it wasn't in session. Jefferson declined to call Congress into special session, feeling no need to obtain a declaration of war even though he was about to dispatch the U.S.

armed forces on a mission that carried a high likelihood of battle. This master of literary craftsmanship finessed the issue through cleverly worded orders. The U.S. ships sent to the Mediterranean, he declared, would not blockade any state that had not declared war on the U.S. and would not attack unless first attacked. But the navy had permission to use force to protect American merchant shipping as well as to enforce existing treaty obligations. And if, upon reaching the Mediterranean, the U.S. squadron found that one of the Barbary States *had* declared war on America, it was authorized "to chastise their insolence by sinking, burning or destroying their ships and vessels."

Jefferson had no way of knowing that immediately after he wrote those orders, one of the Barbary States would commence hostilities. Yusuf Karamanli, the pasha of Tripoli, had been growing more and more restive because he was getting less American tribute than his neighbors. He manifested his displeasure by dispatching one of his *polacres*—a shallow-drafted vessel typical of the boats used in the Mediterranean—to capture the U.S. merchant brig *Catharine*. When the U.S. envoy James Leander Cathcart refused the pasha's demands for more tribute, the aggrieved ruler sent soldiers to the American consulate on May 14, 1801, to chop down the flagpole flying the Stars and Stripes—a traditional method of declaring war in North Africa where wood, of the kind used for flagpoles, was scarce. Thus, even without a declaration of war from Congress (a more limited authorization to use force would be approved later), the U.S. was now committed to its first combat far from home.

The Cautious Commodores

Chosen to command the initial American naval foray into the Mediterranean was Richard Dale, a veteran of the Revolutionary War. At 23, he had been John Paul Jones's first lieutenant aboard the *Bonhomme Richard* and had acquitted himself with great valor. But those adventures were decades in the past, and he had grown more cautious with age. He set sail on June 2, 1801, aboard his flagship, the *President*, one of the elegant 44-gun frigates designed by Joshua Humphreys, leading a squadron that consisted of the 36-gun frigate *Philadelphia*, the 32-gun frigate *Essex*, and the 12-gun sloop *Enterprise*. He reached Tripoli in July and mounted a blockade, one of the more boring and exasperating tasks in a mariner's life.

Nothing much happened for the first month. On August 1, 1801, Commodore Dale ordered Lieutenant Andrew Sterrett of the *Enterprise* to sail off to Malta to bring back fresh water. On the way, Sterrett spotted a sail. He set off in pursuit, hoisting a British flag as he did so. As a *ruse de guerre*, a "false flag" was considered acceptable deceit in those days, but a captain was honor bound to show his true colors before opening fire. This Sterrett did as soon as he ascertained that the other ship was the 14-gun *Tripoli*, belonging to the pasha.

The *Enterprise* rapidly closed in and delivered broadside after broadside with its 12 guns. The *Tripoli* tried to ram the American ship, but Sterrett skillfully maneuvered away and kept up his withering fire. After more than three hours of combat, the *Tripoli's* commander, Rias Mahomet Rous, lowered his flag, but just as Sterrett prepared to accept his surrender he opened fire again. The Tripolitans pulled this trick twice. Sterrett, after almost being lured in, showed no mercy and kept firing until he had smashed the *Tripoli's* masts, holed her hull, and raked her deck. When a boarding party from the *Enterprise*, led by Lieutenant David Porter, finally surveyed the *Tripoli* they discovered total desolation: Out of 80 crewmen, 30 had been killed and 30 wounded. No one aboard the *Enterprise* was injured—an amazing testament to the poor quality of Tripolitan marksmanship. Sterrett, forbidden to take prizes because the U.S. was not formally at war, had all of the *Tripoli's* arms thrown overboard and her mast chopped down before he allowed the battered ship to limp home.

The pasha was not exactly overjoyed to see his defeated captain. He made Admiral Rous ride through the streets of Tripoli mounted backwards on a jackass, with sheep's entrails hanging around his neck. For good measure, the admiral received 500 *bastinadoes*.

By September 1801, Commodore Dale found his supplies exhausted and most of his men nearing the end of their one-year enlistment. He left the *Essex* and *Philadelphia* to continue a desultory blockade of Tripoli and sailed home with the *President* and *Enterprise*.

President Jefferson realized that Dale had accomplished little and a new squadron would have to be dispatched if he wanted to bring Tripoli to heel. Congress would not grant a declaration of war, just as it had refused to vote one during the quasi-war with France. On February 6, 1802, Congress did, however, pass an act authorizing the president to use all necessary force to protect American shipping overseas. With this carte blanche, Jefferson sent six more ships to the Mediterranean: the 36-gun frigates *Constellation* and *Chesapeake*, both of Joshua Humphreys's design, along with the frigates *New York* (36 guns),

Adams (28), and *John Adams* (28), and the smaller *Enterprise* (12*).* They would join the *Essex* and *Philadelphia*, already on station.

After Thomas Truxton refused command of the squadron, Jefferson turned to the next most senior officer, Richard Valentine Morris. He was politically well connected—nephew of Gouverneur Morris, one of the signers of the Declaration of Independence, and brother of a pro-Jefferson congressman from Vermont—but soon proved to be an inept commander.

His expedition got off to an inauspicious start when he sailed aboard the *Chesapeake* on April 27, 1802, carrying some unusual passengers: his wife, young son, and a black nursemaid. Some sailors took to calling Mrs. Morris "the commoderess." Women were not unknown aboard fighting ships in those days, usually during port calls; hence the expression "son of a gun," referring to a baby conceived on the gun deck. But Morris's decision to bring his family along clearly signaled that fighting was not high on his agenda. Instead he dithered in Gibraltar, enjoying the social life of the British garrison.

While he left Tripoli practically unguarded some of the pasha's galleys slipped out and snared an American merchant brig. The American envoy to Tunis, William Eaton, a fiery sort, was driven to distraction by Morris's lassitude. "What have they done but dance and wench?" he demanded.

Morris finally reached Tripoli on May 22, after a fruitless year in the Mediterranean. A few days later the *Enterprise*, now commanded by Lieutenant Isaac Hull, caught some feluccas—shallow draft transports—laden with grain trying to sneak into Tripoli harbor. About 10 of them became grounded about 35 miles west of Tripoli. Morris sent a small expedition to burn the grain boats—50 sailors and marines under the command of Lieutenant David Porter. This small group of Americans was met by a far larger number of Tripolitans, but they doggedly fought their way up the beach until they could set the fellucas on fire. Porter then directed the retreat, staggering on despite being hit in both thighs. Since half of the grain was eventually saved, the mission was only a limited success. Midshipman Henry Wadsworth (uncle of the poet Henry Wadsworth Longfellow) nevertheless declared, "Twas good sport I must confess." His was a fairly typical attitude among the battle-loving officers of his day; no reluctant warriors were they.

Having failed to bring the pasha to bay with the stick, Commander Morris now tried the carrot. He entered Tripoli on June 7, 1803, under a flag of truce, to negotiate terms, but he balked at the pasha's demand for $200,000 in tribute plus annual payments of $20,000. Roared the offended pasha: "Then business is at end!" Morris promptly sailed away to Gibraltar to see his new-born son, leaving Captain John Rodgers in charge of the Tripoli blockade. His squadron managed to blow up one *polacre* trying to run the blockade, but by June 30 Rodgers too had anchored off Malta. On July 11, Morris sailed for America with his family, having achieved nothing. Back home he was censured for his timidity by a court of inquiry and had his captain's commission revoked.

A Pack of Boys

Jefferson was growing increasingly frustrated with the negligible results produced by his naval expeditions. After two years of war, Tripoli had not budged a bit and respect for American power was at a nadir because of its dithering commodores. At long last the president found the right man for the job. His name was Edward Preble.

Look at the well-known Rembrandt Peale portrait of him and you see a man with dark blue, piercing eyes, a beaky nose, a resolute jaw, and red hair carefully combed over his forehead to conceal a receding hairline. Born in Maine (then part of Massachusetts) in 1761, young Preble found working on the family farm not to his liking and wound up enlisting in the Massachusetts navy as a midshipman. During the War of Independence, he was captured and imprisoned aboard an odious British prison ship anchored in New York harbor, but managed to win his release through family connections. Once the war was over, he became a prosperous merchant captain and eventually a shipowner. When the undeclared war with France broke out in 1798, he was commissioned a lieutenant commander and swiftly rose to captain in the new federal navy, being one of only nine kept on the list after the quasi-war.

He had not joined the fighting in the Mediterranean earlier because of ill health. Preble's ailments, aggravated by his stay aboard the British prison hulk, were numerous enough for two men: typhoid fever, malaria, consumption (now known as tuberculosis), and a debilitating digestive disorder, probably ulcers, which made him stick to a milk-and-vegetable diet for long stretches of time.

By the time Richard Morris's expedition to Tripoli was ending in failure, Preble was finally well enough to command again. He received his orders on May 19, 1803: Sail aboard the 44-gun frigate *Constitution* to lead a squadron in making war on Tripoli. By 10 the next morning Preble was aboard his flagship. He ordered the ship to be retrofitted and made sure the work was done in record time. He also set out to recruit a crew, finding out-of-work foreign seamen the most likely catches. "I do not believe I have twenty native American sailors on board," he noted.

His officers, appropriately enough for the navy of such a young country, were young themselves. His oldest commander was William Bainbridge, the 30-year-old captain of the *Philadelphia*. His other officers, the 42-year-old Preble grumbled, were "nothing but a pack of boys." But these boys would blossom into the victorious captains of the War of 1812: Stephen Decatur Jr., Isaac Hull, David Porter, James Lawrence, William Biddle, and others. Eventually they would be known as "Preble's Boys," the American analogue to Horatio Nelson's "band of brothers." Their success should not be altogether surprising. Bold new enterprises, whether navies or software companies, tend to be created by those too callow to know any better.

Preble set sail aboard the *Constitution* on August 12, 1803, the rest of his squadron—the heavy frigate *Philadelphia* (36), three 12-gun schooners (*Enterprise*, *Nautilus*, *Vixen*), and two 16-gun brigs (*Argus* and *Syren*)—having already set out. Though his men would soon develop great admiration for their commanding officer, Preble was not well liked to begin with. He was a martinet, a tyrant of the quarterdeck, whose myriad diseases had not improved his disposition. He drove his men hard, lashing errant seamen with the cat-o'-nine-tails and errant officers with an even more potent weapon—his tongue. Wrote Midshipman Charles Morris: "A very violent and easily excited temper was one of the prominent characteristics of Commodore Preble, from the undue expression of which, when he was greatly excited, no officer could escape. Irresolution, no less than contradiction, was an offense in his eyes, and decision of action as well as obedience of orders was necessary to preserve his favorable opinion."

The men's opinions of their imperious commander improved remarkably just as they were nearing Gibraltar. Late one night the *Constitution* encountered an unknown sail. Preble hailed the stranger, who refused to answer. He then warned: "If a proper answer is not returned, I will fire a shot into you!"

A voice from the other ship announced that she was His Majesty's Ship *Donegal*, 84 guns, and demanded that Preble send a boat out to meet her.

Preble shot back: "This is the United States ship *Constitution*, 44 guns, Edward Preble, an American commodore, who will be damned before he sends his boat on board of any vessel!" Then he theatrically called out: "Blow your matches, boys!"

Hearing the signal to open fire, the other captain sheepishly sent over his own boat and explained that his ship was actually the HMS *Maidstone*, a 32-gun frigate that had been caught unawares by the *Constitution*.

Preble's men were impressed by his unflinching attitude toward danger. And he made clear that his bellicosity was not limited to the British. Wrote Preble,

"The Moors are a designing, artful, treacherous set of villains and nothing will keep them so quiet as a respectable naval force near them."

He quickly acted on that belief during a confrontation with Emperor Muley Soliman of Morocco, who had hitherto been friendly to the U.S. but was now making belligerent noises. When he was presented to the emperor, Preble refused to take off his sword or kneel.

"Are you not in fear of being arrested?" the emperor inquired.

"No, sir. If you presume to do that, my squadron in full view will lay your batteries, your castles and your city in ruins."

Preble's unwavering attitude proved a powerful stimulant to peace. The emperor apologized for any affronts to American ships and reratified the friendship treaty his father had signed with the U.S. in 1768. Morocco had been removed as a threat from the American rear as the navy pressed its attack on Tripoli.[14]

But before Preble could reach Tripoli, he received disastrous news from a passing British frigate: The *Philadelphia* had been captured. Her skipper was William Bainbridge, the Bad Luck Billy who had previously commanded the *George Washington* during her ignominious voyage to and from Algiers. At 9 A.M. on October 31, 1803, the *Philadelphia*, which had been blockading Tripoli alone, spotted a sail to the west and gave chase. Two hours later, still in full pursuit, the ship ran aground on the treacherous Kaliusa Reef, not indicated on Bainbridge's charts. The crew desperately jettisoned water kegs, anchors, and anything else they could find. They even cut down the foremast. But still the ship was stuck fast. The *Philadelphia* lay at the mercy of Tripolitan gunboats swarming around her like jackals pouncing on a wounded wildebeest. Bainbridge called a meeting of his officers and they unanimously decided to surrender rather than die fighting. Before giving up the ship, Bainbridge ordered holes drilled in the bottom to scuttle her. Then the 307 officers and men were ferried ashore, stripped of everything save underwear, and presented before a gloating pasha.

They would spend the next 20 months in Tripoli, hostages of the pasha. The crew members were imprisoned in an old warehouse and made to work as slaves, with nothing but black bread, olive oil, and couscous to eat, and a stone floor for a bed. They were not, however, physically harmed. The officers were much better treated at first—a cause of no small resentment among the crew. They were housed in the spacious old U.S. consulate, and, wrote ship's surgeon Jonathan Cowdery, "we were supplied with fresh provisions that were tolerably good," including camel meat. The officers were even allowed to take escorted jaunts around the countryside, acting for all the world like pleasure travelers. Dr. Cowdery, who ministered to the pasha and his family, became a special favorite of Tripoli's ruler, who "sent word that I should have any thing I wanted, free of expense."

From their comfortable quarters, the officers witnessed a dismaying sight not long after arriving in Tripoli: A storm lifted the *Philadelphia* off the reef. Tripolitan carpenters plugged the holes, while divers recovered its guns, anchors, and other implements tossed overboard. The ship was fully salvaged and made operational again. Bainbridge apprised Preble of this development in secret writing—lemon juice diluted with water that became visible when heated. He urged Preble to do everything within his power to destroy the ship, lest it wreak havoc on the American fleet and commerce.

Although a naval court of inquiry later cleared Bainbridge of any wrongdoing, Preble in private seethed over the captain's surrender. "If it had not been for the capture of the *Philadelphia*, I have no doubt, but we should have had peace with Tripoli in the Spring," Preble wrote. "But I have no hopes of such an event." Instead he had to concentrate his resources on destroying the *Philadelphia*. He gave the coveted job of commanding the *Intrepid* to Stephen Decatur Jr., who had eagerly volunteered. Accompanying the *Intrepid* was the *Syren*, commanded by Lieutenant Charles Stewart, which, as it happens, never got a chance to see action because Decatur chose to proceed alone rather than risk losing the element of surprise.

By Sunday, February 19, 1804, *Intrepid* and *Syren* had been gone two long weeks—far longer than necessary for a round-trip to Tripoli—and Preble was getting anxious in his Syracuse headquarters. He feared the two small ships had been lost in the gale that had recently shaken the Mediterranean. At 10 A.M. two ships hove into sight of Syracuse harbor. The *Constitution* hoisted a signal flag to the *Syren*—a maritime way of asking, "Well???" All eyes in the harbor turned for anxious moments to the *Syren* until it hoisted its reply, signifying that the ships' business had been successfully completed.

While gratifying, the destruction of the *Philadelphia* had hardly won the war. Preble concluded that continuing the blockade would be unlikely to produce results. The commodore decided to press the attack against Tripoli. Since he knew that his larger ships could not get close enough to do much damage, he went to the Kingdom of the Two Sicilies (also at war with Tripoli) and borrowed six gunboats and two bomb-throwing ketches. Preble assembled his armada before Tripoli on July 25 to face a formidable target, a thick-walled city of minarets and white-bleached houses defended by 25,000 troops and 115 cannons in addition to the pasha's navy.

On August 3, 1804, the weather finally cleared and at 2:30 P.M. Preble's flagship, the *Constitution*, hoisted a flag signaling that battle was to commence. The ketches moved in to bombard the city with their 13-inch brass mortars. Meanwhile the six Sicilian gunboats—formed in two squadrons, one led by Captain Stephen Decatur Jr., the other by Lieutenant Richard Somers—engaged the enemy's 19 gunboats. Decatur, as usual, showed the most pluck. His men peppered a Tripolitan gunboat with grapeshot and musket balls, then to the astonishment of the enemy, they borrowed a page from Tripolitan tactics and closed in to board the enemy. "I always thought we could lick them in their own way," Decatur later wrote. He proved as good as his word. Decatur leaped aboard the enemy gunboat with 19 sailors. Wielding cutlasses, axes, dirks, pistols, and tomahawks, the Americans took the boat in 10 minutes of savage hand-to-hand combat with 36 Tripolitans. Three of the Americans were wounded; 16 Tripolitans were killed and 15 wounded. "Some of the Turks died like men," Decatur wrote disdainfully, "but much the greater number like women."

Just as Decatur had secured his prize, he received a blow more stunning than any delivered by an enemy's sword. His brother, Lieutenant James Decatur, had commanded another gunboat. James had been fighting a Tripolitan boat that had struck its flag, but when James boarded her, the captain shot him in the head. Upon hearing the news of his brother's death, Stephen Decatur went into a frenzy. Or, as an early biographer put it more grandly, he was seized by "noble indignation at such base treachery."

Most of his men were still aboard the captured Tripolitan gunboat, so with only nine crew members Decatur went in pursuit of his brother's killer. He found a Tripolitan boat (the right one? who knows?) and boarded her, fighting his way to the captain to commence a mano-a-mano struggle. The gigantic Tripolitan lunged with an iron boarding pike, snapping the American's cutlass. Decatur parried the next thrust with his right arm, tearing the weapon out of his own wound and managing with a sudden jerk to wrest it away from his foe. The two commanders fell to the deck grappling with each other, Decatur on top. Another Tripolitan tried to hit Decatur on the head with a scimitar, but a seaman already wounded in both arms interposed his own skull instead and saved Decatur's life. In the next instant, the Tripolitan captain flipped his weaker adversary and pinned him on the deck with his left hand while with his right hand he prepared to plunge home a *yataghan* (short knife). The American captain desperately grabbed the Tripolitan's thrusting arm with one hand while with the other he reached into his pantaloon pocket, whipped out a pistol, and, wrapping his arm around the captain, fired into his back. "It was just like

Decatur," a brother officer marveled. "The chances were ten to one that the bullet would pass through both their bodies, but luckily it met a bone and the huge barbarian rolled off dead." Thus Decatur had captured his second prize of the day, this time overcoming 24 Tripolitans without losing an American life.

Decatur's bravery that day was matched, if not exceeded, by another officer. Lieutenant John Trippe, just 19 years old, was in command of the sixth gunboat. With 10 sailors, he boarded a Tripolitan vessel. Just as they got aboard, the two ships began drifting apart. The 11 Americans were facing 36 well-armed defenders. It was, as Commodore Preble put it, "conquer or perish." Both sides fought with fierce abandon. As the American lieutenant was about to have his head cleaved open by a Tripolitan, Marine Sergeant Jonathan Meredith bayoneted the enemy sailor. Trippe then grabbed a pike to face the Tripolitan captain, a stout, gallant fellow who wielded a scimitar and had sworn on the Koran to win or die. Trippe suffered 10 scimitar wounds, but he kept advancing. The captain struck him a powerful blow—his eleventh wound—and knocked him to his knees. Trippe ended the battle, and saved his own life, by jabbing his pike into his opponent's genitals, a move not often seen in Errol Flynn movies. The Americans wound up carrying the boat, their third prize of the day. Trippe cried whenever he recalled the event later, so deeply did he regret having to kill the courageous enemy captain who had refused to surrender.

Decatur gathered up the three prizes seized by his squadron and returned to the *Constitution*. "I have brought you three of the enemy's gunboats, sir," the bloodstained warrior proudly announced to Preble.

"Three, sir!" the commodore barked. "Where are the rest of them?"

Though Preble later apologized for his outburst, his frustration was understandable. Only Trippe and Decatur had achieved much. While three other enemy gunboats had been sunk, some of the American vessels never even engaged the enemy. And it was hard to tell what damage the bomb ketches had done to the city. The engagement was hardly decisive. Preble offered the pasha $50,000 ransom for his hostages and when this was turned down, mounted another bold but ultimately futile assault on the city.

Preble had already shown more offensive flair than any of his predecessors, so he was stunned by the arrival of the frigate *John Adams* on the night of August 7, 1804, bearing news, some welcome—President Jefferson had decided to send five more frigates to the Mediterranean—and some not: Samuel Barron, a captain senior to Preble, would take command of the squadron. Jefferson had no idea when he made the appointment how aggressive Preble had been. In his private journal, Preble wrote that "how much my feelings are lacerated [by] this supercedure at the moment of victory cannot be described and can only be felt by an officer placed in my mortifying position."

But Barron had not yet arrived in the Mediterranean and, wrote Preble, "I hope to finish the war with Tripoli first." He upped the ante, ultimately offering $110,000 for the American hostages, but since the pasha's initial demand had been for $1.69 million, no deal was worked out. He mounted another series of attacks on Tripoli on August 25, August 28, and September 28, 1804, even bringing in the *Constitution* to pound the city with broadside after broadside. But the stone and mud buildings of the capital were not easily damaged. "Such attempts served rather to encourage than intimidate the Tripolitans," wrote Dr. Cowdery, one of the *Philadelphia* prisoners, "and the Bashaw [pasha] was in high spirits on the occasion."

As a final, desperate measure, Preble recalled the *Intrepid*, the ship that had burned the *Philadelphia*, to service. He had her packed with tons of explosives and sent sailing into Tripoli harbor. Her all-volunteer crew of 13 men was supposed to dock her alongside the pasha's fortress and then make their escape just before the fireship blew up. The *Intrepid* disappeared into the fog of the harbor at 8 P.M. on September 3. At 9:47 P.M. the ship mysteriously blew up far short of its target, killing all aboard. Midshipman Robert T. Spence described the sight: "Every thing wrapped in dead silence made the explosion loud, and terrible, the fuses of the shells, burning in the air, shone like so many planets, a vast stream of fire, which appeared ascending to heaven portrayed the walls to our view." What caused the explosion has never been determined, though Preble believed, based on scant evidence, that the crew had blown up their ship rather than risk capture by the Tripolitans.

Before Preble could try anything else, Commodore Barron arrived on the scene. Thus it may be said that Preble's expedition ended not with a whimper but with a bang. News of his exploits preceded him home, and by the time Preble arrived back in America he was a national hero. He retired to Portland, Maine, where he made apple cider and built a mansion before dying three years later at age 46. He had not had long to savor the fruits of success.

The Man Who Would Be Pasha

Samuel Barron was even sicker than Preble but considerably less enterprising. He spent most of his time in the Mediterranean fighting liver disease in the naval hospital at Syracuse. Although he now commanded the largest fleet in the young Republic's history—five frigates along with seven smaller ships—he refused to commit it to battle. Instead he kept up a desultory blockade of Tripoli. The initiative now shifted to an early-day Lawrence of Arabia named William Eaton, who had arrived back in the Mediterranean with Barron in the summer of 1804.

The 40-year-old Eaton, son of a Connecticut farmer, had run away from home at 16 and, lying about his age, enlisted in the state militia to fight the British. He left the army as a sergeant, went to Dartmouth, and married a well-to-do (if homely) widow. Eventually he got a captain's commission in the new federal army and fought Indians under General Anthony Wayne in Ohio. Impetuous, headstrong, stubborn, fiery, Eaton possessed all the qualities necessary to be a first-rate leader—and a poor follower. He wound up being court-martialed for insubordination and misusing army funds. Though cleared of the charges, he left the army and the country, finding a job in 1799 as the new U.S. consul to Tunis. Eaton was one of the most undiplomatic diplomats ever; his approach to the Barbary States was more martial than that of most U.S. naval commanders, with the exception of Preble.

It was in Tunis that he met Hamid Karamanli, older brother of Yusuf Karamanli, pasha of neighboring Tripoli. The Karamanli dynasty, founded by an Ottoman cavalry commander, had ruled since 1711. The youngest son of the previous pasha, Yusuf had acceded to the throne by shooting his eldest brother to death in front of their mother. Hamid, the other brother, was out of the capital when this occurred and he prudently fled to the neighboring state of Tunis. Here he met Eaton and they began plotting together to overthrow Yusuf and end Tripoli's war against America. Finally expelled from Tunis, Eaton sailed home to the U.S. to win support for this project. He promised that if placed on the throne Hamid would not only free the hostages but "always remain the faithful friend of the United States." Although most of the military establishment thought this project was too reckless, President Jefferson and Secretary of State James Madison secretly gave Eaton the go-ahead.

This was to be the first of many times that an American president would plot to overthrow a foreign government—a dangerous game but one that the Jefferson administration found as hard to pass up as many of its successors would. Wrote Madison: "Although it does not accord with the general sentiments or views of the United States to intermiddle in the domestic contests of other countries, it cannot be unfair, in the prosecution of a just war, or the accomplishment of a reasonable peace, to turn to their advantage, the enmity and pretensions of others against a common foe."

Hamid and Eaton set up camp outside Alexandria, Egypt, and proceeded to recruit whatever mercenaries they could find among the dregs of the city. The resulting expedition was one of the motliest armies ever assembled under the Stars and Stripes. There were some 70 Christian mercenaries, one of whom claimed to be the bastard son of Marie Antoinette's chambermaid, joined by 90 Arabs (a number that would swell as the expedition progressed) and more than 100 camels. Besides Eaton, who now styled himself a general in Hamid's army and took to wearing bedouin robes, there were only nine other Americans: a midshipman from the *Argus* and seven marines commanded by First Lieutenant Presley Neville O'Bannon, a tough, resourceful Irish-American from the mountains of Virginia who was much devoted to his commander. "Wherever General Eaton leads, we will follow," said he. "If he wants us to march to hell, we'll gladly go there."

Eaton did not ask anyone to march to Hades, but his appointed destination was not much more inviting: Derna, Tripoli's second city, located 500 miles away across the desert. Eaton figured that this would be a good jumping-off point to march on the capital city of Tripoli, another 500 miles to the west. Riding an Arab stallion and waving a scimitar, Eaton led the expedition out of Egypt on March 8, 1805.

The march across the Libyan desert is not an easy one even for an army with modern equipment, as General Montgomery's British 8th Army discovered when it covered roughly the same route during World War II. Eaton did it with nothing speedier than a horse. Although the temperatures were moderate during the springtime, sandstorms pummeled the group as they moved forward at a pace of some 20 miles a day. To add to their problems, the Christians and Muslims were constantly at each other's throats, mutinies among the Arabs being an almost daily occurrence.

By early April of 1805 supplies were running out, with Eaton reporting that "our only provisions [are] a handful of rice and two biscuits a day." They were reduced to eating the rice raw, lacking water in which to boil it. At one point, the Arabs tried to storm the supply tent and were barely held off by the marines and some Greek artillerymen wielding the expedition's lone cannon. Even Hamid talked of going back, but the expedition was driven forward by Eaton's indomitable will. In his frustration Eaton raged that the Arabs "have no sense of patriotism, truth nor honor," though he did praise their "savage independence of soul."

Despite some desertions, more bedouin came into camp, so that eventually the expedition swelled to 600–700 fighting men, along with hundreds of camp followers. Finally, with the expedition out of water, the men marched over some hills on April 15, 1804, and saw before them the Gulf of Bomba sparkling in the Mediterranean sun. Here they restocked provisions from the USS *Argus* and prepared for a final push to Derna, 60 miles away. On April 25 they reached that walled city, defended by 800 of Pasha Yusuf's loyalists. Word spread that another army was marching from Tripoli to reinforce the garrison. They had no time to waste.

Eaton immediately sent an ultimatum demanding Derna's surrender. Its governor made a memorable reply: "My head or yours." The attack took place on April 27, 1804, with three newly arrived U.S. warships firing broadsides into Derna's fort. Eaton was wounded in the battle but managed to drive off the defenders. At 3:30 P.M., the Stars and Stripes was hoisted for the first time in North Africa, or indeed in any part of the Old World.

Eleven days later, Pasha Yusuf's army, 3,000 men commanded by Hassan Bey, finally arrived before Derna and placed Hamid's forces under siege. But Hamid's and Eaton's men managed to hold off two determined attacks. Victory was in sight when the frigate *Constellation* appeared, like a clap of thunder from a clear blue sky, bearing bad news: The war against Tripoli was over.

Peace had been negotiated by Tobias Lear, formerly George Washington's private secretary, now Jefferson's special envoy. The president had been losing faith in the ability of force to compel the pasha to terms. Colonel Lear and Commodore Barron argued that the U.S. should not be supporting Hamid. In their view, the pretender was weak and unreliable and would never be accepted by his own people. Moreover, Yusuf was threatening to retreat into the interior and kill his hostages if Hamid's force got too close to Tripoli. Jefferson decided to let Lear make the pasha an offer he could not refuse.

Although Lear opposed the Eaton expedition all along, he was able to negotiate a treaty only after the fall of Derna, which scared Yusuf into yielding. News of his brother's progress left the pasha "much agitated," reported Dr. Cowdery of the *Philadelphia*, and "he heartily repented for not accepting the terms of peace last offered by our country." The pasha agreed to a ransom of $60,000 for the *Philadelphia* crew—not only far below his initial demand of $1.69 million but less than the amount he had previously rejected, pre-Derna, from Preble. (A number of scholars have argued that, had Lear waited a little longer, the U.S. could have avoided paying ransom altogether.) Of the *Philadelphia's* original crew of 307, 296 were released; six had died during captivity and five had gone "Turk." (When they heard of the crew's imminent release, four of the five Americans who had sworn fealty to Islam tried to switch back, but an irate Yusuf marched them away never to be seen again. The other Americans lodged no complaint.)

Captain Hugh Campbell of the *Constitution* now had orders to take Eaton, the marines, and Hamid away from Derna. A furious Eaton had to break the news to the others; Hamid was crushed. They could not tell the rest of their followers for fear that a panic would ensue during which they would all get slaughtered. On the evening of June 12, 1805, the Americans sneaked out of Derna, rowing out to the *Constitution*, with Hamid and a small entourage. As word spread of their departure their followers melted into the countryside and Yusuf's forces reoccupied the town.

Eaton boiled over with anger at what he viewed as a sellout of his men and America's allies. He would have been angrier still had he known about a secret codicil to the treaty with Tripoli: Yusuf was allowed to keep Hamid's family for several years as hostages to his continuing good behavior. Even without knowing of this secret provision, Eaton raged, "Our too credulous ally is sacrificed to a policy, at the recollection of which, honor recoils, and humanity bleeds." It would not be the last time the U.S. would be charged with selling out putative allies, whether Hungarians in 1956 or Kurds in 1992. The only thing more dangerous than being America's enemy, it is sometimes said, is being its friend.

Commodore Barron had become too sick to exercise command; he never did order a shot fired in anger during his tenure. He turned over control of the U.S. fleet to Captain John Rodgers, who now faced a threat of war from Tunis. Rodgers resolved the situation simply enough by sailing his formidable armada—16 warships—into Tunis and giving the bey 36 hours to choose peace or war. The bey quickly capitulated and agreed to favorable terms for trade with the U.S. He even sent an ambassador to Washington, where the diplomat was lavishly entertained, including government-provided prostitutes that Secretary of State James Madison drolly justified as "appropriations for foreign intercourse."

Having tamed Tunis and treated with Tripoli, the American flotilla sailed home, leaving only three ships in the Mediterranean.

Back home, William Eaton was greeted as a hero, Tobias Lear as practically a traitor. The Barbary general roundly and shrilly denounced the treaty to anyone who would listen. Hamid, for his part, complained of "no article in my favor, no provision for me and my family, and no remuneration for the advantages I had foregone in trusting to American honor." A guilt-ridden Congress voted Hamid $2,400 plus a $200 monthly allowance, though the lawmakers reluctantly ratified the unpopular Tripoli treaty as a fait accompli. Eaton too got an award from Congress but he was not satisfied. He became a nuisance, hanging around the Capitol, buttonholing congressmen to complain about the treaty, even accusing Lear and by extension Jefferson of "treason against the character of the nation."

Having worn out his welcome in Washington City, Eaton returned to Massachusetts and served one term in the state legislature. He became mixed up with Aaron Burr's wild plot to take over the Louisiana territory, then turned against Burr and had his credibility shredded during Burr's trial for treason, where he was the main government witness (Burr was acquitted). By the time he died on June 1, 1811, Eaton was a 47-year-old invalid, drinking heavily, hobbled by gout and rheumatism, having long since faded into "obscurity and uselessness," as he himself acknowledged. The same fiery temperament that made him so adept at guerrilla warfare made him unsuited for civilian life.

1815

The naval commanders of the Barbary Wars—Bainbridge, Hull, Decatur, Porter, and the rest—went on to distinguish themselves during the War of 1812. The frigates built to defeat the corsairs performed admirably against the Royal Navy. As soon as the Treaty of Ghent was signed on December 24, 1814, ending hostilities with Britain, James Madison, now president, turned his attention to dealing with leftover business with the Barbary States. In the years since 1805, Algiers in particular had been a thorn in America's side, seizing several merchantmen and demanding more and more tribute. In 1814 the dey of Algiers had sided with Britain and declared war on America. Now it was time for a reckoning.

Congress voted a declaration of war against Algiers. Two powerful squadrons were organized, one commanded by Stephen Decatur Jr., the other by William Bainbridge. Once again, Decatur outshone his rivals. He sailed first on May 20, 1815, aboard the *Guerriere,* a 44-gun frigate. His 10 warships caught the Algerian ship *Mashuda,* 46 guns, in the Mediterranean on June 17, 1815. Decatur immediately closed in for the kill. His men-of-war fired broadside after broadside, cutting the Algerian commander in half and clearing his decks. The corsair hauled down its flag after 30 men had been killed and more than 130 wounded; 406 were taken prisoner. Only one American was killed and three wounded. Two days later Decatur captured an Algerian brig.

On June 28, Decatur's squadron sailed majestically into Algiers harbor. The commodore laid out his terms starting with the end of the tribute that America had been paying since 1796. "If you insist in receiving powder as a tribute," Decatur warned, "you must expect to receive balls with it." The cowed bey, a Turk named Omar the Aga, tried to stall for time, but Decatur told him to either accept the terms or face the consequences. He accepted. The bey released 10 American prisoners and paid the United States $10,000 in compensation. Decatur next sailed to Tunis and performed the same trick, winning $46,000 in compensation. Final stop: Tripoli, where Yusuf Karamanli was still on the throne. He agreed to pay the U.S. $25,000 and release 10 European captives (he did not have any Americans). The only American unhappy about the outcome was Commodore William Bainbridge, who grumbled, "I have been deprived of the opportunity of either fighting or negotiating."

"To Conquer Upon the Sea"

During the Barbary Wars, 35 American sailors and marines had been killed in action; 64 were wounded. There was also the pecuniary cost: Just between 1802 and 1806 the U.S. had spent $3 million fighting Tripoli. As Treasury Secretary Albert Gallatin had suggested at the time, it would have been cheaper, at least in the short term, simply to pay off the North African states. But the naval operations had established an important principle—freedom of the seas—and helped end for all time the threat to commercial shipping from the corsairs.

Following the end of the Napoleonic Wars in 1815, the European states turned their attention to expanding their empires, and the independence of the North African states was soon imperiled. In 1816, Britain and the Netherlands sent a fleet to bombard Algiers and compel a treaty promising to end "piracy" forever; 14 years later France invaded Algiers and made it part of its empire. Tunisia was conquered by France and became a protectorate in 1881. Morocco did not fall into European hands until 1912. Yusuf Karamanli, a canny survivor, hung on in Tripoli until 1835 when the Ottomans seized power directly; they were replaced by the Italian empire in 1911. Tripoli would not become a threat to international order again until the 1970s, when, now known as Libya, it became a prime sponsor of terrorism under Muammar Gadhafi.

Stephen Decatur Jr., the great hero of the Barbary Wars, suffered a melancholy end. In 1807 he sat as part of the court-martial that found Captain James Barron guilty of negligence for allowing his ship, the *Chesapeake*, to be taken without a shot by HMS *Leopard*. As a member of the Board of Naval Commissioners, Decatur resisted Barron's efforts to be reinstated in the service. An exchange of increasingly vituperative letters followed. Barron challenged Decatur to a duel; Decatur accepted the challenge. They met at Bladensburg, Maryland, on the damp, cold morning of March 22, 1820. It was pistols at eight paces. The two commodores fired simultaneously. Both men were wounded but only Decatur died. He was just 41. His last words, reported a witness, were "that he did not so much regret his death itself, as he deplored the manner of it; had it found him on the quarter-deck, it would have been welcome."

Though Decatur died young, he left an enduring legacy—and not only in the 20 towns named after him. With Decatur and a handful of others in the lead, the United States had taken its first uncertain steps toward becoming the world's policeman, the protector of commercial shipping, and upholder of international laws against piracy and other transgressions. In the nineteenth century, America could be no more than a junior partner to the Royal Navy, but the seeds of American power had been sown. They would be reaped in the centuries ahead. As Archibald Robbins, an American sailor shipwrecked in Africa in 1815, later wrote: "The mention of Tripoli calls up the proud recollection of the infancy of the American Navy. It was upon the coast of that country, that Americans began to learn how to conquer upon the sea."

2

"Butcher and Bolt"

From the Marquesas, 1813, to China, 1859

The American conquest of the seas was a slow and unsteady process, with some odd twists along the way. One of the oddest occurred in 1813 when a representative of the United States tried to adopt into the "great American family" a South Seas island full of cannibals. The story of how this came about is well worth recounting in some detail, as it represents the pattern of many of America's expeditions abroad in the nineteenth century.

The instigator of this colonial plot was Captain David Porter of the U.S. Navy, one of "Preble's Boys," a fine fighting officer whose audacity and independence sometimes bordered on foolhardiness. The son of a naval captain, he had gone to sea at 16 on a merchantman in 1796, joining the U.S. Navy two years later as a midshipman. He was serving under Captain Thomas Truxton on the *Constellation* when it captured the French frigate *L'Insurgente* during the quasi-war with France. Tradition has it that Midshipman Porter was one of only 13 Americans sent to take charge of the battered ship. For three white-knuckle days, this small prize crew had to steer *L'Insurgente* toward port while preventing a mutiny among 173 surly prisoners. As a reward for successfully completing this perilous assignment, Porter was promoted to lieutenant at 19.

He then shipped out as second-in-command of the *Experiment*, a shallow-draft schooner sent to cruise the Caribbean. On New Year's Day of 1800, the *Experiment* was anchored off Haiti when it was attacked by hundreds of pirates in 10 barges. The unnerved skipper wanted to surrender. Porter, never one to fear a charge of insubordination, pushed him aside and directed a vigorous defense that wound up repelling the pirates' attack.

In 1801 he joined the U.S. expedition against the Barbary States, where he covered himself with more glory, and was twice wounded, before languishing in Tripolitan captivity along with the rest of the *Philadelphia*'s crew. The officers, unlike the men, did not have to bust rocks, and he put his 18 months of enforced leisure to good use, furthering his education beyond the nautical areas in which he was already expert. After his return to America, Porter, by now a master-commandant, was given command of the naval station at New Orleans, where he took stern measures to stamp out the banditti of the sea who called the area home. Here he and his wife also adopted an eight-year-old boy named David Glasgow Farragut, whose mother had died.

In 1811 Porter received a captain's commission and command of the 32-gun frigate *Essex*. When the United States declared war on Great Britain the following year because of British harassment of American trade and impressment of American seamen, Porter's primary mission was commerce raiding. During his second cruise, which took him down to Brazil, he decided on his own initiative to swing around Cape Horn, the tip of South America, making his ship the first U.S. man-of-war to reach the Pacific Ocean. Around the Galapagos Islands he captured so many British whalers that he nearly wiped out Britain's whaling industry in those waters. English critics had a field day denouncing Porter, who had once fought the Barbary pirates, for engaging in conduct that they saw as piratical.

By October 1813, the *Essex* had been long at sea and badly needed retrofitting. But Porter was afraid to put into any South American port for fear of being set upon by a British squadron. Lacking a U.S. base in the area, he decided to make the 2,500-mile journey from the Galapagos to the Marquesas, a chain of 14 volcanic islands 850 miles northeast of Tahiti. Here Porter hoped to find "some relaxation and amusement" for his men. He was to get more than he bargained for.

On October 25, 1813, the *Essex* weighed anchor at Nukahiva, an island of 131 square miles with the best harbor in the Marquesas chain, which Porter incongruously dubbed Massachusetts Bay. Here the *Essex* was joined by five of the ships that she had captured, including one christened *Essex Junior*. Herman Melville, who would enter the same horseshoe-shaped harbor three decades later, remarked that "it presented the appearance of a vast natural amphitheater in decay, and overgrown with vines, the deep glens that furrowed its sides appearing like enormous fissures caused by the ravages of time." The bay was

MAP 2.1   Philippines and the Pacific, circa 1900

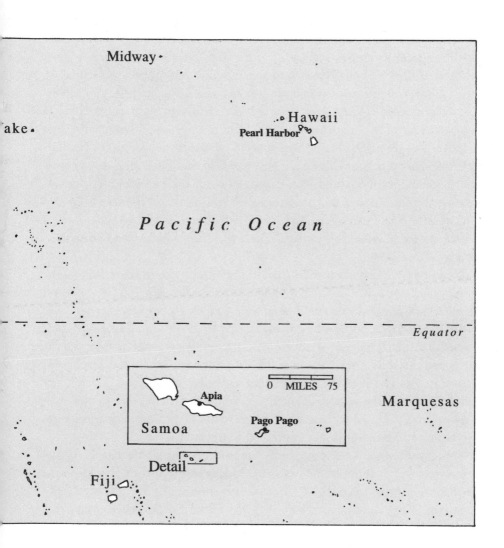

Midway·

ake·

.·◦ Hawaii
Pearl Harbor◦◦
◦

Pacific   Ocean

— —
Equator

0   MILES   75

Apia

Samoa   Pago Pago   Marquesas

Detail

Fiji

the entrance to a land of breadfruit and coconuts, sandalwood and palms—and tens of thousands of Polynesians split into numerous tribes and clans living in valleys separated by 3,000- to 5,000-foot mountain peaks.

The sailors, after so long at sea, devoured the nearly naked Marquesan women with their eyes. Melville would later marvel at "their extreme youth, the light clear brown of their complexions, their delicate features, and inexpressibly graceful figures, their softly moulded limbs"—and, perhaps most welcome of all, their complete lack of sexual inhibitions and venereal diseases. Before long the women swarmed all over the *Essex* and fell into the sailors' arms. The copper-colored men were a less comforting sight, as they stood around the bay clutching massive war-clubs and spears. Wearing only loin clothes and capes made of bark, they sported tattoos from head to toe (including stripes on their faces), feathered headbands, tufts of hair tied around their waists, ankles, and loins, and whale teeth stuck in their earlobes. Porter was astonished to discover as well a rum-soaked, loin-clothed Englishman named Wilson who had been there "for many years" and "had become in every respect, except in colour, an Indian." This expatriate assumed the indispensable role of interpreter.

Gattanewa, the septuagenarian chief of the Taaehs, the tribe controlling the harbor where the *Essex* alighted, took a boat out to the American ship. Porter escorted him around and fired a gun in hopes of impressing him, but Gattanewa, tipsy on an alcoholic drink derived from the kava root, only "complained that it hurt his ears." Porter asked for permission to set up camp on the beach, and the chief agreed, but in return he demanded help in the Taaehs' war against an inland tribe called the Happahs. Porter was trapped: He did not want to get into the middle of a tribal conflict, but he needed Gattanewa's cooperation. What to do? He sent a message to the Happahs offering peace but threatening to make war if they continued to fight the Taaehs.

Not long after the Americans landed and set up camp on the beach, the situation spun out of control. The warlike Happahs renewed their attacks on the Taaehs, calling the Americans "cowards" and threatening to steal their sails. The natives were not impressed by test firings of the visitors' *bouhies* (muskets), so Porter sent Lieutenant John Downes with 40 men and a six-pound cannon into the hills to convince the Happahs "of the folly of resisting our fire arms with slings and spears." Downes's contingent stumbled back later that day, "overcome with . . . fatigue." The small American expedition had confronted some 3,000 to 4,000 Happahs entrenched in a mountain fortress. During the attack Downes was hit with a stone in the stomach and another man took a spear in the neck, but they did manage to take the redoubt, killing five Happahs in the process.

The Americans' Taaeh allies clubbed to death the wounded Happahs, but did not eat them, much to the surprise of Porter, who had heard (correctly) that they were cannibals. They did, however, put their dead enemies' bones to good use by converting them into necklaces and fan handles.

Over the next couple of days, the chiefs of the Happahs and most of the other island tribes arrived to sue for peace. The Americans now turned their attention to building a small village dubbed Madisonville, complete with a fort mounting four guns. When the Stars and Stripes was hoisted over Fort Madison on November 19, 1813, to the accompaniment of a 17-gun salute, Porter informed the natives that they had been admitted "into the great American family, whose pure republican policy approaches so near their own." President James Madison was proclaimed to be their chief, and Britain their enemy. Having asserted a U.S. claim to the islands "founded on priority of discovery, conquest, and possession," Porter buried a flowery proclamation to that effect for future European visitors to find. It was not entirely a romantic gesture. He hoped that the islands would provide a Pacific base of operations for the American navy—an aspiration that was decades ahead of its time.

Although there was work to do, the captain gave his men plenty of opportunity for recreation. There was much feasting, and not only on the abundant pork and breadfruit. "Virtue among them, in the light which we view it, was unknown," Porter wrote of the islanders. "With the common sailors and their girls, all was helter skelter, and promiscuous intercourse, every girl the wife of every man in the mess, and frequently of every man in the ship."

Soon there was more trouble in this Polynesian paradise. The Typees, a more distant tribe renowned for their ferocity (later made famous by Melville's eponymous novel), declared war on the Americans' new allies, the Happahs and Taaehs. The Typees mocked the Americans as "white lizards, mere dirt" and "the posteriors and privates of the Taaehs." "Finding that it was absolutely necessary to bring the Typees to terms, or endanger our good understanding with the other tribes," Porter organized an expedition to the Typee beaches. Some 35 Americans from the *Essex Jr.* landed along with 5,000 Happah and Taaeh warriors in war canoes. The landing was uncontested; their advance was not.

"We entered the bushes, and were at every instant assailed by spears and stones, which came from different parties of the enemy in ambuscade," Porter wrote. "We could hear the snapping of the slings, the whistling of the stones, the spears came quivering by us, but we could not perceive from whom they came." They kept advancing, meeting more and more resistance, until they found the way blocked by a forbidding Typee fortress with seven-foot walls. Porter was low on ammunition, his native allies deserted him, and four of his men were wounded, including Downes, whose leg was shattered by a stone.

There was no choice but to retreat. "We returned to the beach much fatigued and harassed with marching and fighting," Porter wrote, and then they sailed back to Madisonville.

When word spread that the white men had been bested in battle, the Happahs and Taaehs began to turn on their no-longer-invincible allies. Porter feared that his tiny settlement might be overrun and his men massacred. "I had now no alternative, but to prove our superiority by a successful attack upon the Typees," the captain decided. Porter personally organized and led 200 of his men in an inland advance on the Typees' valley designed to circumvent the fortifications that had foiled the first attack from the beach.

The Americans made a treacherous nighttime march to the top of a ridge above the Typee valley. Since his men were "much fatigued" and he did not want to chance a treacherous descent in the dark, Porter put off an attack until daylight. The sailors spent a miserable night on the mountain, drenched by a torrential rainfall and buffeted by shrieking winds. The next morning, the men found that their ammunition was damp, so the attack was delayed for another day. In the meantime, Porter ordered a musket volley fired as a warning to the Typees "to remove their women and children, their hogs, and most valuable effects."

At dawn on November 30, 1813, the Americans, accompanied by Taaeh allies, made the almost vertical descent down a narrow path into the Typees' valley, a placid enclave nine miles long and three miles across, dotted with coconut and breadfruit trees. Before long, "the spears and stones were flying from the bush in every direction." The captain sent a message to the Typees that unless they ceased hostilities at once their villages would be burned. This message being ignored, the sailors marched the length of the valley, fighting every inch of the way, their progress marked by "a long line of smoking ruins." By day's end the battle was over. The Americans had won. Leaving behind "a scene of desolation and horror," Porter and his men returned to Madisonville. Here they received Typee emissaries who came calling with countless hogs as a peace offering.

Porter claimed he took no joy in the blood his men had shed among a "happy and heroic people," but he later reacted indignantly to the charge made in an English magazine that he was guilty of "wantonly murdering unoffending savages." Replied the captain:

> Many may censure my conduct as wanton and unjust. . . . But let such reflect a moment on our peculiar situation—a handful of men residing among numerous warlike tribes, liable every moment to be attacked by them and all cut off; our only hopes of safety was in convincing them of our great superiority over them,

and from what we have already seen, we must either attack them or be attacked. . . . Wars are not always just, and are rarely free from excesses—my conscience acquits me of any injustice, and no excesses were committed, but what the Typees had it in their power to stop by ceasing hostilities.

It was not a justification likely to convince many Typees.

By December 9, 1813, the *Essex* had been retrofitted and stuffed with all the hogs, coconuts and bananas it could carry, and was ready to make sail. But the sailors were not happy about leaving their girlfriends behind. The captain put down an incipient mutiny by informing his crew that, should they resist orders, "I would without hesitation put a match to the magazine, and blow them all to eternity." He never had to make good his bluff. After one troublemaker jumped ship, the remaining crew members subsided and the *Essex* sailed for South America on December 13. To hold the fort, they left behind Marine Lieutenant James Gamble, 2 midshipmen, 19 sailors, and 6 prisoners, including some British sailors from captured vessels. Also left behind were four captured British merchant ships.

All went well, more or less, until the following spring, when the British seamen mutinied. On May 7, 1814, the British mutineers took over the merchant ship *Seringapatam*. As they were sailing away, they wounded Lieutenant Gamble in the foot, and set him and four loyal men adrift in a small boat. At the same time the British beachcomber Wilson was stirring up the Taaehs by informing them that Opotee (Porter) was not coming back. On May 9, a 16-year-old midshipman and three sailors were set upon and butchered on the beach. Two other sailors were wounded in the attack but escaped. Gamble, already wounded in the foot and feverish, was left alone on the merchantman *Sir Andrew Hammond* when two boatloads of Taaehs in war canoes approached. Since all the guns were already loaded, he was able to hobble from one to the next, firing them as fast as possible, and forcing back the attack.

The next morning Gamble and the seven remaining Americans, most ill or wounded, piloted the leaky *Hammond* out to sea. Eventually they reached the Sandwich Islands (Hawaii) and were picked up by a British man-of-war and imprisoned. They finally reached New York in 1815.

Porter fared little better. In March 1814, the *Essex* was attacked by two British warships off Chile. Porter made a desperate fight of it and did not surrender until the decks ran red with blood, three-fifths of the crew being killed or wounded. He was held to have acquitted himself honorably and came home a hero. The *Essex* ended its days as a British prison hulk anchored off the Irish coast.

As for the Marquesas, the State Department simply ignored Porter's attempt to annex them—not surprisingly, for the news of this first overseas conquest arrived while the British were burning Washington. In 1842, when France added the islands to her empire (wherein they remain today, as part of French Polynesia), Washington did not object. The U.S. would not have a Pacific island of its own until the acquisition of Midway twenty-five years later.

"Butcher and Bolt"

The *Essex's* encounter with the tribes of Nukahiva makes a fitting start to a discussion of U.S. small wars in the nineteenth century. Indeed it would serve as a template for many of America's encounters with the world: Yankees arrive with the best of intentions, but soon find themselves sucked into the vortex of war. During the nineteenth century this pattern would repeat itself, from the Falklands to Formosa, from Sumatra to Samoa, from China to Chile. After killing some natives, the Americans seldom stayed long; nor did they usually involve themselves much in local politics. What did they achieve? Sometimes a trade treaty; at other times, simply the satisfaction of having instilled fear of the Stars and Stripes.

The U.S. strategy, if that is the right word for such a haphazard enterprise, might best be characterized as "butcher and bolt"—a bit of slang popular in Britain's Indian Army to describe punitive expeditions against troublemaking tribes, expeditions designed not to occupy territory but to "learn 'em a lesson." Imperialistic officers such as David Porter might be eager to annex territory, but Washington was having none of it, at least not until the latter half of the nineteenth century, when America slowly gained an overseas empire, beginning with the peaceful acquisition of Alaska and Midway Island in 1867 (along with some scattered guano islands) and culminating in a bloody war in the Philippines in 1899. For most of the 1800s Americans' land hunger was sated on the Western frontier.

But even if the U.S. eschewed overseas colonialism, that hardly means the country was isolationist, as the popular myth has it. Any nation that routinely sends warships thousands of miles from home is not exactly cut off from the world. Japan, which was truly isolationist until it was opened in 1854 by an American naval expedition, permitted hardly any contact at all between its citizens and foreign "barbarians." Enterprising Yankee sea captains, by contrast, visited virtually every corner of the globe. And where commercial interests advanced, armed forces were seldom far behind. The flag usually follows trade, not the other way around.

Far from isolationist, American foreign policy in the nineteenth century can best be described as unilateralist, meaning that America usually acted without benefit of formal allies to defend its interests. An in-depth consideration of U.S. foreign policy lies outside the scope of this volume, but suffice it to say that America's early foreign policy was shaped by Washington's farewell address ("steer clear of permanent alliances"), Jefferson's first inaugural address (no "entangling alliances"), and the Monroe Doctrine, a not-always-successful attempt to post a Keep Out sign on the Western Hemisphere. These traditions kept the U.S. from intervening militarily in Europe until 1917, but it was a different matter when it came to the rest of the world. Throughout the nineteenth century, American influence kept expanding abroad, especially in the Pacific and Caribbean.

Much of the growing American role overseas needed no guidance from Washington. It was a result of the restless Yankees' inexorable progress across the North American continent and beyond, a process dubbed "manifest destiny" by journalist John O'Sullivan in 1839. Many of the obstacles in the path of American expansion were summarily knocked aside by military might. The army had the primary job of fighting the Indians, in wars that would drag on until 1890. The army, navy, and marines all pitched in to defeat Mexico in 1846–48 and Spain in 1898. America's small wars abroad were mostly the province of the navy and Marine Corps, and since the marines remained a tiny force throughout the nineteenth century (fewer than 3,000 men until 1896, the Civil War years excepted), the central role in practice was assigned to the U.S. Navy.

The Naval Aristocracy

To understand how America became enmeshed in so many conflicts it helps to understand the era's naval officers. Captain Thomas Truxton wrote that they must be "young men of principle, good education, high sense of honor, manly deportment, prudence, and of respectable connections." Like their cousins in the Royal Navy, many of whose traditions they appropriated, they were largely recruited from the upper- and upper-middle classes (only about 1 percent rose from the ranks); usually lacked formal education, at least until the establishment of the Naval Academy in 1845; trained at sea from boyhood; sometimes acquired a fair amount of riches through prize money; and often married "well" (that is, to wealthy women). The navy inculcated in its officers such putatively un-American traits as obedience to orders and reverence for tradition, as well as more common Yankee virtues such as boldness and pluck. The results were not to the liking of some of their more egalitarian countrymen. Melville complained in the 1840s that "there still lingers on American men-of-war all the stilted etiquette and childish parade of the old-fashioned Spanish court of Madrid."

The navy's way of doing things created a starched, stiff-necked officer corps—imperious, hot-blooded, quick to take offense, and above all brave, sometimes suicidally so. Their ethos was perfectly exemplified by Admiral David Glasgow Farragut's celebrated cry during the 1864 attack on Mobile Bay: "Damn the torpedoes! Full speed ahead." Officers seldom backed down from a challenge, whether from a brother officer (which would result in a duel) or from "natives" (which would result in a punitive expedition). Their code of conduct as an "officer and a gentleman" would not permit any less. This phrase, though still in use, has a musty ring to modern ears, since such rigid notions of manliness and honor have all but died out in the West, except, oddly enough, among young inner-city men who are liable to resort to violence if they feel "dissed." In prior centuries this code of honor was universal among aristocrats, and American naval officers—dubbed a "naval aristocracy" by historian Peter Karsten—were no different.

The enlisted men of the navy, by contrast, were anything but aristocratic. They were closer to the "scum of the earth," as Wellington affectionately described the British "common soldiers" who defeated Napoleon. Unlike the Royal Navy, the U.S. Navy did not resort to impressment to man its ships. All its sailors were volunteers. Yet the pay and working conditions were hardly inviting to most landsmen. So who would sign up under those circumstances? The jack-tars were for the most part uneducated and impoverished, the dregs of the waterfront, many of them sailors who could not find civilian berths. More than half were foreign-born and most of those were not U.S. citizens. Roughly 14 to 18 percent were black freemen—a considerably higher proportion than in the country as a whole (2.5 percent).

One of the marines' main jobs aboard ship was to protect "officer country" from the lower deck rabble; serving in landing parties was a secondary mission the marines acquired as the century progressed. Corporal punishment was a hallmark of shipboard life until flogging was finally outlawed in 1850, much to the regret of old sea dogs. The official grog ration was abolished in 1862, though wine was still allowed in the officers' mess until 1914, but regardless of regulations, seamen (like soldiers) remained a hard-drinking lot. Gambling and whoring were other prime diversions for bluejackets.

To simplify somewhat, the nineteenth-century navy may be described as aristocratic officers spoiling for a fight, leading equally combative, often tipsy enlisted men who were on the fringes of society and, to get to the essence of the matter, would not be missed overmuch if a few died in action. Such men were constantly dispatched by the navy to the far corners of the globe to deal with chaotic situations in politically unstable lands populated by people with little understanding of Western notions such as private property and contracts. Far from home, with no way of communicating in less than a few months' time with their superiors back in Washington, they had almost complete autonomy of action. Is it any wonder, then, that Americans became embroiled in so many small wars abroad? The only wonder, really, is that there were not more.

Pirates of the Caribbean

After the Barbary pirates had been stamped out, the navy next turned its attention to piracy closer to home. The West Indies had long been a haven of privateers and buccaneers stretching back to the sixteenth and seventeenth centuries, when Francis Drake, William Kidd, and Edward "Blackbeard" Teach had preyed on Spanish galleons. Attacks on American merchant ships in the region by French privateers had led to an undeclared war between the U.S. and France from 1798 to 1800. In the 1810s piracy again became a problem in the Caribbean, largely as a result of the revolutions against Spain that broke out in Latin America. The South American rebels gave letters of marque—legal authority for privateers—to all comers interested in intercepting Spanish shipping; many were little more than pirates and preyed on American merchantmen. Spain had little ability to protect U.S. ships—and little interest, either, since many American merchants were trading with breakaway republics that the Spanish navy was trying to blockade.

Thus pirates operated with virtual impunity in the countless coves of Puerto Rico and Cuba, both Spanish colonies. Their vessels ranged from rowboats to large sailing ships, some flying the famous Jolly Roger skull-and-crossbones flag, others under a plain blood-red banner. "There is not a fisherman who is not a pirate, nor a canoe that is not a pirate vessel in miniature," wrote Lieutenant Matthew C. Perry.

By one estimate, more than 3,000 acts of piracy were committed between 1815 and 1823 in the West Indies, an area that, after Britain, was America's biggest trading partner. Many were quite bloody. The crew of one American merchant ship seized in the harbor of Matanzas, Cuba, suffered a particularly gruesome fate: The pirates "murdered all the crew of the brig, opened their entrails, hanged them by the ribs to the masts, and afterwards set fire to the vessel and all were consumed!" Such incidents so close to the United States led to soaring maritime insurance rates and pressure on Washington to respond.

In 1822, President James Monroe created the navy's West India Squadron to work alongside the Royal Navy in suppressing piracy. Fourteen ships—ranging in size from the 36-gun frigates *Congress* and *Macedonian* to specially built 12-gun schooners and gunboats—with 1,300 sailors and marines were dispatched under the command of Captain James Biddle, a wealthy Philadelphian. The squadron, operating out of Thompson's Island (now known as Key West), vigorously pursued and often fought pirate vessels.

It was difficult, dangerous work. The *Shark*, a schooner commanded by Matthew Perry, ran down one outlaw ship off the north coast of Cuba. The American man-of-war could not get close enough to shore to attack the pirates, so the bluejackets took to small boats to board the outlaw vessel. As the Americans grappled over the side with muskets, pikes, and knives, the pirates rushed forward to meet them and, in the words of a midshipman, "a desperate hand-to-hand combat ensued." The deck rang with the clash of steel, an occasional gunshot, and the bestial grunts of men fighting for their lives. The pirates gradually gave way, with many jumping overboard to escape. The Americans pursued them relentlessly, killing some in the water. "In silence they sunk, their throats gurgling the water which was deeply crimsoned with the blood . . ." the midshipman reported. "But few escaped; and destroying what we could not preserve, we gathered our booty, and bore our prize away in triumph."

It was not just pirates who were killed. On November 9, 1822, the *Alligator*, another schooner, discovered a cove in Cuba with five captured merchantmen, three pirate ships, and some 100 pirates. Lieutenant William H. Allen, the skipper, led 40 men in small boats to attack the cutthroats. In the ensuing melee, Allen took a musket ball in the chest. His death sparked widespread anger across the United States.

The West India Squadron's most effective foe, however, turned out to be not a pirate's sword but a mosquito's bite. The link between these pesky insects and yellow fever and malaria was not discovered until the end of the century; until then, it was commonly believed that these tropical diseases were transmitted by night air, filth, and mysterious vapors. Given the primitive state of medicine, these epidemics had a devastating impact. Fully one-third of the 300-man crew of the *Macedonian*, Commodore Biddle's flagship, was killed by "yellow jack" (yellow fever) during the oppressively hot summer of 1822. Biddle was forced to return north.

Chosen to replace him was David Porter, conqueror of the Marquesas, terror of British whalers, former prisoner of the Tripolitans. He was not an ideal choice for a job that would require some diplomatic finesse in dealing with the

Spanish officials who ran Puerto Rico and Cuba. Tact had never been Porter's strong suit. Once, when he was a young midshipman, a hard-drinking, foul-tempered lieutenant bawled him out for some petty infraction, and then slapped him to drive the point home. Porter responded by knocking down his senior with one punch. A few years later, a Baltimore tavernkeeper with an aversion to naval officers ordered Porter out of his establishment. Porter refused to leave until he had finished his drink. Enraged and drunk, the proprietor knocked him down and was preparing to deliver another blow when Porter drew his dirk (a short sword) and buried it in his assailant's chest, killing him on the spot. And then there was the time a drunken English sailor approached Porter's ship, anchored in Malta, and insulted the American flag. Porter had the sailor hauled aboard and flogged, almost setting off a war with Great Britain.

The passage of years might have been expected to dim Porter's fires. Not so. By the time he received the call to return to the Caribbean, he was 42 years old and comfortably ensconced in Washington as a gentleman farmer and one of three members of the Board of Navy Commissioners. (This was the highest authority in the navy after the secretary, performing many of the functions that would be given to the chief of naval operations in 1915.) As he slouched into middle age, he had become a bit of a dandy, sporting a monocle, gilt buttons, and a gold-headed cane. Unfortunately his expensive lifestyle, growing family, and lack of financial acumen left his bank account nearly empty. Hoping to reduce his expenses and escape his creditors, Porter volunteered to go to sea again.

The commodore assembled a 16-ship squadron with some unusual features. He acquired five 20-oared barges that could pursue pirates into coastal waters, as well as the *Sea Gull*, the first steam-powered warship ever to go into battle. This Mosquito Fleet (as it came to be called) was needed, Porter explained, to root out "the freebooters and murderers" in their "haunts . . . among the roaring of breakers and the screams of sea-birds." That was precisely where Porter's eager captains went. In just six weeks nearly all the larger pirate craft in the Caribbean were either captured or driven into hiding. But it was impossible to patrol every inlet, every cove, every lagoon on every island, especially since the Americans were receiving scant cooperation from Spanish authorities.

Porter tried to enlist the help of Puerto Rico's governor, but when he sent the USS *Fox* into San Juan harbor a shore battery fired on the American ship, killing its skipper. Porter reacted with, for him, uncharacteristic restraint; he chose to accept the governor's apology. The next time he would not be so accommodating—much to his subsequent regret.

On October 26, 1824, Lieutenant Charles T. Platt, commanding the three-gun schooner *Beagle*, received word that a warehouse in St. Thomas, one of the

Virgin Islands, had been looted of $5,000 worth of goods. The warehouse belonged to the American vice-consul, and he informed Platt that the robbers had most likely come from Foxardo (now Fajardo), a small town on the eastern tip of Puerto Rico, just 40 miles away. Platt set sail at once. Not wanting to alarm the locals, Platt and another officer changed into civilian clothes before landing. They walked into the village of Foxardo where they met with the local *alcalde* (mayor), who denounced Platt himself as a "damned pirate" and threw him and his colleague in jail. Before long, they were released, and allowed to return to their ship amid the laughter and hisses of the locals.

"Make sail at once for Foxardo!" commanded the quick-tempered Porter when he heard of this "outrage." The commodore determined to exact a personal apology from the *alcalde* that, he hoped, would serve as an object lesson for other island officials. Just after sunrise on November 14, 1824, three ships of the Mosquito Fleet anchored off Foxardo. Porter personally led some 200 men in long boats to shore. The Spaniards fled before them, and Porter's men spiked two port guns. The heavily armed landing party, bristling with "muskets, bayonets, pistols, cutlasses and boarding pikes," marched up the dusty road to the village, the commodore striding in front accompanied by a drummer beating step. Porter sent a message to the *alcalde* demanding his immediate apology "for outrages heaped upon an American officer" and warning that "if any resistance is made, the total destruction of Foxardo will be the certain and immediate consequence." Within 15 minutes, the cowed local officials proffered the demanded apology and the landing party sailed away.

Porter thought he had ably defended "national honor," but President James Monroe and his secretary of state, John Quincy Adams, were not happy when they found out about this violation of Spanish sovereignty. Coming soon after the proclamation of the Monroe Doctrine, which pledged that America would not interfere with Europe's existing possessions in the New World as long as no more were acquired, Porter's actions were a distinct embarrassment to the administration. He was relieved of command, and a court of inquiry was convened.

Porter was livid. He pointed out, correctly, that General Andrew Jackson had been cheered, not jeered, when in 1818 he had invaded Spanish Florida and occupied several forts on his own initiative. The irate commodore compounded his difficulties by publicly and unwisely lashing out against the president and secretary of the navy. This led the navy to convene a court-martial chaired by Captain James Barron—the very same officer who had been convicted of negligence in the *Chesapeake-Leopard* affair 13 years before by a court-martial that had included David Porter!

After a five-week trial in the sweltering summer of 1825, Porter was found guilty of disobedience of orders and insubordination. Even though he received only a six-month suspension with full pay, the commodore's pride was lacerated. In a fit of pique, he renounced his American commission, left his wife behind, and accepted an offer to start a navy for newly independent Mexico. After this short-lived, unhappy assignment, Porter wheedled a job out of newly elected President Andrew Jackson: U.S. envoy to Constantinople. Here the 63-year-old commodore died in 1843, but he would continue to exercise influence on the American navy long after his death: His adopted son, David Glasgow Farragut (who as a 12-year-old midshipman had been part of the Marquesas landing), would become the navy's first admiral. Porter's natural son, David Dixon Porter, would succeed Farragut as the navy's senior officer in 1870 upon his adopted brother's death. And Theodore Roosevelt, preeminent chronicler of the War of 1812, would be inspired by Porter's exploits.

As for the pirates of the Caribbean, their days were numbered when, in 1825, the Spanish governors of Cuba and Puerto Rico finally agreed to cooperate in American suppression efforts. The Spaniards had gotten upset when the pirates had turned from looting foreign ships to banditry on land. Dozens of cutthroats were subsequently hanged. By 1826, the new commander of the West India Squadron could report, "Depredations on our commerce are fortunately unheard of where they were formerly so frequent." Much of the credit for this triumph goes to the U.S. Navy. American records indicate that the Royal Navy captured 13 pirate vessels with 300 men; the U.S. Navy is credited with seizing 80 vessels with 1,300 men. Anglo-American action had ended more than three centuries of piracy in the West Indies.

Falkland Islands

The West India Squadron was only one of five the navy deployed abroad in the 1820s. None was particularly powerful, certainly not to rival the Royal Navy, but the U.S. fleet did show the flag and attempt to protect Americans abroad. The Mediterranean Squadron, a remnant of the Barbary Wars, combated piracy growing out of the Greek War of Independence. The Pacific Squadron sent a warship to the Sandwich Islands (Hawaii) in 1826 and another to Tahiti, while attempting with limited success to protect American merchantmen from both Spanish and Latin American privateers preying on neutral shipping. The Africa Squadron tried to suppress the slave trade.

The Brazil (or South Atlantic) Squadron had its hands full with the first Falkland Islands crisis. Argentina, which seceded from Spain in 1810 (and was formally known as the United Provinces of La Plata), claimed sovereignty over these islands; so did Britain. The Argentine governor, Louis Vernet, asserted his authority by ordering foreigners to stop hunting whales or seals in his domain, which Americans had been doing for years, depleting the herds in the process. In an attempt to enforce his edict, Vernet seized three U.S. schooners in 1831. Buenos Aires refused to comply with the indignant demands of the U.S. consul to return the fishing vessels, so Master Commandant Silas Duncan sailed his 18-gun sloop, USS *Lexington,* to the islands "to render justice to our citizens." He seized property taken from the American ships, released the American seamen, spiked the fort's cannon, captured a number of Argentine colonists, and posted a decree warning that anyone interfering with American fishing rights would be considered a pirate.

The Argentines were so furious by this incursion into their "colony" that they broke diplomatic relations with Washington. A few years before, President John Quincy Adams, a veteran diplomat, cultivated and somewhat prissy, might have been furious too. But the pugnacious and earthy Andrew Jackson, the backwoods general who now occupied the White House, was not perturbed. He heartily approved of Duncan's conduct in defending American interests.

The dispute ended in 1833 when a landing party of Royal Marines raised the Union Jack over the Falklands, a task facilitated by Duncan's actions in weakening the Argentine hold over the islands. President Jackson did not object to this violation of the Monroe Doctrine; these flyspeck islands in the South Atlantic were hardly worth a crisis with London. The U.S. had no more trouble with the Falklands for two decades. In 1854, however, the Royal Navy arrested two American merchant captains in another dispute over seal-hunting rights. The American warship *Germantown* appeared and threatened to bombard the British courthouse where the Americans were imprisoned, whereupon the British authorities let the merchant captains off with a light fine. This was the second Falklands crisis—and the last until 1982.

Pepper and Pirates

The biggest U.S. small war of the 1830s occurred in far away Sumatra, now part of Indonesia. Starting in 1788, merchants from Salem, Massachusetts, had established a flourishing pepper trade with the Sumatrans, trading either cheap trinkets or opium for the popular spice. There were millions of dollars in profits to be made—but also big risks in dealing with the natives. "The people," writes one descendent of the Salem pepper traders, "were tricky, aggressive and brutal but with a good deal of real courage." No doubt the Sumatrans thought the same about the Americans.

Occasionally a merchant ship would let down its guard and be swarmed by Sumatran pirates, who would kill the crew and plunder the vessel. That was the fate suffered by a U.S. merchantman inaptly named *Friendship*, which in 1831 anchored off Quallah Battoo (now Kuala Batu), a village on the northwest coast of Sumatra that was ostensibly ruled by the sultan of Acheen but was in reality autonomous. On February 7 the first officer and two seamen were killed, three others wounded. A handful of crew members, including Captain Charles M. Endicott, who happened to be ashore at the time, escaped the pirates and sought assistance from three other U.S. merchantmen anchored 25 miles away at the port of Muckie (now Muki). After a short gun battle, the sailors recovered the *Friendship* but found its decks bloodstained and its holds ransacked. The property loss, including stolen opium, was valued at over $40,000. None of the pirates was captured, but Endicott warned the rajahs who ran the village, "Within the space of twelve months, a big ship from the United States would most assuredly visit Quallah Battoo and punish the aggressors."

Which is just what happened. The *Friendship*'s owners, who included Senator Nathaniel Silsbee of Massachusetts, persuaded President Andrew Jackson to divert the 44-gun frigate *Potomac*, already scheduled to visit China, to make a stop in Sumatra first. At 2:00 P.M. on February 5, 1832, the *Potomac*, disguised as a Dutch merchant ship, dropped anchor off Quallah Battoo. A couple of hours later, seven officers pretending to be civilian sailors eager to buy pepper were sent in a whaleboat to scout the shoreline. They discovered a town of some 4,000 people defended by a few ramshackle forts. Captain Jack Downes, a bellicose sort who had served as Porter's first "luff" (lieutenant) during the mission to the Marquesas, had heard in Cape Town, South Africa, that the Sumatrans were not to be trusted. So he decided to ignore the first part of his orders—to investigate Captain Endicott's account and, if it was found to be accurate, "demand . . . restitution." Only if the natives "delayed beyond a reasonable time" was he authorized to inflict "ample punishment" on them. Downes decided to skip straight to the punishment.

At 4:15 the next morning, 282 sailors and marines splashed through the surf and advanced on the rajahs' forts under cover of the *Potomac*'s guns. The Sumatrans "raised their war-whoop, and resisted most manfully, fighting with spears, sabres, and muskets," wrote the *Potomac*'s schoolmaster, but the "resistance of the natives was in vain." Three of the forts fell in short order, and the town was set ablaze. This, the first U.S. battle in Asia, left two Americans dead and eleven wounded. The next day, Downes moved the *Potomac* closer to shore and unleashed several broadsides at the remaining fort. The Sumatrans had had enough. A delegation of rajahs rowed out to the *Potomac* and promised they would do no more harm to Americans in the future, though they still refused to pay any restitution. Downes, convinced he could achieve nothing more, sailed away, leaving an estimated 100 Sumatran corpses in his wake.

Back home, with partisan feelings running high and a presidential campaign underway, his actions elicited considerable criticism. Whig opponents of the Andrew Jackson administration, already smarting over the veto of a bill chartering the Second Bank of the United States, denounced Downes for killing men, women, and children with scant provocation—and without winning any indemnity.

They were also upset that Jackson had authorized the expedition without Congress's say-so. "If the President can direct expeditions with fire and sword against the Malays," opined the *National Intelligencer* on July 10, 1832, "we do not see why he may not have the power to do the same in reference to any other power or people." The answer was that Jackson *did* enjoy this authority—just as Jefferson had in ordering the fleet to deal with the Barbary pirates. The pro-administration *Washington Globe*, in chastising "These learned Puffendorffs" at the rival *Intelligencer*, made essentially this point.

The real problem, as Navy Secretary Levi Woodbury pointed out in a private letter to Jack Downes, was that he had disobeyed orders by not having made a "previous demand . . . for restitution and indemnity" before attacking Quallah Battoo. Replied an indignant Downes: "No demand for satisfaction was made previous to my attack because I was satisfied . . . that no such demand would be answered, except only by refusal." It was not an especially convincing argument, but the Jackson administration had no intention of repeating the unpleasantness that had attended the court-martial of Downes's friend and mentor, David Porter, seven years before. While quietly cutting short Downes's naval career—he would never command another ship and would end his days as a lighthouse inspector—the administration publicly praised his mission to Quallah Battoo. "The result of that visit," Secretary Woodbury wrote at the end of 1832, "has been to silence all exultation and menaces of further violence from those sea robbers."

The secretary spoke too soon. In 1833 the U.S. merchantman *Derby* was loading pepper off Trabangunchute, Sumatra, when it was attacked by an armed ship; the crew barely managed to fend off the pirates. The *Eclipse*, which anchored off Trabangunchute five years later, was less lucky. The captain's local agent—a Sumatran named Libbee Sumat who served as an intermediary with the pepper sellers—tipped off his clan that the ship would make a prime target, since some of the men were sleeping ashore and the captain was not feeling well. Libbee Sumat's relatives boarded the ship pretending to be friendly, enjoyed a nice cup of tea with the captain, then pulled out long knives and killed the unsuspecting skipper before driving the rest of the crew overboard. The loot, valued at $20,000, was divided among the villages of Soo Soo, Quallah Battoo, and Muckie. "The Malays are growing so insolent that they will be for taking all vessels where there is the least chance of success," complained one American merchant skipper.

U.S. Navy Captain George C. Read and Commander Thomas W. Wyman heard about the attack while anchored in Ceylon (now Sri Lanka), where they were paying a courtesy call with their ships, the frigate *Columbia* and the sloop *John Adams*, respectively. The ships promptly sailed for the west coast of Sumatra, anchoring off Quallah Battoo on December 19, 1838. Mindful of Downes's example, Read decided to talk first and, if necessary, fight later. But the negotiations did not get far, so on December 24 the American ships opened fire on Quallah Battoo's ramshackle forts, which had been reconstructed since Downes's visit six years before. The U.S. squadron then proceeded to Muckie, where preliminary talks aimed at securing restitution yielded nothing. On January 1, 1839, both U.S. ships opened fire, then landed some sailors and marines, who burned the town and its forts. The local inhabitants had been given ample time to evacuate and apparently only one person was killed. Read was preparing to repeat this operation at Soo Soo but took pity on the villagers and sailed back to Quallah Battoo, whose rajahs offered peace terms. They agreed to pay $2,000 compensation to the owners of the *Eclipse* and to protect American shipping in the future. With this, the second Sumatran punitive expedition—far less bloody than the first—came to an end.

Although a few more attempts were made, no more U.S. ships were captured by Sumatran pirates. Before long, however, there were no more U.S. ships to attack. In 1846 the Dutch took over Sumatra and erected trade barriers that ended the Salem-to-Sumatra pepper trade. It was experiences such as this that gradually convinced Washington that it had better promulgate and enforce an open-door policy, lest the U.S. be locked out of developing markets by European colonialists.

Diplomats Afloat

Even when the navy was supposed to be performing other functions, its ships and men somehow often found themselves the victims of native "outrages" that simply had to be avenged. Consider the United States Exploring Expedition, six ships under the command of Lieutenant Charles Wilkes that performed invaluable work surveying the South Pacific from 1838 to 1842. Many of its 241 charts would be used by American forces in World War II; its vast store of specimens and artifacts would become the foundation of the Smithsonian Institution. But the pursuit of science in those days was hardly a bloodless affair. The Americans clashed with the locals in Fiji, Samoa, and Drummonds Island, burning a number of villages and killing dozens of natives.

It is easy enough with hindsight to condemn Yankee imperialism, but sometimes that high-handedness served an undoubtedly moral end. Consider the small amount of help rendered by the U.S. Navy to one of the Hungarian nationalists who rose up unsuccessfully to challenge the Habsburg Empire in 1848—a liberal revolt that aroused passionate approval in the United States. After the uprising was crushed with the help of the czar's armies, one of the revolutionaries, Martin Koszta, escaped to the U.S. and announced his intention of becoming an American citizen. Before acting on this wish, however, he sailed on personal business to Smyrna (Izmir), Turkey, where he was kidnapped by Austrian agents and imprisoned aboard a Habsburg warship anchored in the harbor.

The U.S. sloop *St. Louis*, 18 guns, happened to be on the scene. Its captain, Duncan N. Ingraham, after consulting with the local U.S. chargé d'affaires and after directing fruitless diplomatic entreaties to the Austrians, issued an ultimatum: Either the Austrians released Koszta, or the Americans would "take him by force." Just 10 minutes before the ultimatum was due to expire on July 2, 1853, and with the *St. Louis*'s guns trained on their ship, the Austrians freed their prisoner. This action, which drew an apoplectic reaction from the Habsburg emperor, was greeted with jubilation and approbation back in America. Ingraham received a gold medal and a promotion from Congress.

Another example of humanitarian action was the effort to stamp out the slave trade, which the U.S. joined intermittently after Congress outlawed the importation of slaves in 1807. The main role in capturing slavers was played by the Royal Navy's West Africa Squadron, but the U.S. Navy contributed a few ships of its own, starting with the *Cyane* in 1820. After the early 1820s, the American effort slacked off until the late 1830s, when the Van Buren administration sent fresh ships to the "Dark Continent." Under the Webster-Ashburton Treaty of 1842, the U.S. and Britain each pledged to maintain a squadron with at least 80 guns off the west coast of Africa. Yet the British remained far more enthusiastic about capturing slavers than the U.S. Navy, a government department often run by Southerners. Between 1842 and 1861, U.S. patrollers captured just 24 slave vessels, to the Royal Navy's 595. The U.S. Africa Squadron tended to place more emphasis on protecting U.S. commerce and the freed-slave settlement of Liberia than on stalking slavers.

One of the commanders of the Africa Squadron in the 1840s was Commodore Matthew C. Perry, brother of the late Commodore Oliver Hazard Perry (victor of the Battle of Lake Erie in the War of 1812). He of course gained immortality not for his actions in Africa but for opening Japan to the West in 1853–55, a project first proposed by David Porter in 1815. This feat, which changed the course of history, lies outside the scope of this narrative since it was a peaceful achievement, not a small war. Nevertheless it is worth noting that it was a representative of the navy, not the State Department, who opened up the land of the rising sun, and he did it by boldly leading an armada of "black ships"—including two steamships—into Edo (Tokyo) Bay and awing the Japanese with Western military technology.

The navy frequently assisted American diplomats in the nineteenth century, helping to negotiate scores of treaties opening new vistas for American commerce. For instance, the cruise of the sloop *Peacock* in 1832–33 resulted in trade treaties with the king of Siam (now Thailand) and the sultan of Muscat, whose domain stretched from Arabia to the African isle of Zanzibar. These were the first such agreements the U.S. concluded in the Far East and Middle East.

The navy's successes were usually peaceful; it was the failures that turned into small wars.

China

Americans had plenty of both in China, where their interests ran the gamut from profiteering to proselytizing. The first American commercial vessel, the *Empress of China*, visited the Middle Kingdom in 1784; the first missionaries arrived in 1830. By the middle of the nineteenth century, Yankee merchants had grabbed a small share of the lucrative opium market dominated by the British (British opium came from India, American opium from Turkey). When the Manchu court tried to crack down on this commerce, Great Britain went to war. The Opium War of 1840–1842 resulted in a decisive British victory. China was forced to sign treaties opening up five ports to British trade, ceding

Hong Kong to British sovereignty, and giving British subjects extraterritorial privileges that made them immune from Chinese laws.

Captain Lawrence Kearny, commander of the U.S. East India Squadron (created in 1835), arrived in China with the aging frigate *Constellation* and the sloop *Boston* after the conclusion of hostilities. Kearney demanded that the Manchus extend to America the same terms they had granted Britain. Peking, hoping to play one set of barbarians off against another, was only too happy to comply. In 1844 U.S. envoy Caleb Cushing negotiated the Treaty of Wanghia which gave the U.S. merchants, like their British counterparts, most favored nation status and admission to five treaty ports. The treaty also stipulated that Americans committing crimes in China could only be tried by U.S. officials under U.S. laws. Thus America cleverly reaped the benefits of Britain's war effort.

In 1850 the Taiping Rebellion broke out, engulfing China in one of the deadliest wars of the nineteenth century. At first the foreigners felt more threatened by imperial troops than by the rebels, who professed an ersatz version of Christianity. Starting in February 1854, Manchu bannermen began harassing and attacking foreigners around Shanghai. Indignity of indignities, they even occupied the foreigners' racecourse. Commander John Kelly ordered 60 marines and sailors put ashore from the U.S. ship *Plymouth*. They joined about 150 British marines and sailors, as well as a number of civilian volunteers from Shanghai, in an assault on the imperial encampment. On April 4, 1854, the Anglo-American force routed the bannermen. Only two Americans were killed and four injured in the Battle of Muddy Flat. Horse racing resumed not long thereafter, much to the foreign settlement's relief.

The biggest U.S. military operation in China prior to 1900 occurred as an offshoot of the Second Anglo-Chinese War, sometimes known as the *Arrow* war, after the name of a small ship seized by Chinese authorities in 1856 on suspicion of piracy. The British, claiming the *Arrow* had Hong Kong registry and a British flag, retaliated by bombarding Canton. When the subsequent fighting began to endanger Americans in the city, landing parties from the sail sloops *Portsmouth* and *Levant* and the steamship *San Jacinto* protected U.S. interests. On November 15, 1856, the *Portsmouth's* skipper, Commander Andrew Hull Foote, was in his launch, with the U.S. flag clearly visible, when he was fired upon by two of the barrier forts on the Pearl River between Whampoa and Canton. (The Chinese gunners probably mistook the Stars and Stripes for the Union Jack.) All five shots missed. But the next day, a cannonball from one of the forts crashed into another American boat, decapitating the coxswain.

Foote was a 50-year-old veteran of the navy who had shown great zeal in the past in combating slave trafficking and would later distinguish himself during the Civil War with his command of Union gunboats in the Western theater. He was also a Puritan who crusaded for temperance and delivered scorching Sunday sermons to his sailors. But he was no turn-the-other-cheek Christian. After consulting with Commodore James Armstrong, who was in charge of the East India Squadron, he ordered an attack on the forts at once.

The Chinese turned out to be tougher opponents than the Fijians or Sumatrans. The barrier forts had European-designed fortifications with seven-foot granite walls and 176 guns manned by 5,000 troops. During the four-day battle that followed (November 16, 20–22, 1856), interrupted by unsuccessful negotiations, the *Portsmouth* and *Levant* were hit 49 times. A launch carrying some sailors ashore was hit and sunk. But these were not serious setbacks; China still had a long way to go before it acquired military parity with the West. A landing party of 287 sailors and marines had little trouble capturing and demolishing all four barrier forts. The final toll: seven Americans dead, 22 wounded. The Chinese loss was reckoned at more than 160 dead. The secretary of the navy lauded the East India Squadron for "the brave and energetic manner in which the wrong was avenged." The Anglophilic Commander Foote received an accolade that might have been even closer to his heart when his warships returned to Whampoa anchorage to the cheers of British sailors.

As a result of the *Arrow* war, China agreed to open up 10 more ports to British trade. As in 1844, America won a parallel concession, the 1858 Treaty of Tientsin which included the Manchus' promise to receive a U.S. minister in Peking and guaranteed missionaries the right to preach Christianity. In China, where the U.S. kept three ships to the Royal Navy's 30 or so, America was almost a free rider, benefiting from British protection without paying much of a price. But in a pinch the Americans were always ready to help their fellow English speakers.

Tensions continued to run high between China and the Western powers since the imperial court never seemed willing to do as much to open up its country as the foreigners demanded. In 1859, a joint Anglo-French force attacked the Taku Bar forts, at the mouth of the Pei-ho River leading to Peking. The European expedition ran into heavy fire and did not have enough steamers to tow the assault boats into position. U.S. Flag Officer Josiah Tattnall, watching the proceedings as an ostensibly neutral observer, lent the U.S. paddle-wheeler *Toey-wan* to help transport the British and French troops toward the forts under heavy fire. He also instructed his men to fire back at the Taku forts. A Southern romantic, Tattnall justified this unneutral stance—or so the legend goes—with a quote from Sir Walter Scott: "Blood is thicker than water." Despite the American help, the Anglo-French assault failed, with heavy losses on the European side, but the next year their armies conquered Peking.

Policing the Globe

Blood is thicker than water. Many's the time that British and American naval officers, dining together in port, would clink their glasses to that toast. There was even some truth to it. Although Britain and the U.S. were on the brink of hostilities numerous times after the War of 1812—over the *Caroline* incident of 1840, the Oregon boundary dispute of 1845–46 ("Fifty-Four-Forty or Fight"), the *Trent* affair of 1861, and the Venezuela border dispute of 1895—relations between their navies often grew quite cozy. At least in foreign waters. Like a family, they might quarrel among themselves, but to the world at large they would present a united face. Among the numerous instances of Anglo-American cooperation:

> In 1845, the U.S. sloop *St. Louis* helped a Royal Navy vessel to evacuate British colonists from the New Zealand town of Kororareka just before it fell to a Maori attack.
> In 1864, while the Civil War still raged at home, a small U.S.-chartered steamboat joined British, French, and Dutch naval forces in an assault on the daimyo of Chosu, an isolationist Japanese warlord who had closed the Shimonoseki Straits to foreign commerce. The USS *Wyoming*, an eight-gun corvette, had exchanged fire with the daimyo's forts the previous year but had failed to silence them. This time the large Western force dismantled the threat. London was so grateful for the (negligible) American help that U.S. Navy Lieutenant Frederick Pearson received a knighthood.
> In 1874, the USS *Tuscarora* and HMS *Portsmouth* put ashore landing parties in Honolulu to help restore order after supporters of a defeated aspirant to the throne stormed the Hawaiian legislature.
> In 1882, the Royal Navy bombarded Alexandria, Egypt, to put down a nationalist uprising. One hundred fifty American sailors and marines landed to stop looting, fight fires, and protect American residents, becoming the first foreign troops to enter the city center.

These joint actions provide a clue to the U.S. Navy's function during most of the nineteenth century. The navy had no difficulty conducting offensive operations in 1846–48 against Mexico, a country with no fleet of its own. But if called upon to confront a European flotilla, the navy would have found itself hopelessly outmatched. But that was not its role. Deploying a powerful armada capable of controlling the seas against all comers would have been a costly undertaking. Congress did not want to spend much money on defense and, with wide expanses of open space on either side of the United States, did not feel that it needed to do so.

Congress maintained only a small navy whose peacetime mission was to police the world, enforcing Western standards of behavior, protecting U.S. commerce, and serving as a general adjunct to U.S. diplomacy. No matter how tiny, the navy had little trouble overawing various pirates and tribesmen with its vastly superior technology and training. With the navy's help, U.S. exports soared from $20 million in 1789 to $334 million in 1860. In short, naval captains were doing more or less the same job performed today by the World Trade Organization: integrating the world around the principle of free trade. It just so happened that trade negotiations in those days were a slightly bloodier affair than they are today; hence "butcher and bolt." Since the Royal Navy was engaged in more or less the same task, it made sense for the two services to cooperate from time to time.

The major difference was that Britons wound up painting the world red, planting the Union Jack on one territory after another. This caused occasional tensions, as when a swaggering Royal Navy captain tried to lay claim to Hawaii in 1843, a move peacefully (and successfully) resisted by two U.S. naval vessels. For most of the nineteenth century, America contented itself with carving out what William Henry Seward called the "empire of the seas"—an informal empire based on trade and influence. David Porter's efforts to annex the Marquesas notwithstanding, America was not interested in a formal overseas empire.

Not yet.

3

EMPIRE EMERGING

From Korea, 1871, to Samoa, 1899

I n 1861 the U.S. Navy was redirected from fighting small wars to focusing its energies on the deadliest conflict in American history. This required a buildup of startling proportions. At the beginning of the Civil War, the Union Navy had deployed just 68 vessels. It emerged from the conflict with 626 ships, including 65 ironclads. If it had desired, the United States could have challenged the Royal Navy for command of the seas. But for the time being, America had its fill of martial splendor.

The pacifist mood that so often takes hold after a big war gripped the country again. The army was demobilized, the navy scrapped. By 1881 only 50 vessels remained in the fleet, most of them obsolete hulks. That was just fine as far as the post–Civil War administrations were concerned. One story that gained wide circulation had Rutherford B. Hayes's navy secretary, upon first boarding a warship, exclaiming in surprise, "Why the derned thing is hollow!" Though undoubtedly apocryphal, this tale accurately conveyed the lack of interest in all matters naval displayed by the politicians of the time.

The crabby, conservative naval establishment, riven by feuds between line and staff officers, and run by autonomous bureau chieftains, did not help its own cause by resisting innovations such as steam power and rifled cannons. Its senior officer from 1869 until his death in 1891 was Admiral David Dixon Porter, an aging relic of the old navy forged by his father and the rest of "Preble's Boys"—a force, it was said, composed of wooden ships and iron men.

As the navy declined, so did the frequency of small wars overseas. In the 20 years between 1841 and 1861, the marines landed abroad 24 times. The next 20 years saw half as many landings—only 12. There was a similar falloff in diplomatic negotiations by naval officers—from 201 in the 20 years before the Civil War, to 101 in the 20 years after. This was related to another trend: While American overseas trade soared in the years after the Civil War, the percentage carried in U.S. flag ships plummeted—and so did the need for naval protection of commerce. Congress subsidized the building of Western railroads as a national priority but did not think the decline of the merchant marine was important enough to warrant much action.

The nation's attention and energy were directed elsewhere: to the Reconstruction of the South, the winning of the West, and the industrialization of the Northeast and Midwest. What little military activity the U.S. engaged in for the next few decades was primarily directed against Plains Indians who had the misfortune to find themselves in the path of Yankee settlers. After 1890, the year when the frontier was officially declared closed, America's attention would once again focus on expansion abroad. In the meantime, one of the few expeditions undertaken in the spirit of Porter and Perry was the foray to Korea in 1871.

Korea

Appropriately enough, the commander of this fantastic voyage was the scion of a great naval dynasty stretching back to the service's early glory days. Rear Admiral John Rodgers was the son of Commodore John Rodgers, who had served in the quasi-war with France, the Barbary Wars, and the War of 1812, and had gone on to become the navy's senior officer from 1821 to 1839. The family was linked by marriage to the illustrious Perry clan; one of John Rodgers Sr.'s sisters married the brother of Commodores Oliver Hazard Perry and Matthew C. Perry.

Young John Rodgers became a midshipman in 1828 at 16 and learned his trade the old-fashioned way—aboard ship. Unlike most naval officers of his era, he attended college, spending a year at the University of Virginia, but he headed back to sea without graduating. Promotion in those days was entirely on the basis of seniority, so a man could wait decades in rank until someone above him died or retired. Rodgers made rear admiral—a new rank—only after the Civil War, where he distinguished himself as a commander of ironclads in the Union navy. (It was by no means certain which side he would fight for, since his father, the commodore, had been a Maryland-born slave owner.)

In 1870, at age 58, stout and white-haired, having already spent 24 years at sea, Rodgers took over the somewhat ramshackle Asiatic Squadron (formerly the East India Squadron), based in Hong Kong. He had three steam-powered iron gunboats—the *Ashuelot*, *Monocacy*, and *Palos*—along with three wooden ships, the *Colorado*, *Alaska*, and *Benicia*, that combined sail and steam power. The navy still had reservations about the new-fangled, steam-belching monsters, and anyway coal was hard to come by, so captains had instructions to use sails whenever possible and resort to steam only when necessary in battle.

As Perry had opened Japan, so Rodgers set as his objective opening Korea. The Hermit Kingdom was nominally a vassal of Peking but in reality had control over its own destiny. Its de facto ruler was the regent, Yi Ha-ung, known as the Taewongun ("Prince of the Great Court"), part of the Choson dynasty that had ruled the peninsula since the fourteenth century. The xenophobic Taewongun was determined to keep Korea closed to the West. In 1866 he launched a campaign to eradicate Christianity, executing nine French missionaries and some 8,000 of their converts. France sent a punitive expedition, but it was repulsed by the Koreans.

The Koreans generally treated shipwrecked mariners more kindly, returning a number of American sailors safely to China. But in 1866, a U.S.-registered merchant schooner, the *General Sherman*, was burned and its 27 crew members (mainly Chinese) killed near Pyongyang. The Koreans later explained that the crew had brought this fate upon themselves by entering interior waters without permission, kidnapping a Korean official, and firing into a crowd on shore. This incident nevertheless prompted the Grant administration to mount a major effort to secure from Korea treaties governing shipwrecks and, if possible, trade. Chosen to carry out this assignment were Rear Admiral Rodgers and the U.S. minister to China, Frederick F. Low.

On May 16, 1871, five ships of the Asiatic Squadron, mounting 85 guns and carrying 1,230 officers and men, set off from Nagasaki, Japan, headed for the great unknown—a land where, it was rumored, the natives diced and pickled unwelcome visitors. "Whether this is positively true or not I can't say," Marine Captain McLane Tilton wrote to his wife, "but you may imagine it is not with a great pleasure I anticipate landing with the small force we have, against a populous country containing 10,000,000 savages!"

The expedition reached Chemulpo (now Inchon), Korea's premier port, by the end of May and tried to open diplomatic negotiations. While this was going on, Rodgers sent small boats to do surveying work on the Han River leading toward Seoul. The Koreans naturally took umbrage at foreigners conducting a military survey of one of their most strategically sensitive waterways.

On June 2, one of these surveying parties was fired upon by forts on Kangwha Island. The USS *Palos* and *Monocacy* promptly returned fire, silencing the fort. Afterward, Minister Low demanded an apology. The proud Koreans refused; they thought it was the foreign barbarians who should apologize. So, in the time-honored fashion of the navy, Rear Admiral Rodgers decided to mount a punitive expedition.

The attack got under way on June 10, 1871, a clear, warm day, with steam launches and cutters landing 542 sailors and 109 marines. The first two Korean forts fell with little trouble. The next day—after becoming the first Western troops to spend the night on Korean soil—the expedition faced its toughest challenge: the hilltop fort known as Kwangsong ("the citadel"). To reach it, the Americans had to race down a hill into a ravine and then back up—straight into the mouth of the Korean cannons. The first man over the parapet was killed, and so was the first who entered the fort, but then the Koreans ran out of time to reload and it became a savage hand-to-hand struggle. "Corean sword crossed Yankee cutlass," wrote a contemporary chronicler, "and clubbed carbine brained the native whose spear it dashed aside." The defenders fought valiantly, but they were no match for the Americans, who had much more modern weapons, and less than an hour later Old Glory was fluttering overhead. Virtually all of the 300 defenders had been killed or wounded, or had committed suicide, while only three Americans were killed and 10 wounded. Nine sailors and six marines won Medals of Honor for their heroism.

Having "avenged" this "insult to the flag," the Americans reboarded their ships and spent three monotonous weeks waiting for the Koreans to answer their requests for trade negotiations. After it became clear that Seoul had no interest in reaching a deal, Rear Admiral Rodgers had no choice but to sail away on July 3, 1871, no treaty in hand.

The Taewongun claimed that the "barbarians" had been repulsed, but the ease with which the Americans had destroyed Korea's most formidable fortifications gave added impetus to pro-Western modernizers, who toppled him two years later. Japan became the first foreign nation to sign a treaty with Seoul, in 1876; the second was the U.S., in 1882, thanks to the skillful diplomacy of Commodore Robert W. Shufeldt. Commander Winfield Scott Schley, Rodgers's adjutant, thought in retrospect that the treaty was made possible by the Koreans' memories of their defeat at the hands of warlike Americans a decade earlier. Perhaps. But the 1871 expedition had at most an indirect influence. And by fostering ill will on both sides, it may actually have delayed the establishment of U.S.-Korean relations.

Panama

The Korean expedition was the second biggest U.S. landing abroad between the Mexican War and the Spanish-American War. The biggest occurred in Panama in 1885. This was the culmination of U.S. landings almost too numerous to list throughout Latin America in the nineteenth century. U.S. sailors and marines landed in Argentina in 1833, 1852, and 1890; Peru in 1835; Nicaragua in 1852, 1853, 1854, 1896, and 1899; Uruguay in 1855, 1858, 1868; Mexico in 1870; Chile in 1891; and in Panama, part of Colombia, in 1860, 1873, 1885, 1895. Many of those countries would see even more numerous American interventions in the twentieth century.

These landings were so frequent in part because U.S. embassies and legations did not have permanent marine guards until the twentieth century; whenever trouble occurred in the nineteenth century, marines had to be put ashore. A familiar pattern developed: A revolution takes place; violence breaks out; American merchants and diplomats feel threatened; U.S. warships appear offshore; landing parties patrol the city for several days; then they sail away. The 1885 landing in Panama differed from the normal pattern only in the size of the landing force, in part a product of the fact that even before the construction of a canal, the U.S. had more pressing interests in the isthmus than in the rest of Latin America.

In 1846 Colombia had signed a treaty giving the U.S. transit rights across Panama. Nine years later, the world's first intercontinental railroad opened, running the 48 miles from Colón on the Caribbean to Panama City on the Pacific. This became a vital transit route between the eastern United States and California, acquired from Mexico in 1848. The Panama Railroad Company and the Pacific Mail Steamship Company, which used the railroad to transport mail under a federal subsidy, were both owned by wealthy New Yorkers who got considerably more wealthy as a result of these lucrative ventures. Unfortunately for them, the government in Bogotá always had a tenuous grip on its Panama province. The resulting revolutions led to frequent marine landings.

In 1885 an insurrection elsewhere in Colombia depleted the Colombian army garrison in Panama, leading two different sets of rebels to try their luck. Former Panamanian president Rafael Aizpuru seized Panama City, killing at least 25 people and disrupting the Panama Railroad. Aizpuru threatened "to kill every American on the isthmus." Meanwhile, a Haitian mulatto named Pedro Prestan, fired by a hatred of all white men, led a small band of followers to terrorize Colón, a small, pestilent town with no proper sewers or bathrooms, garbage piled in the streets, and an abundance of over-sized rats.

On March 29, 1885, a Pacific Mail steamer, the *Colon*, arrived from New York full of arms. Prestan seized six Americans—the Pacific Mail superintendent, the general agent of the steamship line, the American consul, the superintendent of the Panama Railroad, and two officers from the USS *Galena*, a gunboat anchored in the harbor—and threatened to kill them if the arms from the *Colon* were not turned over to him. The American consul gave in and told the Pacific Mail company to release the weapons. Upon hearing this, Prestan released his hostages. But Theodore F. Kane, skipper of the *Galena*, blocked the weapons transfer, leading Prestan to seize two of the Pacific Mail employees once again. The following day, March 31, Kane landed 126 men in Colón to protect American property but, strictly following his orders, he refused to arrest Prestan. Before long Colombian troops also arrived and engaged Prestan's followers in a pitched battle outside of town, during which the two American hostages managed to escape. Prestan retreated into Colón and set it afire, reducing the town to cinders.

The Cleveland administration had just taken office, and the new navy secretary, a corporate lawyer named William C. Whitney, decided enough was enough. Under the terms of the 1848 treaty with Colombia, he ordered the navy and marines to scrape together an expeditionary force consisting of eight ships and more than 2,000 officers and men. This was pretty much the outer limit of what the U.S. could muster in those days. But it was enough. By the end of April 11, 1885, the expeditionary force had control of the entire length of the Panama Railroad, with marine guards in white pith helmets posted along the route.

The marines next captured Panama City without a shot being fired and arrested Rafael Aizpuru. He offered to declare Panama a sovereign state with U.S. backing, but the expedition's commander, Rear Admiral James E. Jouett, declined. Nobody had given him orders to carve out a new country. The rebel leader was turned over to Colombian troops, and by May 25, 1885, less than two months after landing, the entire U.S. force had withdrawn. Rafael Aizpuru received only 10 years in exile; Pedro Prestan was hanged by the Colombian government.

While the U.S. had not exactly been isolationist or even neutral—"It cannot be denied that our presence on the Isthmus was of great value to the Government forces," remarked Admiral Jouett—the Cleveland administration had been determined to avoid a long-term entanglement in Panama. That resolution, harking back to the admonitions of Washington and Jefferson, was now on its last legs.

The New Navy

In the 1880s, the U.S. Navy was sufficient for chastising errant Koreans or Panamanians, but by Great Power standards it was a joke, ranking twelfth in the world in number of ships, behind Turkey and Sweden, among others. One midshipman complained in 1883 that his ship, the *Richmond*, was "a poor excuse for a tub, unarmored, with pop-guns for a battery and a crew composed of the refuse of all nations, three-quarters of whom cannot speak intelligible English." During a crisis in 1891 caused by an altercation between some drunk and unruly American sailors and a Valparaiso mob, the Benjamin Harrison administration was brought to the sobering realization that Chile's navy might be more powerful than America's.

This was an intolerable state of affairs, and the U.S. did not long tolerate it. The creation of the New Navy began in 1883, during the Chester Arthur administration, when Congress approved the construction of three steel cruisers—the *Atlanta*, *Boston*, and *Chicago*—that had partial armor plating and breech-loading, rifled cannons (as opposed to the smoothbore muzzle-loaders of old), though they also retained sails to supplement their steam plants. Three years later, during the first Cleveland administration, the *Maine* and *Texas*, America's first battleships powered exclusively by steam propulsion, were authorized by lawmakers.

In 1890, Captain Alfred Thayer Mahan, a 50-year-old professor at the Naval War College whose long career had hitherto been distinguished only by his hatred of sea duty and his affinity for alcohol and high-church Episcopalianism, published a work that would define an age: *The Influence of Sea Power upon History*. It both grew out of, and contributed to, the revolution in naval thinking. Previously the navy had been designed to protect U.S. shipping and the U.S. coastline and, in wartime, to raid enemy shipping. Now Mahan urged the U.S. to match the Europeans in building an armada capable of gaining control of the seas. There was some opposition, including from the complaisant military establishment, but the critics were pounded into submission by the rhetorical broadsides fired by Mahan and his influential friends, a circle that included Senator Henry Cabot Lodge, philosopher Brooks Adams, Rear Admiral Stephen B. Luce, and, not least, a rising young politician named Theodore Roosevelt, who displayed his genius for invective by denouncing "flapdoodle pacifists and mollycoddlers" who resisted the call of national greatness.

The navalists' triumph has been much written about but remains insufficiently appreciated. It was by no means foreordained. In the late nineteenth century the U.S. faced no outside imperative, certainly no major foreign threat, necessitating the construction of a powerful navy. Some historians argue that economic uncertainties—a recession occurred in 1873, a depression in 1893—gave added impetus to military expansion, as part of a search for overseas markets. But hard times could just as easily have led to a contraction of the armed forces and foreign commitments, as they would in the 1930s and 1970s. Instead, in the 1880s and 1890s, Mahan and his cohorts convinced their countrymen that they should propel themselves into the front rank of world powers. The result was the first major peacetime arms buildup in the nation's history, a buildup that gave America a navy capable of sinking the Spanish fleet in 1898.

If the U.S. was to have a two-ocean, blue-water, steam-powered navy, it would need plenty of coaling depots to supply it. The old sailing navy had enjoyed a degree of freedom from fixed bases that would not be rivaled until the advent of nuclear propulsion. Square-riggers could go wherever the winds carried them, repairing and replenishing themselves in virtually any harbor—even on an undeveloped island like Nukahiva, site of David Porter's 1813 landing. Steamers, by contrast, needed assured access to coal and modern repair facilities. The search for coaling depots had already been a powerful impetus for colonialism by the European powers, as it was believed that no navy could ensure access to this vital fuel supply unless it controlled its own stockpiles scattered around the world. The need for secure coaling stations would likewise spur American annexations overseas.

The U.S. acquisitive impulse had been building for some time and, contrary to the popular impression today, did not arrive full grown, as if by immaculate conception, in 1898. William H. Seward, the great apostle of empire who served as secretary of state in the Abraham Lincoln and Andrew Johnson administrations, succeeded in buying Alaska and acquiring Midway Island in 1867 after it was claimed by Captain William Reynolds of the screw sloop *Lackawanna*. He also tried, unsuccessfully, to acquire British Columbia, Greenland, the Danish West Indies (Virgin Islands), and naval bases at Samaná Bay in Santo Domingo (the Dominican Republic) and at Môle Saint-Nicolas in Haiti. Presidents Ulysses S. Grant, in 1869, and Benjamin Harrison, in 1891, attempted to revive plans to buy Samaná Bay and Môle Saint-Nicolas, respectively, but nothing came of it.

The U.S. was more successful in expanding its control over Hawaii. With the signing of a free-trade treaty in 1875, the islands became so closely integrated economically with the U.S. that they were, in the words of one senator who voted for the pact, "an American colony." In 1887 Hawaii granted the U.S. Navy exclusive use of Pearl Harbor, giving America a strategically vital Pacific base. In 1893, American residents overthrew the native queen and asked to join the United States. The local U.S. consul landed 164 bluejackets and marines from the U.S. cruiser *Boston*, proclaiming the islands a U.S. protectorate and urging Washington to annex them. The outgoing president, Benjamin Harrison, signed the annexation treaty. But newly inaugurated Grover Cleveland looked this gift horse in the mouth; he withdrew the treaty from Senate consideration. The U.S. would not acquire Hawaii for another five years, by which time America had become a full-fledged imperialist power.

Samoa

America's deepening involvement in Hawaii reflected its growing orientation toward the Pacific Ocean. As early as 1875 Congressman Fernando Wood had declared, rather prematurely, "The Pacific Ocean is an American Ocean." Well, not quite. But the U.S. was certainly trying to secure its interests all over the Pacific, and nowhere more so than in Samoa, a chain of 14 volcanic islands conveniently located midway between Hawaii and Australia. These islands, populated by 28,000 people in 1881, became the center of increasingly nasty competition between Britain, Germany, and the U.S. in the last decades of the nineteenth century.

The first U.S. warship had reached Samoa in 1835, but America did not become deeply enmeshed in its affairs until 1872, when Commander Richard W. Meade of the USS *Narragansett* concluded a treaty with local chieftains that, in return for extending a U.S. protectorate over Samoa, granted Washington the right to construct a naval station at the first-rate harbor of Pago Pago on Tutuila Island. The Senate declined the protectorate, but in 1878 agreed to take the harbor in return for mediating Samoan disputes with outside powers. The following year, Germany and Britain demanded and won similar privileges at other Samoan harbors. Not content with this concession, Chancellor Otto von Bismarck tried to extend German control over the entire islands in 1887 by installing a favored candidate on the Samoan throne. When a revolution broke out, German forces landed, only to be repulsed by the Samoans.

The Cleveland administration was so upset by this act of German aggression, which threatened America's Pacific flank, that it sent Rear Admiral Lewis Kimberly to Samoa with three warships from the Pacific Squadron. He arrived at the same time as three German warships and one British. All sides were eyeing one another warily when, on March 15, 1889, a mighty hurricane ravaged Samoa, wrecking almost all the foreign warships in the harbor, including the bulk of America's Pacific Squadron. The war fever was literally blown away, at least temporarily.

Instead of fighting, the three powers negotiated and in 1889 agreed to divide control of Samoa among them, just the sort of "entangling alliance" the U.S. once would have rejected. Nine years later the old king of Samoa died and a civil war broke out pitting the followers of Mataafa, the German candidate, against Malietoa Tanu, the Anglo-American choice. Mataafa gained control of the government—but not for long. Viewing Mataafa's usurpation as a violation of the 1889 Treaty of Berlin, U.S. Rear Admiral Albert Kautz, aboard the cruiser *Philadelphia,* coordinated a counterattack with the Royal Navy. In the interest of unity of command, some American sailors were placed under the command of British officers and some British bluejackets were placed under the command of American officers.

On March 13, 1899, an American landing force was put ashore to begin the occupation of Apia. On March 15 and 16, the USS *Philadelphia* along with HMS *Royalist* and HMS *Porpoise* bombarded the area around the towns of Apia and Vailoa, targeting Mataafa's followers but also hitting, allegedly by accident, the German consulate and a German gunboat. On March 23, wearing an ill-fitting British naval officer's dress uniform and borrowed canvas shoes, Malietoa Tanu was crowned king of Samoa under the protective guns of the Anglo-American force. But far from surrendering, the followers of Mataafa, the German-backed pretender, fired into Apia from the bush and constantly skirmished with U.S. and British troops. The Anglo-American forces found it relatively easy to operate along the shoreline, where they could be covered by naval guns, but on April 1, 1899, they made the mistake of leaving the safety of shore to pursue Mataafa's followers inland.

Sixty Americans joined 62 Britons and at least 100 of Tanu's men on this expedition, commanded by Lieutenant A. H. Freeman of the Royal Navy. They were ambushed by Mataafa's men firing guns from well-prepared positions in the tall grass. The Anglo-American soldiers put great store by their machine gun; in the past, the Samoans had fled in terror before its bark. This time, however, the Colt gun jammed, Westerners began dropping, and it looked likely that the column would be annihilated. U.S. Marine Lieutenant Constantine M. Perkins organized a desperate rearguard action around a wire fence, holding off the Mataafans long enough for the column to retreat to the beach, where it was saved by covering fire from HMS *Royalist.* It was only then that they discovered that two American officers and one British officer were missing. The following day the three men were found buried, their heads and ears cut off. In all, four Americans were killed and five wounded in this expedition. Three marines received the Medal of Honor for their bravery on April 1.

The British and Americans continued their sorties and bombardments against the Mataafans until April 25, 1899, when word arrived that Mataafa had agreed on cease-fire lines. An international commission subsequently ended tripartite rule in Samoa, dividing the islands between Germany and America, with Britain receiving compensation elsewhere. The U.S. won title to the island of Tutuila, where the navy set about building a coaling station. In World War I, an expedition from New Zealand expelled the Germans from western Samoa; the islands became independent in 1962. American Samoa never achieved much strategic importance, but it remains part of the United States to this day.

The larger significance of the Samoan adventure is twofold. First the U.S. was abandoning the old strategy of "butcher and bolt"; now U.S. forces were staying in foreign countries and trying to manipulate their politics, if not annex them outright. Normally this practice is known as imperialism, even though Americans, belonging to a country born of a revolt against an empire, are sensitive about applying this term to their own conduct. There is no doubt that at least one American would have been delighted to see this development, if only he had lived so long. The dreams of Commodore David Porter—America's first, frustrated imperialist—were starting to be realized.

A second and perhaps related point is that American troops in distant lands were now encountering much more substantial opposition than they had in years past, due to the diffusion around the world of Western ideals, such as liberalism and nationalism, and Western technology, such as rifles and cannons. In 1841, Lieutenant Charles Wilkes's men had burned three villages and killed countless Samoans without suffering any casualties. Fifty-eight years later, Admiral Kautz's party was almost annihilated by Samoans firing rifles with great accuracy. After a cease-fire had been declared and a weapon buy-back program instituted, the Samoans turned over 3,631 guns. This was the start of a trend: During the Boxer rebellion, German marines would be killed with Mauser bullets and Krupp artillery. America had the misfortune of joining the imperial game just as it was becoming more dangerous.

Part Two

GREAT POWER

4

RED SUMMER
Boxer Uprising, 1900

Few Americans paid much attention as their navy and Marine Corps made one overseas landing after another during the course of the nineteenth century. In part this was because most of the landings were not very large; in part because Americans were not very interested in imperialism abroad; but also in part because the American press was for most of that time a dull, anemic beast, heavily dependent upon the financial favors of political parties. Mass circulation publications supported by advertising did not come into full flower until the 1890s. It is perhaps no coincidence that this decade also saw a marked increase in popular enthusiasm for overseas expansion. The two trends converged most spectacularly in 1898. William Randolph Hearst, the exuberant owner of the *New York Journal,* was exaggerating when he called the Spanish-American War "the *Journal*'s war," but even if the *Journal* and other penny papers did not cause the conflict, they stirred frenzied public support for it.

Once Spain had been defeated, the "yellow press" had need of fresh crusades to boost circulation. The dirty, inglorious war against the Filipinos—the subject of the next chapter—did not fit the bill. Luckily for the newspaper barons, the perfect story emerged from the exotic depths of the Middle Kingdom, a tale of "savage, bitter, cruel barbarous warfare" pitting "Asiatic" hordes against embattled white Christians. All during the summer of 1900 American newspaper readers, like their counterparts in Europe, thrilled to the daily dispatches describing the Boxer uprising in China, the siege of the foreign legations (or embassies) in Peking, and the large relief expedition organized by the leading nations of Europe along with Japan and the United States.

Suddenly, with cruel finality, all hope was snuffed out: EUROPEANS FIGHT TO THE END BUT ARE OVERWHELMED IN LEGATIONS; MEN, WOMEN AND CHILDREN TORTURED BEFORE AWFUL DEATH! So read the front-page banner headline on Friday, July 13, 1900, in Hearst's *New York Evening Journal,* whose masthead boasted that its "Circulation is Greater Than the Combined Circulation of All the Other New York Evening Newspapers." Similar headlines, albeit less lurid, appeared in leading newspapers across the world. Over the next few days, they provided graphic details for readers. On July 16, the *Evening Journal* reported:

> After killing their wives and children to prevent them from falling into the clutches of the frenzied Chinese, the foreigners in Pekin were mowed down.
>
> The savages slew like beasts.
>
> Pekin ran red with blood. History had a new horror, at which generations will shudder.
>
> Not one of the 1,800 white men, women and children was left alive at Pekin....
>
> Penned in within the narrow walls of the legation buildings, the members of the Diplomatic Corps and their guards fought stubbornly and bravely the besiegement of the Boxers until at length their ammunition was exhausted, huge gaps were made in the walls of their buildings and the mutinous Chinese, with demon yells, poured in upon the gallant band.
>
> But death had come before torture. The last white had died fighting, and the blood-maddened Mongolians had to wreak their hellish ingenuity on corpses.

Various other newspapers ran obituaries for the more notable figures killed in the legations, and a memorial service was arranged at St. Paul's Cathedral in London.

There was only one small problem: None of the reports were true. The legations were still holding out. As the *Evening Journal* reported on July 17, without a trace of embarrassment: CHRISTIANS SAFE IN PEKIN.

The story of the nonexistent massacre apparently had been concocted by a shady American working as a special correspondent for London's *Daily Mail* in Shanghai, far from Peking. That this fraud had been accepted so readily by so many vividly illustrates the vast chasm of ignorance and suspicion that separated (and still separates) China from the West. It was this morass of misunderstanding that had led to the senseless siege of the legations in the first place and to one of the odder expeditions in American military history.

Culture Clash

We have already seen how Britain, followed by the United States, France, and other major powers, bludgeoned China into setting aside treaty ports where foreigners could enjoy extraterritorial privileges. Diplomats, soldiers, and traders flocked to this growing list of ports, while missionaries, Catholic and Protestant, set up shop in the interior. By 1894 there were 2,000 foreign missionaries in China who claimed almost 800,000 native converts. They were a profoundly disruptive influence, for they brought with them not just Western religion but also Western civilization.

What you think of this depends on what you think of Western civilization. Many, perhaps most, Chinese did not think much of it. Modernity is always a disruptive influence on any traditional society. It is bound to be resented all the more when imposed from abroad, at the point of a gun. Tales spread of missionaries making medicines out of children's eyes and hearts, or drinking women's menstrual blood. The Chinese scarcely needed to invent imaginary grievances since the real injuries they suffered were serious enough. British and American traders imported tons of opium, creating millions of Chinese addicts, under the protective guns of the British and U.S. navies. Western imports destroyed the market for Chinese goods, while Western-built railroads ("iron centipedes") put bargemen and porters on the Grand Canal out of work. Even worse, China's defeat in an 1895 war with Japan—the only Asian state that modernized fast enough to attain parity with the West—accelerated the dismemberment of the Middle Kingdom. The Europeans carved out spheres of influence, with Britain taking the Kowloon New Territories and Weihaiwei harbor, Germany Kiaochow and Tsingtao, Russia Port Arthur and the Liaotung Peninsula, and the French Kwangchowan in southern China adjoining Indochina, the spoils of a previous conquest. The final partition of the Celestial Empire appeared imminent.

America alone refused to join the colonial race, although its mariners had helped open China to Western trade. By the turn of the century China still accounted for only 1 percent of U.S. foreign trade, but the dollar value of American exports there had more than tripled during the 1890s and promised to grow further still—as long as the Europeans and Japanese did not bar the way. In 1899 and 1900 Secretary of State John Hay issued his famous Open Door notes, committing the U.S. to maintain China's territorial integrity and, more important from America's standpoint, to preserve free trade for all comers—what Hay called "a fair field and no favor." This policy's genesis stretched all the way back to 1844 when America had demanded, and won, trade concessions from the Manchu court equal to those granted England after the First Opium War.

Not all of China's troubles were the doing of outsiders—unless one counts the Manchu rulers as outsiders to Chinese society, which strictly speaking they were, since they came from Manchuria. By 1900 the decadent, despotic Ching dynasty, which had ruled China since 1644, was on its last legs. The government was so inept and corrupt that by comparison, one historian suggests, czarist Russia was "a model of dynamism and progressive thought." In 1898 the sickly young Emperor Kuang-hsü, hoping to follow in the footsteps of Czar Peter the Great and the Emperor Meiji, launched a series of bold, modernizing reforms. This burst of activity was short-lived. After just 102 days, the emperor was ousted by his aunt, the Empress Dowager Tz'u-hsi, who had ruled on and off since 1861. A vast mythology has accreted around Tz'u-hsi; foreigners, who dubbed her Old Buddha, claimed that she was sexually wanton and morally depraved. Whatever the truth of the more sensational charges, there was no doubt that she was opposed to modernization and openness to the West.

Thus antiforeign elements were now dominant at court at the same time that the I-ho ch'üan, or the "Righteous and Harmonious Fists," were spreading in the countryside. The Boxers, as they came to be known among foreigners because of their martial arts expertise, resembled other millennial movements elsewhere—the Sudanese Mahdists in the 1880s, for example, or the Sioux Ghost Dancers in 1890—among peoples whose traditional way of life was crumbling before the onslaught of modernity. The Boxers fed off hopelessness and despair, and there was plenty of both in north China in 1898–99. Catastrophic floods swept Shantung province in 1898, followed by drought that winter. Millions of peasants were left landless and hungry. They became prime recruits for the Boxers, who blamed all their troubles on the foreigners (Primary Devils), Chinese Christians (Secondary Devils) and collaborators with both (Tertiary Devils).

The Boxers spread placards that read: "Heaven is now sending down eight million spirit soldiers to extirpate these foreign religions, and when this has been done there will be a timely rain." These spirit soldiers were said to possess the Boxers when they chanted magical incantations, supposedly making them invulnerable to bullets. Boxer leaders even fired blunderbusses loaded with blanks at their followers to demonstrate their powers. When Boxers were killed, their leaders invariably declared that the dead men had been insufficiently pious, or blamed some other cause.

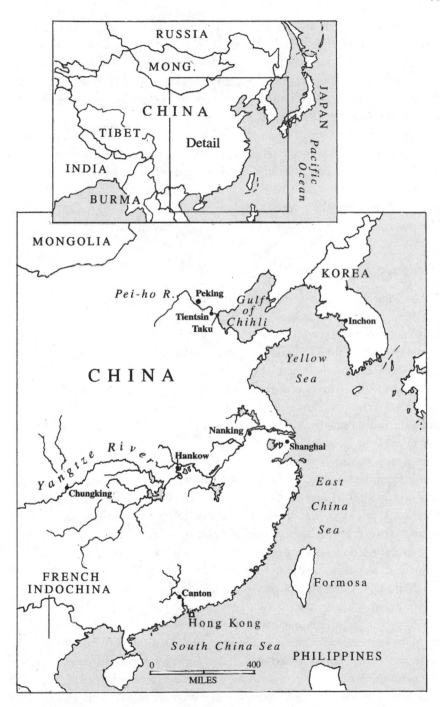

MAP 4.1 China and Korea, circa 1900

The Boxers had few leaders of stature; they were a spontaneous peasant uprising, instantly identifiable by their red banners, sashes, and turbans. Previous secret societies had been anti-Manchu, and some Boxers showed initial inclinations in that direction, but they were co-opted by xenophobic mandarins who particularly resented foreign missionaries. Their slogan became: Support the Manchus, Destroy the Foreign.

Originating in German-dominated Shantung province in 1898, where the Chinese governor was sympathetic, by early the next year the Boxers had spread next door to Chihli province, where Peking was located and where not coincidentally foreign missionaries had made the most inroads. Some governors battled the Boxers, but the reactionary elements at court encouraged the uprising. The Boxers were even incorporated into local government militias.

"Situation Extremely Grave"

By late May 1900, the Boxers were advancing on Peking, slaughtering Chinese Christians, ripping up railway and telegraph lines, burning churches and railroad stations along the way. Even as they drew ever closer to the Legation Quarter—an area three-quarters of a mile square squeezed between the walls of the Tartar City and the Imperial City, where the embassies of 11 nations were located—the diplomats inside were not overly concerned. Herbert Squiers, the American secretary, allowed his wife and children to travel to their summer home 15 miles outside Peking; they made it back just ahead of a Boxer mob that burned the house.

It was not until May 28 that the Western ministers summoned legation guards from the warships anchored off the Taku bar. With grudging permission from the Tsungli Yamen (foreign ministry), some 350 soldiers and sailors—56 Americans among them—made the 80-mile rail journey to Peking. American marines arrived at the train station without incident on the night of May 31, then marched down the streets of the capital past sullen, silent crowds of Chinese to reach the Legation Quarter. "Thank God you've come," exclaimed U.S. Minister Edwin H. Conger. "Now we're safe."

Not quite.

Up to that point only one foreigner had been killed by Boxers—a missionary slain in Shantung province the previous December. After May 31 the Westerners' situation worsened considerably. On June 3 the Boxers cut the railway between Peking and Tientsin. On June 9 they burned the grandstand at the foreigners' racetrack outside Peking; in the ensuing melee an English student killed a Chinese. The next day the British summer legation went up in flames.

On June 11 a Japanese diplomat ventured outside his legation and was hacked to pieces by imperial soldiers. On June 13 Boxers rampaged through Peking, burning foreign churches and Chinese stores and homes amid bloodcurdling chants of "Sha! Sha!" (Kill! Kill!). A pall of gray smoke hung above the ancient city. Missionaries and Chinese Christians sought refuge in Peking and the treaty ports. Young bucks from the legations, as if going on a big-game hunt, would venture outside to "bag" Boxers and rescue Christians. Westerners killed hundreds of Chinese in these forays, sometimes without provocation, further enflaming the situation.

On June 9, Sir Claude MacDonald, the British minister, sent a desperate telegram to Vice Admiral Sir Edward Seymour in Tientsin: "Situation extremely grave. Unless arrangements are made for immediate advance to Pekin, it will be too late."

The Seymour Expedition

Admiral Seymour, who as a midshipman 40 years before had fought in China during the Second Opium War, hastily organized a relief expedition cobbled together from the allied troops in Tangku and Tientsin. On the morning of June 10, the first of four troop trains chugged out of Tientsin, heading for Peking. Aboard were 2,100 officers and men, among them a 29-year-old naval officer named David Beatty who would go on to command the British battle cruiser fleet at the Battle of Jutland in World War I. The American contingent was made up of 112 bluejackets and marines under Captain Bowman McCalla, skipper of the USS *Newark*. The officers took full dress uniforms, expecting to be in Peking no later than the next evening.

The column advanced unopposed until it had almost reached Lang-fang, a railway station halfway between Tientsin and Peking. Just outside Lang-fang, on the afternoon of June 11, the foreign troops were swarmed by Boxers wearing red sashes and waving swords, pitchforks, and clubs. Although Chinese troops generally had up-to-date Western guns, the Boxers did not. What they lacked in firepower they made up in suicidal courage. Henry Savage Landor, a British war correspondent, described how the Boxers, "in a state of hysterical frenzy," dashed straight into the guns of the allied troops, "exposing themselves with bare chests to the bullets of foreign rifles." At least 35 Boxers were killed by the steady cracking of the troops' Maxim guns and rifles.

The expedition never got beyond Lang-fang. Ahead, the tracks were torn up and advance parties were mauled by Boxers. Seymour refused to abandon the trains, and they became a magnet for more Boxer attacks. On June 14, 400 to

500 Boxers armed only with swords and spears charged the column while many of Seymour's men were resting or washing their clothes. The soldiers emptied their magazines at the brave Boxers but still they kept coming. Only a Maxim gun managed to stop the human wave attack, leaving 88 dead Boxers littering the battlefield.

That same day Boxers cut the tracks between Lang-fang and Tientsin, leaving the Seymour column stranded. This happened because the leaders of the French and German contingents had refused Seymour's request to take a train back to the rear to keep open the column's line of communication; they were afraid that if they did so, the British and American contingents would have the honor of entering Peking first.

Finding his advance blocked, his rear harassed, his provisions running out, and his ammunition dangerously low, Seymour was forced to make a fighting retreat. The column fell back on Yangtsun on June 18. Here they found the tracks leading back to Tientsin completely torn up. The Chinese attacks increased, now coming not just from Boxers but also from the better-trained and -armed regulars of General Tung Fu-hsiang's and General Nieh Shih Cheng's army divisions. On the morning of June 19, the Seymour column abandoned the trains and began marching on foot toward Tientsin, 30 miles away, with the supplies and wounded men being transported in four junks down the Pei-ho River. As they slowly retreated, the men of the Seymour expedition had to deal not only with Chinese cavalry, infantry, and artillery attacks but also with blinding dust storms kicked up by savage winds. Casualties quickly mounted. The Americans led by Captain McCalla bore the brunt of the fighting, because they had been given a place of honor in the lead.

On June 21, Seymour's expedition stumbled onto the imperial armory at Hsiku, located just a few miles north of Tientsin. The foreigners had no idea of the existence of this 40-acre complex, which gives some sense of how inadequate their intelligence was. The allied troops stormed the compound early the next morning, or at least the Royal Marines did, assisted by the Americans and Germans; the French and Russians refused to cooperate with Seymour's plan. Inside, Seymour's men discovered copious stores of modern guns and ammunition as well as plenty of rice. Though Tientsin was only a few miles away, the men were tired and the compound was surrounded by Chinese troops, so Seymour elected to hole up and await relief. The would-be rescuers were now in desperate need of rescuing themselves.

Since the telegraph lines had been severed on June 13, Westerners in Tientsin and Peking had no idea where the admiral's forces had gone. These 2,100 men seemed to vanish off the face of the earth; many assumed they had been wiped out. The Chinese concluded, not unreasonably, that they had scored a resounding victory in cutting off this Western advance.

Taku Forts

While Seymour tried in vain to reach Peking, allied warships steamed to the Taku bar, the entrance from the Gulf of Chihli to the Pei-ho River, which leads to Tientsin and then to Peking. It was protected by four forts, two on each side of the river, that had been rebuilt by German engineers after being captured by Franco-British forces in 1860. On June 16, 1900, a council of allied officers met aboard a Russian warship and decided that the forts had to be neutralized in order to begin the relief of embattled Westerners in Tientsin. They demanded that the Chinese surrender the forts within 24 hours, or else. The naval commanders took this precipitous step, tantamount to a declaration of war, entirely on their own authority. When Sir Claude MacDonald, the British minister, learned of it days later he fretted that they had "sounded the death knell of the foreigners in Peking."

Although the allies precipitated the battle, it was the Chinese who fired the first shot. At 12:50 A.M. on June 17, just as the deadline was about to expire, the Taku forts opened fire with their Krupp artillery. A Russian vessel that inexplicably turned on its searchlight suffered heavy casualties in the ensuing nighttime bombardment. Allied gunboats returned fire, but their light cannons made little dent on the thick fortress walls, until a couple of lucky shots blew up two of the forts' powder magazines. At dawn a landing force composed of British, Italian, German, Russian, Austrian, and Japanese sailors and marines landed in the mud flats and marched 1,300 yards to the northwest fort. The first man over the ramparts, a courageous Japanese officer, was killed. But the rest of the allied troops would not be stopped, and just 15 minutes later the first fort fell. By 6:30 A.M., after almost six hours of combat, all the Taku forts had been taken, at a cost of only seven allied dead and 15 wounded (another 24 sailors were killed in the nighttime artillery exchange).

By all rights the poorly planned and badly coordinated allied amphibious attack against entrenched positions should never have succeeded. That it did is a testament to the poor quality of leadership among the Chinese soldiers. Thanks to these troops' failure to hold the strong positions at Taku, the way was now open for the allies to advance into the interior of the Celestial Kingdom.

The U.S. took no part in the attack. Rear Admiral Louis Kempff, the senior U.S. Navy officer in the area, decided that he could not initiate hostilities against a sovereign state without direct orders from Washington. The USS *Monocacy*, an ancient paddle-wheel steamer (she had been part of the Rodgers expedition to Korea three decades earlier), was anchored away from the battle and used as a safe haven for Western women and children. It suffered one hit from a Chinese shell, which didn't cause much damage. After the battle, the *Monocacy*'s skipper complained to Kempff, "I feel a natural regret, shared no doubt by the officers, that duty and orders prevented old Monocacy from giving her ancient smooth-bores a last chance."

Kempff sent off a telegram to Washington requesting permission to join future operations on the grounds that China's government had, in effect, declared war on America by backing the Boxers and firing on the *Monocacy*. President McKinley, then in the middle of a reelection campaign during which imperialism was the major issue, agreed. Without consulting Congress, he committed the U.S. to fighting the Boxers and dispatched some 5,000 troops for that purpose (only about half of them would arrive in time to see any action).

Imperial Council

While the battle of the Taku forts was raging, the Boxers were swarming all over Peking, and the Seymour expedition was floundering away, a momentous meeting had convened amid the faded splendor of the Forbidden City. From June 16 to 19, 1900, Empress Tz'u-hsi met with 100 of her top mandarins, princes, and generals to decide on a course of action regarding the Boxers. There was a sharp division between those, led by General Jung-lu and the Southern viceroys, who wanted to suppress the Boxers and save the foreigners, and the xenophobic mandarins led by the bold and brash Prince Tuan who wanted to wipe out the "foreign devils." Prince Tuan, who had recently been appointed head of the Tsungli Yamen, replacing the anti-Boxer Prince Ching, presented the empress with a high-handed ultimatum that he said came from the Western ministers. It was a forgery, but she had no way of knowing that, and she was angered by the barbarians' supposed impertinence. When news arrived on June 19 of the allies' (real) ultimatum to the Taku forts, this sealed her decision. She decided to declare war on the foreigners.

What had started as an internal rebellion in China now metamorphosed into a war pitting north China against the combined might of the West plus Japan. (Southern and central China remained peaceful; the imperial authorities there simply ignored the empress's decree.) There is much debate among historians over what pushed the empress into this hopeless confrontation. Some argue that she genuinely believed that the Boxers possessed magical powers that would allow them to wipe out the "hairy ones." Others suggest that she feared the Boxers more than the West. Perhaps she reasoned that her troops were incapable of suppressing the Boxers, and that if she did not propitiate them the Ching dynasty would be overthrown. Whatever her reasoning, the empress's decision to support the red-sashed rebels proved catastrophic not only for her family but for China.

There is even more debate over what responsibility the allies must bear for this declaration of war. Some historians suggest that if the legation guards had not been summoned, if the Seymour expedition had not been dispatched, if the Taku forts had not been attacked—*if, if, if*—then a bloody confrontation could have been avoided. Perhaps. Or the legations might have been wiped out. It was not a chance the foreigners in Peking were willing to take. They remembered all too well how the European men, women, and children of Cawnpore had been slaughtered during the 1857 Indian Mutiny.

Following the imperial council's meeting on June 19, 1900, the Tsungli Yamen sent identical notes to each of the legations notifying them that China was breaking diplomatic relations, and that if they didn't evacuate to Tientsin by 4 P.M. the next day, their safety could no longer be assured. There was much confusion inside the Legation Quarter over what to do. Most of the ministers leaned toward following the Tsungli Yamen's demand, even if this meant abandoning countless Chinese Christians to a gruesome fate.

Baron Clemens von Ketteler, the hotheaded, dashing German minister, decided to go to the Tsungli Yamen to stall for more time. He set out at 10 A.M. on June 20, calmly puffing on a giant Havana cigar and perusing a book, as he was borne away in his sedan chair by coolies (as native workers were derisively called). He refused to take any German marines with him and was accompanied only by a couple of servants and his interpreter, following in another sedan chair. Von Ketteler did not seem to care that he had been a marked man for several days, ever since he had thrashed a Boxer he had caught in the Legation Quarter. Just a few minutes after leaving the foreigners' compound, von Ketteler was surrounded by imperial soldiers from the Peking Field Force and shot in the back of the head. He was killed instantly; his interpreter was wounded but made it back alive. (When the allies took Peking, the Germans identified an army corporal named En Hai as the culprit and decapitated him on the spot where von Ketteler had died. He claimed to have acted under orders.)

"When the story of Von Ketteler's murder had been confirmed, a shiver of horror shook each and every foreigner then in Peking," wrote Polly Condit Smith, a young American woman visiting the U.S. legation, "and we realized, perhaps for the first time, the horror of our position." Any talk of evacuation was now abandoned; all feared they would share the baron's fate if they ventured outside. There was also no sign of Admiral Seymour's expedition; one wag in the British legation joked that he should be renamed "Admiral See-no-more." The foreigners had no choice but to dig in and await Chinese attacks.

Sir Claude MacDonald and another man from the British legation were standing near the gate when, at 4 P.M. on June 20, right on schedule, the firing started. "It must have been on the stroke of the hour when 'whiz,' the almost forgotten sound, followed by another and yet another," MacDonald later recalled, "and then some summer leaves from the trees above fell slowly to the ground, then a bullet struck the coping of the canal a few inches from where I stood and with as much dignity as we could command we walked back into the kindly shelter of the main gate." Huberty James, an elderly British professor who had long resided in China, was not as lucky. He wandered outside to the Chinese positions and was shot to death.

The siege of the foreign legations, which would last for 55 days, had begun.

The legation area covered 85 acres, bounded on the south by the Tartar City wall and on the north by the wall of the Forbidden City, the whole bisected by a smelly open sewer canal called the Jade River. Besides legations representing 11 foreign powers, there were also numerous businesses serving the foreign community. Into this compound were jammed almost 900 Europeans—including 148 women and 79 children—plus at least 3,000 Chinese Christians. (Thousands more Chinese Catholics took refuge in Peitang Cathedral outside the Legation Quarter.) The European women and children, along with many of the male missionaries, were moved into the British Legation, which had the biggest and most secure buildings. The Chinese Christians were shuffled off to the mansion and 14 acres of grounds (called the Fu) belonging to Manchu Prince Su, located opposite the British legation, but only after the Europeans had looted the palace of any valuables. It would be the Chinese Christians who would suffer the most during the siege, because the Europeans hoarded the stocks of food.

By the end of the siege, the starving Chinese converts were reduced to eating tree bark and leaves, while the Europeans still enjoyed free-flowing champagne. The chief complaint among the Westerners was that all the fresh meat was consumed in the first few days; thereafter they were forced to dine on tinned foods and fresh horsemeat. The prize racing ponies belonging to the diplomats were carved up at the rate of two or so a day. "The all important question now is not if 'Cochon' will win more cups in the future," joked Polly Condit Smith about a prize horse, "but if his steaks will be tender."

It was almost tolerable if one could ignore the bullets whizzing around, the stifling temperatures (over 100 degrees), and the nauseating smells that emanated from dead dogs, horses, and people. "The temperature is like a Turkish bath without the clean smell," Miss Smith complained. The men constantly puffed cigars and cigarettes to mask the smell and some of the more daring ladies followed suit. The women took care of the young and wounded, prepared food, and sewed sandbags at a feverish pace, many from Prince Su's fine linens. It was one of the few times in history that soldiers would shelter behind sandbags made with lace flourishes.

The defense of the compound fell to 408 soldiers and 125 male volunteers. They had few heavy weapons: the American marines had brought a Colt machine gun, the British a Nordenfelt five-barrel gun, the Italians a one-pound cannon, and the Austrians a Maxim gun. That was all they had to face countless thousands of attackers. The area under defense gradually diminished as the siege wore on but never amounted to less than 2,100 yards of perimeter, which left the defenders stretched perilously thin. Under the direction of a Methodist missionary who had been trained as an engineer at Cornell, the defenders erected elaborate barricades around the legations. After a few days, overall command was given to the British minister, Sir Claude MacDonald, a gaunt-faced, veteran British infantry officer who had fought tribesmen in Africa before joining the diplomatic corps. But though Sir Claude was nominally the commander, he did not always manage to convince the various national contingents to obey his orders.

The most immediate threat was fire. In the first four days of the siege the Chinese tried to burn out the defenders. And indeed they succeeded in ruining the French, Austrian, Italian, Belgian, and Dutch legations. On June 23 they even set ablaze the Hanlin Library, the leading repository of ancient Confucian texts in the world, in an attempt to destroy the British legation next door. This was an act of vandalism so at odds with the Chinese reverence for learning that it shocked the old China hands among the defenders. They tried to save some of the ancient manuscripts, but with little luck. As the defenders passed buckets of water back and forth to douse the flames, Chinese sharpshooters kept up a steady pinging. The flames were put out, just barely, but the gunfire continued unabated.

Every night came what the defenders called "the serenade": steady bulleting into the compound from Chinese rifles and cannons. Since the Chinese abjured using their modern artillery, their firing created a "hellish" noise and commotion but caused relatively little damage. The most dangerous areas were the grounds of the Fu, defended by Japanese and Italian marines, and the Tartar Wall, 40 feet high and 40 to 50 feet thick, held by Americans, Germans, and Russians. If the Chinese commanders had coordinated their attacks they could have overwhelmed these meager defenses. But they never did.

Why the Chinese failed to press home their attack has been a subject of debate for more than a century. We still do not know with certainty what went on at the highest reaches of the imperial government, and likely never will, but the speculation of contemporaries and historians alike is that some of Tz'u-hsi's mandarins were less than eager to slaughter the "foreign devils." The Boxers, who had started all the trouble in the first place, were not involved in the attack on the legations; a U.S. Marine officer trapped inside noted, "I never saw a yellow-sashed, fist-shaking Boxer . . . during the entire siege." The most ferocious and effective besiegers were the Kansu Braves, a Muslim army unit led by General Tung Fu-hsiang. But many of the other Chinese soldiers, under the command of General Jung-lu (said to have been the empress's former lover), often seemed to aim high. They also refused to employ the modern Krupp artillery that could have reduced the legations to rubble in short order. General Yuan Shih-kai, governor of Shantung province and commander of the best-trained division in the entire Chinese army, refused to attack the legations altogether.

This ambivalence on the part of the attackers gave much of the siege a stilted, unreal feel, akin to a Peking opera performance. But if the Chinese soldiers were simply playing with the legations, as a cat does with a mouse, it was nevertheless a dangerous game for all concerned.

On the Tartar Wall

The American contingent of 56 marines was the third largest in the Legation Quarter, behind the British and Russians. Their commanding officer was Marine Captain John Twiggs Myers. Like many officers of his day (and ours), soldiering ran in his family: His grandfather was General John Twiggs, a Revolutionary War hero; his father, Abraham C. Myers, served as quartermaster general of the Confederate army. Jack Myers was born in 1871 while the family was living in exile in Germany following the Civil War. After returning home, he graduated from the Naval Academy.

His postgraduate education included a great deal of colonial fighting. As a second lieutenant Myers was in command of the marine detachment aboard the USS *Charleston* in 1898 when it was dispatched from California to the Philippines to fight the Spanish. Along the way the cruiser stopped at Guam, a Spanish possession. The ship fired a dozen shots at the ancient Spanish fort guarding the capital. There was no return fire. Instead a Spanish officer came out to the cruiser to apologize for not having any powder; otherwise, he declared politely, the fort would reply to the *Charleston's* "salute." When the poor fellow heard that Spain and America were at war, he promptly surrendered. Myers led a landing party that disarmed the Spanish garrison and secured Guam for the United States.

After fighting Filipino *insurrectos*, 29-year-old Jack Myers had been sent to Peking along with the rest of the marine detachment from his new ship, the *Oregon*. He now threw himself into the task of defending the U.S. section of the Tartar Wall. Every day the marines, with the help of Chinese workers, would strengthen their barricades. And every night the attackers would push their own barricades closer to the marine positions. Myers would often stay awake for days at a time directing the defense. A German soldier who served alongside the marine captain later wrote: "He never leaves the barricade, day or night, and in the most critical moments, he is as calm as others are after a good dinner."

That calmness came in handy on Sunday, July 1, 1900, when the Germans, whose position was next to the Americans, were temporarily driven off the wall by a surprise Chinese attack. Seeing their flank exposed the Americans also withdrew, but the Chinese for mysterious reasons did not occupy their positions. Myers led his men back onto the wall an hour later, and they fortified themselves against an attack from the Chinese-occupied German positions in their rear. The next day the Chinese got bolder and pushed their barricades close enough so that they were literally a stone's throw from the Americans. They also began building a tower on the wall that would allow them to fire straight down into the legations. Sir Claude MacDonald decided there was no choice but to destroy the tower, already 15 feet tall.

Captain Myers assembled 23 British marines, 15 Russians, and 15 of his own men for the job. At 3 A.M. on July 3, they scrambled over the ramparts and attacked the Chinese, driving them off in hand-to-hand combat. At least 20 Chinese were killed, at a cost of only three dead allied soldiers. Sir Claude later praised this as "one of the most successful operations of the siege, as it rendered our position on the wall, which had been precarious, comparatively strong."

Myers saw no more combat in the siege of Peking. During the attack he stumbled onto a spear and wounded his leg. Later he contracted typhoid fever and almost died. He recovered, just barely, and went on to have an illustrious career, serving in Cuba, Mexico, World War I, Haiti, and the Dominican Republic. He retired as a major general and died at a ripe old age in Coconut Grove, Florida, in 1952. Charlton Heston portrayed a fictionalized version of the marine captain in the 1962 film *Fifty-Five Days at Peking*.

With Jack Myers out of action, the command of the marines in Peking passed to Captain Newt Hall. He did not command much respect among his hard-drinking and boisterous men; they thought him too timid and dithering. Luckily other marines more than made up for Hall's deficiencies. Chief among them was Dan Daly, who would later be described by Marine Commandant John Lejeune as "the outstanding Marine of all time." A 25-year-old private, he was a tough Irish-American from the streets of Manhattan, where he had sharpened his fighting skills while employed as a newsboy in the days when circulation wars weren't just metaphorical. He was a small man, just 5 foot 6 inches tall and 132 pounds, but he had ramrod straight posture and piercing gray eyes that, wrote an anonymous marine biographer, "looked upon danger without fear." Like many other young men, he had enlisted in order to fight the Spanish but never got a chance. Instead he had been shipped to Peking.

On July 15, 1900, Captain Hall was told by the American minister, Herbert Squiers, to expand the U.S. position on the Tartar Wall by erecting a new barricade 100 yards in front of the marines' current position. He and Private Daly crawled out to reconnoiter the area. They expected that other marines and coolies would then appear with sandbags to fortify the position. But none showed up. Hall decided to go back and get help. He told Daly: "I can't order you to stay here. But if the Chinks can be held back tonight, we can dig in so they'll never break through."

Daly spat a stream of tobacco juice and laconically replied, "See you in the morning, Captain." The private was left alone behind a low stone parapet, clutching his Lee straight-pull 6 millimeter rifle and a bandoleer of ammunition. The Chinese attacked all night in groups of one or two. Daly calmly picked them off, firing at the silhouettes framed by the flames leaping out of nearby houses. At dawn on July 16, Daly was relieved by other marines. He climbed down off the wall and asked his buddies, "Anybody know what 'Quon-fay' means? They were calling me that all night." Someone replied, "It means devil." For his valor Daly won his first Medal of Honor; he would win another one 15 years later in Haiti.

The Japanese, under their outstanding commander, Colonel Goro Shiba, performed even more heroic feats defending the Fu, where the Chinese Christians were camped out, but they were being pushed back by the weight of Chinese attacks. By July 13, they had given up three-quarters of the Fu grounds to the enemy. Everywhere the defenders were being ground down. Casualties mounted (mainly among the Chinese Christians and legation guards), dysentery swept the compound, morale flagged. If the war of attrition continued, the defenders feared, they would not last much longer. The more gloomy men talked of killing their wives and children should the Chinese burst through, in order to spare them "violation" and torture. Polly Condit Smith, not being married, walked around with a pistol to use on herself "if the worst happens."

Rumors of imminent relief or impending disaster swept the compound on a daily basis. Still cut off, they had no idea whether a relief force would reach them in time.

Tientsin

From the West's standpoint things were not much better outside Peking. Southeast China remained calm, but in north China bedlam reigned. In June and July, the Boxers went on a rampage, killing more than 200 missionaries and countless Chinese Christians. A number of European women and children were murdered, but some of the grisliest violence was reserved for the second-class devils. Ai Sheng, a resident of a small town in Chihli province, recalled years later that when Boxers came on June 4 they burned dozens of Chinese Christian families to death. "When one young woman escaped from the flames, her belly was cut open with a sword by the Boxers. One could hear the sound of skin separating from bones. Several Boxers grabbed the woman by the thighs and arms and threw her back into the flames. The savagery was unspeakable."

Those Westerners, mainly missionaries and railroad engineers, who could not reach the Peking legations headed for Tientsin, 84 miles away, which had a sizable foreign concession located south of the walled city. By June 15 the Chinese city of Tientsin had fallen to the Boxers. Two days later Boxers, along with imperial troops, opened a siege of the mile-long concession. At first there were only 1,700 or so Russian troops to defend the settlement against perhaps 50,000 attackers. The Chinese brought up artillery that poured at least 60,000 shells into the Western Settlement. "To show oneself in the streets was to be shot at," wrote British Methodist missionary Frederick Brown, "and only the

fact that these Boxer sympathizers were untrained in the use of arms prevented an immense loss of life."

Help was on the way. Having secured the Taku forts, Western troops set out to
relieve Tientsin. In the vanguard was a U.S. Marine battalion, eight officers and
132 enlisted men, sent from the Philippines under the command of Major
Littleton W. T. Waller. One of his young lieutenants was Smedley D. Butler, of
whom the world would hear much more before long. They landed on June 19,
just two days after the Taku forts had fallen. The next day they entrained for
Tientsin, 31 miles away, with no maps to guide them.

Along the way, they bumped into 400 Russian soldiers marching in the same
direction. The Russians hopped aboard the train, but the journey was a short
one since the bridge ahead was found to be destroyed. They bivouacked on the
night of June 20 about 12 miles from Tientsin. In the distance they could hear
"the dull booming of cannon and the crash of rifle-fire." The Russian colonel
woke up Waller at 2 A.M. the next day and insisted on advancing on Tientsin
immediately. Waller did not feel that 540 men could get through but reluctantly
joined in. By daylight, having reached the outskirts of Tientsin, they found
themselves under attack on two sides from a much larger Chinese force. "I
thought we were finished," Smedley Butler confessed.

The Russians retreated, leaving the 140 marines with one Colt machine gun
to face some 2,000 Chinese. Already three marines had been killed and nine
wounded. The Americans had no choice but to retreat. For the next four hours,
they trudged down the railroad track, pursued by Chinese cavalry. Along the
way Smedley Butler, another lieutenant and four enlisted men rescued a private
who was lying in a mud ditch, severely wounded and about to be killed by the
enemy. They carried the wounded man for 17 miles. The four enlisted men
received Medals of Honor, but until 1914 such medals were not given to naval
and marine officers, so Butler had to be satisfied with a battlefield promotion.
The marines suffered four killed and nine wounded in this ill-fated advance.

Allied reinforcements finally arrived, and at noon on June 24 the marines led
more than 2,000 soldiers through a dust storm into the Tientsin foreign concession. One of the men who greeted them was a 25-year-old American mining engineer named Herbert Hoover who, along with his wife, had taken refuge
in Tientsin. In his memoirs the former president later wrote: "I do not remember a more satisfying musical performance than the bugles of the American
Marines entering the settlement playing 'There'll be a Hot Time in the Old
Town Tonight.'"

The first order of business was to rescue the woebegone Seymour Relief Expedition, trapped at the Hsiku Arsenal, eight miles from Tientsin, since June 21. Seymour tried to communicate with Tientsin by dispatching Chinese messengers through the Boxer lines. After three messengers had failed, a fourth finally made it through. On the morning of June 25 a relief column of 2,000 men (including Waller's marine battalion) set out for Hsiku and escorted Seymour's expedition back to Tientsin. Of 2,100 men who had set out with the admiral, 62 had been killed and 280 wounded. The remainder joined the swelling allied force at Tientsin.

By July 11, more than 12,000 allied troops were in the city, half of them Russian and Japanese, and the allied commanders decided to conquer the Chinese City a half-mile away in order to "silence the pestiferous Boxer batteries." Among the last allied troops to arrive in time for the attack were two battalions of the 9th U.S. Infantry Regiment—15 officers and 575 men—and the 1st Marine Regiment—18 officers and 300 men—both dispatched from the Philippines. Since they were latecomers, Colonel Emerson H. Liscum, the 9th's commander, and Colonel Robert Meade, the new marine commander, had no opportunity to take part in the planning of the attack. This was done by the British, French, Russian, German, and Japanese commanders—not, as it turned out, very well—and they simply told the Americans where to go. The American soldiers, who agreed to operate under British General Arthur Dorward of the Royal Engineers, would soon pay the price for the allies' lack of planning and coordination.

In the early morning hours of July 13 the battle of Tientsin began, pitting 6,000 allied troops against perhaps 30,000 defenders dug in behind 50-foot stone walls. The Americans, French, British, and Japanese moved out to attack the southern gate of the walled city, while the Germans and Russians went around to the east. Coalition warfare proved a mess. The 9th Infantry was supposed to be on the left of the allied attack but due to a mix-up and lack of clear orders, Colonel Liscum led his men to the right. The infantrymen had to advance across open ground, broken by ponds and mudholes, ditches, and embankments. In their dark blue shirts they made excellent targets for Chinese defenders armed with modern Mauser, Mannlicher, and Winchester rifles sold to them by Western arms companies.

Before long the 9th Infantry was pinned in water up to their waists, trapped under the blazing sun, their ammunition running low. "The shelling was more terrific than any I experienced during the Civil War," wrote U.S. Consul J. W. Ragsdale, who observed the attack, "and I served under General Sherman." In the hours that followed almost a quarter of the men in the 9th's two battalions were killed or wounded. One of the casualties was Colonel Liscum, who had survived the Civil War, the Indian campaigns, the Spanish-American War, and the Philippine War. He saw the 9th's standard-bearer fall and rushed to grab the colors, only to be shot in the abdomen. He died clutching the Stars and Stripes. The onset of darkness allowed the 9th to retreat, after 23 men were killed and 73 wounded.

The marines fared little better. Guided by Herbert Hoover, who knew the area and had volunteered to help, they advanced by rushes to support the Royal Welsh Fusiliers on the extreme left of the allied line. Before long their advance was halted by a swamp. Here they sat, being picked off by Chinese gunners. Smedley Butler ventured out of the trench to rescue a wounded man and was wounded himself. He was carried to the rear by another officer, but the rest of the marines would be trapped in the rice paddies till nightfall "with the Chinese guns thundering an unceasing death tattoo." "The bullets came like hail," a marine enlisted man recalled. "I had the heel shot from my shoe and a hole through my hat . . . and that was the hardest five hours I think I ever spent."

The whole allied advance was stalled and might have been thrown back were it not for the daring Japanese. Early on the morning of July 14, Japanese sappers attached explosives to the South Gate of Tientsin. They tried to light the fuse three times but each time it went out. Finally a Japanese engineer ran forward with a box of matches to set off the powder, blowing himself and the gate to pieces. As Japanese and other allied troops poured into the city, Chinese resistance crumbled. Boxers and imperial soldiers alike fled through two gates the allies had left deliberately unguarded for this purpose. It had been a costly victory, however. The allies suffered 750 men killed and wounded, almost half of them Japanese.

After Tientsin was taken, allied troops and civilians launched an orgy of murder, rape, and theft. An American missionary noted that "those who remained have been treated as if they were all Boxers or spies, and have been freely looted, their houses burned, and themselves driven out to any fate that might await them." The Germans and the Russians were the worst offenders; some of them would rape women and bayonet them afterward. British war correspondent Henry Savage Landor noted a breakdown along national lines in the objects of the looting. He thought that the Japanese were the only soldiers who showed "any natural and thorough appreciation of things artistic." The Americans, by contrast, showed no appreciation "for artistic embroideries, nor for rare bronzes and china ware." Like most of the soldiers, they stuck to grabbing gold, silver, and jewelry. "Sweet lessons in 'western civilization' we are giving to the Chinese," one foreigner trapped in Peking later commented.

A Truce

With Tientsin in their hands, the allies could prepare for an offensive to take Peking. But would they be in time? In mid-July 1900, as noted at the beginning of this chapter, newspapers around the world headlined (in the words of the *New York Evening Journal*) ALL WHITE PEOPLE IN PEKIN MASSACRED. Ironically, the news of the legations' fall came just when their position was rapidly improving. Pressure on the Legation Quarter eased almost at once after the fall of Tientsin. There had always been two parties in the Imperial Court, one in favor of destroying the legations, the other opposed. The success of the Western forces at Tientsin gave the upper hand to those forces in the government, especially the southern Chinese governors, determined to spare the legations.

The result was a truce that broke out on July 17. The Westerners were startled to find that the Chinese troops who had been sniping at them the day before were now selling them eggs and even giving tours of their fortifications. The Tsungli Yamen sent over conciliatory messages, as well as fresh fruit and vegetables, and allowed some of the Western ministers to send telegrams, which is how the outside world came to find out that reports of the legations' demise had been much exaggerated.

The truce was short-lived. The anti-Western elements once again won the upper hand in the imperial court and executed five senior mandarins who favored a more conciliatory stance. The firing on the legations had never totally ceased, and by early August it had resumed with a renewed ferocity.

By this time the suffering inside had increased. Condensed milk was running out and babies were dying of malnutrition. The Chinese Christians, who did not have as many provisions as the Westerners, were slowly starving. Still, hope of salvation was increasing. On August 2, the legations received a message from London, relayed by the Tsungli Yamen, informing them that troops were on the way to Peking. "Keep up heart," implored the telegram.

Through the Cornfields

The besieged would have taken less heart if they had known how slowly and chaotically the relief column was being organized. Lack of troops wasn't the problem. Countless Western warships were anchored off the Taku bar, disgorging thousands of men. By the end of July, 28,000 soldiers had arrived in Tientsin. Though few were first-rate—most came from various Asian colonial garrisons: the British troops from India, the French from Indochina, the

Americans from the Philippines—even so, they were better officered, better armed, and better trained than their Chinese foes. But the allied generals, like most generals of every age, never felt they had enough forces available. Some suggested that 60,000 men would be needed to take Peking. The generals were finally stirred into action when they received messages smuggled out of Peking informing them of what dire straits the legations were in.

Some 20,000 men set out for Peking on the afternoon of August 4, 1900. There were 9,000 Japanese, 4,800 Russians, 2,900 Britons, 2,500 Americans, 1,200 French, and a few hundred Austrians, Germans, and Italians. The Rev. Frederick Brown, a missionary attached to the force as an intelligence officer, described the long, narrow column moving out:

> From its winding form it gave one the idea of a serpent wriggling its way along. At its head were the picturesque uniforms of the Generals and staff, followed by the fine Indian soldiers, mounted on their beautiful horses. Then came the gallant Welsh Fusiliers; while the well-set, business-like United States infantrymen marched next, burning to avenge the slaughter the 9th infantry had suffered ten days before. Then came the Japanese general, with his soldiers in white clothes...

And so on. Accompanying the men were 70 field guns and a long line of supplies pulled by horses, ponies, donkeys, mules, even a few camels shipped by the Russians from Central Asia.

The nominal commander of this polyglot force was British Lieutenant-General Sir Alfred Gaselee, a veteran of the Indian army. But all officers of the Allied Expeditionary Force were loath to take orders from any other nation. Some of the national contingents got along fine; the American and British soldiers, for example, affectionately referred to each other as "damned lime juicers" and "damned Yankees." But in general, mutual suspicion was rife. As a result the cardinal military principle of unity of command was violated, the expedition's orders being hashed out every night in a meeting of the various generals.

The American commander was Major General Adna Romanza Chaffee, a dour 48-year-old cavalryman with a fierce countenance, bushy mustache, bronzed skin, and a puffed-out chest festooned with ribbons won in his numerous campaigns. He had enlisted as a Union private in 1861, suffering wounds at Gettysburg and Brandy Station, and had spent much of his career fighting Indians. In 1874, serving as a captain in the 5th Cavalry, he had played a major role in winning the Red River War against Cheyenne, Comanche, and Kiowa warriors. Chaffee had inspired his men with a memorable exhortation: "Forward! If any man is killed I will make him a corporal." Chaffee had been promoted to general officer rank only in 1898 upon the outbreak of the Spanish-American War. One person who met the general noted: "He has a high forehead, deepset dark eyes and high cheek bones slightly scarred from smallpox. His years in the cavalry have caused him to be slightly bowlegged and butt-sprung. He walks with his feet wide apart pointing inward and this gives him a mincing crablike gait. . . . His natural habitat is astride a horse."

His command consisted of the 9th and 14th Infantry Regiments, a marine battalion, a 6th Cavalry troop, and Reilly's Battery (six 3.2-inch guns from Light Battery F, 5th Artillery, commanded by Captain Henry J. Reilly)—about 2,500 men in all. Although these were regular army and marine regiments—all the state-organized volunteers mobilized to fight the Spanish in 1898 had already been disbanded—most of these soldiers had little experience. Colonel A. S. Daggett of the 14th Infantry estimated that only about 10 percent of his men were veterans, but this experience, being concentrated among the officers and noncomissioned officers (corporals and sergeants), was to prove invaluable. It is hard to get an objective impression of how the American troops compared to other nationalities since observers naturally tended to describe their own country's troops in glowing terms and to disparage the others. Several observers praised the Americans for their marksmanship and logistics, but the only universal point of agreement was that the Japanese were the bravest and most disciplined fighters.

The expedition followed the Pei-ho River, the same route the Anglo-French force had taken in 1860. The Chinese army made only two determined stands, the first (at Peitsang) broken largely by Japanese troops, the second (at Yangtsun) by Americans. (After suffering these defeats, the Chinese commanders, Yu-lu and Li Ping-heng, committed suicide.) In the latter battle, the Americans suffered eight men killed and nine wounded when a Russian cannon accidentally shelled their position. It seems that the Russian gunners had asked the British Royal Artillery for the range and were given the number in yards. However the Russians assumed it was in meters, since they used the metric system. This was one of the more costly pitfalls of coalition warfare.

But even if there was little resistance on the 10-day march to Peking, the advance was not easy. The temperature was constantly above 100 degrees during the day, and the men had to march through cornfields 10 to 15 feet high, which eliminated any breeze. Many were prostrated by the heat, dust, and sun. Dysentery and typhoid fever also ravaged the ranks. "It was a nightmare," recalled one marine.

Among those marching in the American contingent was Smedley Butler, the teenage marine captain, who had gotten up off his sickbed and limped along despite a leg wound, sickness from polluted water, and a toothache. Others had less fortitude. One soldier, the war correspondent Henry Savage Landor reported, "who had become a raving lunatic, with his tongue parched and frightfully distorted features, was making gestures to his companions to shoot him, because he could bear the pain no longer." The country across which the troops marched was littered with dead people and dead animals. "These remain unburied," observed Colonel A. S. Daggett, "and were food for dogs and hogs and crows and buzzards."

The advance of the allied column was actually making life rougher for the Legation Quarter, since it was pushing more Chinese troops back into Peking. The Chinese mounted some of the most severe attacks of the entire siege in early August. On the night of August 13, for the first time they even situated a rapid-fire Krupp field gun on the Imperial Wall, where it could fire down into the legations. The gun did more damage in 10 minutes than all the old Chinese smoothbores had done in the past month. Luckily for the legations, counterfire from the American Colt machine gun and the Austrian Maxim gun killed the Chinese gun crew and silenced the Krupp cannon. But what if the Chinese brought up more Krupp artillery? The Westerners feared that the Chinese were making one last push to wipe them out before the relief force arrived.

On August 13, the allied force bivouacked all day at Tungchow, a town only 14 miles from Peking. Here the generals decided upon a plan of action to take the capital, with each of the armies assigned its own objectives. The attack was supposed to start on August 15, but the Russians jumped the gun. On the night of August 13, they sent a patrol in strength toward Peking. Finding the way clear and wanting to get a jump on the other contingents, the Russians attacked at once. This advance had more than a little in common with the Russian race to Berlin in 1945 or to Pristina airport in Kosovo in 1999, both instances of the Russians seeking to beat their ostensible allies to a joint objective. But in 1900 they did not get far. In the confusion of the night, the Russians attacked the Tung Pien gate, which had been assigned to the Americans. After blowing the outer gate with artillery, the Russian troops were pinned down by murderous fire in the courtyard, unable to advance any farther. As soon as the other allied forces realized the Russians were gone from camp, they hurriedly packed up and set out on a mad dash for the glory of being first to reach the legations.

The Americans reached Peking on the morning of August 14, a clear, cloudless day. Unable to advance through the Tung Pien gate with the Russians blocking the way, the U.S. units simply slid south. Here they confronted a section of the Tartar Wall 30 feet high—and no gate in sight. They had no scaling ladders, either, so Colonel Daggett of the 14th Infantry asked for a volunteer to climb the wall. Corporal Calvin P. Titus stepped forward. "I'll try, sir." He was the bugler of Company E, a tall, scrawny kid, just 20 years old. All eyes were on him as he slowly slithered up the wall, finding footholds in the eroded stone. As he prepared to go over the top, Daggett wrote, "All below is breathless silence. The strain is intense. Will that embrasure blaze with fire as he attempts to enter it? Or will the butts of rifles crush his skull?" Luckily for Titus, the Chinese were so disorganized that they had no defenders on this section of the wall. He climbed up and shouted down, "The coast is clear. Come on up."

After a few men had reached the top, they were finally discovered by the city's defenders, who opened fire. But by then it was too late. There were too many Americans on the wall to throw back. At 11:03 A.M., Old Glory was planted atop the wall. "As that flag was unfurled and stood out against the August sky, there went up to heaven a shout of triumph the Spartans might have envied," Daggett wrote. For his exploit, Corporal Titus won a Medal of Honor and an appointment to West Point; he retired decades later as a lieutenant colonel.

It did not take long for the Americans to reach the Tung Pien gate, relieve the Russians, and rout the defenders. The Americans then fought their way through the city streets, with the route being cleared by the horse-drawn artillery of Reilly's Battery. During the attack, Marine Lieutenant Smedley Butler was shot in the chest, but the bullet struck a large brass button and merely knocked him unconscious. He rejoined his unit, coughing up blood. At 4 P.M., the Americans finally reached the legations.

Too late!

No, the legations had not fallen to the Chinese. Almost as galling to American honor, they had fallen to the British.

The American and Japanese attacks on the Tartar City had drawn off most of the defenders, allowing the British to waltz in almost uncontested. They found a water gate leading into the Legation Quarter and at 2:45 P.M. on August 14, 1900, Sikh soldiers wearing khaki uniforms and red turbans crawled through the mud and muck of the sewer to end the siege of Peking. There was quite a contrast between rescuers and rescued. The relief column had been on the march for a week; the men were tired, sweaty, and dirty. Henry Savage Landor noted that some of the nonfighting men in the legations, on the other hand, "wore starched shirts, with extra high glazed collars, fancy flannel suits, and vari-coloured ties. We dirty creatures thought these particular fellows silly and objectionable; they put on such patronising airs that it made one almost feel sorry we had relieved them."

Still there was no mistaking the joy in the legations at finally being rescued. The siege had taken its toll. Sixty-six foreigners had been killed, most of them servicemen (including eight Americans); amazingly enough, only one European woman and six children died. Another 150 foreigners had been wounded. Many more Chinese Christians had perished. Outside Peking 240 missionaries were murdered in north China in 1900, many of them women and children. And some 30,000 Chinese converts died.

Inside Peking, the Legation Quarter had not been the worst hit. The Chinese attacks took an even more fearsome toll in the Peitang Cathedral. Thirty-four hundred Chinese Christians and 55 missionaries clustered inside, protected by just 43 Italian and French sailors commanded by French Sub-Lieutenant Paul Henry. There were more people besieged here than in the legations, and they had less food, faced more determined attacks, and took more casualties. More than 400 died in all, including 75 children, some from wounds, others from starvation and disease. It was truly a miracle that the rest survived. The Boxers rather imaginatively attributed their failure to a "ten thousand woman flag," woven out of pubic hair, that the defenders supposedly draped on the cathedral, thus negating the Boxers' magic.

Reilly's Battery

Having conquered Peking, the allies were uncertain as to how to proceed. What were they to do with the Empress Dowager Tz'u-hsi? If they deposed her, who would rule China? To avoid this choice, the allies insisted on pretending that they had been fighting simply to suppress the Boxer "rebellion"; they refused to acknowledge the empress's declaration of war. It was just as well from their perspective that just as the Allied Expeditionary Force was arriving she slipped out of Peking disguised as a peasant. She then went on a grand "tour of inspection" of the countryside, trying mightily to pretend that her capital was not occupied by smelly barbarians. That still left the question of how to handle the Imperial

City and the Forbidden City. If the allies invaded the empress's domain, they feared she would lose too much face with her subjects; but if they stayed out, they feared she would be able to tell her people that they had not really been defeated.

General Adna Chaffee, apparently on his own initiative, ordered U.S. troops to advance on the Forbidden City before dawn on August 15, the day after he had arrived in Peking. First they had to penetrate the adjoining Imperial City, which required passing through three heavy wooden gates, each one at least 8 inches thick and sealed with enormous padlocks. This was a job for Reilly's Battery. A couple of horse-drawn guns were wheeled into position in front of the first gate to the Imperial City. A lieutenant coolly walked over and chalked an X in the middle, ignoring the bullets ricocheting around him. Then he strolled back and ordered his guns to fire at point-blank range. "The heavy studded ancient doorway creaked and quivered," wrote Henry Savage Landor, "and splinters flew in every direction as each thorite shell hit the gate full." Eventually the gate gave way, and a company of the 14th Infantry poured into the courtyard to clear out the Chinese defenders. This process was repeated with a second gate and a third—all under heavy Chinese fire.

The Americans lost a number of men in this operation, most notably Captain Henry J. Reilly. Born in Ireland, he had enlisted as a Union private in 1862 and won a battlefield commission for bravery. A slight man—he stood 5 foot 11 inches and weighed just 145 pounds—he had blue eyes hidden behind a pince-nez, a close trimmed beard, and a mustache streaked with gray. His 39 years of soldiering had elevated him no higher than captain but along the way his courteous, gentle demeanor had won the affection of his men. Many of them cried when they saw Reilly felled by a bullet to the head. But they kept firing. They were about to blast the final gate leading to the Forbidden City when a messenger arrived from Chaffee to announce: "The general directs that you suspend all further operations."

According to Savage Landor, this order was greeted with a "melody of oaths as only American boys can devise." And no wonder. They had seen their beloved Reilly and five others killed and 19 wounded—and for what? So that they could stop short of their goal? This galling decision had been forced on Chaffee by his fellow allied commanders. When they got wind that the Americans were on the verge of breaking into the Forbidden City, they convened a council of war and demanded that the advance stop at once. Their ostensible justification was that they did not want to insult the empress by entering her lair. But this was nonsense. In fact the allies staged a big ceremony of entering the Forbidden City three days later, with the Russians leading the way. It was not that they were opposed to entering the Forbidden City. They were opposed to the Americans entering first. So Reilly and the others had died in vain.

Reilly's funeral was held on August 16. After the ceremony, the parsimonious U.S. Minister, Edwin Conger, tried to grab the flag from the casket, explaining, "There are so few American flags in Peking, this one can't be spared."

"Don't touch that flag," growled General Chaffee. "If it's the last American flag in China it will be buried with Reilly."

Rape and Pillage

As soon as the allies had secured Peking, the looting began. Everyone, military and civilian, missionary and diplomat, Asian and Westerner, joined in stealing everything of value they could get their hands on. Polly Condit Smith, the young American visitor who had been trapped in the Legation Quarter, found various admirers presenting tokens of their affection: a Russian officer tried to give her a sable coat, a Belgian offered a tortoiseshell bracelet set with pearls, a Sikh presented an expensive clock and two chickens. It was the chickens she valued most. But some of those present became rich from their loot. "It took stronger wills than we possessed not to be tempted by brocades and furs lying in the gutters," Smedley Butler later confessed.

Count Alfred von Waldersee, a German field marshal who had arrived too late to take part in the actual campaign, became the new allied commander. He ensconced himself in one of the empress's palaces with a Chinese concubine to warm his bed, and carried out Kaiser Wilhelm II's orders to behave "just as the Huns a thousand years ago" did. The German troops were particularly enthusiastic in staging grisly reprisals against the Chinese. The countryside was stripped bare for miles around Peking, many temples and pagodas of great value being blown up and countless Chinese being beaten, raped, or murdered— sometimes all three. "It is safe to say," said General Chaffee, "that where one real Boxer has been killed since the capture of Peking, fifty harmless coolies or laborers on farms . . . including not a few women and children, have been slain." As with the looting of Tientsin, the rape of Peking was not a good advertisement for the benefits of Western civilization.

In fairness it should be noted that there was more to the allied occupation than plunder and pillage. The foreign armies split Peking into zones of occupation, as Berlin and Vienna would one day be split. While the Germans and Russians were interested primarily in preying on the natives, the Americans took their administrative duties in the western half of the Chinese City more seriously. American troops enforced sanitary regulations to stop epidemics, opened charities and hospitals, set up a court run by the Chinese, created schools, policed opium dens and gambling houses. The U.S. sector was so well run that people flocked there from other parts of the city.

The U.S. and other nations began pulling their troops out of Peking after September 7, 1901. On this date, the Chinese government signed a protocol containing a variety of punishments for its failure to suppress the Boxers, including a promise to pay the West an indemnity of $335 million over the next 39 years at 4 percent annual interest. (Ever since the Opium Wars, it had become standard practice for the West to make China pay the costs of defeating it.) The full amount would never be paid. Starting in 1908 President Theodore Roosevelt turned over the U.S. share to pay for Chinese students to be educated in the U.S.

By May 1901 the only U.S. ground forces left in north China were five officers and 150 infantrymen guarding the Peking legation.

Rise and Fall

The faction at the imperial court that had wanted to save the legations hoped that doing so would be good for the Middle Kingdom and the Ching dynasty. It did not work out that way. The Boxer Protocol further impinged on Chinese sovereignty by giving foreign powers the right to deploy troops from Peking to the sea, and the vast indemnity weakened the state treasury. Russia used the Boxer uprising as an excuse to temporarily seize all of Manchuria in the summer of 1900. Ching prestige was shattered beyond repair. Tz'u-hsi, Old Buddha, died in 1908. Four years later the last emperor, Hsüan-t'ung (better known as P'u-i), would be overthrown and a republic declared.

Although it marked one of the death knells of the Manchus, the Boxer uprising represented a milestone in the rise of American and Japanese power. Both in the legations and in the relief expedition, the bravest, most disciplined soldiers were Japanese. And, oddly enough, they were also respectful of Chinese lives and property—restraint that would be spectacularly lacking during Japan's invasion of the Middle Kingdom in the 1930s. Japan's reputation would be further enhanced by its thrashing of Russia in 1905. The sun was clearly rising on the Japanese empire.

So, too, U.S. power was ascendant. Ever since the Civil War the U.S. had been an economic juggernaut. But it was a slow process to convert economic carbohydrates into military muscle. Most of the U.S. campaigns abroad in the nineteenth century had been small affairs. That had changed when the U.S. had grabbed the remains of the Spanish empire in 1898. Now something else had changed as well: America had abandoned its old unilateralism. Uncle Sam was now willing to take part in military coalitions with other Great Powers. In this respect the Boxer campaign presaged Washington's entry into World War I in "association" with the Triple Entente.

The Boxer campaign presaged World War I in another respect as well: It showed the difficulties of fielding a multinational army. The bickering was almost nonstop, the coordination virtually nonexistent. A number of American lives were lost—in the badly planned attack on Tientsin, for instance—due to the lack of centralized planning.

Many of the American soldiers who served in the Boxer campaign would get to see plenty more action. Just as many of them had come from the Philippines, so many would return, to suppress a far more determined and better organized guerrilla uprising than the one they had faced in China.

5

"ATTRACTION" AND "CHASTISEMENT"

The Philippine War, 1899–1902

"We are bound for googoo land now," Lieutenant Edward A. Bumpus remarked as the army transport ship steamed through the tropical evening dusk. Aboard were 77 men in heavy blue woolen shirts, khaki trousers, and floppy felt campaign hats. Ahead of them lay a clearing with 200 or so thatch-roofed huts resting on stilts, a church building, and a meeting hall, all squeezed precariously between the vast, forbidding mountainous jungle and the shark-infested Leyte Gulf. This was the village of Balangiga, located at the southernmost tip of Samar, the third largest island in the Philippine archipelago. On August 11, 1901, the men of Company C, 9th U.S. Infantry, splashed ashore to a surprisingly boisterous welcome from the Filipino residents. The troopers expected a spell of routine occupation duty at the tail end of a war they thought was almost over.

More than three years before, the burgeoning power of the United States had dismembered the remains of the Spanish empire and put the Philippines under the Stars and Stripes. The Filipinos stubbornly resisted their new colonial masters, and though successive U.S. generals proclaimed victory at hand, American soldiers kept dying in ambushes, telegraph lines kept getting cut, and army convoys kept being attacked. Among the most stubborn of guerrilla commanders was General Vincente Lukban, scion of a rich family of mixed Chinese and Tagalog origin who directed resistance on Samar. Lukban's men had begun by executing all the Spanish clergy on the island and replacing them with native priests. Afterward they targeted not only Americans but also their collaborators, burying three *americanistas* alive, tying another to a tree and hacking him to bits. The Americans retaliated in kind, occasionally torturing suspected guerrilla sympathizers to elicit information, sometimes killing prisoners, and routinely burning the homes and crops of villagers who harbored *insurrectos*.

It was not at all the kind of conflict that soldiers like. This dirty war offered no heroic charges, no brilliant maneuvers, no dazzling victories. Just the daily frustrations of battling an unseen foe in the dense, almost impassable jungle. For Company C, this was an unwelcome contrast to the excitement of recent years, when the men had fought in Cuba (the Spanish-American War) and north China (the Boxer Uprising), distinguishing themselves at San Juan Hill, Tientsin, and Peking. There was no campaign to be waged in Balangiga, in fact not much to do: no gambling dens, no bars, no bordellos, not even regular mail calls. The men were afflicted with malaria and homesickness and boredom. One private went mad. Another committed suicide.

The most immediate task at hand was sanitation. The Americans were disgusted by what they found. "On the ground beneath the flooring, the natives threw every kind of filth, and it was rarely one could approach a hut without holding his nose," complained Company C's trumpeter. The company commander, Captain Thomas W. Connell, a by-the-book West Pointer and a "young, vigorous, zealous officer," demanded that the Filipinos clean up the mess, which he considered a breeding ground for diseases like cholera. They refused. So he rounded up local men and forced them into "policing" their village at gunpoint. Then he confined them in tents too small to hold so many comfortably. Naturally they resented their involuntary servitude.

The captain was blissfully unaware of the villagers' true feelings. Connell thought that as a fellow Catholic he had special empathy for the villagers, and that he and his men were welcome because Pedro Abayan, Balangiga's *presidente* (mayor), had asked the army to send a contingent to protect the town from "pirates." What Connell did not know was that Abayan had separately written to General Lukban, telling him that he had adopted a "deceptive policy" with "the enemy" and that "when a favorable opportunity arises, the people will strategically rise up against them." That letter was one of many captured by an army raid on Lukban's headquarters on August 13, 1901, but it moved so slowly up the army chain of command that it never reached Company C in time.

The men of Company C had already spent more than a month in Balangiga when on Friday, September 26, 1901, the first of 80 burly laborers mysteriously appeared from the jungle to help with the cleanup. Captain Connell did not suspect that they were actually Lukban's *insurrectos*.

On Sunday, September 28, the bugler sounded reveille at 5:30 A.M., and following roll call the men poured out of the village meeting hall, used as a barracks, to head for the mess tent. Most of them were unarmed; only three sentries were left on duty. The town's police chief, Pardo Sanchez, casually strolled up to one of them, grabbed his rifle, and smashed him on the head with its butt. At that moment the church bells began pealing, the surrounding jungle resonated with the sound of conch shells being blown, the doors of the church flew open, and hundreds of bolomen poured into the streets of Balangiga, "yelling like devils."

Some of them rushed for the convent, which had been converted into officers' quarters. Captain Connell was caught in his room, still in his pajamas. He jumped out of his second-story window and landed in the plaza, only to be hacked to death by at least 20 bolomen. Company C's other two officers were also killed right away.

The men in the mess tent and the barracks were similarly unprepared. A sergeant bending over a vat of boiling water to wash his mess kit was attacked with an ax and pitched head first into the water, with only his legs protruding. Another sergeant's head was cleaved right off his neck and plopped onto his plate. In just 15 minutes, 38 officers and men were killed—and of the 36 survivors, most were wounded, many severely. One private, a survivor later recalled, "was crawling on his hands and feet like a stabbed pig, his brains falling out through the wound he had received."

Those not killed in the initial assault fought ferociously for their lives with whatever came to hand—knives and forks, picks and shovels, rocks and a baseball bat. A cook threw a pot of boiling coffee in the faces of his assailants and then pelted them with canned goods. Some of the men reached the barracks where the company's rifles were stored, grabbed their .30 caliber Krag Jorgensens and "starting pumping lead into the 'googoos.'" They drove the attackers out of Balangiga, at least for the time being, but they knew that to survive they had to reach another U.S. garrison, and the only way to do that was by water. Under the direction of Sergeant Frank Betron, 36 survivors, most wounded, staggered down to the beach and clambered into five *barotos* (wooden canoes with double outriggers), clutching a handful of provisions and the U.S. flag that had been fluttering above their parade ground.

"We at last shoved off, thanking God we were leaving, and thinking the worst of our troubles were over. But our troubles had hardly started," a private wrote. The Americans fired their rifles to hold off Filipinos in pursuing boats, but sharks were not so easy to drive off; a school of them followed the canoes, drawn by the blood dripping into the water. Fresh water ran out about noon. "Words cannot express our state of mind with that tropical sun burning down on our heads, no water to drink, and the salt water causing excruciating pain as it soaked into our wounds. But God favored us with delirium, and I don't think any of us can tell all that happened that afternoon."

Not until dawn the next day did the survivors finally reach the U.S. outpost at Basey, 30 miles up the coast. Just 26 men out of Company C's original roster of 74 survived the ordeal, and all but four of them were wounded.

Stationed at Basey was Company G, also of the 9th Infantry. Their reaction to the news of their comrades killed and wounded can only be imagined. Captain Edwin V. Bookmiller, the Basey commander, set off for Balangiga aboard a steamer with 55 of his men and eight survivors from Company C. They arrived at 12:30 P.M. on Monday, September 29, 1901. As they got to within 500 yards of shore, they opened fire, driving out of the village any remaining Filipinos, who took with them 52 working rifles and 26,000 rounds of ammunition. In Balangiga, they found smoldering buildings and a series of harrowing sights: Corpses stripped naked, some burned or hacked beyond recognition; Lieutenant Bumpus, a bolo slash across his face filled in with strawberry jam to lure ants from the jungle; even the company dog was dead, its eyes gouged out and replaced with stones. The men of Company G gathered up the dead Americans and buried them in a mass grave. There were also some dead natives strewn about, though the Filipinos had taken many of their dead with them, making an accurate count of their losses impossible to calculate (estimates ranged from 50 to 250 dead). "After burying dead," Captain Bookmiller noted laconically in his report, "burned the town and returned to Basey."

The news of the Balangiga "massacre" made front-page headlines in the United States. The press compared it to the Alamo and the Little Bighorn in the annals of the country's military disasters. As they read the gruesome details, more than a few Americans must have wondered what their sons were doing, 7,000 miles from home, still fighting and dying in a war whose conclusion had been officially announced more than once. Subjugating the Philippines was turning out to be a lot harder than promised.

"Splendid Little War"

The conflict in the Philippines was the unwelcome and unforeseen offspring of that "splendid little war," as Secretary of State John Hay famously described the

Spanish-American War. The war against Spain had come about in 1898 in large part because Americans wanted to free the Cubans from the yoke of Spanish oppression. Few realized that the first shots would be fired in the Far East. But that was the logic of war plans drawn up by the Navy Department under the guidance of Assistant Secretary Theodore Roosevelt. Those plans called for the U.S. Asiatic Fleet to head to Manila upon the outbreak of hostilities and destroy the Spanish warships based there.

Commodore George Dewey carried out those instructions to perfection. At 5:45 A.M. on May 1, 1898, Dewey gave the order that would become a catchphrase, "You may fire when you are ready, Gridley," to Captain Charles V. Gridley, captain of the USS *Olympia*. In the next seven hours the more modern U.S. fleet proceeded to sink all but one of the Spanish vessels. Spain suffered 371 casualties, the U.S. only nine wounded and one dead, of heatstroke. Dewey became a national hero overnight, but he was left with one major problem: what to do about the Spanish army still in possession of the Philippines. A naval victory was all very well, but ships could not occupy land.

The Spanish, who had ruled the Philippines for more than 300 years, already had their hands full with a native uprising that had started in 1896, led by a 27-year-old provincial mayor named Emilio Aguinaldo y Famy. A small man of mixed Tagalog and Chinese ancestry, born into a moderately well-to-do family, Aguinaldo had little schooling—he had dropped out at 13 to help run the family businesses, his father having died when he was just nine—but he had no shortage of charisma, shrewdness, and eloquence. With no formal military training, he proved himself to be a talented guerrilla leader, driving the Spanish out of his native Cavite province, at least temporarily. He became the undisputed leader of the independence movement after engineering the execution of a rival, Andres Bonifacio.

Unfortunately, this infighting weakened the independence movement just as the Spanish were stepping up their attacks. Aguinaldo was forced to abandon Cavite, but he displayed considerable skill in evading his Spanish pursuers, establishing an unimpregnable stronghold in the mountains north of Manila. Unable to defeat the rebels, the Spanish tried to buy them off. Aguinaldo accepted an offer of 800,000 pesos in return for his pledge to leave the country, but he had no intention of giving up the struggle. He merely relocated to Hong Kong with some aides and used the Spanish lucre to buy more arms. In Hong Kong and Singapore he sought backing from the local U.S. counsels, offering to help America in its war with Spain. The American envoys were enthusiastic—so enthusiastic that Aguinaldo later claimed that they had pledged U.S. support for Philippine independence. If so, they exceeded their authority.

Having sunk the Spanish fleet, Dewey now sent a cutter to Hong Kong to fetch Aguinaldo. When the two men met aboard Dewey's flagship, the *Olympia*, anchored in Manila harbor, they were a study in contrasts. The young Filipino, not yet 30, was an unprepossessing sight, with his slight stature, face pockmarked by smallpox scars, and rumpled khaki uniform complemented by a captured Spanish sword. Rear Admiral Dewey was equally diminutive, but he was more than twice Aguinaldo's age, sporting silver hair and a mustache to match, resplendent as always in his sharply creased, white dress uniform, and basking in his new-found celebrity and rank. The two men, different in so many ways, also offered sharply different accounts of what occurred that day, May 19, 1898, and in subsequent encounters. Aguinaldo claimed Dewey promised him U.S. support for an independent Philippines; Dewey protested that he had said no such thing. Aguinaldo may have been so desperate for American backing that he read more into Dewey's vague assurances than the admiral intended. All that Dewey wanted was for Aguinaldo's men to engage the Spanish army until American troops arrived. He told the rebel leader, "Go ashore and start your army."

Even before Aguinaldo went ashore, the Filipino army had already sprung into existence, led by capable regional commanders, and before long the Filipinos had won control of almost the entire archipelago, leaving only Manila in Spanish hands. On June 12, 1898, Aguinaldo and other Filipino leaders issued a declaration of independence based on the U.S. model. Dewey refused to attend the ceremonies or to give any recognition to the new government. At the end of June the first U.S. troops began arriving in the Philippines, part of a 12,500-man expeditionary force sent by President McKinley with a vague goal: to "complete the reduction of Spanish power in the archipelago" and provide "order and security to the islands while in the possession of the United States."

The U.S. troops found Filipino forces already entrenched around Manila. After delicate negotiations Aguinaldo agreed to let the *norteamericanos* pass through his lines. The commanders of the 15,000 Spanish soldiers trapped inside the capital had no desire to fight, but feared the consequences should their former subjects take over. So they negotiated an elaborate hoax with Admiral Dewey whereby the U.S. troops would lob a few shells into Manila and then the Spanish could surrender "under fire." The sham "battle" of Manila occurred on August 13, 1898. Unfortunately the troops on the ground had not been let in on the joke. When they heard the firing, some of the Spanish soldiers panicked and started shooting back. Six Americans and 49 Spaniards died before the Spanish governor-general managed to surrender the city as intended. U.S. troops occupied Manila, keeping the Philippine army out at gunpoint.

The Filipinos, who had done the bulk of the fighting and dying, were given no role in the surrender ceremony. They were understandably aggrieved.

Treaty of Paris

Now that the United States found itself unexpectedly in possession of the Philippines, or at least its capital, President McKinley had to figure out what to do with it. Most Republicans were screaming for annexation. But the famously indecisive, inscrutable president temporized and agonized. "I walked the floor of the White House night after night until midnight," he later told a group of Methodist missionaries, "and I am not ashamed to tell you, gentlemen, that I went down on my knees and prayed Almighty God for light and guidance more than one night. And one night late it came to me this way . . . that there was nothing left for us to do but to take them all, and to educate the Filipinos and uplift them and civilize and Christianize them, and by God's grace do the best we could by them, as our own fellowmen for whom Christ also died." Most Filipinos were already Christian, Catholic to be precise, but never mind. McKinley's thinking very much reflected the twin currents of Protestant piety and American jingoism that defined the turn-of-the-century zeitgeist.

There were also more practical reasons for grabbing the Philippines. The race for colonies was in full swing, and Americans feared that they would be locked out of the Asian market. The British already had a naval base at Hong Kong that gave them access to China; many strategists argued the U.S. needed its own base, and what better place than near Manila? But the War and Navy departments warned that it was impractical to confine the U.S. presence to Manila and the naval town of Cavite; if a European empire or Japan gobbled up the rest of the islands those American outposts would become indefensible. As if to confirm those fears, the German navy, dispatched by a kaiser lusting after colonies, was shadowing Dewey's fleet. McKinley feared that if the U.S. did not annex the Philippines, Germany or Japan or some other power would step in, to the detriment of not only American but Filipino interests.

That the Philippines could be self-governing was not a notion seriously entertained in Washington. Based on what scant information he had about life in the islands, McKinley concluded that Aguinaldo was not a popular leader, especially among non-Tagalogs, and that, absent outside rule, the archipelago would sink into chaos and conflict between competing ethnic groups.

The president therefore wired U.S. representatives meeting in Paris with Spanish envoys to demand all of the Philippines as well as Guam and Puerto

Rico as the price of peace. The treaty ending the Spanish-American War was signed on December 10, 1898. The U.S. paid Spain $20 million and thereby acquired title to the Philippines, with its 7,108 islands and some 7 million inhabitants. McKinley issued a proclamation announcing the U.S. goal as "benevolent assimilation."

To make good on the president's pledge, the U.S. occupation army undertook a wide variety of improvements in Manila—cleaning up the unsanitary conditions left behind by the Spanish, vaccinating the inhabitants, repairing roads, building schools, and generally making the city bustle again. This work was only partly altruistic, since its larger purpose was to make Manila more livable for the army of occupation. But most Filipinos had no desire to be "assimilated," benevolently or otherwise. Tensions mounted between the U.S. troops in Manila and the Philippine soldiers who surrounded them. Some of Aguinaldo's men attacked American soldiers; some American soldiers attacked Aguinaldo's men.

Although some historians have hinted that there was an American conspiracy to provoke a clash, the reality is that neither side was eager to commence hostilities. McKinley, with his memories of service as a Union major in the Civil War, had seen enough dying to last him a lifetime. Besides, he hoped that if he waited long enough, Filipino resistance would crumble. Aguinaldo, for his part, hoped that if *he* waited long enough, the U.S. Senate would refuse to ratify the Treaty of Paris.

As the Filipino leader was well aware, there was substantial opposition to annexation in the United States. A virtual who's who of prominent Americans, including Grover Cleveland, Andrew Carnegie, Samuel Gompers, William James, Jane Addams, and Mark Twain, joined the Anti-Imperialist League. Carnegie, one of America's richest men, even offered to buy the islands himself for $20 million in order to set them free. Many of these worthies were old-fashioned "mugwumps" who believed America could best serve the world by setting a shining example at home. Another, less high-minded strain of opposition to annexation came from Southern Democrats such as Senator "Pitchfork Ben" Tillmann who opposed mixing with "Asiatic hybrids" and "inferior races" and feared that Caucasian workers could not compete with "those who live on a bowl of rice and a rat a day."

But those resisting annexation were swamped by a tidal wave of imperialist sentiment. Led by the likes of Theodore Roosevelt, the advocates of annexation represented the coming generation whose "progressivism" at home was matched by imperialism abroad. Although they made appeals to America's security and commercial interests, their primary pitch was idealistic. Albert J. Beveridge, the newly elected senator from Indiana, thundered: "God has not been preparing the English-speaking and Teutonic peoples for a thousand years for nothing but vain and idle self-contemplation and self-admiration. . . . He has made us adepts in government that we may administer government among savage and senile peoples." The English poet Rudyard Kipling joined in, urging the U.S. to "take up the white man's burden" in a poem of the same name, subtitled "The United States and the Philippine Islands."

The Senate did wind up ratifying the Treaty of Paris by one vote more than the two-thirds required (57–27), but only after fighting had already broken out.

"The Ball Has Begun"

On the night of February 4, 1899, Private Willie Grayson, a small-town kid who had enlisted in the First Nebraska Volunteers, was on guard duty in an eastern suburb of Manila whose control was in dispute between the U.S. and Philippine forces. The night was oppressively hot and humid, and the mosquitoes were giving him no rest. Just before 8 P.M., Grayson heard some low whistles, possibly signals, and saw three or four armed Filipinos approaching him, cocking their weapons. "I yelled 'halt,'" Grayson later recalled, "and the man moved. I challenged with another 'halt.' Then he immediately shouted 'Halto' to me. Well I thought the best thing to do was to shoot him. He dropped." Grayson then ran back to camp to alert his comrades that the "niggers are in here all through these yards." Firing quickly spread up and down the line. An aide woke up Colonel Frederick Funston of the First Kansas Volunteers to inform him "the ball has begun."

The U.S. Army was only slightly better prepared for this war than it had been for the previous one, against the Spaniards. Prior to the Spanish-American War, the whole army had comprised just 28,183 officers and men—considerably smaller than the New York Police Department today. Upon the outbreak of hostilities, Congress raised the regular army strength to 56,688 men and McKinley issued a call for the states to recruit 125,000 volunteers for a one-year enlistment. The resulting regiments had little formal military training and generally lacked the equipment necessary for tropical campaigning, but some, the First U.S. Volunteer Cavalry (Rough Riders) most famously, more than compensated for these shortcomings with the formidable shooting and riding skills they brought with them from civilian life. The men were issued blue flannel uniforms that were unsuitable for the tropics and canned provisions that frequently turned out to be rotten.

The regulars were armed with the new Krag-Jorgensen, a Norwegian-made .30 caliber, five-shot rifle firing smokeless powder. But there were not enough Krags to go around, so the volunteers were issued the Civil War-vintage, single-shot Springfield rifle. When fired, the .45 caliber Springfield bucked like a bronco and emitted a smoke screen that blinded its shooter while revealing his position to the enemy. Its only advantage was that one of its shots was guaranteed to fell any adversary short of a rhinoceros. Supplementing these rifles were various early machine guns (Maxim-Nordenfeldt, Hotchkiss, Colt, and Gatling being the most popular brands) and 3.2 inch, breech-loading field artillery.

When the Battle of Manila began on February 4, 1898, 11,000 U.S. soldiers, mainly volunteers, were thinly deployed along 16 miles of front facing Filipino trenches. On paper it appeared that the Filipinos had the upper hand: Their 20,000 men surrounding Manila, part of an army of at least 80,000, outnumbered the Americans, they were well dug in, and they were armed with a combination of antiquated Remington single-shot rifles and more modern Mauser repeating rifles captured from the Spanish that were superior to the Americans' Krags. Moreover, they had excellent intelligence on the U.S. deployments and planned a rising in Manila to attack the Yanquis from the rear.

All these advantages soon proved illusory. The Filipinos had even less training than the U.S. volunteers and they did not have enough shoes, let alone rifles, to go around; many of them were armed only with bolo knives and many of those who had rifles did not know how to use their sights. The Filipinos were courageous—U.S. General Henry Lawton called them "the bravest men I have ever seen"—but they were no match for a modern Western army.

As soon as the sun rose over the rooftops of Manila on Sunday morning, February 5, 1899, following a night of wild shooting in the dark, Major General Elwell S. Otis, the U.S. commander, ordered a general advance. Admiral Dewey's warships peppered the Filipino positions with their heavy guns; then the volunteers charged forward with a "Montana yell" or a "jayhawk cheer." Aguinaldo's army crumpled. Some desperate Filipinos tried to escape by swimming the Pasig River, but the marksmanship of the volunteers ensured that few made it to the other bank alive. One American soldier described the resulting slaughter as "more fun than a turkey shoot." Back in Manila, three alert regiments managed to squelch the planned Filipino rising. The only problem the U.S. commanders encountered was reining in their overeager troops, who quickly overran their objectives and kept going. In the first day's fighting, an estimated 700 Filipinos were killed, to only 44 Americans; another 194 Americans were wounded.

During the next few months, as American reinforcements poured in, U.S. troops advanced steadily. At the end of March, Aguinaldo's capital at Malolos, 20 miles northwest of Manila, fell to General Arthur MacArthur's Second Division, with Colonel Frederick Funston and his Kansans leading the way. But Aguinaldo and his government merely retreated farther north. The U.S. army was unable to consolidate its gains or destroy the Filipino forces. As often as not, victorious U.S. columns would head back to the safety of Manila and the Filipinos would reoccupy the territory they had just lost.

There were simply not enough U.S. soldiers in the Philippines to garrison the islands—only 30,000 men, and more than half were state volunteers whose term of service ended with the signing of the peace treaty with Spain in April 1899. Yet General Otis, convinced that the war was all but over, put off requesting additional manpower.

The initial U.S. offensive petered out in the spring of 1899, and not only because of the expiring enlistments. Spring also marked the beginning of the rainy season. The roads became virtually impassable and most campaigning had to be suspended until the fall. Although the Filipinos had proven easy enough opponents, the elements were harder to overcome. Cholera, dysentery, malaria, venereal diseases, and sheer heat exhaustion ravaged the ranks, depleting some units of 60 percent of their strength. By June 1899 the war in the Philippines had already lasted longer than the one against Spain and still U.S. control extended only 40 miles outside Manila. "We are no nearer a conclusion of hostilities here than we were three months ago," lamented one officer in the field.

The Insurrectos

Luckily for the Americans their enemies were even more disorganized. The independence movement was riven by ethnic and class divisions. On September 15, 1898, just a month after the U.S. occupation of Manila, a national assembly had convened in the market town of Malolos, 20 miles north of the capital, to issue a constitution for the Philippine Republic. *Ilustrados*, as upper-class Filipinos were known, dominated this meeting and crafted a constitution that gave the vote only to the landed gentry. (Of course, at this time most Americans, specifically blacks and women, did not enjoy the franchise either.) Emilio Aguinaldo was given dictatorial powers as the first president of the Philippine Republic. General Antonio Luna, the army commander, and Apolinario Mabini, the disabled, intensely cerebral prime minister, were anxious to win the support of the peasants by challenging the existing power structure in Filipino society. But Aguinaldo went along with the wealthy landowners, effectively foreclosing the possibility of mobilizing the mass of the people against the Americans.

After the setbacks of February and March 1899, a majority of the Malolos Congress voted to end the armed struggle and accept an accommodation with the occupiers. The hotheaded General Luna was so incensed that he arrested most of the cabinet members for "treason"; they were immediately freed by Aguinaldo.

Luna was an upper-class Ilocano, whereas most of the other independence leaders were Tagalogs. As a young man, he had gone to Spain to study chemistry but instead immersed himself in military strategy. He was, according to Aguinaldo, a "fiery and fanatical commander," but his terrible temper was his undoing; he alienated many of his putative allies. On June 5, 1899, Luna was murdered by soldiers loyal to Aguinaldo. There is much circumstantial evidence to indicate that the president at least approved of, if he did not actually order, the assassination. Without Luna to help him, Aguinaldo now assumed personal command of his Army of Liberation. At the same time, some prominent leaders of his government journeyed to Manila and surrendered to the Americans.

"Filipino Thermopylae"

In November 1899 General Elwell Otis, the U.S. commander, mounted an offensive designed to destroy the army of liberation and occupy most of Luzon, the main island in the archipelago. He had at his disposal newly formed federal volunteer regiments, 35,000 men in all, authorized by Congress to replace the state volunteers, who had disbanded. Otis drew up a three-pronged attack designed to capture Aguinaldo and his men before they could escape into the mountains of northern Luzon. The plan called for Major General Arthur MacArthur to pin down the Filipino army on the plains of central Luzon while Brigadier General Loyd Wheaton staged an amphibious landing in the Filipino rear at Lingayan Gulf, 150 miles north of Manila. Major General Henry Lawton's cavalry would close off the mountain passes to the northeast.

It was a good plan, but Wheaton was too cautious in its execution and failed to link up with Lawton's division in time to block Aguinaldo's retreat into the mountains. Nevertheless a "flying column" of 1,100 cavalrymen under Brigadier General Samuel B. M. Young advanced so rapidly north that they almost managed to nab the Filipino leader. In his haste to escape, Aguinaldo was forced to leave behind his wife, mother, sister, and son.

Brigadier General Gregorio del Pilar, the commander of Aguinaldo's bodyguard, volunteered to stay behind with 60 men to block the American advance at Tila Pass, a narrow entrance to the Benguet Mountains. Still in his early twenties, the "boy general" was already a legend: well-born, educated, handsome, dapperly dressed, and a ladies' man, he was also a spectacularly brave soldier, always leading his men from the front. "The Americans could never take this place," he vowed theatrically, "and if they ever take it, it would only be over my dead body."

At dawn on December 2, 1899, a battalion of the 33rd Infantry Regiment under Major Peyton C. March, part of Young's flying column, reached the Tila Pass. Mauser fire from the Filipino barricade killed several of March's men and blocked his advance. On one side of the narrow, zigzagging trail was a deep gorge; on the other, a mountain 1,500 feet high. March ordered a company to climb the mountain in order to flank the Philippine position. Two hours later the Americans reached the summit and opened fire on the Filipinos from above, while March led the rest of his men in a frontal charge. Correspondent Richard Henry Little, watching from a nearby town, described what happened next in a much-quoted passage:

> Then we who were below saw an American squirm his way out to the top of a high flat rock, and take deliberate aim at the figure on the white horse. We held our breath, not knowing whether to pray that the sharpshooter would shoot straight or miss. Then came the spiteful crack of the Krag rifle and the man on horseback rolled to the ground, and when the troops charging up the mountain side reached him, the boy general of the Filipinos was dead.

Maybe it happened like that. Other eyewitnesses closer to the action did not see the white horse—this Homeric touch was probably added by an overly poetic correspondent—but in any case the deaths of del Pilar and 50 of his 60 men at the "Filipino Thermopylae" had bought Aguinaldo just enough time to escape deep into the mountains. The rest of his force did not fare so well. By February 1900 American troops had marched the length and breadth of Luzon, scattering *insurrectos* wherever they went, and breaking the back of Aguinaldo's army.

But the war did not end. It entered a new and more dangerous phase.

Guerrillas

While fleeing from General Young's flying column, Emilio Aguinaldo and his top commanders held a council of war at Bayambang on November 13, 1899. Here they decided to dissolve the Army of Liberation and resort to guerrilla warfare, the traditional strategy of the weak resisting the strong. Guerrillas cannot hope to defeat the enemy in the open field; they must wear down the occupying army until it finally tires of the struggle. To achieve this goal, guerrillas have to alter the odds in their favor, using the element of surprise to attack where they can bring superior numbers to bear against isolated enemy outposts. "The strategy of guerrilla war is to put one man against ten," Mao Tse-tung later explained, "but the tactic is to pit ten men against one."

Though often associated with modern wars of "national liberation," such methods had been employed millennia before Mao's birth. The apocryphal Books of the Maccabees record the hit-and-run tactics employed by Judas Maccabaeus in his attacks against the Syrians. The Romans faced similar challenges not only in Judea but in North Africa, Britain, Gaul, Germany, and elsewhere. Indeed the Roman Empire was ultimately brought down by "barbarian" tribes, the Goths and Huns, who fought in quasi-guerrilla fashion. The most successful guerrillas were really partisans operating in conjunction with regular forces, such as the Spanish irregulars who harassed Napoleon's army from 1808 to 1813. Their campaign, which contributed to the Duke of Wellington's ultimate victory, gave birth to the word *guerrilla*, meaning "small war." But there was no longer a regular Philippine army available to assist in the campaign against the *Americanos*; it was to be purely a struggle waged in the shadows.

It is unclear how much of this history the uneducated Aguinaldo was familiar with. His knowledge of guerrilla war was more practical, gained during the earlier uprising against Spain. Yet his own experience would be of limited use in the coming campaign. Although Aguinaldo remained the titular leader of the independence struggle, he had no way of controlling events across a vast archipelago from his remote mountain hideaway. His subordinate commanders thus had almost complete autonomy. This was both a strength and a weakness: a strength because the capture of one band of guerrillas would not affect the rest, a weakness because it was impossible to coordinate an offensive across the archipelago.

As a result, the nature and intensity of the guerrilla warfare varied considerably from place to place. While some regions, particularly Tagalog-speaking south and central Luzon, were hotbeds of *insurrecto* activity, in nearly half the archipelago's provinces there was no fighting at all. Where the guerrillas were active they tended to operate in 30- to 50-man bands, usually living in the hills. They would attack army patrols, ambush supply wagons, cut telegraph wires, and fire into occupied towns, while avoiding pitched battles. The efforts of these full-time *insurrectos* were complemented by part-time militia who lived in the towns and barrios.

The U.S. Army tried to exert control by appointing Filipinos to act as police chiefs, mayors, and other municipal officials under the supervision of the local U.S. garrison. But in many provinces the guerrillas set up their own parallel government structure, sometimes run by the very same officials the Americans had selected. In this way, the revolutionaries managed to collect taxes from the townspeople, recruit more men, and keep their forces supplied, all under the noses of the American troops.

Even those Filipinos not active in the Katipunan society, as the secret nationalist movement was called, usually refused to aid the army by divulging the names of sympathizers. Those who did share information could expect violent retribution. Some *americanistas* were burned or buried alive; others had their tongues cut out, limbs hacked off or eyes gouged out. The *insurrectos* even burned down whole towns on occasion if they refused to pay "taxes."

Few guerrilla uprisings are easily suppressed, and the Philippine experience was no exception. The *insurrectos* could strike any time at any of the U.S. garrisons thinly sprinkled about the archipelago. On one occasion, an American sentry on duty outside the town of Neuva Caceras was approached by a farmer with a basket of eggs to sell. Before the soldier could look up, the farmer reached into his basket, pulled out a bolo and decapitated him, vanishing before anyone could respond. The guerrillas also concocted the kind of traps that the Vietcong would one day build: pits concealing sharpened bamboo stakes or trip wires that would propel a spear into a man's chest. Most of the patrols sent out to snare the perpetrators wound up catching nothing more than a mouthful of dust. As Brigadier General James F. Wade noted: "The common soldier wears the dress of the country; with his gun he is a soldier; by hiding it and walking quietly down the road, sitting down by the nearest house, or going to work in the nearest field, he becomes an 'amigo,' full of good will and false information for any of our men who may meet him."

Aguinaldo intensified his campaign in the months leading up to the U.S. election of 1900, hoping to deliver a victory for the Democratic candidate, William Jennings Bryan, who had proclaimed his opposition to imperialism. Some of the more outspoken American anti-imperialists even openly wished for Aguinaldo's victory "against our army of subjugation, tyranny and oppression." Many soldiers fighting in the Philippines were bitter about the antiwar rhetoric coming from home. "If I am shot by a Filipino bullet," complained General Henry Lawton, who was in fact killed shortly thereafter, "it might just as well come from one of my own men . . . because . . . the continuance of the fighting is chiefly due to reports that are sent from America."

The perceived link between the *insurrectos* and the Democrats backfired for both. The Republicans were able to paint their opponents as unpatriotic, and Bryan, who had actually abandoned anti-imperialism as an issue just before the election, was trounced by the McKinley-Roosevelt ticket. This was a big setback for Aguinaldo. The U.S. was now in the Philippines to stay and was prepared to do whatever it took to defeat the insurgency. The following year, the U.S. Supreme Court cleared the way for long-term U.S. rule by holding, in the Insular Cases, that the Constitution does not follow the flag and that the U.S. could govern foreign peoples without granting them citizenship and all of its attendant rights. It was these decisions that prompted Mr. Dooley's famous observation that "th' Supreme Court follows th' illiction returns."

Early in 1900 the ineffectual General Elwell S. Otis stepped down as the army commander. He was replaced by General Arthur MacArthur, father of Douglas, and, like his son, a military genius at least in his own mind. In the 1890s, after decades of lobbying, he was finally awarded a Medal of Honor for his Civil War exploits at Missionary Ridge. MacArthur was determined to stiffen what he viewed as Otis's overly lenient treatment of the Filipinos. To back him up he had 70,000 battle-hardened veterans, two-thirds of the entire army, assisted by units composed of Macabebes, Illocanos, and other Philippine ethnic groups suspicious of the Tagalogs who led the independence movement. Enlisting natives as soldiers and scouts was, for the army, a tactic as recent as the just-concluded Indian Wars and as old as William Eaton's expedition to overthrow the pasha of Tripoli in 1805. In the Philippines (as in many other places, including Vietnam six decades later), these locally recruited soldiers, acting out clan and ideological hatreds, were usually harsher than Americans in their dealings with the guerrillas.

MacArthur often butted heads with William Howard Taft, a genial, 325-pound judge from Ohio sent by McKinley as chairman of a commission to supervise the transition from military to civilian rule in pacified areas. Taft associated with pro-American, upper-class Filipinos who told him the guerrillas were mere *ladrones* (bandits). Taft believed this. He called the Filipinos "our little brown brothers" and thought they welcomed U.S. rule. Soldiers campaigning in the wilds far from Manila knew better. They coined a contemptuous song: "He may be a brother of Big Bill Taft/But he ain't no friend of mine!"

Despite the disagreements between Taft and MacArthur, they effectively pursued a complementary two-pronged approach. Taft emphasized the policy of "attraction" that, from the very beginning, had been an integral part of the army's occupation strategy. Soldiers built schools, ran sanitation campaigns, vaccinated people, collected customs duties, set up courts run by natives, supervised municipal elections, and generally administered governmental functions efficiently and honestly. A thousand idealistic young American civilians even journeyed to the Philippines to teach school in a precursor of the Peace Corps. Despite the use of increasingly harsh methods against guerrillas and their suspected sympathizers, most U.S. soldiers remained on good terms with most civilians. Officers frequently socialized with Filipino notables in their area; and, writes one historian, "the vast majority of these daily interactions were civil, even cordial."

On December 23, 1900, with Taft's encouragement, prominent Filipinos, many of them former members of the independence movement, organized the Partido Federal (Federal Party) on a platform calling for eventual statehood for the Philippines. The Federalistas toured the countryside, telling guerrillas to surrender and take a loyalty oath to the U.S. Those who did were generally well treated.

All this was part of the struggle for what a later generation would call "hearts and minds." But it was clear to privates and generals alike that, although such positive steps might help to reconcile the Filipinos to American rule in the long run, the insurgency could only be defeated in the short term by military means. There were plenty of Americans willing to play "bad cop" to Taft's "good cop."

Already the army had displayed considerable cruelty in fighting the Filipinos. Even during the initial campaigns of 1899, there were credible reports of soldiers shooting prisoners "while trying to escape," burning towns, and torturing suspects to elicit information. One interrogation technique, passed down from the Spaniards, was called the "water cure": the victim would be held down, his mouth propped open, and water forced down his throat until his guts felt close to bursting, then a soldier would push on his stomach to clear out the water. American soldiers became more hard-hearted the longer the guerrilla war dragged on. It was common, for example, after guerrillas cut telegraph wires or attacked U.S. supply wagons for the army to burn a nearby town. Abuse of American prisoners of war further inflamed the soldiers; while most POWs were courteously treated, some had limbs hacked off or eyes gouged out or were slow-roasted over a fire. "No more prisoners," wrote one Washington volunteer in the war's early days. "They take none, and they tortured our men, so we kill wounded and all of them."

Senior officers did not usually order such illegal conduct but they often turned a blind eye, in an early version of a "don't ask, don't tell" policy. The prevailing view was summed up by Major General Loyd Wheaton in 1900: "You can't put down a rebellion by throwing confetti and sprinkling perfumery."

General Arthur MacArthur gave official sanction to policies designed to punish the *insurrectos* and their sympathizers, for he saw no other way to end the war quickly. On December 20, 1900, he declared martial law over the islands and invoked General Orders 100 (GO 100). Issued by President Lincoln in 1863 and widely imitated by other countries since, this landmark document envisioned war as a social contract: An occupying army had a duty to be humane in its dealings with civilians; to do otherwise would be stupid as well as immoral, for it would turn potential friends into foes. But likewise civilians had a duty not to resist; if they violated this duty, they would be dealt with harshly. GO 100 held that combatants not in uniform would be treated like "highway robbers or pirates" and, along with civilians who aided them, they could be subject to the death penalty.

General William Tecumseh Sherman had invoked this order as he cut a swathe of destruction through the South, and now MacArthur wanted to do the same in the Philippines. His intent was to force the civilian population, especially the prominent families, to choose sides; neutrality would be considered akin to resistance and punished accordingly. As part of this strategy, MacArthur confiscated the property of some rebel leaders and shipped 38 of them off to exile in Guam. To Taft's consternation, MacArthur increased press censorship so that word of his tough tactics would not leak out.

MacArthur's harshness, combined with Taft's softer approach, helped to blunt the effectiveness of the guerrillas. But the most dramatic blow to the independence movement was delivered by a hard-drinking officer with less than three years' experience in the army.

"Is This Not Some Joke?"

Frederick Funston was a generation younger than the senior army brass at the turn of the century. Born in the last year of the Civil War, he grew up on a Kansas homestead. From his father, Edward, who served in the state legislature and Congress, where he was known as "Foghorn Funston, the Farmer's Friend," Freddie inherited a booming voice and a lifelong allegiance to the Republican Party. He did not inherit his father's imposing height—Freddie never grew taller than 5 feet 4 inches—but in compensation he developed a powerful chest and strong shoulders.

Like his friend Theodore Roosevelt, Funston combined a love of history, literature, and science with a hankering for adventure and a passion for the outdoors. Failing to gain admittance to West Point, he spent a couple of years at Kansas State University, where a fraternity brother described him as "a pudgy, applecheeked young fellow . . . [who] had absolutely no sense of fear, physical or spiritual." After dropping out of college, he got a job working as a field botanist for the U.S. Department of Agriculture, which sent him on long, lonely treks through the Dakota Badlands, Death Valley, and Alaska. When he returned from the wilds, bronzed and fit, Funston quit his job and moved to New York to pursue a writing career.

One spring evening in 1896 Funston happened upon a Madison Square Garden rally staged by supporters of the Cuban guerrillas then fighting the Spanish. He immediately signed up, "I fear as much from a love of adventure and a desire to see some fighting as from any more worthy motive." Along with some other gringo volunteers he was smuggled into Cuba and joined the rebels as an artillery officer. He took part in several battles, was twice wounded, had his legs crushed by a falling horse, and contracted typhoid fever and malaria. When he finally tried to go home, he was caught by a Spanish patrol and barely escaped execution. He returned to the United States on January 10, 1898, weighing just 90 pounds, limping badly, and coughing up blood. Yet his hunger for war was not sated.

As soon as he had healed, Funston accepted the colonelcy of a volunteer regiment being raised in his native Kansas. The unit was sent to the Philippines, where, during the initial offensive in February of 1899, Funston distinguished himself as one of the most reckless and courageous officers in the army. His men were invariably at the front of the U.S. advance, and Funston was invariably in front of his men. For performing "one of the most difficult of military operations"—"forcing the passage of an unfordable river in the face of an entrenched enemy"—Funston won the Medal of Honor. An opportunity for even greater glory would come once the conventional war had ended and the guerrilla campaign had begun.

On January 8, 1901, Funston, by then a 35-year-old brigadier general in command of a district in northern Luzon, was in his headquarters in the town of San Isidro when he received a telegram that created "no little excitement." It informed him that some couriers bearing dispatches from Emilio Aguinaldo had surrendered to a U.S. garrison 60 miles north. Under interrogation, the chief courier, Cecilio Segismundo, told the Americans that Aguinaldo was holed up in Palanan, a village in the Sierra Madre mountains of northeastern Luzon, adding that all the approaches to this remote hideaway were carefully guarded and that it would be impossible for an American force to get close without alerting *el presidente*, who would simply slip away again.

A way out of this dilemma presented itself in Segismundo's coded letters. Working all night, fueled by copious quantities of coffee, Funston and two of his aides were able to decrypt the dispatches. One of them turned out to be an appeal from Aguinaldo to his cousin, asking him to send 400 armed insurgents to his headquarters.

Eureka!

Funston hatched a bold plan: He would use Macabebe Scouts—Filipino natives who belonged to an ethnic minority hostile to Tagalogs like Aguinaldo—to stage an elaborate ruse. Funston and four other American officers would pretend to be prisoners of war. The Macabebes would pretend to be the reinforcements that Aguinaldo had requested. Using "false colors," Funston would penetrate Aguinaldo's lair and capture the guerrilla leader. General Arthur MacArthur approved the scheme but told its designer, "Funston, this is a desperate undertaking. I fear that I shall never see you again."

Funston's force slipped out of Manila Bay on March 6, 1901, aboard a U.S. Navy gunboat. There were 89 men in all, most of them Macabebes in captured rebel uniforms, but also five U.S. officers, four renegade rebels, and a Spaniard named Lazaro Segovia who worked as an intelligence officer for the Americans. So as not to arouse suspicion, they landed 100 miles south of their objective in a wild part of Luzon where no U.S. troops were stationed. They were on their own. Under the laws of war, capture in enemy uniforms meant certain death. Funston sent ahead forged letters to Aguinaldo informing the president that his reinforcements were on the way, and then led his men on their long hike north along the coast. Almost nonstop rain accompanied them as they hacked their way through thick jungle and traversed overflowing streams. They had not brought enough supplies, so that by the end of their weeklong march most of the men were malnourished and reduced to eating snails and limpets.

Just as they were nearing the end, only 10 miles from Palanan, the men were shocked to receive news that could derail their whole scheme: A letter from Aguinaldo instructed them not to bring the American "prisoners" to the rebel headquarters. Funston had hoped to snare the rebel leader himself, but now that might not be possible. He decided to send the Macabebes ahead with Segovia, while he and the four other U.S. officers trailed cautiously behind. At one point the Americans had to dive off the trail to avoid the real insurgents sent by Aguinaldo to take custody of the "prisoners."

Finally, on the afternoon of March 23, 1901, the insurgent "reinforcements" were welcomed to Palanan, a village of 80 thatch-roofed huts neatly arrayed around a square. There was even an honor guard lined up to greet them. Lazaro Segovia and another phony guerrilla leader went to Aguinaldo's headquarters, a one-story structure perched on stilts, where they chatted pleasantly for a few minutes with the Filipino president and his officers.

After a while, Segovia excused himself, stepped outside, and gave the signal to a comrade who yelled, "Now is the time Macabebes. Give it to them!" The "Macs" fired a ragged volley, scattering Aguinaldo's honor guard. Hearing the firing, and thinking it was done in celebration, Aguinaldo leaned out the window and angrily demanded, "Stop all the foolishness. Don't waste ammunition." At that moment, Segovia charged back in, gun drawn, to announce, "You are our prisoners. We are not insurgents. We are Americans! Surrender or be killed!" Aguinaldo was too stunned to put up much resistance. When Funston arrived a few minutes later and introduced himself, Aguinaldo asked, "Is this not some joke?"

The trip back to Manila was uneventful, Funston recalled, with "the pleasantest relations . . . established between captors and captured." A rapturous reception awaited the ruddy-faced, red-bearded commando leader. "To say that the city [Manila] went wild with excitement," wrote Funston, "mildly expresses the condition." The U.S. went wild too. Aguinaldo's captor instantly became a national hero—one of the few to emerge from this inglorious war. The one sour note came from a London magazine that accused "Fighting Fred" of "a piece of sharp practice." As for Aguinaldo, he was well treated by his captors. On April 19, 1901, he issued a proclamation accepting American sovereignty and calling on his former comrades to give up their struggle.

In the months that followed Aguinaldo's announcement, more than 4,000 guerrillas surrendered and turned in 1,363 rifles. "The armed insurrection is almost entirely suppressed," General MacArthur crowed.

And then came the calamity at Balangiga on Samar island, in which 48 men of Company C, 9th U.S. Infantry, were killed in a surprise dawn attack on their garrison by bolo-wielding *insurrectos*. It was the worst setback for U.S. forces during the entire war.

"Kill and Burn"

On July 4, 1901, General Arthur MacArthur stepped down as commander of the Division of the Philippines. His duties were split between Major General Adna Chaffee, the "butt-sprung" old cavalryman fresh from suppressing the Boxer Uprising, who assumed military responsibility for the islands, and William Howard Taft, the portly judge who became the first civilian governor with authority over all pacified areas. To deal with the situation on Samar, Chaffee called in Brigadier General Jacob H. Smith, a short, wizened 62-year-old who had earned the nickname "Hell-Roaring Jake" for the nonstop stream of invective he directed at subordinates in his booming voice.

Smith was given command of the 6th Separate Brigade, a special unit that included a battalion of 315 marines, most of them veterans who had fought in Cuba, Puerto Rico, and north China. Their commander was Major Littleton Waller Tazewell Waller, a short, stout, swaggering, 45-year-old officer from an old Virginia family who had spent better than two decades in the corps. Smedley Butler, his longtime comrade, described him as "a little fellow with a fiery mustache and a distinguished bearing," an "enormous nose," and posture "straight as a ruler." He "dominated the others" and "his men adored him." Another marine said of Waller: "The U.S. Marine Corps was his God. He never let you forget it." Butler, no mean soldier himself, called Waller "the greatest soldier I have ever known." Others have had a less kind assessment of this "ambitious and ruthless officer with a fondness for the bottle."

"Tony" Waller had seen more than his share of hard fighting, but even he was shocked by the orders he received from Hell-Roaring Jake. As he later recalled, the tiny general told him, "I want no prisoners. I wish you to kill and burn, the more you kill and the more you burn the better you will please me. . . . I want all persons killed who are capable of bearing arms."

Waller: "I would like to know the limit of age."

Smith: "Ten years."

Waller, who knew the laws of war as well as any officer, told his subordinates that "we are not making war against women and children," but nevertheless in October 1901 his marines launched an aggressive pacification campaign. The 6th Separate Brigade marched out in two columns along the Samar coast, burning villages and slaughtering carabao (water buffalo) and rebels alike, carrying out Smith's order to turn "the interior of Samar" into "a howling wilderness." Waller achieved a major success when he discovered the location of one of General Vicente Lukban's strongholds atop the Sojoton cliffs overlooking the Cadacan River deep in the interior of Samar.

Two of Waller's columns, commanded by Captain David D. Porter (a descendant of Navy Captain David Porter of Barbary and Marquesas fame) and Captain Hiram I. Bearss, reached Lukban's redoubt by sunset on November 16, 1901, and attacked the next morning without waiting for Waller and the rest of the expedition to arrive. Gunnery Sergeant John H. Quick, a Medal of Honor winner, provided covering fire with a Colt machine gun while Porter and Bearss led the assault team up the 200-foot cliffs using bamboo ladders. The guerrillas had prepared tons of rocks suspended in large bamboo cages attached to vines, ready to drop on any attackers, but they could not spring the trap properly because of Quick's heavy fire. The marines reached the top, and with their Krag rifles and .45 caliber Colt revolvers overpowered the bolo-wielding defenders. No marines were killed in this attack, which resulted in the death of 30 insurgents and the destruction of their headquarters. Bearss and Porter won Medals of Honor for their actions, but not until 33 years later.

Hell-Roaring Jake Smith congratulated Tony Waller on his "brilliant success" and urged him, "Give your command the needed rest, then touch up the enemy again." Instead Waller's next undertaking would "touch up" his own men. He decided, for reasons that have never been satisfactorily explained, to traverse Samar island from Lanang to Basey, a distance of 35 miles through dense jungle.

Waller set off with three officers and 54 enlisted men on December 28, 1901, accompanied by 33 Filipino porters and two Filipino scouts. They found it much harder going than anticipated. The foliage was dense, the leeches aggressive, the trail nonexistent, the rain incessant. The men lacked enough to eat, their clothes and shoes disintegrated in the damp climate, and their feet were swollen and bleeding. With the men weakening, Waller decided to push ahead to Basey with 15 of the stronger ones and 10 porters, and then send a relief column back for the rest. Along the way, Waller claimed he caught a Filipino guide, called Slim by the Americans, stealing his bolo; "Smoke," another of the Filipino guides, later explained that this man was a former *insurrecto* who wanted ed to kill the major. Twenty-nine days after starting out, Waller reached Bassey, his shirt in rags, his eyes feverish, his men "cut, torn, bruised, and dilapidated." He immediately plunged back into the jungle to search for the others, but failed to find them. Nine days later Waller staggered back into Basey, where he collapsed from fever and exhaustion.

The rest of his men, under the command of Captain David Porter, fared worse. "The men's feet were like raw pieces of beef, and their bodies covered with sores," Porter wrote. They were reduced to eating roots. As they got weaker, they became convinced that their Filipino porters were hoarding food from them. A lieutenant claimed he was attacked by three of the porters, one of whom stabbed him with a bolo while the other Filipinos looked on, doing nothing to help. By the time an army patrol from Lanang finally rescued the survivors on January 18, 1902, ten marines had been left to die along the trail, and those who remained alive were half-starved and half-mad.

Before long, eleven of the Filipino porters were arrested and brought to Basey. A feverish and delirious Waller ordered them executed without benefit of trial. He later explained that, given the small size of his garrison—just 45 men fit for duty, to keep an eye on 95 prisoners and 3,000 potentially hostile townspeople—he did not feel safe keeping the supposedly mutinous porters under lock and key. "It became necessary to expend eleven prisoners," he telegraphed matter-of-factly to Hell-Roaring Jake. Waller thought nothing more of the matter until he arrived back in Cavite, near Manila, on February 29, 1902, and found himself charged with murder, an offense punishable by death under the Articles of War.

Filipinos trying to surrender or already taken captive had been killed before without the perpetrators being court-martialed, but most of those transgressions had been committed by individual soldiers in the heat of battle. An officer ordering the cold-blooded execution of 11 civilians was not something the military high command could ignore, especially not with public outrage building in the United States about army conduct in the Philippines.

In January 1902, a Senate committee had begun hearings on atrocities. Despite the best efforts of the pro-imperialist committee chairman, Senator Henry Cabot Lodge, witnesses testified about the "water cure," about villages being burned, and about other extreme steps that had become part of this dirty little war. In response, Mark Twain mordantly suggested that Old Glory be redesigned, with "the white stripes painted black and the stars replaced by the skull and crossbones."

President Roosevelt and his secretary of war, Elihu Root, tried to defend the army as best they could, but they realized that to placate public opinion they had to make at least a show of cracking down on military excesses. Root decided to make an example of Major Waller. On March 17, 1902, a court-martial was duly convened in a Manila army barracks.

Waller took the stand and acknowledged that he had ordered 11 prisoners shot but argued that his actions were authorized under General Orders 100.

Seeking to protect his superior officer, he assumed full responsibility. Six days later, Brigadier General Jake Smith testified. He did nothing to protect Waller, claiming he had ordered prisoners to be treated humanely and generally painting the marine as a rogue officer. Outraged by what he viewed as a betrayal, Waller took the stand again, and this time revealed what orders he had actually received, an account corroborated by other officers. (Waller added that he had disobeyed his orders not to take prisoners, because "I know the laws of war.")

These admissions caused a sensation in the United States. The *New York Evening Journal* covered its entire front page on April 8, 1902, with a banner headline: "KILL ALL": MAJOR WALLER ORDERED TO MASSACRE THE FILIPINOS! (This fit nicely with the previous day's headline: BRITISH GUILTY OF AWFUL ATROCITIES IN BOER WAR). Waller was acquitted of murder, though the Samar campaign stained his record and prevented him from becoming marine commandant. Hell-Roaring Jake did not get off so easily. He was convicted of "conduct to the prejudice of good order and military discipline" and forced into retirement.

Most historians have taken as the lesson of the Waller case that the tactics practiced on Samar were typical of the war as a whole. Even if they were not, the Samar campaign provided ample ammunition for army critics and cast a pall over the entire U.S. war effort in the Philippines.

Batangas

Samar was not the only place where the Philippine War was concluding in a last gasp of ferocity. In Batangas province in southern Luzon, General Manuel Malvar waged a dogged campaign against the American occupation. To end this resistance, General Adna Chaffee turned to Brigadier General J. Franklin Bell, a Kentuckian who vowed that he would "make the existing state of war and martial law so inconvenient and unprofitable to the people that they will earnestly desire and work for the reestablishment of peace and civil government." Bell announced that he would force all law-abiding Filipinos to move with their household goods and livestock into towns controlled by the U.S. Army. Any able-bodied male found outside the "protected zones" without a pass, Bell warned, "will be arrested and confined, or shot if he runs away." All crops, livestock, and dwellings on the outside would "become liable to confiscation or destruction."

Setting up "concentration camps" (not to be confused with death camps) was a traditional counterinsurgency tactic, then being used by the British in

South Africa and previously employed by the U.S. Army in its campaigns against the Indians, where the camps had been called "reservations." The goal was to separate the insurgents from the population base, for as Mao Tse-tung later explained, "the guerrilla moves among the people as the fish through the water." With more than 300,000 people clustering in his "zones of protection," Bell succeeded in drying up the guerrillas' water. To finish off the insurgency, he sent 4,000 soldiers to search "each ravine, valley, and mountain peak for insurgents and for food," destroying all foodstuffs and capturing or killing all able-bodied men. This unrelenting pressure quickly paid off. On April 16, 1902, Miguel Malvar became the last major guerrilla commander to surrender.

American victory came at a high cost for the residents of Batangas. At least 11,000 of them died in the concentration camps from a combination of disease, malnutrition, poor sanitation, and other health problems. The most thorough historical analysis of the Batangas campaign suggests that most of those deaths can be attributed to malaria and cholera epidemics that the Americans tried in vain to stop, but nevertheless J. Franklin Bell came in for a good deal of opprobrium for his brutal tactics. More than a few critics compared him with Valeriano Weyler, a Spanish general whose *reconcentrado* program to put down the Cuban rebellion had led the yellow press to nickname him "Butcher Weyler." "Who would have supposed that the same policy would be, only four years later, adopted and pursued as the policy of the United States in the Philippines?" wondered the *Philadelphia Ledger*.

It was true. Confronted with a native insurgency, the U.S. had resorted to many of the same tactics used by European colonialists. Yes, the U.S. Army was a good deal less brutal than the Belgians in the Congo or the French in Algeria—and less brutal than some critics have charged—but nevertheless the Philippine War was a rude awakening for those Americans who imagined their country always to be morally superior to the sordid Europeans.

"Why Don't They Tyrannize Us More?"

On July 4, 1902, President Roosevelt proclaimed that the Philippine Insurgency was over. All Filipino political prisoners were given an amnesty and civil government was established over the entire archipelago. Earlier declarations of victory had proved premature, but this one was more justified than most. There would be almost no more organized resistance on the main island of Luzon. Most of the campaigning in future years would be confined to the outlying islands of Mindanao and Jolo, whose fierce Muslim Moros the Spanish had never been able to subdue. Moro uprisings occurred with regularity in the first three decades of the twentieth century (as they still do to this day), but as the years went by responsibility for suppressing them shifted from the U.S. Army to the Philippine constabulary, a quasi-military force made up of Filipino enlisted men led by American officers.

The majority of Filipinos became reconciled to U.S. rule or at least not violently opposed to it, and they were granted increasing autonomy by Washington, far ahead of any comparable movement in European colonies. In 1907 the Philippines became the first Asian state to establish a national legislature. In 1935 the archipelago became a domestically autonomous commonwealth ruled by President Manuel Quezon, a former major in Aguinaldo's army, who once complained of the difficulty of fostering nationalism under such a benevolent colonial regime: "Damn the Americans! Why don't they tyrannize us more?" In World War II many Filipinos fought shoulder-to-shoulder with American G.I.s, though some, including Aguinaldo, collaborated with the Japanese invaders. In 1946, the U.S. granted the islands independence.

Among the institutions bequeathed to the Filipinos by the Americans were public schools, a free press, an independent judiciary, a modern bureaucracy, democratic government, and separation of church and state. Unlike the Dutch in the East Indies, the British in Malaya, or the French in Indochina, the Americans left virtually no legacy of economic exploitation; Congress was so concerned about protecting the Filipinos that it barred large landholdings by American individuals or corporations. To one American political scientist, "the American efforts in the Philippines look like a textbook example of good government."

Filipino feelings about the legacy of colonialism remain more ambivalent, as exemplified by protests that led to the closing in 1991 of the U.S. naval base at Subic Bay, the last spoils of Admiral Dewey's epic conquest. One protester waved a placard that read: Yankee Go Home—And Take Me With You.

How the War Was Won

Pacifying the Philippines had proved to be much more difficult than virtually anyone had predicted. Between 1898 and 1902, a total of 126,468 American soldiers served there (though never more than 69,000 at one time) and fought in 2,811 engagements. By July 4, 1902, the U.S. had lost 4,234 dead and suffered 2,818 wounded. By comparison, only 379 Americans were lost in combat in the Spanish-American War. By their own count U.S. forces killed 16,000 Filipinos in battle. As many as 200,000 civilians also died, victims of disease and famine and the cruelties of both sides. Yet in the end the U.S. did triumph. Decisively.

The Yanks' victory can be ascribed in some measure to the mistakes of the enemy. Emilio Aguinaldo was no Ho Chi Minh, and Antonio Luna, his top general, was no Vo Nguyen Giap. Aguinaldo made the fatal mistake of trying to fight the U.S. Army in a conventional war. His forces were chewed up during a series of battles in 1899 that began just outside Manila in February and finished in northern Luzon in December. Thereafter Aguinaldo resorted to guerrilla warfare, but his government, dominated by *ilustrados* (wealthy landowners), never managed to rally most of the Filipino people to their cause.

The eventual U.S. triumph, however, was hardly foreordained. The U.S. had no tanks and no airplanes and not even enough infantrymen. There were an average of only 24,000 U.S. soldiers in the field at any given time to face at least 80,000 insurgents, who thus outnumbered the army by more than three to one. (By comparison, in the First Chechen War of 1994–95 the Russians had a three-to-one manpower advantage and still lost.) The U.S. also did not have much of a technological edge. Aguinaldo's men were armed with Remington and Mauser rifles, certainly no worse than the regular army's Krag-Jorgensens and superior to the volunteers' Civil War-vintage Springfields. The U.S. could bring to bear superior firepower from field artillery and navy gunboats, but even in the war's early days these advantages were to some extent obviated by the archipelago's difficult jungle-and-mountain terrain; later on, heavy weaponry proved almost entirely irrelevant to combating elusive guerrillas. Moreover, while the *insurrectos* were acclimated to local conditions, foul weather and disease ravaged U.S. ranks. Finally, the rebels, with informers in every barrio, possessed better intelligence about the U.S. Army than the Americans did about them.

The U.S. success in pacifying the archipelago, despite all these disadvantages, may be ascribed to the skillful employment of carrot and stick, "chastisement" and "attraction." The U.S. offered real rewards for those who cooperated with the occupation, ranging from political posts and business opportunities for the elites, to peace and security for the peons. Captured rebels were by and large well treated, and the Filipino people were given growing political autonomy. The army generated additional goodwill by running schools, hospitals, sanitation programs, and other charitable works. Eventually more and more Filipinos tired of the war and decided that U.S. rule was not so bad—certainly preferable to the "dons" who had come before and perhaps even to Aguinaldo's oligarchy.

It is the policy of chastisement that attracted unwelcome attention to the U.S. war effort, both in the early 1900s and in the years since. Critics often have attributed the soldiers' actions to racism. Many abuses did occur, and they were wrong, but it is important to place them into proper perspective. In the first place, isolated garrisons had to operate against an unseen enemy who would kill or mutilate their buddies one day and be transformed into smiling "amigos" the next. It is not surprising that in such stressful circumstances U.S. soldiers did not always observe Marquis of Queensberry rules. Then too it is not entirely fair to apply twenty-first-century morality to the actions of nineteenth-century soldiers. This was a more brutal time, when police departments in America routinely used the "third degree" to elicit confessions and U.S. soldiers themselves were subject to harsh hazing and physical punishment that would not be tolerated today. By the standards of the day, the conduct of U.S. soldiers was better than average for colonial wars.

Although wars against guerrillas tend to be particularly savage, atrocities are endemic to all wars, not just colonial ones. When men are thrust into kill-or-be-killed circumstances, the constraints of civilization often slip off with shocking ease. There were, for instance, many instances of Allied troops killing Germans who tried to surrender in World Wars I and II. "No soldier who fights until his enemy is at close small-arms range, in any war, has more than perhaps a fifty-fifty chance of being granted quarter," writes a British military sociologist. "If he stands up to surrender he risks being shot with the time-honored comment, 'Too late, chum.'" When perpetrated by the winning side in a popular war, such as World War II, such incidents are generally hushed up. They only become the focus of public debate when committed in the course of an unpopular conflict like the one in the Philippines or, later, Vietnam. It is a mistake, however, to focus exclusively on misconduct by soldiers at the expense of the larger strategic picture.

In the end, the success of the U.S. counterinsurgency effort was due not to committing atrocities—24,000 soldiers could hardly hope to terrorize 7 million people into submission—but to paying attention to the rudiments of counterinsurgency strategy. In Vietnam, as we shall see, the army squandered its resources on fruitless search-and-destroy missions. In the Philippines, by contrast, it concentrated on cutting off the guerrillas from civilian assistance by garrisoning the countryside. While the men grumbled about the monotony of life in the *boondocks* (an Americanization of the Tagalog *bundok*, meaning "mountain"), their very isolation forced them to become well acquainted with their area and the people who lived there. This in turn gave them good intelligence, the prerequisite for effective counterinsurgency operations.

The army's success may be ascribed in some degree to the invaluable experience its top commanders had gained in fighting Indians, the finest irregular warriors in the world. Out of 30 U.S. generals who served in the Philippines from 1898 to 1902, 26 had fought in the Indian Wars. And of course one of the few generals without Indian-fighting experience was Frederick Funston, who had acquired plenty of firsthand knowledge of guerrilla warfare during his service with the Cuban rebels. Ordinary American soldiers were also of high caliber, no braver than their Filipino counterparts but better trained and disciplined.

The army could not have won without the navy. Not only did its gunboats provide fire support and supplies for isolated army garrisons, but its blockade of the archipelago effectively prevented Aguinaldo from receiving foreign arms shipments or moving supplies and reinforcements. Geography helped too: In the Philippines, there were no sanctuaries and no Ho Chi Minh trails to keep the guerrillas in business.

All these factors combined to make the Philippine War one of the most successful counterinsurgencies waged by a Western army in modern times.

6

CARIBBEAN CONSTABULARY

Cuba
Panama
Nicaragua
Mexico, 1898–1914

With the capture of the Philippines and its growing role in China, the U.S. had established itself as a significant power in Asia—but just one of many. It was only in the Caribbean and Central America, in the years between the Spanish-American War and World War I, that U.S. hegemony, a *Pax Americana,* was created. The U.S. had played an active role in the Caribbean during the nineteenth century (see Chapters 2–3), but American involvement deepened considerably after 1898. No longer would U.S. sailors and marines land for a few days at a time to quell a riot; now they would stay longer to manage the internal politics of nations. The reasons for the growing U.S. role in the area were many—economic, strategic, ideological—and we shall examine them in turn, but we must not lose sight of the larger reality. American power had already filled up the chalice of North America and, overflowing its confines, naturally spilled into the adjacent region where there were no Great Powers to bar the way.

The American preference was to exercise power diplomatically and economically—sometimes in combination, as in "dollar diplomacy"—but when all else failed there was always the military might of the United States, the brass knuckles hidden beneath the velvet glove. And all else failed frequently enough that U.S. sailors and marines wound up fighting a series of "Banana Wars" throughout Central America and the Caribbean in the first decades of the twentieth century.

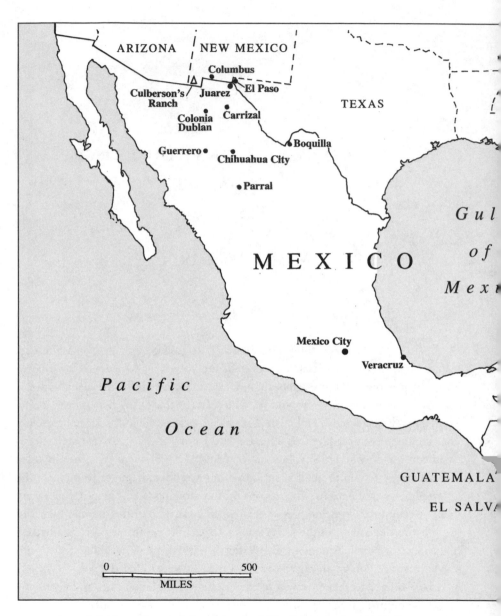

MAP 6.1   Mexico, Central America and Caribbean, circa 1914

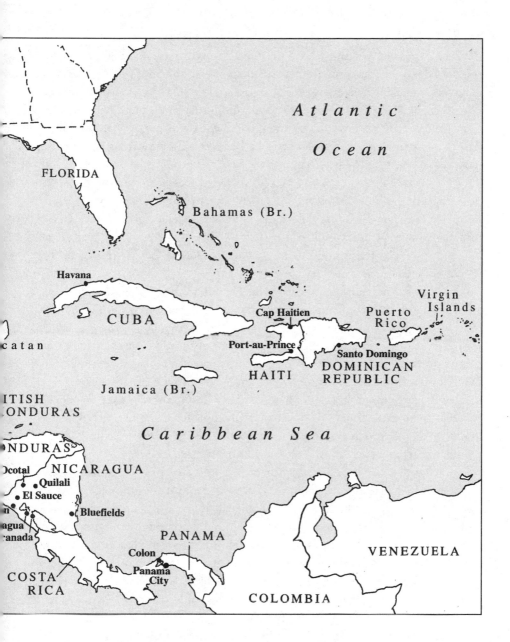

Atlantic

Ocean

FLORIDA

Bahamas (Br.)

Havana

CUBA

Cap Haitien

Virgin
Islands

Puerto
Rico

catan

Port-au-Prince

Santo Domingo

Jamaica (Br.)

HAITI

DOMINICAN
REPUBLIC

ITISH
ONDURAS

Caribbean Sea

NDURAS

Ocotal

NICARAGUA

Quilali

El Sauce

Bluefields

agua

ranada

PANAMA

VENEZUELA

Colon

Panama
City

COSTA
RICA

COLOMBIA

Cuba I

Between January 1899 and May 1902 the U.S. Army ruled Cuba, first under stolid Major General John R. Brooke, then under the more dashing Major General Leonard Wood, erstwhile commander of the Rough Riders. Unlike the Filipinos, the Cubans did not fight U.S. rule, in large measure because they were confident that it would be temporary; with the passage of the Teller Amendment in April 1898, Congress had eschewed any desire to annex the "pearl of the Antilles." The Cuban *insurrectos* took a bonus of $75 a man and duly disbanded. The U.S. Army picked up the pieces after the Spanish left: Soldiers went around distributing food to a hungry populace, staging a sanitary campaign, erecting thousands of public schools (modeled on those of Ohio), rooting out corrupt officials, building roads and bridges, dredging Havana harbor, and generally attempting "to recast Cuban society, such as it was, in the mould of North America."

The occupation's most spectacular achievement occurred when Walter Reed, a U.S. Army doctor, confirmed the intuition of a Cuban physician that yellow fever was not transmitted by general filth or other factors but by one particular variety of mosquito, the silvery *Stegomyia fasciata*. A mosquito-eradication campaign undertaken by the Army Medical Corps produced immediate results: In 1902, for the first time in centuries, there was not a single case of yellow fever in Havana; just two years before there had been 1,400 known cases. Incidence of malaria, another scourge of the city, of all tropical cities, plummeted nearly as much. Such dramatic improvements in public health were to become a commonplace feature of American colonial administration.

Knowing that the U.S. military occupation would be brief, and determined to safeguard American interests in Cuba after the troops went home, Congress passed the Platt Amendment in 1901. Under its terms Cuba would be obligated to obtain Uncle Sam's approval before signing any foreign treaty; maintain low foreign debt; ratify all acts of the U.S. military government; and give the American armed forces the right to intervene at any time to protect life, liberty, and property. In addition, Cuba would have to provide the U.S. long-term leases on naval bases; it was this provision that would lead to the creation of a naval station at Guantánamo Bay in 1903. In short, the Platt Amendment represented a considerable abridgment of Cuban sovereignty.

Havana went along because it had no choice. It was only when the Cubans pledged to honor the Platt Amendment that the U.S. Army left the island, though the U.S. Navy remained a looming presence offshore. Cuba now had its own government headed by Tomás Estrada Palma, a former schoolmaster who had spent years living in New York State, but it was in effect an American protectorate.

Panama

The Platt Amendment, following the outright annexation of Puerto Rico, signaled that the U.S. was intent on turning the Caribbean into an "American lake." This desire grew stronger once an isthmian canal was under way. The story of how the republic of Panama was created is well known and need not be recounted in much detail here. As we have seen, U.S. troops had been frequent visitors to Panama, landing there thirteen times between 1856 and 1902 to guarantee freedom of transit for Americans. Although most of Panama's population had long chafed under the distant rule of Bogotá, in the past U.S. forces had always preserved Colombia's sovereignty over the isthmus. That would change in 1903.

At the time, Colombia's congress and president were balking at the proposed U.S. terms for a canal treaty, demanding more money. The U.S., with its burgeoning power in the Pacific, considered a canal a strategic necessity, and President Theodore Roosevelt was furious at the "homicidal corruptionists" in Bogotá for reneging on their commitments to allow the project to proceed. Although they did not instigate a Panamanian revolution, the president and his secretary of state, John Hay, knew about it beforehand and tacitly encouraged the plotters. The revolutionaries counted on American military intervention and were not disappointed. On November 2, the gunboat *Nashville*, which had just arrived at Colón on Panama's Caribbean coast, received secret orders from the Navy Department to "prevent landing of any armed force with hostile intent, either government or insurgent." The remarkable thing about this telegram is that, when Commander John Hubbard of the *Nashville* received it, the revolution *had not yet broken out*. It would start the next day.

By the time Hubbard received his orders, 500 Colombian soldiers had already landed at Colón, but they still had to traverse the isthmus to reach Panama City, capital of the province. The American railroad superintendent dissembled and told them there were not enough rail cars available to take all of them, but he allowed the Colombian general and his staff to go by themselves. They arrived just in time to be captured by the rebels who took over Panama City on November 3. The success of the revolution was sealed when the USS *Dixie* appeared off Colón on the evening of November 5 and disembarked 400 marines under Major John A. Lejeune. The Colombian army detachment left at Colón decided not to tangle with the marines; instead their colonel accepted an $8,000 bribe from the Panamanian plotters to sail back to Cartagena with his men. Within the next week, eight more U.S. warships arrived at Panama, effectively foreclosing any possibility that Colombia would take the isthmus back by force.

On November 6, 1903, the U.S. government formally recognized the Republic of Panama. One of the new government's first acts was to sign a treaty giving the U.S. permission to build a canal under extremely generous terms that turned the Canal Zone—a 10-mile-wide strip on either side of the waterway—into U.S. territory. It was as brazen—and successful—an example of gunboat diplomacy as the world has ever seen. When Teddy Roosevelt was subsequently accused of having committed (as the *New York Times* termed it) an "act of sordid conquest," he asked Attorney General Philander Knox to construct a defense. "Oh, Mr. President," Knox is said to have replied, "do not let so great an achievement suffer from any taint of legality."

War Plan Black

The isthmian canal, completed in 1914, gave the U.S. an invaluable strategic advantage—the ability to move its fleet quickly between the West and East Coasts, the Pacific and the Atlantic—but also a major headache: protecting the precious waterway. It was the same challenge Britain faced with the Suez Canal. London's response was to assert control over Egypt, the Sudan, and virtually the entire Mediterranean. The U.S. took a similarly sweeping approach with Central America and the Caribbean.

Naval planners looked at the map and realized that there were only a handful of main channels into the Caribbean, the most important being the Windward Passage between Cuba and Hispaniola. Control of Puerto Rico and Cuba gave the U.S. a chokehold over this "strategic center of interest" (to use Alfred Thayer Mahan's words), though the navy remained interested in acquiring bases in Hispaniola as an insurance policy. By 1906 the U.S. Navy was big enough to ensure that no other power would contest control of its own backyard: It deployed 20 battleships, roughly the same number as Germany, and second only to Britain's 49. The extent of American naval might was trumpeted by the cruise of the Great White Fleet around the world in 1907–1909.

Military planners are paid to be paranoid, and despite America's growing power, they constantly saw threats looming, principally from Berlin. The leaders of the War and Navy departments lived in constant fear that Germany would establish bases in the West Indies or South America and then use them to attack U.S. shipping, the Panama Canal or—worst-case scenario—the

American mainland itself. This was the basis of War Plan Black, completed in 1914 by the General Board of the U.S. Navy.

These worries were not entirely farfetched. The German navy, under the command of Admiral Alfred von Tirpitz, was constantly, if unsuccessfully, scheming to acquire a base in the West Indies. The German admiralty staff also drew up war plans between 1897 and 1905 for seizing either Puerto Rico or Cuba as a staging area for an attack on the East Coast of the United States. Operations Plan III, as the German Caribbean strategy was called, was mothballed after 1906, when rising tensions in Europe forced the German navy to focus its attention closer to home. But after World War I broke out, German U-boats did attack some shipping close to the American mainland (though in the Atlantic, not the Caribbean) and the German foreign office did concoct a wild plot for an alliance with Mexico, which would supposedly receive in compensation the return of the southwestern United States. (The Zimmerman Telegram, laying out this plan, was intercepted by British intelligence and helped draw the U.S. into the war.)

The modern-day reader is certainly entitled to doubt in retrospect how much of a threat Germany ever posed to U.S. control of the Caribbean, but the danger loomed large enough at the time and helps to explain American willingness to intervene in the region. These fears were crystallized in the Venezuela crisis of 1902–03.

"International Police Power"

The crisis was precipitated by Venezuela's indebtedness to European creditors. When President Cipriano Castro refused to pay the country's debt, Britain, Germany, and Italy sent warships that shelled a coastal fort, sank a Venezuelan gunboat and blockaded the coast. This was still a time when Europeans viewed defaulting on one's debts as a moral failing and a crime; individual deadbeats were sent to debtors' prisons, while weak foreign states (Egypt in 1876, Turkey in 1881, Serbia in 1895, Greece in 1898, Persia in 1907) were bullied into paying up. But in 1902 the Europeans' designs were frustrated by President Roosevelt, who decided to dust off the hitherto largely moribund Monroe Doctrine.

Roosevelt sent the bulk of the navy (about 50 ships), under the command of Admiral George Dewey, the hero of Manila Bay, on "maneuvers" to the eastern Caribbean and privately informed Berlin that he would use force unless the Venezuela dispute were submitted to international arbitration. Britain and Germany, not wanting to risk a showdown, reluctantly agreed. (The international court at The Hague later ruled for the European powers.) Roosevelt took this action not out of any regard for Venezuela, whose president he derided in private as "an unspeakably villainous little monkey," but in order to make clear that the U.S. would no longer tolerate European military intervention in Latin America.

It soon became clear to Roosevelt that if the U.S. was going to tell the Europeans to stay out, it would have to take steps to police its own backyard. The president thought the Latins incapable of preserving law and order. Some more "civilized" power would have to intervene to make sure that foreign debts were paid and foreign property protected. And in the Western hemisphere henceforward that role would fall to the U.S. "If we intend to say 'hands off' to the powers of Europe, then sooner or later we must keep order ourselves," the president wrote to his secretary of state, Elihu Root, in May 1904.

Seven months later the president announced to Congress: "Chronic wrong-doing, or an impotence which results in a general loosening of the ties of civilized society, may in America, as elsewhere, ultimately require intervention by some civilized nation, and in the Western Hemisphere the adherence of the United States to the Monroe Doctrine may force the United States, however reluctantly, in flagrant cases of such wrong-doing or impotence, to the exercise of an international police power."

This became known as the Roosevelt Corollary to the Monroe Doctrine, and it would govern U.S. policy in the region for nearly 30 years, almost until the day when Roosevelt's cousin, Franklin, was inaugurated as president.

Santo Domingo

The emerging Roosevelt Corollary received an early test in Santo Domingo (the Dominican Republic), a former Spanish colony that had been plunged into chaos in 1899 upon the assassination of its longtime dictator. The resulting revolutionary violence threatened foreign lives and property. The U.S. Navy responded in traditional fashion by frequently intervening to protect foreigners. At one point a Dominican rebel group fired on a U.S. launch and killed a seaman, precipitating an hour-long bombardment of rebel positions by two American warships. In November 1903, a new government led by General Carlos F. Morales consolidated power and promptly stopped payment on foreign debt, including some owed to a New York syndicate, in an attempt to negotiate a more favorable settlement of its outstanding loans. The European bondholders were not receptive and Teddy Roosevelt feared that, as in Venezuela, their governments would resort to force.

Roosevelt denied any interest in extending formal U.S. rule over Santo Domingo: "I have about the same desire to annex it as a gorged boa constrictor might have to swallow a porcupine wrong-end-to." But in order to preserve order and keep the Europeans out, the president agreed to assume a customs receivership. Under a treaty signed in 1905, a retired U.S. army colonel took over customs collection for the Dominican Republic. The agreement called for 55 percent of the revenues to be turned over to foreign bondholders, but because the American collectors were more honest than their predecessors, the Dominican government actually received more money than ever before. The U.S. Senate balked at ratifying the treaty until 1907, but in the meantime Roosevelt simply implemented it by executive fiat.

The Dominican arrangement became a model of how the U.S. could try to use financial rather than military means to establish stability in the Caribbean.

Cuba II

Much as Roosevelt wanted to avoid armed intervention in the region, he found that America's commitments in Cuba made it impossible to stay out. Tomás Estrada Palma won reelection as Cuba's president in a rigged 1905 election boycotted by the opposition Liberal party. (Estrada Palma represented the Moderates, but there were few discernible ideological differences between the parties; like many political parties in the U.S. at this time, they were merely rival gangs of spoilsmen.) The next year, the Liberals raised the banner of revolt, fielding a force of perhaps 24,000 men. The government had no standing army, only an ineffectual Rural Guard that did police work.

Estrada Palma begged Roosevelt to send soldiers to help. The president dispatched some naval vessels to Cuban waters, but after the experience of the Philippines, he had no desire to get involved in another difficult pacification campaign. Instead he sent Secretary of War William Howard Taft and Assistant Secretary of State Robert Bacon to Havana to try to negotiate a truce between Estrada Palma and the Liberals. Estrada Palma and his vice president scotched any hope of a settlement by resigning on September 28, 1906. Cuba now had no government, and as Estrada Palma wanted, the U.S. was forced to intervene.

On September 29, 1906, 2,000 marines under the command of Colonel Littleton W. T. Waller landed, met no resistance, and set up camp just outside Havana. The same day, Taft established a provisional government run by the U.S. Both the Liberals and Estrada Palma were happy with this outcome—the former because Estrada Palma was out of power, the latter because the Liberals were not in power either.

Roosevelt still had no desire to annex Cuba: "I loathe the thought of assuming any control over the island such as we have over Puerto Rico and the Philippines." But for the next 29 months, the 5,000-man Army of Cuban Pacification would administer the island under the direction of a civilian governor general, Charles Magoon. A Nebraska lawyer who had previously run the Canal Zone, Magoon has gotten a vile reputation in Cuban history for tolerating corruption, but he was not personally venal. His sin, if it was that, was to appoint large numbers of Liberal politicians to patronage posts. They acted in the traditional fashion of patronage politicians everywhere, including in the U.S., by stealing from the public purse.

Another presidential election was held in 1908, this one won by the Liberal candidate, José Miguel Gomez. U.S. troops left in January 1909, turning the government of Cuba back to the Cubans. The most lasting legacy of the second U.S. occupation was the creation of a Cuban army trained by U.S. officers—the first of many that Americans would create around the Caribbean.

Dollar Diplomacy

The Roosevelt administration had pursued two complementary policies in the Caribbean: armed intervention under the Platt Amendment and the Roosevelt Corollary, and various peaceful means of exerting control over the region, such as the Dominican customs receivership and a Central American peace conference convened by Secretary of State Elihu Root. President William Howard Taft and his secretary of state, the peppery Philander C. Knox, who took office in 1909, wanted to emphasize economic influence above all, a policy that came to be known as "dollar diplomacy," first by its critics, then by its supporters as well.

Assistant Secretary of State Francis M. Huntington-Wilson explained in 1911 that this meant "the substitution of dollars for bullets . . . taking advantage of the interest in peace of those who benefit by the investment of capital." As part of this policy, the Taft administration encouraged Latin American states to take out loans from Wall Street, not European, banks. The administration also encouraged American investment in the region in the hope that growing prosperity would make revolutionary unrest a thing of the past and hence obviate the need for armed U.S. intervention.

Critics argue that dollar diplomacy represented the subordination of American policy to the interests of Wall Street bankers and American-owned companies such as United Fruit (forerunner of Chiquita) that were bent on exploiting the defenseless peons of Latin America. By extension, critics also argue—echoing the J. A. Hobson/V. I. Lenin thesis that imperialism was driven by a search for markets—that American soldiers and sailors were dispatched to the Caribbean at the behest of American capitalists. There is some truth to both charges—but only some.

The Taft administration, like its immediate predecessors and successors, looked at things in a different way. In their view—an American echo of *civis Romanus sum* (I am a Roman citizen)—American citizens and property abroad were entitled to the same protection that the police provided back home. Thus since the early days of the Republic, marines had been landing to protect Americans from revolutionary violence all over the world. In the Caribbean, this protection was extended not only to Americans but to Europeans as well. Government officials did not view this as a subsidy for profiteering. They saw it as protecting property rights, the cornerstone of civilization. Most of the European states took a similar attitude.

Occasionally the government did more than protect U.S. business abroad by arranging loans for Central American states from Wall Street banks. Washington had no choice but to work through private financial institutions in these days before the existence of the International Monetary Fund and World Bank. But policymakers did not think they were exploiting less-developed countries; they thought that fostering greater American trade and investment would benefit both the U.S. and the target country (a view shared by most U.S. officials to this day). Secretary of State Knox carefully scrutinized loan arrangements to make sure that they were not "unconscionably profitable" for Wall Street. Even when, as in the Dominican Republic in 1904, the U.S. government used its power to help collect payment for U.S. banks, the claims were usually much reduced from their original level and the government was intervening more to forestall European meddling than to satisfy the bankers. In general, the government was using Wall Street at least as much as Wall Street was using the government. As veteran American diplomat Alvey Adee put it: "We are after bigger game than bananas."

This is not to deny that economic motives played a role in U.S. military interventions, merely to suggest that other factors—from protecting the Panama Canal to taking up "the white man's burden"—generally mattered more. It is no coincidence that two of America's most interventionist presidents, Theodore Roosevelt and Woodrow Wilson, were united in their contempt for corner-cutting businessmen, the "malefactors of great wealth," in Roosevelt's cutting phrase.

It is also telling that the greatest level of U.S. investment in Central America prior to World War I was in Guatemala, followed by Costa Rica and Honduras.

The U.S. never intervened militarily in Guatemala and Costa Rica, and in only a very limited way in Honduras (one of those interventions, in 1924, was in opposition to an attempted coup backed by United Fruit). Nor did the U.S. send troops to the large South American republics where Americans had large financial stakes, even though they were hardly models of political stability. "It seems to be a historical fact," wrote one distinguished historian of an earlier generation, "that the more capital a country of the New World has accepted from private investors in the United States the less danger there has been of intervention." There is an obvious explanation for this: Big business was generally quite capable of looking after its own interests without help from Washington, especially in the small states of Central America and the Caribbean that came to be derisively known as "banana republics." It was precisely in those countries where the least American capital was invested— Nicaragua, Haiti, the Dominican Republic—that the U.S. undertook its biggest, most protracted military operations.

Cuba III, IV

The place where U.S. military and economic interests overlapped the most was in Cuba—and yet even there most of the American business community had been either indifferent or outright hostile to the first intervention of 1898, fearing that war would harm an already ailing U.S. economy. After the USS *Maine* exploded in Havana harbor, Teddy Roosevelt exulted to the Washington press corps, "We will have this war for the freedom of Cuba *despite* the timidity of the business world and of financiers" (italics added).

The one section of the business community that favored U.S. intervention was the small number of companies with investments in Cuba. In the years to come, those investments would grow, with large landholdings by United Fruit, the Cuban Cane Sugar Corporation, and other firms. Since most of the Cuban sugar crop went to the U.S., Cuba became almost entirely dependent economically on the *norteamericanos*. And because of its location athwart the Windward Passage and only 70 miles from Florida, Cuba was of great strategic concern to the U.S. Since the Platt Amendment had made it a virtual protectorate, it should be no surprise that U.S. military interventions did not end in 1909.

On May 20, 1912, the Independent Party of Color, representing Cuba's dispossessed black population, staged a revolt against the Liberal government of José Miguel Gomez. The "Negro revolt" was swiftly crushed everywhere except Oriente province, home to many U.S.-owned sugar mills. Secretary of State

Knox worried that the revolutionaries would threaten American-owned sugar estates and mines, so on May 31 U.S. Marines under the command of Colonel Lincoln Karmany landed at Daquiri in Oriente, the very place where 14 years before the American invasion of Cuba began. It turned out that the Cuban army needed no American help in crushing the revolt, and by mid-July the marines were withdrawn.

The final American landing in Cuba came five years later. In 1916 General Mario García Menocal, closely identified with U.S. interests, won reelection to the presidency by fraud. This led to a Liberal uprising the next year. President Woodrow Wilson, with his interest in fostering democracy abroad, might have been expected to look more favorably upon the victims of electoral fraud than his Republican predecessors had done in 1906. But the U.S. had just entered World War I and needed assured access to the Cuban sugar crop. So the Wilson administration backed Menocal's suppression of the revolt and, at the Cuban president's request, landed 2,600 marines in Oriente and Camaguey provinces in 1917. Some marines remained until 1922 to protect American-owned property. As in the 1906–09 and 1912 interventions, no fighting was done by the American forces.

Nicaragua

In Cuba, as in most of Latin America, the U.S. supported the incumbent government against attempts to usurp power by force. But occasionally Washington got angry enough at a Latin government to try and force its ouster. No Latin ruler enflamed passions in Washington more than Nicaraguan dictator José Santos Zelaya, who had been in power since 1893. He was hostile to Yankees and forged closer links with Germany and Japan, whom he tried to entice into financing another isthmian canal to compete with the one planned in Panama. Zelaya also constantly undermined Washington's attempts to impose order and stability in Central America. He overthrew the government of Honduras and openly proclaimed his desire to unite the five Central American republics under his thumb. Since Nicaragua's neighbors did not want Zelaya in control of their region, a general Central American war loomed until Secretary of State Elihu Root convened a peace conference in 1907.

Two years later, in October 1909, General Juan J. Estrada proclaimed a rebellion against his fellow Liberal, Zelaya, in the town of Bluefields. Located on the Mosquito Coast, far from Managua, Bluefields was only nominally part of Nicaragua; it was a center of rubber, banana, and gold-mining companies owned by Americans, Britons, and other foreigners, and had been occupied by

British troops for many years. American residents of Bluefields, including the U.S. consul, backed the revolt because they were fed up with Zelaya, a corrupt and tyrannical ruler with a habit of awarding monopolies on various goods to his (non-American) cronies.

Zelaya sent an army to crush the rebellion. His forces captured two American mercenaries working for the rebels and executed them despite State Department attempts to save their lives. This caused the Taft administration to break off relations with Managua. Secretary of State Knox bluntly told the Nicaraguan chargé d'affaires that the Zelaya regime was "a blot upon the history of Nicaragua."

Under U.S. pressure, Zelaya resigned the presidency on December 17, 1909, turning the job over to a protégé, José Madriz, who renewed the campaign against the Bluefields revolt. With Zelayista forces on the march, Estrada, the rebel leader, told the U.S. consul that he could no longer protect the town. The consul sent out a call for military help—and before long the marines arrived, led by a scrawny young major (just 5 foot 9 inches tall, 140 pounds) "with a hawk's beak of a nose, steel-blue eyes and a thatch of unruly black hair," not to mention a Marine Corps globe-and-anchor emblem tattooed on his chest. His name was Smedley Darlington Butler, and he was already well on his way to becoming a legend.

"If he had been born an Englishman he would have been a Clive or a Rajah Brooke," a fellow marine officer once wrote of Butler. Instead he was born into a prominent Philadelphia Quaker family. Both his father and grandfather were congressmen. Although the Butlers were Hicksite Quakers, they were no pacifists. Smedley's father, Thomas, who was to enjoy a long reign as chairman of the House Naval Affairs Committee (where he would work hand-in-glove with his marine son to protect funding for the navy and marines), was a staunch advocate of a big navy. Once, after making a bellicose speech on the floor of Congress, he encountered in the corridor a pacifist who told him, "Thee is a fine Friend!" The flinty congressman shot back: "Thee is a damn fool!" Smedley was cast very much in that pugnacious mold. "'The fighting Quaker' is what my friends and enemies call me," he wrote in his memoirs, "and I'm proud of both titles—fighter and Quaker."

Another thing Smedley was proud of was his lack of schooling; he would later brag that he was one of the few general officers in the armed forces who had never attended college. When the USS *Maine* blew up in February 1898, the event that would lead to war with Spain, Butler was just 16 years old, a student at Haverford School. "I was determined to shoulder a rifle and help free little Cuba," he recalled, even though he was underage. Turned down by the army, he decided to try the Marine Corps, which had no minimum age for new officers. His mother took him to meet the commandant, Brigadier General Charles Heywood, a friend of his father. Butler lied and told him he was 18. Heywood did not believe him but declared, "Well you're big enough anyway. We'll take you."

Smedley was trained under the eye of an old sergeant major who had fought with Kitchener in the Sudan before retiring and joining the U.S. Marines. After just six weeks' preparation, Smedley was commissioned a second lieutenant, and, with some other young officers, shipped off to Cuba in July 1898. Here he was introduced to soldiering by the "old war birds" who still dominated the corps, many of them aging Civil War veterans. Perhaps because he was so young himself, and in spite of his upper-class background, Smedley began to identify more with enlisted men than with officers—an outlook that he would carry with him all his life, even as he advanced to the rank of major general.

Smedley was lucky to enter the Marine Corps when he did. In the years between 1865 and 1898, the Corps seldom exceeded 2,000 men, and promotion occurred at such a glacial pace that 60-year-old captains were not unusual. Upon the outbreak of the Spanish-American War, however, the corps rapidly expanded, and, with the old veterans retiring, this created lots of opportunities for eager young bucks.

Unfortunately for Butler, the war against Spain was almost over. He saw no action in Cuba and returned home after just eight months. But he liked soldiering and did not want to go back to school. So he accepted a first lieutenant's commission and shipped out for the Philippines. Here he saw his first fighting, leading a company into combat, and became a protégé of L.W.T. "Tony" Waller, whose exploits on Samar would later make him infamous. Butler went with Waller when the marines hastily cobbled together a force to send to China during the Boxer Rebellion. "I am the happiest man alive," Smedley wrote to his mother when he found out he was headed for a real scrap. It was in North China that Butler really blossomed as a soldier. He displayed great heroism on numerous occasions and was twice wounded. The second time, the bullet would have hit his heart were it not for a serendipitous brass button, which Butler carried for years afterward as a souvenir. As a reward for his outstanding performance, he was breveted to captain at age 19 (see Chapter 4).

When he was leaving China in October 1900, Butler contracted typhoid fever, and by the time he reached Manila he weighed just 90 pounds. Catching, and surviving, severe tropical diseases was to be a recurrent theme in his life. In 1902,

while serving on an island near Puerto Rico, he came down with Chagres fever
and for a time he "believed that my end was near." But the indestructible marine
bounced back, as always. In 1905 Captain Butler married Ethel Conway Peters
("Miss Ethel"), a society belle from another old Philadelphia family; Waller was
his best man. The newlyweds were assigned to garrison duty in the Philippines,
where one of Butler's tasks was to supervise the building of gun emplacements on
a remote hill overlooking Subic Bay. Before long the marines had eaten all their
food, and the navy failed to resupply them. An infuriated Butler hopped into a
canoe with a couple of sergeants, intending to row across Subic Bay to get supplies for the men. They were immediately engulfed in a tropical squall that lasted for hours. They got the supplies but almost drowned in the process. The
conservative naval establishment decided, based on his rash actions, that young
Butler might be mentally unstable. A doctor diagnosed him with a "nervous
breakdown," and he was sent home in 1908 on nine months' sick leave.

Smedley did not spend his time lounging around the house in pajamas. He
took a job offered by a family friend to run a coal mine in West Virginia.
Although Butler was almost killed by a drunken mine superintendent, his
tenure in business proved a great success: Production rose and the workers were
satisfied. But even though Smedley had an offer to stay in the mining business,
he could not ignore the siren song of his beloved corps. He accepted a promotion to major and a posting to the Panama Canal Zone, where in 1909 he took
over command of the 3rd Battalion, 1st Regiment.

On the morning of May 27, 1910, Mrs. Butler had taken their two children,
Ethel ("Snooks") and Smedley Jr. ("Tommy"), on a shopping expedition to
Panama City. When she got home at noon she found her husband gone; a note
informed her that he been sent suddenly to Nicaragua and did not know when
he would be back. Butler had received his orders at 8:30 A.M. By 11:30 A.M. he
was on his way with 250 officers and men.

Butler and his battalion landed in Bluefields, a Cape Cod-style village "with
quaint little New England houses with steep roofs and no porches, all built of
wood." The town was held by just 350 rebels who were under siege from 1,500
Zelayistas. But as long as the U.S. Marines were in Bluefields the government
forces were afraid to enter, and U.S. warships commanded by Rear Admiral W.
W. Kimball prevented the government's navy from attacking the town.
Although the U.S. was officially neutral, to Butler "it was plain that
Washington would like the revolutionists to come out on top." Accordingly, the
enterprising marine major wrote a letter to the Zelayista generals besieging

Bluefields to inform them that they could attack—but without firearms, "because their soldiers were poor marksmen and might accidentally hit American citizens." The government generals wrote back: "How are we to take the town if we can't shoot? And won't you also disarm the revolutionists defending the town?" Butler suavely replied: "There is no danger of the defenders killing American citizens because they will be shooting outwards, but your soldiers would be firing toward us."

This act of bravado helped finish the Zelayista government. Since the U.S. armed forces protected Bluefields, the rebels had an invulnerable base of operations. Before long the rebels were in Managua, and, after a personnel shuffle, Adolfo Díaz, a former executive of a U.S.-owned mining company and a leader of the Conservative Party, emerged as president. Díaz agreed to sign a treaty giving the U.S. a customs receivership modeled on the Dominican example. Under State Department pressure, a consortium of New York banks arranged a $1.5 million loan for his government and received in return control of the national bank, railroad, and steamship company. Nicaragua was fast becoming a U.S. protectorate like Cuba.

Predictably, Adolfo Díaz's close relations with the *gringos* did not increase his popularity back home. In July 1912 the Liberal war minister, General Luis Mena, launched a revolution against him. President Taft ordered 100 sailors put ashore from the USS *Annapolis* to protect the U.S. legation in Managua. They arrived in the capital on August 4. Two days later cable and rail lines into the city were cut. On August 11 the rebels surrounded Managua and began an intense artillery bombardment that wound up killing hundreds of people.

President Díaz pleaded for help from Washington, and by now Taft was getting thoroughly alarmed. He thought the situation was "analogous to the Boxer trouble in China" and wanted to send in the U.S. Army. Secretary of War Henry Stimson dissuaded him, arguing that dispatching the army would be tantamount to a declaration of war, whereas the marines, with their long history of landings abroad, could be sent with fewer international repercussions.

Once again the call went out to Major Smedley Butler and his Panama battalion. On August 14, 1912, he reached Managua with his 354 men and found the government garrison in a sorry state. "Poor little fellows," Butler wrote, "they are scared to death, and their faith in me and my men is pathetic, and I would rather lose my life than to fail them." The American major took over informal command of the capital and on his own initiative began issuing orders to the encircled Nicaraguan defenders.

Commander Warren Terhune of the U.S. Navy tried to break out of Managua with 40 sailors and 10 marines. He wanted to get back to his ship, the *Annapolis*, anchored at Corinto, 75 miles away on the Pacific coast. But when Terhune's train reached León, a rebel stronghold, a mob commandeered the train. Terhune and his men had to suffer the ignominy of walking back to Managua, earning the hapless naval officer the sobriquet "General Walkemback." A disgusted Smedley Butler decided that, in order to repair the damage done to American prestige, he had to get the train back and reopen the rail line. The timid Terhune balked at Butler's request, arguing that it was too dangerous, but when the determined marine threatened to resign his commission on the spot, the navy commander gave in.

Butler piled 80 marines and 40 bluejackets onto a train and set out from Managua at midnight on August 25, 1912. The train chugged along slowly, with Butler's men repairing track as they went. Outside León, at about 10 A.M., the train was stopped by a rebel barricade. Butler hopped down, briefly parlayed with "twenty excited soldiers, who threatened all sorts of violence," and then kept on rolling till he reached the port of Corinto. Here he took on reinforcements from a U.S. warship and headed back to Managua. Rebel outposts once again challenged the leathernecks as they were passing through León on the way back, but Butler "waved two little bags of sand in the air yelling 'dynamite.'" The rebels, Butler recalled, "took to the bushes and we sailed serenely on our way." Smedley paused long enough to convince the rebel chiefs to give back the train Terhune had abandoned. He reached Managua on September 1, 1912, without a shot being fired.

Though Butler managed just 17 hours of sleep and lost 10 pounds during his tense, weeklong passage to and from Corinto, he "enjoyed it more thoroughly than any like period of activity since the Boxer campaign." He wrote to his "Darling Bunny Wife": "My passages through León, coming and going, were, I think, the best jobs I ever pulled off. The slightest slip or sign of weakness on my part would have meant a slaughter for, all agree, that my show of verve or bluff was what made the expeditions absolutely bloodless."

Meanwhile, marine reinforcements were pouring into the country. By mid-September there were 1,150 marines in Nicaragua, under the command of Colonel Joseph H. Pendleton, a beloved officer known throughout the corps as "Uncle Joe." His orders, relayed from President Taft by Admiral William H. Southerland, were to reopen the railway line from Managua to Granada and take all rebel-held towns along the rail tracks. Pendleton gave the job to Butler.

The marine major had caught malaria during his previous expedition outside Managua. He lay shivering in bed, chewing on ice to decrease his fever, which spiked up to 104 degrees. When his orders arrived, Butler got off his sickbed and on September 15, 1912, stumbled onto a train loaded with his men and some Red Cross relief supplies. "I wasn't strong enough to stand up," Butler recalled. His feverish appearance earned him a new nickname: "Old Gimlet Eye."

It was to be a perilous journey. While passing through the town of Masaya on September 19, the train was attacked by gunmen on horseback. The marines blazed away at the attackers with machine guns mounted on the roof, but they had some rough moments. One mounted assailant aimed at Butler with a revolver from just 10 yards away but wound up hitting a corporal sitting next to him.

Finally the train reached the outskirts of Granada, headquarters of General Luis Mena, leader of the rebellion. Butler arranged a meeting with Mena's delegates. To impress them, he staged what he later described as an elaborate ruse: He had his men put tent poles into the muzzles of two small field guns to make them look like 14-inch artillery pieces. Then Butler lined up his 250 marines in a tight-packed semicircle so that it would be impossible to see over their heads—and hence to know how many men he had. Mena's delegates were led blindfolded into the middle of this circle, where they found Butler sitting on a wooden camp chair with long legs. From atop this ersatz throne, Old Gimlet Eye grandly demanded that the rebels surrender the entire railroad along with some steamers belonging to the railroad that they had captured on Lake Managua. If they didn't, Butler threatened, he would attack Granada "with my big guns and all my regiments."

Whether or not it happened just as recounted—Smedley's war stories need to be treated with caution—the result was indisputable. The next day, September 22, Mena capitulated. The rebel leader, who was ill, agreed to surrender the railroad and Granada to the Americans. He even agreed to leave the country for exile in Panama. It was a supreme triumph for the Fighting Quaker and a vivid demonstration of how effectively verve and bluff could be deployed as weapons of war.

Although Mena was now out of the picture, the rebellion was not quite over. Another rebel general, Benjamin Zeledón, was still in the field. His men were entrenched atop Cayotepe and Barranca, two fortified hills overlooking the rail tracks just north of Managua. The order went out from Washington: Take those hills! They were a formidable objective, especially Coyotepe, which was 500 feet tall and steep. About 800 rebels were dug in on the two hills with machine guns and rifles.

Colonel Pendleton arrived from Managua with 600 marines; Major Butler came from Granada with 250 more. They gave Zeledón an ultimatum: surrender by 8 A.M. on October 3, 1912—or else. Smedley was worried that Zeledón would give up "and again cheat us out of a scrap." But as Pendleton and Butler anxiously scanned the hills at 8 A.M. they saw no white flags, so they ordered an all-day artillery bombardment to commence. In the predawn darkness of the next day, October 4, the infantry attacked. The Nicaraguan government troops hung back but the marines boldly advanced up Coyotepe, cutting barbed wire as they went. "As we charged up the hill, the rebels opened fire and kept up a devilish hot blazing fire," Butler wrote. "But in exactly forty minutes, we climbed the hill, killed twenty-seven of their men in the trenches at the top, captured nine and put the rest to flight. Then we turned the Coyotepe guns on the Barranca fort opposite, and that garrison fled too."

General Zeledón was killed after the battle, though it was not clear by whom. The official explanation was that his own men shot him trying to escape, but there is some evidence that government forces captured and killed him, while Butler turned a blind eye. Four Americans died and 14 were wounded in this assault, somewhat reminiscent of the Rough Riders' more famous charge up Kettle Hill and San Juan Hill 14 years before in Cuba. Three days later the remainder of the rebellion was snuffed out when sailors and marines occupied León. The total toll of the 1912 intervention: Five marines and two sailors killed, 16 marines wounded, out of 1,150 deployed.

Thanks to this armed intervention, Adolfo Díaz was more secure in the presidency then ever before. In November 1912 presidential elections were held. Since the Liberals (split between competing candidates) boycotted the balloting, Díaz's Conservatives naturally won, even though by all accounts the Liberals enjoyed more popular support. By the end of the month almost all of the marines were withdrawn, leaving only a 100-man legation guard to maintain an American presence in Managua. This force would be sufficient to assure relative peace and stability in Nicaragua for the next 13 years.

Veracruz

Woodrow Wilson's accession to the presidency in 1913 might have been expected to overturn the interventionist trend of the Roosevelt and Taft years. Though he had supported the war of 1898 and the annexation of the Philippines, Wilson had been critical of "gunboat diplomacy" and "dollar diplomacy," often denouncing foreign economic exploitation of Latin America. His first secretary of state, William Jennings Bryan, had been one of the leading opponents of American imperialism. And Senate Democrats had opposed the customs treaties with the Dominican Republic and Nicaragua.

Yet far from renouncing the interventionist policies of his Republican predecessors, Wilson expanded them. The stern Presbyterian professor believed that America had a duty to export democracy abroad, and he was prepared to act on it. "I am going to teach the South American republics to elect good men!" the new president confidently boomed to a startled British envoy, who later declared, "If some of the veteran diplomats could have heard us, they would have fallen in a faint."

A great deal has been written about the differences between Woodrow Wilson and Theodore Roosevelt. It has even been suggested by Henry Kissinger, in his magisterial *Diplomacy*, that the two men were the yin and yang of American diplomacy, Roosevelt representing European-style *Realpolitik* and Wilson the voice of naïve American ideology. This is a misleading assessment. "Roosevelt," concludes the foremost study of his diplomacy, "was prone by instinct to approach issues in terms of right and wrong and . . . he was just as much of a preacher as Woodrow Wilson." Indeed when he was police commissioner of New York, Roosevelt had atop his desk a tablet inscribed with these words: "Aggressive fighting for the right is the noblest sport the world affords." Roosevelt acted on this belief when he helped whoop America into a war to liberate the Cuban people from "murderous oppression," and when he refused to support a pro-American president of Panama who had gained power through election fraud.

The difference between Roosevelt and Wilson was not primarily over ends but means. Wilson believed in the efficacy of international law and moral force. Roosevelt believed that American honor could be protected, and its ideals exported, only by military force. His famous slogan was "Speak softly and carry a big stick." Wilson almost inverted this aphorism. The irony is that Wilson would wind up resorting to force more often than his famously bellicose predecessor had. This may not have been entirely accidental, for Roosevelt believed that his buildup of the military, and his well-advertised willingness to use it, deterred potential adversaries from challenging U.S. power. Wilson, by contrast, he condemned as one of those "prize jackasses" who combined "the unready hand with the unbridled tongue," and hence made war more likely. This may be an overly harsh judgment—there was abundant personal animus between Roosevelt and his successor—but there is little doubt that Woodrow Wilson came into office little realizing how often and how much military force would be required to implement his ideals.

He would find out soon enough.

The first foreign crisis to confront the Wilson administration occurred in Mexico. Since 1876, America's southern neighbor had been ruled by Porfirio

Díaz, a dictator who had established a climate conducive to foreign investment and friendly relations with Washington. By 1910 Mexico was the site of more than a billion dollars in U.S. investment and home to more than 40,000 American expatriates. The 80-year-old Díaz was ousted in 1911, setting off a violent upheaval that would last a decade and permanently transform the face of Mexico.

Díaz's initial successor was the idealistic and ineffectual Francisco I. Madero. In February 1913 Madero was overthrown and murdered by the ruthless General Victoriano Huerta. Woodrow Wilson, who took office just 10 days later, was so offended by the violent takeover of this "desperate brute" that he broke with longstanding tradition that held that a sovereign government would receive international recognition regardless of how it came to power. Wilson not only refused to recognize the Huerta regime, he lifted an arms embargo and allowed U.S. weapons to flow to Huerta's opponents, the Constitutionalists led by Venustiano Carranza. Wilson made it the object of American policy to overthrow the dictator and extend self-government to the Mexican people.

The first open clash between the U.S. and the Hueristas occurred in Tampico, a foreign-dominated Gulf port that was a center of Mexico's oil industry. On April 9, 1914, a party of nine American sailors in a whaleboat flying the U.S. colors was arrested by a Huerista shore patrol for being in a restricted military area without permission. As soon as the Mexican military governor found out, he ordered them released and apologized profusely for the mistake. But this was not good enough for Rear Admiral Henry T. Mayo, the obdurate old cuss who commanded the local U.S. Navy squadron. Lacking a direct radio or telegraph link with Washington, he took the initiative, and in the navy's nineteenth-century tradition (think of David Porter in Puerto Rico), demanded that the Hueristas fire a 21-gun salute to the Stars and Stripes in order to cleanse this stain upon American honor. The local Mexican commander balked at this imperious demand. Wilson, sensing a pretext that he could use to force a showdown with Huerta, made Mayo's intemperate ultimatum his own. "The salute will be fired," he grimly vowed, and ordered both the Atlantic and Pacific Fleets to steam toward Mexico. Huerta finally offered to stage a "reciprocal" salute—first a Mexican battery would salute the U.S. flag, then U.S. ships would salute the Mexican flag—but Wilson deemed this insufficient.

On Sunday, April 19, 1914, Wilson decided to break off a week of negotiations with Huerta, and at 3:00 P.M. the next day he appeared before a joint session of Congress to ask for a blank check to use armed force against Huerta.

The House immediately approved the resolution Wilson wanted, but the Senate adjourned that night without voting.

At 2 A.M. on Tuesday, April 21, the president was awakened and informed that a German cargo ship, the *Ypiranga*, was heading toward Veracruz and would arrive later that morning with a load of munitions for the Hueristas. This would increase Huerta's power and make him harder to dislodge. Wilson did not want to intercept a foreign ship on the high seas; in an odd bit of legal reasoning, he decided it would be better to seize the wharves where it was going to unload. This had the added advantage of denying Huerta customs revenues from Mexico's largest port, which might help to dislodge the dictator. Later that morning, Navy Secretary Josephus Daniels sent a radiogram to Rear Admiral Frank Friday Fletcher, in command of the naval squadron off Veracruz: "Seize custom house. Do not permit war supplies to be delivered to Huerta government or to any other party."

April 21 dawned gray and windy. With a storm brewing, Admiral Fletcher lost no time in executing his orders. Just after 11 A.M., whaleboats were hoisted over the side, and more than 700 marines and bluejackets plowed through the choppy surf toward Pier Four, Veracruz's main wharf. A large and curious crowd of Mexican and American civilians assembled to watch the spectacle. The invaders, organized into a marine regiment and a seaman regiment, encountered no resistance as they clambered out of their boats, formed ranks, and began marching toward their objectives.

From a distance Veracruz looked beautiful, a picture postcard of beaches and pastel buildings surrounded by "indigo waters, sand hills, white walls and coconut palms, mountain peaks piercing the clouds, [and] an island scarred with the grim old fortress of San Juan de Uloa." But upon closer examination the sailors and marines found the narrow cobblestone streets littered with garbage and rotting animal carcasses. Giant black vultures called *zopilotes* circled overhead and mongrel dogs ran wild. A powerful stench pervaded everything in this town of 40,000.

Wilson had counted on a peaceful occupation; he assumed that the Mexican people—"the submerged 85 per cent of the people of that Republic who are now struggling toward liberty"—would welcome American intervention to topple their dictator. This view turned out to be dangerously naive. Veracruz's military commander, General Gustavo Maass, was determined to resist. He distributed arms to local militiamen and convicts from local prisons, and sent 100 of his soldiers to the waterfront with orders to "repel the invasion." Just after they set out, he received orders from Mexico City to withdraw his force without a fight. Maass evacuated most of his 1,000 men, but by then it was too late to prevent a clash.

Just after noon on April 21, 1914, a shot rang out near the railway yard, a U.S. Navy signalman fell dead, and general firing erupted. The battle of Veracruz had begun. Mexican snipers took up positions on rooftops and in windows and began raining bullets down on the Americans. Americans began falling—by 2 P.M. four were dead, 20 wounded—and the sailors, unused to street fighting, bogged down.

Admiral Fletcher hoped to negotiate an armistice but he could find nobody to bargain with. A messenger discovered the mayor of Veracruz cowering in his bathroom, but the mayor said he had no authority over his armed countrymen. On the night of April 21, Fletcher decided that he had no choice but to expand his original mission from simply taking the waterfront to taking all of Veracruz. He was able to accomplish this goal the next day thanks to the arrival of 3,000 marine reinforcements, among them Major Smedley Butler.

"At daylight we marched right through Vera Cruz," Butler remembered. "Mexicans in the houses, on the roofs, and in the streets peppered us from all directions. Some fired at us with machine guns. Since the Mexicans were using the houses as fortresses, the Marines rushed from house to house, knocking in the doors and searching for snipers." Sailors trying to flush out the defenders had been mauled because they had simply walked straight down the middle of the street, but the marines employed sounder tactics. "Stationing a machine gunner at one end of the street as lookout, we advanced under cover, cutting our way through the adobe walls from one house to another with axes and picks," Butler wrote. "We drove everybody from the houses and then climbed up on the flat roofs to wipe out the snipers."

Although the navy also participated in this mission, the sailors proved less adroit at street fighting. A naval regiment led by Navy Captain E. A. Anderson, who had no experience in land warfare, advanced in parade-ground formation upon the Mexican Naval Academy, making his men easy targets for the cadets and other defenders barricaded inside the two-story building. The bluejackets' advance was repulsed with casualties, the situation only being saved by three warships in the harbor that pounded the academy with their long guns for a few minutes, silencing all resistance. The bombardment killed 15 cadets, including José Azueta, the son of a commodore. He became a great Mexican martyr; a monument to him still stands in Veracruz.

By noon on Wednesday, April 22, 1914, the sailors and marines had complete control of Veracruz. In the process, the Americans suffered 22 killed and

70 wounded. The exact Mexican losses are unknown, but at least 126 died and 195 were wounded.

The Navy Department was so ecstatic about this victory that it gave away medals by the bushel. Congress for the first time authorized the Medal of Honor for naval and marine officers as well as enlisted men. Smedley Butler was awarded one of 55 Medals of Honor handed out for this minor two-day engagement, the most for any battle before or since. He was incensed at this "unutterably foul perversion of Our Country's greatest gift," and tried to return his decoration, but the Navy Department insisted he keep it. The irony is that Butler had deserved a Medal of Honor for his actions in the Boxer Uprising, but had never gotten one.

The army and navy brass assumed that the occupation of Veracruz would be a prelude to an advance on Mexico City, as called for in their war plans, and as had actually happened in 1847 during the last war with Mexico. Otherwise, the occupation made no strategic sense in their minds. They had not even drawn up any plans for a military intervention in Mexico short of all-out war. But President Wilson had lost his stomach for more bloodshed, and unlike his European counterparts in that fateful year, he refused to subordinate important political decisions to the demands of military timetables. He decided to head off a war with Mexico by not advancing beyond Veracruz. But he also did not want to relinquish the port, at least while Huerta was still in power. Army and navy officers were perplexed by what Admiral Mayo called a "decidedly strange . . . state of affairs," under which the U.S. could occupy the principal port of a country it was not at war with. But the armed forces followed the commander-in-chief's orders, even if they did not agree with them, and the U.S. Army moved in to administer Veracruz.

Chosen to command the port city was 49-year-old Brigadier General Frederick Funston. His career had languished since his daring capture of the Filipino leader Emilio Aguinaldo 13 years before. He had returned from the Philippines to San Francisco in January 1902 to recuperate from chronic ulcerative appendicitis. He immediately tried to cash in on his fame by going on a lecture tour, but before long a backlash against him set in. Senator Henry Cabot Lodge's committee, investigating the conduct of the Philippine War, heard testimony that Funston had ordered prisoners to be tortured and sometimes shot. Funston did nothing to help his own cause. In one speech he declared that critics of the war ought to be strung up on the nearest lamppost. This caused such a furor that his old friend and admirer, President Theodore Roosevelt, sent word that he should shut up. This he did, but he got into more hot water with Secretary of War William Howard Taft in 1906, who ended his command of the Army of Cuban Pacification almost before it had begun.

Funston's luck did not go permanently AWOL. When the 1906 earthquake struck San Francisco, Funston was deputy commander of the military district of Northern California. Since the commanding officer was out of town, Funston personally took charge of the relief effort. He once again became a hero, but was passed over for further promotion owing to the jealousy of older officers and concerns among his superiors about his temperament. Navy Secretary Josephus Daniels was hesitant to appoint "Fighting Fred" Funston as commander of the Veracruz occupation for fear that "he may do something that may precipitate a war." This worry was reasonable enough but turned out to be unfounded. Funston *was* itching to proceed on to Mexico City—"Merely give the order and leave the rest to us," he begged the secretary of war—but when no such order was forthcoming, he contented himself with running the port city.

Where possible, Funston tried to keep the original Mexican bureaucrats in place, but few of them would serve an army of occupation. Most of the jobs had to be filled by army officers. Their main task, as an American weekly newspaper noted, was fighting "not the Mexicans, but the enemies of the Mexicans and all mankind, the microbe." Veracruz, which suffered from a polluted water supply and lack of adequate sewage, was swept regularly by epidemics of yellow fever, malaria, dysentery, smallpox, tuberculosis, and other diseases. Funston, following the example of the army in Cuba, the Philippines, and elsewhere, imposed sanitation at gunpoint. He even imported 2,500 garbage cans from the United States. As a result the death rate among city residents plummeted, and the vultures left town. In general the *Americanos* proved more efficient and honest than the Huerista officials they replaced; the police, for instance, no longer took bribes and actually cracked down on crime. It was, concludes one American historian, "a benevolent despotism, the best government the people of Veracruz ever had."

The occupation quickly became a boring routine. The thousands of American soldiers had little to do. They marched hither and yon, and spent much time frequenting cantinas, bordellos and cinemas exhibiting new-fangled moving pictures. One of the few Americans to enjoy an adventure was an army captain named Douglas MacArthur, son of old General Arthur MacArthur of Philippine War fame. Assigned to Funston's staff as an intelligence officer, Douglas decided to slip out of Veracruz with a few Mexican railroad workers to bring back some locomotives, which were in short supply in Veracruz.

MacArthur returned with three locomotives—and an amazing tale of having shot it out with a party of Mexican cavalry that had attacked his little band. MacArthur was "incensed" that he did not win a Medal of Honor for this exploit.

Just 10 weeks after the occupation began, on July 15, 1914, the Mexican dictator Victoriano Huerta resigned from office. The occupation of Veracruz—which denied him vital customs revenue—was undoubtedly a factor in his decision, but more important was the thrashing Venustiano Carranza's rebel forces had administered to his army. Carranza replaced him as president, and although he refused to hold elections, Wilson nevertheless pledged on September 16 to withdraw U.S. forces from Veracruz. The actual pullout was delayed for a couple of months until Carranza agreed not to retaliate against civilians who had aided the occupation.

On November 23, 1914, all 7,000 U.S. troops in Veracruz unceremoniously marched down to the piers and boarded transport ships. By 2 P.M. they were gone, leaving behind copious stocks of arms for the Carrancistas, meticulous records of all administrative actions and not a few wailing girlfriends. Constitutionalist troops moved in, and before long the residents were once again tossing garbage into the streets.

What did this seven-month occupation accomplish? It did nothing to stop the delivery of arms to the Huerista regime. The *Ypiranga* simply diverted from Veracruz and offloaded its cargo south of the city on May 27, 1914; Wilson no longer cared. The occupation also did nothing to resolve the incident at Tampico that had started the whole affair. Admiral Mayo never did get his 21-gun salute. Instead he was forced to call on British and German warships to help evacuate all 2,600 American residents of Tampico because of anti-*gringo* rioting. The anti-American reaction was not limited to Mexico; the events of 1914 stirred up rioting across Latin America. An Argentine political cartoon summed up the prevailing Latin view when it depicted a menacing Uncle Sam demanding of a Mexican: "Salute my flag like it deserves or I'll take off your hat with a cannon shot."

For all these reasons the wife of the U.S. chargé d'affaires in Mexico City described the occupation of Veracruz as a "screaming farce." But Wilson had reason to be satisfied anyway, for the occupation had contributed to the downfall of his nemesis, that "brute" Victoriano Huerta. Contrary to the expectations of America's admirals and generals, a limited intervention in Mexico had more or less achieved its purpose.

7

LORDS OF HISPANIOLA

Haiti, 1915–1934
Dominican Republic, 1916–1924

The landing force shoved off at 4:50 P.M. on July 28, 1915. The 340 sailors and marines from the U.S. armored cruiser *Washington* landed two miles west of Port-au-Prince and marched into town. From a distance, Marine Sergeant Faustin Wirkus thought the Haitian capital looked "beautiful" and "romantic," with its sloping hills dotted with "white-walled, tile-roofed houses" surrounded by "green foliage." But on closer inspection, "Fairyland had turned into a pigsty." The marines discovered "evil-smelling offal" and rotting garbage piled up in the streets. "More than that, we were not welcome. . . . " Firkus later wrote. "We marched over the cobblestoned streets of the waterfront through walls of human silence and dead-eyed stares."

But the resistance was mostly passive, and the marines had little trouble occupying Port-au-Prince, notwithstanding occasional sniping. The only two U.S. casualties were the result of "friendly fire" from inexperienced sailors. The U.S. occupation of Haiti, which would last for 19 years, had begun.

"A Wild Orgy of Revenge"

American troops had been drawn into Haiti for much the same reason they had occupied Veracruz: because of political turmoil. It was a pattern that was to be repeated throughout the Caribbean and Central America in the early years of the twentieth century: The more unstable a country, the more likely the U.S. was to intervene. And no country was more unstable than Haiti. Of 22 rulers between 1843 and 1915, only one served out his term of office. During those years there were at least 102 civil wars, coups d'etat, revolts, and other political disorders. The period between 1908 and 1915 was particularly chaotic. Seven presidents were overthrown during those seven years.

Most of these coups followed a familiar pattern. They were orchestrated by the mulatto elite that ran the black republic. (Mulattos, or those of mixed African and European ancestry, were a tiny, educated minority, practicing Catholicism and speaking French. They regarded themselves as a race apart from, and superior to, the Creole-speaking, voodoo-practicing, darker-skinned Haitian masses.) A cabal of *mulatre* (mulatto) plotters in Port-au-Prince, the capital, would become unhappy with the incumbent. They would select an alternative candidate—usually a *noir* (black)—and line up financing for him from the German merchant community, which expected to make a tidy profit on its investment out of public funds once the usurper came to power. The would-be president would journey to the wild, mountainous north of Haiti, where he would recruit to his cause tatterdemalion soldiers of fortune and part-time bandits known as *cacos* (after a local bird of prey) with promises of loot. The *cacos* would march south toward Port-au-Prince, plundering coastal towns as they went. Since the Haitian army was corrupt and ineffectual, there was little to slow their progress. Upon the *cacos'* arrival at the outskirts of the capital, the incumbent president would go quickly and quietly into foreign exile, taking a portion of the treasury with him. His successor would be elected by the National Assembly at gunpoint. The *cacos* would be paid off from the public treasury and happily return home, until a fresh revolutionary leader invited them to march again. It was, boasted one Haitian in 1915, "an efficient revolutionary system. . . . The most intricate and elaborate system in the world."

The last of these genteel coups occurred in February 1915, when Vilbrun Guillaume Sam, a *noir* from the north, seized the presidential palace with *caco* help. Almost immediately upon taking office, Sam found the *cacos* once again in revolt, this time rallying to the banner of Dr. Rosalvo Bobo, a red-haired *mulatre* who had the support of the Dominican Republic's ministry of war. Unlike the previous occupants of his office, Sam was not prepared to go quietly into exile. He ordered Port-au-Prince's police chief, General Charles-Oscar Etienne, to round up 200 members of the mulatto elite, including a former president, and hold them as hostages to be killed in the event of a revolution, presumably backed by their relatives.

The revolution broke out on July 27, 1915. That morning the National Palace was attacked and President Sam sought refuge with his family in the French legation next door. Police chief Etienne and his henchmen proceeded to massacre at least 160 of their prisoners, leaving the prison walls covered with entrails, the gutters running with blood. This was a violation of the "time-honored rules and precedents" of Haitian coups, which held that the mulattos who orchestrated events were to remain inviolate. Mobs of enraged mulattos rose up across Port-au-Prince. Oscar Etienne was dragged out of the Dominican legation where he had taken refuge and torn to bits. His body "was shot at, hacked at, and defiled by every passer-by, and by evening had become an unrecognizable pulp of flesh." The following morning Etienne's remains were doused with cooking oil and set afire.

President Sam suffered a similar fate. On July 28, a mob led by the fathers of his victims dragged him out of the French legation and quickly killed him with machete chops. "Hands, feet and head cut off, eviscerated, the body was dragged through the street by mobs, *elite* mingling with blacks in a wild orgy of revenge. Sam's hands, feet and head were stuck on pickets of the iron fence on our Champ de Mars."

News of this violence, with its violation of French diplomatic immunity, swiftly reached Rear Admiral William B. Caperton aboard the U.S. cruiser *Washington*, anchored just a mile off Port-au-Prince. "A trim, smallish man with the weathered face of a sailor, his hair and mustache silver-gray beneath his gold braided hat," Caperton was a 60-year-old Tennessean and had spent 44 of those years in the navy, rising upward in a steady but unspectacular progression of jobs until in January 1915 he took over the Atlantic Fleet's Special Service Squadron, which handled gunboat diplomacy in the Caribbean. He had been in Haitian waters aboard the *Washington* since the beginning of July, shadowing Dr. Rosalvo Bobo's progress along the coast to ensure that no foreigners were caught up in revolutionary violence.

After President Sam's untimely demise, the American, British, and French ministers journeyed out to Caperton's flagship and begged him to land troops to restore order. On the evening of July 28, 1915, Caperton received a cablegram from the chief of naval operations in Washington: "State Department desires American forces be landed Port-au-Prince and American and Foreign Interests be protected." Caperton had anticipated his orders by a few hours, so that by the time the cablegram arrived U.S. Marines were already in control of Haiti's capital.

The American public, preoccupied with the war ravaging Europe and various news events closer to home, barely noticed. The July 29, 1915, edition of the *New York World*, the mass circulation daily founded by Joseph Pulitzer, relegated the landing to a small item on page nine. Among the more important stories splashed across the front page: "Elsie Ferguson, Actress, Will be a Banker's Bride."

U.S. and Haiti

The occupation of Port-au-Prince was only the culmination of a longstanding U.S. involvement in the affairs of Haiti stretching back to 1800, when a slave revolt had expelled Napoleon's legions and, with a little help from the U.S. Navy, established the second independent nation in the Western hemisphere. In the nineteenth century, several U.S. administrations made unsuccessful attempts to secure use of the excellent port at Môle Saint-Nicolas on the northwest coast. Civil unrest in Haiti led to 19 landings by U.S. Marines to protect foreign residents between 1857 and 1913.

U.S. interest in Haiti grew with the construction of the Panama Canal, since Haiti and Cuba dominate, from opposing sides, the Windward Passage leading to the canal. The State and Naval departments lived in constant fear that some European power would establish a naval base in Haiti that would threaten U.S. preeminence in the Caribbean. These fears were especially acute because Haiti had a flourishing German merchant community, which controlled 80 percent of its foreign trade, and American intelligence reports indicated that these businessmen were active in manipulating Haitian politics. Washington was afraid that Haiti's constant chaos would give the Europeans an excuse to intervene.

As elsewhere in the Caribbean, the Taft administration tried to use dollar diplomacy to stabilize the situation. With scant success. In 1910–11 Secretary of State Philander Knox muscled aside a Franco-German consortium that wanted to grab control of the Banque Nationale de la Republique d'Haiti, and helped Wall Street banks led by National City Bank (forerunner of Citibank) acquire a 50 percent stake in the national bank. Another Wall Street consortium with many of the same participants began building a Haitian national railway. In 1914, fearing that the destitute Haitian government would raid the Banque vaults, the State Department sent a gunboat and some marines to transport gold stocks from Port-au-Prince to New York for safekeeping. (The money was returned five years later with interest.)

The American business community agitated for more military involvement to safeguard their investment. But in the larger scheme of things, the U.S. economic stake in Haiti was insignificant; in 1913 U.S. direct investment in Haiti amounted to $4 million, or one-third of 1 percent of the total U.S.

investment in Latin America. In any case, Woodrow Wilson, according to his navy secretary, refused to put American troops "at the beck and call of the American dollar."

Wilson and his first secretary of state, William Jennings Bryan, continued the policy of their predecessors: trying to create stability by imposing U.S. control over government finances, the model that had been tried in the Dominican Republic next door. But the intensely nationalistic Haitians refused to budge. When Haiti's foreign minister broached the subject of U.S. financial control to the National Assembly, he was almost killed by the enraged legislators. Haiti's financial situation kept deteriorating and Kaiser Wilhelm II's warships kept nosing around its waters, raising the possibility of German intervention in the event of a debt default. Meanwhile, Haiti's worsening political chaos troubled a U.S. president bent on extending constitutional government south of the border.

"Action is evidently necessary and no doubt it would be a mistake to postpone it long," Woodrow Wilson wrote on July 2, 1915. Less than a month later, the bloodbath in Port-au-Prince presented the president with the perfect opportunity to intervene.

The marines were landed for essentially two reasons, as Wilson's second secretary of state, Robert Lansing, later explained. The first was "to terminate the appalling conditions of anarchy, savagery, and oppression which had been prevalent in Haiti for decades." The second was "to forestall any attempt by a foreign power to obtain a foothold on the territory of an American nation." Contrary to the prevailing myth, economic considerations did not play an important role. U.S. business interests, such as they were, had not been directly threatened by the revolution that toppled Vilbrun Guillaume Sam.

"This, I Think, Is Necessary"

To secure the capital, Admiral William Caperton summoned reinforcements. By early August 1915 there were 2,029 marines in Haiti, formed into a brigade commanded by Colonel Littleton W. T. Waller, the 59-year-old colonial soldier who had acquired a certain notoriety on the Philippine island of Samar. Tony Waller's men disarmed the remnants of the Haitian army, paying them off at $2 per head. Some *cacos* tried to make trouble, but their ineffectual attacks on the marines were easily repulsed and they were chased out of town. The marines took over the administration of Port-au-Prince, offering free food to the hungry, free medical care to the sick—and a free kick in the backside to troublemakers.

Acting Secretary of State Lansing, who had just taken over for William Jennings Bryan, was not sure what the next step should be. President Wilson told him: "I suppose there is nothing to do but take the bull by the horns and restore order."

This meant, first of all, picking a new president. The job would be done by the National Assembly, but Washington wanted to make sure the legislators made no mistake. Admiral Caperton and his French-speaking deputy, Captain Edward L. Beach, made a quick survey of the Haitian political scene and decided that Dr. Rosalvo Bobo, the latest revolutionary leader, would not govern in either Haiti's or America's best interests. Captain Beach summoned Dr. Bobo aboard the cruiser *Washington* and peremptorily informed him, "You are not a candidate because the United States forbids it." Instead the U.S. settled on Senate president Philippe Sudre Dartiguenave, a mulatto who promised to cooperate with the American occupation. On August 12, 1915, under the watchful eyes of marines with fixed bayonets and with Beach walking the floor to round up votes, the National Assembly overwhelmingly picked Dartiguenave as president. It was no more brazen a usurpation than that of any previous Haitian president, but neither was it quite the democratic election that the U.S. pretended at the time.

The Americans wasted no time in solidifying their hold on Haiti, a country about the size of Maryland with perhaps 2 million inhabitants. In late August and early September 1915, marines finished occupying Haiti's coastal towns, and navy paymasters began running the government's customs houses. The proud Haitians evinced growing hostility to the *blancs* and their client president. Admiral Caperton responded in early September by declaring martial law and banning "false or incendiary propaganda against the Government of the United States or Government of Haiti."

To give all this a legal gloss, the State Department drafted a Haitian-U.S. Treaty that it presented for Dartiguenave to sign "without modification." The treaty gave the U.S. the right to supervise government finances, control customs collection, create an American-officered constabulary, and, last but not least, intervene militarily to enforce the other treaty provisions. The treaty would last for 10 years, with the option of renewing it for another 10 if *either* party so desired.

At first Dartiguenave balked at signing this accord—until Major Smedley Butler, Old Gimlet Eye, entered the picture. Among the marines, it was said that Smedley was dispatched to the National Palace to obtain Dartiguenave's signature. The president tried to hide in his bathroom. The marine waited outside the door for an hour. Still no sign of the president. Growing impatient,

Butler walked outside, grabbed a ladder, propped it against the palace wall, and climbed up to the window of the bathroom to discover Dartiguenave sitting on a porcelain commode, fully dressed in pinstriped trousers, morning coat, and top hat, smoking a cigar and reading a copy of *Petit Parisien*. Wasting no time, Butler supposedly leaped through the window to present the treaty and a fountain pen to the startled president. "Sign here," he commanded, and the president did.

There is no sense inquiring whether this "gorgeous legend" is literally true; even if only apocryphal, it gives an accurate flavor of how the U.S.-Haiti Treaty of 1915 came into being. "I confess that this method of negotiation, with our Marines policing the Haytian capital is high-handed," wrote Secretary of State Lansing to President Wilson. "It does not meet my sense of a nation's sovereign rights and is more or less an exercise of force and an invasion of Haytian independence. From a practical standpoint, however, I cannot but feel that it is the only thing to do if we intend to cure the anarchy and disorder which prevails in that Republic."

Wilson, whose pure faith in national self-determination was diluted by a generous dollop of *Realpolitik*, wrote back, "This, I think, is necessary and has my approval."

The First Caco War

It did not have the approval of the *cacos*, the wild northern gangs whose lucrative racket—preying on peasants and politicians alike—was threatened by the North American newcomers. In September 1915, the *cacos* rose up to challenge U.S. rule. They besieged U.S.-occupied coastal towns and ambushed marine patrols. Clearly, this was a job for Smedley Butler.

His first stop was Gonaives, a small coastal town under siege by 800 *cacos* led by General Pierre Rameau. Butler and his 108 men had just arrived in Gonaives on September 20, 1915, and were resting after supper when word arrived that Rameau's *cacos* were attacking the railroad tracks. The marines, wearing only underclothes, did not bother to put on uniforms; they simply grabbed their rifles and gunbelts, and, half-naked, chased the *cacos* out of town. Butler later described how he caught up with Rameau, "a weazened up old Negro" on a horse, surrounded by about 450 followers. Butler claimed he walked up to the *caco* general, and when he refused to dismount, abruptly pulled him off the saddle. "This was more humiliating to him than defeat in battle," Smedley wrote. "His prestige with his men was destroyed, and he was no longer the great general."

This story—probably somewhat exaggerated—indicates that Butler had lost none of the brashness that he had displayed in Nicaragua. He chafed under his commanding officer, Colonel Eli K. Cole, who did not show similar flair. Cole was holed up with 700 men in Cap Haitien, the largest town in northern Haiti, and was afraid to move into the interior. The colonel claimed that it was impossible to clean out the *cacos* from the mountains of northern Haiti until he had 3,000 men. At the time, there were not that many marines in the whole country. Both Tony Waller, Cole's commander, and Smedley Butler, his subordinate, thought he was being overly cautious. "Cole was a fine officer, but inclined to be over-educated," Butler fumed. "If you have too much education, you are acutely conscious of the risks you run and are afraid to act." Butler, by contrast, had little formal schooling but lots of experience in what is now called counterinsurgency warfare. His background convinced him that a small number of well-trained Western troops could disperse a large number of guerrillas, as long as they displayed considerable élan and never gave up the initiative.

To prove his theories, Butler set out on October 22, 1915, with just four officers and 37 enlisted men, old-timers all, on a reconnaissance patrol through the heavily forested mountains of northern Haiti. This area, infested with *cacos*, had not been visited by white men since the French had left in 1804. "Oh the wildness of it all," Butler marveled in a letter to his father, "the half-clothed, vicious natives, the wonderful scenery and fine clean air, there is no country like it that I have ever seen."

Two days after starting out, Butler's patrol was wending its way in pitch darkness and driving rain across a river when they came under rifle fire from hundreds of *cacos*. With bullets whizzing through the air, Butler was right in his element. "Isn't this great?" he exulted. Luckily for the marines, the *cacos* were extremely poor shots, but they still put the outnumbered Americans on the run. In their haste to escape, the marines lost their lone machine gun in the river. Gunnery Sergeant Dan Daly, the 47-year-old spitfire who had already won a Medal of Honor defending the Legation Quarter in Peking during the Boxer Uprising, volunteered to retrieve it. He swam the river by himself, found the machine gun strapped to a dead horse, hefted it onto his back and coolly hiked back to the rest of the patrol—all under fire. For this exploit he would win his second Medal of Honor.

The marines spent a miserable night besieged by hordes of *cacos* who blew conch shells and screamed death threats. Smedley was undaunted. "Just go for those devils as soon as it's light," he told his men. "Move straight ahead and shoot everyone you see." That's just what they did, the *cacos* scattering before their onslaught. "The Marines went wild after their devilish night and hunted down the Cacos like pigs," Butler later wrote. Amazingly, only one marine was wounded in this battle. The patrol, hungry and exhausted, finally staggered back to base a couple of days later.

A number of other *caco* forts fell in short order, leaving only one major redoubt in enemy hands: Fort Rivière, an old French stronghold planted atop Montagne Noir, 4,000 feet above sea level. Colonel Eli Cole, cautious as ever, thought it would take an infantry regiment and an artillery battery to conquer the fort. Smedley Butler had other ideas. He told Cole, "Colonel, if you let me pick one hundred men from the eight hundred you have here, I feel I can capture the place at once without wasting more words." Cole was skeptical but offered to let his brash subordinate take a shot.

Butler reached Fort Rivière on the evening of November 17, 1915. Leaving most of his force to provide covering fire, he took 26 men with him, advancing in rushes until they reached the base of the fort's 15-to–25 foot walls. Here they were temporarily safe from being fired on from above. But the only entrance they could find was a drain 4 feet high and 3 feet wide extending about 15 feet into the interior of the fort. It was obvious that anyone crawling through the hole would be an easy target for a defender on the other side. Butler, for once, was "writhing inside with indecision." Sergeant Ross L. Iams stepped forward and declared, "Oh hell, I'm going through." He was followed by Butler's orderly, Private Samuel Gross, and then by Butler himself.

As the three marines were crawling through the drain, a big *caco* on the other side took aim with a rifle, fired . . . and somehow missed. Before he could reload, Sergeant Iams jumped into the courtyard and shot him dead. The three marines quickly found themselves surrounded. "Sixty or seventy half-naked madmen, howling and leaping, poured down upon us," Butler wrote. A few seconds later the rest of the marine company "began to pop out of the hole like corks out of a bottle." In the ensuing hand-to-hand combat, the marines made short work of the *cacos*, who, in their desperation, threw away their rifles and fought with swords, clubs, rocks, and machetes, "which were," Butler noted, "no match for bullets and bayonets."

The battle was over in ten minutes. At least fifty *cacos* were killed, and while some escaped, the marines took no prisoners. The only U.S. casualty was a marine who lost two teeth when he was hit in the face with a rock. Major Butler, Sergeant Iams, and Private Gross all received Medals of Honor (Butler's second) for this engagement, which essentially ended the *caco* threat in the north. Butler had vindicated his own boasts: Relentless pursuit could indeed bring a far more numerous, but ill-trained and badly armed, enemy to heel.

Within a few months, roughly 2,000 U.S. marines had established firm control over a country of 2 million people. The marines suffered three killed, 18 wounded; *caco* casualties are unknown but probably numbered some 200 dead. The marines' success may be attributed to daring patrolling combined with generous treatment of *cacos* who surrendered; they were given amnesty, money to turn in their guns, and consideration for government employment. It was a virtuoso display of counterinsurgency warfare.

In Washington, a fellow cabinet member kidded Navy Secretary Josephus Daniels by hailing him as "Josephus the First, King of Haiti." The jape was not far off.

Governing Haiti

To consolidate its power, the U.S. set up a native constabulary officered by Americans that would combine the functions of an army and a police force. Similar units had been created in the Philippines, Puerto Rico, and Cuba. Smedley Butler, fresh from campaigning against the *cacos*, was appointed the first commandant of the Gendarmerie d'Haiti in December 1915. Newly promoted to the rank of marine lieutenant colonel, Butler became at the same time a major general in the gendarmerie. Along with 114 other marines, he trained a force of 2,553 Haitians. It was an attractive assignment for marines like Butler because they received a higher rank in the gendarmerie and a second salary to supplement their corps paycheck. Most of the junior gendarmerie officers were corporals and sergeants in the corps, though as time went by more Haitians were promoted to the officer ranks.

The recruits tended to be uneducated *noir*s; mulattos generally thought military service beneath them. They proved on the whole to be fiercely loyal to their American officers, though their combat effectiveness was not great in the early years. The marines concentrated their own forces in Port-au-Prince and Cap Haitien, where they lived the easy lives of imperialists, with the usual round of dances, clubs, and social hours. Some officers, including Butler, brought their wives over to join them. The Haitian gendarmes and their American officers were scattered in garrisons across the impoverished countryside.

Although the United States had quickly taken control of Haitian customs and financial affairs, the other so-called treaty services, public works and public health, were slower to get going. Most of those functions wound up being performed by the gendarmes, who administered prisons, roads, bridges, the water supply, telegraph lines, sanitation, and other vital services. Gendarme officers, in the manner of colonial administrators everywhere, ran their districts with virtually unlimited authority, serving as local judges, paymasters, mayors, and tax collectors. While they generally performed far more efficiently and honestly than their Haitian predecessors had, there were some abuses that would cause problems later on.

Smedley Butler, who as gendarmerie commander became one of the most powerful men in Haiti, reflected the attitudes of most marines. He expressed affection for "my little chocolate soldiers" and determined to do his "level best to make a real and happy nation out of this blood crazy Garden of Eden." Other U.S. officers were more disdainful. Colonel Tony Waller, scion of a long line of Virginia slave owners (including some killed in Nat Turner's slave revolt), bragged, "I know the nigger and how to handle him."

Tensions escalated in Port-au-Prince between the undiplomatic marines and the mulatto elite who had been used to living off government largesse. The elites looked down on the occupying *blancs* as uncouth, unschooled clods; most of them did not even speak *francais!* The marines seethed at the mulattos' pretensions and demands for privileged positions. Butler announced that "no preference [will be] shown any negro owing to a supposed superiority due to the infusement of white blood in his veins." Smedley declared that he liked the 99 percent of Haitians who didn't wear shoes; they were "the most kindly, generous, hospitable, pleasure-loving people." It was the other 1 percent, in their "vici kid shoes with long pointed toes and celluloid collars," who drove him to distraction. He felt that they were not trustworthy and, while professing friendship to the Americans, were plotting against them in secret. And so many of them were. Who could blame them?

No mulatto caused more consternation for the Americans than their own hand-picked president, Phillipe Sudre Dartiguenave. With the Americans having defeated the *cacos*, bane of generations of Haitian presidents, he felt free to assert more independence. After U.S.-supervised legislative elections were held on January 15, 1917—the fairest in Haitian history—Washington wanted the new National Assembly to approve a fresh constitution. The State Department demanded that legislators remove the bar on property ownership by foreigners and ratify all acts of the occupation authorities. Both Dartiguenave and the assembly balked. Instead nationalist deputies began writing and adopting their own constitution. The marines decided that they had no choice but to dissolve the assembly. Dartiguenave was quite happy to have this occur—he was not popular with the deputies—but he wanted the *blancs* to do the dirty deed so that no one would blame him.

The marines, however, insisted that the legal niceties be observed. On the morning of June 19, 1917, Smedley Butler, in his capacity as chief of the gendarmerie, marched over to the presidential palace to get the president and a majority of his cabinet to sign a decree proroguing the assembly, as required by law. At first Dartiguenave was reluctant, but Butler browbeat the president and four cabinet members into signing. "The signatures were so small that one needed a magnifying glass to read them," Butler commented.

The only question now was who would present the decree to the assembly. Dartiguenave feared for his life if he did so. Butler went over to the assembly with a handful of gendarmes. Like Cromwell before the Long Parliament, he was met by jeers and hisses. The alarmed gendarmes began cocking their rifles. Butler ordered them to unload, and proceeded to formally enter the decree dissolving the assembly. Dartiguenave would now rule as a virtual dictator, relying on a hand-picked Council of State to carry out his decisions.

The U.S.-written constitution was submitted to a national plebiscite on June 12, 1918. The vote was 98,225 in favor, 768 against. The lopsided margin was no surprise, since 97 percent of Haitian voters were illiterate. They were willing to vote any way the men with guns, in this case the gendarmes, told them to. Wrote one marine: "I blush at the transparent maneuvers to which we resorted to make it appear that the Haitians were accomplishing their own regeneration in accordance with democratic principles as understood in the United States." Blushing or not, U.S. control was now both de facto and de jure.

Dominican Republic

Just as the marines were settling into Haiti, trouble was brewing next door in the Dominican Republic. Though larger in land area than Haiti, occupying two-thirds of the island of Hispaniola, the Dominican Republic had fewer inhabitants. Its population, at a million or so in 1916, was perhaps half that of Haiti. This disparity had made it relatively easy for Haiti to impose brutal colonial rule upon its neighbor from 1801 to 1805 and again from 1822 to 1843. The Hispanic Dominicans liked rule by the francophone Haitians so little that they volunteered to return to Spanish sovereignty from 1861 to 1865. When the Spanish pulled out a second time, the Dominicans tried to interest the U.S. in annexation. The Grant administration was amenable, but the treaty was defeated by the Senate in 1871.

Left to its own devices, the Dominican Republic reverted to weak central government and strong caudillos who held sway over the countryside. Theodore Roosevelt's customs receivership, imposed in 1905, did little to stabilize the situation. Another period of turmoil broke out in 1911 when Dominican President Ramon Caceres was assassinated. In an attempt to end the chaos, Woodrow Wilson demanded that fresh elections be held in October 1914. The winner of the balloting, supervised by the U.S. Navy and Marines, was a wealthy caudillo named Juan Isidro Jimenez. Having overseen his election, the Wilson administration pressured Jimenez to agree to a treaty allowing the U.S. to set up a constabulary and assume financial control, thereby expanding the customs receivership already implemented by Roosevelt into a more wide-ranging protectorate. Jimenez was amenable to some of these demands, but the Dominican Congress was not.

In the spring of 1916, the Dominican Congress began impeachment proceedings against Jimenez at the same time that the powerful war minister, General Desiderio Arias, declared a revolt against him. The president was chased out of his own capital. In Washington, Jimenez was perceived as "our man," while Arias was thought to be pro-German and a conduit of arms to the *cacos* resisting U.S. rule in Haiti. Rear Admiral William Caperton, commander of the navy's Special Service Squadron, was given wide discretion by the Navy and State departments to intervene as he saw fit to prop up Jimenez.

Caperton sent 150 marines by sea from Haiti to Santo Domingo. The marines' commander, Major Frederic Wise, found President Jimenez encamped outside the walls of Santo Domingo with about 800 followers. Jimenez told the Americans that he wanted his presidency back but did not want it with American help, which would discredit him among his own people. He asked Wise and the American minister to visit General Arias and ask him to surrender without a fight. This they did. "Dopey" Wise, a blunt-spoken marine with a volcanic temper, later recounted the conversation:

> I told him that this damned business of having revolutions in San Domingo had to cease; that he must get out and let the President come back into the capital without a row; that the United States meant business and if he didn't do it we were going to put him out.
> "I do not intend to leave," he said.
> "Oh, yes, you will," I told him.

When Wise got back to camp, he told President Jimenez that they would have to take the capital by force. The president was appalled: "I can never consent to attacking my own people." He resigned on the spot, his duties being taken over by a council of ministers. Wise, feeling that American prestige was on the line, was still determined to oust Arias. He waited a few days until 400 marine reinforcements arrived from Haiti under Major Newt Hall (last seen defending the legations in Peking during the Boxer Uprising). Admiral Caperton also showed up to take command personally. Arias was told that he had two days—until 6 A.M. on May 15, 1916—to surrender Santo Domingo. That morning the marines marched into the city expecting to fight it out block by block as they had in Veracruz, only to discover that Arias and his men had slipped out the night before. The marines occupied the capital without a shot being fired.

Arias was still in the countryside with a considerable portion of the Dominican army, ready to resist U.S. occupation. But he proved no match for the marines. It took 1,300 marines little more than a month to occupy the major coastal towns and to seize Arias's stronghold, Santiago de los Caballeros, the country's second-largest city. It was no contest, really. On one occasion, a small party of marines was attacked by 150 of the enemy. "I suppose the eight or nine of us looked easy to them," Dopey Wise wrote. What the Dominicans had not counted on was the Americans' machine gun; they apparently had never seen such a weapon before. Wise let them advance quite close before demonstrating what it could do. "I could see sheer amazement on their faces. The gun was functioning properly. All up and down the line I could see them dropping. Then they turned and ran."

The biggest loss of American lives occurred not in this brief campaign, which concluded with Arias's surrender, but shortly thereafter. A hurricane blew into Santo Domingo harbor in August 1916, causing the cruiser *Memphis* to founder on the rocks and killing 40 U.S. sailors.

In 1917, the Wilson administration purchased the Virgin Islands from Denmark and landed troops in Cuba to quell unrest (see Chapter 6). These moves completed the U.S. strategy, stretching back to the days of Commodore David Porter's campaigns against pirates in the 1820s, of turning the Caribbean into an American lake. The Stars and Stripes now flew over the Panama Canal Zone, Puerto Rico, Haiti, the Dominican Republic, and the Virgin Islands, while the rest of the Central American and Caribbean states were firmly under Uncle Sam's thumb, with the exception of a few islands safe in the hands of America's allies, Britain and France. Germany, and any other power bent on making trouble for the U.S., had been firmly excluded from the region.

Pacification and Administration

Now the U.S. occupation authorities turned to the task of running the Dominican Republic, a country about the size of New Hampshire and Vermont combined. As in Haiti, the Americans preferred to rule through a local president who would accede to U.S. control of government finances and a new constabulary. But unlike in Haiti, no suitable high-level politician was willing to work with the occupiers. President Wilson was told that he could either withdraw U.S. forces or impose martial law. He chose the latter option "with the deepest reluctance," as "the least of the evils in sight in this very perplexing situation."

On November 29, 1916, Rear Admiral Harry S. Knapp, who had replaced Admiral Caperton as commander of the Special Service Squadron, proclaimed U.S. military government of the Dominican Republic with himself as governor. Marines assumed control of the Interior, War, Police and other ministries, though many lower-level Dominican civil servants remained on the job. Under U.S. direction, the educational system was revamped (the number of students enrolled increased five-fold), roads built, jails cleaned up, sanitation imposed, hospitals updated, taxes overhauled. Thanks to American medical improvements, the population rose sharply. As in Haiti, the U.S. created an American-officered constabulary, the 1,200-man Guardia Nacional Dominicana, that was intended to serve as an efficient and apolitical police force and army.

The most immediate problem for the U.S. occupiers was pacifying the wild eastern provinces, El Seibo and San Pedro de Macoris, which had never been brought under the effective control of any central government. As in Haiti and elsewhere, the marines tended to see anyone who challenged their rule as mere *gavilleros* (highwaymen). There were some 600 full-time Dominican fighters in the field, supplemented by many more part-time guerrillas who would blend into the civilian population when necessary. There was no guerrilla leader of transcending importance—no one like Aguinaldo in the Philippines or later Sandino in Nicaragua—but there were a number of potent local chieftains. One of the most effective anti-American caudillos was Vicente "Vicentico" Evangelista. In March 1917 he kidnapped two American civilians and hacked them to death, leaving the remains for wild boars to feast on. He led marine pursuers on a merry chase before surrendering on July 5 of that year. Two days later Vicentico was shot and killed by marines "while trying to escape." The widespread suspicion that he was murdered only deepened anti-American feeling.

When the U.S. entered World War I, all of the marine officers were eager to go to France. Many of the best ones did; those left behind in this backwater tended to be second-raters. And instead of commanding seasoned veterans from the "Old Corps," these officers had to lead inexperienced draftees, many of them practically mutinous when they were not discharged after the armistice of 1918. The incidents of abuse against Dominicans jumped noticeably during 1917–18. A marine captain named Charles F. Merkel became notorious as the Tiger of Seibo; he personally tortured one prisoner by cutting him with a knife, pouring salt and orange juice on his wounds, and then cutting off his ears. Word of these abuses reached Santo Domingo, leading to Merkel's arrest in October 1918. While in prison awaiting trial he blew his brains out. Rumor had it that his suicide was preceded by a visit to his jail cell by two marine officers who left him a gun with one bullet in it.

Patrolling the sprawling Dominican countryside was not easy given how few marines were in the country—never more than 3,000 men, a peak reached in 1919, and of that total only about one-third were out in the field in the rebellious eastern provinces. By 1919 the marines had received radios that made it easier to coordinate their efforts and six Curtiss "Jenny" biplanes that allowed them to expand the reach of their patrolling and even to bomb some guerrilla outposts. Still, as in most guerrilla wars, there was no quick or easy victory to be had; just the wearying slog of garrison duty and incessant patrolling.

Anti-American activity never seriously threatened the U.S. hold on the country, but it was a constant, low-level nuisance. The unrest in the eastern provinces lasted until 1922 when, with independence already in sight, the marines launched a final counterinsurgency campaign under the direction of Brigadier General Harry Lee. The guerrillas finally agreed to surrender in return for amnesty. The countryside was pacified at last. During the course of the campaign between 1916 and 1922, the marines claim to have killed or wounded 1,137 "bandits," while 20 marines were killed and 67 wounded.

The Second Caco War

Matters were more serious in Haiti, where in 1919 another full-blown *caco* revolt erupted. Its roots lay in assorted grievances created by four years of American occupation, principal among them being the corvée. An ancient practice going back to prerevolutionary France, the corvée was a system whereby poor peasants could be forced to work on road gangs in lieu of paying taxes. A Haitian law of 1863 allowed the corvée in Haiti, but it had fallen into disuse—along with the roads—until revived by the marines in 1916. When he was gendarmerie commander, Smedley Butler made large-scale use of the corvée to create a modern transportation system for Haiti. In 1915, when the marines arrived, there had been only two paved streets in the entire country, both in Port-au-Prince. By 1918 the corvée had constructed 470 miles of roads, including the first highway linking Haiti's principal cities, Port-au-Prince and Cap Haitien.

Despite its obvious success, the corvée also caused equally obvious resentment. It was, after all, forced labor—and under the guns of the *blancs* no less. At first the peasants did not mind too much since they got free lodging, meals, and entertainment. But then rumors spread that the road work was a prelude to the reintroduction of slavery. As the corvée became more unpopular, gendarmes used more brutal methods to gather up road gangs, sometimes roping the Haitians together to prevent them from fleeing. Butler's successor as gendarmerie commander, Major Alexander S. Williams, "soon realized that one of the great causes of American unpopularity among the Haitians was the corvée." Williams abolished this practice on October 1, 1918, but by then the damage had been done. Many Haitian peasants were deeply resentful of the occupation. At the same time, the mulatto elites in Port-au-Prince were dissatisfied too, for the occupation had cut them off from the public treasury. In these explosive conditions, only a spark was necessary to ignite a conflagration.

The spark came from Charlemagne Massena Peralte. A mulatto who was a French-trained lawyer and an ally of would-be president Dr. Rosalvo Bobo, Peralte was described by one marine as "handsome, brave and intelligent"; another praised his "gift for flamboyant proclamations and the more inflaming brands of oratory." He had been arrested by the gendarmerie in early 1918 and sentenced to five years' hard labor for allegedly taking part in a plot to attack the home of an American officer. Later that year, while being forced to sweep the streets of Cap Haitien, Peralte escaped custody and took to the northern hills to rally another *caco* uprising "to drive the invaders into the sea and free Haiti." The cry of "Haiti for the Haitians" spread across the land. With old hands like Littleton W. T. Waller and Smedley Butler having been transferred to France, the remaining marines were lethargic in putting down the disturbances. Before long, all of central and northern Haiti was aflame with rebellion. "You couldn't go out of any of the towns in the affected districts without a Cacao taking a shot at you, though he wouldn't hit you," wrote Lieutenant Colonel Frederic Wise, newly arrived from the Dominican Republican and promoted to command of the gendarmerie.

Peralte, with an estimated 5,000 full-time followers (and thousands more occasional volunteers), fought a running series of battles with the marines and gendarmes between April and October of 1919. On October 7, he even raided

Port-au-Prince. This attack was driven off, but the marines and gendarmes could not stamp out the rebellion or capture its leader. Dopey Wise, the gendarmerie commander, instructed a subordinate: "Get Charlemagne."

The job fell to Herman Hanneken, a 26-year-old marine sergeant acting as a captain in the gendarmerie. A strapping blond Missourian with "high cheek bones and lean jaws" and an "eye singularly direct, deep-set, pale and old, like a cat's," "Hard Head" Hanneken was known for being silent and standoffish, cold and calculating. He commanded the garrison at Grande Rivière, a small town in the north, located in an area infested with *cacos*. Hanneken hatched an elaborate plot to lure the elusive *caco* leader out of hiding. Out of his own pocket (no government money being available), he financed his own *"caco"* band, led by Jean-Baptiste Conze, a wealthy mulatto planter who set up headquarters in abandoned old Fort Capois along with a gendarme "deserter," Private Jean Edmond Francois. Hanneken hoped that Charlemagne would take Conze into his confidence and thereby lead the Americans to his hideout.

To complete the ruse, Hanneken staged an attack on Fort Capois that Conze ceremoniously drove off. Hanneken was even "wounded." Or so it seemed to anyone who saw the gendarmerie captain skulking around Grande Rivière with his arm in a sling oozing red ink. As the pièce de résistance, Conze presented Charlemagne with Hanneken's pearl-handled Smith and Wesson pistol, which he claimed the wounded marine had dropped. The local people and Hanneken's own marines muttered about what an embarrassment all this was: The mighty blancs beaten by those ragged nobodys from the hills!

But Charlemagne Peralte, nobody's fool, was suspicious. One night, he stole into Conze's camp and walked up to Conze. According to Dopey Wise's account:

> "Conzee [sic]," he said, "you are not a true Cacao. You are nothing but a spy in the pay of these accursed Americans."
>
> "If you believe that, the best thing you can do is kill me now," he said.
>
> Charlemagne stood over him, pistol in hand. For a moment Conzee's life hung by a hair. Then Charlemagne spoke.
>
> "I'll give you a chance to prove if you're a true Cacao," he said. "All you have done so far is to lead a few small raids against a few small villages. Take me a real town away from the Americans and I'll begin to think you're a true Cacao."
>
> "I'll do it," Conzee told him.

The town picked for the *caco* raid was Grande Rivière. Just before the attack was scheduled to take place on October 31, 1919, Hanneken and his second-in-command, a marine corporal named William Button, slipped into the jungle with 20 gendarmes dressed in *caco* rags. Appropriately enough, this being Halloween, Hanneken and Button darkened their bodies with lamp black so they could pass as *cacos* in the dark. It helped that Hanneken, having spent four years in Haiti, could speak Creole, though Button could not. Hiding in the bushes, they heard hundreds of *cacos* marching by, headed for Grande Rivière, where a nasty trick awaited them: Marine reinforcements had sneaked into town the previous night with a machine gun.

All was going according to plan—except where was Charlemagne? Hanneken had hoped to ambush the rebel leader at a spot just outside Grande Rivière, but Private Jean Edmond Francois, the gendarme "deserter" planted in the rebel camp, arrived to inform him that Charlemagne had not gone along on the raid. He was going to remain on a nearby hill until he received word that the attack had been successful. Hanneken decided that he and his *"cacos"* would deliver the good word to Charlemagne in person. At 10 P.M., he set off with his small contingent into the mountains swarming with hundreds if not thousands of *cacos*. "It was as daring a deed, I think, as men ever undertook," Dopey Wise wrote. "Certain death was the price of failure."

The small party managed to get by four of Peralte's outposts with little trouble, thanks to Private Francois, who was known to the guards and gave them the proper passwords. At the fifth outpost, the charade was almost uncovered. A sentry noticed Button's Browning Automatic Rifle (BAR) and demanded to know where he got such a "fine-looking" weapon. Button just barely managed to bluff his way through. Finally they reached the edge of Charlemagne Peralte's camp. Just 15 feet away they saw the guerrilla leader illuminated by the reflected light of a campfire. Peralte sensed trouble and was on the verge of melting into the night when Hanneken drew his .45 caliber automatic pistol and put a bullet through his heart. Meanwhile, Button opened fire on the milling *cacos* with his BAR. The gendarmes then hurried up and drove off the remaining rebels.

At daybreak on November 1, 1919, the raiding party returned to Grande Rivière, where they discovered that the main body of marines had easily repulsed the attack by Peralte's men the night before. The return of Hanneken's raiders caused no little excitement in the town since, as proof that they had really killed Charlemagne, four gendarmes were carrying his corpse trussed to a door. The marines circulated photographs of the dead man throughout the island nation, but the gesture backfired because the picture gave the mistaken appearance that Peralte had been crucified, helping to turn him into a martyr.

For the time being, however, Peralte's assassination broke the back of the revolution. Hanneken and Button were awarded Medals of Honor for their exploits, so reminiscent of Frederick Funston's raid on Emilio Aguinaldo's camp in the Philippines. Hanneken also received a lieutenant's commission in the corps; he would go on to command a battalion on Guadalcanal in World War II and retire as a brigadier general. Corporal Button was less lucky; he died in Haiti the following year, a victim of malaria.

The only remaining guerrilla leader of any stature was Benoit Batraville, who had perhaps 2,500 followers spread throughout central Haiti. Starting in January 1920, Colonel John Russell, the new marine commander in Haiti, launched an aggressive campaign against him, with 1,300 marines and 2,700 gendarmes. The marines even utilized seven Curtiss HS-2L flying boats and six Curtiss "Jenny" biplanes; 25-pound bombs were loaded into mailbags, strapped between the wheels of a Jenny and released with a tug of rope, turning them into crude bombers.

The marines suffered only one major setback. On April 4, 1920, a small gendarme patrol led by Lieutenant Lawrence Muth was ambushed by a large *caco* force led by Batraville himself. Muth was badly wounded and left for dead by the rest of his patrol, but he was still alive, just barely. Batraville, who was an accomplished *bocor* (wizard), took him back to camp and enacted a grisly voodoo ritual. He decapitated Muth and cut out his heart and liver, toasting them over a fire and passing them around for his men to eat—the heart to steal Muth's courage, the liver for his wisdom. Finally, Benoit and his men rubbed bits of Muth's brain over their weapons and bullets to give them better accuracy.

News of this ritual spread around Haiti, enraging the marines and redoubling their determination to capture Batraville. A marine patrol acting on a peasant's tip finally came upon Batraville's bivouac on May 19, 1920. In the ensuing firefight, Benoit was wounded. As he was struggling to draw his revolver, the *caco* general was finished off by a marine sergeant with a pistol shot to the head. Lieutenant Muth's binoculars were found around Batraville's neck.

The Second Caco War was over. According to the marines' official toll, they killed 2,250 *cacos* between 1915 and 1920, with the bulk of those deaths (1,861) coming in 1919. In addition, 11,600 *cacos* surrendered. The marines lost just 13 men, the gendarmerie 27 men. This huge disparity in casualties should not be taken completely at face value. As in Vietnam decades later, there was undoubtedly some inflation of the body count by glory-seeking soldiers (and *cacos* seldom left their dead behind to be counted and buried). But to the extent that the numbers can be trusted, they can be explained by the superior training of the marines and gendarmes. The disparity in weapons between the two sides was not vast. Though the marines had some machine guns and Browning Automatic Rifles and the *cacos* did not, both sides fought in the main with rifles and pistols. But the *cacos* were notoriously poor shots while the marines, and in later years the gendarmes too, fired with deadly accuracy.

As with any counterinsurgency, much of the marines' success could be attributed to nonmilitary factors. American rule was sufficiently attractive that the vast majority of the population did not rise up in rebellion. Indeed many Haitians were happy to have protection against the predations of the fearsome *cacos*. This helps to explain why a couple of thousand marines succeeded where a century earlier 27,000 of Napoleon's crack troops had failed. The French had been trying to reimpose slavery, and had fought a campaign of extermination, whereas, by Haitian standards at least, U.S. tactics were restrained and U.S. rule quite mild. (The other part of the explanation is that French ranks had been decimated by yellow fever. The link between mosquitoes and this disease was not confirmed until the turn of the twentieth century—knowledge that proved invaluable to the marines in Haiti, as it did to other white troops operating in tropical climes.)

"Practically Indiscriminate Killing"

The marines had no sooner put down the *cacos* than they came under fire on the home front. Rumors of alleged marine atrocities galvanized opposition to the occupation back in the U.S. Though the tales would become much exaggerated in the telling, they did start with a grain of truth: As in all colonial regimes, no matter how benign, some marines, especially those isolated in rural outposts, abused their authority over the natives.

In one remote town, Croix de Bouquet, the local marine commander had two Haitians shot to death just for the excitement of it. He was pronounced insane and confined to a mental institution. When one of his marine subordinates was put on trial, his defense lawyer claimed that killing natives in Haiti was comparatively routine. After reading the trial transcript, General George Barnett, the marine commandant, wrote to the commanding officer in Port-au-Prince, Colonel John H. Russell, that he "was shocked beyond expression to hear of . . . practically indiscriminate killing of natives."

An internal investigation was conducted in Haiti, followed by an outside investigation by two marine generals, John A. Lejeune and Smedley Butler. Both reports concluded that "indiscriminate killings" were the exception, not the norm. That finding was confirmed in a third investigation led by Admiral Henry T. Mayo, who wrote, "considering the conditions of service in Haiti, it is remarkable that the offenses were so few in number"—a conclusion denounced as a "whitewash" by *The Nation* magazine.

The occupation of Hispaniola became election fodder in 1920 when General Barnett's remark about "indiscriminate killing" leaked out and became front-page news. Warren G. Harding, the Republican presidential candidate, appealed for black votes by declaring that he would not "empower an assistant secretary of the navy to draft a constitution for helpless neighbors in the West Indies and jam it down their throats at the point of bayonets." It would have escaped none of his listeners that the assistant secretary in question was Franklin D. Roosevelt, now the Democratic nominee for vice president.

Harding's denunciations of the "rape" of Hispaniola were echoed by the National Association for the Advancement of Colored People and by the Haiti-Santo Domingo Independence Association, which won the support of such prominent Americans as Eugene O'Neill, Felix Frankfurter, H. L. Mencken, and Samuel Gompers. In their efforts to lobby American public opinion for an end to the occupation, these groups were aided by the Union Patriotique and the Union Nacional Dominicana, made up, respectively, of Haitian and Dominican intellectuals and politicians.

These protests spurred a congressional investigation in 1922. A special Senate committee chaired by Republican Senator Medill McCormick of Illinois spent 11 months studying conditions in Hispaniola, taking testimony from both critics and supporters of the occupation and visiting the island. The committee criticized some blunders made by the Wilson administration and a few abuses committed by the marines but did not find evidence of widespread atrocities. Senator McCormick essentially endorsed the policy Washington had been pursuing ever since the Wilson administration, which called for an indefinite occupation of Haiti but for withdrawal from the Dominican Republic in a few years' time. To guarantee stability after the occupation's end, the Wilson administration wanted a treaty that would guarantee U.S. control of Santo Domingo's finances and constabulary, as well as the right to intervene militarily at will.

Harding, despite his caviling during the 1920 election, did little to change this policy once in office. His secretary of state, Charles Evans Hughes, entered into protracted negotiations with Dominican representatives over the terms of an American pullout. In 1922 an agreement was reached: The customs receivership installed by Roosevelt in 1907 would continue until all loans from Wall Street banks were paid off in 1942, but Yanqui officers would no longer boss around the Guardia Nacional. An election was duly held in March 1924, and in September of that year, the winner, Horacio Vasquez, was inaugurated as president. On September 18, 1924, the last marines left Dominican soil, their policing duties being taken over by the newly renamed Policia Nacional Dominicana under the command of Dominican officers. The situation effectively reverted to what it had been prior to 1916: a large measure of U.S. influence but not outright control over Dominican affairs.

Haiti in the 1920s

When it came to Haiti, by contrast, the Harding administration was content to follow the advice of Senator McCormick, who wrote, "We are there, and in my judgment we ought to stay there for twenty years." Why leave one end of Hispaniola but not the other? U.S. rule in Haiti was indirect and hence less burdensome and controversial than the military administration that had proved necessary in the Dominican Republic. As the *New York Times* opined in 1920, "The American administration of Haitian affairs is conducted under the treaty of 1916. . . . In the case of the Dominican Republic, however, there can be no such defense." Washington, moreover, viewed Santo Domingo as better able to run its own affairs than Port-au-Prince.

While refusing to withdraw, Harding did reorganize the U.S. occupation of Haiti, creating at the suggestion of the McCormick Committee an office of high commissioner to coordinate the myriad occupation authorities. Smedley Butler was in the running for the job, but his appointment was torpedoed by the State Department, which feared that he was not diplomatic enough. The appointment went to Marine Colonel John H. Russell, a courtly Georgian who ruled Haiti for the rest of the 1920s in conjunction with Louis Borno, a mulatto who took over as president from Dartiguenave in 1922 in one of the few peaceful transfers of power in Haitian history.

Russell consciously modeled his regime upon that of the British in Egypt between 1882 and 1914. Lord Cromer, a former viceroy, had described the British occupation there: "One alien race, the English, have had to control and guide a second alien race, the Turks, by whom they are disliked, in the government of a third race, the Egyptians." Substitute "Americans" for "English," "mulattos" for "Turks," and "blacks" for "Egyptians," and that sentence forms a fair description of U.S. rule in Haiti.

The 1920s were one of the most peaceful and prosperous decades in Haiti's troubled history. The American administrators, assisted by the increasingly Haitianized gendarmerie (renamed the Garde d'Haiti in 1928), ran the government efficiently and fairly. Graft was radically reduced, and the occupiers did not seek commercial gain for themselves or their countrymen. The occupation authorities were so determined to protect the Haitian people from "exploitation" by large foreign companies that they may even have retarded the republic's economic development.

Haitian elites protested the government's refusal to convene the National Assembly—President Borno ruled through an appointed Council of State—but this body had never been representative of the great mass of the Haitian people; it had served the interests only of the mulatto oligarchy. The major blot on U.S. rule was censorship of the press, which in the absence of effective libel laws tended toward incendiary, sometimes scurrilous, denunciations of the powers-that-be. In general, however, the U.S. regime was more tolerant of dissent and more liberal than any Haiti had seen before or since. The level of force required to support the government was minimal: There were fewer than 800 marines in the country, most concentrated in Port-au-Prince and Cap Haitien.

The first clouds appeared on the horizon in 1929. A dispute over the stipends paid to students at a government-run agricultural college led to a student strike that spread into a general protest against the occupation and against President Borno, who refused to hold elections. Outposts of the Garde d'Haiti were attacked by mobs. General Russell, the high commissioner, responded by imposing martial law. In the town of Les Cayes, some 1,500 protesters armed with stones, clubs, and machetes confronted 20 marines. The marines tried to disperse the crowd by firing over their heads. When a Haitian lunged forward and bit a marine, another American tried to use his bayonet to drive back the attacker. The enraged crowd surged forward and the outnumbered marines, fearing they would be torn to bits, opened fire. Twelve Haitians were killed, 23 wounded. It hardly compared with the Amritsar Massacre in India 10 years earlier, when a British garrison in a similar situation had killed 400 natives and wounded 1,200. Nevertheless opponents of the U.S. occupation were quick to condemn the Les Cayes "massacre." The Communist Party even staged a protest rally in New York.

Within 10 days of the incident at Les Cayes, the civil unrest in Haiti was over and martial law was lifted. But to the new president, Herbert Hoover, who had much else on his mind, the 1929 protests showed that continuing the occupation was more trouble than it was worth. He began the process of withdrawal. In 1930, elections for the National Assembly were held for the first time in a decade. The winners were black nationalists opposed to the occupation, one of whom, Stenio Vincent, became the new president of Haiti. (This outcome offered indisputable evidence that the election had not been rigged by the marines.) What Hoover had started, former Assistant Navy Secretary Franklin D. Roosevelt finished. In 1933 Roosevelt, now president, signed a treaty ending the occupation, though a measure of U.S. financial control would remain until 1947.

On August 14, 1934, the U.S. colors were lowered for the last time at the headquarters of the marine brigade in Port-au-Prince. The next day the marines paraded down to the waterfront and sailed away. Having arrived in Haiti to the sound of gunfire, they left to the tune of the Marine Corps anthem, belted out by the Garde d'Haiti band.

In Retrospect

In later years it became fashionable to focus upon the failures of the U.S. occupation of Hispaniola, and failures there undoubtedly were, but the occupation did accomplish its immediate objectives: to keep the Europeans, especially the Germans, out, and to create stability. Of course there is no way to know whether the Germans would have intervened absent American involvement. From a military standpoint, the Hispaniola campaign showed that American soldiers could wage counterinsurgency warfare with great skill and without suffering significant casualties (26 Americans killed in action, 79 wounded). That a few thousand marines pacified an island of perhaps 3 million people was a tribute to the corps' skill in waging small wars.

The proud American administrators who left Haiti could tick off a list of achievements: 1,000 miles of roads constructed, 210 major bridges, 9 major airfields, 1,250 miles of telephone lines, 82 miles of irrigation canals, 11 modern hospitals, 147 rural clinics, and on and on. (The Dominican occupation, being shorter, resulted in less construction.) All built by the occupiers, and at little cost to U.S. taxpayers; in these days before the Agency for International Development, the administrators of Hispaniola were expected to finance their governments out of customs revenues. Even critics were forced to concede the occupation's material benefits. But the effects of occupation did not last long. After the marines left, the roads decayed, the telephones stopped functioning, and thugs once again took control of the machinery of government.

In the Dominican Republic, Rafael Trujillo, commander of the Guardia Nacional, seized power in 1930 and kept it until 1961, when he was assassinated in a CIA-backed coup. Four years later, in 1965, U.S. troops were back in the Dominican Republic to put down a leftist revolt. While the U.S.-created guardia proved indispensable to consolidating Trujillo's rule, in Haiti, the garde, or army, was less important. Its commander failed in a 1938 coup attempt to seize power for himself. A parade of presidents of varying degrees of corruption and despotism ruled until 1957, when the black nationalist Francois "Papa Doc" Duvalier began a long reign. Duvalier distrusted the army and relied on his own secret police, the Tontons Macoutes. Upon his death in 1971, he was succeeded by his son, Jean-Claude "Baby Doc" Duvalier, who held power until 1986. In 1994 the U.S. armed forces were back in Haiti, traveling down many of the roads built by Smedley Butler's gendarmerie, in another attempt to introduce constitutional government to the island nation.

Critics of American intervention later charged that the U.S. had deliberately installed dictatorships in Hispaniola and elsewhere in the Caribbean. Very nearly the opposite is true. The marines had tried hard to plant constitutional government but found it would not take root in the inhospitable soil of Hispaniola. The only thing that could have kept a Trujillo or Duvalier from seizing power was renewed U.S. intervention—precisely the course that critics of American "imperialism" had deplored in the first place. Taking those criticisms to heart, Franklin Roosevelt inaugurated the "Good Neighbor" policy under which Washington would eschew intervention and befriend whoever was in power in Latin America. Unfortunately, those who came to power often were not of the highest moral caliber. The only thing more unsavory than U.S. intervention, it turned out, was U.S. nonintervention.

8

THE DUSTY TRAIL

The Pancho Villa Punitive Expedition, 1916–1917

The American interventions in Haiti and the Dominican Republic had been more or less voluntary; they had not been forced upon the Wilson administration, save by the president's own conscience. The U.S. was not so lucky with its next small war, which came about because of an invasion of American soil—as Second Lieutenant John P. Lucas was among the first to discover.

Lucas had graduated from West Point in 1911 and promptly been dispatched to the Philippines. He liked his tour of duty there and was dismayed when three years later, at age 24, he found himself transferred to the 13th U.S. Cavalry Regiment based at Camp Furlong, New Mexico, near the international border. Life in neighboring Columbus (population 350) did not compare with the excitement of the Orient. "There was little to do and plenty of time to do it in," he later recalled, amid "the sand storms, the heat and monotony of existence in this sun-baked little desert town," with its "cluster of adobe houses, a hotel, a few stores and streets knee deep in sand." All around was the vast desert with its "cactus, mesquite and rattle snakes."

In search of excitement, he went off for a week's leave in March 1916 to El Paso, Texas, where he played polo against fellow cavalry officers. "On a hunch" Lucas decided to return to Columbus on the last train of the night, known as the "Drunkard's Special," on March 8 rather than wait till morning. He reached Columbus at midnight and stumbled to his quarters in the dark; the town had no electricity. He found his tiny adobe shack empty; his roommate, another young officer, was away. His .45 caliber revolver was empty—his roommate had taken the ammunition—and on another hunch Lucas decided to reload before falling asleep.

He was awakened at 4:30 A.M. on March 9 by "some one riding by the open window" of his room. He looked outside and saw a man with a black sombrero on horseback. The night air rang with shouts of "Viva Mexico" and "Viva Villa." Lucas instantly realized the invaders were followers of Francisco "Pancho" Villa, the legendary Mexican revolutionary and outlaw who had lately been carrying out a vendetta against the United States. "I got hold of my gun and stationed myself in the middle of the room where I could command the door, determined to get a few of them before they got me." Lucas was saved when a sentinel on duty opened fire on the Mexicans, distracting them from Lucas's house. The guard was killed, but Lucas took advantage of the opportunity to dash out in search of his men.

Columbus had been caught completely by surprise. There had been unconfirmed reports that Villa intended to attack a border town, but Colonel Herbert J. Slocum, the 13th Cavalry's experienced commander, had not been able to learn much about Villa's movements because standing orders from Washington forbade him from sending scouts south of the border. Slocum had only 500 men to cover 65 miles of border, and just 350 of them were in camp. No one had sounded the alarm when, earlier on the night of March 9, more than 400 Villistas had slipped across the border and headed for Columbus. The *pistoleros* had divided into two parties, one group attacking the town of Columbus, the other heading for Camp Furlong, located just south of the town across the railroad tracks.

The raiders cut a swathe of destruction through the Columbus business district. Some of them ran into the Commercial Hotel, the only one in town, where they grabbed what loot they could and shot five guests. They set fire to the grocery store across the street, and the flames quickly engulfed the hotel as well. The Mexicans also fired into private homes, killing and wounding more residents of Columbus.

Many of the officers with families lived nearby, outside Camp Furlong. Captain Rudolph E. Smyser barely managed to get himself, his wife, and two children out the back while Villistas battered down his front door. The Smysers hid in an outhouse until it was safe to come out. Lieutenant William A. McCain, his wife, and little girl hid in the mesquite behind his house, along with his orderly. Before long, they were joined by Captain George Williams. The sounds of battle seemed to be dying down when an isolated Mexican stumbled upon this little clump of Americans. Before he could do anything, McCain shot him with a shotgun, but the birdshot didn't kill him. The men grabbed the wounded Mexican and realized he had to be silenced before he could give the alarm. They tried to cut his throat with a pocket knife, but it proved too dull. They finally killed him by hammering his head with a pistol, as a distraught Mrs. McCain and her young daughter watched in horror from only a few feet away.

Aside from a few sentries, the only Americans who were already awake in Camp Furlong were the cooks. The Villistas who tried to invade the kitchen shack were in for a nasty surprise. The cooks fought them off with pots of boiling coffee, axes, and shotguns normally used for hunting up meat. Meanwhile, the stable hands fought back with pitchforks and baseball bats.

There were only two officers in camp that night—2nd Lieutenant Lucas and 1st Lieutenant James P. Castleman, the officer of the day. Castleman had just put down a book around 4 A.M. when a bullet smashed through his window. He grabbed his revolver, flung open his door, and came face to face with a Mexican pointing a rifle at him. The Mexican fired and missed. Castleman made no mistake; he practically blew the Mexican's head off with a heavy .45 caliber slug. Then he ran to the barracks where he began to round up the men of his outfit, Troop F. The soldiers advanced toward town in the dark, firing at muzzle flashes. When the troopers entered Columbus, they found that the burning hotel illuminated the silhouettes of Mexican attackers, and their rifle fire began to take a deadly toll.

Before long, Troop F bumped into the only other organized group of defenders, Machine Gun Troop, commanded by John Lucas. Running over the rough ground barefooted, Lucas had managed to reach the guard tent, where the machine guns were kept. With two men, he set up a Benet-Mercier machine gun. After a few rounds, the weapon—which had a history of unreliability—jammed, but they simply grabbed another gun. Lucas's men eventually set up four of the bipod-mounted machine guns. Together with Castleman's riflemen, they delivered a withering cross fire that drove the Villistas out of Columbus just as dawn was breaking, three hours after the attack had begun.

Colonel Slocum, the 13th Cavalry's commander, climbed atop Cootes Hill to watch the retreat. Major Frank Tompkins, itching for revenge, approached the colonel and asked for permission to pursue the raiders. Permission was granted, and within 20 minutes Tompkins had 29 men from Troop H riding for the border, soon to be joined by 27 more men from Troop F led by Lieutenant Castleman. Villa's rearguard tried to stop the pursuit by digging in on a hill, but Tompkins simply ordered his men to charge. Amid the roar of horse hoofs and the crackle of gunfire and the screams of men, the cavalry broke the Mexican line and killed many of the retreating Villistas.

Tompkins soon realized that he was in Mexican territory and wrote back to Slocum for permission to continue. Slocum told him to use his own discretion. Tompkins did not hesitate: He continued chasing the Villistas until they were about 15 miles into Mexico, by which time both men and mounts had grown too exhausted to continue. The weary troopers returned to camp, having killed 70–100 Villistas. No Americans were killed in the pursuit, though both Major Tompkins and his horse received slight wounds and a bullet passed through Tompkins's hat.

Despite having the element of surprise, Villa's attack on Columbus had been a disaster. He lost some 100 men killed and 30 captured (some of whom were hanged following a New Mexico state trial)—at least one-third of his command in all. On the American side, eight civilians and ten soldiers had died; another seven soldiers and two civilians were wounded.

What had motivated Villa to undertake this seemingly foolhardy assault, the most serious invasion of American soil since the War of 1812? That question remains hotly debated to this day; it is one of many mysteries that still swirl around the enigmatic figure of Pancho Villa.

Pancho Villa

The man who would become Pancho Villa was born Doroteo Arango in 1878 in the Mexican state of Durango. His parents were poor sharecroppers on a giant hacienda, and his father died at an early age, leaving his mother to support five children. As a teenager Doroteo turned to banditry. Legend (probably created by Villa himself) has it that he was forced to become an outlaw after he killed a rich man who raped his sister. Francisco Villa—the name he adopted to elude the authorities—proved a successful bandit. He robbed mainly from the rich and, he later claimed, gave some of his proceeds to the poor. Historians differ on the extent of his generosity, but about his ruthlessness there is little dispute. Villa did not hesitate to murder those who crossed him.

When the Mexican revolution broke out in 1910, Villa was 32 years old and living in the northern state of Chihuahua, next door to his native Durango, supporting himself with a combination of legitimate jobs and cattle rustling. Here he was recruited by an emissary of Francisco Madero, the wealthy, slightly otherworldly idealist who was leading the rebellion against the aging dictator Porfirio Diaz. It is not clear why Villa joined the revolution, but it is a good bet that the rebels promised him amnesty for all the criminal acts he had committed. He may also have been motivated by hatred of the ruling oligarchy, by a desire to help the downtrodden from whose ranks he sprang, and by loyalty to his idol, Madero. A desire for booty probably did not motivate him; he took greater care to prevent his men from looting than did most other revolutionary leaders, and he did not acquire significant riches during his political career. Power he did acquire. It did not take this onetime bandit long to become one of the leading men in Mexico.

His rise was due entirely to his native magnetism, shrewdness, and energy, for he had little ideology and less education; though he displayed great reverence for learning, he himself was virtually illiterate. E. Alexander Powell, an American author who met him in 1911, described Villa as "stockily built and of medium height—not over five feet ten, I should guess—with the chest and shoulders of a prize fighter and the most perfect bullet-shaped head I have ever seen." His black hair was "as crisp and curly as a negro's" and "a small black mustache serves to mask a mouth which is cruel even when smiling." Observers agreed that his most extraordinary feature was his prominent brown eyes. "Indeed," wrote Powell, "they are really not eyes at all, but gimlets which seem to bore into your very soul."

Villa epitomized the Mexican ideal of *macho*. Although he did not drink or smoke, he was a world-class womanizer, marrying one woman after another without bothering to divorce his previous wife. He also had a reputation as a superb horseman—he came to be known as the "Centaur of the North"—and as one of the best gunfighters in Mexico. His cruelty (to his enemies) and his generosity (to the poor) added to his legend. Highly emotional, he could weep publicly one minute, and the next instant be gripped by cold, murderous rage. Writers who met him often compared him to a "wild animal," a "lion," or a "jaguar."

His men loved him and feared him in equal measure; and he in turn was devoted to their welfare. Starting out with just 14 followers, Villa swiftly rose to become one of the top military leaders of the revolution, helping Madero assume the presidency in 1911. Villa then took a break from politics to run, of all things, a string of butcher shops. His incongruous foray into the bourgeois society of Chihuahua City, the provincial capital, did not last long. In 1912 he was summoned back to the colors to help the Madero government and the federal army put down a counterrevolution. Villa, the passionate man of the people, clashed with the ambitious and imperious army general Victoriano Huerta, a holdover from the Diaz regime who viewed him as a dangerous rival. Huerta had Villa arrested and nearly executed. After seven months in prison, Villa managed to escape by sawing through the bars of his cell with a saw smuggled in by a sympathetic court clerk. Francisco Madero was not so lucky. In 1913 the president was overthrown and murdered in a military coup led by the blood-thirsty General Huerta.

Many of the forces that had originally risen up to overthrow Diaz now took up arms against Huerta. While the revolution was a complex sociopolitical phenomenon, and ideological debates often took a backseat to clashing personal ambitions, three major strands stand out. First, dispossessed peasants in southern Mexico led by Emiliano Zapata. The most radical of all the major revolutionaries, he was determined to break up the giant haciendas (some owned by Americans) and redistribute their land. Second, poor farmers, miners, cowboys, and Indians in northern Mexico led by Pancho Villa, who pressed for regional autonomy as well as land reform. And third, progressive members of the middle and upper classes ("men who have always slept on soft pillows," in Villa's contemptuous phrase) who had turned against the oligarchy. They constituted the most moderate elements of the revolution. Madero had been one of these disillusioned *hacendados* (landlords); the new leader of the revolution, Venustiano Carranza, was another. Carranza, the white-bearded, 53-year-old governor of the northern state of Coahuila, refused to recognize Huerta's usurpation. To unite the opposition, he organized the Constitutionalist Party and appointed himself its *Primer Jefé* (First Chief).

Pancho Villa nominally recognized Carranza's leadership, but this was nothing more than a marriage of convenience. After briefly taking refuge in El Paso, Texas, Villa returned to northern Mexico to organize a formidable new army, the División del Norte (Division of the North), built around the ultra-brave, ultra-loyal *dorados* (men of gold), his version of Napoleon's Old Guard. His men soon proved their worth by routing the *federales* in Chihuahua. The unlettered guerrilla leader spent the tumultuous month of December 1913 running the state personally. He expropriated the largest landowners, turning over much of their property to his followers. But he was no wild-eyed Bolshevik. He protected the middle class and foreign property owners, and kept his troops firmly under control. After four weeks of surprisingly effective administration that sent his prestige soaring, Villa set off again to make war against the Hueristas.

In 1914, the Constitutionalists, with a little assist from the U.S. occupation of Veracruz, finally succeeded in toppling Huerta. But with victory in their grasp, the revolutionaries fell out among themselves, setting the stage for the greatest bloodletting of the entire civil war. The conflict pitted the peasant *caudillos* Zapata and Villa against the patrician Carranza. Villa and Zapata occupied Mexico City (the First Chief took refuge in Veracruz after the American evacuation), but they had little desire to govern the country themselves and before long evacuated the capital. In 1915 Villa's División del Norte fought a series of four climactic battles against Carranza's army, led by General Álvaro Obregón, a self-taught soldier with a genius for organization. Time after time, the overconfident Villa launched reckless frontal attacks on Obregón's carefully prepared defenses, modeled with the help of German advisers on those of the Western Front in Europe. But horses were little use against machine guns, and the División del Norte was shattered in the ensuing slaughter. At the beginning of 1915, Villa had commanded some 40,000 to 100,000 men organized in a regular army with infantry, cavalry, and artillery. By year's end he was left with no more than a few hundred guerrillas.

This was not the only transformation Villa underwent that year. At one time, he had been the most pro-American of all the major Mexican revolutionaries. Unlike Carranza, he did not protest Woodrow Wilson's occupation of Veracruz; Villa told his followers, "It is Huerta's bull that is being gored." Many Americans, especially those of a liberal bent, in turn admired Villa. The journalist John Reed dubbed him the "Mexican Robin Hood" and Secretary of State William Jennings Bryan described him as "a Sir Galahad." Hollywood even glamorized him in a movie filmed on location with Villa's cooperation. But then the gringos turned on Villa. President Wilson decided that the U.S. had to have stability south of the border, and the man most likely to deliver it was Venustiano Carranza, notwithstanding his well-advertised antipathy to the U.S. On October 19, 1915, Wilson extended de facto recognition to the Carranza government and placed an embargo on all arms shipments to anti-Carrancista forces.

Two weeks later, on November 1, 1915, Villa's forces attacked Agua Prieta, in the state of Sonora, just across the border from Douglas, Arizona. Villa thought that this isolated Carrancista garrison would be easy picking. He was dismayed to find a powerful force entrenched behind barbed wire and machine gun nests. His men were repulsed with heavy losses. He later learned that President Wilson had allowed the Carrancistas to move reinforcements into Agua Prieta across U.S. territory. Pancho Villa began to focus his formidable faculty for hatred on the Colossus of the North.

As usual, Villa's rage found murderous expression. On January 10, 1916, a band of Villistas stopped a train near the town of Santa Isabel, Chihuahua. They robbed all the passengers but did not harm the Mexicans. Seventeen American mining engineers aboard the train were executed. Less than two months later came the raid on Columbus.

Villa's reasons for the attack remain mysterious. Multiple explanations have been mooted: He was driven by irrational hatred of Americans; he was trying to punish Sam Ravel, owner of Columbus's Commercial Hotel, to whom he

Stephen Decatur, one of America's early naval heroes (lower right), locked in combat with a Tripolitan captain in 1804. Note the sailor interposing his head to block a scimitar chop aimed at his commander. Early accounts credited Reuben James, but it was probably Daniel Frazier. (Library of Congress)

Burning of the U.S. frigate Philadelphia, *Tripoli harbor, 1804. Admiral Nelson called Decatur's raid to destroy this captured warship "the most bold and daring act of the age." (Library of Congress)*

Edward Preble, the most offensive-minded of the commodores dispatched by President Jefferson to wage undeclared war against the Barbary Pirates. His proteges, "Preble's Boys," would go on to greater glory in the War of 1812. (Naval Institute)

David Porter, one of Preble's Boys, in 1813 tried to claim the Marquesa Islands in the South Pacific as America's first overseas possessions—and wound up in the middle of brutal tribal warfare. He was the prototype of the nineteenth century naval officer: imperious, hot-blooded, quick to take offense, and, above all, brave. (Naval Institute)

Porter's sketch of a warrior he encountered in the Marquesas, where head-to-toe tattooing was customary for the men. He belongs to the Taaeh tribe, Porter's allies in fighting the fierce Typees. (Naval Institute)

Bombardment of Quallah Battoo, 1832. After the plundering of an American merchant ship engaged in the pepper trade, President Andrew Jackson dispatched a warship to remote Sumatra to seek revenge. This was typical of the missions the navy undertook during the nineteenth century. (Naval Institute)

Marines guarding the U.S. consulate, Samoa, 1899. Anglo-American troops fought German-sponsored tribesmen to put their own candidate on the island's throne. Washington wound up annexing one of the Samoan islands. (Naval Institute)

Boxers on the march. In the summer of 1900, this mystical sect rampaged through north China, killing foreigners (first class devils) and native Christians (second class devils). (Library of Congress)

An American cavalryman and two British Sikh soldiers near a dead Boxer. To rescue diplomats besieged in Peking, a multinational expedition had to make a suffocating march through cornfields ten to fifteen feet high. (National Archives)

Ninth U.S. Infantry camped in the Forbidden City. After liberating the legations, foreign troops occupied Peking. Some of them, especially the Germans, committed atrocities against innocent Chinese. (Library of Congress)

U.S. troops in the Philippines meet civilians. An unforeseen outcome of the Spanish-American War, President McKinley's annexation of the Philippines in 1899 led to armed resistance from Filipinos who wanted independence. The U.S. Army pacified the islands with a combination of policies designed to win popular support and punish insurrectos. *(Library of Congress)*

Marine Major Littleton W. T. Waller led a campaign to turn the Philippine island of Samar into a "howling wilderness" in revenge for the massacre of an army infantry company. He wound up being court-martialed for brutality. (National Archives)

Emilio Aguinaldo, leader of the Philippine independence movement. He fought first the Spanish and then the Americans. He made the mistake of trying to match the U.S. in conventional warfare before resorting to guerrilla tactics. (Library of Congress)

Army officer Frederick Funston led a daring commando raid, employing native troops disguised as insurrectos, *to capture Aguinaldo in his remote jungle hideaway. He was one of the few American heroes to emerge from this inglorious war. (Library of Congress)*

Horse-drawn artillery, Veracruz, 1914. Woodrow Wilson ordered the port occupied in an attempt to topple Mexico's dictator. The military high command wanted to march on Mexico City, as called for in their war plans, but the president restrained them. (National Archives)

A U.S. Marine in full field pack, preparing to go ashore at Veracruz. The marines proved much more adroit at street-fighting than U.S. sailors did. (National Archives)

Smedley Butler, "the Fighting Quaker," played a prominent role in every small war fought by the marines between 1898 and 1929. After winning two Medals of Honor and retiring as a major general, he became one of the country's most outspoken pacifists and anti-imperialists. This picture was taken when he was a major. (Library of Congress)

A marine sentry in Cuba, 1919. U.S. troops landed repeatedly in Cuba in the first three decades of the twentieth century. The Roosevelt Corollary to the Monroe Doctrine committed the U.S. to policing the Caribbean and Central America. (National Archives)

Marines on a firing line in the Dominican Republic, 1916. Woodrow Wilson occupied the island of Hispaniola as part of an effort "to teach the South American republics to elect good men." (National Archives)

A marine (foreground) drills native recruits of the Dominican National Guard. The U.S. set up similar units in many of the countries it occupied. They were supposed to be apolitical, but often plunged into politics after American officers were withdrawn. (National Archives)

Two marines with a caco prisoner. The cacos—mercenaries and part-time bandits—had been overthrowing Haitian governments at the rate of more than one a year when marines occupied the country in 1915. The cacos tried to challenge the marines but were swiftly suppressed in a virtuoso display of counterinsurgency warfare. (National Archives)

Marine patrol, Haiti, 1919. In fighting small wars, marines learned to rely on small-unit patrols, eschewing the kind of big-unit tactics that the army later employed in Vietnam. (National Archives)

Francisco "Pancho" Villa, originally a bandit, rose to become one of the leading figures in the Mexican revolution that broke out in 1911. His eyes, an observer said, were "gimlets which seem to bore into your very soul." (Library of Congress)

Villa's 1916 attack left much of Columbus, New Mexico, in ashes. Although the small U.S. garrison was caught by surprise, the troops quickly rallied and drove off the pistoleros. *(National Archives)*

General John J. Pershing personally led more than 10,000 U.S. soldiers deep into Mexico in pursuit of Villa and his band. The punitive expedition almost sparked a second war between the U.S. and Mexico, but it was good training for World War I. (Library of Congress)

The army employed motorized transport in the field for the first time during the Pershing expedition. Small wars have often been a testing ground for new equipment and tactics. (National Archives)

Foreign troops on parade, Vladivostok, 1918. After the Bolsheviks seized power and took Russia out of the Great War, soldiers from the U.S., Japan, Britain, and other Allied nations were dispatched to north Russia and eastern Siberia. Tensions ran high in Siberia between American and Japanese forces. (National Archives)

Supply convoy, north Russia, January 1919. American troops spent a hard winter trying to beat back Bolshevik attacks in subzero temperatures. Their efforts were in vain. Britain and America sent just enough soldiers to allow Lenin to claim he was fighting foreign aggression—but not enough to win. (National Archives)

Augusto C. Sandino (in middle, with checked jacket), a Nicaraguan guerrilla leader, eluded U.S. Marines from 1927 to 1933. He became a hero to leftists around the world, but he never managed to capture a major city or disrupt elections held under U.S. supervision. (National Archives)

Sandino's seal shows a Sandinista decapitating a prone Marine. Sandino, who changed his middle name to César from Calderon because of his admiration of Julius Caesar, had a flair for theatrical gestures. (National Archives)

Lewis "Chesty" Puller was one of the most decorated Marines of all time, a hero of World War II and the Korean War. He learned his trade battling Haitian and Nicaraguan guerrillas. This picture was taken when he was a second lieutenant. (National Archives)

A marine biplane in Nicaragua, next to the squadron mascot. The marines staged what may have been the first organized dive-bomb attack in history during a 1927 battle against the Sandinistas. (National Archives)

Marines guarding Shanghai. The U.S. military presence in China lasted roughly a century, ending in 1941. During the 1910s–1920s, U.S. soldiers helped defend Shanghai's International Settlement from Chinese warlords and nationalists. In the 1930s, the threat came from Japanese invaders. (National Archives)

The Panay, *a U.S. gunboat, was sunk in 1937 by Japanese warplanes near Nanking, China—an attack later seen as a harbinger of Pearl Harbor. It was the first Yangtze Patrol boat lost to enemy action. For the most part, U.S. soldiers in China accomplished their policing mission without killing or being killed. (National Archives)*

A British warship signaling an American gunboat on the Yangtze River. The two navies worked together to protect foreign businesses and missionaries. During the Nationalist revolution of 1926–1928, many foreigners feared (prematurely) that China was about to go Red. (Naval Institute)

General William Westmoreland compiled a distinguished record in World War II. But nothing in his training or background prepared him for counterinsurgency warfare in Vietnam. (National Archives)

Big-unit "search and destroy" raids were a main focus of the U.S. effort in Vietnam. But even with the use of "vertical envelopment" tactics, seen here, they usually failed to pin down the elusive Vietcong guerrillas. (National Archives)

The key to pacifying the countryside lay with the South Vietnamese militia, such as this village guard. But most American officials—with the notable exception of some marine veterans of past small wars—underestimated their importance. (National Archives)

had given money to buy arms that had never been delivered; he was hoping to steal war supplies and loot from Columbus; he was a pawn in a German conspiracy to provoke a war between the U.S. and Mexico (there is evidence that such a German plot did exist, but no evidence that it influenced Villa's actions). There is probably some truth in most of these explanations, but his foremost biographer, Friedrich Katz, argues that Villa's dominant motive may have been more cunning: He apparently wanted to provoke the U.S. into a limited intervention. Villa figured that such an incursion would discredit the Carranza regime just as the occupation of Veracruz had discredited Huerta, and allow Villa to rally patriotic sentiment to his side. As a captured Villista officer told an Irish correspondent, Villa "said he wanted to make some attempts to get intervention from the gringos before they were ready and while we still had time to become a nation."

If this was Villa's intent, the attack worked as planned.

"In Pursuit"

News of the Columbus raid was flashed across the country almost immediately by an Associated Press correspondent who happened to be in town. Woodrow Wilson heard about it late on the morning of March 9, 1916. The president was reluctant to intervene in Mexico, for he did not want the U.S. distracted with a German threat looming, but he realized that this was an election year and the public would demand a strong response to this violation of American soil. Accordingly, Wilson announced that an army expedition "will be sent at once in pursuit of Villa with the single object of capturing him and putting a stop to his forays."

This public statement from the president was to cause considerable confusion about the actual mission of the expedition. When the newly installed Secretary of War Newton Baker relayed this order to the army, the army chief of staff, grizzled old Major General Hugh Scott, asked him, "Mr. Secretary, do you want the United States to make war on one man? Suppose he should get into a train and go to Guatemala, Yucatan, or South America; are you going to go after him?"

"Well, no, I am not."

"That is not what you want then," General Scott explained. "You want his *band* captured or destroyed."

"Yes, that is what I really want."

Accordingly the orders sent to Major General Frederick Funston, commander of the army's Southern Department, specified that the expedition's mission "will be regarded as finished as soon as Villa's band or bands are known to be broken up." But the public remained under the impression that the expedition's goal was, as the Hearst papers screamed, GET VILLA ALIVE OR DEAD—a considerably more difficult task.

To give an air of legality to this invasion of another country, President Wilson invoked an old U.S.-Mexico treaty that gave each side the right of "hot pursuit" into each other's territory on the trail of bandits. First Chief Carranza agreed to allow American troops to enter Mexican territory as long as the United States would agree to let Mexican troops enter U.S. territory in a similar situation in the future. Despite this tentative agreement, there was considerable risk that the American incursion could trigger a second war with Mexico. The Punitive Expedition accordingly needed a leader with tact to match his military skills. "Fighting Fred" Funston, the hot-blooded Philippine War hero, was out. The man selected for this delicate mission was a 55-year-old, ramrod-straight brigadier general popularly known as "Black Jack."

Pershing

John J. Pershing was born in rural Missouri in 1860 of what he described as "upstanding, though humble, European stock." His earliest memories were of the Civil War. Young Jack, son of a stalwart Unionist store owner, worshipped the bluecoats who rode through town, but he would probably never have joined their ranks if it had not been for the Panic of 1873, which wiped out his father's business. The only way Jack could afford to attend college was to win a position at West Point. His academic record at the Point was mediocre—he finished thirtieth out of a class of 71. But his soldierly bearing and leadership qualities were unsurpassed. He became first captain of the Corps of Cadets, the same post that Robert E. Lee held before him and that Douglas MacArthur would hold after him.

Upon graduation in 1886, 2nd Lieutenant Pershing was assigned to the 6th Cavalry at Fort Bayard, New Mexico. This provided him with a good introduction to the Old Army, 25,000 Indian-fighting, whisky-drinking, poker-playing, expletive-spewing men scattered in dusty outposts along the Western frontier. The officer ranks were still dominated by graying Civil War veterans. The era of the Old Army, designed for constabulary work in Indian territory, was drawing to a close. Young Pershing got to participate in its last campaigns, first against the Apaches and then against the Sioux Ghost Dancers in 1890.

In the next few years Pershing shuttled through a number of assignments, including a stint with the 10th Cavalry, a unit whose enlisted men were black, before winding up as an instructor at his alma mater. His martinet manner so grated on the cadets that they called him "Nigger Jack"—a nickname that stuck, though it was later softened to a more genteel "Black Jack." When the Spanish-American War broke out, Pershing wrangled an assignment back with the "Buffalo Soldiers" of the 10th Cavalry and helped storm San Juan Hill. A commanding officer said he was "cool as a bowl of cracked ice" under fire.

Afterward he was assigned to the Philippines, and it was here that Jack Pershing made a name for himself. He was sent to the island of Mindanao, populated by Muslim Moros who had never really been subdued by the Spanish. The Moros still practiced polygamy and slavery and fiercely defended their way of life, even unto death, with suicidal charges with razor-sharp weapons known as the *kris* and *barong*. Captain Pershing preferred to win over the Moros with outstretched hand rather than mailed fist. So successful was his campaign that he was made a *datto*, or chieftain. When he left the Philippines in 1903, suffering from malaria, he was already one of the most famous officers in the army.

Pershing was 45 years old, and though he had a reputation as a ladies' man and a fine dancer, he had never been married. In his next posting, Washington, he met an enchanting, if plain-looking, 25-year-old woman named Helen Frances Warren, who happened to be the daughter of Francis Warren, not only the richest man in Wyoming but also chairman of the Senate's Military Affairs Committee. Jack fell in love with "Frankie" at first sight. They were married in 1905 at a ceremony attended by Theodore Roosevelt, who pronounced it a "bully match."

The next year, Black Jack received a belated wedding present. President Roosevelt promoted him straight from captain to brigadier general over the heads of 862 more senior officers. Roosevelt explained that it was the only way he could reward merit; in those days all promotions short of general officer rank had to be done on strict seniority. But seeing the son-in-law of a powerful senator promoted out of turn caused no end of resentment in the officer corps. It even led to the publication of rumors, adamantly denied by Pershing, that he had fathered children out of wedlock with a Filipino woman while serving in the archipelago. His young bride stood by the newly minted general, and he survived the storm.

Brigadier General Pershing was sent back to the Philippines in 1907, where he became commander of the Department of Mindanao and civil governor of Moro Province, giving him dictatorial authority over 500,000 people. He spent five happy years mainly preoccupied with the tasks of civil administration. When military action was called for, he showed himself capable of acting with restraint. He stormed one Moro stronghold with a loss of only a dozen Moro lives. His predecessor, General Leonard Wood, the old Rough Rider, had accomplished the same feat only by killing hundreds of men, women, and children.

The Pershings, who by now had four children, left the Philippines in 1914 and set up house at the Presidio near San Francisco. Pershing was in command of the 8th Brigade, which was soon transferred to Fort Bliss, near El Paso, Texas, because of growing unrest in northern Mexico. His family stayed behind at the Presidio.

Before dawn on August 27, 1915, the phone rang at Pershing's Fort Bliss headquarters. The general picked it up himself. It was an Associated Press correspondent calling with news of a fire at the Presidio. "Oh, God!" Pershing cried. "My God! My God! Can it be true?"

Earlier that morning, a blaze had broken out in the general's home. In the flames and smoke, Pershing's 35-year-old wife and his three young girls, the oldest only eight, were killed. Only his six-year-old son, Warren, survived.

Pershing—who had once written to his wife, "I cannot live without you. And I shall not try. It is only half a life. It's so incomplete, so aimless"—cried in anguish as he journeyed to San Francisco to bury his family. Though he soon resumed his stony facade, his grief was almost unbearable. He was still plagued by loneliness and melancholy when, seven months later, he received orders to organize an expedition into Mexico.

Hard Riding

Trying to bury himself in his work, the general wasted no time. At noon on March 15, six days after the Columbus raid, an army column crossed into Mexico from Columbus, with Major Frank Tompkins, who had earlier pursued the Villistas, given a position of honor in the lead. Just after midnight, another column crossed over the border from Culberson's Ranch, New Mexico, this one led personally by Black Jack Pershing on horseback. The two columns were supposed to meet at Colonia Dublan, a Mormon colony 85 miles south of the border, and then fan out in search of Pancho Villa. On its face it appeared to be a hopeless task: Pershing initially had only 4,800 men (his force would eventually exceed 12,000 men) to search the state of Chihuahua, 94,000 square miles of rough, arid land that Villa knew intimately. The Americans, by contrast, did not even have adequate maps.

They found it tough going. The days in the desert were broiling, the nights freezing. The War Department had not equipped the men properly; nobody seemed to have realized that they would need warm coats in this "tropical" climate. It had not rained for nine months, so dust was everywhere, often kicked up by sandstorms. "Disagreeable, dusty march," noted one major. A sergeant wrote that "dust hung over the road like a curtain. The alkali got in our eyes and down our throats, it sifted into our shoes and through our clothing."

The striking arm of the expedition was its four cavalry regiments—the 7th, 10th, 11th, and 13th Cavalry. Also along were two infantry regiments (the 6th and 16th), mainly to protect supply lines. Extra firepower was provided by the 6th Field Artillery with its eight Vickers-Maxim mountain guns. Once at Colonia Dublan, Pershing unleashed his cavalry in a series of "flying columns" cut off from supply trains. He was using essentially the same tactics and over the same ground that his army precursors had used in pursuit of Apaches.

Pershing pushed his commanders mercilessly, and they in turn pushed their men to the edge of endurance. Colonel George A. Dodd, an indefatigable, cigar-chomping 63-year-old who had spent his career chasing Indians, marched the 7th Cavalry—Custer's old outfit—400 miles over 14 days. This despite low rations and difficult conditions. Along the way, Dodd got information that Villa was camped 230 miles south of Columbus in the small town of Guerrero, where the Mexican warlord had defeated a Carrancista garrison on March 27. The 7th Cavalry's 370 officers and men picked their way gingerly over icy trails through the Sierra Madre mountains, but, misled by unhelpful Mexican guides, did not find the most direct route to Guerrero. It was not until 8 A.M. on March 29 that Dodd, after riding all night, could begin his attack. His troopers charged into town. Many of the Villistas escaped into the mountains but 56 were killed, including one of Villa's generals, and 35 wounded. Only five Americans were wounded, none killed.

At first blush, the battle of Guerrero looked like a triumph for the Yanks, but later it was seen as a disappointment. For Pancho Villa had almost certainly been in Guerrero just before the 7th Cavalry entered. He had received a nasty leg wound during his battle against the Carrancista garrison a few days earlier (some said it was one of his own men who shot him). If the 7th had not been misled, probably deliberately, by its guides, it could have captured Villa and ended the Punitive Expedition in triumph after only a week. As it was, Villa and some 150 men escaped from Guerrero. Villa lay up for two months thereafter, hiding in a well-concealed cave high in the Sierra Madres while his leg healed. One day he was able to watch some of Pershing's troopers ride by in the valley below. He even claimed to have heard them singing, "It's a Long Way to Tipperary." The Punitive Expedition never got close to him again, though not for lack of effort.

Planes, Trains, Automobiles

It is hard to exaggerate the difficulties encountered by the various columns as they embarked on some of the fastest and longest marches ever recorded by the U.S. cavalry. "I have been in three wars, and for unmitigated hardship, the Punitive Expedition was the worst of all," one veteran wrote years later.

The flying columns, by definition, could not take with them more than what the men could carry on their backs. They lived on bacon, hardtack, coffee, and sugar for days on end. Orders from Washington forbade them from seizing supplies from the locals, and the cavalry columns were not given money to purchase supplies, forcing many of the officers to dip into their own pockets to buy provisions for their men. The peons were amazed to find an army actually paying for its supplies; this was quite a change from the normal practice of the warlords who had ravaged northern Mexico.

The logistics of the widening search became a monumental headache for Pershing. First Chief Carranza officially denied permission to the Punitive Expedition to use the Mexican national railroad, and President Wilson denied permission to seize it. Some supplies were shipped via the railroad anyway—Carranza turned a blind eye to shipments addressed to civilians in the area—but to supplement this the army for the first time called on motorized transport. There were not enough trucks in army hands to do the job, so General Hugh Scott, the chief of staff, dispatched purchasing agents across the country to buy what they could. He then informed Secretary of War Newton Baker what he had done: "You will have to use your good offices with the President, Mr. Secretary, to keep me out of jail. . . . I had just expended $450,000 of public money that had not been appropriated by Congress, which was a penitentiary offense."

"Ho!" replied Baker. "That's nothing! If anybody goes to jail I'll be the man—I'll go to jail for everybody."

Thanks to Scott's initiative, a motley collection of vehicles streamed into Columbus. There were White and Jeffrey Quad trucks and all manner of cars—Dodges, Fords, Chevys, Studebakers. But while the army had lots of experts in shoeing horses, maintaining saddles, and all the other requirements of animal transportation, it had precious few mechanics. Just about the only soldiers who knew anything about engines were members of the 1st Aero Squadron. Before long they went from maintaining airplanes to maintaining trucks.

The airplane contingent—the first the U.S. had ever deployed—proved a bust otherwise. The 1st Aero Squadron, attached to the Signal Corps, was commanded by Captain Benjamin Foulois, a 34-year-old aviation enthusiast who had been taught by Orville Wright himself. Though he and his men were fine fliers, their equipment was inferior. Their eight Curtiss JN–2 Wright planes, dubbed Jennies, were dangerously unstable except in completely calm air. Unfortunately, 50 miles south of Columbus began the Sierra Madre Mountains, with peaks as high as 12,000 feet. The Jennies could not get beyond the foothills because of strong wind currents. In any case, the Jennies, unlike European warplanes, were not equipped with machine guns, so the only purpose they served for Pershing was to deliver messages to his scattered units. But after just one month's operation, all of the Jennies were out of service, and replacements did not arrive in time to be of any use.

Lacking good radio equipment, Pershing had little choice but to command from the front. At Colonia Dublan, Black Jack rented a Dodge touring car that became his traveling headquarters. He traveled south with a staff officer or two, a clerk, an orderly, and a cook; sometimes some riflemen would accompany him, sometimes not. Trailing behind were two cars filled with American war correspondents. On March 29, 1916, this small party reached San Geronimo Ranch, almost 200 miles south of the border and 7,500 feet up in the Sierra Madres. Here they camped out. "The wind-driven sand and snow cut like a knife," wrote Frank B. Elser of the *New York Times*. "The horses stood miserable and dejected at the picket lines like cattle drifting before a blizzard. Pershing had no tent, no table, not even a folding chair."

This headquarters was not only uncomfortable but dangerous—as became evident when 200 Carrancista cavalrymen galloped into camp. If they had been so inclined, they could easily have captured the commander of the Punitive Expedition. But Pershing managed to parley with them and convinced them to go on their way. He thought it was just like dealing with Moros.

Parral

Major Frank Tompkins, who had already shown his mettle in pursuing the Villista raiders out of Columbus, sought out Pershing at San Geronimo Ranch and asked for permission to take two troops of the 13th Cavalry on a lightning-fast strike deep into Mexico. The general agreed, and Tompkins's 100 men made fast time, covering 85 miles in 50 wearying hours. "We were rapidly losing all outward resemblance to regular troops," Tompkins wrote. "We were ragged, shoes almost gone and nearly everyone had a beard. We certainly presented a hard-boiled, savage appearance." The men were looking forward to resting a little in the town of Parral (population 20,000), where they would be welcomed— or so they were informed by a Carrancista officer they met on the way.

But when the 13th Cavalry reached Parral just after noon on April 12, 1916, they found the reception far from friendly. Major Tompkins was ushered into the office of General Ismael Lozano, a Constitutionalist officer who told him that he should never have entered the town and demanded that he leave at once. As Tompkins led his men out of town, they were pursued by a large crowd shouting "Viva Villa" and "Viva Mexico." Tompkins drew a laugh by shouting "Viva Villa" back at them.

Outside Parral, Carrancista soldiers began firing on the retreating Americans. A sergeant standing next to Tompkins was hit and killed. The major dismounted a rear guard and had them take up position on a small hill. From here they let loose accurate rifle fire, killing an estimated 25 of their pursuers. Then the troopers set off again, until they had to make their next stand, killing another 45 Mexicans. The running battle, during which two Americans were killed and six wounded (including Tompkins), continued late into the afternoon, until the Americans finally marched into the fortified village of Santa Cruz de Villegas, eight miles from Parral. Although they had found temporary shelter, the situation still looked grim—about 100 American troopers were surrounded by 500 to 600 Carrancistas.

Tompkins sent out scouts to find reinforcements. One of his troopers located a squadron of the 10th Cavalry a few miles away. The 10th Cavalry had scattered about 150 Villistas in the village of Agua Caliente (not far from Guerrero) on April 1 and had been moving south at a somewhat slower pace. Now Major Charles Young, one of the few black officers in the army, spurred his Buffalo Soldiers toward Santa Cruz. They arrived just before 8 P.M. on April 12.

Tompkins was so elated that he shouted, "I could kiss every one of you."

"Hello Tompkins!" Young grinned. "You can start in on me right away."

Though no one knew it at the time, the battle at Parral was a turning point: It marked the Punitive Expedition's furthest penetration into Mexico, 516 miles, and the first time Americans had clashed with Carrancistas. Though there would be more battles to fight, the expedition would now begin a slow-motion pullout from Mexico.

Pershing was camping in a cornfield near Satevo two days later when he heard about what had happened 80 miles south at Parral. "He was mad as hell," according to Frank Elser of the *New York Times,* and demanded that the Mexican government punish the instigators of the attack. No apology was forthcoming. Pershing now realized the magnitude of the task before him: He would have to deal not only with hostile Villistas but with much more numerous Carrancistas. "It is very probable that the real object of our mission to Mexico can only be attained after an arduous campaign of considerable length," Pershing wrote to his commanding officer, General Frederick Funston. As a first step he asked for permission to seize the "City and State of Chihuahua" and "all railroads therein."

This was of a piece with the army's traditional, all-or-nothing approach to warfare; army officers seldom had much patience for limited interventions. But President Wilson, who was keeping an uneasy eye on the war raging across the Atlantic, refused to order a full-scale invasion and occupation of Mexico. Nor did he simply withdraw the expedition. Instead, he wanted Pershing to consolidate his forces near Colonia Dublan, so as to lessen the risk of hostilities with the Mexican government but maintain pressure on the Villistas.

Pershing was loath to give up the chase so soon ("it would have been considered by the Mexicans a positive defeat") and won permission to retreat north at a snail's pace. As a first step, he moved his traveling HQ to Namiquipa, about 180 miles north of Parral and 90 miles south of Colonia Dublan.

Patton

Meanwhile the pursuit of the Villistas continued. On April 22, Colonel George Dodd led his 7th Cavalry into the small village of Tomochic and scattered some Villistas, killing 30. The 11th Cavalry, under Colonel Robert Howze, attacked Villista bands on April 11 in the town of Santa Cruz de Herra, on May 4 in Cusihuiriachic, and on May 5 in Ojos Azules. This last engagement was the greatest American success of the campaign. The cavalry troopers caught the Villistas with their pants down—literally. The Mexicans were still asleep when the cavalry charged into their camp. In a two-hour running fight, 61 Villistas were killed; there were no American deaths.

An even more improbable success was achieved by one of the junior members of Pershing's staff. George S. Patton Jr., a 30-year-old 2nd lieutenant who was one of the richest officers in the army, had wangled an appointment as one of Pershing's aides. (It did not hurt that the newly widowed general was sweet on Patton's 29-year-old sister, Nita.) While the Punitive Expedition's headquarters was at Namiquipa, Patton was sent with 10 soldiers from the 6th Infantry and two civilian guides to buy corn for the men. The enterprising young officer decided to make a detour to visit the San Miguelito Ranch owned by one of Villa's most trusted generals, Julio Cárdenas.

The Americans drove up around noon on May 14, 1916, in three Dodge touring cars. Patton deployed the vehicles and his riflemen to block the exits to the hacienda, then boldly walked up to the front door of the house, accompanied only by his interpreter and a corporal. Just as they were approaching, the hacienda doors swung open and three horsemen galloped out. They tried to escape, but seeing the exits blocked, they turned around and headed for Patton, opening fire as they did so, their bullets kicking up gravel around his feet. Patton, known as a crack shot, leveled his ivory-handled Colt .45 revolver and with several shots knocked one of the Mexicans off his horse. A general shootout ensued during which all three Mexicans were killed.

It later turned out that the horseman Patton had shot was none other than General Cárdenas. The other two Mexicans were his subordinates in Villa's army. Patton had the three corpses lashed like deer to the fenders of his cars and drove back to camp with his trophies. His reward came with a promotion to 1st lieutenant and Pershing's affectionate description of him as "my bandit."

Another of Villa's generals, Candelario Cervantes, who was said to have personally led the attack on Columbus, New Mexico, was killed when he and some of his men stumbled into a gunfight with a small U.S. Army party on a mapping expedition.

Mobilization

All these victories—the slaughter at Ojos Azules, the deaths of the two generals—did little to change the larger picture, which was hardly favorable to Pershing's expedition. The expedition's prime goal was to protect American territory, but Mexican attacks into the U.S. had not ceased. On May 5 and 6, 1916, Mexican gunmen attacked the border towns of Glenn Springs and Boquillas, Texas. Similar forays took place on June 10 and June 15. Several Americans were killed and kidnapped in these attacks. The raiders were never positively identified, but rumor had it that there was a connection between these attacks and a fantastic document, the Plan of San Diego, drawn up by some Mexican conspirators who wanted to start a rebellion in the American Southwest that would return to Mexico the territory it had lost in the 1840s. As news of the attacks and the Plan of San Diego spread, alarmed southwesterners screamed for more protection from Washington.

Tensions were running high between the American and Mexican governments. General Hugh Scott met with General Álvaro Obregón on April 30, 1916, to try to reach an agreement over the course of Pershing's expedition, but the talks were repudiated by the Carranza government. A couple of weeks later, General Jacinto B. Trevino, commander of the Carrancista garrison at Chihuahua City, telegrammed Pershing that he had orders "to prevent the

American forces that are in this state from moving to the south, east, or west of the places they now occupy. . . . Your forces will be attacked by the Mexican forces if these indications are not heeded." Black Jack testily replied, "I shall . . . use my own judgment as to when and in what direction I shall move my forces." Similarly bellicose exchanges were taking place between Mexico City and Washington.

President Wilson was alarmed enough to mobilize the National Guard. By the end of July 1916, 112,000 guardsmen were assembled along the southern frontier. War seemed to be imminent.

Carrizal

Under the circumstances Pershing decided to consolidate his command around Colonia Dublan, rather than risk having his scattered forces wiped out by the Mexican army. The general figured that his expedition, now numbering some 10,000 men, would be strong enough to beat off any attack, but he was nonetheless eager for information on Mexican army movements. On June 17, 1916, Pershing summoned Captain Charles T. Boyd and told him to take Troop C of the 10th Cavalry on a reconnaissance mission 75 miles to the south. He knew that sending any units south, in violation of General Trevino's warning, might spark hostilities, but he instructed Boyd "to avoid a fight if possible." Pershing had faith that the captain, a West Pointer with 20 years' experience in the army, would be the right man for this delicate mission.

Boyd set out at once. Along the way he linked up with Troop K of the 10th Cavalry, another African-American unit. As the senior officer present, Boyd assumed command of the combined force of 79 enlisted men, two civilian guides, and three officers. On the morning of June 21, the Americans reached the village of Carrizal and found some 400 Carrancista soldiers drawn up in battle formation. There was no good reason not to bypass the town, and that is precisely what Boyd's civilian guides advised, but for some mysterious reason Boyd insisted on going through it. He was not deterred even when the Mexican general commanding the Carrizal garrison informed him that if he advanced "he would have to walk over the dead bodies of Mexican soldiers." Boyd was said to have instructed a messenger, "Tell the son of a bitch that we're going through!"

Boyd dismounted his cavalry and ordered them to advance across a grassy field toward an irrigation ditch where the vastly superior Mexican force was dug in. When the Americans were about 250 yards from their position, the Carrancistas opened fire with rifles and a machine gun. Nearly all the men in

Troop C were wounded. The Buffalo Soldiers fought bravely, but with bullets "falling like rain," and their own ammunition running out, they had no chance of prevailing. All the officers, including Captain Boyd, were killed quickly. The troopers, left leaderless, were routed by Mexican cavalry. Twelve Americans were killed that day, 10 wounded, and 24 captured. The rest ran away. The Mexicans lost more men—at least 30 killed, 40 wounded—but the battle of Carrizal was an unmitigated disaster for the U.S. Army.

War fever was already raging in the U.S. and Mexico—generals of both armies were eager to attack each other—and the battle of Carrizal might have been expected to provide a casus belli. It did not happen, for both President Wilson and First Chief Carranza kept cool heads. Neither wanted war, Carranza because he feared he would lose, Wilson because he did not want to be distracted while U.S. intervention in the European war was looking increasingly likely. When Wilson demanded the release of the American prisoners taken at Carrizal, Carranza was quick to comply. Twenty-four "ragged and gaunt" troopers were released at El Paso, Texas, just eight days after the battle. Tempers cooled further in the U.S. when survivors of the battle blamed Captain Boyd for provoking the hostilities, in apparent violation of General Pershing's orders. The battle of Carrizal resulted not in a war but in protracted negotiations between representatives of the Mexican and U.S. governments. These talks did not produce an agreement, but as Winston Churchill later remarked, "jaw jaw is better than war war."

"Sitting Here"

The battle of Carrizal represented the last fighting that would be done by the Punitive Expedition—although it was not quite the last American attempt to "get" Pancho Villa. In September 1916, the head of Pershing's intelligence department recruited some Japanese living in Mexico in an attempt to poison Villa's coffee. Like most assassination plots hatched by the U.S. government, this one ended in failure and coverup. More conventional military means were ruled out because Wilson did not want to risk another Carrizal. But the president did not want to simply withdraw the expedition because he figured that its presence in Mexico would be an added inducement for the Carrancistas to hunt down Villa. (In fact, the First Chief needed no encouragement to pursue his mortal enemy.) The upshot was that the Punitive Expedition spent more than half a year—from July 1916 to January 1917—doing little while bivouacked mainly around Colonia Dublan, about 85 miles south of Columbus, New Mexico.

"The camp was most uncomfortable," complained Major Frank Tompkins, "due to the high winds, frequent dust storms, tropical heat of summer, freezing cold of winter, deep mud in the tropical downpours, and swarms of flies." The men sought shelter in hastily erected adobe huts. There was little to do beyond the age-old soldiers' occupations: athletics (principally baseball and boxing), drilling, drinking, gambling, and whoring. Pershing tried to look after the welfare of his men. He even reserved an enclosure—popularly known as the "Remount Station"—just for prostitutes. All the women were inspected for venereal disease, a uniform rate of $2 was established, and all men entering the premises were issued a prophylactic. This helped to dramatically reduce the rate of sexually transmitted diseases, a major concern in these pre-penicillin days. The hookers, for their part, were so grateful for this cozy arrangement that they cooked Thanksgiving dinner for the men. Christmas dinner was less inviting: Big sides of beef were being slow-roasted over open fires when a sandstorm blew through camp, leaving all the meat inedible.

While 10,000 American soldiers were sitting in the middle of Chihuahua, their old nemesis was on the warpath not far away. Pancho Villa, after undergoing surgery on his leg without anesthetic, came out of his cave and assembled a fresh army. He prudently avoided attacking the Americans, instead concentrating his energies on the Carrancistas. His renewed offensive got under way in early July 1916. In the following months he mauled a number of isolated outposts. In mid-September, he invaded Chihuahua City, freed all the government prisoners and spent over seven hours in the provincial capital before retreating.

Villa returned to attack Chihuahua City on Thanksgiving Day. After several days' siege, the city fell and 2,000 men of the Carrancista garrison joined the rebel army (the alternative being execution on the spot). For a brief moment Pancho Villa was once again master of Chihuahua. He felt confident enough to issue a "Manifesto to the Nation" calling on all Mexicans to rally to his side to oppose twin evils: "the unjustified invasion by our eternal enemies, the barbarians of the North" and "the most corrupt Government we have ever had."

Observing events from close by, Pershing ached to intervene. "I can but feel the embarrassment of sitting here while Villa is cavorting about only a few miles south of our position," he wrote to his father-in-law on December 4, 1916. "A swift blow should be made at once against this pretender," he urged his commander, General Funston, five days later. "Our own prestige in Mexico should receive consideration at this time. In the light of Villa's operations during the past two weeks, further inactivity of this command does not seem desirable." But the president refused to authorize any action. Many in the Punitive

Expedition privately raged at Wilson's caution. "He has not the soul of a louse nor the mind of a worm or the backbone of a jellyfish," Lieutenant George S. Patton wrote to a friend, referring to the president of the United States.

Instead of pursuing Villa once again, the Punitive Expedition was finally ordered home in January 1917. On February 5, Pershing's command—10,690 men, 9,307 horses—began crossing the border at Columbus, New Mexico. They were accompanied by 2,030 Mexicans and 533 Chinese seeking refuge from Villa's wrath; the Chinese in particular had reason to be fearful because the xenophobic warlord had a habit of killing Chinese immigrants wherever he encountered them. Within three months, Black Jack Pershing would be headed to France, leading many of his veterans into a far bigger fight.

Aftermath

There is still considerable debate over whether, and to what extent, the Punitive Expedition was a success. Many historians suggest it was successful if only because it gave the army invaluable preparation for fighting in World War I. On this reckoning, the pursuit of Pancho Villa was to the army what the exhibition season is to the National Football League: an opportunity to prepare for real competition. There is some justice to this view. The army gained experience in using trucks, airplanes, machine guns, and other modern technologies, as well as in mobilizing, drilling, and maneuvering large bodies of troops. "When the command left Mexico it was probably more highly trained than any similar force of our army had ever been before," wrote General Pershing.

The most obvious grounds for branding the Punitive Expedition a failure was its inability to capture Pancho Villa. In his own defense, Pershing could reply that this had never been his mission; his job was only to break up or destroy the Villista bands. How well did he accomplish this objective? The Punitive Expedition killed 135 Villistas, wounded 85, captured 19. This was enough for many historians, and General Pershing himself, to label the expedition a success. There is little doubt that, as called for in Pershing's original orders, Villa's bands had indeed been "broken up." But only temporarily.

In the fall of 1916 Villa staged a remarkable resurgence. When Pershing entered Mexico, Villa had no more than 400 demoralized men. When he left, Villa had some 5,000 confident fighters and was more powerful than at any time since early 1915. Moreover, his resurgence may be attributed, at least in part, to his skill at playing on nationalist resentment of the armed *gringos* in their midst.

Villa's success was short-lived—but it was not the Punitive Expedition that would bring him down. Starting in early January 1917, a large Constitutionalist army engaged in a running series of battles with the Villistas. By April 1917, General José Murguia had repeatedly battered Villa and broken his power once again. But Pancho Villa had more lives than a cat. He mounted yet another comeback in 1919.

Just after midnight on June 14–15, 1919, some 1,200 Villistas attacked the Carrancista garrison at Juárez. By the next night, stray shots from the battle had killed and wounded some Americans in next-door El Paso, Texas. Brigadier General James B. Erwin, in command at Fort Bliss, Texas, decided to cross the border and disperse the Villistas. His artillery bombarded the Juárez racetrack, where the Villistas were concentrated, killing many of them. Then Colonel S.R.H. "Tommy" Tompkins—older brother of Major Frank Tompkins and himself a veteran of the Punitive Expedition—led the 2nd Cavalry Brigade (composed of units from the 7th and 5th Cavalry Regiments) across the Rio Grande just south of Juárez. At the same time, infantrymen from the 24th Infantry Regiment poured into Juárez across the Santa Fe Street bridge. Caught in a pincer movement, the Villistas "scattered like quail," in Tompkins's words. The U.S. troops immediately returned to American soil.

Francisco Villa would never raise another substantial fighting force. In 1920 he retired from politics and accepted the government's offer of a 500,000-peso yearly pension and a spacious hacienda. The great revolutionary who had once challenged the power of the *hacendados* became one himself, but not for long. Too dangerous to the government to remain alive, Villa was gunned down in 1923. Virtually all the other major revolutionary figures suffered a similarly violent end. Zapata was killed in 1919, Carranza the following year. The survivor was the one-armed general Álvaro Obregón, who in 1920 became the new president of Mexico, the last to take power by force. (It was his government that was responsible for Villa's death.) The Mexican Revolution, which from 1910 to 1920 ravaged vast stretches of the countryside and resulted in a million deaths, was over. Its lasting legacy was the paradoxically named Partido Revolucionario Institucional (Institutional Revolutionary Party), which ruled without interruption until 2000.

Pershing capped his triumphant command of the American Expeditionary Force in France with promotion to "general of the armies"—the first and last in U.S. history. He served a stint as army chief of staff, provided useful advice to America's military leaders in World War II, and died at age 87 at Walter Reed Army Hospital in 1948. The old cavalryman who had once chased Geronimo lived long enough to see the dropping of an atomic bomb. Major General Frederick Funston was not so lucky. He died of a heart attack on February 19,

1917, just weeks after the Punitive Expedition ended. Had he lived, the command of U.S. forces in France might have gone to him, not Pershing.

Pershing might never have won his starring role in World War I if, unlike MacArthur during the Korean War, he had not kept quiet in public about what he saw as the ineptitude of his political masters. But in private he seethed about the unsatisfying outcome of the Punitive Expedition, which he blamed on the restrictions imposed by President Wilson. "Having dashed into Mexico with the intention of eating the Mexicans raw," Pershing wrote to his father-in-law, Senator Francis Warren, in early 1917, "we turn back at the very first repulse and are now sneaking home under cover like a whipped cur with his tail between his legs." Many years later, in the twilight of his life, the old general revised his opinion and concluded that "the policy of the Commander-in-Chief with regard to Mexico . . . was substantially right" after all, because "the country did not want war with the neighboring state."

9

Blood on the Snow

Russia, 1918–1920

Less than a month after "Black Jack" Pershing and his men arrived home from Mexico, Woodrow Wilson summoned Congress into special session "to receive a communication concerning grave matters of national policy." On the night of April 2, 1917, the president got into a car for the short drive down Pennsylvania Avenue to the Capitol. A cavalry escort surrounded his automobile as it rolled past throngs of spectators waving placards and flags. It was pouring rain ("the soft fragrant rain of early spring"), and a cabinet member recalled how "the illuminated dome of the Capitol stood in solemn splendor against the dark wet sky." The ornate House of Representatives chamber was packed not only with members of Congress but also with Supreme Court justices, cabinet members, foreign ambassadors, leading journalists—just about everyone who mattered in Washington.

All eyes were on the gaunt president as he began to read, at first with little emotion, then hitting one crescendo after another like the expert orator that he was. "Wilson had words that were the equivalent of ten-inch guns," one observer marveled, "others the equivalent of lances, not omitting yet others that were the equivalent of submarine torpedoes, poison-gas, and tear-bombs." By the time he reached his stirring peroration—"America is privileged to spend her blood and her might for the principles that gave her birth and happiness and the peace which she has treasured. God helping her, she can do no other."—the audience was crying and cheering and clapping.

Within a week, Congress would respond to Wilson's appeal with a declaration of war. This time America would be facing not a ragged bunch of Villistas or Haitian *cacos* but the combined might of the German and Austro-Hungarian Empires. One of the unforeseen consequences of the president's fateful speech was that America would also be drawn, within a year's time, into a small war on the soil of its ally, Russia.

Russia had not been far from Wilson's thoughts as the president grappled with the decision of whether to go to war. He had waited and agonized, despite one provocation after another from Imperial Germany, not only because he was genuinely loath to join the slaughter on the Western Front, but also because he did not want to align the republic of Washington, Jefferson, and Madison—his fellow Virginians—with the despotic regime of the czars. Wilson had been exhilarated when, on March 17, 1917, he had received news that a liberal revolution had deposed Nicholas II. The former president of Princeton joked with his cabinet that Russia's new provisional government must be a good one; after all, its leader was a professor.

Now the European war could be depicted as a struggle between tyranny and freedom, and America's participation justified as part of a crusade to make the "world safe for democracy." In his April 2 speech to Congress, Wilson alluded to "the wonderful and heartening things that have been happening within the last few weeks in Russia," developments that had made Russia "a fit partner for a League of Honor." Wilson backed up his rhetoric by sending assistance in the form of loans and advisers to the provisional government.

The idealistic president, who claimed, based more on wishful thinking than anything else, that Russia had "always been in fact democratic at heart," was dismayed at how little time it took that country to revert to its illiberal ways. In November of 1917, the Bolshevik Party overthrew Premier Alexander Kerensky, dissolved the Constituent Assembly, and proclaimed a dictatorship of the proletariat.

Wilson had mixed feelings about foreign revolutions. He was sympathetic to uprisings that espoused liberal ideas, such as those of Madera in Mexico and Kerensky in Russia. On the other hand, notwithstanding his proselytizing for the creed of "national self-determination," Wilson had used military force to affect the outcome of revolutions in Mexico, Haiti, the Dominican Republic, and Cuba. He justified this seeming discrepancy by reasoning that U.S. forces were acting against despotic cliques and laying the foundation of liberty in those countries. Wilson viewed Vladimir Lenin much as he had viewed

Victoriano Huerta—as a strongman with no legitimacy. The president called Bolshevism "the poison of disorder, the poison of revolt, the poison of chaos," and "the negation of everything that is American." In neither Mexico nor Russia did Wilson want a conservative dictatorship resurrected, whether of the Diaz or Romanov dynasty. He wanted to aid liberal democrats who had briefly held power before being toppled—Maderistas in Mexico, Social Revolutionaries and Constitutional Democrats in Russia. This, he felt, was in the best interests of Mexican peons and Russian peasants alike.

The analogy between Wilson's views of the Mexican and Russian revolutions is not one imposed after the fact by historians; Wilson himself was conscious of it. "My policy regarding Russia is very similar to my Mexican policy," the president declared. Just as he had refused to recognize Huerta, so now Wilson refused to recognize the Soviet government. And just as he had given covert aid to Huerta's enemies, so now he authorized secret assistance to anti-Bolshevik forces in Russia. But would the U.S. intervene militarily in Russia, as it had in Mexico in 1914 and 1916?

Not at first. But on March 3, 1918, the Soviet government signed the one-sided Treaty of Brest-Litovsk with Germany, taking Russia out of the Great War and ceding vast tracts of land—the Baltic provinces, Ukraine, southern Russia—to Berlin. Russia's abandoned allies, France and Britain, were apoplectic. The end of the Eastern Front meant that Germany could transfer a million soldiers to throw against their exhausted armies on the Western Front. They also feared that the Bolsheviks would turn over to the German army vast quantities of war supplies they had shipped to Russia. Rumors were rife that Lenin, who had been returned to Russia from foreign exile in a sealed German train car "like a plague bacillus," was an agent of the kaiser.

Just three days after the Treaty of Brest-Litovsk, 160 British Royal Marines disembarked at the northern Russian port of Murmansk. They landed, oddly enough, at the request of the local soviet (or workers' council), which wanted protection from the German army massing in nearby Finland. Before long, several thousand British troops were occupying Murmansk. The British government asked its allies—France, the U.S., Japan—to send reinforcements not only to north Russia but also to eastern Siberia. The British hoped to keep war supplies out of German hands, to aid anti-Bolshevik Russians (known as the Whites) and to reestablish an Eastern Front.

Opinion was divided in the U.S. government. The American ambassador to Russia, David R. Francis, and Secretary of State Robert Lansing, both conser-

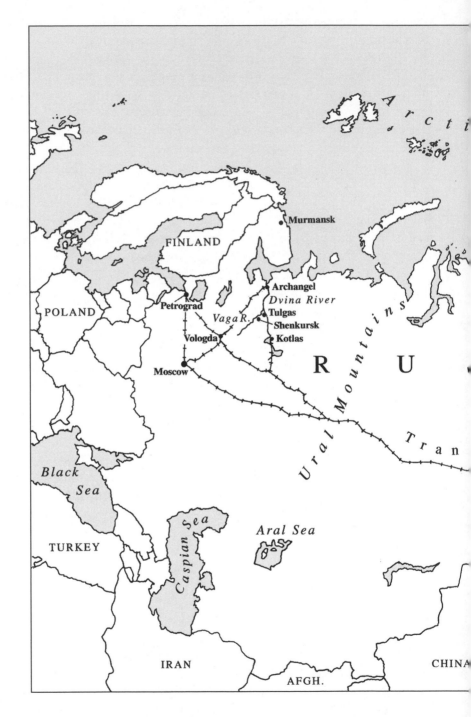

MAP 9.1   Russia, circa 1918

vative Democrats, were staunchly anti-Bolshevik and inclined to intervene. On the other side, General Pershing, commander of the American Expeditionary Force in France, and General Peyton C. March, army chief of staff, opposed any involvement in Russia as an unnecessary and unwinnable diversion from the Western Front. Theirs was the narrow view of military professionals focused on a narrow military problem—defeating Germany. They ignored the larger question of what the postwar world would look like and failed to realize how damaging the existence of a "Red" regime in Russia would be to America's hopes to "make the world safe for democracy." (Some of their successors took a similarly blinkered view of U.S. war aims in 1945 and did not perceive the need to occupy more of Central Europe before the Red Army arrived and the iron curtain descended.)

Woodrow Wilson was more concerned about events in Russia, but he too was reluctant at first to intervene. While he would have been happy to see the Bolsheviks overthrown, he feared that sending foreign soldiers into Russia, especially Japanese, would trigger a nationalist backlash. Wilson eventually agreed to an intervention, albeit a very limited one, for a variety of reasons: to restrain the Japanese in eastern Siberia; to placate the Allies; to combat Germany; to rally anti-Bolshevik Russians into action. The pivotal factor, however, was the plight of the plucky Czechoslovak Legion.

The legion was made up of some 70,000 Czechs and Slovaks, prisoners of war and deserters from the Austro-Hungarian army who had volunteered to fight for the Allied cause in order to secure independence for their homeland. Now that Russia was no longer in the war, the legion planned to make its way across Siberia to Vladivostok, and then sail to France to fight on the Western Front. At first the Bolsheviks permitted them to go on their way, but then, fearing that the Czechs would link up with the Whites, they tried to disarm the legion. War Commissar Leon Trotsky issued an order that any armed Czech should be shot on sight. The Czechs would not give up their weapons and, after a series of small clashes, full-scale fighting broke out on May 25, 1918—often cited as the starting date of the Russian Civil War.

The Czechs were virtually the only organized military force left in Russia. It did not take them long to seize the Trans-Siberian Railway from the Pacific Ocean to the Volga River, which gave them mastery of two-thirds of Russia's land area. Their success caught everyone off guard. The Allies' Supreme War Council decided to take advantage of the situation by asking the Czechs to remain in place for the time being in order to form the nucleus of an Eastern Front. Having issued those orders, the Allies, including the U.S., felt a moral responsibility to safeguard the legion. This was uppermost on Wilson's mind when, on July 17, 1918, the president sat down at his typewriter and typed out a famous aide-mémoire:

> Military action is admissible in Russia, as the Government of the United States sees the circumstances, only to help the Czecho-Slovaks consolidate their forces and get into successful cooperation with their Slavic kinsmen and to steady any efforts at self-government or self-defense in which the Russians themselves may be willing to accept assistance. Whether from Vladivostok or from Murmansk and Archangel, the only legitimate object for which American or allied troops can be employed, it submits, is to guard military stores which may subsequently be needed by Russian forces and to render such aid as may be acceptable to the Russians in the organization of their own self-defense.

These ambiguous instructions were to cause no end of confusion: *Which* Russian forces could U.S. troops assist in their efforts at "self-government or self-defense," and to what extent? Those questions would be answered by America's men in the field, who enjoyed a large degree of autonomy from Washington.

Siberia

The biggest U.S. force sent to Russia was under the command of Major General William S. Graves. A Texan who had previously served in the Philippines and with the Pershing Punitive Expedition, before taking a succession of staff jobs in Washington, Graves had recently been placed in command of the 8th Division at the Presidio in California and hoped to join the fighting on the Western Front. On August 2, 1918, he received a telegram urgently summoning him to a meeting in Kansas City with Secretary of War Newton Baker. Graves grabbed the first train he could. At the Kansas City train station, Baker told him that his destination would be Siberia, not France, and handed him an envelope containing Wilson's aide-mémoire. "This contains the policy of the United States in Russia which you are to follow. Watch your step; you will be walking on eggs loaded with dynamite. God bless you and goodbye."

That was all the instruction Graves was to receive before sailing for Siberia. With "no information as to the military, political, social, economic, or financial condition in Russia," the general reached the Bay of the Golden Horn on

September 1, 1918. He discovered that Vladivostok had earlier been occupied by the Allies and was now under a White government. (The "White" label was applied to all foes of the Bolsheviks—the "Reds"—including czarists, socialists, liberal democrats, and various ethnic minorities.) Before long he had more than 8,000 men under his command, drawn from his own 8th Division based in California and from the 27th and 31st Infantry Regiments based in the Philippines. A bluff sort with little patience for the complexities of diplomacy, Graves found himself aggravated by the maneuvering of America's supposed allies. The British, Italians, and French had token forces in Siberia (829, 1,400, and 107 men, respectively), but the Japanese, who were supposed to have no more than 12,000 men, had actually sent more than 70,000. They were there not to further the Allied war effort but as part of an attempt to grab Russia's maritime provinces.

Britain and France were eager to secure American cooperation in moving west and helping the Czech Legion and the White Army fight the Bolsheviks. This Graves refused to do. He interpreted his vague orders to mean that his men should remain neutral in the Russian Civil War. While he later agreed to have U.S. soldiers guard sections of the Trans-Siberian Railway—an act that wound up drawing them into battle against Red partisans—he refused to engage in an offensive against the Bolsheviks, or even to confiscate weapons from suspected Communists. Graves was more appalled by the actions of Whites than of Reds. Two Japanese-sponsored Cossack warlords, Ataman Kalmykov and Ataman Semenov, terrorized the Siberian countryside, killing, torturing, and robbing countless innocents whom they accused of Bolshevik sympathies. "I am well on the side of safety when I say that the anti-Bolsheviks killed one hundred people in Eastern Siberia, to every one killed by Bolsheviks," Graves wrote. (The general apparently was not aware that in the areas under their control, Lenin's secret police, the Cheka, were executing hundreds of thousands of "class enemies.")

Graves's refusal to help the Whites caused no end of consternation among the other Allied governments and among the pro-White State Department representatives in Siberia, who demanded that Washington relieve the general. But the Wilson administration stood behind Graves—even as other American soldiers in North Russia were doing what Graves would not: fight the Bolsheviks. Years later, Graves wondered: "If these two expeditions had the same instructions, how is it possible that the Archangel expedition was used in hostile combat against the Soviet forces, while the Siberian expedition was not?" To answer that question, we must examine how the mission to Archangel developed.

North Russia

The first Americans in North Russia reached Murmansk aboard the *Olympia*, Admiral Dewey's old flagship from the Spanish-American War, at the end of May 1918. From here, they joined a small expedition under the command of British Major General Frederick C. Poole, who had been ordered by the Supreme War Council to seize Archangel, a port on the White Sea not far from the Arctic Circle. Unlike Murmansk, Archangel offered a rail connection to the Trans-Siberian Railway. If Allied troops grabbed Archangel and the railroad, they could "establish communications with the Czechs." That, in turn, was supposed to be the prelude to rallying the Russian people to reenter the Great War.

On August 1, 1918, the Allied armada seized Mudyug Island just north of Archangel in an amphibious assault assisted by seaplanes. The next day, anti-Bolshevik forces organized with the aid of the Allies overthrew the Archangel Soviet. When Allied troops disembarked at Archangel on August 2, they were met by cheering locals. A new government was installed under Nikolai K. Chaikovsky, an elderly socialist intellectual who had spent years plotting against the czar.

Fifty American sailors from the *Olympia* landed on August 3 to help police Archangel. Twenty-five of them proceeded to the railroad yard, where they got in a gun battle with some Red Guards who were just leaving town. An ensign named Donald Hicks was wounded in the exchange, making him the first American casualty in Russia—but far from the last.

When the Bolshevik leaders in Moscow heard that Allied troops were landing in Archangel—presumably sent by the capitalist imperialists to stamp out the workers' revolution—they began packing their archives. First the revolt of the Czech Legion, now this. The cause seemed lost. Even War Commissar Leon Trotsky despaired: "More and more, the front of the Civil War was taking the shape of a noose that seemed to be closing tighter and tighter around Moscow. The soil itself seemed to be infected with panic. Everything was crumbling. There was nothing to hold on to. The situation seemed hopeless."

The Bolsheviks would have cheered up considerably if they had realized how inconsequential the Allied force actually was. Poole gamely tried to advance south, but he had barely enough men, fewer than 1,500, to occupy the town of Archangel. Seizing the whole province, an area almost the size of France and Germany combined, was out of the question. Prime Minister David Lloyd George and President Wilson were willing to send some reinforcements but hardly enough to march to Moscow. Both Lloyd George and Wilson were ambivalent about the intervention—the president called it "modest and experimental"—and so limited their exposure. The British sent some 5,000 infantrymen who had been declared unfit for active duty, along with two squadrons from the Royal Air Force. (Its biplanes and monoplanes, with their open cockpits, proved of limited use in the harsh winter conditions.) The U.S. Army sent the 339th Infantry Regiment accompanied by the 337th Ambulance Corps, the 337th Field Hospital, and a battalion of the 310th Engineers—about 5,700 men in all.

The 339th, "Detroit's Own," was composed mainly of men from Michigan and Wisconsin. Some of them were the sons of recent immigrants from Eastern Europe and therefore had the advantage of speaking Russian, but neither officers nor men had much military experience. They had been drafted in May 1918, given less than two months' training at Fort Custer, Michigan, and shipped to England at the end of July. A month later, they were on their way to Archangel. An influenza epidemic broke out aboard the crowded transport ships. By the time the ships docked in Archangel on September 5, 1918, many of the men were sick and about 100 were either dead or dying.

"Mud, filth and dark skies were our welcome. We were disappointed, disgusted and disheartened," wrote a private. "Our welcome was unpleasant. Our prospects, gloomy."

British General Poole, acting under orders from the Supreme War Council, hoped to seize the two railroads running to Kotlas and Vologda, towns about 400 miles south of Archangel and 350 miles north of Moscow. From there, he could hook up with the Trans-Siberian Railway controlled by the Czech Legion. This was a considerably more ambitious goal than merely guarding Allied war supplies, and to accomplish it, Poole would need the cooperation of American troops.

The U.S. ambassador to Russia, David Francis, had by this time arrived in Archangel. Francis heartily approved of Poole's mission. In fact, he asked President Wilson for up to 100,000 reinforcements to help "suppress bolshevism." This extra force was not forthcoming, but Francis allowed U.S. troops to participate in Poole's offensive. Unlike General Graves in Siberia, the 339th Regiment's commanding officer, Lieutenant Colonel George E. Stewart, was also amenable to offensive action. Stewart, an up-from-the-ranks officer who had won the Medal of Honor in the Philippines, pretty much gave up all responsibility for his troops. He holed up in Archangel for the duration of the campaign, much to his men's disgust. Since he raised no objections, two of the 339th's three battalions were rushed from Archangel to the front, where they would fight under British command. (The third battalion remained behind to guard Archangel.)

Poole split his force into two major columns, one following the Archangel railroad south to Vologda, the other the Dvina River to Kotlas. The Allied advance was unopposed at first, but before long the Anglo-Americans found themselves skirmishing against an enemy they called "Bolos," a combination of the Red Guard militia and the newly formed Red Army. Their offensive bogged down, literally. The soldiers did not have adequate maps and kept running into unmarked swamps. The most successful force turned out to be two platoons of Company A, 339th Infantry, under Captain Otto "The Viking" Odjard. They managed to capture the popular summer resort of Shenkursk (sometimes spelled Shenkhurst) and to advance a bit farther south—about 200 miles from Archangel—before turning back.

By mid-October 1918, the Allied offensive had stalled out, swallowed up in the vast depths of Mother Russia like most invasions throughout history. Already 30 Americans had been killed and 76 wounded. The chances of achieving General Poole's original objective—reaching Vologda and Kotlas and linking up with the Czechs and Whites on the Trans-Siberian Railway—had evaporated. The only goal left for the Allied expeditionary force was to survive its visit to Russia.

Poole was left holding an area bigger than the Western Front—about 500 miles—with fewer than 10,000 men thinly spread out to face an enemy growing stronger by the day. The Red Army would reach almost a million men by the end of 1918, 3 million a year later. Luckily for the Allies, most of the Communists' energy was expended fighting the White armies in Siberia, South Russia, and the Baltics. But the Red Army was still able to throw numerically superior forces against the Allied and White armies in northern Russia.

And in mid-October 1918 came the first flakes of snow, the first of many that would paralyze the region for the remainder of the winter.

Ironside

Into this dismal scene stepped a giant called Tiny. William Edmund Ironside had earned that nickname because he was a hulking 6 feet 4 inches tall and weighed 270 pounds. He had joined the British army as a subaltern in 1899 and had rapidly advanced to the temporary wartime rank of brigadier general at age 38. His most notable characteristic, apart from his size, was his linguistic ability. Over a career that took him from South Africa to India, he had picked up knowledge of 16 languages ranging from Urdu to Russian. In September 1918, he was commanding an infantry brigade in France when a telegram summoned him to London. Here he met the chief of the Imperial General Staff, who told Ironside that he would be going to Archangel as chief of staff of the Allied force. "You are to prepare for a winter campaign. No joke that!"

It became even less of a joke when Ironside arrived in Russia, just 12 days after leaving France. Though he expected to serve under General Poole, Poole told him that he was leaving immediately for England. Ironside was thrust into command of the Allied expedition, which he would retain since Poole would never return from his leave. (He was recalled due to clashes with David Francis and other Allied ambassadors, who felt that Poole was too high-handed in his dealings with the White Russians.)

Ironside found the situation dismaying. He had been told that the Allied troops were there merely to assist the efforts of the legitimate government of Russia. But the Whites were in a sorry state. When Ironside called on Nikolai Chaikovsky, the head of the provisional government in Archangel, he found "a placid old gentleman of over seventy years of age, very tall and thin, but surprisingly active in body. He spoke fluent English, having spent long periods of exile in England and the United States, interspersed with several terms of imprisonment in Russia." Ironside urged Chaikovsky to organize a formidable army, but he found the old revolutionary unresponsive. "The old man was completely and utterly unmilitary, and did not seem to realize that force would be necessary to defeat the Bolsheviks. He was living quietly in the past, and he was the same old plotter he had always been."

As it turned out, Chaikovsky had little control over the White army under his ostensible command. In early September 1918 the army, led by czarist officers, had briefly ousted him in a coup that was at least winked at by General Poole. Only through the intervention of David Francis and other Allied ambassadors was Chaikovsky reinstated in power. The northern White Army was good for little more than political intrigue, at least in the beginning. Ironside urged Chaikovsky to replace the army's leadership, which was done, but it took a while to find competent officers to take over. In the meantime the Slavo-British Legion was formed—a force composed of Russian enlisted men under British officers.

Ironside discovered that there were not even adequate maps of the Allied positions. So he set out to tour the front himself, traveling by pony-drawn sleigh, often accompanied only by his faithful servant, Piskoff. What he found was not encouraging.

The general remembered his first meeting with an American unit: "The whole company was lined out, peering into the forest with their arms at the ready. No clearings had been made for even a modest field of fire. I explained to the company commander what he should do, so that a few sentries should watch while the remainder of his men rested or took their meals. He stared at me with obvious amazement and then burst out with, 'What! Rest in this hellish bombardment!'"

Ironside looked around to see the "hellish bombardment." All he noticed were "a few shells . . . falling wide in the forest." The American soldiers clearly had a long way to go before they measured up to the standards of the Western Front.

"Tiny" tried one last, limited offensive to gain more defensible quarters for the winter. After this petered out he went on the defensive. Since it was impossible to build Western Front-style trenches in the frozen tundra of northern Russia, Ironside ordered the erection of log blockhouses. The 310th U.S. Engineers tackled the task with enthusiasm and skill. Eventually they would build 316 blockhouses that were so sturdy as to be impervious to anything short of a direct artillery hit.

"The Ground Trembled"

It did not take long for these defenses to come in handy. In early November 1918 the Reds launched an offensive. The brunt of the attack fell on Tulgas, a "group of low, dirty log houses huddled together on a hill" near the Dvina River, about 200 miles south of Archangel. This village was held by one company of U.S. infantry, one company of the Royal Scots infantry, and one section of the Canadian Field Artillery—about 600 men altogether, commanded by a U.S. Army captain with all of one year's service. On the morning of November 11, 1918, a carefully planned Bolshevik assault caught Tulgas by surprise. More than a thousand Russian infantrymen charged out of the forest and fell upon the Allied positions from the rear.

The Reds immediately overran a field hospital full of Allied wounded. A curious drama ensued. A giant commissar named Melochofski wearing a big black fur hat loudly ordered his men to kill all the patients. He was momentarily distracted by a quick-thinking British NCO who offered him rations and two bottles of rum. A young Russian woman then marched in and announced that she would shoot any Soviet soldier caught harming the wounded. This turned out to be Melochofski's mistress. Faced with her displeasure, he countermanded his order and, grumbling, left the hospital to continue the battle. She stayed behind to care for the wounded, as the fighting swirled in all its fury around the hut. No more was seen of Melochofski until he staggered into the field hospital a few hours later, fatally wounded, to die in the arms of his lover.

This woman's name is lost to history, but to the wounded men whose lives she saved she was known as Lady Olga.

The delay in the hospital—as well as a few minutes spent by Red troops ransacking part of Tulgas—proved to be the turning point of the battle. It gave the Canadian gunners just enough time to wheel around their two field pieces, which had been facing the wrong direction, and load them with shrapnel. When the Russians renewed their attack, they were stopped at point-blank range by muzzle blasts that "shattered them into ghastly dismembered corpses and hurled blood and human flesh wide in the air in sickening, spattering atoms." Some 100 Soviet soldiers, Melochofski among them, were killed and many more wounded in the first day of the Battle of Tulgas.

The fighting did not abate during the next three days. Bolo gunboats anchored in the Dvina River kept up a steady bombardment of Allied positions. U.S. Army Lieutenant John Cudahy later remembered how "the air was stabbed by the sibilant, vindictive snarl of the shells" and how "the ground trembled in quaking travail." Among those who fell victim to the shelling were the village priest, "the crown of his head cut clean as with a scalpel, exposing the naked brains," and his two children, who had been sleeping alongside him. By the end of the third day of battle, Cudahy wrote, "A quarter of the little company had been hit, and those who remained were hollow-eyed from fatigue, so weary that they staggered like drunken men."

Relief came on November 14, the fourth day of the battle. Cudahy, heir to a meat-packing fortune and a graduate of Harvard, took a few men into the forest and blew up a Bolshevik arms dump. The resulting explosions of ammunition "sounded like the musketry of a regiment," Cudahy wrote, "and the tired and discouraged Bolsheviks thought it was a fresh regiment firing unseen from the unknown depths of the forest." This caused panic among the raw Red troops, most of whose commissars had been killed. The weather finally sealed the Bolsheviks' fate. The Dvina froze, forcing their gunboats to depart, and the infantry retreated with them.

By the time the Bolos gave up the attack, 300 had been killed, with many more wounded. The Allied losses were 28 men killed, 70 wounded, with the brunt of the casualties falling among the Royal Scots. As on the Western Front, the side on the defensive had prevailed, but it was a near thing.

"Filth and Cooties"

The irony of the Battle of Tulgas is that it began on the day the World War ended—November 11, 1918. "It was hard for our men to realize," wrote

General Ironside, "why they, of all the great armies which had fought so well and so long, should have to go on fighting in a cause which they understood so little."

There was no good answer. The original objectives that had led to the sending of expeditionary forces to Russia—saving the Czechs, reviving the Eastern Front, preserving war supplies—no longer applied. The Allies decided to retain their forces mainly because they were loath to abandon their White Russian allies. By mid-November, retreat was impossible in any case. Archangel was iced in.

Spirits sank among the troops when they realized that they would be trapped in Russia for the winter. French colonial troops chanted "the war is over" and refused to fight, as did portions of the Slavo-British Legion and the White Army. All these mutinies were put down at gunpoint, but clearly morale was plunging, along with the thermometer.

The north Russian winter did not help. In December and January, there were no more than four hours of daylight. Life seemed to be enveloped in a cold, gloomy twilight, with temperatures frequently plunging to 40 or 50 degrees below zero Fahrenheit. "The wind howled and blew," wrote U.S. Private Donald E. Carey, a 25-year-old school teacher from rural Michigan. "It caught one's breath; chilling through in almost no time, shooting its intense cold to the very marrow."

The extreme cold made it difficult to perform even the simplest task outdoors. Frostbite was a constant menace, and anyone who touched a gun barrel with his bare hand felt as if he were holding red hot metal. But the extreme cold also had its positive aspects: Sanitation was good and wounds were antiseptic since anything outside froze instantly.

The men stationed in Archangel had a relatively easy time of it, frequenting the town's cafés, theaters, and bordellos and getting plenty of rations, even if they had to steal them from the warehouses that they were supposed to be guarding. Next down the hardship scale were troops on the railroad front; they were quartered in relative luxury inside railroad cars. Those on the river front had the hardest time; they had to make do in Russian peasant huts.

Relations between Americans and Russians were generally good, but the doughboys did not enjoy being quartered in these primitive dwellings. "Our small, dingy, unventilated room was overrun with cockroaches and harbored a stench. . . . " Private Carey complained. "The filth and cooties produced such irritation that at times it seemed I would become insane."

Another major irritation to the Yanks was the British officer corps, the hearty Tiny Ironside excepted (the Americans applauded him as "the soldier's type of commanding officer"). Stories spread that the British were hoarding medical supplies and shipping crates of Scotch to their officers instead of food to the doughboys. The Americans were thoroughly irritated by the British rations they did receive—bully beef (akin to corned beef), hard biscuits, dehydrated vegetables, and, worst of all for these coffee-drinkers, black tea.

"The 'limeys' as they were contemptuously called—when not designated by some foul names—were anathema to most of our troops. The snobbish self-assurance and patronizing air of English soldiers, even in colonial times, never met favorably with Americans. . . . " Carey wrote. "One E Company corporal told me he said to an English officer, 'We licked you twice and can do it again.'"

No doubt such remarks did not endear American soldiers to British officers. Luckily ordinary Tommies and doughboys generally got along better. They had to. If they did not cooperate, neither would leave Russia alive.

"Valley of Death"

After the November assault on Tulgas, the next major Red assault was aimed at driving the Allies out of Shenkursk, which stuck out from the Allied lines like a toe dangling in shark-infested waters. This summer resort, located on the Vaga River, was protected mainly by Company A, 339th Infantry, under the command of Captain Otto "The Viking" Odjard, the same men who had captured it back in the fall of 1918. The doughboys were deployed about 18 miles south of the city with the most outlying U.S. position, in the village of Nijni Gora, occupied by 46 men under Lieutenant Harry Mead.

At dawn on January 19, 1919, Bolo artillery concealed in the surrounding forest opened up "a terrific bombardment" of Nijni Gora. An hour later the shelling stopped and swarms of white-clad infantry some 1,000 strong rose out of the snow and charged into the village with fixed bayonets. Seeing that the situation was hopeless, Lieutenant Mead decided to make a hasty retreat. But the Bolshevik machine guns made it suicide to go down the village's streets. Mead wrote:

> To withdraw we were compelled to march straight down the side of this hill, across an open valley some eight hundred yards or more in the terrible snow, and under the direct fire of the enemy. There was no such thing as cover, for this valley of death was a perfectly open plain, waist deep in snow. To run was impossible, to halt was worse yet and so nothing remained but to plunge and flounder through the snow in mad desperation, with a prayer on our lips to gain the edge

of our fortified positions. One by one, man after man fell wounded or dead in the snow, either to die from the grievous wounds or terrible exposure.

Only seven men of the original 46 were unwounded by the time they reached Visorka Gora, the village where the main body of Company A was quartered. Yet even the entire company—about 200 men—was pitifully too small to stand and fight against the onslaught they now faced. Retreat was the only option. The next five days would be a nightmare of fighting and marching, freezing and bleeding, with the men receiving little food and less sleep. One by one they were picked off, this man from a rifle bullet, that man from artillery shrapnel, a third from the icy, unrelenting grip of the Russian winter. Among those severely wounded was their commanding officer, The Viking, Captain Odjard. By the time the remains of Company A staggered into Shenkursk on the afternoon of January 24, some soldiers were so weary that they fell asleep on the spot.

They did not have long to rest.

Shenkursk's 1,100 defenders were practically surrounded by more than 3,000 Red Army troops. General Ironside, anxiously monitoring events from Archangel, ordered the garrison evacuated before it was wiped out. The only escape route not yet blocked by the Red Army was over an old logging trail that snaked through the forest. Yet what if the Bolsheviks knew about this trail too? What if they were playing a game, drawing the garrison out, only to slaughter them on the narrow path where they would be easy targets for marksmen waiting in the woods? They would have to take that chance. To stay in Shenkursk any longer would mean either death or surrender.

The weary men were told to get ready to move by midnight on January 24. As the appointed hour arrived, chaos gripped the streets of Shenkursk. One hundred of the worst wounded were packed on sleighs, wrapped tightly against the sub-zero temperatures, and sent ahead, pulled along by ponies. Behind the sleighs trudged 1,000 soldiers, British, Americans, and White Russians, accompanied by 500 civilians who feared falling into Bolshevik hands. Many of the marchers had carried along too many possessions, and as they progressed the trail became littered with horded treasures. And with tired men. "Time after time that night," recalled Lieutenant Mead, "one could hear some poor unfortunate with his heavy pack on his back fall with a sickening thud upon the packed trail, in many cases being so stunned and exhausted that it was only by violent shaking and often by striking some of the others in the face that they could be sufficiently roused and forced to continue the march."

The Shenkursk garrison had not experienced much luck so far. Now fate smiled on these tired, downtrodden men as they marched mechanically through the black forest. No Red Army snipers appeared out of the woods to pick them off. Nothing blocked their way. They were 10 miles out of Shenkursk, when, at 8 A.M. on January 25, they heard "the roar of cannon . . . far behind us." The Bolsheviks were bombarding Shenkursk, unaware that the garrison had slipped out the previous night.

The Allied troops kept marching for another two days, with only a few hasty stops along the way, until they reached the village of Vistavka. Here they dug in and finally, one assumes, got a little sleep. Company A stayed in Vistavka for two months, enduring numerous attacks, until the spring thaw finally forced the Reds to suspend their offensive.

The men of the Shenkursk garrison no doubt cast up more than a few thanks heavenward for their narrow delivery. Yet if they were happy, the Bolsheviks had reason to smile as well. They had not wiped out the garrison, but perhaps that was just as well; killing so many English and American soldiers might have backfired by enflaming Western public opinion. The Reds had accomplished something more important than a massacre: They had succeeded in driving the Allies farther north at a critical moment when a large White army was advancing west from Siberia. By routing the Allies out of Shenkursk, the Reds had prevented any possibility of a linkup between these two "bourgeois" forces. It was a significant victory for the newly formed Red Army.

Paris

The future of the Allied expeditionary force would be decided not in the blood-stained snows of Russia but in the gilded conference halls of Paris. Here, in January 1919, the Allied leaders convened to shape the postwar world. A sharp difference of opinion developed over what to do about the Bolsheviks.

Winston Churchill, the newly appointed British secretary of state for war, joined with French Field Marshall Ferdinand Foch to urge a more wide-ranging Allied intervention. Churchill "agreed that none of the Allies could send conscript troops to Russia"—such a move would not be popular with any electorate—but he "thought that volunteers, technical experts, arms munitions tanks, aeroplanes, etc., might be furnished." Even if the Allies did not choose to send more soldiers, Churchill and Foch urged the conference to repatriate Russian prisoners of war held by Germany to White-controlled areas, where they could join the anti-Bolshevik armies. In addition, Churchill and Foch suggested, the Allies should mobilize the states bordering Russia, especially

Finland, Poland, and the Baltics, to cooperate with the Whites in crushing the Reds.

Churchill argued adamantly and eloquently for his position before, during, and after the Paris conference. "Of all the tyrannies in history, the Bolshevist tyranny is the worst, the most destructive and the most degrading," he declared, warning that if it was not stamped out there would be "a union between German militarism and Russian Bolshevism . . . which would be unspeakably unfriendly to Britain and to the United States and France, and to all that those free democracies stand for." But Churchill's prophetic warnings fell on deaf ears—much as his warnings about the Nazis would be ignored in the 1930s.

It was not that the Allied leaders were sympathetic to the Bolsheviks. But British Prime Minister David Lloyd George and President Woodrow Wilson were convinced that further intervention would be counterproductive. They did not think foreigners could suppress a revolution, even though Britain and America had successfully suppressed revolutions from India to the Philippines. They thought the Bolsheviks would fall from power on their own if they were unpopular; and if the Reds were winning, it must be because they had popular support. It did not occur to them that the Communists' success might be due, as it largely was, to purely military factors—the Reds had better and more unified leadership, more materiel and men, and greater willingness to brutalize the population into acquiescence than the Whites did. This more than compensated for the fact that in 1917 the Bolsheviks had won only 24 percent of the vote in the last elections for the Constituent Assembly. Nor did it occur to these Western statesmen that, although many of the White leaders were hardly democrats, the Reds were imposing upon the Russian people a regime that would make Ivan the Terrible's look almost benign by comparison. Finally, there was little awareness of the danger posed to the West by Bolshevik rule in Moscow. Lloyd George was more fearful of the supposed threat that a czarist Russia would pose to British India. The sorely mistaken British prime minister argued, in all seriousness, that the "Bolsheviks would not wish to maintain an army, as their creed was fundamentally anti-militarist."

Behind all these arguments lay a simple fact: The Allies were war-weary, and their leaders thought there would be no popular support for further action in Russia. Back in Congress, Senator Hiram Johnson, a leading Republican isolationist, kept introducing resolutions calling for the troops to be recalled from Russia. His last resolution, on February 14, 1919, was defeated by the narrowest possible margin, with the vice president casting the deciding vote. Other congressional leaders—including House Speaker Champ Clark and Senators William Borah and Robert LaFollette—joined the get-out-of-Russia chorus.

While some prominent Republicans like Senator Henry Cabot Lodge were prepared to support a serious intervention that looked likely to topple the Bolsheviks, they were not enthusiastic about the inconsequential deployment that was actually being undertaken.

Wilson, for his part, had allowed himself to be talked into a half-hearted intervention mainly to help the Czechs, satisfy the Allies, and stymie the Germans. With the war over, none of those reasons applied anymore. On February 16, 1919, the president told Secretary of War Newton Baker to call off the expedition to North Russia. The British War Cabinet followed suit. The actual withdrawal could not occur until the spring—until then the North Russia expedition was iced in—but the end was in sight. The Western policy toward Communist Russia was metamorphosing from attempted overthrow to the creation of a "cordon sanitaire."

Withdrawal

The American troops in North Russia learned of their imminent pullout in late February 1919 from their newspaper, *The American Sentinel,* which had picked up the news from the *New York Times.* The War Department did not bother to officially notify the 339th Regiment's commander, Colonel George Stewart. The men were happy to be going, but felt dejected that the withdrawal was months away. As with U.S. forces in Vietnam after 1968, morale, never high to begin with, plunged as it became clear that they were only marking time and that their commanders had no intention of seeking victory. An anonymous typed sheet circulated among the U.S. troops claiming "We have no heart for the fight."

The situation was even worse among other nationalities. There had already been mutinies among the Slavo-British Legion and the French colonial troops. Much to General Ironside's distress, the infection had spread to his own countrymen. At the end of February 1919, the newly arrived Yorkshire Regiment was ordered to the front. Two sergeants stepped forward to announce that the men would not fight. The mutineers were court-martialed and given life sentences. The Yorks did eventually fight, however reluctantly, which was a good thing from Ironside's perspective. He needed every man he could muster to hold off the Reds' incessant attacks. In March 1919, Tiny even had to rush 500 rear-unit soldiers, ranging from clerks to bakers, from Archangel to the front to prevent a Bolshevik breakthrough.

In the end the Allies were rescued by the weather. The onset of spring in April 1919 turned the roads into mud and forced the Reds to suspend their offensive.

In mid-April 1919 U.S. Brigadier General Wilds P. Richardson, a veteran of Alaskan service, arrived to supervise the withdrawal of American forces. General Ironside, still in command of the Allied expedition, had the doughboys pull out slowly, turning over their defensive positions to White Russians. One of the positions handed over to the Russians was Tulgas. A few weeks later, on April 25, 1919, Tulgas's White Russian garrison murdered its officers and surrendered the town to the Bolsheviks. It was not easy for the American troops, who had fought so hard to hold Tulgas the previous November, to hear of this setback. (British and White Russian troops recaptured the town in mid-May.)

By early June 1919 practically all the U.S. troops were gone from Archangel. During the North Russia campaign, the Yanks lost 244 men—144 from battle, the rest from disease and accident. Three hundred and five Americans were wounded in battle. The British lost even more men. Allied casualties would have been higher still were it not for the fact that they spent most of the campaign on the defensive. That the Reds suffered far greater losses was scant consolation.

General Ironside remained behind after the Yanks left. His ranks were swollen by some 8,000 volunteers sent from Britain to help extricate his soldiers from North Russia. Ironside decided to give the Reds one last hard blow in order to allow a clean withdrawal of his men and to leave the White Army in a defensible position. On August 10, 1919, 3,000 British and White Russian soldiers attacked an estimated 6,000 Red troops on the Dvina River. The attack was a smashing success: The Anglo-Russian force inflicted 1,300 casualties and took 2,000 prisoners. That was the British army's last hurrah in Russia. In early September 1919, the British began evacuating Archangel, taking with them 5,500 Russian refugees. The northern Whites managed to hold out by themselves for only a few months. On February 21, 1920, the Red Army marched into Archangel. Murmansk fell two days later.

Suchan Valley

The Allied mission to Siberia would last longer. It will be recalled that General William Graves, the U.S. commander in Siberia, was unwilling to commit his men to battle. He focused his energy not on fighting the Bolsheviks but on dissuading the Japanese, with their 70,000 men in Siberia, from simply seizing Russia's Pacific provinces. Graves was, for the most part, simply a spectator to the White Army's efforts to fight the Reds.

The initial White government in Siberia, based in Omsk, 3,000 miles west of Vladivostok, had been headed by Social Revolutionaries. The White Army, run by czarist officers, was not in sympathy with these socialists. On November 17, 1918, Cossacks and White officers staged a coup that overthrew the Omsk government and installed in power Alexander Kolchak, an admiral in the czar's navy. Kolchak was designated Supreme Ruler in command of all White armies, but his command did not really extend beyond Siberia, since there was no effective communication with the three other White armies—the north Russia forces under General Eugene Miller, the Baltic contingent under General Nikolai Yudenich, and the Transcaucasus command under General Anton Denikin.

The Czech Legion—the initial reason for the Allied intervention—was exhausted by the fall of 1918. The legionnaires just wanted to go home, and they stopped fighting once the Social Revolutionary government, with whom most of the Czechs sympathized, was overthrown. It was left to Kolchak to organize an indigenous force to attack the Reds. He turned out to be a poor organizer. Nevertheless, the White Army staged a Siberian offensive in March 1919 with 100,000 men and managed to get to within 500 miles of Moscow. (It was just as this White advance was reaching its peak in April 1919 that the Red Army attacked Allied troops at Shenkursk in north Russia in order to prevent the two forces from joining.) The Whites' success was short-lived. In mid-June 1919 the Red Army counterattacked and drove Kolchak back. It was the beginning of the end for the supreme ruler.

The U.S. troops in Siberia were far from the front but not entirely removed from the action, since numerous Red partisans were operating behind White lines. A flash point became the Suchan Valley, a region 75 miles east of Vladivostok that produced coal needed to keep the Trans-Siberian Railway running. In May 1919, at Communist instigation, the Suchan miners went on strike, dealing a major blow to the White Army. General Graves refused Admiral Kolchak's request that U.S. troops put down the strike, but American soldiers could not entirely avoid being drawn into the conflict because they guarded the railway to the Suchan Valley. The local Red partisan leader, Yakov Ivanovich Triapitsyn, a former sergeant in the czarist army, threatened to run the Yanks out of the Suchan Valley by force if necessary.

On June 22, 1919, five U.S. soldiers fishing on the Suchan River were captured by Triapitsyn's partisans. A patrol from the 31st Infantry that set out to free the prisoners came under fire from hidden Red partisans. The doughboys flushed out the snipers, but not before five of them had been killed.

Worse was to come.

On the night of June 24, 1919, Company A of the 31st Infantry Regiment, under the command of Lieutenant Lawrence Butler, bivouacked at the base of a hill in Romanovka, an important spur on the railroad between the Suchan Valley and Vladivostok. A guard was posted at the top of the hill with orders to remain there until sunrise. The newly arrived Butler probably did not realize that at this time of the year the sun rose in Siberia at 4 A.M., long before reveille. The sentry duly returned to camp at that hour, while his mates were still snoring in their tents.

A few minutes later several hundred Red partisans slithered undetected through the tall grass on the hill to open fire on the camp below, catching the 76 Americans by surprise. Nineteen doughboys were killed in the first few minutes of shooting, many still in their beds. Lieutenant Butler had the lower part of his jaw shot away and his leg wounded but nevertheless managed to use hand gestures to get the remainder of his men into a firing line. The surrounded Americans, outnumbered three or four to one, retreated behind a large woodpile and then behind a log house, all the while keeping up a steady fire.

In desperation, Butler sent a corporal to sneak through the Red lines and get help. The messenger was shot but managed to flag down a passing U.S. supply train. Lieutenant James Lorimar took half a platoon from the train to relieve Company A. He found the shattered remnants of Butler's command huddled together, with Butler himself passed out by some ammunition boxes. Thirty men wound up dying; another 20 were wounded.

It was a heavy price to pay for a badly positioned camp site and a careless guard detail, but at least the surviving Americans learned their lesson. "From then on we remained on alert at all times," recalled a soldier, "slept with our clothes on, with rifle in reach."

Triapitsyn eventually released the five captured American fishermen in exchange for five partisans. But the Reds continued to wage guerrilla war against the Americans in the Suchan area, forcing General Graves to abandon his policy of strict neutrality. American troops, many employing counterinsurgency tactics learned in the Philippines, set out to suppress the partisans in cooperation with Japanese and White units. Each town in the valley fell in turn, though a few Yanks would be killed or wounded during each skirmish. The campaign climaxed on August 7, 1919, when a U.S. combat patrol wiped out 30 partisans in a gunfight, finally convincing Triapitsyn to withdraw from the area. In all, Allied forces killed 500 guerrillas in this running series of battles.

The doughboys' success had no strategic significance. The Red Army continued to push back Kolchak's increasingly disorganized White forces. In August

1919, the Allies decided to cut off the flow of supplies to the Siberian Whites, deeming them to be a lost cause. Three months later, on November 14, 1919, Omsk, the White capital, fell, and Siberia disintegrated into chaos. The White army joined a flood of refugees fleeing the Bolsheviks. A typhus epidemic killed 60,000 people. Banditry became rampant. The remainder of the Czech Legion joined the pell-mell scramble to escape. Along the way they captured Admiral Kolchak, who was trying to escape aboard a train with the imperial gold reserves. The Czechs traded Kolchak and his gold to the Bolsheviks in return for safe passage for themselves. The supreme ruler was executed on February 7, 1920.

With the Reds sweeping toward Vladivostok, Secretary of State Robert Lansing warned President Wilson, "If we do not withdraw we shall have to wage war with the Bolsheviki." On January 16, 1920, the gravely ill president ordered the withdrawal of U.S. forces from Siberia. General Graves and his staff were the last to evacuate; they left in April 1920. As their ship pulled away from the dock, a Japanese band struck up, "Hard Times Come Again No More."

By September 1920, the Czech Legion too was gone, leaving behind 13,000 dead countrymen. The Japanese stayed until 1922, when a more liberal government in Tokyo gave up hope—at least for the time being—of carving out an empire on the mainland of Asia.

Although Graves had tried to prevent his soldiers from fighting, they had suffered their share of casualties. In Siberia, the U.S. lost 160 killed in action (as well as an additional 168 deaths from accident and disease) and suffered 52 wounded. The expedition was not entirely in vain: While the U.S. intervention did nothing to stop the Bolshevik advance, it did help dissuade Japan from annexing eastern Siberia.

Opportunity Lost

The futility of the Allied intervention in Russia has often been noted. Less commented upon has been the opportunity lost. Historian Richard Ullman writes: "If the initial landings at Archangel could have been carried out by two or three divisions—the number which [British envoy R. H. Bruce] Lockhart and the military attaches at Moscow had insisted was the bare minimum necessary for success—instead of the 1,200 troops who actually occupied the port at the end of July [1918], there is little doubt that they could have forced their way to Moscow and overthrown the Bolshevik regime." Winston Churchill seconded this view. Two or three divisions—24,000 to 36,000 men—was hardly a huge commitment for the Allies, given that they had 150 divisions fighting on the Western Front with little to show for it.

And there was no shortage of opportunities when even such a small commitment might have made all the difference. Historian Martin Malia has identified three points of "mortal danger" for the nascent Bolshevik regime during the 18 months from mid-1918 to the end of 1919: "The first . . . was the summer of 1918, when the Germans occupied the west and the south, and the Whites advanced from the east. The second was the spring of 1919, when Admiral Kolchak advanced out of Siberia towards the new capital, Moscow. And the third occasion was the fall of that year, when General [Anton] Denikin advanced from Ukraine to within two hundred kilometers of the capital, and General [Nikolai] Yudenich moved on Petrograd from Estonia."

Given how close the outnumbered and outsupplied Whites got to victory on their own, it is hardly outlandish to assume that, with a little nudge from the Allies at one of these crucial junctures, the Russian Civil War might have had a different outcome. If the Bolshevik Revolution had been strangled in its crib, there would likely have been no Stalinist terror, no great famine in Russia, no Cold War, no Communist takeovers in China or Eastern Europe—and quite possibly no World War II, since if Russia had not had a Soviet government, it might have joined with the West to nip Nazi expansionism in the bud (no Molotov-Ribbentrop pact). Tens of millions of people might have been spared an early death. This is only speculation, but there is little doubt that the Bolshevik hold on power was precarious and that concerted foreign intervention might have made the difference. Instead, Britain and America sent just enough soldiers to allow Lenin to claim that the Bolsheviks were fighting foreign aggression—but not enough to win. The story of the Anglo-American expedition to Russia in 1918, then, is a story of one of the great lost opportunities of history.

Yet it would be wrong to dwell only on the expedition's failure. The campaigns in Siberia and especially north Russia stand as a monument to the courage and endurance of the American fighting man in the face of almost unbearable adversity. They were not as important in their repercussions as the winter of 1777–78 that the Continental Army spent in Valley Forge, a winter that made American independence possible. They were not as tragic as the 1942 Bataan Death March, an ordeal that resulted in the deaths of up to 10,000 American and Filipino prisoners of war. They were not as epic as the breakout from the frozen Choisin Reservoir in 1950, when 15,000 marines had to escape a Chinese army many times more numerous. Yet the Siberian and north Russian expeditions shared something of the stoic spirit of those more famous events. And the Russia veterans, the "Polar Bears," as they later called themselves, had the death toll to prove it. Tulgas, Shenkursk, and Romanovka—names now all but forgotten in the annals of U.S. military history—deserve to be mentioned whenever fortitude under fire is discussed.

10

CHASING SANDINO

Nicaragua, 1926–1933

Once the boys came home from France—and Russia—many Americans exhaled a sigh of relief and muttered, "Never again." Disillusionment set in almost at once. The slaughter in the trenches, the skirmishing in the snow had not made the world safe for democracy. It had produced a defeated Germany eager for revenge and a ravaged Russia pledged to export revolution. Britain, the old guarantor of international order, had been drained by the exertions of the Great War. America alone had the power to police the globe. The power, but not the desire. The Senate, in large part because of Woodrow Wilson's stubbornness and inflexibility, refused to ratify the Treaty of Versailles or to join the League of Nations.

It would be an exaggeration to say that America turned isolationist, but there is no question that before the Great War, America's military commitments had been expanding, whereas afterward they contracted. The Harding administration ended the occupation of the Dominican Republic, if not Haiti, and undertook no fresh interventions in Latin America. Anything smacking of "imperialism" was in bad odor with enlightened opinion. America resorted once again to dollar diplomacy, with private companies extending loans and investment to Europe, Latin America, the Middle East, Asia, even to the Soviet Union. In the security realm, the Republican administrations of the 1920s placed their faith in disarmament conferences and international treaties, culminating in the quixotic Kellogg-Briand Pact of 1928, which outlawed war "as an instrument of national policy."

Americans put aside the cares of the world, preferring to concentrate on other things—on Jack Dempsey's fights, Babe Ruth's home runs, Charlie Chaplin's movies, Rudy Vallee's songs. Events in Nicaragua would soon make plain, however, that America's attempts to withdraw from an active security role in the world could backfire.

"Disastrous Results"

The U.S. had been landing troops in this Central American republic since 1853 and had been the dominant force there since at least 1910. It was of abiding interest to Washington because of its proximity to the Panama Canal. In 1912, led by Smedley Butler, the marines put down a Liberal revolt and installed as president the Conservative Adolfo Díaz (see Chapter 5). Most of the marines left shortly thereafter, but a "legation guard" of 100 men remained behind in Managua, a vital source of support for the government, though a cause of friction with some locals. As in other countries, the U.S. also set up a constabulary officered by marines.

The U.S. involvement in Nicaragua was financial as well as military. The Wall Street banks Brown Brothers and J. & W. Seligman took control of both the railroad and national bank of Nicaragua, while a U.S.-dominated high commission was set up to administer the government's finances. The Bryan-Chamorro Treaty of 1916 gave the U.S. the exclusive right to build a second trans-Isthmian canal in Nicaragua, as well as various naval bases, in return for a payment of $3 million. All this made Nicaragua in effect a U.S. protectorate, and ensured peace and stability for the next 13 years under the auspices of Conservative governments either headed, or dominated by, the pro-American strongman General Emiliano Chamorro.

By 1924, however, President Calvin Coolidge and his powerful secretary of state, Charles Evans Hughes, were determined to pull out. Early in that year Managua finished repaying its foreign loans and completed the process of resuming control over its national railroad and bank. In October, a fair election, held under partial U.S. supervision, was won by a fusion ticket of Liberals and Conservatives opposed to Chamorro. On August 3, 1925, over the protests of the new government, the marine legation guard marched out of Managua and sailed away.

"Seldom if ever," wrote a *New York Times* correspondent four years later, with unnecessary exaggeration, "has a nation, having full knowledge of the danger, taken deliberately a step whose disastrous results were more thoroughly a mathematical certainty than the United States took in ordering this withdrawal."

Those disastrous results manifested themselves within a month of the marines' departure. Chamorro refused to accept the election's verdict and overthrew the government in a bloodless coup. Though the U.S. had spent a decade backing Conservative regimes, President Coolidge refused to recognize Chamorro's usurpation. The Liberals, meanwhile, raised the banner of revolt. They seized much of Nicaragua's Atlantic coast, including the town of Bluefields, home to a sizeable American business community. In 1926, U.S. Marines landed in Bluefields to protect foreign lives and property. Once again America was being drawn into a civil war between Liberals and Conservatives—an ancient division in Nicaragua, one based less on ideology than on blood and soil, pitting two of the country's principal cities (Liberal León versus Conservative Granada) against each other.

The State Department maintained relentless pressure on Chamorro to resign; the U.S. chargé d'affaires even telephoned the president regularly to taunt him. Chamorro finally agreed to transfer power to an interim government led by fellow Conservative Adolfo Díaz, who had once been the American-backed president. But the Liberals would not accept this outcome. Dr. Juan Sacasa, a Liberal who had been vice president in the government overthrown by Chamorro, proclaimed himself the rightful ruler—a claim recognized by Mexico, which also supplied Sacasa's forces with weapons.

This raised alarms in Washington, for Mexico's government was then veering left, threatening to nationalize American oil interests. Anonymous administration officials were quoted in the newspapers worrying that "a Bolshevist wedge" would be driven "between the continental United States and the Panama Canal." When during the winter of 1926/27 it became obvious that the Liberal revolt was gaining ground and the Díaz government could not survive on its own, the Coolidge administration decided to intervene. "The action of Mexico in the Nicaraguan crisis is a direct challenge to the United States. . . ." wrote Undersecretary of State Robert Olds on January 2, 1927. "Nicaragua has become a test case. It is difficult to see how we can afford to be defeated."

Within a couple of months, 2,000 "devil dogs"—as the marines were now proudly calling themselves—had been dispatched. They seized the principal Pacific and Atlantic ports and declared them "neutral zones"; they reestablished a Legation Guard in Managua; and they policed the railway line between

Corinto and Managua. The Liberal insurgent army, led by General Jose Maria Moncada, carefully avoided clashes with the Americans but continued to push back the Conservative forces.

The Coolidge administration had little interest in being drawn into another war in Nicaragua. For one thing, even the limited intervention already under way was drawing criticism in Congress, with isolationist Senator William E. Borah denouncing it as a "mahogany and oil policy" undertaken at the behest of Wall Street plutocrats. (Actually the U.S. economic stake in Nicaragua was fairly small.) To "straighten the matter out" and facilitate a timely withdrawal, Coolidge decided to send a personal envoy to Nicaragua.

The man chosen for the job was Henry L. Stimson, an American aristocrat if ever there was one: A graduate of Philips Andover, Yale (where he made Skull and Bones), and Harvard Law School; a big-game hunter; a prominent Wall Street lawyer; a moderate Republican internationalist; a pillar of rectitude (he once denounced spying, proclaiming that "gentlemen do not read each other's mail"); and one of the original "wise men." Stimson was a pivotal figure in twentieth century American diplomacy, a protégé of the men (like Theodore Roosevelt and Elihu Root) who launched the Spanish-American War and a mentor to those (like Robert Lovett and John McCloy) who shaped the post–World War II world. Stimson had already been secretary of war in the Taft administration; he would go on to serve as governor-general of the Philippines, secretary of state under Herbert Hoover, and secretary of war again during World War II.

When called upon to resolve the crisis in Nicaragua, "The Colonel"—as he liked to be called, because of a brief stint as a 50-year-old volunteer artillery officer in World War I—quickly showed why he inspired trust in presidents and CEOs alike. Though he knew little about the country—he pronounced it *Nic-a-rag-yew-a*—when he sailed there in April 1927, it took this consummate negotiator only a month to complete his mission.

Stimson and his wife found a land ravaged by war. "A large portion of the city of Chinandega was in ashes," he wrote. "Almost every man or boy whom one met either in the country or the cities was armed." Within a few days, he formulated a proposal to end the fighting: Adolfo Díaz would remain as president until U.S.-supervised elections were held in 1928; both sides would turn over their arms to American forces; Díaz would appoint Liberals to his government; and marines would stay in the country until a new national guard, organized by

American officers, could take over policing duties. Díaz and the Conservatives immediately accepted this plan. To win the Liberals' concurrence, on May 4, 1927, Stimson journeyed 15 miles north of Managua to the village of Tipitapa to confer with the rebels' military commander, General Jose Maria Moncada.

The colonel and the general sat down on a riverbank in the shade of a large blackthorn tree. "Peace is imperative," Stimson bluntly told Moncada. "I have instructions to attain it willingly or by force." Moncada hated to see Díaz continue in office, but he had no intention of fighting the United States. So he promised to abide by Stimson's terms, provided that his subordinate commanders agreed. "In less than thirty minutes, we understood each other and had settled the matter," Stimson wrote.

By mid-May 1927, when Stimson left for the United States, the fighting had ceased and both Liberals and Conservatives were surrendering their weapons to the U.S. Marines. There were a few scattered clashes between marines and Liberal bands, but in general both parties were happy to have an American presence to keep their ancient enemies in line. Just before leaving Managua, the Colonel told the *New York Times,* "The civil war in Nicaragua is now definitely ended."

In reality it was just beginning.

Sandino

Only one Liberal commander refused to accept the Peace of Tipitapa: Augusto C. Sandino. He was born around 1893, the illegitimate son of a well-to-do plantation owner and an Indian servant girl. As a young boy he was a reader and a dreamer; after learning of the glories of Rome he changed his middle name from Calderon to César. His father was a dedicated Liberal and young Augusto inherited his politics. He was no doubt dismayed to see the Liberal government ousted and replaced in 1912 by the American-backed Conservatives, but he took no active part in politics in his youth. In 1920 Sandino shot a man in a fight (the causes are obscure) and fled the country, going first to Honduras, where he worked at a U.S.-owned sugar refinery; then to Guatemala, where he worked briefly on a United Fruit banana plantation; and finally to Tampico, Mexico, where he found work at an American oil company. Tampico at the time was a hotbed of radical thinking, ranging from communism to syndicalism. Here Sandino became a Freemason and a firm believer in Latin American nationalism of the anti-Yanqui variety.

In 1926, at age 33, he returned to Nicaragua and briefly took a job with the American-owned San Albino gold mine. It did not take him long to join the

Liberal revolt against the Chamorro government. A superb orator, he raised a band of 29 men and on November 2, 1926, launched his first, unsuccessful attack on a government garrison at Jicaro. He then went to link up with the main Liberal army but found that its commander, General Moncada, greeted him "disdainfully" and refused his requests for arms. Thus was born a grudge against Moncada that was to motivate Sandino at least as much as his antipathy toward the gringos.

Sandino managed to acquire weapons nevertheless, and a swelling band of followers. He won some notable victories against larger Conservative forces and was calling himself "general" by the time the Peace of Tipitapa was signed. He had no sympathy with a treaty signed by that "traitor," Moncada. Refusing Moncada's offer to appoint him governor of the department of Jinotega, Sandino gathered up 200 of his men and marched off to the wilds of northern Nicaragua. "I decided to fight," he explained, "understanding that I was the one called to protest the betrayal of the Fatherland."

Oddly enough, this revolutionary who would become a hero of the anti-American left launched his movement by asking for *more* U.S. intervention. Sandino's initial demand was that the U.S. establish a military government immediately, kick out all Conservative and Liberal office holders, and then hold an election. After his demand was rebuffed by Washington, Sandino holed up in Nueva Segovia, a remote region of soaring mountains and thick jungles located along the border with Honduras, establishing his capital in the village of Jicaro, which he renamed Sandino City.

It was not long before Sandino's fury focused not just on the government but on its American defenders.

"Marines Do Not Know How to Surrender"

The first marines—just 50 men—set out for the province of Nueva Segovia from Managua on May 31, 1927. They occupied the provincial capital, Ocotal, about 110 miles north of Managua, but since there were only 1,800 marines in the whole country there were hardly enough men to garrison the entire province. (As we shall see in the next chapter, marine strength was being siphoned off by a concurrent crisis in China.) The marines were reinforced by the Guardia Nacional, 1,136 Nicaraguan enlisted men officered by 93 marines, under the command of Marine Colonel Elias Beadle.

The government forces were surprised to learn on June 30, 1927, that Sandino had seized the American-owned San Albino mine, where the rebel leader had once worked. From here he issued the first of many florid manifestos, denouncing the Americans as "morphine addicts" who had come to "kill us in our own land," and vowing that "my sword will defend the national honor and redeem the oppressed." The marines had paid little attention to Sandino until this point, but now he had their attention. On July 15, 1927, Brigadier General Logan Feland, the marine commander in Nicaragua, dispatched a force of 75 marines and 74 guardsmen with orders to disarm Sandino and his followers. Through his excellent intelligence network, the rebel chieftain found out that these reinforcements were on the way and decided to attack before they arrived.

Ocotal was a town of 1,400 people, located not far from the Honduran border in a valley ringed by mountains on all sides. Until the arrival of reinforcements, its garrison consisted of 48 Nicaraguan guardsmen and 41 marines under the command of Captain Gilbert Hatfield. Sandino had been taunting Hatfield via telegram and letter for weeks. The rebel decorated one of his letters with a crude drawing of a guerrilla brandishing a machete over the neck of a prostrate marine—this became his seal—and closed with a flourish: "I remain your most obedient servant, who ardently desires to put you in a handsome tomb with beautiful bouquets of flowers."

"Bravo! General," the Spanish-speaking Hatfield wrote back. "If words were bullets and phrases were soldiers, you would be a field marshal instead of a mule thief."

Sandino tried to make good on his threats by attacking Ocotal. His nucleus consisted of some 60 full-time fighters wielding rifles, machine guns, and dynamite bombs; to aid them, he recruited hundreds of local peasants, many armed only with machetes. He began infiltrating his men, perhaps 600 in all, into Ocotal in the early evening hours of July 15, 1927, dispatching one company to attack the marine barracks, located in the two-story adobe town hall, and another to the National Guard barracks, located in a church across the plaza.

At around 1 A.M. on July 16, an alert marine sentry spied a movement in some bushes near Ocotal's city hall. A startled Sandinista opened fire, ruining Sandino's hopes to surprise the garrison. The next few minutes were chaotic. Attackers rushed out of the night screaming "Viva Sandino" and "Death to the Yanquis" and firing rifles and machine guns at the marine and National Guard barracks. The defenders were almost instantly at their battle stations and returned as good as they got. After a few hours of desultory firing, the Sandinistas launched three foolhardy frontal assaults on the marine headquarters, all repulsed with heavy losses by the Americans' rifles and automatic weapons.

Just after 8 A.M. Sandino dispatched a messenger under a flag of truce to deliver a message to the marines. He promised they would not be harmed if they surrendered within the hour, but if they did not, he vowed to put the town to the torch. Captain Hatfield's answer was not quite as pithy as "Nuts!"—Brigadier General Anthony McAulliffe's reply to a Nazi demand for his surrender 17 years later during the Battle of the Bulge. But it was in the same spirit. "Go to hell. . . ." Hatfield replied. "Marines do not know how to surrender."

As soon as the messenger had returned to the Sandinista lines, the shooting resumed, with more intensity than ever. Not even a tropical rainstorm in the afternoon could dampen the firefight. As the day wore on, the outnumbered defenders probably would have been ground down and defeated were it not for the help they received from the skies.

At around 10 A.M. on July 16, two marine airplanes had appeared over Ocotal. Seeing that a battle was raging, the pilots briefly strafed Sandinista positions before returning to Managua to report to headquarters. Four hours later, airborne reinforcements arrived over Ocotal: a flight of five DH-4 biplanes, each carrying two machine guns (one mounted in a fixed position at the front, operated by the pilot; the other on a swivel in the rear, operated by the observer) and four 25-pound bombs. The squadron leader, Marine Major Ross "Rusty" Rowell, formed his planes into a tight V formation and led them toward the ground from 1,500 feet, strafing Sandinista positions as they dived and loosing bombs at the end of their arc, sometimes from just 300 feet above the deck.

Dive-bomb attacks on a much larger scale would play a major role in the success of the German blitzkrieg that kicked off World War II. In sheer firepower, five relatively primitive biplanes could not compare with the hundreds of Stukas later employed by the Luftwaffe to shatter Polish and French resistance. But the shock and terror spread by the marines' British-designed DeHavillands was every bit as great; the Nicaraguans had never seen anything like it. In fact the world had never seen anything like it. The marines' attack that day at Ocotal may have been the first organized dive-bombing raid in history.

As the marine aviators made one pass after another, the frightened attackers "threw away their rifles, jumped over fences, and raced wildly through the streets. . . ." Rowell reported. "I never saw such a wild rout, and probably never will again."

By the time the DeHavillands were forced to return to Managua, their fuel having run low after 45 minutes of action, the battle of Ocotal was over. It had lasted 16 hours. Captain Hatfield later estimated that 300 Sandinistas had died (the real figure was probably closer to 60). The marines lost just one man killed and suffered one wounded; the National Guard had three wounded and four captured.

Ocotal showed Sandino the folly of punching it out toe-to-toe with American forces in a conventional battle.

Hot Pursuit

After the battle's end, Marine Major Oliver Floyd set off in pursuit of the retreating guerrillas with 78 marines and 37 guardsmen mounted on horses and mules. Sandino planned to ambush his pursuers in the town of San Fernando, 10 miles from Ocotal, but the plan went awry when Sandino's sentry disappeared into a shack with an Indian girl, allowing the marine column to reach the center of town undetected. A sharp firefight ensued in which one marine private was killed, but the Sandinistas fled after suffering 11 casualties, Sandino himself just barely escaping. Major Floyd grimly marched on, defeating another Sandinista ambush, killing an estimated 30 guerrillas, and occupying both Sandino's "capital," the town of Jicaro, and his primary source of funds, the San Albino mine.

During his pursuit, Floyd concluded that the ordinary Nicaraguans he met were "unquestionably strong for Sandino." To suppress the rebellion, therefore, "I will have to wage a real blood and thunder campaign and I will have casualties every day. . . . I will be involved in a small real war." Yet marine headquarters was fooled by Floyd's momentary success into thinking that, as an intelligence report declared, "Sandino's power is broken."

Far from broken, Sandino turned now to the classic guerrilla tactic of staging hit-and-run attacks while avoiding confrontations on equal terms with the enemy. His method manifested itself after a marine Vought Corsair biplane was shot down on October 8, 1927, by small arms fire in the jungle near Jicaro. The pilot and navigator were captured by the Sandinistas, tried before a court-martial and shot. Sandino and 200 of his men then set a trap for the marine patrol they knew would be coming to rescue the aviators.

Sure enough, within a few hours Marine Lieutenant George O'Shea was leading 19 men from the Jicaro garrison toward the scene of the crash. As they were marching uphill along a narrow jungle trail, dynamite bombs started exploding all around them and they discovered a large Sandinista force emerging from the foliage. Using grenades and a Thompson submachine gun, the marines and guardsmen managed to blast their way out of the trap, but they had no choice but to retreat. They spent the next day engaged in a running gunfight with the Sandinistas until they finally reached their base at

Jicaro, "suffering from exposure and complete exhaustion, bruised, cut up by thorns and bitten by insects." Four National Guardsmen were killed on this expedition, and O'Shea thought "it is a miracle that we did not suffer more casualties."

There were to be numerous similarly frustrating encounters in the months ahead. The terrain of northern Nicaragua was ideally suited for guerrilla warfare; indeed this area would be utilized to great effect by American-backed contras in their fight against the Sandinista government in the 1980s. As one visitor observed: "On every hand loomed height after height, great crags and ridges, profound valleys and enormous precipices, all blanketed in the densest tropical vegetation, some days simmering under the hot, open tropical sky, at other times almost invisible in the whirl of tropical storms."

Amid this dense wilderness stood a 5,000-foot mountain known as El Chipote. This was the Sandinistas' headquarters, and the marines devoted much of their energy to pinpointing its location. On November 23, 1927, a marine airplane finally found it. For weeks to come, marine aviators launched regular bombing runs against El Chipote but their ordnance, so devastating against the Sandinista ranks in Ocotal, had little effect against the dug-in positions atop the mountain. With their explosives being swallowed up by the jungle, the marines decided they had no choice but to mount a ground assault on the rebels' mountain lair.

On December 19, 1927, two columns set off on converging routes toward El Chipote. They did not get far. Each was ambushed in turn and "slaughtered," a lieutenant wrote, "like rats in a trap."[13] They barely managed to stagger into the town of Qualili, but this offered scant relief. Located at the base of a dozen hills, Qualili was virtually indefensible, and before long it was under siege from perhaps 400 Sandinistas. Of 174 officers and men who had set out, eight were dead and 31 wounded, including every surviving officer. Eighteen of the wounded were in such bad shape that they would die if they did not receive immediate help, but they were unlikely to survive a trip on muleback; their only hope was relief from the air. A few decades later, a helicopter would have been dispatched, but although the marines in Nicaragua would later experiment with an "autogyro," an operational model did not yet exist. That made it a job for fixed-wing aviation.

The troops tore down houses, hacked through bush, and pulled down trees to create a small, rough landing strip in the middle of town. Marine 1st Lieutenant Christian F. Schilt volunteered to fly into the beleaguered town in his Vought O2U-1 Corsair biplane. From January 6 to January 8, 1928, he made ten trips to Quilali, bringing in 1,400 pounds of relief supplies and taking out 18 wounded men, the whole time under heavy fire. Every time he land-ed, marines had to rush out and grab the Corsair's wings to keep it from over-shooting the abbreviated landing strip. The plane had no brakes.

Schilt won the Medal of Honor for what a journalist called "one of the most gallant and skillful exploits in aviation," but his bravery only facilitated the evacuation of Quilali. It did nothing to stamp out the Sandinista uprising, or make up for the guerrillas' skillful ambushes of the marine/guard columns. The marines' "stupidly criminal blunder" had allowed Sandino to claim "a moral vic-tory," in the estimation of one lieutenant who was in Quilali.

Later that month (January 1928), the marines renewed their assault on El Chipote. Major Rusty Rowell stepped up his air attacks, this time with new Vought Corsairs and Curtiss Falcons that carried more bombs than the old DeHavilands. These raids resulted in more substantial Sandinista casualties, including the wounding of Sandino's mistress. Faced with this withering assault, the Sandinistas slipped away, leaving straw dummies to occupy their positions. By the time a marine battalion reached the summit of El Chipote on January 26, 1928, having blasted the jungle with mortars and rifle grenades all the way up the mountain in order to ward off ambushes, they found the guer-rillas' fabled hideaway deserted.

Catching Sandino was proving to be about as easy as grabbing a fistful of water.

A Hero to the Left

To the marines he may have been nothing more than a "bandit," but to leftist critics of America, Augusto César Sandino was fast becoming a hero. Admirers from across Latin America flocked to his red-and-black banner. In early 1928, the radical American journalist Carleton Beal journeyed overland from Honduras, dodging marine air raids along the way, to meet the elusive rebel chieftain at his new hideout. "Sandino is short, probably not more than five feet," Beals recorded:

> On the morning of our interview he was dressed in a new uniform of almost black khaki, and wore puttees, immaculately polished. A silk red and black hand-kerchief was knotted about his throat. His broad-rimmed Stetson, lower over his forehead, was pinched into a shovel-like shape. Occasionally, as we conversed, he shoved his sombrero far back on his head and hitched his chair forward. The ges-

ture revealed his straight black hair and full forehead. His face is straight-lined from temple to sharp-angled jawbone, which slants to an even firm jaw. His regular curved eyebrows are high above liquid black eyes without visible pupils, eyes of remarkable mobility and refraction of light—quick intense eyes.

Beals was much taken by his host, whom he described as "a man utterly without vices, with an unequivocal sense of justice, a keen eye for the welfare of the humblest soldier." He published a series of articles about his trip in *The Nation* and later a book—a small part of a growing campaign to lionize the Nicaraguan rebel.

Pro-Sandino committees sprang up across Latin America. In Moscow, the Communist International, or Comintern, sent "fraternal greetings to the workers and peasants of Nicaragua, and the heroic army of national emancipation of General Sandino." In China, the Kuomintang renamed one of its divisions after him. In New York, the All American Anti-Imperialist League, a Comintern front group, rallied to his defense carrying signs that read: Wall Street and not Sandino is the Real Bandit. At one such rally, editors from the *Daily Worker* and *The Nation* solicited money to send "medical supplies" to the Sandinistas.

Sandino was happy to have the communists' support, and he had some communists in his staff, most notably the Salvadoran Agustín Farabundo Martí, but he never toed the party line. Eventually he broke with Martí, who complained that Sandino "did not embrace the communist program for which I was fighting." Precisely what Sandino was fighting for always remained murky; he was fired by hatred of "that traitor" Moncada and the "machos"—as he derisively called the Americans—but he lacked a well-thought-out political agenda.

The 1928 Election

Embarrassed by their setbacks, the marines rushed more men to Nicaragua, but they were unprepared for Sandino's next stratagem. The guerrillas swung south, capturing and looting several American-owned mines and coffee plantations. (Sandino impishly suggested that the owners send President Coolidge a bill for the damages.) Yet while able to elude the marines and win admirers around the world, Sandino was having trouble rallying his own countrymen to his cause. This became evident in the election of 1928.

Balloting was scheduled for November 4, 1928, in accordance with the Peace of Tipitapa. Much to the marines' chagrin, President Coolidge appointed Army Brigadier General Frank Ross McCoy—"one of those iron-willed, super-logical, single-track types whose stern jaw carries not an ounce of compromise"—

to run the electoral commission. Sandino denounced the election as illegal and urged voters to boycott it, even staging terrorist attacks to disrupt the voting. But his campaign of intimidation did not work. The U.S. flooded the country with more than 5,000 servicemen—the most it has ever stationed in Nicaragua—to ensure that voting occurred peacefully and fairly. Nearly 90 percent of registered voters went to the polls, and even in Sandino's stronghold of Nueva Segovia, 82 percent voted. Sandino's archenemy, the Liberal candidate Jose Maria Moncada, won a decisive victory in an election that was generally acknowledged, even by the defeated Conservatives, to be the cleanest in the country's history.

After the voting, both the Liberal and Conservative parties pleaded with Washington to retain a military presence in Nicaragua, and the outgoing Coolidge administration agreed, a decision to which the new president, Herbert Hoover, reluctantly acceded, at least for the time being. The guerrilla war dragged on in a series of small-unit actions deep in the bush, some won by the guerrillas, others by the government.

A few months after the election, the marines received an unexpected bonus. One morning in early February 1929, an exhausted General Manuel Maria Giron, Sandino's chief of staff, was riding alone, half asleep in the saddle, when he had the misfortune to bump into a marine patrol bathing in the river. Or rather four of the eight marines were bathing; the other four were standing guard. They spotted the lone rider and immediately apprehended him. The commander of this alert detail was none other than 1st Lieutenant Herman "Hard Head" Hanneken, who a decade earlier had killed the rebel leader Charlemagne Peralte in Haiti to help end the Second Caco War. Giron was turned over to Nicaraguan government troops, who held a kangaroo court-martial and sentenced him to death. Just before he was hanged, Giron was asked if he had any last words. His reply: "No, you son of a bitch!"

Giron's death was a blow to Sandino. The rebel leader must have realized that he needed foreign help if he was to prevail against the *Yanquis*. In May 1929 Sandino and some trusted lieutenants slipped across the border into Honduras and headed north to Mexico.

Sandino had reason to hope that Mexican president Emilio Portes Gil would offer him aid. But he was denied permission to proceed to Mexico City, instead being shunted off to a guest villa on the Yucatan Peninsula. U.S. ambassador Dwight Morrow—Charles Lindbergh's father-in-law—applied strong and skillful pressure on the Mexican government not to offer Sandino much support. Not until January 1930, after he had been waiting for more than six months, did Sandino receive an audience with Mexico's president, and nothing significant came of this meeting. Sandino returned to his villa and made a great show of resuming his routine, since he knew that Mexican and American agents were watching. Once he had lulled his watchers to sleep, he and his aides slipped away. By mid-May 1930, after a year away, they were back in Nicaragua with little to show for their Mexican sojourn.

"The Perfect Soldier"

After the 1928 election, the U.S. began drawing down its military strength in Nicaragua, leaving only about 1,500 marines by 1929. Most of the marines garrisoned the large cities; combat operations in the hinterlands were generally turned over to the Guardia Nacional, assisted by marine aviators. Under the direction of marine officers, this force developed into the most competent of the constabularies created by the U.S. throughout Central America and the Caribbean. Despite 10 mutinies that left five American officers dead, its enlisted men remained for the most part loyal to their gringo leaders. Its most feared unit was Company M, commanded by a marine named Lewis Burwell Puller.

There is a paradox about the Marine Corps. The marines, as a group, are America's best-known fighting men, immortalized in the most famous image of American warfare, the flag-raising at Iwo Jima. Yet no individual marine is particularly celebrated. To the men who fought with him, "Chesty" Puller would become perhaps the most admired marine in history, but who now remembers him outside the corps? To the extent that he is known at all among the general public, it is probably as the father of a marine who returned from Vietnam a quadriplegic and wrote a best-selling book about his ordeal before committing suicide. Dozens of army generals—and even a few army enlisted men, such as Alvin York and Audie Murphy—are more famous. This may be a tribute to the corps' collective ethos. Or it may simply be that relatively few marines have commanded an organization bigger than a division in battle; and none were wartime theater commanders like Grant, Pershing, Eisenhower, MacArthur, or Schwartzkopf.

Certainly Chesty Puller did not attain the eminence of these more senior generals, but his life was every bit as colorful. Before retiring in 1955 as a lieutenant general, he would win a record five Navy Crosses—the service's second highest decoration—for his actions during World War II and the Korean War. In 1950, as a colonel commanding the 1st Marine Regiment, 1st Marine Division, he landed at Inchon and then participated in the hellish retreat from

Choisin Reservoir—an epic of endurance for the marines, who had to ward off numerically superior Chinese attackers in subzero cold. Told at one point during this retreat that his position was surrounded, Puller was said to have replied, "Those poor bastards. They've got us right where we want 'em. We can shoot in every direction now." A marine commandant reportedly later said of Puller, "He's about the only man in the Corps who really loves to fight. I'll go further: He's the only man in any of the services who loves fighting." Recent research has cast doubt on these and many other tales that have accumulated around Puller's life, but their continual telling and retelling among marines testifies to the attraction that Chesty still exercises on the "mystic chords of memory."

"The perfect soldier"—as he was described by a combat correspondent on Guadalcanal—was born in small-town Virginia in 1898. His grandfather had died fighting for the Confederacy, and young Lewis's (pronounced "Lewie's") heroes were Robert E. Lee and "Stonewall" Jackson. He grew up on a steady diet of hunting, fishing, and horseback riding; after his father, a traveling salesman, died of cancer when he was 10, Lewie took to trapping muskrats before school to supplement his mother's income. "Those days in the woods saved my life many a time in combat," he later recalled.

Puller grew into a young man "with a chest like a pouter pigeon [hence his nickname] and a sort of bullet-shaped head." After graduating from high school with a mediocre record, he entered the Virginia Military Institute in 1917. But he was so desperate to see action in France that he dropped out after a year to enlist as a private in the marines. With the Corps rapidly expanding because of the war in Europe, Puller was sent straight from boot camp to be trained first as an NCO, then as an officer. But much to his regret, the World War ended before he could make it to France.

After the armistice, the corps was downsized and Puller found himself denied an officer's commission. In 1919 he and a pal named Lawrence Muth enlisted as marine privates and requested duty in Haiti, where they could serve as officers with the gendarmerie. The 21-year-old Puller arrived just in time to fight the second *caco* uprising. It was in the Haitian outback that he gained his advanced education in soldiering. Not long after landing he was leading patrols deep into the bush, commanding men who spoke no English, while he spoke no Creole. During four months in combat, he learned to live off the country, operate at night, and move fast; one of the few French words he knew at first was *vite!* (hurry).

Puller enjoyed his service with the gendarmerie but was eager to become a regular marine officer. After several unsuccessful attempts, he finally pinned on a second lieutenant's gold bars in 1924. He spent the next four years in America, engaged in the normal routines of garrison life. He tried to become an aviator but flunked out of flight school and then requested reassignment to overseas expeditionary duty. In 1928 his wish was granted. At first he was assigned to desk duty with the guardia in Managua, but by constantly badgering his superiors he got out into the field where he could again see action. He would be in the bush almost nonstop during two tours of duty in Nicaragua between 1929 and 1933, interrupted by a year off (July 1931–June 1932) to attend the Army Infantry School at Fort Benning, Georgia.

Puller was an impressive presence, with "a lantern jaw, a mouth like a proverbial steel trap" and a face that looked "as though it were carved out of teak wood." His "normal speaking voice was somewhere between a rasp and a growl and when he wanted to get your attention he could bark like a howitzer." He and his adjutant—William A. Lee, a marine gunnery sergeant who was commissioned a guardia lieutenant—certainly got their men's attention. They turned Company M, the Mobile Company, into a fearsome long-range patrolling unit.

Its three dozen men were mostly locally recruited Indians who had intimate knowledge of the terrain of Jinotega province where they operated. They were armed with only five automatic weapons—three Thompson submachine guns and two Browning Automatic Rifles—and six grenade launchers mounted on Springfield rifles. The rest of the men had to make do with the old Krag-Jorgensen rifle that had been used in the Philippines three decades before. Puller understood the secret of effective counterinsurgency: "you've got to keep moving"—patrolling nonstop, often at night, to keep the guerrillas on the run. Company M averaged 30 miles a day on foot over winding mountain trails. They kept slogging right through the rainy season, spending 20 days of every month in the field, even as the trails turned to mud and their uniforms disintegrated into rags. Puller and his men carried only a handful of supplies on sturdy native mules, and for the most part subsisted on a diet of rice, beans, coffee, and some occasional wild game or beef. Whenever a chow line formed, Puller and Lee made sure they were at the back; their men got fed first. If a man was wounded or killed, he often had to be evacuated by hand or in a cart up to 100 miles over jungle trails. Puller subscribed to the old marine ethos to never leave a man, dead or alive, on the battlefield.

Company M might occasionally receive assistance from marine airplanes—to evacuate wounded, say, or conduct reconnaissance—but for the most part the men were on their own; if they got into trouble, help was not likely to arrive in time. This did not faze Puller. He was careful but not overly cautious; Company M loved a good scrap and would willingly walk into an ambush if Puller and Lee thought this was the only way to draw the enemy into battle. When the firing started, the two officers ran right into the thick of it. Thanks to the guardsmen's discipline and shooting accuracy, they suffered few casualties while inflicting many.

As news of Company M's exploits got around, Puller became known as El Tigre, and rumors spread that his men carried on their belts the ears of slain Sandinistas. Sandino even put a price of 5,000 pesos on the stocky Virginian's head. It would never be collected.

1932 Election

Despite the success of Company M—and a comparable, all-marine unit led by Captain "Red Mike" Edson that patrolled the Coco River separating Honduras from Nicaragua—the guardia's campaign was hardly sufficient to end the Sandinista threat. The major problem was the 500-mile border with Honduras. There were simply not enough guardsmen (just 2,350 officers and men in 1931) and marines (fewer than 1,500) to police this sparsely settled frontier. The guerrillas could always avoid decisive defeats and slip over the border if need be. From the other direction, supplies flowed through Honduras to the Sandinista bands. In many cases their weapons came from the United States, bought on the open market by Sandino's agents and shipped from Mexico. Sandino sometimes even got higher-quality rifle ammunition than the marines were issued.

And his men knew how to use their weapons. Unlike Haitian *cacos,* who for the most part fired wildly and inaccurately into U.S.-held towns, the Sandinistas conducted skillful attacks on isolated marine contingents. On New Year's Eve 1930, Sandino's men ambushed 10 marines outside Ocotal, killing eight and wounding two. This brought home to President Hoover and his secretary of state, Henry Stimson, the price of the Nicaraguan intervention. They determined to pull out after the 1932 election, provided the marines could leave without the collapse of the Managua government. In the meantime, they reduced the marine presence even further, to fewer than 1,000 men.

In 1931 Sandino shifted his base of operations to Nicaragua's Atlantic coast, where the guerrillas raided a series of American-owned businesses, including a lumber company and banana plantation controlled by the Standard Fruit Company. American businessmen screamed for protection from Washington but it was not forthcoming. Secretary Stimson had no sympathy for this "pampered lot of people." He announced that the U.S. was abandoning its traditional policy of protecting American civilians and businesses in Nicaragua: "The Department recommends to all Americans who do not feel secure under the protection afforded them by the Nicaraguan government . . . to withdraw from the country, or at least to the coast towns whence they can be protected or evacuated in case of necessity." Stimson's declaration emboldened the Sandinistas, who stepped up their raids in the countryside north of Managua.

Augusto Sandino took some pains to win the allegiance of the peasants by treating those who cooperated with his forces well, but those who did not pay "taxes" or provide other help to the Sandinistas—or, worse, those who helped the National Guard—could expect a terrible vengeance. The Sandinistas administered various *cortes*, or cuts, to those they sought to punish. There was the *corte de chaleco*, or vest cut: The victim's head was chopped off with a machete, the arms were amputated, and a design etched into the chest with a machete; the *corte de cumbo*, or gourd cut: A machete was used to slice off a portion of the offender's skull, exposing his brain to the sun and leaving him to die a lingering, agonizing death; and the *corte de bloomers*: The victim's legs were chopped off at the knees, leading him to bleed to death.

The National Guard and marines, as in most counterinsurgency operations, responded with a combination of measures designed to attract civilian support and punish those who helped the guerrillas. On the punitive side, the National Guard was accused of using the "water cure" to elicit information, roughing up prisoners, and mutilating dead guerrillas (one American *guardia* lieutenant posed for a photograph holding a severed guerrilla head). On a more positive note, the *guardia* took over civil administration in many parts of the country and generally did a better job than the patronage appointees who came before and after. The *guardia's* doctors, on loan from the U.S. Navy, launched nationwide immunization programs to combat smallpox and typhoid fever.

Uncle Sam's helping hand was especially visible after a devastating earthquake and fire ravaged Managua on March 31, 1931. The marines, Chesty Puller among them, took the lead in salvage, rescue, and recovery operations. Medical supplies flown in by the navy and marines prevented epidemics. More than 1,400 Nicaraguans died in this catastrophe, but the death toll undoubtedly would have been much higher without U.S. aid.

Still, despite the *guardia's* and marines' best efforts, the Sandinistas were able to continue operating, which would have been impossible if the bulk of the civilian population in northern Nicaragua were cooperating with government forces.

By the time of the 1932 election, America was deep in the Depression and the U.S. Congress was turning increasingly isolationist. Will Rogers expressed the sentiments of many when he asked, "Why are we in Nicaragua and what the hell are we doing there?" In 1929 congressional critics tried and failed to attach a rider to the naval appropriations bill cutting off all funding for the marines in Nicaragua. In 1932, they succeeded in blocking funding for American troops to supervise that year's balloting. President Hoover and Secretary Stimson nevertheless managed to scrape up enough personnel using existing appropriations to supervise a minority of the polling stations.

Like the 1928 election, this one was probably fairer than many big-city elections held in the U.S. during this period. The winner was the Liberal candidate, Dr. Juan Sacasa, who had once raised the banner of revolt against a previous Conservative government and its American patrons. But now Washington gladly recognized his government.

El Sauce

Jose Maria Moncada, the outgoing Liberal president, determined on one last grand flourish to mark the end of his administration: He would drive a golden spike to commemorate the completion of a railway line from León to El Sauce. Guardia intelligence officers received word that Sandinistas would try to disrupt the ceremony, scheduled for December 28, 1932. The day after Christmas, Chesty Puller with seven guardia lieutenants, including Bill Lee, and 64 handpicked National Guardsmen, boarded a train to El Sauce. They arrived just in time to find 250 Sandinistas looting the construction company commissary. What happened next recalls the 1969 movie *Butch Cassidy and the Sundance Kid*: The outlaws are happily looting a mail train when out of nowhere approaches another locomotive . . . and out tumble the lawmen, horses' hoofs thundering, guns blazing. The Sandinistas must have been as startled as Butch and Sundance.

The guerrillas deployed on either side of the railroad tracks and opened up on the train with a machine gun. Half the guardsmen jumped out with Puller on the right side, the others following Lee to the left. Lee's men took cover from the Sandinistas' machine gun fire in a dry creek bed, while Puller's contingent circled around to turn the enemy's flank. After slightly more than an hour's battle, they drove off the Sandinistas, who left behind 31 dead guerrillas and 63 live horses. The guardia casualties: three killed and three wounded. It was the worst defeat suffered by the Sandinistas since the battle of Ocotal five years earlier. Moncada was so impressed that as one of his last acts in office he promoted Chesty Puller to major and Bill Lee to captain in the guardia.

The officers did not have long to enjoy their new rank. As scheduled, the marines withdrew from Nicaragua at the beginning of 1933.

Somoza

The new government, feeling vulnerable without U.S. protection, immediately entered into negotiations with Augusto Sandino. On February 2, 1933, the guerrilla chieftain journeyed to Managua to sign a ceasefire. With his arch-enemies, the Americans, gone, he was willing to agree to the "gradual abandonment of his arms." Under the agreement, Sandino was allowed to retain 100 armed men on a tract of land in the remote Coco Valley. Over the following month 1,800 Sandinistas were officially demobilized—yet only 361 weapons were turned in, leading to the suspicion that Sandino retained a secret weapons cache.

Though the war was officially over, the animosity between the Sandinistas and the National Guard hardly abated. As long as the marines were running the guardia, it remained a relatively professional and neutral force. But on January 2, 1933, the guardia was denuded of all American officers. Since the Nicaraguan Military Academy had opened only three years before, there were few Nicaraguans qualified to take over the senior posts. The Liberals turned to political appointees, who quickly politicized the force. Its *jefe director* became Anastasio "Tacho" Somoza, who had been war minister under Moncada and was a fluent English speaker (which helped make his selection popular at the American legation).

Sandino was unsparing in his verbal attacks on the guardia, which he denounced as a criminal institution. The guardia officers, not unnaturally, perceived Sandino as a threat to their well-being. The ineffectual Sacasa government was caught in the middle, equally afraid of both the guardia and the Sandinistas.

In mid-February 1934, while Sandino was visiting Managua for a round of meetings and receptions, General Somoza and the other senior guardia officers gathered in a secret meeting where they signed a resolution titled "The Death of César." On the night of February 21, 1934, Sandino attended a farewell dinner at the presidential palace. The guerrilla leader and some other Sandinistas left in a car around 10 P.M., only to find their way blocked by a guardia patrol, which took Sandino and two of his generals to a military airfield. Here they were joined by Sandino's brother, who had also been abducted at gunpoint, and mowed down with a machine gun. The next morning, the guardia surrounded a Sandinista camp in the north, killing a number of the guerrillas and disarming the rest. The Sandinistas finally had been crushed; the National Guard was triumphant.

Two years later, in 1936, Somoza deposed President Sacasa and became president in his own right. His dynasty would rule the country until rebels calling themselves Sandinistas overthrew Somoza's son in 1979.

Leftists charged for years afterward that Somoza had been given an American go-ahead to kill Sandino and usurp power—an impression that Tacho himself was happy to foster. The evidence does not support this contention. The U.S. minister, Arthur Bliss Lane, was shocked and upset when he heard about Sandino's assassination. He wanted to support the democratically elected Sacasa government. But there was little he or his successor could do. President Franklin Roosevelt's "Good Neighbor" policy, an extension of the Hoover approach, committed Washington not to interfere in Latin America's internal affairs.

Since the early days of the twentieth century, the U.S. had refused to recognize Nicaraguan rulers who came to power by unconstitutional means—even the pro-American Emiliano Chamorro. But now Washington was willing to extend the hand of friendship to all Latin rulers, regardless of how they came to be called "el presidente." Of Somoza, Franklin Roosevelt famously (and perhaps apocryphally) said, "He's a sonofabitch but he's our sonofabitch." But make no mistake: Somoza did not attain power because of U.S. support; he attained power because of U.S. indifference.

Ironically, many of the same critics who later attacked the U.S. for supporting tyrannical regimes had earlier criticized the U.S. for interfering in Latin America's internal affairs. Yet those interventions were the only way that nations such as Nicaragua were likely to see free and fair elections with the losers honoring the outcome (as in 1928 and 1932). Once the marines left, those countries reverted to dictatorships. It was hardly Washington's fault. Yes, the National Guard in Nicaragua made possible Somoza's tyranny, but there had been no shortage of dictators in the country's past—nothing but, in fact—and all had come to power without benefit of a U.S.-trained constabulary. Dictatorship was indigenous; democracy was a foreign transplant that did not take, in part because America would not stick around long enough to cultivate it.

"The Best School"

From a purely military standpoint, the U.S. intervention must be judged a limited success. Forty-seven marines were killed in action; another 66 were wounded. Counting casualties from all causes—disease, accident, suicide, homicide—136 marines lost their lives in Nicaragua. The U.S. casualties were heavier than in the Dominican Republic (17 killed in action) or Haiti (10 killed in action) because the Sandinistas were more skilled in guerrilla warfare than their Hispaniola counterparts. But even when combined with the death toll among native National Guardsmen (75 were said to have died in action, though the actual figure may be higher), those losses are still relatively low for five years of almost nonstop warfare. Writes one historian, "The total number of Marine combat fatalities during the entire intervention was probably less than the Sandinista losses in the single battle of Ocotal."

Of course, as the U.S. learned a few decades later, body counts can hardly be the measure of success in a guerrilla war. On one level, the Nicaraguan adventure was frustrating; after all, the marines never managed to catch Sandino or stamp out his movement. Nevertheless they did keep Sandino on the run. The Sandinistas continued to operate, primarily in the northern wilderness, but they never came close to seizing a major city, much less the whole country.

Certainly by big war standards—by the standards of World War II, where the Allied goal was unconditional surrender—the Nicaragua intervention was a flop. But in small wars, the military's role is akin to that of a police department; it is expected to keep the criminals at bay, not to stamp out criminality altogether. The armed forces do not necessarily have to win a counterinsurgency; sometimes it is enough not to lose. By that standard, the Nicaraguan intervention achieved its goals.

And the marines reaped plenty of collateral benefits from their five years spent chasing Sandino. A generation of marines gained invaluable experience in small unit operations, combat patrolling, close air support, the use of automatic weapons, and jungle fighting. "The Constabulary Detachment, where I saw it in both Haiti and Nicaragua, was the best school the Marine Corps has ever devised," Chesty Puller proclaimed near the end of his life.

A few years later many of the Nicaragua veterans—Puller, "Red Mike" Edson, Herman Hanneken, and others—would put those lessons to good use on Guadalcanal, in the first major U.S. offensive of World War II. If, as the Duke of Wellington once claimed, the Battle of Waterloo was won on the playing fields of Eton, then it might be said with equal justice that the Pacific campaign in World War II was won in the jungles of Nicaragua.

11

"BY BLUFF ALONE"
China, 1901–1941

Revolutions in Nicaragua were a normal, almost routine, occurrence. Not so in China, among the oldest and most unchanging of nations, a land shaped by reverence for ancestors and respect for tradition. At the dawn of the twentieth century, absolute power was still exercised by mandarins clad in satin robes and skullcaps; women of good breeding still bound their feet, a ritualized torture that caused excruciating lifelong pain but was necessary in order to become a well-to-do wife or concubine; men from high-status families still studied the Confucian classics and calligraphy in order to take the series of examinations that would open the door to lucrative bureaucratic appointments; and countless peasants in blue cotton garb still eked out a meager living from the jade green earth, much as their ancestors had millennia ago, always one flood or drought away from starvation. Here and there, signs of a more modern (if perhaps less civilized) world could be glimpsed—steamboats on the Yangtze, a few railroads sprouting in the northern provinces, telegraph wires snaking between some major towns—but, for the most part, the Middle Kingdom clung to its old ways. China was like an exquisite porcelain doll, lovingly crafted by skilled artisans and carefully preserved over the centuries in a beautiful old lacquer cabinet that was growing musty with age and could not remain locked much longer.

The nineteenth century had brought momentous change. A growing Western and Japanese presence coincided with—and probably contributed to—major domestic upheavals, the biggest being the Taiping Rebellion from 1850 to 1864. The Ching dynasty was unable to respond effectively. An initial burst of governmental reform in 1898 had ended after just 100 days, setting the stage for the xenophobic Boxer Uprising in 1900. In the decade after the foreigners' suppression of the Boxers, the ruling Manchus tried halfheartedly to reform their government, to make it more "modern" and constitutional, but as in Russia, the monarchy's reform efforts only spurred revolutionary upheaval. Anti-Manchu nationalism was on the rise among a younger generation of students trained in Western and Japanese learning. Most prominent among the intellectuals calling for a republic was Sun Yat-sen, a physician educated in Hawaii and Hong Kong who preached the virtues of the "Three People's Principles," nationalism, democracy, and socialism.

On October 10, 1911, a military mutiny against the Manchu authorities broke out in the industrial town of Hankow and quickly spread across the country. Just 83 days later, the abdication of the boy emperor Pu-yi ended two and a half centuries of Ching rule. Men across the land cut off their queues, worn as a symbol of subjugation to the Manchus. After more than two millennia of dynastic rule, the Chinese people had embarked on a brave, if short-lived, experiment in self-government.

The inspiration for the newly proclaimed republic came from Sun Yat-sen but its president became Yüan Shih-kai, an ambitious military commander who had previously served the Manchus. Yüan created a dictatorship and even tried to proclaim himself emperor, but his attempt to claim the Altar of Heaven failed. After his death in 1916, no strongman emerged to take his place. Sun Yat-sen briefly tried to establish his own regime in Canton but he was run out of the city by warlords. He died in 1925 a disappointed man, having seen his dream of a republican China dissolve into endless squabbling and warfare among competing regional warlords.

As we have seen, the U.S. had been drawn into the two other great revolutions that occurred during the second decade of the twentieth century—the Mexican revolution of 1911 and the Russian revolution of 1917. So too would America be drawn in by the ripples emanating from the overthrow of China's imperial system in 1912. But like most things in the Middle Kingdom, the full implications of these events would take time to make themselves apparent.

Treaty Ports

For the most part, at least in the beginning, the clashes between warlords and the virtual dissolution of central government had little impact on foreigners, who lived in a world isolated from that of most Chinese. With the exception of some missionaries in the interior, most foreigners resided in "treaty ports" and "concessions" created by the treaties imposed by the West in the nineteenth century. The most important of these outposts was Shanghai, little more than a small, sleepy port surrounded by malarial wasteland when the Manchus had first turned over the area as a residence for foreigners in 1842. By the 1920s, it had become one of the great cities of the world, rich and cosmopolitan, with its stately Bund running along the waterfront, grand hotels and apartment houses, vast department stores and varied food shops, foreign and domestic banks, trading houses and factories, elegant clubs and seedy watering holes, opium dens and bordellos. Living here by 1930 were perhaps 3 million Chinese and 50,000 to 70,000 foreigners, 3,000 Americans among them, making this China's largest city.

Like the other treaty ports and concessions, Shanghai was not technically a colony, but foreign residents could be forgiven for thinking it was. As a result of the unequal treaties, certain foreigners, Britons and Americans among them, enjoyed immunity from Chinese laws; they could be tried only by their own countrymen. (Germans and Russians were stripped of this privilege after the First World War.) They also had their own government, or rather two governments—one in the International Settlement (formed in 1863 by joining the American and British settlements), another next door in the French Concession, both run by municipal councils elected by a handful of foreign property owners. The Chinese remained in control of the parts of the city bordering the foreign settlements. Thus Greater Shanghai was split between three different governments, each with its own police force.

Chinese residents of Shanghai's foreign settlements paid taxes but, until the late 1920s, had no representation on the city councils. Except for *amahs* (nannies) with their foreign charges, Chinese were not even permitted into the Public Gardens across from the British consulate (though, contrary to legend, there was no sign that proclaimed, No dogs or Chinese allowed). This naturally caused no end of resentment among Chinese nationalists, but they and their countrymen also benefited from Shanghai's extraordinary economic success. It served much the same function as Hong Kong did until its handover to Beijing in 1997, providing a haven where the rule of law prevailed, taxes were low, government services worked, entrepreneurial energies could be unleashed, and a vigorous political and intellectual debate could take place. More daily newspapers were published in the International Settlement in the 1920s than in the rest of the country combined. Notwithstanding the usual urban problems—crime, poverty, pollution, racial tensions—millions of Chinese flocked to this bustling metropolis. So did countless refugees from across the world, ranging from White Russians fleeing the Bolsheviks in the 1920s to German Jews fleeing the Nazis in the 1930s.

The other treaty ports were smaller, tamer versions of Shanghai: the Chinese city a crowded maze of bustling alleys and lanes, full of noise and smells, shanties and food stalls, dirt and beggars, lepers and wild dogs; and nearby, separated by high walls and iron gates, the foreign concession: broad, tree-lined avenues, clean and quiet, solid brick buildings, spacious houses with large verandahs, and pleasant parks, with only the omnipresent "coolies" pulling rickshaws or carrying food baskets, to remind a foreigner that this was not Birmingham or Baltimore.

"By Bluff Alone"

Connecting the treaty ports in central China was the Yangtze River, 3,500 miles long, originating in Tibet and flowing a winding course to empty in the muddy waters of the Yellow Sea near Shanghai. The Yangtze watershed contained almost half of China's population. And patrolling it were foreign warships, including the U.S. Navy's Yangtze River Patrol. Though the YangPat, as it was known in navy jargon, was not officially organized until 1919, U.S. warships had been regularly navigating the Middle Kingdom's largest and most important waterway since the pioneering voyage of the USS *Susquehanna* in 1854.

Until 1925 the YangPat relied on six ramshackle gunboats captured from the Spanish by Admiral Dewey in 1898. Because the Yangtze became shallower the farther one went inland, only two of the vessels, the *Palos* and *Monocacy*, were able to navigate the entire length of the river in winter when the water was at its lowest. All were underpowered and lightly armed. In 1925 Congress authorized the construction of six new gunboats specifically designed for the Yangtze: the *Guam*, *Tutuila*, *Oahu*, *Panay*, *Luzon*, and *Mindanao*, all named for American colonial possessions in the Pacific. There were also some destroyers and a few other sundry vessels assigned to regular duty in China.

They were part of the U.S. Asiatic Fleet, which in 1925 consisted of one heavy cruiser, 20 destroyers, 12 submarines, 11 gunboats, and various tenders and transports. The fleet spent the fall and winter at Cavite in the Philippines, the summer cruising along the coast of China. The Asiatic Fleet's primary mission was to prepare for war against Japan. Under War Plan Orange, first begun in 1904 and revised constantly during the 1920s, it was supposed to shield the

Philippines and America's other Pacific possessions long enough for the main U.S. battle fleet to steam across the Pacific and defeat the Japanese navy.

The Yangtze River Patrol, a bunch of tin buckets with pop guns, obviously could do little against the Imperial Japanese fleet. Its task was simply to police the river, protecting the lives and property of American traders, civilian sailors, and missionaries—and keeping the Open Door from slamming shut. Unlike other nations, the U.S. did not seek to carve out its own quasi-colonial sphere of influence; the U.S. policy, first articulated in two famous diplomatic notes in 1899 and 1900, was to preserve the "Chinese territorial and administrative entity" and safeguard "for the world the principle of equal and impartial trade with all parts of the Chinese Empire." Commerce with China amounted to less than 4 percent of U.S. foreign trade during the 1920s, but Washington felt responsible for securing American treaty rights. "It is our wish," said Rear Admiral William Phelps, YangPat commander in 1923, "to make every American feel perfectly safe in coming to the Yangtze Valley to live or to transact business."

This was no easy job given the weak central government in China and the corresponding rise in lawlessness. The gunboats would often land parties of armed sailors to protect foreign settlements from bandits and warlord troops, categories that were frequently indistinguishable. The handful of U.S. merchant ships on the Yangtze were also in constant danger. The Yangtze Rapids Steamship Company, the C. R. Cox Company, and the Dollar Steamship Company ran passenger and cargo service along the river, while the Standard Oil Company of New York (forerunner of Mobil) operated a number of refineries and tankers to supply kerosene and oil for Chinese lamps. Some warlords would try to requisition these U.S.-flagged vessels at gunpoint to transport their troops. Others would try to exact "taxes" on the stretch of the river they controlled.

In response, bluejackets sometimes served as guards aboard merchant vessels; at other times a gunboat would escort merchantmen. A typical incident: On July 20, 1920, the SS *Alice Dollar*, a U.S.-owned steamer, is heading for the treaty port of Chungking, 1,400 miles from Shanghai, when she is fired on from shore by warlord troops seeking to collect a toll. The following day the USS *Monocacy* takes her under escort; the gunboat in turn receives a steady round of fire from the riverbanks, which she returns with her six-pound cannon and .30 caliber machine gun. Two *Monocacy* men are lightly wounded in this half-day operation. Often in this type of escort operation, the YangPat cooperated closely with the Royal Navy, which had 15 gunboats of its own on the river. These missions usually involved no combat; it was simply a matter of showing the flag and deterring any violence against Americans. The only fighting the U.S. bluejackets regularly engaged in were brawls with other nations' sailors in waterfront dives.

For a sense of what it was like to be a "river rat"—as the Yangtze patrollers called themselves—there is no better source than the novel *The Sand Pebbles*, written by Richard McKenna, a navy enlisted man who served on the river in the late 1930s. (It was made into a 1966 movie starring Steve McQueen.) The action is set in 1925 aboard the USS *San Pablo*, nicknamed the *Sand Pebbles*, a decrepit old gunboat captured from the Spanish in 1898—just like its real-life counterpart, the USS *Villalobos*. "She looked stubby and blocky and topheavy . . . more like a house than a ship," and did not have much by way of armor, ordnance or speed. But the old *Sand Pebbles* had other compensations, as petty officer Jake Holman, the novel's protagonist, discovers. The bunks are softer and wider than normal in the navy and are spaced farther apart. Quite a contrast to a typical fleet vessel where "Somebody's rump sagged in your face and someone else's feet were next to your pillow."

Better still: "Just about everything a sailor had to do for himself on other ships was done for him on this one." Chinese laborers ran the engine room, swabbed the decks, shaved the men, cleaned their clothes, cooked their meals. Jake is amazed to discover how fresh and plentiful and delicious the food is. There are even fresh eggs—as many as a man can eat. "Any chow on here's better than a holiday dinner in the Fleet," he crows. And all these delicacies cost the sailors relatively little; they merely turn over 10 percent of their monthly paychecks to Lop Eye Shing, the ship's "number one boy," actually an old, partially paralyzed man, who pays all the laborers and takes enough "squeeze" off the top to make himself wealthy in the bargain.

While Chinese laborers take care of the normal tasks of running a ship, the bluejackets concentrate on strictly military functions: training to repel boarders, fire the ship's guns, and serve as landing parties. It is not unusual for the *San Pablo's* 50 men to confront a mob of thousands of Chinese threatening some foreign concession—and to carry the day without firing a shot. "As a fighting machine, *San Pablo* was a joke," acknowledges its skipper, Lieutenant William Collins. "In a genuine battle he could not whip even General Pan's ragtain army, let alone 40 million Hunanese. He was a man with a kitchen chair in a cage full of tigers." So what made the *San Pablo*, and its real-life counterparts, effective tools of policing? "Faith made *San Pablo* invincible in Hunan. Faith kept the tigers believing that they were house cats." Faith in the power represented by the Stars and Stripes flying prominently on the *San*

Pablo's mast. Some Chinese mothers were so convinced that the U.S. had the Mandate of Heaven that, legend has it, they embroidered crude American flags on their babies' shoes to ward off devils. Thus the Yangtze Patrol's mission was to maintain "face" by making a display of military prowess while doing everything possible to avoid being put to the test of battle. Not unlike a big-city police force, which flourishes firearms but tries to use them only as a last resort.

The U.S. garrisons in Tientsin and Peking played a similar role. They had been established under the Boxer Protocol, signed in 1901, which gave the Western powers and Japan the right to permanently station troops in those two cities. Even after the bulk of the military forces sent to rescue the foreign legations went home, the U.S. kept a marine guard in Peking that, by the mid-1920s, numbered 400 to 500 men. Starting in 1912, another 700 to 1,000 men from the army's 15th Infantry Regiment were stationed in Tientsin, putting them in position to rush to Peking and rescue the legations in case of another outbreak of antiforeign violence.

In 1924–1925, as fighting between warlord troops raged across north China, leaderless soldiers streamed toward Tientsin. The 15th Infantry sent out small detachments to make sure that none entered the foreign concession. One such detail, 28 men under the command of Sergeant Karl Grahlberg, was armed to the teeth with Springfield rifles, Browning Automatic Rifles, Colt .45 automatic pistols—but no ammunition, save for five rounds for the sergeant's own sidearm. Instead they were given baskets of rice, tea, and cabbages to hand out to the warlord soldiers in exchange for their firearms. "The high command didn't want Karl to initiate a war of his own there in the hinterland," wrote a 15th Infantry veteran. "If he was to carry out his mission, he would have to carry it out by bluff alone." In this instance, as on so many others, the 15th Infantry lived up to its pidgin English motto: Can Do. The warlord soldiers accepted their rations and gave Tientsin a wide berth.

This policing mission—today it would be called peacekeeping—had little in common with the type of service experienced by millions of draftees in the First or Second World Wars, but it was perfectly amenable to the volunteer soldiers and sailors serving on the China station. Many were long-term enlistees from the margins of society. Jake Holman himself was there only because a judge gave him the choice of the navy or reform school—a not uncommon situation.

In the navy, Jake and his real-life counterparts found a home. While the duty was largely a boring routine, as it so often is in peacetime, there were plenty of opportunities for R&R in the bars and whorehouses of treaty ports. ("The most of it goes for likker and wimmen," one sailor wrote of his pay. "The rest I spend foolishly.") Some River Rats even settled in China after retirement, opening a bar and shacking up with a "pig," as the sailors affectionately referred to Chinese girls. Life in China with the navy was in many ways more pleasant than their existence back home.

Northern Expedition

This free and easy life was interrupted in 1925 by the outbreak of the Nationalist revolution; from 1927 to 1928, when the revolution was at its height, the Yangtze Patrol would be involved in no fewer than 37 skirmishes. Nationalist sentiment had been building among China's students and intellectuals for some time, nationalism being a nineteenth-century European import that had finally taken root. The students were doubly disgusted by native warlordism and foreign imperialism. These impulses were channeled by two powerful new forces: the National People's Party, or Kuomintang (KMT), organized by Sun Yat-sen, and the Chinese Communist Party, organized under Moscow's guidance. In 1923–24 the KMT and the Communists joined together in a common front. Their immediate goal was to solidify their rule in the area around Canton, but in the meantime, agitators stirred up outbreaks against foreign domination further north.

A series of worker strikes and demonstrations in Shanghai led on May 30, 1925, to a march by some 2,000 demonstrators shouting, "Down with imperialism!" A British officer feared that his police station would be stormed, and just a few seconds after shouting a warning to disperse, he ordered his Chinese and Sikh constables to open fire. Eleven protesters were killed, 20 wounded— few enough deaths given the violence racking China at this time, but these were deaths caused by foreigners, and that made all the difference. The May 30th Incident, as it became known, sparked strikes, protests, and boycotts across the country. A month later, on June 23, another serious incident occurred in Canton. Thousands of protesters, including armed military cadets, tried to storm a bridge leading from the city proper to the foreign settlement on Shamian Island. In the ensuing melee, British troops killed 52 demonstrators and wounded 100. This poured more fuel on the fires of Chinese nationalism, enough to singe foreigners standing too close to the flames; Hong Kong was practically paralyzed by strikes for 16 months.

Unlike in the past, most of the anger this time was directed at Britons and Japanese, viewed as the most oppressive imperialists in China, but Americans living in the same concessions could hardly remain aloof. After a general strike was declared in Shanghai the State Department agreed to land American sailors and marines "to afford adequate protection to American lives and property," though ostensibly not to defend the International Settlement itself, which was seen in Washington as an unfortunate relic of imperialism. By early June 1925, the U.S. had more than 400 servicemen ashore and 13 warships at anchor in Shanghai, the second largest military force in the area after the British.

Amid all this turmoil, the Nationalist army surged out of its Canton base. Its leader was Chiang Kai-shek, a protégé of the late Sun Yat-sen who had visited the Soviet Union to study Red Army methods and then opened the Whampoa Military Academy to train a new generation of Chinese officers. In July 1926, at the head of 6,000 Whampoa cadets and 85,000 troops, assisted by Soviet advisers and supplies, Chiang embarked on his long-planned Northern Expedition to defeat the warlords and unify all of China.

Because of the KMT's alliance with the Communists, many Westerners, especially businessmen and soldiers, viewed the Northern Expedition as Bolshevism on the march and Chiang as a tool of the Comintern. Others, mainly missionaries, idealized it as the last, best hope for good government in China. Neither view would be vindicated by events.

Nanking Incident

By the fall of 1926, having met little resistance from the poorly organized warlords in their path, Chiang's surging armies had reached the Yangtze. Fighting now swirled around cities with sizable foreign populations. Early in January 1927, the British abandoned the Hankow and Kiukiang concessions to Chinese mobs, being careful to avoid another May 30th Incident but suffering in the process a great loss of "face." Or so crusty old China hands told one another over tumblers of whisky in their Shanghai clubs.

On the night of March 23, 1927, the Nationalist army entered Nanking, which had no foreign concession but was the center of American missionary activity in the Yangtze River valley. Several days earlier small parties of U.S. sailors had landed to evacuate the American community, but a number of long-time residents had refused to leave. Among those still trapped inside the city were Pearl Buck and her family. Not yet a famous novelist, Buck was the daughter of Protestant missionaries and had lived most of her life in China. She spoke fluent Mandarin and had always gotten along well with the Chinese but now, for the first time, she feared for her life. And with good reason. The American vice president of Nanking University, a Christian college where she taught, was killed; an American woman, a missionary, was seriously wounded. In all, six foreigners would be killed in Nanking. The future author of *The Good Earth* narrowly avoided their fate.

Buck's gray brick house was broken into and looted by a mob while she and her family scuttled into a kindly Chinese neighbor's mud hut. Here they hid, trying desperately to keep their small children from making a sound, while Nationalist soldiers marched through the neighborhood. At any moment, she feared they would be dragged out and murdered. "In the midst of this desperate waiting suddenly we heard a frightful noise, a thunder, rumbling over the roof," Buck wrote. "What was it? It came again and again. It could only be cannon. But what cannon? The Chinese had no such cannon as this, deafening us, roaring above the human shouts and cries." It took her a moment to realize: "Foreign cannon—the warships in the river!"

And so it was.

The U.S. destroyers *Preston* and *Noa* had arrived off Nanking several days before to evacuate the American community. British and Japanese warships came on a similar mission. This did not deter KMT troops from attacking both the Japanese and British consulates; several Britons and the Japanese consul were wounded. Despite the protection afforded by a small party of U.S. sailors, U.S. Consul John K. Davis decided that the consulate building was no longer safe. On March 24, 1927, he and his wife set out, accompanied by a small party of sailors and some missionaries, to seek refuge two-and-a-half miles away in the hilltop house occupied by the local representative of the Standard Oil Company of New York (Socony). They were attacked along the way, with a navy enlisted man and a Chinese servant being wounded and the sailors shooting two of the attackers in return. Finally they reached Socony Hill and joined other Americans and some British consular officials trapped inside—52 foreigners in all.

Throughout the day Chinese soldiers bent on loot and perhaps worse approached the house. The foreigners handed over all their money and valuables but soon there was no more left to give, and still the soldiers kept coming. At 2:53 P.M., three navy signalmen atop Socony Hill braved sniper fire to send a message by semaphore to the foreign warships anchored in the river: "We are being attacked. Open fire. SOS SOS SOS."

The skipper of the USS *Noa*, Lieutenant Commander Roy C. Smith, saw the signal. Like most captains in the Yangtze Patrol, isolated a long way from headquarters, he did not have the time or means to get orders before acting. He knew that Washington did not want its representatives starting a war in China, but he also knew he could not simply leave the Americans in Nanking to their fate. He told his gunnery officer, Lieutenant Benjamin Franklin Staud, "Well, I'll either get a court martial or a medal out of this. Let her go, Bennie!" With that, the *Noa's* 4-inch guns unleashed a salvo into the hills of Nanking, soon to be joined by the *Preston* and the British cruiser *Emerald*. It was this gunfire that Pearl Buck, hiding in the city, heard as distant thunder. Three Japanese destroyers moored nearby did not open fire, but at each blast from the Anglo-American vessels their crews yelled a loud "Banzai!"

"The gunfire was most effective and undoubtedly saved all our lives," wrote Ensign Woodward Phelps, one of the Americans trapped on Socony Hill. "Missionaries in the interior who were being looted stated that all looting ceased when the bombardment commenced. At Socony Hill the soldiers ran like scared rabbits, but not until we had killed three or four of them ourselves." As soon as the soldiers disappeared, the Socony Hill refugees made ropes out of sheets and lowered themselves down the 60-foot wall at the foot of the hill. Then the ragtag party—48 men, two women, two children—walked a mile to the river, commandeered three sampans, and finally reached the safety of the American warships.

That still left some 90 American men, 40 women, and 20 children trapped inside Nanking. The senior British and American naval officers on the spot issued an ultimatum to the Chinese authorities: either produce the refugees or Nanking would be shelled. All the Americans, including Pearl Buck and family, were delivered safely by the evening of March 25, 1927. It was a bittersweet salvation for the missionaries, many of whom had long resented the quasi-colonial foreign military presence in China and had sympathized with the aspirations of Chinese nationalists. "All my life I had seen those gunboats in the river, and I had wished that they were not there. I had felt they should not be there, foreign warships in Chinese interior waters," Pearl Buck wrote. "Now such a ship was saving me and mine and taking us to a refuge."

For unleashing the *Noa's* guns, Lieutenant Commander Smith received neither a court-martial nor a medal, but his "cool-headed judgment" was applauded by his boss, Rear Admiral H. H. Hough, commander of the Yangtze Patrol.

General Duckboard

Admiral Clarence Williams, commander of the Asiatic Fleet, wanted to exact revenge for the Nanking "outrage" by pounding various KMT military installations in cooperation with the British, French, and Japanese. A few decades before, Theodore Roosevelt would no doubt have jumped at the opportunity. But America's chief executive was now a reserved, taciturn New Englander whose cautious personality was far removed from Roosevelt's high spirits and love of warfare for its own sake. The world situation, too, was different from Roosevelt's day. Imperialism was on the wane, and the Middle Kingdom, teeming with Chinese soldiers armed with modern weapons, was no longer the pushover for Western militaries that it once had been. Calvin Coolidge had no desire to be drawn deeper into a war in China; he refused Admiral Williams's request to teach the KMT a lesson. Instead the Yangtze Patrol was ordered to evacuate American civilians and diplomats from all treaty ports below Hankow, and to bring the refugees to Shanghai.

President Coolidge did, however, reluctantly agree to dispatch the 4th Marine Regiment from San Diego to help defend Shanghai's International Settlement from the advancing Nationalist armies. By mid-1927, the U.S. had more than 5,600 soldiers in China. To command the marines, the president summoned Old Gimlet Eye, Brigadier General Smedley Butler, ballyhooed by *Time* magazine as the "Premier 'Fighting Devil' Among 'Devil Dogs.'"

It is worth taking a moment to catch up on Butler's doings since we last encountered him commanding the Gendarmerie d'Haiti (after having already fought in the Spanish-American War, Philippine War, Boxer Uprising, Nicaragua, and Veracruz). As soon as America entered World War I, Butler became desperate to fight on the Western Front. For almost a year his urgent entreaties were ignored by marine headquarters, which, much to his chagrin, deemed him irreplaceable in Haiti. He was not sent to France until September 1918, just a couple of months before the armistice, and even then he was not ordered to the front but assigned to run Camp Pontanezen, a supply base on the French coast for the American Expeditionary Force.

Though disappointed, Butler tackled this job with his customary verve. When numerous requests through "channels" failed to produce the wooden duckboard needed to cover the camp's sea of mud, he simply marched his men to an army warehouse and liberated what he needed. Thus he gained a new nickname: General Duckboard. By the time he left France in July 1919, Butler had earned plaudits and a promotion to brigadier general for his skill in reorganizing the AEF's main transit and supply depot.

Back in the States, Butler took over command of the marine base at Quantico. Peacetime duty could not satisfy this warrior, however. When the mayor of Philadelphia asked him to take over the police department of his crime-ridden hometown, Butler jumped at the chance. President Coolidge granted him leave from the corps and in 1924 he was installed as Philadelphia's Director of Public Safety. The teetotaling Quaker general proved to be an indefatigable and incorruptible enforcer of Prohibition. Too indefatigable and incorruptible. He caused a backlash among prominent citizens who did not want their vices interfered with and wound up being fired by the same mayor who had hired him.

In 1926 Smedley returned to the corps as commander of the San Diego barracks only to find himself in the middle of another high-octane controversy. After his second-in-command, Colonel Alexander S. Williams, showed up visibly drunk at a hotel, Butler ordered him court-martialed—to hoots of derision from "wets" across the country. Smedley's public reputation did not improve when Williams was convicted, demoted, and transferred to San Francisco, where he drove his car off a pier and drowned in a possible suicide. But Butler bulled on, taking command of 2,500 marines called out to guard mail trains in the western United States after a series of violent robberies. He had just successfully completed this assignment when early in 1927 he received orders to sail to China.

"Shanghai Has Become Red"

Brigadier General Butler arrived in Shanghai on March 25, 1927, the day after the siege of Socony Hill had been lifted in Nanking, 160 miles away. Panic was running high among the foreign residents of Shanghai. Communist workers had already staged a general strike and armed insurrection in the Chinese part of the city. The local warlord troops, poorly trained peasant conscripts, fell apart; in panic some of them tried to force their way into the International Settlement, only to be mowed down by British rifle and machine gun fire. By the time Nationalist troops marched into the Chinese sections of Shanghai on March 22, the city was already in the hands of the Communist labor union. Posters screamed, Exterminate the feudal forces!, workers paraded with red armbands, and any Chinese who cooperated with foreigners was denounced as an "imperialist running dog." "Shanghai has become red," exclaimed a French nun.

The Shanghai Municipal Council, which governed the International Settlement, responded by declaring a state of emergency, calling out the Shanghai Volunteer Corps (1,500 militiamen under British command), and requesting additional assistance from the dozens of foreign warships anchored offshore. Some 20,000 foreign troops were landed, the largest contingent being 13,500 British soldiers. They crouched behind barbed wire and sandbags, ready to repel any attack on the International Settlement.

Admiral Williams agreed to land 1,500 marines but would not permit them to man the perimeter, in keeping with the Coolidge administration's policy of protecting American lives and property in China but not "the integrity of the [International] Settlement." In practice this was a distinction without a difference, but it was an attempt, however clumsy, to suggest that the U.S. was not an imperial power like the others. The U.S. also offered to renegotiate the unequal treaties, though little was done to match words to deeds. In keeping with administration policy, Smedley Butler limited his marines to patrolling the interior of the International Settlement, "prepared to frustrate any attempts on the part of our own servants to murder us in bed."

The attempt never came. Instead it was the Communists who were murdered. Chiang Kai-shek had been willing to make common cause with the Communists, but now that all of southern and central China was in his grasp he decided to double-cross his putative allies before they could double-cross him. Starting on April 12, 1927, Nationalist soldiers and their underworld allies attacked the Reds, beginning in Shanghai and moving on to other towns, killing thousands and arresting more. They dealt the Communists a series of swift, hard blows that left them reeling.

To replace his Communist backing, Chiang sought and found support among wealthy bankers, industrialists, and organized crime figures in Shanghai. He also shed his movement's xenophobic rhetoric and appealed for help from Western and Japanese governments. In the eyes of the American public, Chiang's transformation into a sympathetic figure was completed in December 1927 when he married Soong Mei-ling, the Wellesley-educated daughter of a prominent Chinese financier, in a Christian ceremony in Shanghai.

With the consolidation of Chiang's power along the Yangtze and his purge of the Communists, the foreigners in Shanghai could finally afford to exhale. Life returned to its normal round of cocktail hours and dances, race meets and tennis matches. The marines' major concern shifted from the Communist threat to the British threat, the threat being that the "limies," as Smedley Butler called them, might outshine U.S. troops in spit and polish displays. The leathernecks rose to the challenge by nickel plating their weapons, burnishing entrenching tools, polishing helmets, and "secretly" training a band. At a review of all the foreign troops in the city they won top honors.

Mission accomplished!

Northern China

More serious work awaited the marines in China. Anticipating that Chiang Kai-shek would march north with the ultimate objective of seizing Peking, in June 1927 Butler and his men shifted their operations from Shanghai to the Peking-Tientsin corridor. Both cities had sizable foreign populations and, as a result of the Boxer Protocol, garrisons of foreign troops to protect them. In Peking there were 500 "horse marines"; in Tientsin, 900 men from the army's 15th Infantry Regiment. Butler brought more than 3,000 marine reinforcements to Tientsin, accompanied by artillery, machine guns, light tanks, and 20 airplanes. This gave the U.S. a formidable force in the area but greatly annoyed the 15th Regiment's officers, who were to be placed under Butler's command in the event of hostilities.

Chiang's much-anticipated march north was delayed; he was still distracted mopping up Communists and warlords in the south. This left the marines, camped out under the pitiless summer sun on Woodrow Wilson Boulevard in the Tientsin Foreign Concession, with little to do. Butler drilled his men to a high state of readiness so that they would be able to reach Peking and evacuate U.S. diplomats if another Boxer-like incident occurred. As part of this task, the marines worked on improving the roads between Tientsin and Peking—a job that Butler, drawing on his road-building experience in Haiti, tackled with gusto. One Chinese village was grateful enough for the marines' help to present Butler with a Ten Thousand Blessings Umbrella, a scarlet silk canopy on 12-foot poles that was traditionally given to great public benefactors.

When, on Christmas Eve 1927, the Standard Oil installation outside Tientsin caught fire, the marines pitched in to help put out the flames, with Butler playing fire chief. This firefighting was not entirely altruistic, since the ability of marine trucks and airplanes to operate depended on having access to Socony's gasoline.

But for the most part the marines' mission was aptly characterized by Smedley Butler as "grueling monotony." It was quite a contrast from the last time Butler had visited Tientsin, during the Boxer Uprising. Then the emphasis had been on daring offensive action. Now the marines had an even more difficult task: to restrain their eagerness for battle. "I continually lectured the men that our purpose now was peaceful and that we weren't carrying any chips on our shoulders that might lead to fighting," Butler wrote. "I was tolerating no clashes with the Chinese people. I warned them that if a Marine so much as laid a hand on a rickshaw coolie he would be court-martialed." Despite some incidents of rowdyism, the marines generally obeyed Butler's edict and carried out their mission peacefully.

Things got more exciting early in 1928, when Chiang Kai-shek's armies finally resumed the last phase of the Northern Expedition. On May 3–5 the advancing KMT armies clashed with Japanese troops around Tsinan, capital of Shantung province. Ostensibly the Japanese troops were merely protecting their fellow countrymen living in Tsinan; in reality, the Japanese were becoming alarmed about the prospect of a strong China united under the Kuomintang and were trying to stymie Chiang Kai-shek. Though the Japanese held onto Tsinan and the rest of the province, the Nationalist armies simply took a detour and reached Tientsin a week later.

With the arrival of the KMT army, most of the warlord soldiers withdrew north, leaving considerable chaos in their wake. Smedley Butler estimated that for about a week 150,000 Chinese troops of various factions were within 10 miles of the Tientsin concession. But all gave it a "wide berth" because of the presence of 15,000 foreign troops. The general in charge of the Japanese garrison at Tientsin, apparently itching for a replay of Tsinan, urged joint international action that would be likely to precipitate a confrontation with the Chinese. The U.S. vetoed this plan. Instead Butler maintained cordial relations with the various Chinese generals and made sure they respected American lives and property. "Had we not been in such strength we would have had trouble," Butler wrote.

Thanks in part to the American role in blocking Japanese interference, Chiang Kai-shek took Tientsin and Peking peacefully. China was now at least nominally united under KMT rule. Although Chiang's hold was very tenuous, northern China did quiet down for the time being. By early 1929 the marines were withdrawn from Tientsin, leaving behind the army's 15th Infantry Regiment.

Smedley Butler basked in the success of his marines in preserving the peace but privately griped to the corps commandant, his friend John Lejeune, that "the American government is wasting its biggest ammunition"—the marines—"on sparrows." Although "we can do this traffic duty better than anyone else," he suggested that it should be turned over to "inferior forces," meaning the army, and that the devil dogs should be reserved "for real 'rough and tumble' service such as we are now having in Nicaragua." Butler's complaint again underlined the fact that even soldiers with vast experience in peacekeeping operations preferred, if possible, warfighting.

"I Was a Racketeer for Capitalism"

Butler returned home in 1929 and was promoted to major general, becoming at 48 the youngest major general in the U.S. armed forces. But he never became marine commandant, a failure that Butler, who had not attended college, blamed on a clique of Naval Academy graduates. The job went instead to a bland organization man who was an Annapolis graduate. Butler was consigned once again to running the Quantico base, which left him plenty of time to make extra money on the lecture circuit. During one of his speeches in 1931 Smedley told a disparaging story about the Italian dictator Benito Mussolini, igniting an international incident. The Italian government complained, Secretary of State Henry Stimson apologized, and President Hoover had Butler arrested, making him face the prospect of a court-martial. This unleashed a storm of pro-Butler publicity, forcing the administration to settle for giving him a letter of reprimand. The 50-year-old major general thereupon retired from the corps, if not from public life.

In 1932 citizen Butler ran unsuccessfully in the Republican U.S. Senate primary in Pennsylvania. The following year, he went public with an accusation that a shadowy cabal of Wall Street financiers had tried to recruit him for a plot to overthrow President Roosevelt and establish a fascist dictatorship. An investigation by the House Un-American Affairs Committee confirmed that Butler had indeed been approached, but all indications were that the alleged conspiracy was never very serious. In any case Butler's denunciations established his reputation as an anti-Wall Street firebrand. In 1935, just before his assassination, presidential candidate Huey Long named Butler secretary of war in his shadow cabinet. Smedley, who had voted for Roosevelt in 1932, moved further and further left. He voted for socialist candidate Norman Thomas in 1936 and did not hesitate to share speaking platforms with leaders of the American Communist Party.

By the mid-1930s America's leading imperial soldier had become a pacifist and anti-imperialist. In a 1935 magazine article he wrote that he had spent most of his time as a marine "being a high-class muscle man for Big Business, for Wall Street and the bankers. . . . I helped in the raping of half a dozen Central American republics for the benefit of Wall Street. . . . In short I was a racketeer for capitalism." The same year he published a book, *War Is a Racket*, a very short, very crude exposition of an economic determinist viewpoint which held that all wars, whether the occupation of Haiti or World War I, were launched by capitalist cabals for their own benefit. Most of this was already a cliché by the 1930s, but it had more credibility coming from a retired major general than from the average street-corner orator.

Butler's views have been cited over the years by critics intent on "proving" that the Banana Wars were undertaken at the behest of big business. The reality is that Butler was not involved in the decisions to use force; he carried out his orders, and carried them out well, but he often did not know precisely why they were issued. The credibility of his wilder charges should also be viewed in light of the other intemperate views he expressed at the time.

In his last years, Old Gimlet Eye became a leading critic of any military buildup. He thought the U.S. armed forces should be restricted by constitutional amendment to homeland defense only, excluding even Alaska and Hawaii. "Not a single drop of American blood should ever again be spilled on foreign soil," he thundered on August 31, 1939. Hitler's invasion of Poland the next day did not change his mind. Right up to his death, from cancer in June 1940, this self-proclaimed "military isolationist" was warning Americans not to get involved in trying to stop the Axis powers.

Smedley Darlington Butler was sui generis, no doubt, but his end-of-life outbursts do indicate something of the American military's ambivalent attitude toward imperialism. Butler was hardly the only soldier who felt disdain for money-grubbing businessmen and thought that the warrior ethos should not be corrupted by commercial considerations. Nor was he the only soldier to feel that small wars overseas were a waste of time. He took these views to a more radical extreme, however, than just about any officer of such high rank before or since. One cannot help but suspect that Butler's Quaker pacifist beliefs, so long suppressed during his military career, came back with a vengeance upon his retirement.

Shanghai in the 1930s

Back in China, the nature of the threat faced by American troops changed after Butler's departure in 1929. From the start of the Chinese revolution in 1911 until the completion of the KMT's Northern Expedition at the end of 1928, the primary challenge had been to protect American lives and property from warlord troops and various anti-foreign uprisings. In the 1930s the U.S. military's focus changed to protecting Americans, and to a lesser extent Chinese, from the depredations of Japanese troops embarked on a savage campaign of conquest.

The threat had been presaged by the 1928 clash between KMT and Japanese troops at Tsinan. Three years later the Japanese army annexed Manchuria and set up a puppet regime under the last Manchu emperor, P'u-yi, a government not recognized by Washington. Generalissimo Chiang Kai-shek, more worried about the Communist threat, did not attempt a military response, but the anger of the Chinese people could not be contained. On January 18, 1932, a Chinese mob attacked five Japanese Buddhist monks in Shanghai, providing a pretext for the Japanese armed forces, eleven days later, to attack the slums of Chapei outside Shanghai's International Settlement. The Chinese Nineteenth Route Army put up a surprisingly stout resistance, and warfare soon raged around the foreign community.

The defense of the International Settlement had previously been divided into sectors, with U.S. troops guarding its western third, which turned out to be next door to the fighting. The U.S. garrison—1,624 men of the 4th Marines and 1,100 men from the army's 31st Infantry Regiment—were under strict orders not to fight the Japanese. But at the same time, they had to stop the Japanese from sending troops through the Anglo-American sectors of the city in an attempt to outflank Chinese defensive lines. This delicate task required as much diplomatic as military savvy. Unlike in the past, this time U.S. soldiers manned the perimeter defense of barbed wire, machine gun nests, and sandbagged emplacements strung out along the bank of Soochow Creek. It was a hazardous assignment, with stray shells often landing in the U.S. zone, but not nearly as hazardous as life in neighboring Chapei, which was leveled by Japanese airplanes and artillery, causing mass civilian casualties. By March 8, 1932, the Japanese had conquered Chapei, and the generalissimo had withdrawn the Nineteenth Route Army from the area. An armistice was arranged in May, easing the strain on the American defenders for the time being.

The Japanese militarists were encouraged by the feeble international response to this aggression. Five years later, on July 7, 1937, Japanese troops provoked a clash with Chinese soldiers at the Marco Polo Bridge just outside Peking, signaling the start of the Sino-Japanese War, which would not end until Japan's surrender to Allied forces in 1945.

It did not take the Japanese long to conquer both Peking and Tientsin, which had U.S. garrisons of 528 marines and 814 soldiers, respectively. The fighting reached Shanghai in August 1937, and once again the approximately 2,500 marines were nervous bystanders. During the ensuing battle, four Chinese bombers, aiming for a Japanese battleship in the harbor, instead dropped their bombs in the middle of the International Concession, killing approximately a thousand civilians, mostly Chinese. Later that afternoon, more Chinese bombs narrowly missed the USS *Augusta*, flagship of the Asiatic Fleet, also moored in Shanghai harbor. A week later a shell burst on the *Augusta's* well deck, killing one sailor and wounding 17 others.

The Nationalist army put up a brave fight but, after suffering staggering casualties, was driven out of Shanghai by a Japanese amphibious assault that threatened an envelopment of their positions. On November 11, 1937, Chinese troops began retreating in the direction of Nanking, the Nationalist capital located 160 miles west of Shanghai, with Japanese forces not far behind. Chiang Kai-shek's hold on the entire lower Yangtze Valley, China's industrial heartland, was in peril.

"Get Under Cover"

After Japanese airplanes had begun bombing Nanking in September 1937, one of the Yangtze Patrol gunboats, the *Panay*, had been dispatched to protect and assist the Americans who still remained in the city. On Saturday, December 11, just two days before the brutal Rape of Nanking began, the *Panay* left the city carrying, in addition to its normal crew of five officers and 54 men, 15 evacuees—American newsmen, businessmen, and diplomats, as well as a couple of Italian correspondents. The gunboat steamed slowly up the Yangtze; at dusk it anchored 12 miles from the city. Three Standard Oil tankers—the *Mei Ping*, *Mei An*, and *Mei Hsia*—clustered around the gunboat for protection.

The next day, December 12, 1937, a Japanese army boat briefly came alongside and demanded to inspect the *Panay*, but when its captain, Lieutenant Commander Joseph Hughes, refused, the soldiers left. The *Panay* and the three tankers steamed a few more miles and anchored in the broad, muddy river 27 miles away from Nanking. An American diplomat aboard the *Panay* radioed their location to various U.S. consulates and asked them to inform the Japanese command of their position.

It was a clear, calm, lazy day, and the men aboard the *Panay* went about their normal Sunday routine. At 1:35 P.M., a sailor on the deck spotted some airplanes flying high overhead. Without warning, six planes suddenly dived toward the gunboat, their Rising Sun emblems clearly visible. Three minutes later, the chief quartermaster shouted: "They're letting go bombs! Get under cover." Then the ominous whistling sound, followed by an explosion. Some of the Japanese planes got within a hundred feet of the ship, close enough for the Americans to see the pilots' faces. How could the pilots miss the giant U.S. flags prominently displayed in three places around the ship?

Yet the bombs kept falling, dropped by a squadron of 24 Japanese naval airplanes, a combination of medium bombers, dive bombers, and fighters. All the ship's officers, except the surgeon, were wounded right away. The captain had his leg fractured and his face badly cut. His executive officer, Lieutenant Arthur "Tex" Anders, was wounded in the throat and, unable to speak, took to scribbling orders on the bulkhead and various scraps of paper, blood speckling his words. Some of the crew members, including one petty officer who did not have time to put his pants on, ran over to fire the ship's .30 caliber machine guns at the marauding airplanes, but to little effect.

Unable to defend itself, the *Panay* also could not flee; one of the first blasts had punctured the fuel line, leaving the ship sitting in the water like a dummy target at a shooting range. About 20 minutes after the start of the attack, 20 bombs had been dropped on or near the *Panay*, and water was a foot-and-a-half deep below deck; the pumps could not keep up. At 2:05 P.M., the order was given to abandon ship. The men lowered two motor sampans and ferried themselves to shore as Japanese warplanes strafed them, creating more casualties.

The crew, many of them wounded, hid in some reeds along the river bank and took stock of their situation. They saw a couple of Japanese patrol boats approach the *Panay* and spray the sinking ship with machine gun fire. They saw the four Socony oil tankers ablaze after also having been attacked by the Japanese aircraft. They saw, a little before 4 P.M., their ship slide beneath the water, the first U.S. Navy vessel ever lost to enemy aircraft and the first Yangtze Patrol boat lost to enemy action of any sort. The men feared that the Japanese might set out to exterminate the survivors, if only to hide the evidence of the attack.

The *Panay*'s crew straggled along the shore. They reached a village and then the nearby town of Hohsien, where they managed to telephone word of their predicament to the outside world. On December 14, 1937, two British gunboats and an American gunboat, accompanied by Japanese warships, arrived to rescue them. By the time their 60-hour ordeal was over, two navy enlisted men, an Italian journalist, and a civilian American oil-tanker captain were dead; 74 men on the *Panay* and the three oil tankers were injured.

In the days to come, the Japanese government apologized profusely for this "very regrettable incident" and paid $2.2 million in reparations. The official line from Tokyo was that the Japanese warplanes mistook the gunboat and oil tankers for Chinese ships ferrying troops out of Nanking. President Franklin D. Roosevelt, not yet ready to declare war on Japan, accepted this explanation.

He even asked an American newsreel cameraman who had been aboard the *Panay* to suppress part of his film which showed Japanese planes attacking the ship from virtually deck level—a distance from which the pilots could not have failed to spot its giant American flags.

If the attack was no accident, what had caused it? The most probable explanation, though one that in all likelihood can never be proved, is that an ultranationalist Japanese army officer, Colonel Kingoro Hashimoto, who was in the area, tricked the Japanese navy into bombing the *Panay* in the hope of either provoking a confrontation or humiliating America. Like the attack on the USS *Stark* by Iraqi warplanes in 1987, another ostensible accident, the *Panay* incident did not provoke an immediate war but did foreshadow hostilities in the near future.

Surrounded

The American press reacted with predictable fury to the *Panay* attack, but many newspapers also suggested that, as the *St. Louis Post-Dispatch* put it, "American military forces must be withdrawn from the Japanese-Chinese battle zone." The War Department seconded this view. No withdrawal occurred, however, because the State Department feared that the removal of U.S. military forces would give Japan a green light for further aggression.

But the small number of American servicemen left in China could do little to resist the Japanese advance. Tokyo now controlled all of the important cities of northern and eastern China and much of the land in between. Chiang Kai-shek's government was forced to seek refuge first in Hankow and then in Chungking, deep in the interior vastness of China, 1,400 miles from Shanghai. There was no longer any need for the Yangtze Patrol since by mid-1938 the river had become a war zone and commercial traffic had ground to a halt. The U.S. garrisons in Tientsin and Shanghai were tiny islands stranded in a sea of hostile Japanese troops.

The Japanese were greatly irritated to see how these Western outposts aided Chiang. Since the Western powers did not recognize the puppet governments set up by the Japanese to rule occupied territories, they continued to let Nationalist officials operate in the Shanghai International Settlement, collecting customs duty and operating a post office, radio and telegraph offices, and a central bank. The revenue generated here helped keep the government of Free China afloat.

Protecting this enclave was the puniest of forces. The U.S. maintained only about 1,000 men from the 4th Marines in Shanghai. The British had another

2,500 men in their garrison, but they were withdrawn in August 1940, after the collapse of France, rendering its 4,000-man garrison useless. The 750 Italian troops were of no value in defending the settlement's neutrality following Mussolini's alliance with Japan, formally announced in June 1941 when Italy entered World War II on Germany's side.

It was not these tiny forces that maintained the neutrality of Shanghai's International Settlement; it was simply that Tokyo was not yet ready to make war on Britain and America. But there was always a danger that extremist nationalists in the Japanese army would invade the settlement regardless of the consequences. There were constant incursions by Japanese patrols into the American-controlled sector, all turned back peacefully by the marines. On one occasion, 80 Japanese soldiers entered the U.S. zone after dark and began rounding up 200 Chinese for "trial." When Chesty Puller, the Haiti and Nicaragua veteran who was now executive officer of the 2nd Marine Battalion, heard about the incident, he wasted no time in leading 22 marines out to confront the Japanese. Puller drew his pistol and told a Japanese officer, "I'll give you five minutes to free those men and get your troops back across Soochow Creek where you belong." This time, the Japanese complied, but it was clear that war was looming, and that the little garrisons in Shanghai and Tientsin could only come to grief.

The 15th Infantry, the "Can Do" Regiment, was withdrawn from Tientsin in 1938. All Asiatic Fleet dependents, some 2,000 women and children, were sent home late in 1940. The 4th Marines did not leave Shanghai until November 28, 1941, going from the frying pan into the fire: They wound up in the Philippines where their fate would be either death or capture on Corregidor and Bataan. On December 5, 1941, the Yangtze Patrol was officially dissolved. When Japanese forces attacked Pearl Harbor two days later, only one of the U.S. gunboats, the *Wake*, was left in Shanghai. Manned by a skeleton crew, it was taken without a shot by the Japanese. Three other Yangtze gunboats managed to brave the choppy open seas to escape to the Philippines, but within six months all three had been sunk. It was an inglorious end to the longest continuous military operation in American history.

The Legacy of Imperialism

The U.S. presence in China was resented over the years by many Chinese, and repented of by many guilt-ridden Americans, because it carried the taint of imperialism. Many Chinese felt as affronted by the U.S. Navy being on the Yangtze as Americans would have felt had the Chinese navy tried to patrol the

Mississippi River; as offended by the garrisons in Shanghai, Peking, and Tientsin as Americans would have been by Chinese garrisons in Washington, New York, and Baltimore. Perhaps even more galling to many Chinese were the petty slights and indignities—the stray look, the odd word, the sudden outburst of violence—by which the white man made plain that he did not regard the "yellow" race as his intellectual or social equal. All this is undeniable and understandable, yet much can be said in defense of the U.S. role.

To start with, the U.S. did not carve out its own quasi-colonial sphere of influence, as Japan and the European powers did. Instead America helped prevent the Europeans from dividing China into formal colonies. The Open Door policy was codified in international law through the Nine Power Treaty of 1922. The U.S. also pushed for a reduction in the number of treaty ports; the total shrank from a high of almost 80 to 13 by 1937. The unequal treaties were not finally nullified until 1943, but by then this was a mere formality. The Europeans and Americans had long ceased to be a threat to Nationalist China; they were now Chiang Kai-shek's allies in his fight against the Japanese and the Communists.

The primary mission of American forces in China was not aggressive, though it may have seemed that way to many Chinese; "their primary function," as the State Department stated in 1937, "is protecting American nationals, secondarily, American property." This would not have been necessary if China had had an effective national government capable of enforcing law and order, but it did not. One could argue that repeated foreign interventions helped undermine the legitimacy of China's governments, and there is some truth to this. But for the most part foreigners merely revealed the rot in the Celestial Empire's institutions; they did not cause it. Japan, though considerably smaller in land area and population than China, had stronger political and social structures that allowed it to withstand European and American bullying.

The Western missionaries and businessmen who rushed into China under the protection of Western navies unsettled its traditional society but also provided real benefits to the Chinese people. By the 1920s the old missionary impulse to win "China for Christ" had been largely channeled into running medical, educational, and social-welfare programs, much as the Peace Corps would later do. Americans helped set up numerous schools and colleges, such as Nanking University and Yenching University, that provided a Western education to thousands of Chinese scholars, women included. The Rockefeller Foundation created Peking Union Medical College, China's premier research and training hospital. YMCAs and YWCAs sprouted across the land, offering, among other programs, public health seminars and anti-opium campaigns.

Ironically, many of these educational institutions fostered nationalist and xeno-phobic feelings by exposing Chinese students to Western ideology. The most fervent supporters of both the Kuomintang and the Communist Party were some of the most Westernized Chinese.

Like the missionaries, the businessmen who flocked into the Middle Kingdom were resented by many Chinese, and understandably so. Even after they stopped importing vast quantities of opium (London outlawed the export of opium from India to China in 1913), the foreigners remained for the most part immune from Chinese taxes and laws. But the treaty ports where the busi-nessmen flocked were more boon than bane.

Part of the benefits were political: The treaty ports provided neutral areas where Chinese out of favor with the current regime—whether deposed warlords or radical students—could live, write, and speak in safety. Many of the denunci-ations of the unequal treaties were written in the very treaty ports they made possible. After being driven out of Canton in 1918, Sun Yat-sen settled in Shanghai's French Concession; three years later, the Chinese Communist Party held its first congress there. All this was most unusual since China had no his-tory of tolerating anti-government publications or organizations. In the 1930s these treaty ports became a vital haven that helped keep Free China afloat.

But most of the cities' benefits were economic. These settlements, especial-ly Shanghai, gave China the genesis of a modern banking and industrial sys-tem. The historian Immanuel C. Y. Hsu writes:

> Foreign investors introduced modern technology and the entrepreneurial spirit, and financed many modern industries. . . . Their success created an environment in which profit from industrial undertakings was demonstrably possible, thereby prompting the Chinese to follow their example. Additionally, the employment and training of Chinese in foreign factories and business establishments pro-duced a native pool of technical knowledge of production and managerial skills which later were to be profitably tapped by and for the Chinese. . . . Nor should one lose sight of the fact that foreign-leased areas and treaty ports provided a cer-tain degree of peace and order necessary for industrial growth; and that foreign establishments had already borne most of the cost of 'social overhead,' such as public utilities, roads, and communications facilities, which eased the develop-ment of Chinese industry.

Many of these achievements would be forgotten during the horrors that engulfed China in the decades that followed—civil war, famine, the Cultural Revolution—but in the 1980s capitalism would experience a resurgence, building on the almost-forgotten foundations of the distant past. From the perspective of the twenty-first century, then, Western imperialism could be seen as neither a blind alley nor a crippling burden but as a promise delayed, an opportunity deferred.

It goes without saying that Western businessmen did not provide these benefits in a spirit of altruism; that is not how capitalism works. But while Americans did reap some profits in China, it was never as much as either boosters of China trade or its critics would suppose. From 1890 to 1920, China represented just 3.5 percent of U.S. exports and 1.4 percent of U.S. foreign investment. For Britain, businessmen were the driving force behind its China policy; but in the case of America, it was the missionaries who were more important. This hardly supports the theories of a Smedley Butler that all military policy is driven by pursuit of material gain.

What is most striking is how long the American military stayed in China—and how successfully. The sinking of the *Panay* was the only military disaster suffered by the United States during almost a century of peacekeeping duty in the Celestial Kingdom, from the 1840s to 1941. That the mission went so smoothly is, in retrospect, remarkable. There were seldom more than a handful of U.S. sailors, soldiers, and marines on the China station, far from home, and surrounded by all manner of potential enemies: various Chinese armed forces, the militaries of other foreign powers, and of course the Chinese people themselves, 400 million strong in the early twentieth century, who, if aroused, easily could have expelled the small number of intruders from their midst.

The U.S. armed forces in China were never adequate to deal with a determined foe. They could perform only a policing role, and that mainly through bluff and swagger. There is no shortage of examples in American history of similar missions that came to a sad end; one thinks of the marines being blown up in their Beirut barracks in 1983. In China, by contrast, the Americans' bluff worked almost until the very end.

Part Three

SUPERPOWER

12

LESSONS LEARNED
The Small Wars Manual

With the end of the mission to China, a chapter in American military history had come to a close. The nation now girded itself for an epic, globe-spanning struggle that would demand the conscription of millions of soldiers and total mobilization of the home front, a struggle that would not end until the enemy's unconditional surrender. It was a far cry from the small, cheap, limited interventions routinely undertaken by professional soldiers on the fringes of America's prewar empire. After the signing of the armistice on the deck of the battleship *Missouri* in Tokyo Harbor on September 2, 1945, Americans had only the briefest interlude to savor peace before being plunged into the maelstrom of another major war, this one on the Korean peninsula, part of a larger struggle against communism that would consume the nation's energies for more than four decades. There would still be a few small wars—U.S. troops were landed, for instance, in Lebanon in 1958 and the Dominican Republic in 1965, both times at the behest of the local government, both times successfully—but for the most part the nation's preferred method of waging the Cold War was through covert operations.

In actions that harked back to William Eaton's attempts to overthrow the pasha of Tripoli in 1805, America's secret agents helped topple left-leaning governments in countries ranging from Guatemala to Iran. (Sometimes, as in the landing at Cuba's Bay of Pigs in 1961, such efforts went spectacularly awry.) And in operations that recalled the establishment of constabularies in the

Philippines, Cuba, Haiti, the Dominican Republic, and Nicaragua, U.S. military advisers helped train government forces in the 1940s and 1950s to put down communist insurgencies in countries ranging from Greece to the Philippines. Many of these interventions involved small war methods, but they did not, for the most part, call on American troops, save for scattered advisers.

This left the American armed forces free to concentrate on their primary mission—preparing to wage World War III. Dwight D. Eisenhower, army general turned president, instituted a "New Look" for American strategy that eschewed an ability to fight limited wars in favor of escalating any conflict through the use of atomic weapons, an area in which the U.S. then had a preponderance of power.

The armed forces, the army especially, were not happy with the doctrine of "massive retaliation," which minimized their conventional war-fighting role. But this in no way implied that the army wanted to engage in small wars. Soldiers preferred World War II-style conflict that was limited only in the sense that it did not involve strategic nuclear weapons. For the most part they were glad to be free of the headaches associated with lower-intensity conflicts, in which both the means and ends were usually severely circumscribed. These interventions had seldom been popular with those called upon to carry them out. It should not be hard to see why. True, many of these operations offer some chance of glory, an opportunity eagerly seized by the likes of Stephen Decatur, Frederick Funston, and Herman Hanneken. But such glory is more fleeting than most. Whereas the generals who lead big armies in big wars—from Sherman to Schwartzkopf—remain household names, who now remembers Smedley Butler, John Rodgers, or J. Franklin Bell?

Professional soldiers naturally want to prove their mettle fighting against other professional soldiers. True warriors would like nothing better than to take part in a clash of armies on empty plains or fleets on the high seas or airplanes in the blue skies, all spheres where martial skill can be displayed in its "pure" form, without worrying about nettlesome political complications. The primary characteristic of small wars is that there is no obvious field of battle; there are only areas to be controlled, civilians to be protected, hidden foes to be subdued. Soldiers must figure out who the enemy is before killing him; make a mistake and, like Major Littleton W. T. Waller or later Lieutenant William Calley, you are likely to face a court-martial. There is little satisfaction in winning such a war—would the New York Yankees rejoice after beating a Little League team?—but much grief if you lose, as the army found out after Russia in 1919 and in Vietnam. Even if you do everything right, what is your reward? Often it means staying and assuming unfamiliar and probably unwelcome duties as administrators and tax collectors, road builders and agricultural advisers, police officers and judges, garbage collectors and public health workers. Most professional soldiers have no desire to be politicians.

Small wonder then that most military services conceive their role in big war terms—closing with and annihilating the armed forces of the enemy. Many professional soldiers share the disdain of Antoine-Henri Jomini, the Swiss-born military strategist of the nineteenth century, who wrote that wars involving nonprofessional combatants were "dangerous and deplorable," because "they always arouse violent passions that make them spiteful, cruel, terrible." Jomini's considered view was that professional soldiers should simply avoid this sort of "organized assassination" in favor of more "chivalresque" violence. That seems to be the view of many American officers too.

Even though its chief occupation throughout much of the nineteenth century was fighting Indians, the army never bothered to develop a doctrine of anti-guerrilla warfare because the generals always viewed the Indian Wars as a temporary diversion from their "real" job—preparing to fight a conventional army. Likewise, the army made little attempt to draw lessons from its operations against Philippine *insurrectos*, Mexican Villistas, and Russian Bolsheviks—not "real" wars either. The navy, too, despite its long-standing role in gunboat diplomacy, preferred to think of its mission as sinking enemy fleets, a role laid out by the apostle of sea power, Alfred Thayer Mahan. Even in the Marine Corps, which became known in the early years of the twentieth century as "State Department troops," many longed for the greater glory of major wars. The marines jumped at the chance to fight in World War I, and in the interwar period marine strategists developed amphibious warfare techniques that would be employed in the Pacific theater during World War II.

In the history of the American military there have of course been some exceptions to the big war mindset—a handful of Americans, such as Francis Marion (the Swamp Fox) and John Singleton Mosby (of Mosby's Rangers), who relished the role of guerrillas, and a few, like the Indian-fighters Nelson Miles and George Crook and the communist-fighter Edward Lansdale, who showed talent and aptitude for anti-guerrilla warfare. But the first military service to view counterinsurgency and other forms of small war fighting as an integral part of its mission was the Marine Corps. Based on their own experiences in the early years of the twentieth century, and on a handbook that grew out of Britain's colonial experience, the marines in the 1930s wrote *The Small Wars Manual.*

Much of this book consists of now-archaic tactical advice—the best way to load a mule, for instance, complete with helpful illustrations—but, especially in its early chapters, the manual is an unparalleled exposition of the theory of small wars.

The *Small Wars Manual* begins with a definition: "As applied to the United States, small wars are operations undertaken under executive authority, wherein military force is combined with diplomatic pressure in the internal or external affairs of another state whose government is unstable, inadequate or unsatisfactory for the preservation of life and of such interests as are determined by the foreign policy of our Nation." While the army might view such missions as an unwelcome diversion from its main business, the manual states that "small wars represent the normal and frequent operations of the Marine Corps."

How do small wars differ from big? "In a major war, the mission assigned to the armed forces is usually unequivocal—the defeat and destruction of the hostile forces," the manual states. "This is seldom true in small wars." In these encounters, U.S. forces have a more ambiguous mission: "to establish and maintain law and order by supporting or replacing the civil government in countries or areas in which the interests of the United States have been placed in jeopardy."

In trying to achieve these vague objectives, the nation's civilian authorities do not simply set the armed forces free to do whatever they feel necessary. "In small wars, diplomacy has not ceased to function and the State Department exercises a constant and controlling influence over the military operations." Nor do these missions rely on the military's traditional approach: using maximum firepower to blast the enemy into oblivion. Instead the *Small Wars Manual* recommends trying to achieve U.S. objectives "with the minimum of troops, in fact, with nothing more than a demonstration of force if that is all that is necessary and reasonably sufficient."

The manual is keenly aware of the limits of military power in general. "Peace and industry cannot be restored permanently without appropriate provisions for the economic welfare of the people," the manual says. In keeping with this attitude, the manual suggests that the "hatred of the enemy" usually inculcated among troops in major wars is entirely inappropriate in these circumstances. "In small wars, tolerance, sympathy and kindness should be the keynote to our relationship with the mass of the population."

Such operations are harder, in many ways, than a military's traditional duty. After all, "in small wars no defined battle front exists and the theater of operations may be the whole length and breadth of the land." U.S. troops are sent out on policing functions, where the main task is simply to figure out who the enemy is. American soldiers will be facing "members of native forces [who] will suddenly become innocent peasant workers when it suits their fancy and convenience." The enemy will always have better intelligence and knowledge of the countryside than the Americans will—and they can choose the best moment to ambush small American detachments. "It will be difficult and hazardous to wage war successfully under such circumstances," the *Small Wars Manual* warns. And time consuming: Such operations can drag on indefinitely and never result in a clear outcome such as Appomattox. Yet as the manual makes clear, there is no alternative. Small wars cannot be fought with big war methods.

The final edition of the *Small Wars Manual* was published at the most inopportune of times, 1940. It seemed to have little application to World War II, though what is often forgotten is that along with the clash of big armies the 1939–1945 conflict saw plenty of guerrilla operations by forces as disparate as the Yugoslav partisans and the French *maquis*—not to mention America's own Office of Strategic Services (OSS), forerunner of the Central Intelligence Agency (CIA). By the time America found itself embroiled in a small war in a place called Vietnam, however, the *Small Wars Manual* and its lessons had been all but forgotten.

13

LESSONS UNLEARNED
Vietnam, 1959–1975

The marines landed on Monday morning, March 8, 1965, splashing ashore through the heavy surf of the South China Sea onto the hot beaches just north of Danang, South Vietnam's second-largest city. They were part of a contingent of 3,500 men assigned to provide security for an American airbase being used to stage bombing raids against North Vietnam. The troops, in full battle rig, accompanied by M-48 medium tanks and self-propelled artillery, were ready for trouble. "We thought there was a gook behind every tree and a land mine every three feet," a private recalled. Instead, they were met by the mayor of Danang, who delivered a brief speech, and some schoolgirls who placed flowered wreaths around their necks and held up a sign proclaiming: "Welcome to the Gallant Marines."

As with most landings of marines abroad, the public back home barely noticed. It might as well have been Haiti, 1916, or Nicaragua, 1912. The *New York Times* ran a front-page photo of marines rushing off a landing craft—an image that could have been taken straight from the John Wayne classic *Sands of Iwo Jima*—but it only warranted a small story on an inside page. Dr. Martin Luther King Jr.'s planned march on Selma, Alabama, was much bigger news that day, as was a new crime control package proposed by President Lyndon Johnson. The landing at Danang has acquired great significance in retrospect. Those marines were part of the first U.S. combat unit—the 9th Marine Expeditionary Brigade—to land in Vietnam. The first of almost 3 million men (though never more than 540,000 at one time) who would fight and bleed and, 58,000 of them, die, in the jungles and mountains and paddies of South Vietnam in a futile crusade to keep a communist dictatorship from extending its grip from Hanoi to Saigon.

The conflict in Vietnam—the longest in American history and one of the costliest—might seem a curious candidate for inclusion in a book about "small wars." But a discussion of what occurred in Indochina between 1959 and 1975 is unavoidable. "Small wars" refers more to a style of warfare—clashes with guerrilla or irregular forces—than to the scale of combat. For the American armed forces, Vietnam would be the ultimate test of their ability to fight this kind of unconventional conflict. Their failure to rise to the challenge would have profound consequences for U.S. military policy in the decades to come, shaping the armed forces' approach to future small wars. One cannot understand what followed—the small wars of the 1990s, for instance—without understanding what happened in Southeast Asia. Nor can one gain a proper appreciation for the achievements of America's small war soldiers of the past— the Butlers and Hannekens and Pullers—without seeing what happened when all their hard-won experience, their painfully accumulated battle lore, was tossed away as casually as a spent bullet casing.

Bad Advice

The origins of America's involvement in Vietnam continue to spark debate, and no doubt will for generations to come. That is not our primary concern here. Suffice it to say that after the French pulled out in 1954, having lost the pivotal battle of Dienbienphu, Vietnam was split between a Communist government in Hanoi led by Ho Chi Minh and a non-Communist one in Saigon led by Ngo Dinh Diem. The former aligned with Moscow and Peking, the latter with Washington. Ho Chi Minh and his colleagues in the North Vietnamese Politburo spent a few years consolidating their rule over the North—which involved a reign of terror against "enemies of the people"—before undertaking the task of "liberating" the South and reunifying the country. On May 13, 1959, the 15th Plenum of the Party Central Committee voted to resume *dau tranh vu trang* (armed struggle) in the South. But it did not launch an outright invasion, as North Korea had invaded South Korea in 1950. Instead, trained cadres— southerners who had gone north in 1954—began infiltrating South Vietnam to organize a secret Communist infrastructure, building a political base for guerrilla war. The following year, Hanoi announced the formation of the National

Liberation Front, a front group for the Communist effort to conquer the South. The People's Liberation Armed Forces—popularly known as the Vietcong— launched a campaign of assassination and intimidation aimed at officials of the Saigon government. Before long they were making inroads in the Mekong Delta, the Highlands, the coastal plains—almost everywhere in the South outside the major cities.

President John F. Kennedy had come to office pledging "to bear any burden, meet any hardship, support any friend and oppose any foe to assure the survival and success of liberty." The front line of the battle appeared to be in Southeast Asia. But Kennedy and his advisers, remembering the unhappy, bloody stalemate on the Korean Peninsula, were afraid of getting embroiled in another land war in Asia. Instead of sending combat troops, Kennedy sent more aid to the Diem government, along with an increasing number of military advisers. The advisers, some piloting U.S.-supplied helicopters, found themselves drawn into combat operations against the Vietcong, and the U.S. began suffering its first casualties; 32 Americans died in combat in 1961 and 1962.

By 1963 there were 12,000 U.S. military advisers in the South; a year later the figure had almost doubled, to 23,000. Superficially the advisers' work resembled that of the Americans who trained native constabularies in the Philippines, Haiti, the Dominican Republic, and elsewhere. But there were crucial differences that would have important long-term ramifications. The marines who had served as advisers in the Caribbean had created constabularies—part army, part police force—that emphasized internal defense. In Vietnam, by contrast, U.S. advisers organized a miniature version of their own armed forces, complete with heavy armor, artillery, air force, navy, marines, rangers. The goal was to create a force capable of fighting a conventional conflict, because the advisers figured that the most likely threat to the South would come from a Korean War-style invasion. In the late 1950s this was not an unreasonable bet, but it turned out to be wrong. Disastrously wrong. The main challenge to Saigon would come not from regular armies but from guerrillas. Their American advisers did not prepare the South Vietnamese soldiers for this challenge.

What made things worse was another major difference between the U.S. role in the Banana Wars and in Vietnam. In the Caribbean, and in the Philippines, U.S. officers had been in direct command of locally recruited soldiers. Likewise, during the Korean War, South Korean forces reported to U.S. commanders, who had the power to remove incompetent or corrupt officers. In Vietnam that was not in the cards. Washington did not want to ask for American field command, and Saigon would not grant it, because to do so would have given credence to the communist claim that the Americans were "neocolonialists" come to replace the French. As a result, command of the South Vietnamese armed forces was turned over to officers usually chosen less for their professional competence than for their political allegiance to, and often family links with, the ruling oligarchy.

The combination of inappropriate training and poor leadership severely hobbled the South Vietnamese armed forces. When the South Vietnamese army mounted big-unit operations in pursuit of the Vietcong, the guerrillas usually gave them the slip as easily as ants evading elephants. On those few occasions when they did manage to bring the Vietcong to battle, the South Vietnamese army suffered humiliating defeats. The major effect of these operations was to expend a great deal of firepower, killing innocent civilians and making fresh converts to the Communist cause. "Guerrilla warfare requires the utmost discrimination in killing," Lieutenant Colonel John Paul Vann, an outspoken American adviser, wrote in a 1963 briefing intended for the Joint Chiefs of Staff. "Every time we killed an innocent person we lost ground in our battle to win the people." But Vann's army superiors refused to listen; his briefing to the Joint Chiefs was canceled.

Ngo Dinh Diem knew that more had to be done. At the urging of the local CIA station and Sir Robert Thompson, a British counterinsurgency expert, he attempted to implement a political agenda to deny the Communists control of the countryside. The centerpiece of his efforts was a program designed to fortify local villages for self-defense, called Strategic Hamlets. A promising idea, it did not get far, in part because the bulk of the South Vietnamese army was diverted to conventional operations, in part because of the ineffectiveness of the Saigon regime. Still, it is possible that Diem's initiatives might have shown greater success over time, were time not running out for Diem himself.

The Kennedy administration increasingly viewed Diem as a liability in the struggle against the communists. It did not help that Buddhist monks were immolating themselves in the streets of Saigon to protest against the Catholic-led regime. Such heavily publicized embarrassments reinforced American officials' tendency to accentuate the negative about Diem—he was an authoritarian ruler with a penchant for rigging elections and squelching dissent—while ignoring his strong nationalist credentials and the lack of credible alternatives. In early November 1963 South Vietnamese army officers, acting with the tacit encouragement of the U.S. government, overthrew and murdered Diem and his brother. Three weeks later Kennedy, too, would lie dead, felled by an assassin's bullet in Dallas. Although Lyndon Baines Johnson quickly emerged as a strong—if often insecure, bombastic, and deceitful—successor in Washington, the Saigon government was left rudderless. One president succeeded another with dizzying rapidity, each worried more about holding onto power than about stopping the Communists. It took three long years before Nguyen Van Theiu finally emerged as the next strongman of the South.

Hanoi was delighted. A National Liberation Front official history calls the coups "gifts from heaven for us." The communists took advantage of the situation, infiltrating more men south along the Ho Chi Minh Trail, a network of trails and roads that ran parallel to South Vietnam through the adjoining nations of Laos and Cambodia. Starting in April 1964, those transiting the trail included regular North Vietnamese soldiers armed with mortars, rocket launchers, automatic rifles, and machine guns. Working in close cooperation with the Vietcong they stepped up their attacks, including terrorist strikes in Saigon aimed at American targets. The South Vietnamese armed forces seemed powerless before this onslaught. Some of his advisers urged Johnson to introduce U.S. combat troops. But he had an election to win, and a Great Society to run, so he hesitated—until a curious incident gave him an excuse to act.

On August 2, 1964, North Vietnamese patrol boats attacked the *Maddox*, a U.S. destroyer operating in the Gulf of Tonkin on a mission to gather intelligence and support South Vietnamese commando raids against the North. The next day the *Maddox* and another destroyer, the *C. Turner Joy*, reported being attacked again. The *Maddox*'s skipper concluded afterward that the second attack was probably a phantom, which he attributed to "freak weather" and an "overeager" young sonar technician. Nevertheless the president seized on this incident to seek from Congress authorization to use whatever force he deemed necessary to protect South Vietnam and America's other allies in Southeast Asia.

The Gulf of Tonkin resolution, which was approved unanimously by the House and with only two dissenting votes in the Senate, has since been attacked by numerous commentators on two somewhat contradictory grounds. First, it is alleged, Johnson tricked Congress, luring America into Vietnam by a deception. Second, it is charged, he did not go far enough; he should have asked for a full-fledged declaration of war. Neither accusation stands up to close scrutiny. While the second Gulf of Tonkin attack probably did not occur, the larger reason why Congress approved the resolution was very real: Communist fighters controlled by Hanoi were indeed trying to conquer a U.S. ally, South Vietnam. Did this require a declaration of war? Not if history is any guide. As we have seen, numerous American presidents had committed U.S. armed forces to battle in the past without even this much congressional authorization. Declarations of war—voted against Britain in 1812, Mexico in 1846, Spain in 1898, the Central Powers in 1917, the Axis in 1941—were the exception, not the norm, when the U.S. committed its armed forces to combat overseas.

In retaliation for the Gulf of Tonkin incident, Johnson ordered limited air strikes against North Vietnam. But with an election looming, he was in no hurry to get any more deeply involved in Vietnam. Once he had won a landslide victory over Barry Goldwater in November 1964, the gloves could come off. An initial series of bombing strikes called Flaming Dart soon turned into a prolonged air campaign, known as Rolling Thunder, aimed at North Vietnam and at infiltration routes in Laos.

Rolling Thunder lasted for three and a half years—March 1965 to November 1968. But its duration was the only resemblance between it and the strategic bombing that had devastated German and Japanese cities in World War II. Rolling Thunder was a limited bombing campaign of "slowly ascending" escalation designed to bring the North Vietnamese to the negotiating table. Johnson and his secretary of defense, Robert McNamara, personally decided what targets would be hit and what munitions would be dropped. "They can't even bomb an outhouse without my approval," the president bragged.

The most important targets were placed off-limits. Johnson refused to strike Hanoi, North Vietnam's capital; Haiphong, its most important harbor; the overland supply routes from China; or the Red River dikes, destruction of which could have flooded the area around Hanoi and killed hundreds of thousands, possibly millions, of civilians. (By contrast, U.S. warplanes in the Korean War had destroyed North Korea's dike system, with devastating results.) The bombing was punctuated by numerous pauses designed to signal to North Vietnam, and the world, Washington's goodwill. Instead, Hanoi read this (rightly) as a sign of the Johnson administration's weakness and irresolution. The North Vietnamese used bombing pauses to rebuild and to improve their air defenses, which took a growing toll on American fliers as the years went by. It is a sign of Rolling Thunder's futility that—although the operation dropped roughly 800 tons of bombs a day for three and a half years—imports reaching North Vietnam by sea more than doubled during this period. Henry Kissinger's verdict rings true: The bombing campaign was "powerful enough to mobilize world opinion against us but too half-hearted and gradual to be decisive."

Limited as it was, Rolling Thunder could not be carried out by jets operating from aircraft carriers alone. The U.S. Air Force needed bases in South

Vietnam—bases that would be vulnerable to enemy attack. The danger was vividly demonstrated on February 7, 1965, when the Vietcong struck a U.S. airfield in the Highlands, in Pleiku, destroying 10 aircraft, wounding more than 100 Americans, and killing eight. This led President Johnson to land marines to protect the largest U.S. airbase, at Danang.

General William Westmoreland, head of the U.S. Military Assistance Command, Vietnam, wasted little time in asking for more troops—and for expanding their mission beyond base security. By June 1965, he wanted 44 "maneuver" battalions—200,000 men—available for offensive operations. The Joint Chiefs of Staff eagerly backed him up, and President Johnson approved the request at the end of July. The alternative, he feared, was a communist victory, and he was not about to go down in history as another president who had "lost" an Asian country to communism, as Truman had "lost" China. Not even a "damn little pissant country," as he called Vietnam.

Now that U.S. combat troops were being introduced, the question was, How would they be used? The answer rested in large part with a tall, handsome, thick-browed officer who sported six rows of decorations on his chest and radiated a "can-do" attitude.

A Clash of Strategies

It is hard not to sympathize just a bit with William Childs Westmoreland, one of the great tragic figures in American military history. A southern aristocrat, born into a wealthy South Carolina family, he went on to West Point where, like Robert E. Lee, John J. Pershing, and Douglas MacArthur before him, he attained the honor of becoming first captain of cadets. Westy entered World War II a first lieutenant and emerged a colonel, having fought with the 9th Infantry Division in North Africa, Sicily, Normandy, the Bulge, Remagen. Identified as one of the army's brightest young officers, he won his first star in Korea. In 1958 came command of the 101st Airborne Division, followed by the prestigious post of superintendent of the U.S. Military Academy at West Point (again following in MacArthur's footsteps). It was at West Point that he suffered the first blot on his heretofore spotless record: He failed to sign up Vince Lombardi as the head football coach. The candidate whom he hired produced a losing record, much to the chagrin of such West Point alumni as Dwight Eisenhower and Douglas MacArthur. But that was his only slip-up. Westy was the army's Golden Boy, and so he was sent to the scene of the action. If the action had been a replay of World War II or Korea he would no doubt have emerged a hero, perhaps even one of the all-time greats. Instead he was sent to fight a war for which nothing in his training or experience had prepared him.

Initially assigned as deputy commander of the U.S. Military Assistance Command, Vietnam, Westmoreland, by now nearly 50 years old, took over in 1964 as the senior U.S. officer in the country. It was his job to figure out how to defeat the Vietnamese Communists. No easy task, that. The obvious solution, from the Pentagon's perspective, would have been to invade the North and make Ho Chi Minh cry "uncle." But that was off the table. Johnson was afraid that an invasion of the North would divert attention from his Great Society programs and might even spark a war with China—a concern that, as newly released documents reveal, was well-founded. For similar reasons, the president ruled out cutting the Ho Chi Minh Trail by occupying Laos, or even inflicting unlimited punishment from the air against North Vietnam. Westmoreland was discouraged by these limitations but undaunted. He simply resolved to fight the war his way within the parameters laid down for him. And his way was the army way, the American way, the World War II way: Find the enemy, fix him in place, and annihilate him with withering firepower.

John F. Kennedy had been a great enthusiast for low-intensity conflict. He changed the nation's official military strategy from Massive Retaliation to Flexible Response, pledging to meet aggression at any level without instantly hauling out nuclear weapons. As part of this policy (and over the objections of the brass), he bestowed the green beret on the Special Forces and expanded their budget. The army was happy to have more funding, but it adamantly resisted attempts to move its focus away from preparing for a conventional conflict in Europe. The generals had no intention of letting a bunch of Harvard whiz kids tamper with the formula that had won World War II. Kennedy tried to overcome this resistance, but he was unable to effect any fundamental reform before his death, and Johnson did not share his interest in the subject.

Westmoreland was one of the pillars of the army establishment that had successfully resisted fundamental change. He was a by-the-book man—and his book was not the *Small Wars Manual*. The army's *Field Manual of Operations* preached that "wars can be won only by offensive action," and that was precisely what Westmoreland set out to do. He organized his forces for large-unit "search and destroy" missions designed to root out and annihilate the enemy in the spooky terrain of the Highlands, "a run of erratic mountain ranges, gnarled valleys, jungled ravines and abrupt plains" that stretched across the spine of Vietnam. Westmoreland wanted "a well-balanced, hard-hitting force designed to fight in sustained combat and just grind away against the enemy on a sustained basis." The task of pacification—of preventing the Communists from gaining control of the South's people—he relegated to the South Vietnamese army, which, being created in the U.S. Army's own image, had no enthusiasm for the job either. Thus the really hard, vital work of keeping the Vietcong out of the South's population centers was left for the most part to the ill-equipped, ill-trained South Vietnamese militia, who did not even have access to modern rifles.

Never mind that search-and-destroy tactics had been attempted by the South Vietnamese armed forces for years on the advice of their American trainers—with scant success. Westmoreland and other American generals convinced themselves that the problem lay with the South Vietnamese army, not with its doctrine and force structure. If only the Americans could implement the same strategy with more firepower, more mobility, more gusto, victory would be theirs. At a press conference, Westmoreland was asked what the answer to counterinsurgency was. His one-word reply: "Firepower."

That would have been the right answer if South Vietnam were facing a conventional invasion, but it was not. "People's war," as preached by Mao Tse-tung and waged by General Vo Nguyen Giap, commander of the North Vietnamese armed forces, was designed to avoid a test of the enemy's strength. The struggle of "national liberation" progressed through three phases. Phase 1: send out loyal cadres to propagandize the peasants and create in the countryside "a protective belt of sympathizers willing to supply food, recruits, and information." Phase 2: launch a protracted guerrilla struggle, during which "collaborationists and 'reactionary elements' are liquidated" and "vulnerable military and police outposts" are ambushed. Once the government has been sufficiently weakened, it is time for phase 3: the formation of conventional armies (main forces) that, in conjunction with a general popular uprising, will finish off the enemy and create a "people's republic."

Westmoreland was well aware of all this; his bedside reading included Mao Tse-tung's Little Red Book on guerrilla warfare. But with the clarity of hindsight, it is obvious that he misjudged the situation in 1965. He thought the Communists were progressing to phase 3—conventional war—whereas in reality Hanoi was still for the most part in phase 2—guerrilla war. (The North did escalate to phase 3 in 1968, 1972, and 1975.) His mistake was understandable because starting in 1965, North Vietnamese army units *were* infiltrating the South. But the communists were placing the bulk of their efforts elsewhere. In 1966 there were only 38,000 People's Army of North Vietnam soldiers in the South, while the Vietcong, most of them southerners, numbered at least 220,000. (North Vietnamese did not dominate the ranks of Communist forces in the South until after 1968.) Moreover, most Communist main force units used essentially guerrilla-style, hit-and-run tactics. U.S. military studies showed that the number of Communist attacks in battalion size or greater actually *decreased* between 1965 and 1966—from an average of 9.7 per month in the final quarter of 1965 to 1.3 per month in the final quarter of 1966. The number of small-scale attacks jumped 150 percent during this period.

Because the Communists were still in phase 2, the Ho Chi Minh Trail did not loom as large in reality as it did in Westmoreland's calculations. He was desperate to close this supply conduit, and U.S. forces expended vast amounts of munitions in a futile attempt to achieve this goal. But the Vietcong did not need much aid from the North; most of their supplies and manpower were appropriated from peasants in the South. A 1965 CIA study estimated that the Vietcong needed no more than 12 tons a day of supplies from outside—an amount that, in U.S. terms, could be carried in one tractor-trailer rig or 15 pickup trucks.

There was little hope that Westmoreland's conventional strategy could stop this guerrilla threat. More likely his approach would simply wear down the U.S. forces—just what General Giap was counting on.

From the start, this strategy had a number of critics, primarily officials from the CIA, the marines, and the State Department, along with guerrilla warfare experts such as Air Force General Edward Lansdale and Sir Robert Thompson, as well as a handful of renegade army officers such as John Paul Vann. They urged Washington to adopt the methods employed by the Marine Corps in the past, the tactics immortalized in the *Small Wars Manual*, but they did not get very far.

Marine Major General Victor H. Krulak later recalled his frustrations in lobbying for a "spreading inkblot" strategy—expanding American control slowly from the seacoast by pacifying one hamlet after another, as the U.S. had done in the Philippines six decades before. Although not physically imposing (he was just five feet five, 138 pounds, so small that he needed an exemption from physical requirements to obtain his commission), "Brute" Krulak was a first-rate fighter and thinker. His nickname derived from his days at the Naval Academy, when he had been a ferocious wrestler despite his diminutive size. In the late 1930s, he served with the 4th Marines in Shanghai, where he helped develop a type of landing craft that was widely employed during World War II. Then he won a Navy Cross, the service's second-highest decoration, fighting the Japanese in the Pacific. Along the way, he had been steeped in the Corps' small wars tradition, learning from, and serving alongside, many of the veterans of Haiti, the Dominican Republic, and Nicaragua. The plan he developed for winning in Vietnam drew on those experiences.

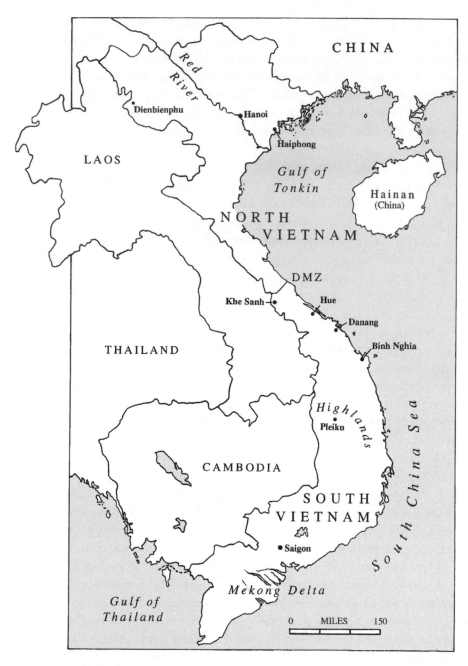

MAP 13.1   Indochina, circa 1965

Under his scheme, which was similar to that of other counterinsurgency experts, U.S. forces would concentrate on cutting off the Vietcong from the population centers along the Mekong Delta and the coastal plain, where most of the South Vietnamese population was located. Eighty percent of the people, he observed, lived in 10 percent of the country, the bulk of them in small farming communities. The key to winning the war was to provide security for these villagers, to reassure them that it was safe to side with the government and to resist the Vietcong's attempts to "tax" them, seek information from them, and enlist their young men to carry arms against the government. It would be virtually impossible to hunt down and eliminate the communist forces in their jungle lairs, but if the U.S. could cut them off from the civilian population, they would wither away. Krulak liked to quote General Giap: "Without the people we have no information. . . . They hide us, protect us, feed us and tend our wounded."

Denying the Vietcong access to the people would call for few big-unit operations. It would take aggressive small-unit foot patrolling, especially at night, to gather intelligence and disrupt guerrilla operation. Above all, it would mean training local people to defend themselves. That was the only way to ensure the long-term security of the country. U.S. forces could not totally forgo big-unit operations; they would sometimes be necessary to expel enemy main forces from a region and prevent them from coming back. But the chief thrust had to be on pacification, not search-and-destroy. Krulak wanted to combine this pacification strategy with the bombing and mining of Haiphong harbor, the entry point for much of the North's war materiel.

In December 1965, less than a year after the first U.S. combat troops had landed in South Vietnam, Krulak sat down in his office, situated on a mountain overlooking Pearl Harbor, and wrote a 17-page "strategic appraisal" in which he pointed out the futility of pursuing a conventional strategy. Gaining possession of the Highlands—where Westmoreland was focusing his efforts—was pointless, Krulak argued, because the people and the food in South Vietnam were located on the coastal plain. "A key point is this:" he wrote, "the conflict between the North Vietnamese/hard core Vietcong, on the one hand, and the U.S. on the other, could move to another planet today and we would not have won the war. On the other hand, if the subversion and guerrilla efforts were to disappear, the war would soon collapse, as the enemy would be denied food, sanctuary and intelligence."

Krulak, then the commander of the Fleet Marine Force, Pacific, and the third-ranking general in the entire Corps, took his memo to Washington in an attempt to win over the U.S. government to his view. Brute was no naïf when it came to Beltway politics. He had known John F. Kennedy from World War II and had become friendly with Bobby Kennedy during a previous assignment as special assistant to the Joint Chiefs of Staff and the secretary of defense for counterinsurgency. He instantly got in to see Robert McNamara, but the defense secretary was not very receptive to his views. "Why don't you talk to Governor Harriman?" he suggested, palming him off on the assistant secretary of state for Far Eastern affairs.

They met for lunch at W. Averell Harriman's Georgetown mansion. Over the soup course, Krulak complained about all the munitions being wasted in fruitless bombing of the Ho Chi Minh Trail. Then he got around to his plan of action, beginning with a proposal to "destroy the port areas, mine the ports, destroy the rail lines, destroy power, fuel and heavy industry." Harriman wrinkled his forehead, waved a sterling silver soup spoon at him, and demanded, "Do you want a war with the Soviet Union or the Chinese?" End of conversation. (In fact, when the kind of bombing Krulak advocated was undertaken seven years later, no war with either the Soviet Union or China resulted.)

Krulak found the army establishment no more receptive. "Many people applauded the idea, among them army generals Maxwell Taylor and James Gavin," Brute recalled. "General Westmoreland told me, however, that while the ink blot idea seemed to be effective, we just didn't have time to do it that way. I suggested to him that we didn't have time to do it any other way; if we left the people to the enemy, glorious victories in the hinterland would be little more than blows in the air—and we would end up losing the war."

Which is exactly what happened.

The Big-Unit War

By 1968, the Free World forces (as they were known) consisted of 536,000 soldiers from the U.S., 66,000 from allied countries (Korea, Australia, New Zealand, Thailand, the Philippines), and 670,000 men in the armed forces and militia of South Vietnam. And still it was not enough.

Westmoreland sent his forces thrashing through the rainforests and mountains on big-unit search-and-destroy missions with fancy code names like Cedar Falls and Junction City. But "Charlie" would not cooperate. The Vietcong refused to play the *Wehrmacht* to Westmoreland's Patton. Even with extensive use of "vertical envelopment" by helicopter, the American forces seldom managed to pin down enough of the Vietcong to bring their overwhelming firepower to bear. Thanks to their agents and informants, the communists usually knew when the Americans were coming. The U.S. forces, on the other hand, were usually ignorant of enemy strengths and locations. On those rare occasions when the Vietcong were caught off guard, the Americans would helpfully announce their presence with the roar of helicopters arriving and the thump of artillery shells crashing down. Suitably alerted, the enemy would disappear, only to return a few days later, by which time they knew the G.I.'s would be gone. The official report on Junction City and Cedar Falls—two attempts to destroy communist base camps in 1967—concluded, "It was a sheer physical impossibility to keep him [the enemy] from slipping away whenever he wished if he were in terrain with which he was familiar—generally the case. The jungle was just too thick and too widespread to keep him from getting away."

U.S. soldiers never lost a battle, but neither did they manage to pin down enough of the enemy so that a victory meant something. The Vietcong had the initiative. They could either accept battle or not, carefully calculating how many casualties they could afford to lose. The U.S. military estimated in 1967 that 88 percent of all engagements were initiated by the enemy, clearly implying that the U.S. was fighting on the enemy's terms.

A large part of the problem was that the Pentagon did not field a force designed for counterinsurgency operations. Anti-guerrilla operations place a premium on highly skilled light infantry with a flair for dealing with civilians. The U.S. once had plenty of such soldiers, men like Smedley Butler and Chesty Puller who spent decades in the bush. By the 1960s, Butler was dead, Puller was in retirement, and such skills had been all but lost. Young American draftees in Vietnam had little training in counterinsurgency. By the time they learned the ropes they had departed, since soldiers rotated "in country" on one-year tours. As John Paul Vann quipped, "The United States has not been in Vietnam for nine years, but for one year nine times."

The situation was even worse among officers above the platoon level. Most of them served no more than six months with a field unit—a system designed to allow as many ambitious career officers as possible to "punch their ticket" in combat. In late June 1966, Colonel Harold Moore's tour as commander of the 1st Cavalry Division's 3rd Brigade ended while his men were engaged with the enemy. "It would have been criminal, in those circumstances, to relinquish command to a man who was still pissing Stateside water, and I flatly refused to do so," Moore recalled. But the change of command was delayed by only 10 days. A month later his successor made a mistake that the more battle-hardened Moore might have avoided. A mistake that cost 25 men their lives.

It was not that American soldiers in Vietnam were inferior to those in previous U.S. wars; many were just as dedicated, just as heroic as the G.I.s immortalized in *Saving Private Ryan* and *The Longest Day*. What they lacked was experience—experience that the army's perverse personnel policies ensured that they did not acquire. A Vietcong guerrilla, on the other hand, did not fight for six months or one year and then go home. Like U.S. servicemen in World War II, he served "for the duration"—or until he was killed.

The U.S. high command tried to make up for its shortcomings in jungle fighting by flexing America's industrial muscles. The disparity in technology between the two sides was so vast that it almost seemed as if the Jetsons were fighting the Flintstones. On the communist side were guerrillas in black "pajamas" and tire-tread sandals armed with homemade booby traps and perhaps AK-47 assault rifles or mortars. The U.S. side had sensors, ground radar, infrared equipment, defoliants, herbicides, cluster bombs, missiles of various varieties, tanks, armored personnel carriers, artillery of various calibers, naval vessels ranging from small patrol boats to giant nuclear-powered aircraft carriers, and of course all the aircraft—everything from B-52 bombers to UH-1 Huey helicopters to specially fitted C-47 airplanes known as Puff the Magic Dragon equipped with automatic machine guns capable of spitting out 6,000 rounds a minute. To say nothing of the infantryman's tools—M-16 and M-14 assault rifles, mortars, machine guns, flame throwers, grenade launchers, claymore mines, C-4 plastic explosives, rocket launchers.

Sometimes the search for a technological solution reached comic proportions. U.S. soldiers can't track down the Vietcong in the jungle? No problem. The XM-2 Personnel Detector will do the job. An electrochemical device carried on a helicopter, the XM-2 was supposed to detect the presence of human urine, on the assumption that where there's urine there must be Vietcong. But the Vietcong quickly learned how to "spoof" this device by hanging buckets of urine in trees. Another, equally futile idea was Defense Secretary Robert McNamara's proposal, borrowed from a Harvard law professor, to build an electronic fence to seal off South Vietnam from infiltration. The military nicknamed this plan the McNamara Line, in homage to another series of fortifications—the Maginot Line which had failed to protect France from German invasion in 1940. The McNamara Line, which was supposed to consist of barbed wire, mines, and acoustic and seismic detection devices, did not get very far.

But by and large the Pentagon's concepts of high-tech warfare *were* implemented. Much of what the military accomplished was simply miraculous. Deep-water ports and airfields, roads and supply depots, base camps and headquarters buildings, telephone networks and post exchanges (PXs)—all sprang into existence virtually overnight, thanks to the ingenuity and hard work of military engineers and civilian contractors. When not in the field, U.S. soldiers had access to hamburgers and ice cream, air conditioning and cold beer, movie theaters and bowling alleys. All this logistical effort tied down vast numbers of American personnel, however, leaving relatively few available for field service. "For every man who lived in a grubby bunker on a remote firebase," wrote one Vietnam veteran, "four or five slept between sheets and, likely as not, in air conditioned rooms."

Nothing was more impressive (or depressing, depending on one's perspective) than the sheer amount of firepower expended by U.S. forces. The U.S. dropped more than 8 million tons of bombs over Vietnam—twice the amount dropped by British and American bombers during all of World War II. This statistic is amazing enough, but more startling still is that at least half of these bombs, and almost all of the millions of tons of artillery shells fired by U.S. forces, were expended not over the enemy, North Vietnam, but over America's ally, South Vietnam.

Most air strikes and artillery bombardments were not conducted in support of U.S. ground forces in combat but were designed to interdict enemy supplies and personnel. U.S. artillery batteries were in the habit of routinely unleashing "harassment and interdiction" fire, just blazing away with no real target, in the hope of hitting some unseen enemy. H&I fire—which was supposed to be limited to "free-fire zones" devoid of civilians—accounted for nearly two-thirds of all artillery shells fired and bombs dropped in 1966. "The batteries fired their allotments every opportunity they had," said one U.S. artillery officer, "whether there was actually anything to shoot at or not."

All this firepower took a growing toll on the enemy and (though it was not usually intended) on civilians too. But it did little to draw the U.S. closer to victory. The Vietcong became expert at dodging American firepower, often by tunneling underground or hiding in the forest, sometimes by "hugging" U.S. troop formations so tightly that air strikes could not be called in without risking "friendly" casualties. The Vietcong even learned to turn American munitions against their makers, converting artillery shells into lethal mines and booby traps.

The courage of the American fighting man could not be doubted. But as the war progressed, it dawned on the grunts that their heroism was for naught. The war's glorious futility was exemplified by one senseless siege.

Khe Sanh was located in the far northwest corner of South Vietnam, near the border with Laos, a rugged, isolated wilderness of dark green mountains and dense jungle frequently soaked by heavy rainfall and often enshrouded by thick fog. The French had established a dirt airstrip on a plateau here, an outpost that was reachable from the coast only by a single narrow road. Westmoreland insisted on garrisoning Khe Sanh over the vociferous objections of Brute Krulak and other marine commanders, who pointed out that adequately defending it would require a commitment of manpower out of all proportion to its importance. No matter how large the U.S. garrison became, it would not cut the Ho Chi Minh Trail; Communist infiltrators could always bypass Khe Sanh to the south. While Westmoreland gave a number of reasons for garrisoning Khe Sanh, some marines began to suspect that his primary motive was this: He hoped that sticking a battalion of marines in the middle of the wilderness would draw large numbers of North Vietnamese troops, who could then be slaughtered by U.S. firepower.

Giap was happy to oblige, for he saw an opportunity to catch the Americans at a disadvantage. In April 1967 North Vietnamese units occupied the hills surrounding Khe Sanh, giving them direct line-of-sight into the U.S. base. The marines had no choice but to root them out, assaulting uphill straight into withering fire delivered from a cunningly constructed network of bunkers and trenches. To marine commanders this was distressingly similar to the bloodlettings they had suffered on one Pacific atoll after another two decades earlier. As in World War II, the marines took their objectives but at high cost—155 dead, 425 wounded in two and a half weeks of battles. Worse was to come.

Giap did not give up on Khe Sanh after his men were pushed off those hills. He simply moved in more regulars, 30,000 to 40,000 men in all. On January 20–21, 1968, they opened fire on the Khe Sanh base with their mortars and field pieces, signaling the start of a siege that would last 77 days. Westmoreland was delighted; he had his climactic battle at last. He airlifted in reinforcements—more than 6,000 U.S. Marines and 600 South Vietnamese Rangers were now defending this grimy fire base miles from anywhere. The outnumbered defenders had one advantage: virtually unlimited firepower from field artillery and airplanes, including the all-mighty B–52s, which would unleash more than 75,000 tons of explosives during the siege. Standing in Khe Sanh, "you could watch mortar bursts, orange and gray-smoking, over the tops of trees three and four kilometers away, and the heavier shelling from support bases further east along the DMZ, from Camp Carrol and the Rockpile, directed against suspected troop movements or NVA [North Vietnamese army] rocket and mortar positions. . . . And at night it was beautiful." Less beautiful were the shells the North Vietnamese sent in return. Downright ugly, from the marines' standpoint, was the fact that no amount of U.S. shelling could drive the communists off the nearby hills.

The marines had no choice but to burrow into their foxholes and hastily constructed bunkers to await relief. If it came in time. As January 1965 turned into February and February into March, the American press worked itself into a lather comparing Khe Sanh with Dien Bien Phu—another fortified garrison whose fall could drive another foreign army out of Vietnam. Losing Khe Sanh therefore became unthinkable. Westmoreland organized a 30,000-man expedition—Operation Pegasus—to relieve the marines. But by the time the cavalry arrived—in this case, the 1st Cavalry Division (Airmobile)—there was nothing left for them to do. The North Vietnamese attackers, having suffered heavy losses, simply disappeared back into the vast jungles whence they came.

It was a glorious victory, but to what end? Having held Khe Sanh, at an official cost of 205 American lives and 852 wounded, the marines promptly abandoned it, dynamiting their bunkers before they left. The entire battle had been simply a diversion from the real job—gaining control of the Vietnamese population centers. It eventually dawned on some American officers that Communist attacks in the Highlands were designed expressly to lure American troops away from the coastal areas. Giap later acknowledged this: "The primary emphasis," he said, is "to draw American units into remote areas and thereby facilitate control of the population of the lowlands." Westmoreland's strategy meshed perfectly with Giap's.

Desperate to come up with some measure of progress, Westmoreland turned to the infamous body counts. He thought that killing the enemy in great numbers would force them to give up the struggle, just as soon as he reached the "crossover point" when the enemy could no longer replace its casualties. It did not work out that way. North Vietnam was ruled by a dictatorship impervious to the pressure of popular opinion. Its leaders could tolerate staggering casualties with equanimity; after the war, Hanoi admitted losing 1.1 million dead and 300,000 missing, out of a population base of 20 million (North Vietnam and areas of the South controlled by the Communists in 1965). "The communist side in Indochina during the Vietnam War suffered proportional military losses equivalent for the United States in the mid-1990s of 13 million Americans killed and 3.9 million missing in action," a historian writes. "Put another way, in terms of military dead, the communist side sacrificed thirty-six times more of their own soldiers to unify Vietnam than did the Federal government to defeat the secessionist Confederate states." By contrast, American casualties of 58,000—roughly equal to the death toll on America's highways during one year, 1970—were enough to help drive the U.S. out of the war.

Westmoreland's "attrition" strategy worked, but in the wrong country. It broke the will not of North Vietnam but of America.

The Small War

The American war in Vietnam was not exclusively a big-unit, conventional boxing match. There was also "the other war," the pacification struggle, waged, on the American side, by an alphabet soup of agencies: the Central Intelligence Agency, the Agency for International Development, the U.S. Information Agency, the State Department. In 1967 the Johnson administration unified all these programs under CORDS (Civil Operations and Rural Development Support), a joint civil-military office headed by a pugnacious bureaucrat named Robert Komer. Many of the pacification programs concentrated on the struggle for "hearts and minds," spending millions of dollars to build schools and hospitals, resettle refugees, improve rice production, electrify rural areas, spread pro-government propaganda. As in the Philippines six decades before, it soon became obvious that, while development aid could make the people more friendly to the U.S. side, that was a long-range project. The most immediate need was to provide villagers with security against the guerrillas who came around demanding food, shelter, intelligence, draftees. This was a job for soldiers, and the precious few of them who were assigned this task achieved impressive results. The most notable example was the Combined Action Program begun in 1965.

This was a marine initiative modeled on the constabularies the Corps had founded in Haiti, the Dominican Republic, and Nicaragua. There was a direct line of descent, for after chasing Sandinistas around the wilds of Nicaragua in the 1930s Chesty Puller had become an instructor at the marines' Basic School, where one of his pupils was 2nd Lieutenant Lewis Walt, who as a general in Vietnam would go on to create CAP. "The Caribbean campaigns had many lessons applicable to Vietnam forty five years later," Walt wrote. Trying to apply those lessons, the marines organized CAP in 1965. Each Combined Action Platoon consisted of a marine rifle squad under the command of a sergeant—all volunteers chosen for their ability to work with the locals. The 12-15 marines were paired with a platoon from South Vietnam's Popular Forces militia, about 30 men from the local community. Together, the marines and militiamen worked on securing a village from the Vietcong, the Americans providing military know-how, the Vietnamese invaluable knowledge of local conditions.

The classic account of CAP in action remains "The Village," published by a marine captain named Francis J. West Jr. in 1972. It recounts the efforts of a

dozen marine volunteers who worked side by side with Popular Forces militiamen to pacify the coastal village of Binh Nghia, located 300 miles north of
Saigon and 400 miles south of Hanoi. When the marines first arrived in June
1966, Binh Nghia's seven hamlets, with their 5,000 inhabitants, were virtually
run by the Vietcong. The guerrillas could come and go at will, taxing the inhabitants to support themselves and killing any South Vietnamese officials who got
in their way. The Popular Forces who were supposed to be protecting the villagers were too scared to do anything.

The marines quickly changed that. A dozen of them—from Company C, 1st
Battalion, 7th Marines—arrived on June 10, 1966. They "left behind an
American base camp with its thick barbed wire and canvas cots, solid bunkers,
soupy ice cream and endless guard rosters." In Binh Nghia they lived no better
and no worse than the Popular Forces. The Americans and the Vietnamese
slept side by side in a ramshackle fort, ate the same food, smoked the same cigarettes, drew the same patrol assignments.

By day the marines and Popular Forces interacted in a friendly manner with
the villagers, winning their trust and confidence. By night, they patrolled
aggressively, often clashing with the Vietcong—70 firefights in their first couple of months. As they continued patrolling night after night, the marines' jun-
gle-warfare skills rapidly improved. Before long they were moving as stealthily,
and becoming as adept at setting ambushes, as their enemies. The Popular
Forces also experienced a rapid improvement in their skills and confidence,
thanks to the training they received from the marines. Together, their efforts
drove the Vietcong out of Binh Nghia.

Army critics worried that CAP's small marine outposts would be vulnerable
to annihilation by Communist main forces, which could throw hundreds of
attackers against a couple of dozen defenders. A valid concern. The Vietcong,
seeing the success the marines were having in Binh Nghia, decided that if they
did not want to be pushed out of the area altogether they would have to wipe
out the Americans. To achieve this task, the local guerrillas were reinforced by
a company from the 409th North Vietnamese Battalion—about 140 men in all.

On the night of September 14–15, 1965, the Communists struck the combined forces compound at Binh Nghia, known as Fort Page. After midnight,
North Vietnamese sappers expertly cut through a single strand of barbed wire
and plucked out sharpened wooden stakes designed to discourage unwelcome
visitors. Six of the marines were not home that night; they were out patrolling.
That left only six Americans and 12 PFs to hold the fort. The defenders, grown
complacent, were caught completely by surprise. Almost before they had time
to react, the Communist soldiers were inside the compound. Amid the din of

explosives and the chatter of automatic weapons fire, the marines were cut down, one by one. Their desperate resistance gave some of the PFs just enough time to huddle together and prevent the attackers from overrunning them too. Stymied, the Communist commander gave the order to retreat about an hour after the attack began. It was only then that a marine squad from a nearby base—supposed to act as Fort Page's emergency reserve—arrived, too late to do anything but succor the wounded and bury the dead. Six Vietnamese defenders and five Americans, including Sergeant Joseph Sullivan, the squad commander, were killed on that grim night. Only one American survived the attack, and he was badly wounded. (The attackers lost at least 15 men.)

"At first light," writes West, "General Lowell English, commander of the 1st Marine Division, entered the smoldering fort and called aside the six surviving marines who had been out on patrol that night. Speaking softly, he said they had a choice. They could stay or they could go." Given the chance to evacuate, the remaining marines refused. "We couldn't leave," one of the marine privates said. "What would we have said to the PFs after the way we pushed them to fight the Cong? We had to stay. There wasn't one of us who wanted to leave. The only people we wanted out was that worthless reaction squad that didn't get to the fort until after it was overrun."

How many other American soldiers would have volunteered to remain in a dangerous post in Vietnam if given the chance to leave? That the combined action marines wanted to stay was a testament to their morale and esprit de corps. Their close involvement with the daily life of Binh Nghia gave them a stake in the war; by contrast, most American soldiers had little friendly interaction with ordinary Vietnamese other than prostitutes, taxi drivers, and bartenders.

The CAP unit continued its mission at Binh Nghia with six replacements, volunteers all, and they enjoyed increasing success. The 409th North Vietnamese Battalion went back to the hills, and the local Vietcong had been too badly hurt in the attack on Fort Page to present much of a menace. As the dozen Americans continued with their efforts to integrate into village life, they came to feel "that the five thousand villagers accepted them. They ate in their houses, went to their parties, and to their funerals." No doubt their welcome was improved by the fact that no air or artillery strikes were called in on Binh Nghia. The combined action platoon skirmished at night with the Vietcong in the nearby rice paddies, but the villagers were largely spared the horrors of war.

Good relations with the villagers paid off. By the time another main force attack was organized on Fort Page, in March 1967, the defenders were ready, thanks to intelligence supplied by their informants. Knowing that an attack was on the way, their battalion commander ordered the combined action marines to evacuate before they were hit by some 300 enemy soldiers. The dozen marines gathered together and decided that they would not go—even if this meant risking a court-martial for disobeying orders. "I'm going to stay here and blast them," vowed one private. "They're not getting *this* fort. They're not getting *this* ville." And they did not. After one of the Communist scouts was detected and killed by an alert Popular Forces militiaman, the rest of the main force scuttled away, knowing that the defenders were on their guard.

The Communists never again seriously threatened Binh Nghia. By the time the marines pulled out in October 1967, the village, once a Vietcong haven, was so secure that "the PFs were patrolling . . . in teams of two, like cops on a beat." There were some setbacks after the marines left, but the Popular Forces were for the most part able to keep the Vietcong out. A few years later even the PF were no longer necessary. "By 1970 Binh Nghia was so peaceful that the new American district adviser had termed it a 'R&R' (Rest and Recreation) center."

This success—achieved with assault rifles, not tanks or warplanes or artillery— was not unique. Despite (or, more likely, because of) its lack of firepower, CAP produced results. "No village protected by a Combined Action Platoon was ever repossessed by the Vietcong," Brute Krulak wrote, "and 60 percent of the marines serving in Combined Action units volunteered to stay on with their marine and Vietnamese companions for an additional six months when they could have returned to the United States." Moreover, contrary to the army's fears that the program was too dangerous, CAP casualties were 50 percent lower than in search-and-destroy operations. "The use of CAPS is quite the best idea I have seen in Vietnam, and it worked superbly," said Sir Robert Thompson, the British counterinsurgency expert.

Although successful, the Combined Action Program was never more than a sideshow to the army's conventional campaign. At its peak the program involved fewer than 2,500 marines. General Westmoreland claimed in his memoirs that "I simply had not enough numbers to put a squad of Americans in every village and hamlet." Actually it would not have been necessary to put a squad in every village, only in those not yet pacified. But even putting a squad "in every village and hamlet" would have required no more than 167,000 U.S. troops—a fraction of the 540,000 eventually deployed.

Westmoreland's big war stymied pacification efforts not only by sapping much needed manpower, but also in other, more insidious ways. If you're trying to win the hearts and minds of the peasants, you don't want to napalm their

huts. Yet that is what was happening as the search-and-destroy missions proceeded. This is not to suggest that the U.S. armed forces were routinely and
deliberately killing civilians, as some critics claimed. In fact they often took
great care to avoid non-combatant casualties, despite Vietcong attempts to lure
U.S. forces into firing into occupied villages. But there is little doubt that the
emphasis on body counts encouraged commanders to shoot first, ask questions
later. Whether deliberately or not, all this firing caused a large number of civilian casualties. It also left an ugly, indelible scar on the landscape. Parts of South
Vietnam began to resemble pictures of Verdun in World War I. General Harold
K. Johnson, army chief of staff, later acknowledged that firepower was applied
"on a relatively random basis" and that the U.S. "just sort of devastated the
countryside."

Vast seas of refugees were sent pouring into Saigon and other major cities
where they took up residence in hastily erected shantytowns. By 1968, 5 million of the South's 17 million people had been forced to flee their villages.
Many of them no doubt would have been surprised to learn that the *Small Wars
Manual* counseled U.S. soldiers that "tolerance, sympathy and kindness should
be the keynote to our relationship with the mass of the population."

Westmoreland and the army doggedly stuck with their big-unit strategy. Then
came the Tet Offensive.

On January 30–31, 1968, in violation of a truce called during the lunar New
Year (Tet) celebrations, the Vietcong and the North Vietnamese army assault-
ed most of the major towns and cities in the South simultaneously. The defenders were caught by surprise, and the attackers, perhaps 100,000 strong, scored
some initial successes. Commandos penetrated the grounds of the U.S. embassy
in Saigon. The North Vietnamese army occupied the ancient city of Hue. But
these gains were fleeting; the Communists were quickly pushed back. By
February 24, following three weeks of bloody street fighting, even Hue was
retaken. The Communists lost an estimated 50,000 men killed. (The U.S. losses amounted to about 2,000 men.) The Vietcong were virtually wiped out as an
effective fighting force. No popular uprising ever occurred. Instead, the barbarous behavior of the Communists during the brief period they occupied Hue
(at least 3,000 people, classified as "reactionary elements," were executed)
helped turn many South Vietnamese more firmly against their cause.

By any objective measure, the Tet Offensive was a disaster for the
Communists. But that was not how it was perceived in the United States.
Americans were shocked by the Vietcong's ability to mount such an extensive

offensive. For months they had been assured by their leaders that there was "light at the end of the tunnel." Now they perceived nothing but darkness—an impression reinforced by misleading news coverage that portrayed Tet as a defeat for the United States. CBS anchorman Walter Cronkite concluded a post-Tet broadcast by declaring, "It seems now more certain than ever that the bloody experience of Vietnam is to end in a stalemate." Johnson reportedly turned to an aide and exclaimed, "that it was a turning point, if he had lost Walter Cronkite he had lost Mr. Average Citizen."

In the months that followed, Johnson refused a request from Westmoreland for an additional 200,000 troops and then relieved Westy of command, kicking him upstairs into the job of army chief of staff. Nine days later, on March 31, 1968, Johnson stunned America by announcing that he would not seek reelection. The public impression, right or wrong, was that both Westmoreland and Johnson had been driven from office by their failures in Vietnam. Their departure set the stage for a shift of strategy that brought the U.S. to the brink of an improbable success.

One War

Lyndon Johnson was succeeded by Richard M. Nixon, William Westmoreland by his deputy, General Creighton Abrams. Abrams, like Westmoreland, had a conventional army background: He graduated from West Point and commanded an armored battalion in World War II under Patton. Among other achievements, he led the breakout from Normandy after D-Day and commanded the joint tank-infantry force that relieved the embattled paratroopers at Bastogne during the Battle of the Bulge. Along the way, "Abe" Abrams developed a reputation as one of the smartest officers in the army, not an intellectual exactly, but an officer who knew how to get at the heart of a problem and could present his conclusions with a disarming wit and sly humor—unless he was provoked, in which case his temper was terrible to behold.

By the time he took over in Vietnam, there was plenty for this cigar-chomping general to be furious about. The failure of the big-war strategy had become glaringly obvious, antiwar protests were mushrooming back home, and U.S. troops levels were falling—along with morale. After it became clear that victory was no longer the U.S. objective in Vietnam, that support on the home front was dwindling, and that a slow-motion pullout was beginning, unit discipline and cohesion crumbled. (Much the same thing happened on a smaller scale among Allied troops in north Russia in the winter of 1918–1919.) Hardened professionals might be able to soldier on under such desperate circumstances, but it was asking too much of young draftees led by equally inexperienced junior officers and NCOs. Drug use, racial tension, insubordination, and even fragging—enlisted men murdering their officers or NCOs—all skyrocketed. It was obvious to Abrams, and his new superiors in the White House, that the military could not continue to do business as usual.

Much to the annoyance of some of his subordinates, Abrams shifted the emphasis from big-unit "search-and-destroy" missions to population control. He refused to see pacification as "the other war." Under his new approach, which he called the "one-war" strategy, he broke up divisional forces and sent them on extensive patrol and night operations in platoon and company strength. Big-unit operations continued after 1968—for instance, the bloody, futile battle of Hamburger Hill in May 1969—but the dominant U.S. strategy, dubbed "clear and hold," was now more in line with what the marines and some army mavericks like John Paul Vann had advocated all along. "The strategy of search and destroy was officially dead," wrote one high-ranking army officer.

Working alongside Abrams was William Colby, a CIA veteran who took over pacification operations in late 1968. Having operated as a guerrilla himself in World War II, working for the OSS in occupied France and Norway, Colby understood the nature of the problem; and having been CIA station chief in Saigon in the early 1960s (he had argued against toppling Diem), he understood the country too. Under his direction, the Phoenix program, working with South Vietnamese security forces, helped identify and eradicate the Communist political apparatus in the South's villages. Phoenix has often been caricatured as a program of organized assassination, but in fact the bulk of cadres that it "neutralized" were captured or induced to defect, not killed. The program is credited with killing roughly 26,000 Vietcong cadres, capturing 33,000, "turning" 22,000. General Tran Do, Communist deputy commander in the South, later admitted that Phoenix was "extremely destructive."

Another, equally important part of the pacification effort was the added support given by the U.S. and South Vietnamese governments to local militias— the Regional Forces, Popular Forces, and People's Self-Defense Forces—on the front lines of village protection. In the past they had often operated with ancient weapons left over from the French. For the first time, Colby ensured that most of them at least had surplus M-16s.

The final piece of the pacification puzzle was land reform undertaken by President Nguyen Van Thieu—giving farmers legal title to the fields they tilled, in order to give them a bigger stake in Southern society. Ironically, Thieu was implementing some of the programs that had originally been started by Diem, only now he was doing it with U.S. support.

The Vietcong, already hard hit in the failed Tet Offensive of 1968, never recovered. "For practical purposes the PLAF [Vietcong] had been destroyed," writes a leading expert on the Vietnamese communists. By 1970, more than 90 percent of the South's population was under Saigon's control. Sir Robert Thompson, the British counterinsurgency expert, wrote in 1970 that he was "able to visit areas and walk through villages which had been under Viet Cong control for years. There was a much greater feeling of security, and the people were ready to take up arms for the government because they sensed that the Viet Cong were weaker. . . . Existing roads are kept open, and more are being repaired and opened monthly."

At the same time, the U.S. military targeted North Vietnamese sanctuaries that had previously been off-limits. In 1970 President Nixon authorized the "secret invasion" of Cambodia by U.S. and South Vietnamese units—actually an incursion that wiped out key Communist base camps. This had the disadvantage of sparking fresh antiwar protests back home, including the infamous shooting at Kent State that left four students dead, but it struck an effective blow against the enemy infrastructure. In addition to killing or capturing 13,000 enemy soldiers, this operation captured 23,000 individual weapons, more than 16 million rounds of small arms ammunition, 14 million pounds of rice, and so on.

A 1971 incursion designed to cut the Ho Chi Minh Trail in southern Laos was less successful, in no small part because this raid, near the village of Lam Son, was undertaken by the South Vietnamese with only American air and artillery support. (By this time, Congress had forbidden participation by U.S. ground troops.) The poor showing by South Vietnamese forces at Lam Son, coupled with the increasing success of the pacification campaign, led Hanoi to abandon guerrilla warfare for the time being. The North would now move to phase 3: conventional war.

Starting on March 30, 1972, 125,000 North Vietnamese regulars, backed by hundreds of Russian-supplied tanks and howitzers, slashed into the South from bases in North Vietnam, Laos, and Cambodia. General Giap's goal was nothing less than the military conquest of the South—or failing that, to at least embarrass Richard Nixon badly enough to drive him out of office in the 1972 election and end American support for Saigon. The Philippine *insurrectos* had tried a similar stratagem in an attempt to defeat McKinley in 1900. Giap's ploy worked no better than Aguinaldo's had.

The South Vietnamese army fell back but would not break. Once they stopped retreating, the southerners counterattacked with the help of American air support, including B-52 raids that pulverized the advancing northern columns. (Finally U.S. warplanes had a target in the open!) The air force was also given permission to blast the area around Hanoi, and the navy to mine Haiphong harbor. The North wound up gaining some territory from the Easter Offensive, but in most respects it was a failure, costing Hanoi perhaps 50,000 dead and 450 tanks destroyed. The North's defeat may be ascribed to a combination of Giap's mistakes (he had never tried an armored blitzkrieg before), U.S. air supremacy, and South Vietnamese fighting prowess. The only missing element: U.S. combat troops. By now there were virtually none left in Vietnam (though southern units still had American advisers). "By God," General Abrams marveled, "the South Vietnamese can hack it!"

Nixon and his national security adviser, Henry Kissinger, skillfully exploited the failure of the Easter Offensive. Using their openings to Moscow and Beijing, they convinced Hanoi's key allies to apply pressure for a diplomatic solution. The Politburo had no choice but to return to the negotiating table. When negotiations again stalled, Nixon ordered Operation Linebacker II, the "Christmas bombing" of the North in 1972. (The U.S. did not actually bomb on Christmas Day.) This was not a repeat of Rolling Thunder, the highly restricted bombing campaigns of the Johnson administration. This time B-52s were unleashed against Haiphong and Hanoi, though they were careful to avoid civilian targets. The 12 days of raids caused major damage to North Vietnamese industry and infrastructure—and lifted the spirits of American POWs imprisoned in Hanoi, who cheered as bombs burst near their compound.

Prodded by the Christmas bombing, the North Vietnamese came to terms. On January 27, 1973, Henry Kissinger and Le Duc Tho signed the Paris Peace Accord. Although the Nixon administration, beset by domestic difficulties, was so desperate for an agreement that it allowed some North Vietnamese troops to remain in the South, nevertheless this should have signaled a conditional U.S. victory. True, South Vietnam was incapable of defending itself alone. But so was South Korea after the Korean War, or West Germany after World War II. Only the continuing presence of U.S. troops saved Seoul and Bonn. There would be no more U.S. troops, or even supplies, for South Vietnam. Fed up with the war in Indochina, Congress drastically reduced aid to the South and prohibited any U.S. combat action, direct or indirect, in Indochina.

When the final northern offensive started in 1975, the South Vietnamese armed forces were critically short of supplies; even bandages had to be taken off corpses and reused. Much has been written about the failures of the southern forces, about low morale, poor leadership, cowardice, corruption, incompetence. Much of it true. But it is important to remember that, when properly supplied and backed by air power, as in 1972, the South Vietnamese showed they could fight and fight well. No army, by contrast, can operate effectively if it is critically short of vital materiel, as South Vietnam was in 1975. Only U.S. aid could have saved the day. Because it was not forthcoming, North Vietnamese T-54 tanks soon rumbled into Saigon.

Military and CIA helicopters evacuated all the remaining Americans and many of their Vietnamese friends. But there was not enough room to take everyone who wanted to leave. The pictures of Vietnamese fighting in vain to squeeze onto overcrowded helicopters are among the saddest images in U.S. history, a tragic coda to America's longest and least successful war.

Why America Lost

The only subject more contentious than why America got into Vietnam is why it lost. Some, of course, deny that America lost at all, claiming, as Richard Nixon did, that the U.S. won on the battlefield and went home. It was South Vietnam, not America, that was defeated. This view—and its rebuttal—may be summarized in a famous exchange that the late Colonel Harry Summers had with a North Vietnamese colonel after the war. "You know you never defeated us on the battlefield," Summers said. "That may be so," the North Vietnamese colonel replied, "but it is also irrelevant." The North Vietnamese colonel was right. Whatever happened on the battlefield, there is no denying that Saigon wound up falling. Hanoi achieved its strategic objectives; Washington did not.

Roughly speaking, there are three schools of thought about why this happened.

The first holds that the war was unwinnable. The North was too dedicated to victory, the South too weak. There was nothing America could have done to prevail at a reasonable cost. Even some who believe the war was a noble effort subscribe to the unwinnable hypothesis, though mostly it is held by those who think that U.S. involvement was disgraceful. During the war, some in the West even hailed the Vietcong as "liberators" whose takeover of the South would be welcomed by its people. Given unified Vietnam's long, dreary record of economic stagnation and political repression, few would make such claims today. Although glamorization of the Communists has faded, many still demonize the Saigon government. Without a more popular government in place, they assert, the struggle was unwinnable.

This view may be right, but it has several shortcomings. Admittedly, the parade of southern strongmen who succeeded Ngo Dinh Diem—overthrown and killed in a U.S.-backed coup in 1963—suffered a certain lack of legitimacy. And the quality of leadership within the South Vietnamese army was often appallingly low. Still, most South Vietnamese evidenced little desire to be ruled from Hanoi. There was never a popular communist uprising in the South; instead more than a million "boat people" fled the North's advance in 1975. And when properly supplied, as it was in 1972, the South Vietnamese army fought reasonably well. In short, there was no evidence that South Vietnam was not a viable state absent conquest from the North. In all likelihood, if left alone it would have evolved into a prosperous democracy, as Taiwan and South Korea have done under U.S. military protection.

Moreover, it is simply hard to believe that the U.S.—which in cooperation with its allies had defeated the combined might of Fascist Italy, Nazi Germany, and Imperial Japan a scant two decades earlier—could not defeat a tiny, preindustrial society on the edge of Asia. Advocates of the unwinnable-war school reply that the North Vietnamese were masters of guerrilla tactics, a type of warfare that is virtually impossible to defeat. Indeed, thanks to Mao Tse-tung, Ho Chi Minh, Che Guevara, and other famed leaders of "national liberation" struggles, the word *guerrilla* has acquired an almost mystical connotation. It is all too easy to overlook the fact that most guerrilla campaigns do not succeed. Since World War II, guerrillas have been stymied in Northern Ireland, Israel, Italy, Germany, Spain, Greece, the Philippines, Malaya, Turkey, Kenya, El Salvador, Peru, Guatemala, Mexico, and numerous other countries. Even the famous Che Guevera was hunted down and killed in 1967 by a Bolivian unit assisted by American Special Forces advisers. And as we have seen, the U.S. in the past had considerable success against guerrillas in the Philippines, the Dominican Republic, Haiti, Nicaragua, and elsewhere. It is quite possible that Vietnam was sufficiently different from all these prior instances that the U.S. could not have won. But at the very least, this assumption needs to be treated skeptically, especially since the U.S., despite all the mistakes made along the way, came tantalizingly close to winning at least a conditional victory.

The second school of thought holds that only a conventional war against North Vietnam could have delivered victory. According to advocates of this approach, pacification was a diversion. The real threat came from North Vietnamese troops, not Vietcong guerrillas. As Air Force General Curtis LeMay put it, memorably if crudely, "We should stop swatting flies and go after the manure pile." Ignoring the teaching of the *Small Wars Manual* that armed forces often have to limit their operations because of political necessities, this school blames President Johnson's restrictions for costing America victory. No invasion of the North. No occupation of Laos to cut the Ho Chi Minh Trail. Not even any bombing of Hanoi or Haiphong, the harbor through which the

North received supplies from the Soviet Union. Instead, Johnson pursued an ineffectual bombing campaign punctuated by pauses that gave the North time to rebuild. No wonder America lost! Advocates of this view, including Westmoreland himself, also sharply criticize Johnson for not calling up the reserves and for failing to rally the American people behind the war effort. One influential army historian blames the Joint Chiefs of Staff for not confronting Johnson and threatening to resign en masse unless he allowed the use of "the *total force* they believed would ultimately be required in Vietnam" (italics added).

This view calcified into something of an orthodoxy throughout much of the U.S. armed forces, especially in the army, in the years after 1975. As we will see, the notion that America erred by not waging total war against North Vietnam would shape the strategic approach of the U.S. armed forces for decades to come.

The conventional critique has much to recommend it. If the U.S. armed forces were going to pursue an orthodox strategy, they should have invaded the North or at least Laos; otherwise the big-war approach had no chance of working. Yet the conventional school overlooks some important facts. First, Johnson's concern that an invasion of the North would have triggered a Chinese response is quite plausible; as noted earlier, Mao Tse-tung was apparently willing to send the People's Liberation Army into battle if U.S. ground troops crossed the DMZ. Second, the conventional critique overstates the importance of outside support to the Communist insurgency in the South—a misconception fueled by Hanoi's official accounts. Whereas during the war itself, the North downplayed its involvement in the revolutionary struggle in the South, in the years after the war, Communist historians have exaggerated the role of the North Vietnamese army, seeking to deny the southern guerrillas any credit for the final victory. "The fact is that at least until 1968," writes the leading American historian of the North Vietnamese army, "the burden of combat was carried by the PLAF. It comprised chiefly southern recruits." Thus cutting the Ho Chi Minh Trail probably was not the "silver bullet" needed to end the war. Even occupying North Vietnam might not have sufficed to guarantee an American victory. The French had done that and had nevertheless been defeated by Ho Chi Minh's guerrillas.

The third and final approach can be called the "small war" school. Its proponents hold that the neglect of pacification by the army high command was a fatal error. The conventional school replies that pacification was irrelevant because, even though the South was ultimately pacified, it made no difference. The North simply staged an armored invasion, showing that the conventional war was the most important one all along. But why was the North able to win a conventional conflict in 1975, whereas previous attempts in 1968 and 1972 had failed? The obvious answer was the absence of U.S. troops. And why were U.S. troops absent? Because the American people and their congressional representatives had become fed up with the war, forcing the executive branch to pull out. And why did the American people tire of the war? Because of the futility and high cost of the attrition strategy employed by Westmoreland from 1965 to 1968.

In short, the Communist insurgency really did win the war. Not by defeating U.S. forces on the battlefield—but that was never its goal. As General Giap later explained, "We were not strong enough to drive out a half-million American troops, but that wasn't our aim. Our intention was to break the will of the American Government to continue the war." Westmoreland's attrition strategy helped Giap achieve this goal by wearing out the U.S. armed forces on all those fruitless "search-and-destroy" missions, generating heavy casualties and squandering public support for the war. Hanoi had accurately concluded that the war's center of gravity was American public opinion; Washington did not come to the same realization until it was too late. "The fundamental truth," writes one retired American general, "is that the United States had won the irrelevant war in Vietnam, and had lost the real one—the war for the 'hearts and minds' of the American people."

A small-war approach, if pursued from the beginning, might have retained popular support for a longer, lower-intensity commitment. Such an approach should have utilized volunteers, as the U.S. did in almost all its previous small wars, instead of the draftees sent to Vietnam. The American people are naturally impatient to see victory in any conflict fought by half a million conscriptees who suffer heavy casualties; in smaller skirmishes of the past, they were more patient if only a relatively small number of professional soldiers were sent overseas, and if they did not suffer crippling losses. These troops could have concentrated on protecting South Vietnam's population centers and building up indigenous security structures modeled on the constabularies of Haiti, the Dominican Republic, and so on. They could not have ignored Communist main forces altogether, but they could have put their emphasis on cutting off the guerrillas from their population base instead of chasing the main forces all over the Highlands.

The success this approach might have had should not be exaggerated. Vietnam was far bigger than any previous "small war" in U.S history. The Vietnamese Communists were far better armed, trained, organized, and motivated than any previous guerrillas fought by American soldiers. And they enjoyed an invaluable advantage: safe havens in neighboring countries. No one can know if a small-war approach, pursued from the beginning, would have resulted in a U.S. victory. But it probably would not have produced results any worse than the big-war strategy the army employed. Even if America had still lost the war, the defeat would have been considerably less costly and less painful. It is hard to avoid the conclusion that the American armed forces paid a high price in Vietnam for neglecting to study the *Small Wars Manual*.

14

In the Shadow of Vietnam
The Powell Doctrine and Small Wars in the 1990s

M uch of the army, indeed much of the U.S. armed forces, drew a curious lesson from Vietnam. Instead of concluding that they should employ better strategy and tactics in fighting small wars, they concluded, á la Jomini, that they should avoid fighting them altogether. As far as most officers were concerned, the bitter experience of Vietnam, when the military suffered abuse back home and plummeting morale and discipline in the ranks, reinforced the validity of Douglas MacArthur's complaint about the Korean War: "In war there is no substitute for victory." Never mind that to most people, the outcome of the Korean War *does* look like a pretty adequate substitute for victory—especially if total victory required going to war against Communist China and Russia. Nevertheless, a generation of young officers who received their baptism of fire in Indochina vowed: Never again! "Many of my generation, the career captains, majors and lieutenant colonels seasoned in that war," wrote one Vietnam veteran, "vowed that when our turn came to call the shots, we would not quietly acquiesce in halfhearted warfare for half-baked reasons that the American people could not understand or support."

That veteran made good on his pledge, or at least tried to. His name was Colin Powell, and in the 1980s he became the top military aide to Secretary of Defense Caspar Weinberger. Together they produced what became known as the Weinberger/Powell Doctrine, or simply the Powell Doctrine. This consisted of severe preconditions that must be met before U.S. forces are committed to battle: (1) "the United States should not commit forces to combat overseas unless the particular engagement or occasion is deemed vital to our national interests or that of our allies"; (2) if the U.S. does commit troops, "we should do so wholeheartedly, and with the clear intention of winning"; (3) the armed forces should have "clearly defined political and military objectives"; (4) the relationship between ends and means "must be continually reassessed and adjusted if necessary"; (5) "there must be some reasonable assurance we will have the support of the American people and their elected representatives in the Congress"; (6) "finally, the commitment of U.S. forces to combat should be a last resort." In succeeding years, another precondition became widely accepted as part of the Powell Doctrine—all U.S. deployments must have an "exit strategy."

The Powell Doctrine, which grew out of the debacle of Vietnam and was nourished by the military's traditional distaste for small wars, has come to stand for an all-or-nothing approach to warfare, with the ideal war being one in which the U.S. wins with overwhelming force, suffers few casualties, and leaves immediately. This has become the conventional wisdom in some corners. Presidential candidate George W. Bush declared in his acceptance speech at the 2000 Republican convention: "A generation shaped by Vietnam must remember the lessons of Vietnam. When America uses force in the world, the cause must be just, the goal must be clear, and the victory must be overwhelming."

It sounds like common sense. And sometimes the Powell Doctrine makes perfect sense. The U.S. invasion of Grenada in 1983 and of Panama in 1989 succeeded in removing rulers objectionable to the U.S. government through the use of overwhelming force. The failure of Desert One—the Iranian hostage rescue mission in 1980—and the tragedy of the peacekeeping mission to Lebanon three years later, which ended in the deaths of 241 marines, seemed to further confirm the wisdom of the Powell approach. Neither mission used sufficient force for the ambitious objectives it was trying to achieve, and both ended ignominiously.

Yet it is all too easy to overlook more successful applications of limited force; low-intensity operations that achieve their goals are apt to be ignored by the public, whereas failure is endlessly fascinating. (This helps explain why George Armstrong Custer is one of the most famous figures in American military history.) Even leaving aside covert U.S. support for insurgencies trying to overthrow foreign governments (e.g., the contras in Nicaragua or the *mujahadeen* in

Afghanistan) and foreign governments trying to put down insurgencies (e.g., El Salvador in the 1980s and Peru in the 1990s), there has been no shortage of successful peacetime operations by U.S. troops.

Starting in 1982, U.S. troops have been part of a peacekeeping force deployed in the Sinai desert to serve as a buffer between Egypt and Israel. In 1986 U.S. warplanes bombed Libya in retaliation for a terrorist attack on U.S. servicemen in Berlin. On numerous occasions, U.S. Marines have successfully evacuated U.S. diplomats and civilians from war zones—for instance, from Liberia in 1990, 1992, and 1996, Sierra Leone in 1997, the Central African Republic in 1996, and Congo in 1997. Many of these missions, in the spirit of the Chinese Relief Expedition of 1900, involved a surprising amount of combat, often necessary to secure the grounds of U.S. legations from trigger-happy revolutionaries.

Perhaps the most successful, if least known, small war of recent decades occurred in 1987–1988. As part of the Iran–Iraq War, Tehran targeted oil tankers belonging to the Gulf Arab states, which were providing financial support to Baghdad. The Reagan administration responded by putting Kuwaiti tankers under the U.S. flag and sending U.S. armed forces to protect them. The navy and marines wound up engaging in numerous battles with Iranian gunboats and missile platforms. To reinforce the point that failure is more memorable than success, the Tanker War is best known for the accidental shoot-down of an Iranian passenger jet by the USS *Vincennnes* and the Iraqi attack on the USS *Stark*, instead of for its overall success in keeping open a strategically vital waterway.

Iraq

None of these missions, from the Sinai peacekeeping to the Persian Gulf escort duty, fit neatly into the all-or-nothing paradigm. So few missions short of World War II satisfy the Powell checklist that, if strictly applied, it becomes a recipe for inaction. Indeed, General Powell, as Joint Chiefs of Staff chairman, even opposed a show of force that might have deterred Saddam Hussein from invading Kuwait on August 1, 1990. In the months that followed, he displayed deep reluctance to launch Desert Storm, preferring to wait indefinitely for sanctions to take effect. Early on, Powell told Defense Secretary Dick Cheney: "The American people do not want their young dying for $1.50 a gallon oil."

With the benefit of hindsight it is obvious that Powell and other senior generals overestimated Iraqi capabilities. They insisted that no offensive operation could be undertaken unless the U.S. deployed 500,000 troops. President

George Bush did not flinch. He approved the troop request and decided to fight exactly as the post-Vietnam army thinks wars should be fought: using massive, overwhelming firepower to pulverize the enemy and minimize U.S. casualties. The result, as the world well knows, was one of the most lopsided victories in military history—a triumph that the elder Bush claimed had buried "the Vietnam syndrome once and for all."

Yet the Vietnam mindset—characterized by excessive caution about open-ended, low-intensity operations—was very much alive in the war's aftermath. President Bush, at General Powell's urging, decided to end the ground war after just 100 hours, allowing at least half of the Iraqi Republican Guard to escape destruction and Saddam Hussein to hold on to power. A decade later, when Bush's son became president, the Iraqi dictator was still developing weapons of mass destruction, still thumbing his nose at America, still destabilizing the region.

Why didn't the U.S. armed forces go all the way to Baghdad in 1991, as some at the time had suggested? There were a plethora of explanations—it would generate unwelcome images of U.S. forces slaughtering fleeing Iraqis (e.g., the "Highway of Death"), it was not part of the U.N. mandate, it would fracture the allied coalition, it would lead to the dismemberment of Iraq, it would not result in a "desert democracy where people read *The Federalist Papers* along with the Koran" (in Powell's sarcastic words)—but underlying all of them seemed to be the reluctance of the Pentagon and the administration to undertake an occupation of Iraq—precisely the sort of nebulous political mission the military was desperate to avoid after Vietnam. President Bush, Powell writes, "had promised the American people that Desert Storm would not become a Persian Gulf Vietnam, and he had kept his promise."

Instead, it turned into a Persian Gulf Hungary, a replay of 1956, when the U.S. encouraged a rebellion against the Soviets and then stood by as the rebels were crushed. At least in Hungary the Eisenhower administration had the excuse that its military options were severely limited, for fear of starting World War III. Not so in Iraq, where the triumphant, all-powerful U.S. armed forces easily could have crushed the remnants of Saddam's army. Instead the U.S. did nothing as Saddam's men slaughtered the Shiites and Kurds who had risen up to challenge his rule at American instigation.

In April 1991, after the initial revolts had been suppressed, the U.S. finally stepped in to provide relief for Kurdish refugees in the north and to establish a no-fly zone over northern Iraq. A year later a no-fly zone was added over southern Iraq. The U.S. Air Force spent the next decade patrolling these no-fly zones, sparring with Iraqi air defenses and launching occasional punitive strikes as part of an effort to contain the regime in Baghdad. It was a poor substitute for toppling Saddam when the opportunity presented itself.

Somalia

In November 1992, a year and a half after Operation Provide Comfort in northern Iraq, General Powell and the other senior brass reluctantly acceded to another humanitarian mission, this time to feed the starving of Somalia. The generals went along in no small part because they wanted to deflect attempts to involve U.S. armed forces in stopping ethnic cleansing in the former Yugoslavia, a mission they viewed as a hopeless "quagmire." Somalia, by contrast, appeared to offer a chance to burnish America's do-gooder credentials without risking serious combat. Just deliver relief supplies and leave. Simple. Or so it seemed.

A joint army–marine task force, backed by an aircraft carrier battle group offshore and working in cooperation with other foreign contingents, had little trouble securing control over much of Somalia in December 1992. It quickly became apparent, however, that merely delivering bags of food would not be enough. Long-term relief would require bringing order to Somalia's chaotic political situation, dominated by warring clans.

The Pentagon and administration had no intention of getting U.S. troops involved in long-term "nation building." Having long since forgotten U.S. interventions in the Philippines, Haiti, the Dominican Republic, and Nicaragua, and conveniently overlooking more recent experiences in Germany and Japan, the generals thought of only one thing when they heard this dread term: another Vietnam. Thus the armed forces did little or nothing to disarm Somalia's heavily armed political factions when they had the chance—a decision that one U.S. Army officer on the scene called "the critical mistake of the intervention." The second critical mistake was to pull out the bulk of the 26,000 U.S. troops in May 1993 and turn over the difficult tasks that remained to a United Nations force that included a small U.S. contingent. "This was like a doctor going home once the cancer patient was sedated but before the tumor was removed," wrote the army officer.

The U.N. was not up to the job and the cancer quickly metastasized. The emboldened warlords, previously cowed by American soldiers, especially the marines, were not bashful about challenging the U.N. troops that remained. A month after the handover to the U.N., 24 Pakistani soldiers were killed and 50 wounded by gunmen loyal to warlord Muhammed Farah Aidid. The U.N. Security Council authorized Aidid's arrest, and U.N. troops, including

Americans, went after him and his clan. Trying to nab a warlord in Mogadishu proved no easier than trying to capture one in northern Mexico eight decades earlier. As frustrations grew, the local U.S. commander requested the dispatch of a Special Forces team to aid in the hunt. The Clinton administration and General Powell, the Joint Chiefs chairman, departed from his doctrine long enough to agree to send Task Force Ranger, consisting of the elite Delta Force reinforced by army Rangers.

A month and six frustrating (but well-executed) raids later, it all went awry. On October 3, 1993, the hunters became the hunted in the back streets of Mogadishu. After two MH-60 Black Hawk helicopters were downed by rocket-propelled grenades, Task Force Ranger was besieged by thousands of Somalis firing rocket-propelled grenades and AK-47 assault rifles. The Special Forces troopers remained trapped until the next morning, when the U.S. 10th Mountain Division organized a relief expedition by borrowing tanks and armored personnel carriers from the Pakistani and Malaysian U.N. contingents. Eighteen Americans were killed, 82 injured, one captured, making this the costliest single day of combat for the army since Vietnam.

Americans were horrified to see, in the days that followed, television footage of American corpses being abused and dragged through the streets by jubilant Somalis. President Clinton, embarrassed by this debacle so early in his administration, quickly announced that the U.S. was pulling out of Somalia within six months.

On one level this episode seemed to reinforce the validity of the Powell Doctrine by showing what happens when it is not followed. The U.S. had gone to war against Aidid and his clan but had refused to publicly acknowledge what it was doing, or to send sufficient forces to win. The scapegoat became Defense Secretary Les Aspin, who was sacked in part because he had refused local U.S. commanders' requests for tanks. Yet General Powell, while supportive of the armor request, had opposed sending powerful AC-130 gunships that might have helped rescue Task Force Ranger. He and others in the Pentagon had also been intent on pulling out the bulk of the initial U.S. expedition as quickly as possible.

Much of this decisionmaking was premised on a fear of "mission creep" and "gradual escalation," catchphrases that have become ubiquitous in military discourse since the Vietnam War. The Special Forces raid was seen as a quick, painless alternative to the slow, hard grind of a pacification campaign. "It seemed to promise victory without much of a commitment," writes an army officer, "a short-cut to success, an almost nonmilitary surgical strike, the mythical grail sought by many in Washington's policy elite."

The irony of Somalia was the opposite of what it had been in the Gulf War. In the Gulf, fear of a small war (the occupation of Iraq) had prevented a big war from being carried out to a completely satisfactory conclusion; in Somalia fear of a big war prevented a small war from being waged effectively. These are the yin and yang of the Vietnam Syndrome, still a prominent part of U.S. military thinking decades after the fall of Saigon.

Haiti

The Gulf War and the Somalia debacle shaped the conduct of U.S. small wars for the rest of the 1990s. In the popular imagination, the former taught that war could be waged successfully with few if any casualties, while the latter seemingly demonstrated that the American people and their leaders had no stomach for deaths suffered in a merely "humanitarian" expedition.

American skittishness in asserting its power was on full display eight days after the battle of Mogadishu. The USS *Harlan County*, loaded with Special Forces and Canadian soldiers, approached the piers of Port au Prince, Haiti, and was turned away by a small mob threatening "another Somalia." This shows what happens when a superpower cuts and runs: Its next mission becomes much harder to accomplish.

President Clinton subsequently decided to occupy Haiti in order to restore deposed President Jean Bertrand Aristide, but this invasion had little in common with its 1915 predecessor. Eight decades before, U.S. forces had moved quickly and decisively to pacify the entire country and impose a government that, for all its problems, gave Haiti a measure of peace and stability that it had seldom known before or since. In 1994, by contrast, the U.S. occupiers were told not to get their hands dirty with the hard work of governance. The author Bob Shacochis, who spent time with a Special Forces "A Team" in the countryside, recounted how these tough troopers were forbidden from disarming FRAPH (Front for the Advancement and Progress of Haiti) paramilitaries and taking other steps to establish the rule of law. The Green Berets were frustrated that, as one sergeant put it, they couldn't "take care of the bad guys, like we were supposed to be doing."

What accounts for this reluctance? Fear of taking any casualties on a merely "humanitarian" mission. The commanders of the 10th Mountain Division, Shacochis found, "weren't letting any of their boys outside the gates of Cap [Haitien] unless they traveled in a reinforced platoon—about forty guys, with mortars and armored vehicles—and were accompanied by either a battalion commander or an executive officer." Quite a contrast from the swashbuckling days of Smedley Butler and Herman "Hard Head" Hanneken. The irony is that during the second invasion of Haiti in 1994, the U.S. deployed more than 20,000 combat troops, versus a maximum of 3,000 during the 1915 invasion. Yet American troops, or at least their commanders, were far more cautious the second time around. In Shacochis's paradoxical, but accurate, formulation, "U.S. soldiers had invaded Haiti for the primary purpose of protecting themselves."

Not surprisingly, a mission designed above all to minimize casualties accomplished little else. Aristide was restored to power, but it was a hollow victory. The U.S. left behind a cesspool of corruption, incompetence, and violence— and a president who turned out to be no democrat. The situation in Haiti deteriorated further in the years that followed.

Bosnia

America's political and military leaders were even more reluctant to get involved in the Balkans, another situation that did not fit neatly with the Powell Doctrine's win-and-get-out-quick approach. In the early 1990s many voices, in and out of government, pushed for a "lift and strike" policy—lifting the arms embargo to the Bosnian Muslims and using air power to hit Serbian positions. The Pentagon, in the person of General Powell, was adamantly opposed. "No American President could defend to the American people the heavy sacrifice of lives it would cost to resolve this baffling conflict," Powell wrote of Bosnia in 1995. And in part because Powell's stature was so vast, overshadowing a president who had never served in the military, nothing was done—at least not until the general retired. Finally in 1995, after some 300,000 people had died, NATO told Serbian forces to stop their aggression in Bosnia or face air strikes. Many senior U.S. generals and admirals opposed this limited use of force. But it took remarkably few sorties by NATO, principally U.S, warplanes—combined with a Croatian ground offensive—for the Serbs to agree to a peace treaty that, for all its faults, ended the killing in Bosnia.

Even after the signing of the Dayton Peace Accord, which called for the dispatch of peacekeepers, the U.S. military remained reluctant to get "bogged down" in the Balkans "quagmire." U.S. troops sent to Bosnia received the most restrictive rules of engagement possible. "When I received my written mission from Division," recalls a battalion commander from the 1st Armored Division, "absolutely minimizing casualties was the mission prioritized as first, so I in turn passed it on in my written operations order to my company commanders."

But what happens if the dictates of "force protection" clash with the job at hand? "If mission and force protection are in conflict, then we don't do the mission," an army major recalled being told by his brigade commander in Bosnia. In keeping with this ethos, the U.S. military was reluctant to arrest Bosnian war criminals or undertake the tasks of civil administration, making it much harder to forge a lasting peace—and, ironically, making it less likely that the U.S. troops could be brought home soon.

Kosovo

The easiest way to minimize casualties is to not send troops at all. Hence in the 1990s cruise missiles became America's preferred instrument of waging war. In 1998 President Clinton launched these unmanned weapons against Sudan and Afghanistan in retaliation for the bombings of two U.S. embassies in Africa. These strikes, which resembled a navy bombardment of native villages in the nineteenth century, achieved little beyond demolishing a Sudanese pharmaceutical plant and turning Osama bin Laden into a worldwide celebrity. This ineffectual raid may have emboldened bin Laden's al Qaeda network to undertake its deadly attack against the Pentagon and World Trade Center three years later.

The trend toward push-button war reached its zenith in Kosovo. "The Services were against any commitment there," General Wesley Clark later wrote. When the order to begin bombing was given on March 23, 1999, Clark, the supreme Allied commander in Europe, told his subordinates that the top priority was "not to lose aircraft"; "impact[ing] the Yugoslavian military and police activities on the ground" was a secondary concern. While NATO pilots were flying safely out of anti-aircraft range, the Kosovars they were supposed to be protecting were at the mercy of Serb ethnic-cleansing squads. It is a curious morality that puts greater value on the life of even a single American pilot—a professional who has volunteered for combat—than on hundreds, even thousands, of Kosovar lives. This has led some to suggest that the safest people on a modern battlefield are those who wear an American uniform.

Whatever its morality, this strategy was not particularly effective, notwithstanding some attempts to paint Kosovo as the first war won by air power alone. Seeing that high-altitude bombing was having little effect on the dug-in Yugoslav armed forces, and knowing that ground troops were out of the question, General Clark requested the dispatch of tank-busting AH-64 Apaches, the best combat helicopters in the world. The senior Pentagon brass disapproved; they viewed this as step closer to a Vietnam-like quagmire. To dissuade the White House, they made outlandish claims that Task Force Hawk, as the chopper unit was called, would suffer 50 percent casualties in a few days of battle. (Clark later wrote that this estimate reflected "a plain lack of knowledge" and that "this was just a way of saying, 'Don't do the mission.'")

When Task Force Hawk was finally dispatched, the generals insisted that 6,200 troops and 26,000 tons of equipment, including 14 ultra-heavy M1A1 Abrams tanks, be sent along to safeguard the unit's base in Albania. The pilots were eager to fly, judging the risks acceptable, but the Pentagon dragged its feet so long that the Apaches never went into combat. Slobodan Milosevic decided to pull out of Kosovo anyway, but only after the KLA guerrillas had launched a ground offensive—which forced Yugoslav units out into the open where they could be hit by NATO air power—and after Western leaders had threatened a major ground war.

In the aftermath of the bombing campaign, a multinational peacekeeping force was sent to occupy Kosovo, including a U.S. contingent. As in Bosnia, the U.S. Army's risk-averse mentality impeded attempts to establish a durable peace. American troopers seldom ventured outside their fortified compound, Camp Bondsteel, without wearing their forbidding "battle rattle"—body armor, Kevlar helmets, the works. This impeded their ability to interact with local civilians, gather intelligence, and spread goodwill—prerequisites for a successful occupation. British soldiers, by contrast, looked more confident and approachable in their green berets and rolled-up sleeves.

Although dressed for battle, U.S. forces shied away from any confrontation. They did little to stop Albanian militants from using Kosovo as a base from which to stage an uprising in 2001 against the multiethnic government of neighboring Macedonia—an insurgency that threatened to imperil the tenuous peace of the Balkans.

In the Balkans the U.S. was trying to play the role of imperialist on the cheap, an imperialist unwilling to act as forcefully and decisively as the U.S. had in years gone by. And much of the explanation can be found in a "no casualties" mindset.

The Body Bag Syndrome

The impulse to avoid indiscriminately sacrificing the lives of American servicemen and women is noble, and it is certainly preferable to the callous attitude of the Russian military toward its rank and file, whether in Chechnya or aboard the *Kursk*, the submarine that sank in 2000. But in the immediate post–Cold War era America's political leaders were more careful to husband the lives of volunteers—men and women who have sought out combat and its risks—than their predecessors were with the lives of draftees in years past.

Sometimes this policy can backfire cruelly: If foreign enemies know that killing a few Americans will drive the U.S. out of their country, they are far more likely to target American soldiers or civilians. And their task will be facilitated by force protection strategies—as at Khobar Towers in 1996 or in Beirut in 1984—that conveniently group American service members in one building. Every time U.S. forces flee some country after suffering casualties, it makes it less likely that the U.S. will be able to accomplish its objectives in the future *without* using force.

Those whose lives are on the line do not ask for a no-casualties policy. In one survey of 12,500 service members conducted by the Center for Strategic and International Studies, 86 percent agreed with this statement: "If necessary to accomplish a combat/lifesaving mission, I am prepared to put my own life on the line." The CSIS study also found that "excessive aversion to casualties has . . . led to some confusion in the military, where self-sacrifice and the willingness to accept casualties in military operations has always been a key part of the ethos." Nor are most of the rank and file intrinsically opposed to "humanitarian" missions; many report that they like helping people and, like the sergeant in Haiti, express frustration with force protection policies that keep them from doing more.

Political and military leaders justify this preference for sanitized, high-tech warfare by arguing that the American people simply will not tolerate casualties anymore, at least not in a "small war," that as soon as the body bags start coming home support for a mission will evaporate. This is said to be a fact of life in the television age. The military analyst Edward Luttwak has even mounted an elaborate justification for the "body bag syndrome": He claims that families are more reluctant to lose sons than they once were because they have fewer children today. (Actually the decline in family size predates casualty-phobia.)

What evidence is there to support this thesis? Three examples are usually cited: Vietnam, Beirut, and Somalia. Consider each in turn.

Support for the Vietnam War did not decline until after 1968—until, that is, after more than three years of intense combat with little to show for it. Even as late as 1968, roughly as many Americans favored escalation (37 percent) as withdrawal (39 percent). Afterward public sentiment shifted in favor of withdrawal, but a plurality still favored only a gradual pullout.

Support for the peacekeeping mission in Beirut was never high to begin with, even before the blast that killed 241 marines on October 23, 1983. If anything, this calamity caused a temporary *spike* in support; many enraged

Americans wanted revenge. Before long, public sentiment returned more or less to where it had been before the suicide truck bombing.

Support for the relief mission to Somalia was so high in its early days that the public barely noticed eight fatalities suffered by U.S. forces. Popular enthusiasm had waned, however, well before 18 Rangers were killed on October 3, 1993. Even after this tragedy, the public did not demand *immediate* withdrawal, the option chosen by the Clinton administration. "Had the administration chosen instead to galvanize public opposition to Somali warlord Mohamed Farah Aideed," write two political scientists, "our research suggests that Americans would have tolerated an expanded effort to catch and punish him."

These examples suggest that casualties are hardly the dominant factor in public attitudes toward most military expeditions. Social scientists and pollsters find that other factors—such as the odds of success and the stakes involved—count much more. This helps explain why the American public favored a pullout from Somalia but not from Saudi Arabia, where 19 airmen were killed in the 1996 Khobar Tower bombing. The U.S. stake in Saudi Arabia was obviously much greater.

Moreover, polling data suggests that if the elites in government and the media are united in favor of a mission—as they were, for instance, during the early days of Somalia—the public is willing to go along, even if the mission does not conform to the dictates of "national security," narrowly defined. A Triangle Institute for Security Studies report found that for missions such as peacekeeping in Congo "the mass gives substantially higher estimates of acceptable casualties than do civilian or military elites." In fact, suffering casualties can actually increase American public support for a military operation, so as to ensure that their soldiers did not die "in vain." Thus when leaders choose not to enter a war or choose to fight with the most antiseptic means possible, they should not cite "public opinion" as an alibi for their actions.

This is not to suggest that the American people are insensitive to casualties. They are not, nor should they be. Few foreign policy objectives are worth buckets of blood; ends and means must be in balance. Small wars, by definition, have relatively small rewards, and they must be conducted accordingly. But even the best-run operations will suffer some losses. In the Banana Wars of the 1910s and 1920s, the marines lost 79 men in combat. Not bad for occupying three countries (Haiti, the Dominican Republic, Nicaragua) for a combined total of 48 years—but presumably too costly by today's standards.

Would things be different today, now that television cameras are available to beam to the public back home every detail of their troops' involvement overseas? Not necessarily. To be sure, a frisson of excitement courses through the body politic when soldiers are committed abroad—the first SEALs and marines to land in Mogadishu in 1992 found more foreign cameramen than Somalis to greet them—but interest usually wanes as the entanglement drags along. In the decade following the Gulf War, the U.S. Air Force conducted combat operations daily over Iraq, with hardly any notice taken back home.

The American military knows that it cannot ignore the power of pictures. In the media age it is impossible for U.S. soldiers to employ some of the brutal methods that were common, for instance, in the Philippine War. (Just imagine one of the victims being interviewed on network television.) Americans today are not necessarily any more sensitive than were their early twentieth-century compatriots about having their soldiers kill large numbers of foreigners, even foreign civilians—no one knows or much cares, it seems, exactly how many Somalis were slain in the Battle of Mogadishu—as long as the events are not brought home to the living room in vivid color. The Pentagon is aware of this, and since Vietnam it has taken pains to ensure that the U.S. press is not given unfettered access to the modern battlefield.

Television has necessarily modified how U.S. forces conduct operations, but it has hardly made it impossible to wage small wars effectively. Indeed, the British army, representing a society every bit as media-saturated as the United States, has shown far less sensitivity to casualties in its small wars (e.g., in Sierra Leone and Kosovo) than its overly cautious cousins across the Atlantic do.

America's no-casualties mindset was finally jettisoned in the wake of the September 11, 2001, attacks on New York and Washington. America's leaders decided that the country was ready to support military action that risked sending body bags home. It is sobering to speculate what might have been achieved if this conclusion had been reached earlier. Might Osama bin Laden have been prevented from launching these bloody attacks if the U.S. had done more than lob a few cruise missiles at him in 1998?

The Big-War Force

It is hard to say exactly who was responsible for the military's no-casualties mindset, demanded neither by ordinary civilians nor by ordinary soldiers. Political leaders blame the generals and admirals, claiming they are still psychologically traumatized by the scars of Vietnam. The generals and admirals blame political leaders, claiming that the men and women in uniform are unwilling to take risks because if something goes wrong, they will be left to twist in the wind by their political masters. Both explanations have merit, insofar as military policy is set through a complex interaction between the Pentagon, White House, and Capitol Hill.

A similarly complicated process—with the added lobbying clout of defense contractors thrown in—produces the structure and equipment of the armed forces. In the 1990s and early 2000s, that structure often proved ill-suited to the demands of "contingency operations," the newest argot for "small wars." "Still trying to fight our kind of war—be it World War II or Desert Storm—we ignore the real war-fighting requirements of today," says retired Marine General Anthony Zinni. "My generation has not been well prepared for this future, because we resisted the idea."

The future of small wars requires pretty much what the past did—well-trained infantry. Although high-tech gadgets can come in handy and close air or light armor support can be invaluable, many of the expensive weapons systems the U.S. armed forces have come to rely on are neutralized in small war settings—unless the war in question consists of nothing but punitive strikes. Seventy-ton M1 Abrams tanks are too big to make it down the streets of a Third World city. (The 1st Armored Division found its tanks more hindrance than help when it was sent to Bosnia in 1995.) There are few targets for B-2 stealth bombers to hit when fighting guerrillas. Aegis guided-missile cruisers cannot separate warring factions. Yet in the armed services, most careers are built around such technologies.

In the 1990s, even as it grumbled about the expense of too many deployments, the Pentagon continued ordering superexpensive new weapons systems such as the VSNX aircraft carrier and the Crusader self-propelled howitzer, as well as both the F-22 fighter plane *and* the Joint Strike Fighter. This is not to suggest that these systems are useless or unnecessary; the military must continue to prepare for big wars and small, and some costly platforms (such as B-52 bombers) can readily be adapted for lesser contingencies. But the military has placed too much emphasis on these systems at the expense of technologies (e.g., unmanned aerial vehicles such as the Predator and Global Hawk) that hold great promise but have little constituency inside the Pentagon.

The bigger concern is that the military found itself badly configured for the missions it was called on to undertake after the end of the Cold War. The problem was especially acute in the army, organized in a divisional structure that has changed little since Napoleon's day. Although the army had plenty of heavy divisions, there was not enough fast sealift or airlift to deploy them to a battle zone quickly. It took six months to assemble an army during the Persian Gulf War; in the future the armed forces are unlikely to have so long. When it had to assemble a small-war force, the army often had to mix and match parts from various commands because it did not have self-contained units ready for the job at hand. This disrupted training routines, lowered combat readiness, and created hardship for those left behind, who had to pick up the workload of the soldiers who were deployed. Hence complaints about an excessive "operations tempo."

Sometimes there simply were not enough of the right people in the regular forces—especially in specialties such as military police and intelligence—to get the job done, forcing the army to call up reservists. Over 95 percent of the army's civil affairs and psychological warfare specialists are in the reserves.

This was, at least in part, another legacy of Vietnam. In the 1970s the army restructured itself to make large-scale conflict virtually impossible without reservists, on the assumption that no president would call up the reserves for an unpopular war. But this policy has made smaller-scale deployments overly dependent on part-time soldiers, who grumble, rightly, that they signed up with the understanding that they would be deployed only in a major emergency.

By the end of the 1990s, the U.S. armed forces had begun to recognize that they were not properly configured for the challenges ahead. The air force reorganized itself into expeditionary units. The army set up an experimental medium-weight brigade designed to deploy anywhere in the world within 96 hours. But the armed forces need to change more than their organizational chart; they need to change their outlook. Their mindset remains that of a mass army composed of conscripts mobilized to win a big war, but that is not the role of the armed forces early in the twenty-first century. They are a smaller, all-volunteer force, one of whose duties is policing the Pax Americana.

"The mentality of an imperial army is, of necessity, utterly different from that of a mass army," writes strategist Eliot Cohen. "The former is composed of soldiers; the latter crusaders. The former accepts ambiguous objectives, interminable commitments and chronic skirmishes as a fact of life; the latter wants a definable mission, a plan for victory and decisive battles. In the imperial army the trooper finds fulfillment in the soldier's life; in the mass army in the belief that he exists to 'fight and win America's wars.'"

The incompatibility between the armed forces' big war mindset and their small war missions accounts for a good deal of the angst suffered by the services, especially the army, since the end of the Cold War.

The Small-War Force

The American armed forces—1.4 million strong as of 2001—are a wide and variegated lot, so it stands to reason that not everyone in uniform will be resistant to small-war missions. The two most notable exceptions have been the Special Operations forces and the marines.

Although technically a part of the army, the Special Operations forces are almost a fifth branch of the armed forces. The army's Special Operations Command, headquartered at Fort Bragg, North Carolina, is composed of some 26,000 soldiers, including the Rangers (light infantry), the Delta Force commandos, an air support squadron known as the Night Stalkers, civil affairs and psychological warfare groups, and the Special Forces. (These forces in turn report to the U.S. Special Operations Command, which also encompasses navy and air force commandos.) The civil affairs/psy-ops and Special Forces are especially focused on political, peacetime missions.

At any one time, there are 1,200 to 1,500 Special Forces operators—popularly known as Green Berets—deployed in dozens of countries around the world, working on missions ranging from removing land mines to training friendly foreign militaries. The Special Forces' basic unit is the A Team, typically composed of a dozen hand-picked veterans—one captain, one warrant officer, ten sergeants. These tough operators pride themselves on being "culturally sensitive," "linguistically able," and proficient in surviving without the elaborate infrastructure the U.S. military customarily lugs overseas, using their wiles to accomplish a wide range of tasks far removed from conventional warfare. Their nickname—the "snake eaters"—sums up their ethos.

In preparation for overseas assignments, the psy-ops and civil affairs specialists receive even more extensive language and cultural training than do the Special Forces. This author visited one classroom at Fort Bragg where an African-born professor teaches a course on his native continent that would not be out of place in America's leading graduate schools.

The psy-ops soldiers are the military's experts in marketing and advertising. Their job is to undermine enemy morale, smooth the path for American troops, and achieve U.S. objectives with a minimum of bloodshed. Civil affairs specialists undertake the essential task of governance wherever American troops may find themselves—otherwise known as imperialism (a term that, needless to say, they never use). Psy-ops and civil affairs soldiers, wearing distinctive red berets, are an essential element of U.S. occupations in countries ranging from Haiti to Kosovo—as their predecessors were in Germany and Japan, and in the Philippines before that. Without their work, a battlefield triumph may amount to little. Hence the civil affairs motto: "Secure the Victory."

Unlike the army's civil-affairs units, the marines are not known for their tact or diplomacy, yet they too embrace small-war missions, so much a part of their tradition as the "911 Force." In the 1980s the marines even reprinted the *Small*

Wars Manual and made it part of the curriculum at the Basic School, where all newly commissioned officers are trained. In the 2000s, they set about writing an updated *Small Wars Manual*.

What makes the marines suited for these missions? Traditionally they (like the Special Forces) have focused on people, not weapons systems. They see themselves less as "tank drivers" or "fighter pilots" than as warriors. Their famous credo: Every marine a rifleman. The marines are also flexible in organization. Marine expeditionary units can be formed quickly by drawing on infantry, air power, artillery, armor—whatever is appropriate for the job at hand. Within these units, marines stress flexibility and initiative down to the lowest ranks, a vital requirement in the chaotic and fast-shifting environment of a small war.

The marines are far from perfect. In Beirut in 1983, because of overly restrictive rules of engagement, they were caught unprepared and lost 241 servicemen. But by and large they have been far better at small wars than the army. The contrast was on vivid display in Somalia.

The marines took an aggressive attitude. They patrolled actively and always bristled with firepower, letting Somalis know they were not to be messed with. Paradoxically the marines wound up killing far fewer Somalis—some 500—than the army, which tried a more diplomatic approach but ended up killing 5,000. After the marines left, the warlords, especially Muhammed Farah Aidid, became bolder in challenging U.N. and U.S. forces. Casualties ensued. As special U.S. envoy Robert Oakley said, "The departure of the heavily armed, aggressively patrolling marines from south Mogadishu obviously had a much greater psychological effect on the Somalis, especially the SNA (Aidid's Somali National Alliance), than the continued presence of the QRF (Quick Reaction Force) from the (army's) 10th Mountain Division." The ultimate result was the death of 18 U.S. soldiers.

By contrast, the marines read their *Small Wars Manual*, which counsels that "the morale effect of tanks and armored cars is probably greater in small wars operations than it is in a major war." They brought in armored vehicles to surround warlord compounds and did not suffer any disasters. (The marines employed light armor, well suited for the situation, not the heavy armor that the army tried to take into the Balkans with little success.)

Although sometimes caricatured as homicidal Neanderthals (see, e.g., *Full Metal Jacket*), the marines have shown themselves to be the most intellectually supple of the services. A visitor to Camp Lejeune, North Carolina—East Coast base for marine expeditionary forces—finds the marines practicing not only traditional amphibious assaults but also newer missions such as crowd control in urban areas. The marines know that the world is becoming heavily urbanized and realize they had better develop a strategy for urban warfare; otherwise they will suffer as heavily as the army did in Mogadishu. The army by contrast takes the approach that it doesn't "do" cities; it prefers to go around, rather than through, urban areas. Just as in earlier days the army preferred not to "do" counterinsurgency. Alas, America's enemies are seldom obliging enough—Saddam Hussein being a notable exception—to fight the kind of wars many in the Pentagon would prefer. Indeed the costliest foreign attack on American soil—the September 11, 2001, airliner hijackings—came from terrorists utilizing box cutters and knives, not the kind of foes the regular military establishment has spent most of its energy preparing to fight.

15

In Defense of the Pax Americana

Small Wars in the Twenty-First Century

The past is an uncertain guide to the future, but it is the only one we have. What can it teach us about small wars and how to fight them?

The most obvious point, but one well worth making, is that the types of missions that the armed forces found themselves undertaking after the end of the Cold War—missions at odds with the military's traditional conception of its own role, as embodied in the Powell Doctrine—are nothing new. Specifically, there is absolutely nothing novel about:

• *Wars without a declaration of war.* There is a myth prevalent in some quarters that the Korean War was America's first "undeclared war," and that presidents since then have been traducing the Constitution to deploy military forces abroad on their own initiative. Congress even passed the War Powers Act after the Vietnam War to limit presidential war-making authority.

True, Korea was America's biggest undeclared war up to that point, but it was hardly the first. All the wars chronicled in this book were undeclared, starting with the Tripolitan War, when Thomas Jefferson initially sent a naval squadron to the Mediterranean without bothering to ask for congressional approval. As the *Small Wars Manual* states, "small wars are operations undertaken under executive authority." On those few occasions when a president sought congressional authorization, he usually made clear that it was nonbinding. Woodrow Wilson, for instance, ordered the marines to land in Veracruz in 1914 *before* the Senate had finished debating the matter. The Philippine War, too, broke out before the Senate ratified the Treaty of Paris annexing the archipelago. Congress has generally voted a declaration of war only in the event of hostilities with another major industrialized power and sometimes not even then; witness the quasi-war with France in 1798–1800. Military operations in Third World nations have seldom been seen to require a formal declaration of war.

That doesn't mean Congress has no role to play; it can cut off funding for an operation it finds objectionable. Various lawmakers tried to do precisely that during the U.S. intervention in Nicaragua from 1926 to 1933. Although these attempts never completely succeeded, they encouraged the Hoover administration to hasten the withdrawal of troops. Four decades later, Congress was more successful in cutting off funding for any further U.S. involvement in Indochina.

• *Wars without exit strategies.* The U.S. military stayed continuously in Haiti for 19 years, in Nicaragua for 23 years, in the Philippines for 44 years, in China for almost 100 years. These long-term deployments should be no surprise. After all, the U.S. still has not found an "exit strategy" from World War II or the Korean War; American troops remain stationed in Germany, Japan, Italy, and South Korea more than a half century after the end of the wars that brought them there. As of this writing, U.S. troops remain in the Middle East to contain Iraq a decade after the Gulf War ended, a mission that results in regular air attacks against Iraq and some U.S. casualties (in the Khobar Towers and USS *Cole* bombings).

This runs counter to the assumption implicit in the Powell Doctrine that U.S. troops should win a battle and go home. But home where? To bases in Europe and Northwest Asia—themselves the legacy of prior wars? Or to bases back in the U.S.A.? If the latter, why station troops on the mainland? This puts them farther from any likely action, makes life more boring (would you rather live in the Mojave Desert or Europe?), and does not save much money. Stationing troops abroad can actually be cheaper if Washington duns American allies, as it should, to pay part of the bill. Moreover, imposing an artificial exit deadline prior to any U.S. intervention severely limits its effectiveness by encouraging America's enemies to await its departure.

• *Wars that are fought less than "wholeheartedly."* Most of the wars chronicled in this book were fought for extremely limited objectives—to free hostages (Barbary War, Boxer Uprising), to exact revenge (Canton 1854, Korea 1871, Pershing Punitive Expedition), to overthrow a dictator (Veracruz 1914). Some had more ambitious objectives, such as annexing the Philippines or pacifying Haiti, but even where the ends were unlimited, the means remained severely circumscribed. Even in the biggest of the small wars chronicled here, the Philippine War, there was no mass mobilization. Only 70,000 soldiers were sent, and they were all volunteers. More typical was Haiti, which never had more than 3,000 U.S. Marines and little if any heavy weaponry.

The notion that U.S. troops must be deployed only in overwhelming force was alien to the armed forces of the past. In China, except for a brief period during the Boxer Uprising in 1900 and the Nationalist Revolution of 1927–1928 (when the U.S. had about 5,000 servicemen in the country), the U.S. never fielded forces remotely capable of dealing with any serious adversary.

• *Wars in which U.S. soldiers act as "social workers."* This phenomenon, said to be prevalent in the 1990s, raises hackles among veterans who complain, "It wasn't like that in my day. Our job was fighting wars, period." It is true that during World War II and the Cold War the U.S. military concentrated for the most part on its conventional war-fighting capabilities, and for good reason. But this is far from the norm in American history, and it was not even exclusively true during the 1941–1989 period (witness the 101st Airborne Division escorting African-American students to school in Little Rock, Arkansas, in 1956).

Soldiers follow orders, and presidents have often found it convenient or necessary to order the armed services to perform functions far removed from conventional warfare. Throughout U.S. history, marines at home and abroad have found themselves providing disaster relief, quelling riots, even guarding mail trains. Soldiers also have often acted as colonial administrators—in the Philippines, Haiti, Nicaragua, and Veracruz, to say nothing of post–World War II Germany and Japan or the post–Civil War South.

In fact occupation duty is generally necessary after a big war in order to impose the victor's will on the vanquished. If ground forces win a battle and go home, as the Powell Doctrine advocates and as actually happened in the Gulf War, the fruits of victory are likely to wither on the vine. Only boots on the ground can guarantee a lasting peace.

• *Wars in which America gets involved in other countries' internal affairs.* It is often said that the Kosovo War marked a new departure: the first time the West tampered with the supposedly sacred principle of sovereignty, embodied in the 1648 Treaty of Westphalia, which held that countries should be free to run their own affairs without outside interference. In reality, Westphalian principles were often traduced in Europe and seldom considered binding by either Europeans or Americans in their dealings with less developed parts of the globe.

The U.S. has been involved in other countries' internal affairs since at least 1805, when, during the Tripolitan War, William Eaton tried to topple the pasha of Tripoli and replace him with his pro-American brother. The rest of this book is a record of U.S. involvement in the internal affairs of other states, from Samoa to Nicaragua to China. Although the U.S. wanted to preserve the Open Door and protect China from being carved up into colonies by the Europeans and Japanese, American respect for Chinese sovereignty was far from absolute. What else explains America stationing troops in three of China's largest cities and sending gunboats to patrol its largest river?

• *Wars without a "vital national interest."* The search for a "vital national interest" was not much of an issue during the Cold War because almost every regional intervention (e.g., Grenada in 1983 or the Dominican Republic in 1965) could be linked, rightly or wrongly, to the fight against communism. But since the end of the Cold War, this has become a prime source of controversy. Various critics assert that U.S. armed forces should not be in Kosovo or Haiti or Somalia because, they claim, there is no national interest there. It all depends of course on how one defines "national interests." Isolationists like Patrick Buchanan say that U.S. interests are not threatened unless someone attacks American territory. Interventionists like Richard Holbrooke assert that U.S. interests are threatened even by AIDS in Africa. Who is right? It's a matter of individual judgment, but history suggests that the U.S. has never confined the use of force to situations that meet the narrow definition of American interests preferred by realpolitikers and isolationists.

A few small wars, like those against the Barbary pirates or the Boxers or Villistas, were fought to protect American nationals or territory and presumably would meet a narrow definition of self-interest. But it would be a stretch to claim that most of these interests were "vital." How vital were most of the "wrongs" avenged by hot-blooded nineteenth-century naval captains? Or how vital was it to protect U.S. trade with China, which never amounted to more than 4 percent of the total? U.S. policy toward China was driven less by businessmen than by missionaries, predecessors of today's human rights lobby.

What about American interventions in Latin America during the gunboat diplomacy era? Surely they were undertaken for material gain. A myth has flourished around these interventions—that they were conducted, as Smedley Butler later claimed, at the behest of Wall Street banks and banana companies. But in fact, as I argue in Chapters 6–7 and 10, the desire to protect American economic interests was only one of the motives behind the Banana Wars, and often not the most important one. Strategic and, yes, moral concerns played a vital role, especially in the actions of Woodrow Wilson, who vowed "to teach the South American republics to elect good men." "The interventions by U.S. Marines in Haiti, Nicaragua, the Dominican Republic, and elsewhere in those years," writes the political scientist Samuel P. Huntington, "often bore striking resemblances to the interventions by Federal marshals in the conduct of elections in the American South in the 1960s: registering voters, protecting against electoral violence, ensuring a free vote and an honest count."

The moral component is sometimes hard to discern from the vantage point of the twenty-first century because the terms in which it is expressed have changed. In the early twentieth century, Americans talked of spreading Anglo-Saxon civilization and taking up the "white man's burden"; today they talk of spreading democracy and defending human rights. Whatever you call it, this represents an idealistic impulse that has always been a big part in America's impetus for going to war. When its leaders try to present the case for war in purely strategic or economic terms—as Secretary of State James Baker III famously did when he said the Gulf War was about "job, jobs, jobs"— Americans are likely to be left cold. It is usually the moral component—in this case, Iraqi atrocities against Kuwaitis—that convinces Americans to take up arms.

Few wars are waged for *purely* humanitarian reasons. Most are fought for a combination of causes, moral, strategic, and economic. Sometimes the balance is heavily tilted toward moral factors—the Spanish-American and Kosovo Wars are good examples—but geopolitical considerations are rarely absent altogether. The U.S. fought Spain in part to assert an American leadership role in the Western Hemisphere, and it fought Serbia in part to assert an American leadership role in Europe.

• *Wars without significant popular support.* Few of the wars chronicled in this book aroused much enthusiasm among the American public. Just as few nineteenth-century Britons thought much about the thin red line safeguarding their interests on the Indian frontier, few Americans paid attention to what their troops were doing on the periphery of empire. Americans who glanced at their newspapers on July 29, 1915, might have noticed reports that the marines had landed in Port-au-Prince the day before. But if they were interested in overseas developments at all, they were probably more concerned with the war then raging in Europe. (The *New York Times* featured a small page-one item under the pithy headline, "Haitians Slay Their President; We Land Marines," but that day's lead story concerned the imminent execution of a policeman convicted of murder.)

When small wars aroused any notice back home, it was usually due to opposition mobilizing—particularly notable in the case of the Philippine War, the

1918 deployment to Russia, the occupation of Haiti and the Dominican Republic, and the Sandinista war in Nicaragua. But small numbers of professional soldiers were able to function well far from home even in the face of domestic sniping.

Mass mobilization of public opinion is needed for big wars, especially those like Vietnam that call on legions of conscripts. It is much less necessary when a relatively small number of professional soldiers are dispatched to some trouble spot. This has been especially true of marines. Whereas the presence of the army signaled to American and world opinion that a war was in progress, the marines were known as State Department troops and landed with little public fuss.

• *Wars in which U.S. troops serve under foreign command.* This became a sore point with those who tried to blame the United Nations for the debacle that occurred in Mogadishu on October 3, 1993, although the U.S. combat troops involved remained under U.S. control (only a small number of American logisticians served under U.N. auspices). In the past, however, there have been several instances of U.S. troops serving under the effective command of British officers—for instance, in Samoa (1899) and north Russia (1918–1919). History also offers examples of how unwillingness to subordinate to a multinational command structure can backfire—witness the disorganized march to Peking in the summer of 1900. The issue should not be whether American soldiers are serving under foreign officers, but whether they are serving under competent officers.

On-the-Job Training

It is clear, then, that many deeply held shibboleths about the American way of war—which can be summed up in the misconception that the job of the armed forces is limited to "fighting the nation's wars" in defense of "vital national interests"—have little historical basis. Nor, it must be added, is history kind to the warnings of post-Vietnam alarmists that America risks disaster every time it asks the armed forces to stray into other types of duties. Not all the operations chronicled in this book were totally successful—U.S. troops never caught up with Pancho Villa or Augusto Sandino—but the only real military failure was the mission to Russia in 1918–1920, and it was a pretty small-scale failure, hardly comparable to the grand disaster that unfolded in Indochina.

In most cases the armed forces, however ill-prepared for the job at hand, quickly adapted, figured out what they had to do, and did it with great success. The Philippine War stands as a monument to the U.S. armed forces' ability to fight and win a major counterinsurgency campaign—one that was bigger and uglier than any America is likely to confront in the future. Their experience in China showed that the armed forces are quite capable of muddling through even when they have to rely on bluff and swagger rather than overwhelming force.

In most of these operations the U.S. suffered relatively few casualties. The most costly was the Philippine War, which resulted in 4,200 American combat deaths—a tragedy but not on the scale of Vietnam, which cost 58,000 American lives. No casualties—the mantra of the 1990s—is almost impossible to achieve, but few casualties is the norm in these types of operations.

Perhaps this surface success was deceptive; perhaps fighting small wars incurred deeper, less obvious costs in lost military effectiveness. Surely these wars eroded the armed forces' ability to fight big wars and hurt their ability to attract recruits. Such are the refrains often heard in the post–Cold War era from critics, in uniform and out, who complain about the supposedly excessive pace (the "ops tempo") of small-scale deployments. History suggests we need not worry unduly.

In the early years of the twentieth century, the marines filled their ranks with those who wanted to be "soldiers in the sun." "We have a class of men in our ranks far superior to those in any other service in the world and they are high-spirited and splendid in every way," Brigadier General Smedley Butler wrote in 1928. "They joined because of our reputation for giving them excitement, and excitement from a marine's standpoint can only be gained by the use of bullets and the proximity to danger." Today the marines are having similar success filling their ranks with such recruits even as other services go begging. Across the armed services, reenlistment rates are actually higher in forward-deployed units (the army reports its highest reenlistment rates are in Bosnia and Kosovo), and many soldiers say they enjoy helping people in peace operations.

Such operations may cause disaffection among some who joined the armed forces during the Cold War and view peacekeeping duty as an unwelcome deviation from their preferred mission. But as the Cold War recedes further into history, the bulk of recruits and officers will have a clearer understanding that policing the Pax Americana is a central part of their mission.

Nor do such operations necessarily diminish U.S. readiness for a major war. Units engaged in peace operations may lose their edge at large-scale combined arms operations, says retired marine General Bernard Trainor, "but the service of young NCOs and lieutenants is enhanced. They're not drilling; they're dealing with real world situations." One survey of U.S. troops in Kosovo found that only 14 percent thought this peacekeeping duty would degrade their combat capability; the rest said their battle skills would be either improved or unaffected. Experience bears out this belief. The marines in the 1920s and 1930s were able to fight banana wars *and* prepare for amphibious operations in World War II; fighting the Sandinistas in the jungles of Nicaragua turned out to be excellent preparation for fighting the Japanese in the jungles of the South Pacific. Likewise, Pershing prepared for World War I by chasing Mexican Villistas and Philippine Moros, while the naval heroes of the War of 1812 learned their trade battling the Barbary Pirates.

British history offers further confirmation of this point. Queen Victoria's army spent most of its time on imperial policing duties. Then it was thrust into the biggest war the world had yet known. When British Tommies first landed in France and brushed up against advance units of the Kaiser's army on August 23, 1914, the Germans were startled by the rat-tat-tat rapidity of the fire coming at them. Surely the British must be employing machine guns, a German officer decided. In fact it was nothing more than rifle fire from expert marksmen schooled in the little wars of empire. The British cut the Germans to pieces that day at the Battle of Mons. True, the peacetime British army was too small to engage in all-out warfare against European opponents and had to be rapidly expanded, but its quality was not in doubt.

What Force Can Achieve

Having established, I hope, that small-war missions are militarily doable—and in fact have been done by the U.S. armed forces since the earliest days of the Republic—we turn now to tougher questions: Are they politically desirable? What have small wars of the past achieved?

American success is easy enough to see when the U.S. goal was seeking a strategic or economic concession, whether trade treaties with China, Japan, and smaller nations, or naval bases at Subic Bay in the Philippines and Guantanamo Bay, Cuba, or the right to build an isthmian canal in Panama. So too with missions designed to protect American life and property, such as the navy's efforts to suppress piracy in the Mediterranean and Caribbean in the early years of the nineteenth century, and the army's effort to rescue the legations in Peking during the Boxer Uprising. There is no question that these operations produced results. Equally clear, on the other side of the ledger, is the failure of the mission to Russia in 1918–1920, in large measure because it was unclear why the doughboys were sent. Was it to protect Allied war supplies and the Czech Legion or to overthrow the Bolsheviks? Woodrow Wilson himself was not sure, and the mission achieved little.

It is more difficult to judge the long-term success of punitive expeditions. Whether the expedition was being undertaken by gunboats or gunships, it generally hit its target—but to what effect? In 1986 Ronald Reagan dispatched warplanes to bomb Libya in retaliation for a terrorist attack on American servicemen in West Berlin. Subsequently the State Department claimed that Libyan support for terrorism declined, but there is also considerable evidence that two years later Muammar Gadhafi's agents blew up Pan Am flight 103 over Lockerbie, Scotland, killing 270 people. Was the 1986 raid on Libya really a success?

It is just as difficult to judge the consequences of past punitive expeditions, such as the 1871 mission to Korea. Rear Admiral John Rodgers had the forts around Inchon razed after one of them fired on his ships. Then his naval squadron sailed away. Eleven years later America became the first Western nation to sign a trade treaty with the Hermit Kingdom. The relationship between these two events must remain a matter of conjecture.

In some significant sense, however, such speculation is beside the point. Even if their ultimate consequences are unclear, punitive raids serve an important function. Much like punishments meted out by the criminal justice system, they satisfy the human impulse to see wrongdoers punished. The courts would not stop putting felons in jail even if this were proved to have no deterrent effect, and likewise Washington will not cease ordering retributive strikes for attacks on American citizens.

Finally, we come to those small wars whose success or failure is most difficult to assess—pacification campaigns. This book describes how the United States has occupied for varying lengths of time Samoa, Wake Island, Cuba, Puerto Rico, the Philippines, Panama, Nicaragua, Veracruz, Haiti, the Dominican Republic, and the Virgin Islands, to say nothing of Alaska and Hawaii. Most of these occupations achieved immediate American objectives—keeping the Europeans out, creating stability, protecting foreign lives and property, furthering free trade, and safeguarding strategically important real estate such as the approaches to the Panama Canal.

Many of these interventions also delivered tangible benefits to the occupied peoples. Although American imperial rule was subject to its share of abuses, U.S. administrators, whether civilian or military, often provided the most honest and efficient government these territories had ever seen. Haiti offers a particularly dramatic example. The 1920s, spent under marine occupation, saw one of the most peaceful and prosperous decades in the country's long and troubled history.

Of course U.S. administrators, in the manner of colonialists everywhere, usually received scant thanks afterward. As Kipling wrote:

Take up the White man's burden –
And reap his old reward:
The blame of those ye better,
The hate of those ye guard.

But the bulk of the people did not resist American occupation, as they surely would have done if it had been nasty and brutal. Many Cubans, Haitians, Dominicans, and others may secretly have welcomed U.S. rule—if not while the occupation was going on, then afterward, when local thugs took over from the Americans.

Although U.S. rule was generally benign, its effects often wore off quickly. The two most lasting legacies of American interventions in the Caribbean may be a Latin resentment of the *Yanquis*, now somewhat fading, and a love of baseball, still passionately felt, especially among Dominicans who provide a disproportionate share of the roster of Major League baseball. Most of the physical manifestations of the American empire—roads, hospitals, telephone systems—began to crumble not long after the marines pulled out. This should be no surprise; it has been true whenever technologically advanced imperialists leave a less sophisticated area, whether it was the Romans pulling out of Britain or the British out of India. Veracruz provides a vivid illustration of this phenomenon. The U.S. Army cleaned up the city and reduced the death rate from infectious diseases. Before long the *zopilotes* (vultures) that had made the city their home disappeared. But as soon as the army left, the residents resumed throwing garbage into the streets and back came the vultures.

More significantly, the American track record of imposing liberal, democratic regimes by force is mixed. The most notable successes are Japan, Germany, and Italy. The U.S. tended to be less successful in what later became known as the Third World, with the intriguing exception of the Philippines, which has been for the most part free and democratic except for the 1972–1986 period when Ferdinand Marcos ruled by fiat. Intriguing because the Philippines was the site of one of the longer U.S. occupations, which suggests that if the army stays long enough it leaves a lasting impact. Short-term (or even medium-term) occupations, on the other hand, are unlikely to fundamentally alter the nature of a society. It is not true, as some critics later charged, that in the Caribbean and Central American countries the U.S. deliberately installed dictators such as Duvalier or Somoza. But it is true that the marines could not create institutions strong enough to prevent their being usurped by a Duvalier or Somoza in the absence of American intervention.

That does not mean that U.S. administration is entirely futile. American troops can stop the killing, end the chaos, create a breathing space, establish the rule of law. What the inhabitants do then is up to them. If the American goal is to re-create Ohio in Kosovo or Haiti, then the occupiers are doomed to be disappointed. But if the goals are more modest, then American rule can serve the interests of occupiers and occupied alike. Put another way, "nation building" is generally too ambitious a task, but "state building" is a more realistic objective. The apparatus of a functioning state can be developed much more quickly than a national consciousness.

Successful state building starts by imposing the rule of law—as the U.S. did in the Philippines and the British in India—as a precondition for economic development and the eventual emergence of democracy. Merely holding an election and leaving is likely to achieve little, as the U.S. discovered in Haiti after 1994.

An analogy may help illuminate what U.S. troops can and cannot do. No one expects a big city police department to win the "war on crime." The police are considered successful if they reduce disorder, keep the criminal element at bay, and allow decent people a chance to live their lives in peace. In the process a few cops are likely to die, and while this is a tragedy to be mourned, no one suggests that as a result the police should go home and leave gangsters to run the streets.

It is easy to be fatalistic about the prospect that vigorous policing, at home or abroad, will do much good. But this cheap and easy cynicism has been repudiated by events time and again. In the early 1990s it was common wisdom that New York City was doomed to a downward slide. Crime and disorder were rampant and seemingly ineradicable. But Mayor Rudolph Giuliani showed that the situation was far from hopeless, that effective law enforcement could make a difference. And if it could work in New York City (sections of which, Rick Blaine warned a Nazi officer in *Casablanca*, "I wouldn't advise you to try to invade"), then why not elsewhere?

The Price of Nonintervention

In considering whether, based on the lessons of the past, we should undertake small wars in the future, we ought to remember not only the price of a botched intervention—Vietnam, Beirut, Somalia—but also the price of not intervening, or not intervening with sufficient determination. Two examples come to mind: Nicaragua and Russia.

In the former case, President Coolidge in 1925 withdrew from Managua the legation guard of 100 marines that had helped preserve stability for 13 years. Within a few months, Nicaragua was once again embroiled in revolution, and many more marines returned for a much longer stay.

In revolutionary Russia, Woodrow Wilson and David Lloyd George missed a prime opportunity in 1918–1919 to help topple the nascent Bolshevik regime. There is reason to believe that with slightly more Western help the Whites could have won the civil war—and in all likelihood changed the course of twentieth-century history immeasurably for the better. These examples are worth balancing against the Vietnam analogies that inevitably, tiresomely pop up whenever the dispatch of American forces overseas is contemplated.

The Butcher's Bill

So far I have considered mainly the benefits of intervention. But the costs must never be forgotten. Although it is a mistake to think that every intervention risks becoming another Vietnam-style disaster, it is equally wrong to suppose that every intervention can be as painless as the Kosovo War, which produced no casualties (and only two lost airplanes) among NATO forces. The "no casualties" mantra can work for purely punitive missions, where the job at hand consists of discharging cruise missiles from afar, just as in earlier days a gunboat could shell a native village at no risk to itself. But this no-risk mindset can be fatal for any mission more ambitious. Somalia presents the worst-case scenario: Americans arrive full of vim and vigor, only to leave, tails between their legs, after 18 soldiers die. This sends a message of American irresoluteness that can only cause trouble later.

Any nation bent on imperial policing will suffer a few setbacks. The British army, in the course of Queen Victoria's little wars, suffered major defeats with thousands of casualties in the First Afghan War (1842) and the Zulu War (1879). This did not appreciably dampen British determination to defend and expand the empire; it made them hunger for vengeance.

If Americans cannot adopt a similarly bloody-minded attitude, then they have no business undertaking imperial policing. I am not suggesting that Americans prepare themselves to suffer thousands of casualties for the sake of ephemeral goals, but policymakers should recognize that all military undertakings involve risk and should not run away at the first casualty. More important,

Washington should not structure these operations with the prime goal of producing no casualties. That is a recipe for ineffectiveness.

In any combat operation, blood will be shed, not only on the U.S. side but also among the enemy. This is an elementary truth, yet it was often overlooked in the 1990s when cruise missile strikes were planned to hit buildings after their occupants had gone home. Despite advances in modern weaponry, war can never be a clean, surgical business. Especially not urban and counterinsurgency warfare of the sort the U.S. finds itself undertaking in places ranging from Somalia to the former Yugoslavia. Sometimes, as in the Philippine War, it can be a very ugly business indeed. If the U.S. is not prepared to get its hands dirty, then it should stay home.

Policing the World

Most small wars the United States is likely to wage in the future are not highly controversial *in principle*, even if specific circumstances are likely to arouse debate. By this I mean punitive and protective missions, those designed to safeguard American citizens or punish those who attack them. This role for the armed forces is likely to grow in importance, since the world is littered with American targets—civilian, diplomatic, military—sure to tempt any young man with a gun and a grudge. It is likely that the September 11, 2001, attacks on the World Trade Center and the Pentagon are only a taste of what America can expect in the future. Few except the most obdurate isolationists would begrudge the U.S. the right to hit back or snatch citizens out of harm's way. Humanitarian missions are not very controversial, either, as long as they involve no prospect of combat—providing hurricane relief in Venezuela in 2000, for instance, or earthquake relief in Turkey in 1999. It is pacification missions, especially those billed as "humanitarian," that continue to cause controversy.

Should the United States involve itself in others' civil wars? Should America try to save foreigners from the cruelties of their neighbors or rulers? I believe the answer is yes, at least under certain circumstances. But it is not an easy question to answer and, based on the evidence presented here, I would not be surprised if some readers drew a different conclusion.

Such interventions offend the sensibilities of those who argue, as former Secretary of State James Baker did about Yugoslavia, that "we don't have a dog in that fight." Self-styled realists want U.S. forces to keep their powder dry until North Korea invades the South, Saddam Hussein makes another lunge for Kuwait, or China goes for Taiwan. (Some isolationists think even these contingencies would not warrant American action.) Ignore two-alarm fires, the "realists" and isolationists advise, and await the five-alarm blaze that may (or may not) come.

This cautious attitude, shared by many at the Pentagon, flies in the face of recent history. Democracy, capitalism, and freedom have spread across North America, Europe, Latin America, and to many parts of Asia—everywhere except Africa. At the same time, many parts of the world are being ravaged by tribalism and gangsterism. It is, to borrow the title of a book, *Jihad vs. McWorld.* The United States has an obvious stake in promoting the latter and stymieing the former. A world of liberal democracies would be a world much more amenable to American interests than any conceivable alternative.

Contrary to the dreams of some economic determinists, capitalism and freedom do not spread inexorably on their own. The nineteenth-century free trade system was protected and expanded by the Royal Navy. The only power capable of playing a comparable role today is the United States of America. Like Britain in the nineteenth century, the United States in the twenty-first century has power to spare. In fact the U.S. has more power than Britain did at the height of its empire, more power than any other state in modern times. It deploys the world's only blue-water navy of any significance and the world's most powerful air force; its armed forces have expeditionary capability undreamed of by any other power; its economy, powered by unceasing technological innovation, is the biggest and most dynamic on earth; its language has achieved a ubiquity unrivaled by any tongue since Latin; its culture permeates distant lands; and its political ideals remain a beacon of hope for all those "yearning to breathe free." The U.S. is so far ahead of any rival "in all the underlying components of power: economic, military, technological or geopolitical" that scholars describe the international scene as unipolar.

When it exercised a lesser degree of international hegemony, Britain battled the "enemies of all mankind," such as pirates and slave traders, and took upon itself the responsibility of keeping the world's oceans and seas open to navigation. Today America faces equivalent tasks—battling terrorists, narco-traffickers, and weapons proliferaters, and ensuring open access to not only the oceans but also the skies and space. Britain acted to preserve the balance of power wherever it was endangered, coming to the aid of weak nations (such as Belgium or Turkey) being bullied by the strong (Germany or Russia). America has played a similar role in protecting Bosnian and Kosovar Muslims against Serbs, and Kuwaitis against Iraq.

Many of the steps Britain took, such as stamping out the slave trade or the murderous thug cult in India, were hard to justify on a narrow calculus of self-interest. It acted simply out of a sense that it was the right thing to do. It is doubtful that American leaders can resist the call for similar humanitarian interventions in an age when the public back home knows far more about horrors being perpetrated in the far corners of the world than it did in the Victorian era. And why should America not "do something," assuming the cost of action is not high? Why not use some of the awesome power of the U.S. government to help the downtrodden of the world, just as it is used to help the needy at home? As Theodore Roosevelt said, "A nation's first duty is within its borders, but it is not thereby absolved from facing its duties in the world as a whole; and if it refuses to do so, it merely forfeits its right to struggle for a place among the people that shape the destiny of mankind."

Roosevelt committed the United States "to the exercise of an international police power" in the Caribbean, the one region where America was then the predominant power. Today America has as much power in many parts of the world—for starters, in northeast Asia, Europe, and the Persian Gulf—as it once had only in the Caribbean. Many Americans cringe at the notion that their country should play globocop. But this is not a purely altruistic exercise. Without a benevolent hegemon to guarantee order, the international scene can degenerate quickly into chaos and worse. One scholar argues, with great plausibility, that the 1930s turned out as badly as they did because Britain abdicated its international leadership role, and Uncle Sam refused to don the mantle. Another scholar argues, with equal persuasiveness, that the post-1945 era turned out as well as it did in large measure because America was willing to underwrite the security of the global economy—and that the entire world will suffer if America fails to exert leadership in the years to come.

That does not mean that the armed services should be redirected exclusively toward a constabulary role. This would be as misguided as not preparing for such missions at all. Though no major power threat confronted America at the dawn of the twenty-first century, the odds are that one will emerge in the years ahead; one always has. In the meantime, however, the military cannot simply turn its back on "peace" operations that hold out the promise of resolving small problems before they fester into major crises. The costs of engaging in places like Afghanistan are much lower than allowing them to become breeding grounds for terrorists such as those who struck America on September 11, 2001.

Some say the United States cannot afford to prepare for wars both big *and* small, that America might strangle its economy by the exertion needed to police the nether reaches of the globe. This is an enduring argument, stretching back to the days of Albert Gallatin, Jefferson's Treasury secretary, who insisted that America would be stronger in peacetime if it paid off its debts rather than field a large standing military. This view made sense for a country like the Soviet Union, which spent perhaps 25 percent of its meager GDP on the armed forces—clearly an unsustainable level. But it does not apply to nineteenth-century Britain or twenty-first-century America.

The British Empire did not collapse because its defense drained the Exchequer. It collapsed because Great Britain exhausted itself in fighting and winning two world wars, conflicts that might have been averted if Whitehall had deployed a larger military capable of deterring German aggression. Britain spent an average of 3.1 percent of GDP on defense during its imperial heyday, 1870 to 1913, and kept about 1 percent of its population under arms—hardly a crippling burden. In 2001 America spent just 2.9 percent of GDP on defense, the lowest level since before Pearl Harbor, and approximately 0.5 percent of its population was on active duty. Of course Uncle Sam's military is considerably larger in absolute numbers and infinitely more powerful than Queen Victoria's. But if America needs to spend a little more to accomplish its dual military missions—policing its virtual "empire" and deterring major-power adversaries— then this is still a small price to pay, considering the alternatives.

No nation, no matter how rich, can afford to wage war without end. It makes sense for the U.S., wherever possible, to use non-military means to achieve its objectives. American culture and American economic strength are especially potent tools for spreading American influence abroad. When force is required, the U.S. can often seek help from ad hoc "coalitions of the willing," as in Kosovo, or make use of the United Nations, especially to legitimate its interventions. It is doubtful, however, that this organization will be capable of fielding an effective, independent military force anytime soon. The really big challenges can be resolved only through American leadership, which means a willingness to commit troops if necessary. Often, however, the mere threat is enough. The Roman writer Vegetius's advice, *Qui desiderat pacem, praeparet bellum* (Let him who desires peace, prepare for war), applies as much to small wars as to big.

When the United States does act, it ought to get it right. Sometimes U.S. troops can achieve a great deal by a quick in-and-out operation, as in Panama in 1989, when the U.S. toppled the drug thug Manuel Noriega. But when dealing with collapsing countries—and such states are increasingly common as the artificial boundaries drawn by European statesmen dissolve in places ranging from Indonesia to Congo to Yugoslavia—only a long-term commitment is likely to do much good. The 1994 U.S. intervention in Haiti achieved little beyond restoring the morally dubious Jean-Bertrand Aristide to power.

It is doubtful that America can or should unilaterally occupy countries for as long as it once did. Some system sanctioned by the U.N. may need to be worked out that will allow the international community to place failed states like Afghanistan or Sierra Leone into a state of receivership. A possible model can be found in the "mandates" granted by the League of Nations in the 1920s to European states to run various colonies, in theory for the good of their inhabitants. In the 1990s, Bosnia, Kosovo, Cambodia, and East Timor became wards of the international community; this may be a harbinger of things to come.

In debating the merits of intervention, Americans ought to be wary of arguments that say, "If you intervene in X, why not in Y?" The U.S. was accused of racism for going into Bosnia but not Rwanda. But there is nothing wrong with saving a few people in one place even if you cannot save everybody everywhere. The essence of statesmanship is making difficult choices, weighing costs and benefits, and committing limited resources where they can do the most good. No universal rule to govern American use of force—no alternative to the Powell Doctrine—is possible or desirable. Interventions must be decided on a case-by-case basis. In reaching their decisions, however, policymakers should keep in mind not only the U.S. interests at stake but also how much a proposed mission can accomplish, and at what cost. Even if the U.S. stake is not very great—and it seldom is great, when it comes to small wars—military intervention may still make sense if the costs are low enough or the potential good that American troops can accomplish great enough.

One final bit of advice, based on the lessons of history. In deploying American power, decisionmakers should be less apologetic, less hesitant, less humble. Yes, there is a danger of imperial overstretch and hubris—but there is an equal, if not greater, danger of undercommitment and lack of confidence. America should not be afraid to fight "the savage wars of peace" if necessary to enlarge the "empire of liberty." It has done it before.

NOTES

Preface: Another American Way of War

xii   "Foggy, swamped bottomed": Shacochis, *Immaculate Invasion*, xv.

xiii   "Campaigns undertaken": Calwell, *Small Wars*, 21.

xiv   "Perdicaris alive, or Raisuli dead": The whole affair was settled by negotiation, with Roosevelt's secret encouragement. See Morris, *Theodore Rex*, Chapter 21.

xv   Economic and military power: For an intriguing argument about the origins of American military power see Zakaria, *From Wealth to Power*.

xviii   "The hidden hand of the market": Friedman, *Lexus and Olive Tree*, 373.

Chapter 1: "To Conquer Upon the Sea"

3–5   Burning the *Philadelphia*: U.S. Office of Naval Records, *Naval Documents*, vol. 3, 376–418; Tucker, *Dawn Like Thunder*, 269–283; Lewis, *Romantic Decatur*, 38–52; MacKenzie, *Life of Decatur*, 61–82; Whipple, *To the Shores of Tripoli*, 130–140; McKee, *Edward Preble*, 189–201; Fowler, *Jack Tars and Commodores*, 99–102; Guttridge and Smith, *The Commodores*, 86–91.

5   Quasi-war: The John Adams administration fought an undeclared war against France from 1798 to 1800, because French privateers were seizing American ships carrying British goods (Britain and France were then at war; America was neutral).

6   "Every scheme": MacKenzie, *Life of Decatur*, 11.

6   Decatur: An early, hagiographic biography, MacKenzie's *Life*, remains useful, especially for the documents in the appendix. See also Lewis, *Romantic Decatur*; Tucker, *Dawn Like Thunder*, 265–269; Decatur Biographical File, NHC.

6   "America's first ... hero": Ellis, *American Sphinx*, 204. For more on Decatur's reception, see Allison, *Crescent Obscured*, 190–193.

6–8   Background on Barbary States: Hallett, *Africa to 1875,* 111–132; Fisher, *Barbary Legend;* Abun-Nasr, *History of the Maghrib,* 159–202; Dearden, *Nest of Corsairs,* 1–24; Rogerson, *A Traveler's History of North Africa,* 221–239; Flint, *Cambridge History of Africa,* vol. 5, 99–104.

9   Until 1776: Some American ships were captured by North African corsairs even in pre-Revolutionary times, the first one being taken by Morocco in 1625. In 1645 a Massachusetts ship fought an Algerian raider in what was believed to be the first American naval battle. See Allison, *Crescent Obscured,* xiv.

10   Barbary slaves: For Cathcart's account, see Cathcart, *The Captives, Eleven Years a Prisoner in Algiers,* compiled by his daughter, J. B. Newkirk, in Baepler, *White Slaves, African Masters,* 103–146. For Foss, see Foss, *A Journal of the Captivity and Sufferings of John Foss* in ibid., 71–102; Fowler, *Jack Tars and Commodores,* 4–8. Most, though not all, Americans conveniently overlooked the fact that many more slaves were held by the United States than by the Maghrib states—and, as U.S. diplomat William Eaton noted in 1799, "the Christian slaves among the barbarians of Africa are treated with more humanity than the African slaves among the professing Christians of civilized America." See Allison, *The Crescent Obscured,* 93.

11   U.S. Navy launched and peace signed: U.S. Office of Naval Records, *Naval Documents,* vol. 1, 68–140; Whipple, *To the Shores of Tripoli,* 44–51; Tucker, *Dawn Like Thunder,* 57–95; Sprout and Sprout, *Rise of American Naval Power,* 25–38.

11–12   Bainbridge's voyage: U.S. Office of Naval Records, *Naval Documents,* vol. 1, 375–436; Tucker, *Dawn Like Thunder,* 11–37; Fowler, *Jack Tars and Commodores,* 63–64.

13   Jefferson's decision to fight: Whipple, *To the Shores of Tripoli,* 62–67; Tucker and Hendrickson, *Empire of Liberty,* 294–299; Allison, *Crescent Obscured,* 24–27. For general background on Jefferson, the most exhaustive account remains Malone's two-volume *Jefferson the President,* but the most incisive is Ellis, *American Sphinx.* See also the excellent sketches in Winik, *April 1865,* 4–12; Johnson, *History of the American People,* 201–214; and Leckie, *From Sea to Shining Sea,* 23–28.

13–14   Dale's expedition: U.S. Office of Naval Records, *Naval Documents,* vol. 1, 440–648, vol. 2, 1–82; Whipple, *To the Shores of Tripoli,* 65–81; Tucker, *Dawn Like Thunder,* 131–148; Fowler, *Jack Tars and Commodores,* 66–70.

14–16   Morris's expedition: U.S. Office of Naval Records, *Naval Documents,* vol. 2, 82–531; Whipple, *To the Shores of Tripoli,* 83–104; Tucker, *Dawn Like Thunder,* 148–189; Fowler, *Jack Tars and Commodores,* 72–82.

16–18   Background on Preble and early part of his expedition: McKee, *Edward Preble;* Whipple, *To the Shores of Tripoli,* 105–114; Tucker, *Dawn Like Thunder,* 189–210; Fowler, *Jack Tars and Commodores,* 82–92; Pratt, *Preble's Boys,* 13–39.

18 Couscous: The sailors considered it a great hardship to be forced to eat this grain, which was unfamiliar to the typical eighteenth-century American.

19 Capture of the *Philadelphia* and treatment of crew: U.S. Office of Naval Records, *Naval Documents*, vol. 3, 175–257; Ray, *Horrors of Slavery*, in Baepler, *White Slaves, African Masters*, 188–203; Cowdery, *American Captives in Tripoli*, in ibid., 161–185; Tucker, *Dawn Like Thunder*, 210–251; Whipple, *To the Shores of Tripoli*, 114–130.

20 Noble indignation": MacKenzie, *Life of Decatur*, 91.

20 A seaman: The heroic sailor was probably Daniel Frazier, though early accounts credited Reuben James.

21 John Trippe: He died just six years after his heroics, a victim of yellow fever. See McKee, *A Gentlemanly and Honorable Profession*, 409.

21 Preble's first attack on Tripoli: U.S. Office of Naval Records, *Naval Documents*, vol. 4, 263–347; MacKenzie, *Life of Decatur*, 86–100; McKee, *Edward Preble*, 252–271; Whipple, *To the Shores of Tripoli*, 147–158; Lewis, *Romantic Decatur*, 60–65; Tucker, *Dawn Like Thunder*, 291–307.

22 End of Preble's expedition: Cowdery, *American Captives in Tripoli*, in Baepler, *White Slaves, African Masters*, 173; Whipple, *To the Shores of Tripoli*, 147–169; McKee, *Edward Preble*, 272–346; Tucker, *Dawn Like Thunder*, 307–333; Fowler, *Jack Tars and Commodores*, 110–113.

23 Eaton's background: Edwards, *Barbary General*.

23 Hamid: His name is also spelled as Ahmed and Hamet. Yusuf's name is sometimes converted to Joseph.

24 O'Bannon: For background see Lewis, *Famous American Marines*, 39–54.

25 Eaton's expedition: Eaton Papers, Boxes 7–8; U.S. Office of Naval Records, *Naval Documents*, vol. 5, 348–561, vol. 6, 1–117; Whipple, *To the Shores of Tripoli*, 177–243; Tucker, *Dawn Like Thunder*, 347–415; Edwards, *Barbary General*, 158–224; Wright and Macleod, *First Americans*, 151–196; Fowler, *Jack Tars and Commodores*, 113–119.

27 Eaton and peace with Tripoli: Cowdery, *American Captives in Tripoli*, in Baepler, *White Slaves, African Masters*, 183; Whipple, *To the Shores of Tripoli*, 243–276; Tucker, *Dawn Like Thunder*, 415–448; Edwards, *Barbary General*, 224–266; Fowler, *Jack Tars and Commodores*, 119–123; Malone, *Jefferson: Second Term*, 35–44; Allison, *Crescent Obscured*, 195–201.

28 Decatur's expedition in 1815: Guttridge and Smith, *The Commodores*, 269–288; Whipple, *To the Shores of Tripoli*, 276–281; Lewis, *Romantic Decatur*, 160–183; MacKenzie, *Life of Decatur*, 273–291; Tucker, *Dawn Like Thunder*, 448–426.

28 Cost of Barbary Wars: Fowler, *Jack Tars and Commodores*, 124.

28 End of North African independence: M. H. Cherif, "New Trends in the Maghrib: Algeria, Tunisia and Libya," in Ajayi (ed.), *General History of Africa*, vol. 6, 455–458.

28 James Barron: Brother of Commodore Samuel Barron, who had succeeded Edward Preble as commander of the fleet attacking Tripoli.

29   Decatur's death: Guttridge and Smith, *The Commodores*, 289–299; Whipple, *To the Shores of Tripoli*, 281–282; Lewis, *Romantic Decatur*, 190–230; Tucker, *Dawn Like Thunder*, 426.

29   "Mention of Tripoli": Quoted in Baepler, *White Slaves, African Masters*, 32.

Chapter 2: "Butcher and Bolt"

30–31   Porter background: Long's biography, *Nothing Too Daring*, supercedes Turnbull's earlier *Commodore David Porter*. Also useful: Porter, *Memoir;* Pratt, *Preble's Boys*, 199–240.

31   "It presented the appearance": Melville, *Typee*, 24.

34   "Their extreme youth": Melville, *Typee*, 15.

31–38   Marquesas expedition: Captain Porter recounted his adventures in Porter, *Journal of a Cruise*, and Porter, *Memoir*, 167–253—the source of all quotations attributed to him. For secondary accounts, see Long, *Nothing Too Daring*, Chapter 5; Robotti and Vescovi, *USS Essex*; Werstein, *Cruise of the Essex*, 109–143; Turnbull, *Commodore David Porter*, 183–224; Ellsworth, *One Hundred Eighty Landings*, 112–113.

38   "Butcher and bolt": Gann, *Guerillas in History*.

38   Guano islands: See Skaggs, *The Great Guano Rush*.

39   "Young men": Quoted in McKee, *A Gentlemanly and Honorable Profession*, 167.

40   "There still lingers": Melville, *White-Jacket*, 157.

40–41   Navy officers and men: Karsten, *Naval Aristocracy*; McKee, *A Gentlemanly and Honorable Profession*, 219; Shulman, *Navalism*, 39–45; Bolster, *Black Jacks*.

41   "Murdered all the crew": From a "private letter" dated September 27, 1821, cited in Allen, *Our Navy and the West Indian Pirates*, 22.

43   Porter's temper: Long, *Nothing Too Daring*, 7, 18–19, 33.

44   "Muskets, bayonets": Allen, *Our Navy and the West Indian Pirates*, 68.

45   Roosevelt impressed: Roosevelt, *Naval War of 1812*, 92–93.

45   Caribbean piracy: There are three general histories: Wheeler, *In Pirate Waters;* Allen, *Our Navy and the West Indian Pirates;* and Bradlee, *Piracy in the West Indies*. For Porter's role, see Porter, *Memoir*, 270–345; Long, *Nothing Too Daring*, Chapters 8–9; Turnbull, *Commodore David Porter*, 253–282. The court-martial proceedings were published in U.S. Navy, *Minutes of Proceedings*. For Perry's actions, see Morison, *Old Bruin*, 77–81.

45–46   Falklands: Belohlavek, *Let the Eagle Soar*, 181–190; Schroeder, *Shaping a Maritime Empire*, 28–30; Long, *Gold Braid and Foreign Relations*, 151–155; Remini, *Andrew Jackson*, 197–198; Love, *History of the U.S. Navy*, 159, 229; Hagan, *People's Navy*, 103–104; Offutt, *Protection of Citizens Abroad*, 21–22.

46–47   "The people": Phillips, *Pepper and Pirates*, 5.

47 "Raised their war whoop": Warriner, *Cruise of the . . . Potomac*, 79. This is the memoir of the *Potomac's* schoolmaster.

48–49 Sumatra: A firsthand account of the 1832 expedition may be found in Warriner, *Cruise of the . . . Potomac*, 75–113. See also Phillips, *Pepper and Pirates*; Long, *Gold Braid*, 252–260; Schroeder, *Shaping a Maritime Empire*, 25–28, 45; Belohlavek, *Let the Eagle Soar*, 152–162; Paullin, *American Voyages to the Orient*, Chapters 6, 9; Love, *History of the United States Navy*, 154–158; Remini, *Andrew Jackson*, 192–193; Ellsworth, *180 Landings*, 151–154; Offutt, *Protection of Citizens Abroad*, 22–24; Hagan, *People's Navy*, 102–103; Tucker, *Andrew Foote*, 27–28.

50 Wilkes Exploring Expedition: The commander's account may be found in Wilkes, *Autobiography*, 456–472. See also Long, *Gold Braid*, 291–298; Johnson, *Thence Around Cape Horn*, 52–53; Ellsworth, *180 Landings*, 72–74, 77–82, 144–146; Offutt, *Protection of Citizens Abroad*, 25–26.

50 Kossuth: Klay, *Daring Diplomacy*; Long, *Gold Braid*, 185–190; Hagan, *People's Navy*, 143.

51 Africa: Thomas, *Slave Trade*, 616–620, 661–662, 727–728, 763; Morison, *Old Bruin*, 69, 164–174; Long, *Gold Braid*, 308–320; Ellsworth, *180 Landings*, 5–7; Love, *History of the U.S. Navy*, 174.

51 Naval diplomacy: The two most up-to-date studies are Long's *Gold Braid and Foreign Relations* and Schroeder's *Shaping a Maritime Empire*. Paullin's older *Diplomatic Negotiations* remains useful.

51 China: Here and in subsequent chapters I employ the traditional Wade-Giles method of transliterating Chinese names, which was in use at the time, instead of the more modern Pinyin system. Hence Peking, not Beijing; Canton, not Guangzhou; Tientsin, not Tianjin; etc.

54 China: For the role of the U.S. Navy, see Johnson, *Far China Station*, 19–31, 73–103; Tucker, *Andrew Foote*, 82–101; Nalty, *Barrier Forts*; Paullin, *American Voyages to the Orient*, Chapter 13; Ellsworth, *180 Landings*, 21–30; Leavenworth, *Arrow War*, 34–39. For general background I have relied on two standard histories: Hsu, *The Rise of Modern China*, 139–257, and Spence, *Search for Modern China*, 143–215.

54 Anglo-American cooperation: Karsten, *Naval Aristocracy*, 107; Johnson, *Far China Station*, 115–120; Offutt, *Protection of Citizens Abroad*, 42–48, 65–66; Long, *Gold Braid*, 298–300.

55 U.S. exports: Millett and Maslowski, *For the Common Defense*, 140.

Chapter 3: Empire Emerging

57 Falloff: The figure for landings abroad comes from Ellsworth, *180 Landings*, ii-iii; the diplomatic negotiations figure derives from Long, *Gold Braid*, 416.

57 Post–Civil War navy: Long, *Gold Braid*, 338–341; Shulman, *Navalism*, 26–27; Hagan, *People's Navy*, 175–186.

58   Koreans took umbrage: As Senator A. A. Sargent of California noted on the Senate floor in 1876, reflecting back on the Rodgers expedition, "We may not allow any foreign vessel of a nation with which we even might have a treaty to come and survey our James or any other river." See Lee, *Diplomatic Relations*, 28.

59   "Corean sword": Griffis, *Corea*, 415.

59   Korea: Officers' reports may be found in U.S. Secretary of the Navy, *Annual Report* 1871. McLane Tilton's letters to his wife Nan are in the Tilton Papers. See also Long, *Gold Braid*, 374–380; Johnson, *Far China Station*, 154–166; Johnson, *Rear Admiral Rodgers*, 308–331; Han, *History of Korea*, 364–370, 385–385; Oliver, *History of the Korean People*, 42–54; Griffis, *Corea*, 403–419; Ellsworth, *180 Landings*, 57–59; Offutt, *Protection of Citizens Abroad*, 54–60; Lee, *Diplomatic Relations*, 19–49.

60–61   Panama: Hagan, *American Gunboat Diplomacy*, 152–185; McCullough, *The Path Between the Seas*, 175–179; Panama Geographical File, MCHD.

62   "Poor excuse for a tub": Quoted in Karsten, *Naval Aristocracy*, 279.

63   Economic pressures: See, e.g., LaFeber, *Cambridge History*, vol. 2, *American Search*, 103.

64   New navy and overseas possession: Hagan, *American Gunboat Diplomacy*, 4–26, 40–50; Shulman, *Navalism*; Sprout and Sprout, *Rise of American Naval Power*, 165–222; Morris, *Rise of Theodore Roosevelt*, Chapter 22; LaFeber, *Cambridge History*, vol. 2, *American Search*, 12–20, 66, 81; Healey, *Drive to Hegemony*, 30–32; Stevens, *American Expansion in Hawaii*; Zakaria, *From Wealth to Power*.

66   Medal of Honor: Prior to 1916 the Medal of Honor was the only medal given to American servicemen, and the standard for receiving one was merely "gallantry in action, or other soldierlike qualities." Starting in 1916 the Medal of Honor was limited to those who showed "conspicuous gallantry or intrepidity, at the risk of life, *above and beyond* the call of duty" (emphasis added). See Roth, *Muddy Glory*, 171.

66   Samoa: The most detailed accounts of the April 1, 1899, battle—from the reports of Lt. C. M. Perkins and Assistant Surgeon G. A. Lung—may be found in U.S. Secretary of the Navy, *Annual Report* 1899. See also Craven, "A Naval Episode"; Millett, *Semper Fidelis*, 149–150; Ellsworth, *180 Landings*, 146–149; and Offutt, *Protection of Citizens Abroad*, 83–85. For general background, see Kennedy, *Samoan Tangle*, and Ryden, *The Foreign Policy of the United States in Relation to Samoa*, 191–574.

66   Becoming more dangerous: I am indebted for this point to Millett, *Semper Fidelis*, 149-150.

Chapter 4: Red Summer

69   Hearst and the War of 1898: Nasaw, *The Chief*, Chapter 7, provides a good account.

69   "Savage, bitter": *New York Evening Journal,* July 17, 1900.

72   "Model of dynamism": Keown-Boyd, *Boxer Rebellion,* 4.

71–74   Background on China and Boxers: Esherick, *Origins of the Boxer Uprising;* Fairbank, *United States and China,* 158–205; Cohen, *History in Three Keys,* 14–44, 69–146; Hsu, *Rise of Modern China,* 355–393; Spence, *Search for Modern China,* 216–238; Preston, *Boxer Rebellion,* 12–32; O'Connor, *Spirit Soldiers,* 7–32; *Shanghai Mercury, Boxer Uprising,* ii; LaFeber, *Cambridge History,* vol. 2, *American Search,* 172.

75–77   Seymour relief expedition: The commander of the American contingent left an unpublished memoir in the McCalla Papers; Chapter 27 concerns the Seymour expedition. See also MacCloskey, *Reilly's Battery,* 92–94; Savage Landor, *China and the Allies,* vol. 1, 96–106; O'Connor, *Spirit Soldiers,* 105–106; Keown-Boyd, *Boxer Rebellion,* 64–67, 83–85, 93–99; Preston, *Boxer Rebellion,* 89–104.

77–78   Attack on Taku forts: Savage Landor, *China and the Allies,* 113–124; *Keown-Boyd,* 75–83; Preston, *Boxer Rebellion,* 108–113.

81   Hanlin fire: Seagrave, in *Dragon Lady,* argues that Westerners actually destroyed the library and then blamed it on the Chinese. Preston, in *Boxer Rebellion,* 383, demolishes this conspiracy theory.

82   "I never saw": From an unpublished, undated memoir by Captain Newt Hall, 17. Hall Papers.

82–84   Captain Myers: Myers's report is in U.S. Secretary of the Navy, *Annual Report* 1900. For background on him, see Biographical File; Lewis, *Famous American Marines,* 175–186.

84–85   Dan Daly: Daly Biographical File; Hall Papers; Hall's report in U.S. Secretary of the Navy, *Annual Report* 1900.

85   Peking siege to early July: A firsthand account: Hooker, *Behind the Scenes,* 46–126. See also O'Connor, *Spirit Soldiers,* 167–199; Preston, *Boxer Rebellion,* 124–164; Keown Boyd, *Boxer Rebellion,* 85–93, 104–111, 130–134; MacCloskey, *Reilly's Battery,* 78–84; *Shanghai Mercury, Boxer Uprising,* 87–99; Hsu, *The Rise of Modern China,* 392–396.

85   "When one young woman escaped": Cohen, *History in Three Keys,* 172.

85–86   Siege of Tientsin: A firsthand account comes from Brown, *From Tientsin to Peking,* 32–36. See also O'Connor, *Spirit Soldiers,* 142; Preston, *Boxer Rebellion,* 104–107, 113–123.

86   Marine advance on Tientsin: The more valuable accounts written by participants include Butler and Thomas, *Old Gimlet Eye,* 44–54; Daggett, *America in the China Relief Expedition,* 18–21; Hoover, *Memoirs of Herbert Hoover,* 52. Officers' dispatches may be found in U.S. Secretary of the Navy, *Annual Report* 1900, and in the Butler Papers, Box 4, Folder 1. See also MacCloskey, *Reilly's Battery,* 99–101; Schmidt, *Maverick Marine,* 12–16.

88   Tientsin taken: "Those who remained" quote is from *Shanghai Mercury, Boxer Uprising,* 30. See also Savage Landor, *China and the Allies,* vol. 1,

132–217; Brown, *From Tientsin to Peking*, 32–39; U.S. Secretary of the Navy, *Annual Report* 1900, 1901; Preston, *Boxer Rebellion*, 184–189; O'Connor, *Spirit Soldiers*, 148–155; Keown-Boyd, *Boxer Rebellion*, 134–143; MacCloskey, *Reilly's Battery*, 109–115; Daggett, *America in the China Relief Expedition*, 24–42; Schmidt, *Maverick Marine*, 17–20; Cohen, *History in Three Keys*, 184.

89   Temporary truce: Keown-Boyd, *Boxer Rebellion*, 143–155; Preston, *Boxer Rebellion*, 190–212.

91   "He has a high forehead": Luke E. Wright, vice governor general of the Philippines, in Schott, *Ordeal of Samar*, 169. For more on Chaffee, see Utley, *Frontier Regulars*, 223, and Roth, *Muddy Glory*, 23–24.

91   "It was a nightmare": Wise and Frost, *A Marine Tells It to You*, 55.

94   Relief expedition: Firsthand accounts are contained in Daggett, *America in the China Relief Expedition*, 55–95, and Savage Landor, *China and the Allies*, vol. 1, 324–381, vol. 2, 172–190. See also O'Connor, *Spirit Soldiers*, 216–243; Keown-Boyd, *Boxer Rebellion*, 156–182; Preston, *Boxer Rebellion*, 217–249; Schmidt, *Maverick Marine*, 23.

94   Peitang Cathedral: O'Connor, *Spirit Soldiers*, 253; Keown-Boyd, *Boxer Rebellion*, 191–204; Preston, *Boxer Rebellion*, 262–274; Cohen, *History in Three Keys*, 132.

94–96   Reilly's Battery: Savage Landor, *China and the Allies*, vol. 2, 199–207; MacCloskey, *Reilly's Battery*, 156–169; Daggett, *America in the China Relief Expedition*, 96; Hooker, *Behind the Scenes*, 184.

97    $335 million: Worth roughly $4.35 billion in today's dollars.

97   Allied occupation: Daggett, *America in the China Relief Expedition*, 106–141; Keown-Boyd, *Boxer Rebellion*, 205–219; Butler and Thomas, *Old Gimlet Eye*, 76; Schmidt, *Maverick Marine*, 23; Preston, *Boxer Rebellion*, 283–311.

97   Consequences of Boxer rebellion: Hsu, *Rise of Modern China*, 404–406.

Chapter 5: "Attraction" and "Chastisement"

99   "We are bound for googoo land": Recollection of Private H. W. Manire, in Taylor, *Massacre at Balangiga*, 21.

100   "On the ground": G. E. Meyer, in ibid., 3.

100   "Young, vigorous, zealous": Edwin Bookmiller to Adjutant General, Visayas, September 30, 1901, in U.S. Secretary of War, *Annual Report* 1902, 607.

101   "Yelling like devils": Recollection of company musician G. E. Meyer, quoted in Taylor, *Massacre at Balangiga*, 6.

101   Survivors: The company strength at the time of the attack was 74 officers and men; out of the original 77, one had committed suicide, one had deserted, and one had gone insane and been evacuated.

101   "Stabbed pig": G. E. Meyer, in Taylor, *Massacre at Balangiga*, 7.

101   "Started pumping lead": Ibid., 6.

101–102 "We at last shoved off" and "Words cannot express": From the diary of Private Walter James Bertholf, reprinted in *Infantry,* May 5, 1998, 16.

102   Balangiga massacre: It is not easy to separate fact from fiction regarding this once-famous episode. The most popular account is Schott, *Ordeal of Samar,* which is vivid—perhaps too vivid. It is hard to escape the suspicion that portions of Schott's narrative are fictionalized. For instance, Schott, at 55, claims that Captain Bookmiller gathered up some Filipino prisoners and allowed the survivors of Company C to execute them. But, as Linn points out, in his superb history, *The Philippine War,* 396, this tale is based entirely on one vague line in an account told years later by a soldier who in the meantime had suffered a nervous breakdown. No mention of the killing was made by other eyewitnesses. Karnow, *In Our Image,* 189–191, and Miller, *Benevolent Assimilation,* 200–204, closely follow Schott. This account is based on the officers' reports, found in U.S. Secretary of War, *Annual Report* 1902; Taylor, *Massacre at Balangiga* (a compendium of American survivors' accounts); Brown, *History of the Ninth U.S. Infantry,* 575–593 (the official regimental history); the recollections of Private Adolph Gambiss, in Spanish-American War Survey, 28th U.S. Volunteers, Harry M. Foot File; the diary of Private Walter James Bertholf; Sexton, *Soldiers in the Sun,* 268–272; and Taylor, *Philippine Insurrection,* vol. 5, 689 (for Abayan's letter to Lukban), 703–705. An interesting footnote to the Balangiga massacre is the continuing controversy over the bells of the village church. They eventually wound up at an air force base in Wyoming, and the Philippines wants them back. See Tomsho, "Tarnished Chimes."

104   Dewey: Morris, in *The Rise of Theodore Roosevelt,* 578, has a particularly vivid description of the admiral: "With his beaky nose and restless, caged strut, Dewey looked like a resplendent killer falcon, ready to bite through wire, if necessary, to get at a likely prey."

102–105 Events leading up to U.S. capture of Manila: Linn, *Philippine War,* 15–26; Linn, *U.S. Army and Counterinsurgency,* 6; Karnow, *In Our Image,* 74–126; Bain, *Sitting in Darkness,* 66–72, 154–179; Gates, *Schoolbooks and Krags,* 3–21.

106   Some 7 million inhabitants: Estimates of the Philippines' population at the turn of the twentieth century range from 6 million to 7.5 million.

106   Events leading up to annexation: Sexton, *Soldiers in the Sun,* 42–58; Linn, *Philippine War,* 29–31; Linn, *U.S. Army and Counterinsurgency,* 9; Leech, *In the Days of McKinley,* 323–348; Karnow, *In Our Image,* 107–130; Miller, *Benevolent Assimilation,* 13–16, 31–37; Gates, *Schoolbooks and Krags,* 21–26. There is considerable debate between historians who paint McKinley as pursuing a consistent policy of annexing the Philippines and those who portray him as vacillating for more than

five months until it was clear most Americans favored annexation. For a summary of the debate, see May, *Battle for Batangas*, 74–75.

106   Rising tensions: Sexton, *Soldiers in the Sun*, 50–61, 70–76; Linn, *U.S. Army and Counterinsurgency*, 10; Karnow, *In Our Image*, 130–139; Miller, *Benevolent Assimilation*, 46–60; Roth, *Muddy Glory*, 43–45; Bain, *Sitting in Darkness*, 72–77, 181–185; Gates, *Schoolbooks and Krags*, 27–70.

106   Mugwumps: The term was first used to describe liberal Republicans who defected to Democrat Grover Cleveland in the 1884 election. "Their mugs are on one side of the fence," it was said, "their wumps on the other."

106–107 Debate over annexation: Karnow, *In Our Image*, 136–137; Linn, *U.S. Army and Counterinsurgency*, 11; Miller, *Benevolent Assimilation*, 22–30, 105–120; Roth, *Muddy Glory*, 16; Bain, *Sitting in Darkness*, 77–79, 181–183.

107   Grayson incident: There are numerous competing versions of this pivotal event. A Filipino account claims the Americans fired on three Philippine soldiers standing peaceably in a doorway.

107–108 Background on U.S. Army: Trask, *The War with Spain*, Chapter 7; Linn, *Philippine War*, 8–12; Sexton, *Soldiers in the Sun*, 21–25, 83; Roth, *Muddy Glory*, 39–43.

108   "More fun than a turkey shoot": Such unseemly sentiments are typical of all wars, not just the Philippine conflict. A British soldier in World War II, for instance, compared the "exhilaration" of killing Germans to going "deer hunting." An Australian soldier in World War I compared shooting Turks to "potting kangaroos in the bush." Holmes, *Acts of War*, 377.

109   Initial offensive: Sexton, *Soldiers in the Sun*, 87–126; Linn, *Philippine War*, 45–117; Linn, *U.S. Army and Counterinsurgency*, 12–14; Wilcox, *Harper's History*, 109–230; Karnow, *In Our Image*, 139–146; Miller, *Benevolent Assimilation*, 60–73; Roth, *Muddy Glory*, 45–55; Bain, *Sitting in Darkness*, 79–81, 90–93; Funston, *Memories of Two Wars*, 174–314; Gates, *Schoolbooks and Krags*, 70–76.

109   "We are no nearer": Matthew Batson to wife, June 15, 1899, in Batson Papers.

110   Tensions within independence movement: Linn, *Philippine War*, 33–36, 136–137; Linn, *U.S. Army and Counterinsurgency*, 11, 14; Karnow, *In Our Image*, 156; Bain, *Sitting in Darkness*, 180, 186–191–191; May, *Battle for Batangas*, 67–70; Gates, *Schoolbooks and Krags*, 92–95.

111   "Flying column": One that leaves its supply train behind.

111   Del Pilar's age: Varying accounts give his age as 22 or 24.

111   U.S. offensive and Tila Pass: March's dispatch describing the battle of Tila Pass may be found in U.S. Secretary of War, *Annual Report* 1900, vol. 1, part 6, 330. See also Sexton, *Soldiers in the Sun*, 173–221; Linn, *Philippine War*, 139–159; Wilcox, *Harper's History*, 297–334; Miller, *Benevolent Assimilation*, 96–98; Coffman, *Hilt of the Sword*, 20–21; Karnow, *In Our Image*, 157–159; Bain, *Sitting in Darkness*, 192–198;

Linn, *U.S. Army and Counterinsurgency*, 14–16, 32–33; Miller, *Benevolent Assimilation*, 96–98; Gates, *Schoolbooks and Krags*, 110–112. Most of these accounts accept without reservation correspondent Little's account of the battle, white horse and all. Little also claims that American soldiers stripped del Pilar's body. Linn, *Philippine War*, at 156, has done more digging and found Little's report at odds with the accounts of soldiers on both sides. Another correspondent on the scene, John T. McCutcheon, reported that del Pilar was killed while "preparing to mount" a horse, not while on it. Wilcox, *Harper's History*, 317–320.

112 Guerrillas: There is a vast literature on this subject. I found three excellent books particularly helpful: Laqueur, *Guerrilla*; Joes, *Guerrilla Warfare;* and Asprey, *War in the Shadows*.

113 "The common soldier": Linn, *U.S. Army and Counterinsurgency*, 40.

113–114 Guerrilla campaign: Sexton, *Soldiers in the Sun*, 237–240, 253; Linn, *Philippine War*, 185–244; Linn, *U.S. Army and Counterinsurgency*, 16–18, 39–41, 72, 94–102; Karnow, *In Our Image*, 178–179; Miller, *Benevolent Assimilation*, 98–99; Roth, *Muddy Glory*, 55; Gates, *Schoolbooks and Krags*, 156–186.

114 1900 election and Insular Cases: The Boxer campaign also strengthened McKinley's hand, demonstrating the strategic importance of having a base near China. LaFeber, *Cambridge History*, vol. 2, *American Search*, 178–180; Sexton, *Soldiers in the Sun*, 253–257; Miller, *Benevolent Assimilation*, 128–145; Gates, *Schoolbooks and Krags*, 99–101, 162–163; Sullivan, *Our Times*, vol. 1, 533–553.

115 "Daily interactions": May, *Battle for Batangas*, 155.

115–116 Water cure and other U.S. tactics: Excerpts from the 1902 Senate hearings, which exposed many of these abuses, were published in Graff, *American Imperialism*. See also Sexton, *Soldiers in the Sun*, 240–242; Linn, *Philippine War*, 219–224; Karnow, *In Our Image*, 179; Miller, *Benevolent Assimilation*, 181–187; Roth, *Muddy Glory*, 87; Bain, *Sitting in Darkness*, 84–90.

116 "Throwing confetti": Quoted in Karnow, *In Our Image*, 179.

116 GO 100: For its origins, see Birtle's outstanding book, *U.S. Army Counterinsurgency*, 32–36.

116 Tactics of MacArthur and Taft: Sexton, *Soldiers in the Sun*, 251–257; Linn, *U.S. Army and Counterinsurgency*, 23–26; Karnow, *In Our Image*, 168–181; Miller, *Benevolent Assimilation*, 157–167; Gates, *Schoolbooks and Krags*, 128–149. There is still considerable debate over how much of an impact the policies of "attraction" had. Establishing schools and municipal governments "had a minimal impact on the war effort," writes May in *Battle for Batangas*, xx. By contrast, Gates, in *Schoolbooks and Krags*, 277, argues: "The American policy of benevolence and the many humanitarian acts of the army throughout the war played a much more important role in the success of the pacification campaign than fear did."

117   "Pudgy, applecheeked fellow": William Allen White, quoted in Millett, *Politics of Intervention*, 3.

117   "I fear": Funston, *Memories of Two Wars*, 4.

117   "One of the most difficult military operations": Funston, *Memories of Two Wars*, 272.

116–119 Funston biography and his capture of Aguinaldo: Funston's dispatch describing the capture is in U.S. Secretary of War, *Annual Report* 1901, vol. 1, part 5, 122–130. See also Funston's memoir, *Memories of Two Wars*, 4–149, 385–427; Segovia's memoir, *Aguinaldo's Capture*; Aguinaldo, "The Story of My Capture"; Bain, *Sitting in Darkness*, 14–81, 91–93, 284–385; Sexton, *Soldiers in the Sun*, 145, 259–264; Linn, *Philippine War*, 274–276. After accepting U.S. sovereignty, Aguinaldo retired from politics and became a prosperous farmer. During World War II he cooperated with the Japanese troops who invaded the Philippines. He died in 1964, at 95, having long outlived Funston and most of the other participants in the Philippine War.

120   Description of Waller: Butler and Thomas, *Old Gimlet Eye*, 36–37; Wise and Frost, *A Marine Tells It to You*, 6.

120   "Ambitious and ruthless:" Linn, *Philippine War*, 315.

120   Slaughtering carabao and bolemen: Linn, *Philippine War*, 313, writes: "By 6th Brigade estimates, between 10 October and 31 December 1901, soldiers and sailors killed or captured 759 insurrectos and 58 carabao, and destroyed tons of rice, 1,662 houses, and 226 boats."

121   "Cut, torn": From Waller's report, in U.S. Secretary of the Navy, *Annual Report* 1902, 971.

121–122 "The men's feet": Porter to Waller, February 8, 1902, in U.S. Secretary of the Navy, *Annual Report* 1902.

123   Samar campaign and court-martial: The officers' reports are in U.S. Secretary of the Navy, *Annual Report* 1902, 1903. Hiram Bearss described the campaign in an unpublished memoir: Bearss Papers, Box 1, Folders 12–17 in Porter Papers. The court-martial transcript is in RG 125, Box 235, Entry 27, NARA. For secondary accounts, see Schott, *Ordeal on Samar*, 65–276; Miller, *Benevolent Assimilation*, 204–249; Sexton, *Solders in the Sun*, 272–275; Karnow, *In Our Image*, 191–194; Gates, *Schoolbooks and Krags*, 253–256. Most of these accounts paint Waller as a victim of an army bureaucracy in search of a scapegoat. By contrast, the most comprehensive recent account of the war—Linn's *Philippine War*—argues, at 312–321, that Waller was guilty of incompetence and war crimes and should have been punished accordingly. Linn also argues, in contrast to earlier histories, that Waller's conduct was atypical.

123   Concentration camps: Unlike the concentration camps later set up by the Nazis, the camps established by the Americans were meant to hold civilians, not to kill them.

124 Malvar and Bell: In the years to come, Malvar would become a wealthy farmer who would send four of his sons to U.S. universities. Bell became army chief of staff in 1906.

124 Most thorough analysis: May, *Battle for Batangas*.

124 Batangas campaign: May, *Battle for Batangas*, 249–285; Sexton, *Soldiers in the Sun*, 279; Linn, *U.S. Army and Counterinsurgency*, 59, 152–160; Karnow, *In Our Image*, 187–189; Roth, *Muddy Glory*, 81–84; Gates, *Schoolbooks and Krags*, 257–262. Most historians denounce Bell's tactics as barbaric but Linn, *U.S. Army and Counterinsurgency*, at 160, concludes: "Bell's methods seem, on balance, to have been economical and moderate."

124–125 Moro uprisings: John J. Pershing and Leonard Wood were the principal U.S. commanders who fought the Muslim Moros. Even today Moros engage in intermittent guerrilla war against the Manila government. See Roth, *Muddy Glory*, 26–35, 136–151; Goldhurst, *Pipe Clay*, 103–151.

125 "The American efforts": Smith, *America's Mission*, 46.

125 "Yankee Go Home": Kiester and Kiester, "Yankee Go Home."

125 Casualties: LaFeber, *Cambridge History*, vol. 2, *American Search*, 165; Karnow, *In Our Image*, 194; Sexton, *Soldiers in the Sun*, 19. All casualty figures for the Filipino side are very rough estimates since no accurate census had been taken before the U.S. occupation.

127 "Too late chum": Holmes, *Acts of War*, 382.

127 Indian Wars: LaFeber, *Cambridge History*, vol. 2, *American Search*, 165.

128 Why the U.S. won: For the best summary, see Joes, *Guerrilla Warfare*, 47–51.

Chapter 6: Caribbean Constabulary

132 "Recast Cuban society": Thomas, *Cuba*, 436.

132–133 Cuba, 1899–1902: Thomas, *Cuba*, 417–470; Healey, *Drive to Hegemony*, 49–57; Langley, *U.S. and the Caribbean*, 17–22; Langley, *Banana Wars*, 12–20; Munro, *Intervention and Dollar Diplomacy*, 24–37; Millett, *Politics of Intervention*, 19–58; Sullivan, *Our Times*, vol. 1, 432–454.

133–134 Panama: McCullough, *The Path Between the Seas*, 329–386; Lejeune, *Reminiscences of a Marine*, 152–158; Roosevelt, *Autobiography*, 526–543; Healey, *Drive to Hegemony*, 77–94; Langley, *U.S. and the Caribbean*, 30–38; Munro, *Intervention and Dollar Diplomacy*, 37–65; Challener, *Admirals, Generals and American Foreign Policy*, 148–163; Yerxa, *Admirals and Empire*, 20–22. Morris, *Theodore Rex*, 301, gives a slightly different version of Knox's famous quip ("I think it would be better to keep your action free from any taint of legality"). Most historians have viewed the Panama episode as a "black mark" on U.S. history, but Marks offers a more sympathetic portrayal of Roosevelt's actions in *Velvet on Iron*, 97–105.

135 Strategic planning and Germany: Healey, *Drive to Hegemony*, 97–100; Challener, *Admirals, Generals and American Foreign Policy*, 28–67, 87–103; Yerxa, *Admirals and Empire*, 9–15, 53–66. War Plan Orange, which laid out a strategy for fighting Japan in the Pacific, also depended upon control of the Panama Canal and hence the Caribbean, since it called for the U.S. Atlantic Fleet to rush to the Pacific Ocean. See Yerxa, *Admirals and Empire*, 56.

135–136 Venezuela crisis and Roosevelt Corollary: Healey, *Drive to Hegemony*, 100–106; Langley, *U.S. and the Caribbean*, 22–27; Munro, *Intervention and Dollar Diplomacy*, 65–77; Yerxa, *Admirals and Empire*, 16–20. There is considerable debate over how far Roosevelt actually went in the Venezuela crisis. After leaving office, the former president let slip that he had threatened Germany with war. There is no record of this threat in U.S. or German archives, but Roosevelt's foremost biographer believes that the records were deliberately purged. Morris, *Theodore Rex*, 625.

136–137 Dominican customs receivership: Pons, *The Dominican Republic*, 279–303; Healey, *Drive to Hegemony*, 110–125; Langley, *U.S. and the Caribbean*, 27–30; Langley, *Banana Wars*, 27–30; Munro, *Intervention and Dollar Diplomacy*, 78–111, 118–125; Yerxa, *Admirals and Empire*, 22–23; Perkins, *Constraint of Empire*, 40–45; Knight, *Americans in Santo Domingo*, 14–39; Welles, *Naboth's Vineyard*, 601–639.

137–138 Cuban occupation, 1906–09: Thomas, *Cuba*, 471–493; Millett, *Politics of Intervention*, 59–270; Musicant, *Banana Wars*, 53–63; Langley, *Banana Wars*, 34–49; Langley, *U.S. and the Caribbean*, 38–44; Healey, *Drive to Hegemony*, 126–133; Perkins, *Constraint of Empire*, 12–20.

140 "It seems to be a historical fact": Bemis, *Latin American Policy*, 166.

140 Dollar diplomacy: The latest treatment, as of this writing, is Rosenberg, *Financial Missionaries to the World*. This account also draws on Munro, *Intervention and Dollar Diplomacy*, 160–164, 535–538 (written by a U.S. diplomat involved in Latin American affairs during the period he describes); Langley, *U.S. and the Caribbean*, 59–53; Healey, *Drive to Hegemony*, 144–152; Challener, *Admirals, Generals and American Foreign Policy*, 265–292; Bemis, *Latin American Policy*, 165–166; Pearce, *Under the Eagle*, 17.

140–141 Cuba, 1912, 1917–23: Thomas, *Cuba*, 514–535; Musicant, *Banana Wars*, 71–72; Healey, *Drive to Hegemony*, 198–199, 214–219; Munro, *Intervention and Dollar Diplomacy*, 477–529.

142 "Hawk's beak of a nose": Craige, *Cannibal Cousins*, 51.

142 "If he had been born": Ibid. Baron Clive was one of the architects of British power in India in the eighteenth century. Sir James Brooke was the English ruler of a state on the island of Borneo in the nineteenth century.

142–144 Butler background: Butler and Thomas, *Old Gimlet Eye*, 3–125; Schmidt, *Maverick Marine*, 1–37; Venzon, *Letters of a Leatherneck*, 1–60; Butler Papers; Butler Biographical File.

144   Description of Bluefields: Butler to his mother, June 4, 1910, in Venzon, *Letters of a Leatherneck*, 82.

145   "Poor little fellows": Butler to wife, Managua, August 19, 1912. Butler Papers, Box 5, File 5.

146   "My passages through León" and "enjoyed it more thoroughly": Butler to wife, Managua, September 5, 1912. Butler Papers, Box 5, File 5.

148   Nicaragua intervention, 1910–1912: Butler quotes unless otherwise noted come from Butler and Thomas, *Old Gimlet Eye*, 125–168; Venzon, *Letters of a Leatherneck*, 95–133; and Schmidt, *Maverick Marine*, 39–56. See also the memoir of a lieutenant who served under Butler (he would go on to become marine commandant), Vandegrift, *Once a Marine*, 35–43; Nicaragua Geographical File; Langley, *Banana Wars*, 54–76; Musicant, *Banana Wars*, 140–144; Healey, *Drive to Hegemony*, 152–164; Musicant, *Banana Wars*, 144–156; Munro, *Intervention and Dollar Diplomacy*, 204–216; Challener, *Admirals, Generals and American Foreign Policy*, 294–306; Millett, *Semper Fidelis*, 168–171; Perkins, *Constraint of Empire*, 21–39; Bermann, *Under the Big Stick*, 144–166; Schoonover, *United States in Central America*, 130–149.

149   Kissinger: Kissinger, *Diplomacy*, Chapter 2.

149   "In terms of right and wrong": Marks, *Velvet on Iron*, 90.

149   "Aggressive fighting": Ibid., 92.

149   "Unready hand": Roosevelt, *Autobiography*, 552. "Prize jackasses": Brands, *Last Romantic*, 750.

149   Wilson and Roosevelt: The best comparison is Cooper, *The Warrior and the Priest*. For more on Wilson's diplomacy see Link, *The New Freedom*, 277–280, 319–320; Yerxa, *Admirals and Empire*, 35–39. For more on Roosevelt's diplomacy see Marks, *Velvet on Iron*; Brands, *The Last Romantic*; and Morris, *Theodore Rex*.

151   "Indigo waters": Butler and Thomas, *Old Gimlet Eye*, 170.

153   "Foul perversion": Butler to his mother, February 21, 1916, in Venzon, *Letters of a Leatherneck*, 163.

153   Battle of Veracruz: There are several accounts by marines who took part: Lejeune, *Reminiscences of a Marine*, 206–211; Butler and Thomas, *Old Gimlet Eye*, 178–180; unpublished memoir in Bearss Papers, Box 1, Folder 23. See also Quirk, *Affair of Honor*, 78–103; Sweetman, *Landing at Veracruz*, 51–132; Eisenhower, *Intervention!*, 109–124; Schmidt, *Maverick Marine*, 68–73; Mexico Geographical File.

153–154 Funston background: Bain, *Sitting in Darkness*, 385–395. For details of Funston's 1906 clash with Taft in Cuba (it was over the handling of insurgents' horses, of all things), see Millett, *Politics of Intervention*, 104–107.

154   "Benevolent despotism": Quirk, *Affair of Honor*, 154.

154–155 MacArthur's adventure: James, *Years of MacArthur*, vol. 1, 115–127; Perret, *Old Soldiers Never Die*, 70.

155   Occupation of Veracruz: There are two book-length studies—Quirk, *Affair of Honor*, and Sweetman, *Landing at Veracruz*. See also Eisenhower, *Intervention!*, 125–138; Clendenen, *Blood on the Border*, 157–174; Langley, *Banana Wars*, 93–113; Challener, *Admirals, Generals and American Foreign Policy*, 379–397; Yerxa, *Admirals and Empire*, 35–39; Millett, *Semper Fidelis*, 171–174; Smith, *America's Mission*, 69–71; Lejeune, *Reminiscences of a Marine*, 211–218; Birtle, *U.S. Army Counterinsurgency*, 192–199; Munro, *Intervention and Dollar Diplomacy*, 269–274; Healey, *Drive to Hegemony*, 171–175. In addition, two Wilson biographies are handy—Link, *The New Freedom*, 347–416, and Heckscher, *Woodrow Wilson*, 328–329.

Chapter 7: Lords of Hispaniola

156   Description of Port-au-Prince: Wirkus, *White King*, 15–18.
157   "Efficient revolutionary system": The remark is attributed to a Haitian lawyer named De Beaufort. Craige, *Cannibal Cousins*, 35. Craige was a U.S. Marine officer who served in the late 1920s as chief of police in Port-au-Prince.
158   "Time honored rules": Ibid.
158   "It was shot at": British counsel, quoted in Heinl and Heinl, *Written in Blood*, 398.
158   "Hands, feet and head cut off": Quoted in Craige, *Cannibal Cousins*, 47.
158   Description of Caperton: Healey, *Gunboat Diplomacy*, 8. For more on the admiral, see Caperton Papers.
158   Special Service Squadron: Also sometimes called the Cruiser Squadron, it consisted of 14 mostly aged vessels. The navy had set up the squadron in 1914 to avoid disrupting the combat-readiness of its larger fleets for frequent deployments to the Caribbean on missions that were mostly diplomatic in nature. See Yerxa, *Admirals and Empire*, 39.
158   U.S. intervention in Haiti: I found the following sources especially helpful: Haiti Geographical File, an invaluable repository of documents, including the official gendarmerie history, *History of the Garde d'Haiti*; the Butler Papers; Heinl and Heinl, *Written in Blood*, the best general history of the country; Davis, *Black Democracy*, an older but still valuable history; Schmidt, *United States Occupation of Haiti*, the definitive work on the occupation; Healey, *Gunboat Diplomacy*, a good monograph on the start of the occupation; Link, *Struggle for Neutrality*, the standard account of Wilson's decision making; Langley, *Banana Wars*; Musicant, *Banana Wars*; several memoirs by marines, especially Butler and Thomas's *Old Gimlet Eye*, Wise and Frost's *A Marine Tells It to You*, and Craige's *Cannibal Cousins*; and two books by Dana Munro, a former State Department official—*Intervention*

and Dollar Diplomacy and *U.S. and the Caribbean Republics*. Unless otherwise noted, the sections on Haiti are based on these sources.

160 "At the beck and call": Daniels, "The Problem of Haiti." Figures on U.S. investment come from Schmidt, *United States Occupation*, 41.

161 Two million: Population estimates vary, there being no accurate census of Haiti at this time. The 2 million figure comes from Schmidt, *United States Occupation*, 19. Other sources cite a population of 1.5 million.

162 Signing of the U.S.-Haiti Treaty: This account of Butler's role may be found in Craige, *Cannibal Cousins*, 51–56. Craige describes it as a "gorgeous legend" he heard from an ex-sergeant of Butler's, as well as from a dozen other sources. Similar accounts of Butler's role are found in other publications. No doubt the story was embellished in the retelling.

162 "More humiliating": Butler and Thomas, *Old Gimlet Eye*, 186. While numerous contemporary sources attest to the *caco* attack on Gonaives and Butler's pursuit, the only source I have been able to find for the story of Butler pulling Rameau off his horse is Butler's own memoir. This should be treated with caution, especially since his coauthor, Lowell Thomas, was the same journalist who spread some of the unreliable legends about Lawrence of Arabia.

163 "Cole was a fine officer": Butler and Thomas, *Old Gimlet Eye*, 198.

165 *Caco* revolt suppressed: Butler quotes come from *Old Gimlet Eye*, 189–209; Venzon, *Letters of a Leatherneck*, 149–163; and Schmidt, *Maverick Marine*, 74–81. Also see Butler Papers, Box 6, File 5–7; Haiti Geographical File, 1915–16 Folder (especially reports of Cole, Butler, and Waller); Vandegrift, *Once a Marine*, 46–60 (by Butler's adjutant); and general Haiti sources listed previously.

166 Butler and Waller on Haitians: Quoted in Schmidt, *Maverick Marine*, 84.

166 "No preference" and shoeless Haitians: Ibid., 87–88.

167 "I blush": Craige, *Cannibal Cousins*, 60.

169 Quotes from Wise: Wise and Frost, *A Marine Tells It to You*, 138–144.

167–169 Occupation of the Dominican Republic: I found these sources especially helpful: Dominican Republic files, especially Wise's and Pendleton's reports; two marine memoirs—Major Hiram Bearss's unpublished autobiography in the Bearss Papers, Box 1, Folders 24–25, and Wise and Frost's *A Marine Tells It to You*; Knight, *Americans in Santo Domingo*, an account by a socialist critic; Welles, *Naboth's Vineyard*, a long history by a State Department official; Yerxa, *Admirals and Empire*; Pons, *The Dominican Republic*, the best modern history of the country; Calder, *The Impact of Intervention*; two Marine Corps publications—Fuller and Cosmas, *Marines in the Dominican Republic*, and Condit and Turnbladh, *Hold High the Torch*; the two Munro volumes, *Intervention and Dollar Diplomacy* and *U.S. and the Caribbean Republics*; Musicant, *Banana Wars*;

Langley, *Banana Wars*. Unless otherwise noted this and future sections on the Dominican Republic are based on these sources.

170   Schools revamped: The number of rural public schools jumped from 30 in 1916 to 647 in 1920. The number of students enrolled jumped from 20,000 in 1916 to over 100,000 in 1920. This was the occupation's biggest achievement. See Calder, *Impact of Intervention*, 35, and Pons, *The Dominican Republic*, 326.

172   Mulatto: Technically Peralte was a *griffe*—one-quarter white, three-quarters black—while a mulatto is half black, half white. This book uses the general term *mulatto* for all those of mixed ancestry.

172   "Handsome, brave": Craige, *Cannibal Cousins*, 64.

172   "Gift for flamboyant proclamations": Thomason, *Salt Wind*, 309.

173   Description of Hanneken: From Thomason (a fellow marine officer) in *Salt Winds*, 300.

173–175 Charlemagne's capture: In addition to the standard sources, Hanneken's Biographical File and Oral History provide crucial details.

175   Airplanes: See Mersky, *U.S. Marine Corps Aviation*, 20–21.

175   Casualty count: *History of the Garde d'Haiti*, 67, in Haiti Geographical File.

176   Napoleon: For an excellent comparison of the U.S. and French campaigns in Haiti, see Joes, *Guerrilla Warfare*, Chapter 3.

177   Marine atrocities: In addition to the standard sources, see U.S. Senate, *Inquiry into Occupation and Administration*. Many other documents, including Admiral Mayo's report, can be found in Barnett Papers, Box 1, Folder 10.

178   "The American administration": "The Haiti-Dominican Scandal" (editorial), *New York Times*, October 14, 1920.

179   No commercial gain: See Calder, *Impact of Intervention*, 85–86; Davis, *Black Democracy*, 200; Schmidt, *U.S. Occupation of Haiti*, 175–176. Schmidt writes: "Protracted efforts to induce Sinclair Oil and United Fruit companies to invest in Haiti failed because neither company would agree to terms deemed conscionable by the State Department."

180   Critics of the occupation: "No careful observer can deny that the Military Government did some material good in Santo Domingo." Knight, *Americans in Santo Domingo*, 97. Knight was a socialist critic of U.S. imperialism.

Chapter 8: The Dusty Trail

182–185 Attack on Columbus: The indispensable account is Tompkins, *Chasing Villa*, 48–65, written by the officer who commanded the pursuit. This contains Lieutenant Lucas's account of the attack, from which his quotes are drawn, as well as numerous other key documents. See also Clendenen,

Blood on the Border, 202–210; Clendenen, *United States and Villa*, 234–246; Stout, *Border Conflict*, 33–39; Mason, *Great Pursuit*, 30–21; Eisenhower, *Intervention*, 217–227. John Lucas, one of the two lieutenants who helped drive the Villistas out of Columbus, rose to the rank of major general in World War II. He commanded U.S. forces at Anzio and later led the last U.S. military mission to China.

187   Three strands: Based on the analysis of McLynn, *Villa and Zapata*, 401.

185–188   Background on Villa: The definitive account is Katz's monumental study, *Pancho Villa*. See also Krauze, *Mexico*, 305–333; Johnson, *Heroic Mexico*, 157–310; Clendenen, *Blood on the Border*, 121–202; Clendenen, *United States and Pancho Villa*, 10–234; Stout, *Border Conflict*, 4–32; Mason, *Great Pursuit*, 53–64; Eisenhower, *Intervention*, 46–216; McLynn, *Villa and Zapata*, 53–71. All of these books also recount the history of the Mexican Revolution. For a succinct summary, see John Mason Hart, "The Mexican Revolution, 1910–1920," in Meyer and Beezley, *Oxford History of Mexico*, 435–467.

189   Motives for Columbus attack: Katz, *Pancho Villa*, 550–557. There were even wild conspiracy theories that American capitalists, hoping to precipitate a war with Mexico, had paid Villa to stage his raid. See Clendenen, *United States and Pancho Villa*, 242–245.

190   Orders for expedition: Pershing report to Funston, October 10, 1916, Pershing Papers, Box 372, Folder 1; Scott, *Some Memories*, 519–521 (for Scott-Baker conversation); Link, *Confusions and Crises*, 206–217; Clendenen, *United States and Pancho Villa*, 247–257. Congress adopted a joint resolution approving the use of armed force to capture Villa and his band. This resolution was adopted on March 17, by which time Pershing had already crossed the border.

190   "Upstanding, though humble": Pershing, *Memoirs*, Chapter 1, 1. Pershing Papers, Box 380.

192   Pershing background: Pershing, *Memoirs*, Chapters 1–22, Pershing Papers, Box 380; Vandiver, *Black Jack*, vol. 1; Smith, *Until the Last Trumpet Sounds* (especially acute on his emotional life); Smythe, *Guerrilla Warrior*; Goldhurst, *Pipe Clay*; Mason, *Great Pursuit*, 76–80.

193   Battle of Guerrero: Katz, *Pancho Villa*, 572–573; Johnson, *Heroic Mexico*, 312–313; Tompkins, *Chasing Villa*, 81–88.

194   Logistics: Scott, *Some Memories*, 530–532; Clendenen, *Blood on the Border*, 218–231; Tompkins, *Chasing Villa*, 246–254.

195   Aero Squadron: Mason, *Great Pursuit*, 103–117; Tompkins, *Chasing Villa*, 236–245; Smythe, *Guerrilla Warrior*, 232–233.

195   Pershing headquarters: Pershing, *Memoirs*, Chapter 23. Pershing Papers, Box 379. Mason, *Great Pursuit*, 121–124; Smythe, *Guerrilla Warrior*, 227–229.

196   Battle at Agua Caliente: Tompkins, *Chasing Villa*, 145–157.

197   All or nothing approach: An Army War College report written five days before Villa's attack on Columbus stated that "it is axiomatic that an overwhelming force" should be used in "vigorous field operations. . . . Our war plans accept this axiom. . . . To reject these plans, to use only a part of these plans, or to curtail the forces outlined in these plans, can but invite local disasters and delays." Birtle, *U.S. Army Counterinsurgency*, 202.

197   Battle at Parral and aftermath: Pershing, *Memoirs*, Chapter 23, 10–14, Pershing Papers, Box 379; Tompkins, *Chasing Villa*, 128–144 (the source of quotes from Tompkins); Link, *Confusions and Crises*, 282–286; Smythe, *Guerrilla Warrior*, 241–249.

198   Patton at San Miguelito: D'Este, *Patton*, 172–177; Mason, *Great Pursuit*, 184–188; Williams, *Lieutenant Patton*, 69–71.

199   Border tension and National Guard mobilization: Pershing, *Memoirs*, Chapter 23, 15–18, Pershing Papers, Box 379; Stout, *Border Conflict*, 81–84; Mason, *Great Pursuit*, 196–206; Link, *Confusions and Crises*, 291–303.

199–200 Battle at Carrizal and aftermath: Pershing, *Memoirs*, Chapter 23, 17–20, Pershing Papers, Box 379; Mason, *Great Pursuit*, 206–218; Stout, *Border Conflict*, 84–92; Eisenhower, *Intervention*, 288–300; Clendenen, *United States and Pancho Villa*, 278–285; Link, *Confusions and Crises*, 303–318; Smythe, *Guerrilla Warrior*, 256–260.

200   Plot to poison Villa: Harris and Sadler, *Border and Revolution*, 7–23.

201   "The camp was most uncomfortable": Tompkins, *Chasing Villa*, 214.

201   "I can but feel the embarrassment": Pershing to Sen. F. E. Warren, December 4, 1916. Pershing Papers, Box 426.

202   End of the Punitive Expedition: Mason, *Great Pursuit*, 218–233; Katz, *Pancho Villa*, 604–614; Link, *Campaigns for Progressivism and Peace*, 328–339; Smythe, *Guerrilla Warrior*, 261–282. Katz, in *Pancho Villa*, 612, argues that the failure of the Punitive Expedition made American entry into World War I more likely. It helped convince many in the German government that there was nothing to be lost in unleashing unlimited submarine warfare against the U.S., since its armed forces were so clearly incompetent.

202   "When the command left Mexico": Pershing, *My Experiences*, 1, 10.

202–203 Villa from mid-1916 to 1923: Katz, *Pancho Villa*, 583–794; Johnson, *Heroic Mexico*, 315, 358–364, 372–377; Clendenen, *United States and Villa*, 305–314; Clendenen, *Blood on the Border*, 352–355. There has been much speculation over the years about who ordered Villa's murder (for which only one of the killers served any time in jail—three months). Katz concludes, "There can, on the whole, be little doubt that the Mexican government was not only implicated in but probably organized the assassination of Villa" (p. 780).

204   "Having dashed into Mexico": Pershing to Sen. F. E. Warren, January 20, 1917. Pershing Papers, Box 426.

204   "The policy of the Commander-in-Chief": Pershing, *Memoirs*, Chapter 22, 2. Pershing Papers, Box 17.

Chapter 9: Blood on the Snow

205   April 2 speech: The cabinet member quoted is Williams Gibbs McAdoo; the observer is Sullivan. Sullivan, *Our Times*, V: 272–285. See also the April 3, 1917, *New York Times*; Heckscher, *Woodrow Wilson*, 436–441.

207   "My policy regarding Russia": Quoted in Somin, *Stillborn Crusade*, 108.

207   "Like a plague bacillus": Churchill, *World Crisis: Aftermath*, 63.

210   Czech Legion: For an in-depth account, see Unterberger, *United States, Revolutionary Russia*.

210   The only military force in Russia: "The training of the Red Army at this time," Winston Churchill wrote, with only mild exaggeration, "had not progressed beyond a knowledge of Communism, the execution of prisoners and ordinary acts of brigandage and murder." Churchill, *World Crisis: Aftermath*, 86.

211   Wilson's decision to intervene: The most nuanced account is Foglesong, *America's Secret War*, 11–51, 143–164, 188–225. See also Heckscher, *Woodrow Wilson*, 435–436, 462–465; Goldhurst, *Midnight War*, 3–73; Halliday, *Ignorant Armies*, 15–26; White, *Siberian Intervention*, 139–141. As with all of Wilson's actions, there is considerable debate among historians over his motives. Most historians friendly to Wilson, e.g., Betty Miller Unterberger and George Kennan, argue that anti-Bolshevism did not play a role in his decision making. Radical historians critical of Wilson, e.g., William Appleman Williams, argue anti-Bolshevism was the dominant consideration in Wilson's policy. For a summary of the debate, see Somin, *Stillborn Crusade*, 11–21.

212   Lenin's secret police: The most authoritative estimate is that from 1917 to 1921 the Cheka alone executed 140,000 people, ten times as many people as the czarist government had executed during the previous 50 years. In addition, at least 5 million people died of famines that were mainly the result of Bolshevik agricultural policies. The Whites committed atrocities, too, but on a much smaller scale. Leggett, *The Cheka*, 359.

212   Graves in Siberia: Quotes are from Graves, *America's Siberian Adventure*. See also Goldhurst, *Midnight War*, 73–85; White, *Siberian Intervention*, 271–273.

213   Trotsky despaired: Quoted in Lincoln, *Red Victory*, 187.

214   "Mud, filth and dark skies": Carey, *Fighting the Bolsheviks*, 42.

215   Poole's offensive: A firsthand account of Odjard's advance (written by Lieutenant Harry Mead, who served under him) may be found in Moore et al., *History of the American Expedition*, 55–87. A modern account:

Rhodes, *Anglo-American Winter War*, 21–45. See also Goldhurst, *Midnight War*, 98–113; Halliday, *Ignorant Armies*, 49–70.

215–217 Ironside: This section is based mainly on Ironside's memoir, *Archangel*, 11–45. See also Goldhurst, *Midnight War*, 135–137; Halliday, *Ignorant Armies*, 70–84.

217 "Group of low, dirty log houses": Moore et al., *History of the American Expedition*, 105.

218 Battle of Tulgas: This account is based mainly on the history written by John Cudahy, who was there. Unless otherwise attributed, quotes are from Chronicler (Cudahy), *Archangel*, 138–158. For other accounts see Moore et al., *History of the American Expedition*, 105–114; Gordon, *Quartered in Hell*, 241–251; Halliday, *Ignorant Armies*, 1–12; Goldhurst, *Midnight War*, 143–147; Rhodes, *Anglo-American Winter War*, 71–72.

218–219 "It was hard for our men": Ironside, *Archangel*, 54.

219–220 "The soldier's type": Moore et al., *History of the American Expedition*, 235.

220 Life in North Russia: This section is based mainly on a private's diary: Carey, *Fighting the Bolsheviks*, 128–166. See also Halliday, *Ignorant Armies*, 109–124; Rhodes, *Anglo-American Winter War*, 49–52.

220–222 Retreat from Shenkursk: Based mainly on Lt. Harry Mead's description of the battle. Quotes, unless otherwise attributed, are from Moore et al., *History of the American Expedition*, 135–150. For other soldiers' accounts sees Chronicler (Cudahy), *Archangel*, 181–187, and Gordon, *Quartered in Hell*, 111–124. See also Halliday, *Ignorant Armies*, 125–148; Goldhurst, *Midnight War*, 172–179; Rhodes, *Anglo-American Winter War*, 83–90.

222 Churchill "agreed": Quotes are from the conference proceedings. See Somin, *Stillborn Crusade*, 51.

222–224 Paris Peace Conference and Russia: For Churchill's own account see *World Crisis: Aftermath*, 170–186. For historians' accounts, see Pipes, *Russia Under the Bolshevik Regime*, 63–76; Somin, *Stillborn Crusade*, 44–53, 108–124; Halliday, *Ignorant Armies*, 163–175.

225 U.S. casualties: U.S. Secretary of War, *Annual Report* 1919, 1, part 1, 24. In North Russia British forces lost 326 killed, 656 wounded. Churchill, *World Crisis: Aftermath*, 252.

225 End of the North Russia expedition: Moore et al., *History of the American Expedition*, 198–298; Rhodes, *Anglo-American Winter War*, 99–124; Goldhurst, *Midnight War*, 194–210, 224–232; Halliday, *Ignorant Armies*, 185–210; Churchill, *World Crisis: Aftermath*, 248–254.

227 Sent a corporal: Some accounts say it was Corporal Valeryan Brodnicki, others Corporal Louis Heinzman. Dupuy writes in *Perish by the Sword*, 228, that both were sent. Army records do not clear up this ambiguity.

227 Romanovka "massacre": "Report of Intelligence Patrol No. 2," June 25, 1919, in Yarborough Papers, Box 5; "The Prelude and aftermath of the

Romanovka Massacre, as told to Virginia Cooper Westall by Russell C. Swihart," (n.d.) in Longuevan Papers, Box 1; Sgt. Alan Ferguson to Joseph Longuevan, June 25, 1969, in Longuevan Papers, Box 1; Longuevan letter, September 1968, in Longuevan Papers, Box 1; Paul, *Regimental History*, 20; Kindall, *American Soldiers in Siberia*, 56–58; Dupuy, *Perish by the Sword*, 227–228.

227 "From then on": Swihart, in Longuevan Papers, ibid.

225–228 Siberian campaign: The basic documents may be found in AEF Historical File, RG 395, NARA. See also Robert Eichelberger's dictated, unpublished memoirs in Eichelberger Papers, File 13. For secondary accounts, see Goldhurst, *Midnight War*, 213–269; White, *Siberian Intervention;* Mead, *Doughboys*, 269–284, 378–395; Dupuy, *Perish by the Sword*, 211–271; Kindall, *American Soldiers;* Birtle, *U.S. Army Counterinsurgency*, 218–226.

228–229 "If the initial landings": Ullman, *Anglo-Soviet Relations*, 1, 333.

229 Churchill: "Still I suppose that twenty or thirty thousand resolute, comprehending, well-armed Europeans could, without any serious difficulty or loss, have made their way very swiftly along any of the great railroads which converged on Moscow; and have brought to the hard ordeal of battle any force that stood against them. But twenty or thirty thousand resolute men did not exist or could not be brought together." Churchill, *World Crisis: Aftermath*, 243.

229 Points of "mortal danger": Malia, *Soviet Tragedy*, 121.

Chapter 10: Chasing Sandino

232 Friction with locals: In 1921, some marines trashed the offices of a Managua newspaper that had printed an article accusing them of being "the principal means of transmitting venereal diseases [in Managua] for it is well known that they cohabit with the lowest women." The marines also brawled with the police, killing three of them. The marines involved were court-martialed, and the entire garrison was replaced.

232 "Seldom if ever has a nation": Denny, *Dollars for Bullets*, 201–202.

233 "Devil dogs": Legend has it this moniker was given to the marines by German soldiers in World War I.

233 Occupation: For a sailor's firsthand account, see Pagano, *Bluejackets*.

232–234 Background on Nicaragua: Munro, *U.S. and Caribbean*, 157–221; Macaulay, *Sandino Affair*, 19–47 (the best history of the U.S. intervention); Langley, *Banana Wars*, 180–192; Millett, *Guardians of the Dynasty*, 33–56; Bermann, *Under the Big Stick*, 160–192; Kamman, *A Search for Stability*, 1–54.

235 Peace of Tipitapa: For background on Stimson, see Hodgson's biography, *The Colonel*. Quotes from Stimson are from *The Colonel* and Stimson's

own accounts, *American Policy in Nicaragua* and *On Active Service*, 110–116. See also Kamman, *A Search for Stability*, 97–117.

235–236 Sandino: Macaulay, *Sandino Affair*, 48–61; Langley, *Banana Wars*, 192–197; Millett, *Guardians of the Dynasty*, 63–67; Bermann, *Under the Big Stick*, 192–194; Ramirez and Conrad, *Sandino*, 25–74 (a collection of Sandino's writings).

238 "Threw away their rifles": Rowell, "Experiences with the Air Service," Rowell Papers.

238–239 Battle of Ocotal: Rowell offers his account in the Rowell Papers, the source of the quote attributed to him. For the rest of the battle, see Macaulay, *Sandino Affair*, 70–82; Denny, *Dollars for Bullets*, 312–317; Musicant, *Banana Wars*, 309–310; Langley, *Banana Wars*, 195–197; and, for Sandino's perspective, Ramirez and Conrad, *Sandino*, 74–89.

239 Floyd's expedition: Floyd's report is in the Nicaragua Geographical File.

239–240 Expedition after downed airplane: Quotes are from O'Shea's account of the expedition. Nicaragua Geographical File.

240 "On every hand": Beals, *Banana Gold*, 239.

240 "Slaughtered like rats": Thomas J. Kilcourse diary. Kilcourse Papers.

241 "One of the most gallant . . . exploits": Denny, *Dollars for Bullets*, 322.

241 "Stupidly criminal blunder": Kilcourse diary. Kilcourse Papers.

241 From Ocotal to El Chipote: The Kilcourse diary, in the Kilcourse Papers, provides an invaluable account of the expedition to Qualali. See also Nicaragua Geographical File, MCHC; Macaulay, *Sandino Affair*, 83–104; Denny, *Dollars for Bullets*, 320–328; Musicant, *Banana Wars*, 315–335; Langley, *Banana Wars*, 197–199; Millett, *Semper Fidelis*, 248–250.

241–242 Beals on Sandino: Beals, *Banana Gold*, 264.

242 Machos: Central American slang for blonds; used by Sandino and other Nicaraguans as a pejorative reference to North Americans. Ramirez and Conrad, *Sandino*, 69.

242 International support for Sandino: Macaulay, *Sandino Affair*, 83–84, 112–114; Munro, *U.S. and the Caribbean*, 238–254; Millett, *Guardians of the Dynasty*, 117–120; Kamman, *A Search for Stability*, 136–137, 140–142. For Sandino's writings, see Ramirez and Conrad, *Sandino*.

242 Description of McCoy: Beals, *Banana Gold*, 293. For more on McCoy's role in Nicaragua, see Bacevich, *Diplomat in Khaki*, 119–137.

243–244 From the 1928 election to Sandino's trip to Mexico: Macaulay, *Sandino Affair*, 125–160; Langley, *Banana Wars*, 202–212; Kamman, *A Search for Stability*, 143–191.

244 His son's book: Puller, *Fortunate Son*.

245 Recent research: The definitive account is Hoffman's impressively researched *Chesty*. For the doubts he raises about these quotations, see 399 and 537.

246   Description of Puller: From a 1978 speech to the Fairfax Optimists Club by Brigadier General (ret.) Edwin H. Simmons, in the Puller Biographical File.

245–247   Chesty Puller: For background, see Hoffman, *Chesty*, which supersedes Burke's *Marine*, a quasi-memoir written with Puller's cooperation. For his Nicaragua experience, see Puller Biographical File and oral history; William Lee oral history.

247   Coco River patrols: See the only biography of Edson, Hoffman's *Once a Legend*, 50–94.

247–249   Sandinista campaign up to 1932 election: Macaulay, *Sandino Affair*, 161–218; Munro, *U.S. and the Caribbean*, 255–269; Millett, *Guardians of the Dynasty*, 94–97; Langley, *Banana Wars*, 214–218; Kamman, *A Search for Stability*, 193–216; Bickel, *Mars Learning*, 155–178.

249–250   Battle of El Sauce: Hoffman, *Chesty*, 96–99; Burke, *Marine*, 82–86; William Lee oral history. Puller emerged unscathed from his time in Nicaragua. Lee was wounded twice, once in the head, once in the arm, but survived to become a Japanese prisoner in World War II. He survived that too, to retire as a colonel in 1950.

250–251   Somoza's rise to power: Macaulay, *Sandino Affair*, 239–258; Munro, *U.S. and the Caribbean*, 269–279; Millett, *Guardians of the Dynasty*, 120–145; Langley, *Banana Wars*, 218–221; Bermann, *Under the Big Stick*, 216–226; Kamman, *A Search for Stability*, 217–236.

252   "The total number of Marine . . . fatalities": Macaulay, *Sandino Affair*, 239.

252   "Best schools": Lewis Puller Oral History.

Chapter 11: "By Bluff Alone"

254   Chinese revolution: I have drawn heavily on three standard works: Fairbank, *U.S. and China*, 196–219; Hsu, *Modern China*, 452–486; and Spence, *Search for Modern China*, 245–300. See also Roberts, *Concise History of China*, 203–217. Modern scholarship has established that central government in China during the "warlord period" was more effective than previously supposed.

255   Bund: An Anglo-Indian word for quay. It was usually used to refer to the main street of any treaty port, in this case Huangputan Road. Waldron, *From War to Nationalism*, 18.

255–256   Shanghai: Clifford, *Spoilt Children*, 1–78, provides a captivating description of life in the 1920s. See 68 for the figure on daily newspapers; 26 for the truth about "No dogs or Chinese allowed." For other views of the city, see Buck, *My Several Worlds*, 64; Sergeant, *Shanghai*; Carpenter, *China*, 57–68 (a contemporary traveler's account); Powell, *My 25 Years in China*, 18–28 (by an American newspaperman in Shanghai).

256   Life in treaty ports: For an evocative description, see Tuchman, *Stilwell*, 35.

257   "It is our wish": Quoted in Cole, *Gunboats and Marines*, 29.

257–258 Protecting the SS *Alice Dollar*: Tolley, *Yangtze Patrol*, 89. For general background on Yangtze Patrol, see ibid.; Cole, *Gunboats and Marines*, 24–40; and the memoir of a former YangPat commander, Stirling, *Sea Duty*, 206–223.

259   "By bluff alone": Finney, *Old China Hands*, 105.

258–260 Life aboard the *San Pablo*: McKenna, *The Sand Pebbles*, 13–155. The "likker and wimmen" quote—possibly apocryphal—is from Tolley, *Yangtze Patrol*, 85. For a sociological treatise on U.S. soldiers and sailors in China, see Noble, *The Eagle and the Dragon*.

261   Unlike in the past: In 1905, Chinese merchants had organized a boycott of American goods to protest U.S. restrictions on Chinese immigration.

261   U.S. and Nationalist movement, 1925–26: Fairbank, *U.S. and China*, 220–240; Cole, *Gunboats and Marines*, 53–84; Tolley, *Yangtze Patrol*, 123–133; Hsu, *Rise of Modern China*, 514–525, 531–534; Clifford, *Spoilt Children*, 97–176; Tuchman, *Stilwell*, 90–98; Spence, *Search for Modern China*, 334–348; Roberts, *Concise History of China*, 222–226.

263   Attack on Nanking: Pearl Buck quotes are from Buck, *My Several Worlds*, 205–218. For the rest of the siege, see Tolley, *Yangtze Patrol*, 144–165; Hoyt, *Lonely Ships*, 101–111; Cole, *Gunboats and Marines*, 111–120.

264–265 Butler background: Schmidt, *Maverick Marine*, 96–172; Butler and Thomas, *Old Gimlet Eye*, 242–287; Butler Papers; Butler Biographical File; Venzon, *Letters of a Leatherneck*, 203–259.

265   "Shanghai has become red": Quoted in Clifford, *Spoilt Children*, 220.

266   "Integrity of the Settlement": Secretary of State Frank Kellogg, quoted in Condit and Turnbladh, *Hold High the Torch*, 127.

266   "Prepared to frustrate": Butler to Lejeune, Shanghai, April 5, 1927, in Butler Papers, Box 8, File 1927 L.

266   Shanghai, 1927: Clifford, *Spoilt Children*, 194–256; Condit and Turnbladh, *Hold High the Torch*, 110–141; Cole, *Gunboats and Marines*, 98–111, 127–134; Tolley, *Yangtze Patrol*, 165–167; Powell, *My 25 Years*, 141–160; Hsu, *Rise of Modern China*, 526–531; Spence, *Search for Modern China*, 348–354; Sergeant, *Shanghai*, Chapter 3.

267   "Grueling monotony": Butler to Lejeune, Tientsin, July 23, 1928, in Butler Papers, Box 8, File 1927 L.

267   "I continually lectured": Butler and Thomas, *Old Gimlet Eye*, 291.

268   "Wide berth" and "Had we not been": Butler to Lejeune, Tientsin, July 23, 1928, in Butler Papers, Box 8, File 1927 L.

268   "The American government is wasting": Ibid.

268   Marines in Tientsin: For Butler's role, see Schmidt, *Maverick Marine*, 182–201; Butler Papers; Butler Biographical File; Butler and Thomas,

Old Gimlet Eye, 287–299; Venzon, *Letters of a Leatherneck*, 259–294. For a wider picture, see Cole, *Gunboats and Marines*, 135–169; Condit and Turnbladh, *Hold High the Torch*, 141–144; Spence, *Search for Modern China*, 361–364.

270   End of Butler's life: Schmidt, *Maverick Marine*, 202–250; Butler Papers; Butler Biographical File; Venzon, *Letters of a Leatherneck*, 295–312; Archer, *The Plot to Seize the White House.*

270–271 Shanghai, 1932: Condit and Turnbladh, *Hold High the Torch*, 152–164; Sergeant, *Shanghai*, Chapter 5; Hsu, *Rise of Modern China*, 546–553; Spence, *Search for Modern China*, 391–394.

271–272 Shanghai, 1937: Condit and Turnbladh, *Hold High the Torch*, 167–176; Hsu, *Rise of Modern China*, 579–585; Spence, *Search for Modern China*, 443–448; Hoffman, *Once a Legend*, 111–120; Tolley, *Yangtze Patrol*, 239–244.

272   Rape of Nanking: During the period from December 1937 to January 1938, Japanese troops killed some 50,000 residents and raped tens of thousands of women. See Chang, *Rape of Nanking*, for the gruesome details.

272–274 *Panay* attack: The definitive account is Perry, *Panay Incident*. Koginos, *Panay Incident*, focuses more on the background and repercussions. See also Tolley, *Yangtze Patrol*, 245–252; Hoyt, *Lonely Ships*, 3–25.

275   Puller incident: There are other variations of this tale, though all agree on the basic facts. See Hoffman, *Chesty*, 128.

275   Last days in China: Condit and Turnbladh, *Hold High the Torch*, 176–195; Davis, *Marine*, 102–121; Tolley, *Yangtze Patrol*, 252–292; Spence, *Search for Modern China*, 450–456; Sergeant, *Shanghai*, Chapter 8.

276   Treaty ports: Different sources give different numbers. These are from Waldron, *From War to Nationalism*, 12.

276   "Their primary function": Quoted in Koginos, *Panay Incident*, 11.

277   "Foreign investors": Hsu, *Rise of Modern China*, 437.

278   Impact of U.S. on China: Hsu, *Rise of Modern China*, 430–437; Spence, *Search for Modern China*, 379–388; Fairbank, *U.S. and China*, 327–335; Thomson, Stanley, and Perry, *Sentimental Imperialists*, 31–61. Figures on trade and investment are from Thomson, Stanley and Perry, *Sentimental Imperialists*, 103.

Chapter 12: Lessons Learned

282   "New Look" and limited war: See Gacek, *Logic of Force*, Chapter 5. The army's preferred type of war has been called mid-intensity, to contrast it with high intensity (using nuclear weapons) and low intensity (small wars).

283   Jomini's views: John Shy, "Jomini," in Paret, *Makers of Modern Strategy*, 143–186.

283   Army and counterinsurgency: There *was* an informal tradition passed down over the years. See Birtle's excellent study, *U.S. Army Counterinsurgency*, 271–282.

283   *Small Wars Manual*: For the story of how it came to be written, see Bickel, *Mars Learning*, 205–235.

284–285 Quotations: From U.S. Marine Corps, *Small Wars Manual*.

Chapter 13: Lessons Unlearned

286   "Gook behind every tree": Private First Class Bill Brocksieker, quoted in Lehrack, *No Shining Armor*, 18.

286   Landing at Danang: For the memoir of a marine who landed in Vietnam the same day, but by airplane not landing craft, see Caputo, *A Rumor of War*, 51–53. Also see the *New York Times*, March 9, 1965.

287   Origins of Vietnam War: Helpful recent books include Kaiser, *American Tragedy*; McMaster, *Dereliction of Duty*; Logevall, *Choosing War*.

288   Vietcong: Vietcong literally means "Vietnamese communist"—a term used by Washington and Saigon, never by Hanoi.

289   "Guerrilla warfare requires": Quoted in Krepinevich, *Army and Vietnam*, 84. For more on Vann's role, see Sheehan's brilliantly written *Bright Shining Lie*.

290   "Gifts from heaven": Quoted in Gibson, *Technowar*, 88.

290–291 Gulf of Tonkin resolution: This interpretation is inspired by Lind, *Vietnam—The Necessary War*, 186-191.

291   "Slowly ascending": From National Security Memorandum no. 328, April 6, 1965, quoted in Gibson, *Perfect War*, 328.

291   "Outhouse": Quoted in Karnow, *Vietnam*, 430.

291   Imports doubled: Karnow, *Vietnam*, 471.

291   "Half-hearted": Kissinger, *White House Years*, 232.

292   "Pissant country": Quoted in Karnow, *Vietnam*, 411.

292–293 Westmoreland: Davidson, one of Westmoreland's former staff officers, provides a largely admiring sketch in *Vietnam at War*, 369–385. See also Zaffiri, *Westmoreland*, and Westmoreland's memoir, *A Soldier Reports*.

293   China: See Chen, "Personal-Historical Puzzles"; Zhai, "Beijing and the Vietnam Peace Talks" and "Beijing and the Vietnam Conflict." These articles, drawing on newly opened Chinese and Vietnamese archives, reveal that Mao Tse-tung promised to respond with combat troops if the U.S. Army crossed into North Vietnam. Although this promise was never put to the test, from 1965 to 1973, 320,000 Chinese engineering and antiaircraft artillery troops were present on North Vietnamese territory; 1,100 of them died, 4,200 were wounded.

293   "Erratic mountain ranges": The description comes from Herr, *Dispatches*, 93.

293 "Grind away": Westmoreland interview, quoted in Krepinevich, *Army and Vietnam*, 165.

294 "Firepower": Quoted in Krepinevich, *Army and Vietnam*, 197.

294 Three stages of guerrilla war: From Mao Tse-tung, *On Guerrilla Warfare*, quoted in Asprey, *War in the Shadows*, 254–255.

294 Bedside reading: Westmoreland, *A Soldier Reports*, 277. He added, however, that "I was usually too tired in late evening to give the books more than occasional attention."

294–295 Statistics on North Vietnamese offensive: Krepinevich, *Army and Vietnam*, 177–193; Gibson, *TechnoWar*, 338–339.

295 Inkblot: Also known as an "oil stain" strategy. The analogy was invented by the nineteenth-century French general Joseph Gallieni, who successfully pacified Senegal, Tonkin, and Madagascar. See Joes, *Guerrilla Warfare*, 185.

297–298 Krulak: These and subsequent quotations are from his memoir, *First to Fight*, 181–205. Krulak had initially supported the big-war strategy before changing his mind in 1964–1965. This description of Krulak's background and behavior also derives from Sheehan, *Bright Shining Lie*, 292–305, 629–633. Marine Colonel William Corson in *The Betrayal*, 177, called Krulak "the fallen unsung hero of the Other War."

298 Cedar Falls and Junction City: Cedar Falls, in January 1967, sent two full infantry divisions plus other units into the Iron Triangle, an enemy base area 20 miles north of Saigon. U.S. forces reported killing over 700 communist soldiers and capturing 280 prisoners. Junction City, from February 22 to May 14, 1967, used the 1st Infantry Division, the 173rd Airborne Brigade, the 11th Armored Cavalry Regiment, and a brigade of the 9th Infantry Division against War Zone C, another communist sanctuary near the Cambodian border. U.S. forces reported killing 2,700 Vietcong and capturing vast amounts of rice, ammunition, and medical supplies.

298 Charlie: The name derives from the radio call sign for Vietcong: Victor Charlie. The enemy was also sometime called Mr. Charles or the Cong or simply the Gooks.

299 "Sheer physical impossibility": Cited in Davidson, *Vietnam at War*, 428.

299 Eighty-eight percent initiated by the enemy: Krepinevich, *Army and Vietnam*, 188. Gibson, in *The Perfect War*, 11, gives the figure as "over 80%."

299 Moore: Moore and Galloway, *We Were Soldiers Once*, 344.

300 XM–2: Dunnigan and Nofi, *Dirty Little Secrets*, 236.

300 Fence: Davidson, *Vietnam at War*, 391; Palmer, *Summons of the Trumpet*, 152–153; Krepinevich, *Army and Vietnam*, 184–185.

301 "For every man": Palmer, *Summons of the Trumpet*, 156. Luttwak, *Pentagon and the Art of War*, 32, writes that fewer than 80,000 of the

536,000 U.S. soldiers in Vietnam in 1968 were serving in infantry battalions.

301   Dropped on South Vietnam: U.S. fixed-wing aircraft flew 2.6 million sorties over the South and just 528,000 over the North. A sortie is one mission by an airplane. Almost all the millions of helicopter sorties were in South Vietnam. Dunnigan and Nofi, *Dirty Little Secrets*, 108. For figures on bomb tonnages, see Record, *Wrong War*, 91; Gibson, *Perfect War*, 136. Different sources give slightly different numbers.

301   "Every opportunity they had": Quoted in Krepinevich, *Army and Vietnam*, 202.

302   "You could watch": Herr, *Dispatches*, 132. Herr was a writer for *Esquire* who frequently visited Khe Sanh during the siege.

303   "The primary emphasis": Cited in Krulak, *First to Fight*, 217.

303   Khe Sanh: Krulak, *First to Fight*, 205–222; Sheehan, *Bright Shining Lie*, 640–649, 703–708, 710–712; Hammel, *Khe Sanh*; Herr, *Dispatches*, 86–167; Pisor, *The End of the Line*. For media coverage, see Braestrup, *Big Story*, 256–334.

303   "Proportional military losses": Record, *Wrong War*, 37.

304   Casualties: In addition to 58,000 deaths (47,000 of them in combat), 362,000 U.S. service personnel were wounded, sick, or injured. In terms of deaths, Vietnam was the fourth-costliest war in U.S. history, behind the Civil War (558,500 dead), World War II (407,300), and World War I (116,800). The figures for other wars: Revolutionary War (4,400), War of 1812 (2,300), Mexican War (13,300), Spanish-American War (2,500), Philippine War (5,000), Korean War (55,000), Gulf War (300). Dunnigan and Nofi, *Dirty Little Secrets*, 240–244.

304   "The Caribbean campaigns": Walt, *Strange War*, 29.

307   Binh Nghia: This section summarizes West's gripping book, *The Village*, the source of all quotations.

307   "Quite the best idea": Quoted in Krepinevich, *Army and Vietnam*, 174.

307   "I simply had not enough": Westmoreland, *A Soldier Reports*, 166.

307   CAP: The estimate of 167,000 U.S. troops comes from Krepinevich, *Army and Vietnam*, 176. See also Walt, *Strange War*, 105–112; Corson, *The Betrayal*, 174–199, by a marine colonel who commanded CAP. Peterson's *Combined Action Platoons* is of limited value.

308   "Relatively random basis": Quoted in Krepinevich, *Army and Vietnam*, 199.

308   Five million refugees: Record, *Wrong War*, 86. Some strategists argued that creating refugees was good for the U.S. war effort because it would deny peasant backing to the Vietcong, but it also helped destabilize South Vietnam.

309   Tet: For a critique of the media coverage, see Braestrup, *Big Story*. The author notes on 601 that there is controversy over whether Johnson in fact made the remark about Walter Cronkite, and if so when.

309　　Abrams: For an excellent description by one of his staff officers, see Davidson, *Vietnam at War*, 575–585. For a biography, see Sorley, *Thunderbolt*.

310　　Fragging: The term came from "fragmentation grenade," a weapon often used in such attacks.

310　　Hamburger Hill: The battle began on May 11 when a battalion of the 101st Airborne Division attacked a sizable enemy force entrenched on Ap Bia Hill in the A Shau Valley near the Cambodian border. Three more battalions were required to take this objective, which became known as Hamburger Hill. Fifty-six Americans paid with their lives for this real estate, of no strategic value; more than 600 of the enemy were killed. The battle further enraged antiwar demonstrators in America. See Davidson, *Vietnam at War*, 614.

310　　"Search and destroy was . . . dead": Davidson, *Vietnam at War*, 615. Lt. Gen. Davidson was MACV's chief intelligence officer from 1967 to 1969.

310　　Phoenix: The statistics are from Moyar, *Phoenix*, 236, the most comprehensive account of the program. The author rightly notes that all such figures should be treated with extreme caution.

310　　"Extremely destructive": Quoted in Karnow, *Vietnam*, 617.

311　　"PLAF had been destroyed": Pike, *PAVN*, 49.

311　　More than 90 percent: The Hamlet Evaluation Survey of June 1970 reported that 91 percent of South Vietnamese hamlets were "secure" or "relatively secure," 7.2 percent were contested, and just 1.4 percent were under Vietcong control. By the end of 1971, 97 percent of villages were classified as secure or relatively secure. Of course the seeming exactitude of these statistics masked considerable guesswork, and no doubt some fraud, by those who compiled them. But this was a more useful measure of the war's progress than body counts. Davidson, *Vietnam at War*, 634, 661.

311　　"Able to visit": Cited in Walt, *Strange War*, 166. For Colby's account of his pacification programs, see *Lost Victory*, chaps. 15–19.

313　　As Nixon did: See Nixon, *No More Vietnams*.

313　　"You never defeated us": Summers, *On Strategy*, 21.

313　　Even some who think the war was noble: See, e.g., Podhoretz, *Why We Were in Vietnam*, 62: "The only way the United States could have avoided defeat in Vietnam was by staying out of the war altogether." See also Lind, *Vietnam*.

313　　Unwinnable: For a forceful exposition of this view, see Record, *The Wrong War*.

314　　Post–World War II insurgencies: For an overview, see Asprey, *War in the Shadows*.

314　　"Stop swatting flies": Quoted in Record, *Wrong War*, 103.

315   "Total force": McMaster, *Dereliction of Duty*, 328. For the best exposition of the conventional warfare view, see Summers, *On Strategy*. Summers, unlike some others of this school, holds the military more at fault than civilian policymakers.

315   "Burden of combat": Pike, *PAVN*, 46.

316   "We were not strong enough": Quoted in Karnow, *Vietnam*, 20.

316   "Fundamental truth": Davidson, *Vietnam at War*, 732.

317   Small-war approach: The best exposition of this view is Krepinevich's important book, *The Army and Vietnam*, on which this chapter draws heavily. See also Sorley, *A Better War*, a compelling reinterpretation of the war's final years; Colby, *Lost Victory*, a memoir by the former CIA director; Corson, *The Betrayal*, written in 1968 by a marine colonel disgusted with the high command's neglect of "the other war"; Hunt, *Pacification*; Joes, *America and Guerrilla Warfare*, 209–259; Blaufarb, *Counterinsurgency Era*; Asprey, *War in the Shadows*; Cable, *Conflict of Myths*; and Lind, *Vietnam—the Necessary War*. Not all these authors would agree with every argument presented here. For instance, there remains sharp disagreement over whether Abrams initiated a new strategy. Sorley argues he did, Krepinevich disagreed (in an interview with the author).

Chapter 14: In the Shadow of Vietnam

318   "Many of my generation": Powell, *An American Journey*, 149. Weinberger Doctrine is discussed on 303.

320   Liberia evacuations: Bolger, *Death Ground*, chap. 6.

320   Tanker War: See Palmer, *Guardians of the Gulf*, chaps. 6–7, for a detailed account.

320–322 Gulf War: For Powell's account, see *My American Journey*, chaps. 18–19; "Persian Gulf Vietnam" is at 526, "Desert democracy" at 527. For an illuminating account of Powell's role, see Gordon and Trainor, *The Generals' War*. For Powell's opposition to deterring Saddam's invasion, see 18; for Powell's comment about "$1.50 gallon oil," see 33.

322   "Critical mistake" and "doctor going home": Stanton, *Somalia on $5.00 a Day*, 106. Stanton served as a major with the 10th Mountain Division.

323–324 "It seemed to promise": Bolger, *Savage Peace*, 329.

324   Somalia disaster: For a superb account of the Battle of Mogadishu, see Bowden, *Black Hawk Down*. For a broader picture, see Bolger, *Savage Peace*, chap. 7. Powell's account is in *My American Journey*, 564–566, 580, 583–584, 586, 588–589.

324   "Take care of the bad guys": Shacochis, *Immaculate Invasion*, 331.

324–325 Haiti: Shacochis, *Immaculate Invasion*. "Any of their boys outside the gates": 218. "For the primary purpose": 254. While Haiti's population in 1994 (approximately 6.5 million) was considerably greater than in 1915 (2 million), the number of U.S. troops sent was proportionately much greater in 1994. In 1994 the ratio of U.S. soldiers to Haitians was 1 to 325; in 1915, it was 1 to 666.

325   "No American President": Powell, *My American Journey*, 577.

325–326 Quotes about Bosnia: From Snider, Nagl, and Pfaff, "Army Professionalism."

325–326 Bosnia: Holbrooke's *To End a War* provides a first-rate, firsthand account by the chief U.S. negotiator at Dayton. Holbrooke constantly clashed with admirals and generals who wanted to take a minimal approach to implementing the peace treaty. See 336–337 for one particularly egregious example: U.S. troops stood by in 1996 as Serbian thugs forced Serb residents of Sarajevo to burn their homes and leave the city.

326–327 Kosovo: Clark's memoir, *Waging Modern War*, is invaluable. "The Service was against": 165. "Not to lose aircraft": 182. "Lack of knowledge": 289. "Don't do the mission": 230. For more on Apaches, see Priest, "Army's Apache Helicopters Rendered Impotent in Kosovo."

327   "Battle rattle": Gordon, "Looking Like War to Keep the Peace." This section on Kosovo is also based on the author's visit there in October 1999.

328   86 percent: Center for Strategic and International Studies, *American Military Culture*, 66.

328   "Excessive aversion": CSIS, *American Military Culture*, 22.

328   The rank and file: See Moskos, "Peacekeeping Improves Combat Readiness." Moskos is a sociologist who surveyed U.S. troops in Kosovo.

328   Declining family size: Luttwak, "Where Are the Great Powers?" For a critique, see Burk, "Public Support for Peacekeeping."

328   Vietnam: Larson, "Casualties and Consensus."

328–329 Beirut: Burk, "Public Support for Peacekeeping."

329   "Had the administration": Feaver and Gelpi, "A Look at Casualty Aversion." For more on Somalia, see also Kohut and Toth, "Arms and the People"; Larson, "Casualties and Consensus"; and Burk, "Public Support for Peacekeeping."

329   "Substantially higher estimates": Feaver and Kohn, "Digest of Findings and Studies."

331   Zinni quote: From a speech to the U.S. Naval Institute, March 2000. http://www.usni.org//Proceedings/Articles00/prozinni.htm.

332   "The mentality of an imperial army": Cohen, "Why the Gap Matters."

333   Special Forces: This section is based on the author's visit to Fort Bragg, May 10–11, 2001.

334   Marines in Somalia: See Ricks's justly acclaimed *Making the Corps*, 182–184.

335   Marine doctrine and training: The author visited Camp Lejeune, North Carolina, on October 4, 2000, and May 9–10, 2001. For background on marine training of enlisted men, see Ricks, *Making the Corps*; for marine officer training, see Freedman, *Corps Business*.

Chapter 15: In Defense of the Pax Americana

337   Declaration of war: Britain—upon whose precedents the Founders based their understanding of federal powers—also routinely went to war in the seventeenth and eighteenth centuries without declaring war, or sometimes not declaring war until several years after hostilities had started. See Yoo, "Continuation of Politics."

338   Westphalian principles traduced in Europe: There are numerous examples. In 1815 the allied powers toppled Napoleon and installed a monarchy in France; in 1848 the Russian czar dispatched 400,000 troops to help crush a liberal uprising in Hungary.

340   "The interventions": Huntington, *American Politics*, 250–251.

342   "We have a class of men . . . ": Butler to Gen. John Lejeune, Tientsin, China, July 23, 1928, in the Butler Papers, Box 8, File 1927 L.

342   "Service . . . is enhanced": Comment made at Foreign Policy Research Institution conference on humanitarian interventions, Philadelphia, February 12, 2001.

342–343 Survey of Kosovo soldiers: Moskos, "Peacekeeping Improves Combat Readiness."

343   British army in France: Keegan, *First World War*, 97–100.

345   Philippines: A number of Philippine elections have been characterized by accusations of fraud, but the same might be said of American elections.

348   Realists: A school of international affairs scholarship whose leading theoreticians were Hans Morgenthau and Kenneth Waltz, and whose leading practitioner in recent years has been Henry Kissinger. Realists believe that the international system is made up of states pursuing their own material self-interest in an anarchic environment. They generally discount the importance of ideology in motivating state action or the ability of international institutions to limit state power.

349   "Components of power": Wohlforth, "The Stability of a Unipolar World."

350   "A nation's first duty": Quoted in Beale, *Theodore Roosevelt*, 34.

350   1930s: Kindleberger, *World in Depression*.

350   Post–1945 era: Gilpin, *Challenge of Global Capitalism*.

351   Defense spending: Figure for U.S. defense spending comes from www.csbaonline.org. The British figure comes from Ferguson, *Cash Nexus*, 45, 48. This paragraph also draws on Ferguson's last chapter.

BIBLIOGRAPHY

Abbreviations

AMHI: Army Military History Institute, Carlisle, Pennsylvania
HL: Huntington Library, San Marino, California
LC: Library of Congress Manuscripts Division, Washington, D.C.
MCHC: Marine Corps Historical Center, Washington Navy Yard, Washington, D.C.
MCRCA: Marine Corps Research Center Archives, Quantico, Virginia
NARA: National Archives and Records Administration, Washington, D.C., and College Park, Maryland
NHC: Naval Historical Center, Washington Navy Yard, Washington, D.C.

Unpublished Sources

American Expeditionary Force in Siberia, 1918–1920, historical files. Records of U.S. Army Overseas Operations and Commands. NARA, Record Group 395
George Barnett Papers, MCRCA
Matthew A. Batson Papers, AMHI
Hiram I. Bearss Papers, MCRCA, includes typescript of unpublished memoir (cited as Bearss, *Memoir*).
James Franklin Bell Papers, AMHI
Smedley D. Butler Biographical File, MCHC
Smedley D. Butler Papers, MCRCA
William B. Caperton Biographical File, NHC
William B. Caperton Papers, LC
China Geographical File, MCHC
Daniel Daly Biographical File, MCHC
Stephen Decatur Jr. Biographical File, NHC
Dominican Republic Geographical File, MCHC
John Downes Biographical File, NHC

William Eaton Papers, HL
Merritt A. Edson Biographical File, MCHC
Robert L. Eichelberger Papers, AMHI
Haiti Geographical File, MCHC
Newt Hall Papers, MCRCA, includes partial typescript memoir of siege of Peking legations in 1900 (cited as Hall, *Memoir*).
Herman H. Hanneken Biographical File, MCHC
Herman H. Hanneken Oral History, MCHC
Thomas J. Kilcourse Papers, MCRCA
Harry Knapp Biographical File, NHC
William A. Kobbe Papers, AMHI
Victor H. Krulak Oral History, MCHC
William A. Lee Oral History, MCHC
Joseph B. Longuevan Papers, AMHI
Bowman Hendry McCalla Papers, LC, includes typescript "Memoir of a Naval Officer" finished in 1910 (cited as McCalla, *Memoir*).
Mexico (Vera Cruz) Geographical File, MCHC
John T. Myers Biographical File, MCHC
Nicaragua Geographical File, MCHC
Douglas Osborn Papers, AMHI
Panama Geographical File, MCHC
Frank A. Paul, ed. *Regimental History Thirty-First U.S. Infantry July 1916-July 1920*, AMHI
Joseph H. Pendleton Biographical File, MCHC
John J. Pershing Papers, LC, includes typescript of an unpublished memoir (cited as Pershing, *Memoirs*).
Pershing expedition records. Office of the Adjutant General, Mexican Border. NARA, Record Group 94, Boxes 8127–8147
Porter Family Papers, LC
Lewis B. Puller Biographical File, MCHC
Lewis B. Puller Oral History, MCHC
John Rodgers Biographical File, NHC
Major Ross E. Rowell, "Experiences with the Air Services in Minor Warfare," Lecture Delivered at the Army War College, Washington, D.C., January 12, 1929. Ross E. Rowell Papers, MCRCA.
Samoa Geographical File, MCHC
Christian F. Schilt Oral History, MCHC
Julian C. Smith, et al., "The Guardia Nacional de Nicaragua, 1927–1933," typescript of report prepared by Guardia officers, in Julian C. Smith Papers, MCRCA
Spanish-American War Survey: 9th U.S. Infantry, 33rd U.S. Infantry, 28th U.S. Volunteer Infantry, AMHI
Sumatra Geographical File, MCHC
McLane Tilton Biographical File, MCHC

McLane Tilton Papers, MCRCA
Littleton W. T. Waller court-martial transcript. Records of the Office of the Judge Advocate General, Proceedings of General Courts Martial 1866–1902. NARA, Record Group 125, Box 235, Entry 27
Littleton W. T. Waller Sr. Papers, MCRCA
Faustin Wirkus Biographical File, MCHC
Frederic May Wise Biographical File, MCHC
Word War I survey: American Expeditionary Force, Siberia, AMHI
Leroy Yarborough Papers, AMHI

Newspapers

New York Daily Tribune
New York Evening Journal
New York Sun
New York Times
New York World

Published Sources (Including the Internet)

Abun-Nasr, Jamil M. *A History of the Maghrib*. Cambridge: Cambridge University Press, 1971.

Aguinaldo, Emilio. "The Story of My Capture." *Everybody's Magazine* 5, no. 24 (August 1901).

Ajayi, J. F. Ade, ed. *General History of Africa*. Vol. 6, *Africa in the Nineteenth Century until the 1880s*. Berkeley: University of California Press, 1989.

Allen, Gardner W. *Our Navy and the West Indian Pirates*. Salem, Mass.: Essex Institute, 1929.

Allison, Robert J. *The Crescent Obscured: The United States and the Muslim World, 1776–1815*. New York and Oxford: Oxford University Press, 1995.

Alter, Robert Edmond. *First Comes Courage*. New York: G. P. Putnam's Sons, 1969.

Archer, Jules. *The Plot to Seize the White House*. New York: Hawthorn Books, 1973.

Asprey, Robert B. *War in the Shadows: The Guerrilla in History*. Revised and updated. New York: William Morrow and Company, 1994.

Bacevich, A. J. *Diplomat in Khaki: Major General Frank Ross McCoy and American Foreign Policy, 1898–1949*. Lawrence: University Press of Kansas, 1989.

Baepler, Paul, ed. *White Slaves, African Masters: An Anthology of American Barbary Captivity Narratives*. Chicago and London: University of Chicago Press, 1999.

Bain, David Haward. *Sitting in Darkness: Americans in the Philippines*. Boston: Houghton Mifflin, 1984.

Barber, Benjamin R. *Jihad vs. McWorld: How the Planet is Both Falling Apart and Coming Together and What This Means for Democracy*. New York: Times Books, 1995.

Bartlett, Merrill L. *Lejeune: A Marine's Life, 1867–1942.* Columbia: University of South Carolina Press, 1991.

Beale, Howard K. *Theodore Roosevelt and the Rise of America to World Power.* Baltimore: Johns Hopkins University Press, 1956.

Beals, Carleton. *Banana Gold.* New York: Arno, 1970. Reprint of 1932 edition.

Bearss, Hiram I. *Memoir.* See Unpublished Manuscripts: Hiram I. Bearss Papers, MCRCA.

Beede, Benjamin R. *Intervention and Counterinsurgency: An Annotated Bibliography of the Small Wars of the United States, 1898–1984.* New York: Garland, 1985.

Belohlavek, John M. *"Let the Eagle Soar!": The Foreign Policy of Andrew Jackson.* Lincoln: University of Nebraska Press, 1985.

Bemis, Samuel Flagg. *The Latin American Policy of the United States: A Historical Interpretation.* New York: Harcourt, Brace & Company, 1943.

Bermann, Karl. *Under the Big Stick: Nicaragua and the United States Since 1848.* Boston: South End, 1986.

Bickel, Keith B. *Mars Learning: The Marine Corps' Development of Small Wars Doctrine, 1915–1940.* Boulder: Westview, 2001.

Birtle, Andrew J. *U.S. Army Counterinsurgency and Contingency Operations Doctrine, 1860–1941.* Washington: Center of Military History, 1998.

Blaufarb, Douglas S. *The Counterinsurgency Era: U.S. Doctrine and Performance, 1950 to the Present.* New York: Free Press, 1977.

Bolger, Daniel P. *Death Ground: Today's American Infanty in Battle.* Novato, Calif.: Presidio, 1999.

———. *Savage Peace: Americans at War in the 1990s.* Novato, Calif.: Presidio, 1995.

Bolster, W. Jeffrey. *Black Jacks: African American Seamen in the Age of Sail.* Cambridge: Harvard University Press, 1997.

Bowden, Mark. *Black Hawk Down: A Story of Modern War.* New York: Atlantic Monthly Press, 1999.

Braddy, Haldeen. *Pershing's Mission in Mexico.* El Paso, Texas: Texas Western Press, 1966.

Bradford, James C., ed. *Admirals of the New Steel Navy: Makers of the American Naval Tradition, 1880–1930.* Annapolis, Md.: U.S. Naval Institute Press, 1990.

Bradlee, Francis B. C. *Piracy in the West Indies and Its Suppression.* Salem, Mass.: Essex Institute, 1923.

Bradley, John. *Allied Intervention in Russia.* New York: Basic Books, 1968.

Braestrup, Peter. *Big Story: How the American Press and Television Reported and Interpreted the Crisis of Tet 1968 in Vietnam and Washington.* Abridged edn. Novato, Calif.: Presidio, 1994.

Brands, H. W. *Bound to Empire: The United States and the Philippines.* New York: Oxford University Press, 1992.

———. *T.R.: The Last Romantic.* New York: Basic Books, 1997.

Brinkley, George A. *The Volunteer Army and Allied Intervention in South Russia, 1917–1921.* Notre Dame, Ind.: University of Notre Dame Press, 1966.

Broder, Jonathan. "Tangier," *Smithsonian* 90 (July 1998).

Brown, Frederick. *From Tientsin to Peking with the Allied Forces*. [London: Charles H. Kelly, 1902.] Reprinted New York: Arno, 1970.

Brown, Fred. *History of the Ninth U.S. Infantry, 1799–1909*. Chicago: R. R. Donnelley & Sons, 1909.

Buck, Pearl S. *My Several Worlds: A Personal Record*. New York: John Day, 1954.

Burk, James. "Public Support for Peacekeeping in Lebanon and Somalia: Assessing the Casualties Hypothesis." *Political Science Quarterly* 53 (April 1999).

Butler, Smedley D., and Lowell Thomas. *Old Gimlet Eye: The Adventures of Smedley D. Butler, As Told to Lowell Thomas*. New York: Farrar & Rinehart, 1933.

Butler, Smedley D. *War Is a Racket*. New York: Round Table, 1935.

Cable, Larry E. *Conflict of Myths: The Development of American Counterinsurgency Doctrine and the Vietnam War*. New York: New York University Press, 1986.

Calder, Bruce J. *The Impact of Intervention: The Dominican Republic During the U.S. Occupation of 1916–1924*. Austin: University of Texas Press, 1984.

Calwell, C. E. *Small Wars: Their Principles and Practice*. 3rd edn. Reprinted East Ardsley, U.K.: EP Publishing Ltd., 1976. Originally published 1906, first edition 1896.

Caputo, Philip. *A Rumor of War*. New York: Ballantine Books, 1977.

Carey, Neil G., ed. *Fighting the Bolsheviks: The Russian War Memoir of Private First Class Donald E. Carey, U.S. Army, 1918–1919*. Novato, Calif.: Presidio, 1997.

Carpenter, Frank G. *China*. Garden City, N.Y.: Doubleday, Doran & Company, 1930.

Carr, Caleb, ed. *The Book of War*. New York: Modern Library, 2000.

Carter, Ashton, and William J. Perry. *Preventive Defense: A New Security Strategy for America*. Washington, D.C.: Brookings Institution, 1999.

Cathcart, James Leander. *The Captives: Eleven Years a Prisoner in Algiers*. Compiled by his daughter, J. B. Newkirk [La Porte, Ind.: Herald Print, 1899]. In Paul Baepler, ed., *White Slaves, African Masters*. Chicago: University of Chicago Press, 1999.

Center for Strategic and International Studies. *American Military Culture in the Twenty-First Century*. Washington, D.C.: CSIS, 2001.

Challener, Richard D. *Admirals, Generals, and American Foreign Policy, 1898–1914*. Princeton: Princeton University Press, 1973.

Chang, Iris. *The Rape of Nanking: The Forgotten Holocaust of World War II*. New York: Basic Books, 1997.

Chen Jian. "Personal-Historical Puzzles About China and the Vietnam War." Unpublished Working Paper no. 22, Cold War International History Project. Washington: Woodrow Wilson Center for Scholars, May 1998.

Cherif, M. H. "New Trends in the Maghrib: Algeria, Tunisia, and Libya." In J. F. Ade Ajayi, ed., *General History of Africa*. Vol. 6, *Africa in the Nineteenth Century until the 1880s*. Berkeley: University of California Press, 1989.

Christopher, Warren. *Chances of a Lifetime*. New York: Scribner/Lisa Drew, 2001.

Chronicler [John Cudahy]. *Archangel: The American War with Russia*. Chicago: A. C. McClurg, 1924.

Churchill, Winston S. *The World Crisis, 1918–1928: The Aftermath*. New York: Charles Scribner's Sons, 1929.

Chwialkowski, Paul. *In Caesar's Shadow: The Life of General Robert Eichelberger*. Westport, Conn.: Greenwood, 1993.

Clark, Wesley. *Waging Modern War*. New York: PublicAffairs, 2001.

Clendenen, Clarence C. *Blood on the Border: The United States Army and the Mexican Irregulars*. New York: Macmillan, 1969.

_____. *The United States and Pancho Villa: A Study in Unconventional Diplomacy*. Ithaca, N.Y.: Cornell University Press, 1961.

Clifford, Nicholas R. *Spoilt Children of Empire: Westerners in Shanghai and the Chinese Revolution of the 1920s*. Hanover and London: Middlebury College Press, 1991.

Coffman, Edward W. *The Old Army: A Portrait of the American Army in Peacetime, 1784–1898*. New York: Oxford University Press, 1986.

_____. *The Hilt of the Sword: The Career of Peyton C. March*. Madison: University of Wisconsin Press, 1966.

Cohen, Eliot A. "Why the Gap Matters." *The National Interest*, Fall 2000.

Cohen, Paul A. *History in Three Keys: The Boxers as Event, Experience, and Myth*. New York: Columbia University Press, 1997.

Cohen, Warren I. *Empire Without Tears: America's Foreign Relations, 1921–1933*. Philadelphia: Temple University Press, 1987.

Colby, William, with James McCargar. *Lost Victory: A Firsthand Account of America's Sixteen-Year Involvement in Vietnam*. Chicago: Contemporary Books, 1989.

Cole, Bernard D. *Gunboats and Marines: The United States Navy in China, 1925–1928*. Newark: University of Delaware Press, 1983.

Coletta, Paolo E. *Bowman Hendry McCalla: A Fighting Sailor*. Washington, D.C.: University Press of America, 1979.

Collins, John M. *America's Small Wars: Lessons for the Future*. Washington: Brasseys, 1991.

Condit, Kenneth W., and Edwin T. Turnbladh. *Hold High the Torch: A History of the 4th Marines*. Washington: Historical Branch, G–3 Division, Headquarters, U.S. Marine Corps, 1960.

Connaughton, R. M. *The Republic of the Ushakovka: Admiral Kolchak and the Allied Intervention in Siberia, 1918–20*. London and New York: Routledge, 1990.

Cooper, John Milton. *The Warrior and the Priest: Woodrow Wilson and Theodore Roosevelt*. Cambridge, Mass.: Belknap, 1983.

Corson, William R. *The Betrayal*. New York: W. W. Norton, 1968.

Cowdery, Jonathan. *American Captives in Tripoli; or, Dr. Cowdery's Journal in Miniature*. 2nd edn. [Boston: Belcher and Armstrong, 1806]. In Paul Baepler, ed., *White Slaves, African Masters*. Chicago: University of Chicago Press, 1999.

Craige, John Houston. *Cannibal Cousins*. New York: Minton, Balch & Co., 1934.

Craven, T. T. "A Naval Episode of 1899." U.S. Naval Institute Proceedings (March 1928).

Daggett, A. S. *America in the China Relief Expedition*. Kansas City: Hudson-Kimberly Publishing Co., 1903.

Daniels, Josephus. *The Wilson Era: Years of Peace—1910–1917*. Chapel Hill: University of North Carolina Press, 1944.

———. *The Cabinet Diaries of Josephus Daniels, 1913–1921*. E. David Cronon, ed. Lincoln: University of Nebraska Press, 1963.

———. "The Problem of Haiti," *Saturday Evening Post,* July 12, 1930.

Davidson, Phillip B. *Vietnam at War: The History, 1946–1975*. Novato, Calif.: Presidio, 1988.

Davis, Burke. *Marine! The Life of Lt. Gen. Lewis B. (Chesty) Puller, USMC. (Ret.)* Boston: Little, Brown 1962.

Davis, H. P. *Black Democracy: The Story of Haiti*. New York: Dial, 1928.

Dearden, Seton. *A Nest of Corsairs: The Fighting Karamanlis of Tripoli*. London: John Murray, 1976.

Denny, Harold Norman. *Dollars for Bullets: The Story of American Rule in Nicaragua*. New York: Dial, 1929.

D'Este, Carlo. *Patton: A Genius for War*. New York: HarperCollins, 1995.

DeMontravel, Peter R. *Hero to His Fighting Men: Nelson A. Miles, 1839–1925*. Kent, Ohio: Kent State University Press, 1998.

Dobson, Christopher, and John Miller. *The Day They Almost Bombed Moscow: The Allied War in Russia, 1918–1920*. New York: Atheneum, 1986.

Dohrman, Richard. *The Cross of Baron Samedi*. Boston: Houghton Mifflin, 1958.

Dunnigan, James F., and Albert A. Nofi. *Dirty Little Secrets of the Vietnam War: Military Information You're Not Supposed to Know*. New York: St. Martin's, 1999.

Dupuy, Ernest R., and William H. Baumer. *The Little Wars of the United States*. New York: Hawthorn Books, 1968.

Dupuy, R. Ernest. *Perish by the Sword: The Czechoslovakian Anabasis and Our Supporting Campaigns in North Russia and Siberia, 1918–1920*. Harrisburg, Pa.: Military Service Publishing Co., 1939.

Edgerton, Robert B. *Warriors of the Rising Son: A History of the Japanese Military*. New York: W. W. Norton, 1997.

Edwards, Samuel. *Barbary General: The Life of William H. Eaton*. Englewood Cliffs, N.J.: Prentice-Hall, 1968.

Eisenhower, John S. D. *Intervention! The United States and the Mexican Revolution, 1913–1917*. New York: W. W. Norton & Co., 1993.

Ellis, Joseph J. *American Sphinx: The Character of Thomas Jefferson*. New York: Alfred A. Knopf, 1997.

Ellsworth, Harry Allanson. *One Hundred Eighty Landings of United States Marines, 1800–1934*. Washington, D.C.: History and Museums Division, Headquarters, USMC, 1974. Reprint of 1934 mimeograph.

Esherick, Joseph W. *The Origins of the Boxer Uprising*. Berkeley: University of California Press, 1987.

Evans, Ernest. *Wars Without Splendor: The U.S. Military and Low-Level Conflict*. Westport, Conn.: Greenwood, 1987.

Fairbank, John King. *The United States and China*, 4th Edition. Cambridge: Harvard University Press, 1979.

Feaver, Peter D., and Christopher Gelpi. "A Look at Casualty Aversion: How Many Deaths Are Acceptable? A Surprising Answer." *Washington Post*, November 7, 1999.

Feaver, Peter D., and Richard K. Kohn. "Digest of Findings and Studies," Project on the Gap Between the Military and Civilian Society, Triangle Institute for Security Studies. June 2000. www.poli.duke.edu/civmil/survey.html

Fehrenbach, T. R. *This Kind of War: A Study in Unpreparedness*. New York: Macmillan, 1963.

Ferguson, Niall. *The Cash Nexus: Money and Power in the Modern World, 1700–2000*. New York: Basic Books, 2001.

Finney, Charles G. *The Old China Hands*. Garden City, N.Y.: Doubleday & Co., 1961.

Fisher, Godfrey. *Barbary Legend: War, Trade and Piracy in North Africa, 1415–1830*. Oxford: Clarendon, 1957.

Flint, John E., ed. *The Cambridge History of Africa*. Vol. 5, *From c. 1790 to c. 1870*. Cambridge: Cambridge University Press, 1976.

Foglesong, David S. *America's Secret War Against Bolshevism: U.S. Intervention in the Russian Civil War, 1917–1920*. Chapel Hill: University of North Carolina Press, 1995.

Forester, C. S. *The Barbary Pirates*. New York: Random House, 1953.

Foss, John D. *A Journal of the Captivity and Sufferings of John Foss* [Newburyport, Mass.: n.p., 1798]. In Paul Baepler, ed., *White Slaves, African Masters*. Chicago: University of Chicago Press, 1999.

Fowler, William M., Jr. *Jack Tars and Commodores: The American Navy, 1783–1815*. Boston: Houghton Mifflin, 1984.

Freedman, David H. *Corps Business: The Thirty Management Principles of the U.S. Marines*. New York: HarperBusiness, 2000.

Friedman, Thomas L. *The Lexus and the Olive Tree*. New York: Farrar Straus and Giroux, 1999.

Fuller, Stephen M., and Graham A. Cosmas. *Marines in the Dominican Republic, 1916–1924*. Washington: History and Museums Division, U.S. Marine Corps, 1974.

Funston, Frederick. *Memories of Two Wars: Cuban and Philippine Experiences*. New York: Charles Scribner's Sons, 1911.

Gacek, Christopher M. *The Logic of Force: The Dilemma of Limited War in American Foreign Policy*. New York: Columbia University Press, 1994.

Gann, Lewis. *Guerillas in History*. Stanford, Calif.: Hoover University Press, 1971.

Gates, John Morgan. *Schoolbooks and Krags: The United States Army in the Philippines, 1898–1902*. Westport, Conn.: Greenwood, 1973.

Gibson, James William. *The Perfect War: Technowar in Vietnam*. Revised edn. New York: Atlantic Monthly Press, 2000.

Gilbert, Martin. *Winston S. Churchill*. Companion Volume 4, Part 1, *January 1917–June 1919*. Boston: Houghton Mifflin, 1978.

Gilpin, Robert. *The Challenge of Global Capitalism: The World Economy in the Twenty-First Century.* Princeton: Princeton University Press, 2000.

Goldhurst, Richard. *The Midnight War: The American Intervention in Russia, 1918–1920.* New York: McGraw-Hill, 1978.

_____. *Pipe Clay and Drill: John J. Pershing: The Classic American Soldier.* New York: Reader's Digest Press, 1977.

Gordon, Dennis. *Quartered in Hell: The Story of the American North Russian Expeditionary Force, 1918–1919.* Missoula, Mont.: Doughboy Historical Society, 1982.

Gordon, Michael R., and Bernard E. Trainor. *The Generals' War: The Inside Story of the Conflict in the Gulf.* Boston: Little, Brown, 1995.

Gordon, Michael. "Looking Like War to Keep the Peace." *New York Times,* February 4, 2001.

Graff, Henry F., ed. *American Imperialism and the Philippine Insurrection: Testimony Taken from Hearings in the Philippine Islands before the Senate Committee on the Philippines—1902.* Boston: Little, Brown, 1969.

Graves, William S. *America's Siberian Adventure, 1918–1920.* New York: Jonathan Cape & Harrison Smith, 1931.

Griffis, William Elliott. *Corea: The Hermit Nation.* 6th edn. New York: Charles Scribner's Sons, 1897.

Gruppe, Henry E. *The Frigates.* Alexandria, Va.: Time Life Books, 1979.

Guttridge, Leonard F., and Jay D. Smith. *The Commodores: The U.S. Navy in the Age of Sail.* New York: Harper & Row, 1969.

Haas, Richard N. *Intervention: The Use of American Military Force in the Post-Cold War World.* Revised edn. Washington: Brookings Institution, 1999.

Hagan, Kenneth J. *American Gunboat Diplomacy and the Old Navy, 1877–1889.* Westport, Conn.: Greenwood, 1973.

_____. *This People's Navy: The Making of American Sea Power.* New York: Free Press, 1991.

Haley, P. Edward. *Revolution and Intervention: The Diplomacy of Taft and Wilson with Mexico, 1910–1917.* Cambridge, Mass.: MIT Press, 1970.

Hall, Newt. *Memoir.* See Unpublished Manuscripts: Newt Hall Papers, MCRCA.

Hallett, Robin. *Africa to 1875: A Modern History.* Ann Arbor: University of Michigan Press, 1970.

Halliday, E. M. *The Ignorant Armies.* New York: Harper & Brothers, 1958.

Hammel, Eric. *Khe Sanh: Siege in the Clouds.* New York: Crown, 1989.

Han, Sung-joo, ed. *After One Hundred Years: Continuity and Change in Korean-American Relations.* Seoul: Asiatic Research Center, Korea University, 1982.

Han, Woo-Keun. *The History of Korea.* Trans. Kyung-Shik Lee. Honolulu: East-West Center Press, 1971.

Harris, Charles H. III, and Louis R. Sadler. *The Border and the Revolution: Clandestine Activities of the Mexican Revolution, 1910–1922.* Silver City, N.M.: High-Lonesome Books, 1988.

Healey, David. *Drive to Hegemony: The United States in the Caribbean, 1898–1917.* Madison: University of Wisconsin Press, 1988.

_____. *Gunboat Diplomacy in the Wilson Era: The U.S. Navy in Haiti, 1915–1916*. Madison: University of Wisconsin Press, 1976.

Heckscher, August. *Woodrow Wilson: A Biography*. New York: Charles Scribner's Sons, 1991.

Heinl, Robert Debs Jr., and Nancy Gordon Heinl. *Written in Blood: The Story of the Haitian People, 1492–1971*. Boston: Houghton Mifflin, 1978.

Hemmingway, Albert. *Our War Was Different*. Annapolis: Naval Institute Press, 1994.

Herr, Michael. *Dispatches*. New York: Alfred A. Knopf, 1977.

Hill, Howard C. *Roosevelt and the Caribbean*. New York: Russell & Russell, 1965.

Hodgson, Godfrey. *The Colonel: The Life and Wars of Henry Stimson, 1867–1950*. New York: Alfred A. Knopf, 1990.

Hoffman, Jon T. *Once a Legend: "Red Mike" Edson of the Marine Raiders*. San Marin, Calif.: Presidio, 1994.

_____. *Chesty: The Story of Lieutenant General Lewis B. Puller, USMC*. New York: Random House, 2001.

Holbrooke, Richard. *To End a War*. Revised edn. New York: Modern Library, 1999.

Holmes, Richard. *Acts of War: The Behavior of Men in Battle*. New York: Free Press, 1985.

Hooker, Mary. *Behind the Scenes in Peking: Being Experiences During the Siege of the Legations*. London: John Murray, 1910.

Hoover, Herbert. *The Memoirs of Herbert Hoover: Years of Adventure, 1874–1920*. New York: Macmillan, 1951.

Howarth, Stephen. *To Shining Sea: A History of the United States Navy, 1775–1991*. New York: Random House, 1991.

Hoyt, Edwin P. *America's Wars and Military Excursions,*. New York: McGraw-Hill, 1987.

_____. *The Lonely Ships: The Life and Death of the U.S. Asiatic Fleet*. New York: David McKay Company, 1976.

Hsu, Immanuel C. Y. *The Rise of Modern China*, 3rd edn. New York: Oxford University Press, 1983.

Hunt, Richard A. *Pacification: The American Struggle for Vietnam's Hearts and Minds*. Boulder, Colo.: Westview, 1995.

Huntington, Samuel P. *American Politics: The Promise of Disharmony*. Cambridge, Mass.: Belknap, 1981.

Ireland, Bernard. *Naval Warfare in the Age of Sail: War at Sea, 1756–1815*. New York: W. W. Norton & Company, 2000.

Iriye, Akira. *The Cambridge History of American Foreign Relations*. Vol. 3, *The Globalizing of America, 1913–1945*. Cambridge: Cambridge University Press, 1993.

Ironside, Edmund. *Archangel, 1918–1919*. London: Constable, 1953.

James, D. Clayton. *The Years of MacArthur*. 2 vols. Boston: Houghton Mifflin, 1970.

Joes, Anthony James. *Guerrilla Warfare: A Historical, Biographical, and Bibliographical Sourcebook*. Westport, Conn.: Greenwood, 1996.

_____. *America and Guerrilla Warfare*. Lexington: University Press of Kentucky, 2000.

Johnson, Paul. *A History of the American People*. New York: HarperCollins, 1998.

Johnson, Robert Erwin. *Rear Admiral John Rodgers, 1812–1882*. Annapolis: U.S. Naval Institute Press, 1967.

_____. *Thence Around Cape Horn: The Story of the United States Naval Forces on Pacific Station, 1818–1923*. Annapolis, Md.: U.S. Naval Institute Press, 1963.

_____. *Far China Station: The U.S. Navy in Asian Waters, 1800–1898*. Annapolis, Md.: U.S. Naval Institute Press, 1979.

Johnson, William Weber. *Heroic Mexico: The Violent Emergence of a Violent Nation*. Garden City, N.Y.: Doubleday & Co., 1968.

Kagan, Robert. *A Twilight Struggle: American Power and Nicaragua, 1977–1990*. New York: Free Press, 1996.

Kaiser, David. *American Tragedy: Kennedy, Johnson, and the Origins of the Vietnam War*. Cambridge: Belknap Press of Harvard University Press, 2000.

Kamman, William. *A Search for Stability: United States Diplomacy Toward Nicaragua, 1925–1933*. Notre Dame, Ind.: University of Notre Dame Press, 1968.

Karnow, Stanley. *In Our Image: America's Empire in the Philippines*. New York: Random House, 1989.

_____. *Vietnam: A History*. Revised edn. New York: Penguin, 1997.

Karsten, Peter. *The Naval Aristocracy: The Golden Age of Annapolis and the Emergence of Modern American Navalism*. New York: Free Press, 1972.

Katz, Friedrich. *The Life and Times of Pancho Villa*. Stanford, Calif.: Stanford University Press, 1998.

Keegan, John. *The Price of Admiralty: The Evolution of Naval Warfare*. New York: Viking, 1988.

_____. *The First World War*. New York: Vintage, 2000.

Kennedy, Paul M. *The Samoan Tangle: A Study in Anglo-German-American Relations, 1878–1900*. New York: Barnes and Noble Books, 1974.

Kennan, George F. *American Diplomacy, 1900–1950*. Chicago: University of Chicago Press, 1951.

Keown-Boyd, Henry. *Boxer Rebellion: An Illustrated History of the Boxer Uprising in China, 1900*. New York: Dorset, 1991.

Kiester, Edwin, Jr., and Sally Valente Kiester. "Yankee Go Home and Take Me with You." *Smithsonian*, May 1, 1999.

Kindall, Sylvian G. *American Soldiers in Siberia*. New York: Richard R. Smith, 1945.

Kindleberger, Charles P. *The World in Depression, 1929–1939*. Berkeley: University of California Press, 1986.

Kissinger, Henry. *The White House Years*. Boston: Little, Brown, 1979.

_____. *Diplomacy*. New York: Simon & Schuster, 1994.

Klay, Andor. *Daring Diplomacy: The Case of the First American Ultimatum*. Minneapolis: University of Minnesota Press, 1957.

Knight, Melvin M. *The Americans in Santo Domingo*. New York: Vanguard, 1928.

Koginos, Manny T. *The Panay Incident: Prelude to War*. Lafayette, Ind.: Purdue University Studies, 1967.

Kohut, Andrew, and Robert Toth. "Arms and the People." *Foreign Affairs* 47 (December 1994).

Krause, Enrique. *Mexico: Biography of Power: A History of Modern Mexico, 1810–1996*. Trans. Hank Heifetz. New York: HarperCollins, 1997.

Krepinevich, Andrew J. Jr. *The Army and Vietnam*. Baltimore and London: Johns Hopkins University Press, 1986.

Krulak, Victor H. *First to Fight: An Inside View of the U.S. Marine Corps*. Annapolis, Md.: U.S. Naval Institute Press, 1984.

LaFeber, Walter. *The New Empire: An Interpretation of American Expansion, 1860–1898*. Ithaca, N.Y.: Cornell University Press, 1963.

_____. *The Cambridge History of American Foreign Relations*. Vol. 2, *The American Search for Opportunity, 1865–1913*. Cambridge: Cambridge University Press, 1993.

Langley, Lester D. *The United States and the Caribbean in the Twentieth Century*. 4th ed. Athens: University of Georgia Press, 1989.

_____. *The Banana Wars: An Inner History of American Empire, 1900–1934*. Lexington: University Press of Kentucky, 1983.

Laqueur, Walter. *Guerrilla: A Historical and Critical Study*. London: Weidenfeld & Nicolson, 1977.

Laroui, Abdallah. *The History of the Maghrib: An Interpretive Essay*. Trans. Ralph Manheim. Princeton: Princeton University Press, 1977.

Larson, Eric V. "Casualties and Consensus: The Historical Role of Casualties in Domestic Support for U.S. Military Operations." www.rand.org/publications/MR/MR726

Leavenworth, Charles S. *The Arrow War with China*. London: Sampson, Low, Marston & Co., 1901.

Leckie, Robert. *From Sea to Shining Sea: From the War of 1812 to the Mexican War, the Saga of American Expansion*. New York: HarperCollins, 1993.

Lee, Yur-Bok. *Diplomatic Relations Between the United States and Korea, 1866–1887*. New York: Humanities Press, 1970.

Leech, Margaret. *In the Days of McKinley*. New York: Harper & Brothers, 1959.

Leggett, George. *The Cheka: Lenin's Secret Police*. Oxford: Clarendon, 1981.

Legro, Jeffrey W., and Andrew Moravcsik. "Is Anybody Still a Realist?" *International Security* 24 (Fall 1999).

Lehrack, Otto J. *No Shining Armor: The Marines at War in Vietnam, an Oral History*. Lawrence: University Press of Kansas, 1992.

Lejeune, John A. *The Reminiscences of a Marine*. Philadelphia: Dorrance & Co., 1930.

Lewis, Charles Lee. *The Romantic Decatur*. Philadelphia: University of Pennsylvania Press, 1937.

_____. *Famous American Marines*. Boston: L. C. Page & Co., 1950.

Lincoln, W. Bruce. *Red Victory: A History of the Russian Civil War*. New York: Simon and Schuster, 1989.

Lind, Michael. *Vietnam: The Necessary War—A Reinterpretation of America's Most Disastrous Military Conflict*. New York: Free Press, 1999.

Link, Arthur S. *Wilson: The New Freedom*. Princeton: Princeton University Press, 1956.

_____. *Wilson: The Struggle for Neutrality, 1914–1915*. Princeton: Princeton University Press, 1960.

_____. *Wilson: Confusions and Crises, 1915–1916*. Princeton: Princeton University Press, 1964.

_____. *Wilson: Campaigns for Progressivism and Peace, 1916–1917*. Princeton: Princeton University Press, 1965.

Linn, Brian McAllister. *The U.S. Army and Counterinsurgency in the Philippine War, 1899–1902*. Chapel Hill: University of North Carolina Press, 1989.

_____. *The Philippine War, 1899–1902*. Lexington: University Press of Kentucky, 2000.

Logevall, Fredrik. *Choosing War: The Lost Chance for Peace and the Escalation of War in Vietnam*. Berkeley: University of California Press, 1999.

Lone, Stewart, and Gavan McCormack. *Korea Since 1850*. Melbourne: Longman, 1993.

Long, David F. *Nothing Too Daring: A Biography of Commodore David Porter, 1783–1843*. Annapolis, Md.: U.S. Naval Institute Press, 1970.

_____. *Gold Braid and Foreign Relations: Diplomatic Activities of U.S. Naval Officers, 1798–1883*. Annapolis, Md.: U.S. Naval Institute Press, 1988.

Love, Robert W. Jr. *History of the U.S. Navy*. Vol. 1, *1775–1941*. Harrisburg, Penn.: Stackpole Books, 1992.

Lovette, Leland P. *Naval Customs: Traditions and Usage*. Annapolis, Md.: U.S. Naval Institute Press, 1939.

Luttwak, Edward. "Where are the great powers? At home with the kids." *Foreign Affairs* (July 1994).

_____. *The Pentagon and the Art of War: The Question of Military Reform*. New York: Simon & Schuster, 1985.

Macaulay, Neill. *The Sandino Affair*. Micanopy, Fla.: Wacahoota, 1998. Reprint of 1967 edition.

MacCloskey, Monro. *Reilly's Battery: A Story of the Boxer Rebellion*. New York: Richards Rosen, 1969.

MacKenzie, Alexander Slidell. *Life of Stephen Decatur, A Commodore in the Navy of the United States*. Boston: Charles C. Little and James Brown, 1846.

Machado, Manuel A., Jr. *Centaur of the North: Francisco Villa, the Mexican Revolution and Northern Mexico*. Austin, Tex.: Eakin, 1988.

Malia, Martin. *The Soviet Tragedy: A History of Socialism in Russia, 1917–1991*. New York: Free Press, 1994.

Malone, Dumas. *Jefferson the President: First Term, 1801–1805*. Boston: Little, Brown and Company, 1970.

_____. *Jefferson the President: Second Term, 1805–1809*. Boston: Little, Brown and Company, 1974.

Manning, Clarence A. *The Siberian Fiasco*. New York: Library Publishers, 1952.

Marks, Frederick W. III. *Velvet on Iron: The Diplomacy of Theodore Roosevelt.* Lincoln: University of Nebraska Press, 1979.

Martin, Tyrone G. *A Most Fortunate Ship: A Narrative History of "Old Ironsides."* Chester, Conn.: Globe Pequot, 1980.

Masefield, John. *Sea Life in Nelson's Time*. New York: Macmillan, 1925.

Mason, Herbert Molloy, Jr. *The Great Pursuit: General John J. Pershing's Punitive Expedition Across the Rio Grande to Destroy the Mexican Bandit Pancho Villa*. New York: Random House, 1970.

Maugham, W. Somerset. *On a Chinese Screen*. New York: George H. Doran Company, 1922.

Mawdsley, Evan. *The Russian Civil War*. Boston: Allen & Unwin, 1987.

May, Glenn Anthony. *Battle for Batangas: A Philippine Province at War*. New Haven: Yale University Press, 1991.

McCalla, Bowman Hendry. *Memoir*. See Unpublished Manupscripts: Bowman Hendry McCalla Papers, LC.

McCullough, David. *The Path Between the Seas: The Creation of the Panama Canal, 1870–1914*. New York: Simon & Schuster, 1977.

McKee, Christopher. *Edward Preble: A Naval Biography, 1761–1807*. Annapolis, Md.: U.S. Naval Institute Press, 1972.

_____. *A Gentlemanly and Honorable Profession: The Creation of the U.S. Naval Officer Corps, 1794–1815*. Annapolis, Md.: U.S. Naval Institute Press, 1991.

McKenna, Richard. *The Sand Pebbles*. New York: Harper & Row, 1962.

McLynn, Frank. *Villa and Zapata: A History of the Mexican Revolution*. New York: Carroll & Graf, 2000.

McMaster, H. R. *Dereliction of Duty: Lyndon Johnson, Robert McNamara, the Joint Chiefs of Staff, and the Lies That Led to Vietnam*. New York: HarperCollins, 1997.

McNamara, Robert S. *In Retrospect: The Tragedy and Lessons of Vietnam*. New York: Times Books, 1995.

Mead, Gary. *The Doughboys: America and the First World War*. Woodstock, N.Y.: Overlook, 2000.

Means, Howard. *Colin Powell: Soldier/Statesman, Statesman/Soldier*. New York: Donald I. Fine, 1992.

Melville, Herman. *White-Jacket: Or, the World in a Man-of-War*. Boston: L. C. Page & Co., 1950. Reprint of 1850 edition.

_____. *Typee: A Peep at Polynesian Life*. New York: Penguin, 1996. Reprint of 1845 edition.

Mersky, Peter B. *U.S. Marine Corps Aviation, 1912 to the Present*. Baltimore: Nautical and Aviation Publishing Company of America, 1983.

Meyer, Michael C., and William H. Beezley, eds. *The Oxford History of Mexico*. New York: Oxford University Press, 2000.

Miller, Nathan. *Broadsides: The Age of Fighting Sail, 1775–1815*. New York: John Wiley & Sons, 2000.

Miller, Stuart Creighton. *"Benevolent Assimilation": The American Conquest of the Philippines, 1899–1903*. New Haven and London: Yale University Press, 1982.

Millett, Allan R. *Semper Fidelis: The History of the United States Marine Corps*. New York: Macmillan, 1980.

_____. *The Politics of Intervention: The Military Occupation of Cuba, 1906–1909*. Columbus: Ohio State University Press, 1968.

Millett, Allan R., and Peter Maslowski. *For the Common Defense: A Military History of the United States of America*. Revised and expanded. New York: Free Press, 1994.

Millett, Richard. *Guardians of the Dynasty*. Maryknoll, N.Y.: Orbis Books, 1977.

Moore, Harold G., and Joseph L. Galloway. *We Were Soldiers Once . . . and Young: Ia Drang—The Battle That Changed the War in Vietnam*. New York: Random House, 1992.

Moore, Joel R., Harry H. Mead, and Lewis E. Jahns. *The History of the American Expedition Fighting the Bolsheviki: Campaigning in North Russia, 1918–1919*. Detroit, Mich.: Polar Bear Publishing, 1920.

Morison, Samuel Eliot. *"Old Bruin": Commodore Matthew C. Perry, 1784–1858*. Boston: Atlantic Monthly Press, 1967.

Morris, Edmund. *The Rise of Theodore Roosevelt*. New York: Ballantine, 1979.

_____. *Theodore Rex*. New York: Random House, 2001.

Moskin, J. Robert. *The U.S. Marine Corps Story*. 3rd edn. Boston: Little, Brown, 1992.

Moskos, Charles. "Peacekeeping Improves Combat Readiness." *The Wall Street Journal*, April 26, 2001.

Moyar, Mark. *Phoenix and the Birds of Prey: The CIA's Secret Campaign to Destroy the Viet Cong*. Annapolis, Md.: U.S. Naval Institute Press, 1997.

Munro, Dana G. *Intervention and Dollar Diplomacy in the Caribbean, 1900–1921*. Princeton: Princeton University Press, 1964.

_____. *The United States and the Caribbean Republics, 1921–1933*. Princeton: Princeton University Press, 1974.

Musicant, Ivan. *The Banana Wars: A History of United States Military Intervention in Latin America from the Spanish-American War to the Invasion of Panama*. New York: Macmillan, 1990.

Nalty, Bernard C. *The Barrier Forts: A Battle, a Monument, and a Mythical Marine*. Washington: Historical Division, U.S. Marine Corps, 1962.

Nasaw, David. *The Chief: The Life of William Randolph Hearst*. Boston: Houghton Mifflin, 2000.

Nixon, Richard. *No More Vietnams*. New York: Avon, 1985.

Noble, Dennis L. *The Eagle and the Dragon: The United States Military in China, 1901–1937*. Westport, Conn.: Greenwood, 1990.

O'Connor, Richard. *The Spirit Soldiers: A Historical Narrative of the Boxer Rebellion*. New York: G. P. Putnam's Sons, 1973.

Offutt, Milton. *The Protection of Citizens Abroad by the Armed Forces of the United States*. Baltimore: Johns Hopkins Press, 1928.

Oliver, Robert T. *A History of the Korean People in Modern Times, 1800 to the Present.* Newark: University of Delaware Press, 1993.

Oliver, Roland, and Anthony Atmore. *Africa Since 1800.* 3rd edn. New York: Cambridge University Press, 1981.

O'Shaughnessy, Edith. *A Diplomat's Wife in Mexico.* New York: Harper & Brothers, 1916.

Pagano, Dom Albert. *Bluejackets.* Boston: Meador Publishing, 1932.

Palmer, Bruce Jr. *The Twenty-five Year War: America's Military Role in Vietnam.* New York: Simon & Schuster, 1984.

Palmer, Dave Richard. *Summons of the Trumpet: U.S.-Vietnam in Perspective.* San Rafael, Calif.: Presidio, 1978.

Palmer, Michael A. *Guardians of the Gulf: A History of America's Expanding Role in the Persian Gulf, 1833–1992.* New York: Free Press, 1992.

Paret, Peter, ed. *Makers of Modern Strategy: From Machiavelli to the Nuclear Age.* Princeton: Princeton University Press, 1986.

Paullin, Charles Oscar. *American Voyages to the Orient, 1690–1865.* Annapolis, Md.: U.S. Naval Institute Press, 1971.

_____. *Commodore John Rodgers: Captain, Commodore, and Senior Officer of the American Navy, 1773–1838.* Annapolis, Md.: U.S. Naval Institute Press, 1967. Reprint of 1909 edition.

_____. *Diplomatic Negotiations of American Naval Officers, 1998–1883.* Baltimore: Johns Hopkins Press, 1912.

_____. *Paullin's History of Naval Administration, 1775–1911: A Collection of Articles from the U.S. Naval Institute Proceedings.* Annapolis, Md.: U.S. Naval Institute Press, 1968.

Pearce, Jenny. *Under the Eagle: U.S. Interventions in Central America and the Caribbean.* Boston: South End, 1982.

Perkins, Bradford. *The Cambridge History of American Foreign Relations.* Vol. 1, *The Creation of a Republican Empire, 1776–1865.* Cambridge: Cambridge University Press, 1993.

Perkins, Dexter. *A History of the Monroe Doctrine.* Boston: Little, Brown and Company, 1963.

Perkins, Whitney T. *Constraint of Empire: The United States and the Caribbean Interventions.* Westport, Conn.: Greenwood, 1981.

Perret, Geoffrey. *Old Soldiers Never Die: The Life of Douglas MacArthur.* New York: Random House, 1996.

Perry, Hamilton Darby. *The Panay Incident: Prelude to Pearl Harbor.* New York: Macmillan, 1969.

Pershing, John J. *My Experiences in the World War.* 2 vols. New York: Frederick A. Stokes, 1931.

_____. *Memoirs.* See Unpublished Manuscripts: John J. Pershing Papers, LC.

Peterson, Michael E. *The Combined Action Platoons: The U.S. Marines' Other War in Vietnam.* Westport, Conn.: Praeger, 1989.

Phillips, James Duncan. *Pepper and Pirates: Adventures in the Sumatra Pepper Trade of Salem.* Boston: Houghton Mifflin, 1949.

Pike, Douglas. *PAVN: The People's Army of Vietnam*. Novato, Calif.: Presidio, 1986.

Pipes, Richard. *The Russian Revolution*. New York: Alfred A. Knopf, 1990.

_____. *Russia Under the Bolshevik Regime*. New York: Alfred A. Knopf, 1993.

Pisor, Robert. *The End of the Line: The Siege of Khe Sanh*. New York: W.W. Norton & Co. 2002. Reprint of 1982 edition.

Podhoretz, Norman. *Why We Were in Vietnam*. New York: Simon and Schuster, 1982.

Pons, Frank Moya. *The Dominican Republic: A National History*. New Rochelle, N.Y.: Hispaniola Books, 1995.

Porter, David. *Journal of a Cruise*. Annapolis, Md.: U.S. Naval Institute Press, 1986. Reprint of 1815 edition.

_____. *Memoir of Commodore David Porter of the United States Navy*. Albany, N.Y.: J. Munsell, 1875.

Powell, Colin L., with Joseph E. Persico. *My American Journey*. New York: Random House, 1995.

Powell, John B. *My Twenty-five Years in China*. New York: Macmillan, 1945.

Pratt, Fletcher. *Preble's Boys: Commodore Preble and the Birth of American Sea Power*. New York: William Sloane Associates, 1950.

Preston, Diana. *The Boxer Rebellion: The Dramatic Story of China's War on Foreigners that Shook the World in the Summer of 1900*. New York: Walker & Company, 2000.

Priest, Dana. "Army's Apache Helicopters Rendered Impotent in Kosovo." *The Washington Post*, December 29, 1999.

Puller, Lewis B. *Fortunate Son: The Autobiography of Lewis B. Puller Jr.* New York: Grove Weidenfeld, 1991.

Quirk, Robert E. *An Affair of Honor: Woodrow Wilson and the Occupation of Veracruz*. Lexington: University of Kentucky Press, 1962.

Ramirez, Sergio, and Robert Edgar Conrad, eds. *Sandino: The Testimony of a Nicaraguan Patriot, 1921–1934*. Princeton: Princeton University Press, 1990.

Ray, William. *Horrors of Slavery, or the American Tars in Tripoli* [Troy, N.Y.: Oliver Lyon, 1808]. In Paul Baepler, ed., *White Slaves, African Masters*. Chicago: University of Chicago Press, 1999.

Record, Jeffrey. *The Wrong War: Why We Lost in Vietnam*. Annapolis, Md.: U.S. Naval Institute Press, 1998.

Remini, Robert V. *Andrew Jackson and the Course of American Democracy, 1833–1845*. Vol. 3. New York: Harper & Row, 1984.

Renda, May A. *Taking Haiti: Military Occupation and the Culture of U.S. Imperialism, 1915–1940*. Chapel Hill: University of North Carolina Press, 2001.

Rhodes, Benjamin D. *The Anglo-American Winter War With Russia, 1918–1919*. Westport, Conn.: Greenwood, 1988.

Ricks, Thomas R. *Making the Corps*. New York: Scribner, 1997.

Roberts, J.A.G. *A Concise History of China*. Cambridge: Harvard University Press, 1999.

Robotti, Frances Diane, and James Vescovi. *The USS Essex and the Birth of the American Navy*. Holbrook, Mass.: Adams Media Corp., 1999.

Rogerson, Barnaby. *A Traveller's History of North Africa*. New York: Interlink Books, 1998.

Roosevelt, Theodore. *The Naval War of 1812*. New York: Modern Library, 1999. Reprint of 3rd edition, 1883.

_____. *Theodore Roosevelt: An Autobiography*. New York: Da Capo, 1985. Reprint of 1914 edition.

Rosen, Stephen Peter. *Winning the Next War: Innovation and the Modern Military*. Ithaca, N.Y.: Cornell University Press, 1991.

Rosenberg, Emily S. *Financial Missionaries to the World: The Politics and Culture of Dollar Diplomacy, 1900–1930*. Cambridge: Harvard University Press, 1999.

Roth, Russell. *Muddy Glory: America's "Indian Wars" in the Philippines, 1899–1935*. West Hanover, Mass.: The Christopher Publishing House, 1981.

Ryden, George Herbert. *The Foreign Policy of the United States in Relation to Samoa*. New York: Octagon Books, 1975. Reprint of 1933 edition.

Savage Landor, A. Henry. *China and the Allies*. 2 vols. New York: Charles Scribner's Sons, 1901.

Schley, Winfield Scott. *Forty Five Years Under the Flag*. New York: D. Appleton & Co., 1904.

Schmidt, Hans. *Maverick Marine: General Smedley D. Butler and the Contradictions of American Military History*. Lexington: University Press of Kentucky, 1987.

_____. *The United States Occupation of Haiti, 1915–1934*. 2nd edn. New Brunswick, N.J.: Rutgers University Press, 1995.

Schoonover, Thomas D. *The United States in Central America, 1860–1911: Episodes of Social Imperialism and Imperial Rivalry in the World System*. Durham, N.C.: Duke University Press, 1991.

Schott, Joseph L. *The Ordeal of Samar*. Indianapolis: Bobbs Merrill, 1964.

Schroeder, John H. *Shaping a Maritime Empire: The Commercial and Diplomatic Role of the American Navy, 1829–1861*. Westport, Conn.: Greenwood, 1985.

Scott, Hugh Lenox. *Some Memories of a Soldier*. New York: Century, 1928.

Seagrave, Sterling, with the collaboration of Peggy Seagrave. *Dragon Lady: The Life and Legend of the Last Empress of China*. New York: Alfred A. Knopf, 1992.

Segovia, Lazaro. *The Full Story of Aguinaldo's Capture*. Trans. Frank de Thomas. Manila: MCS Enterprises, 1969. Reprint of 1902 edition.

Sergeant, Harriet. *Shanghai: Collision Point of Cultures, 1918/1939*. New York: Crown, 1990.

Sexton, William Thaddeus. *Soldiers in the Sun: An Adventure in Imperialism*. Harrisburg, Pa.: Military Service Publishing, 1939.

Shacochis, Bob. *The Immaculate Invasion*. New York: Viking, 1999.

Shafer, D. Michael. *Deadly Paradigms: The Failure of U.S. Counterinsurgency Policy*. Princeton: Princeton University Press, 1988.

Shanghai Mercury. The Boxer Rising: A History of the Boxer Trouble in China. New York: Paragon Book Reprint, 1967.

Shannon, Magdaline W. *Jean Price-Mars, the Haitian Elite and the American Occupation, 1915–1935*. New York: St. Martin's, 1996.

Sheehan, Neil. *A Bright Shining Lie: John Paul Vann and America in Vietnam*. New York: Random House, 1988.

Shulman, Mark R. *Navalism and the Emergence of American Sea Power, 1882–1893*. Annapolis, Md.: Naval Institute Press, 1995.

Skaggs, Jimmy K. *The Great Guano Rush: Entrepreneurs and American Overseas Expansion*. New York: St. Martin's, 1994.

Smith, Gene. *Until the Last Trumpet Sounds: The Life of General of the Armies John J. Pershing*. New York: John Wiley & Sons, 1998.

Smith, Tony. *America's Mission: The United States and the Worldwide Struggle for Democracy in the Twentieth Century*. Princeton: Princeton University Press, 1994.

Smythe, Donald. *Guerrilla Warrior: The Early Life of John J. Pershing*. New York: Charles Scribner's Sons, 1973.

_____. *Pershing: General of the Armies*. Bloomington: Indiana University Press, 1986.

Snider, Don, John Nagl, and Tony Pfaff. *Army Professionalism, the Military Ethic and Officership in the 21st Century*. Carlisle, Penn.: Strategic Studies Institute, U.S. Army War College, 1999.

Somin, Ilya. *Stillborn Crusade: The Tragic Failure of Western Intervention in the Russian Civil War, 1918–1920*. New Brunswick, N.J.: Transaction, 1996.

Sorley, Lewis. *A Better War: The Unexamined Victories and the Final Tragedy of America's Last Years in Vietnam*. New York: Harcourt Brace & Co., 1999.

_____. *Thunderbolt: General Creighton Abrams and the Army of His Times*. New York: Simon & Schuster, 1992.

Spence, Jonathan D. *The Search for Modern China*. New York: W. W. Norton, 1990.

Sprout, Harold, and Margaret Sprout. *The Rise of American Naval Power, 1776–1918*. Princeton: Princeton University Press, 1939.

Stanton, Martin. *Somalia on $5.00 a Day: A Soldier's Story*. Novato, Calif.: Presidio, 2001.

Stevens, Sylvester K. *American Expansion in Hawaii, 1842–1898*. Harrisburg, Penn.: Archives Publishing Co. of Pennsylvania, 1945.

Stimson, Henry L., and McGeorge Bundy. *On Active Service in Peace and War*. New York: Harper & Brothers, 1948.

Stirling, Yates. *Sea Duty: The Memoirs of a Fighting Admiral*. New York: G. P. Putnam's Sons, 1939.

Stout, Joseph A. Jr. *Border Conflict: Villistas, Carrancistas and the Punitive Expedition, 1915–1920*. Fort Worth: Texas Christian University Press, 1999.

Sullivan, Mark. *Our Times: The United States, 1900–1925*. 6 vols. New York: Charles Scribner's Sons, 1926–1935.

Summers, Harry G. Jr. *On Strategy: A Critical Analysis of the Vietnam War*. New York: Dell, 1984.

Sweetman, Jack. *The Landing at Veracruz: 1914*. Annapolis, Md.: U.S. Naval Institute Press, 1968.

Taylor, James O. *The Massacre at Balangiga*. Joplin, Mo.: McCarn Printing, 1931.

Taylor, John R. M., ed. *The Philippine Insurrection Against the United States: A Compilation of Documents.* 5 vols. Pasay City, Philippines: Eugenio Lopez Foundation, 1971–73.

Thomas, Hugh. *The Slave Trade: The Story of the Atlantic Slave Trade, 1440–1870.* New York: Simon & Schuster, 1997.

———. *Cuba, Or the Pursuit of Freedom, Updated Edition.* New York: Da Capo, 1998.

Thomason, John W. *Salt Winds and Gobi Dust.* New York: Scribner's, 1934.

Thomson, James C., Jr., Peter W. Stanley, and John Curtis Perry. *Sentimental Imperialists: The American Experience in East Asia.* New York: Harper & Row, 1981.

Tolley, Kemp. *Yangtze Patrol: The U.S. Navy in China.* Annapolis, Md.: U.S. Naval Institute Press, 1971.

Tompkins, Frank. *Chasing Villa: The Last Campaign of the U.S. Cavalry.* Silver City, N.M.: High-Lonesome Books, 1996. Reprint of 1934 edition.

Tomsho, Robert. "Tarnished Chimes: Bells of Balangiga Resound Anew in Manila, Cheyenne." *The Asian Wall Street Journal,* November 24, 1997.

Trask, David F. *The War with Spain in 1898.* New York: Macmillan, 1981.

Tuchman, Barbara W. *The Zimmerman Telegram.* New York: Viking, 1958.

———. *Stilwell and the American Experience in China, 1911–45.* New York: Macmillan, 1970.

Tucker, Glenn. *Dawn Like Thunder: The Barbary Wars and the Birth of the U.S. Navy.* Indianapolis: Bobs Merrill, 1963.

Tucker, Robert W., and David C. Hendrickson. *Empire of Liberty: The Statecraft of Thomas Jefferson.* New York: Oxford University Press, 1990.

Tucker, Spencer C. *Andrew Foote: Civil War Admiral on Western Waters.* Annapolis, Md.: U.S. Naval Institute Press, 2000.

Turnbull, Archibald Douglas. *Commodore David Porter, 1780–1843.* New York: The Century Co., 1929.

Tyson, Carolyn A. *Marine Amphibious Landing in Korea, 1871.* Washington: Headquarters, U.S. Marine Corps, 1967.

Ullman, Richard H. *Anglo-Soviet Relations, 1917–1921: Intervention and War.* Princeton: Princeton University Press, 1961.

Unterberger, Betty Miller. *The United States, Revolutionary Russia, and the Rise of Czechoslovakia.* Chapel Hill: University of North Carolina Press, 1989.

———. *America's Siberian Expedition, 1918–1920.* New York: Greenwood, 1956.

United States Marine Corps. *Small Wars Manual.* Washington: U.S. Government Printing Office, 1940. Reprinted 1990.

U.S. Navy. *Minutes of Proceedings of the Courts of Inquiry and Court Martial in Relation to Captain David Porter, Convened at Washington, D.C., on Thursday, the Seventh Day of July, A.D. 1825.* Washington: Davis & Force, 1825.

U.S. Office of Naval Records and Library, Navy Department. *Naval Documents Related to the United States Wars With the Barbary Powers.* 7 vols. Washington: Government Printing Office, 1939–1944.

U.S. Secretary of the Navy. *Annual Report*. Washington: Government Printing Office, 1871–1872, 1899–1904.

U.S. Secretary of War. *Annual Report*. Washington: Government Printing Office, 1900–1902, 1919–1920.

U.S. Senate, Select Committee on Haiti and Santo Domingo. *Inquiry Into Occupation and Administration of Haiti and Santo Domingo*. 2 vols. Washington: Government Printing Office, 1922.

Utley, Robert M. *Frontier Regulars: The United States Army and the Indian, 1866–1891*. New York: Macmillan, 1973.

Vandegrift, A. A., as told to Robert B. Asprey. *Once a Marine: The Memoirs of General A. A. Vandegrift, USMC*. New York: W. W. Norton, 1964.

Vandiver, Frank E. *Black Jack: The Life and Times of John J. Pershing*. 2 vols. College Station: Texas A&M University Press, 1977.

Venzon, Anne Cipriano, ed. *General Smedley Darlington Butler: The Letters of a Leatherneck, 1898–1931*. Westport, Conn.: Praeger, 1992.

Waldron, Arthur. *From War to Nationalism: China's Turning Point, 1924–1925*. Cambridge: Cambridge University Press, 1995.

Walt, Lewis W. *Strange War, Strange Strategy: A General's Report on Vietnam*. New York: Funk & Wagnalls, 1970.

Ward, John. *With the "Die-Hards" in Siberia*. New York: George H. Doran Company, 1920.

Warriner, Francis. *Cruise of the United States Frigate Potomac Round the World During the Years 1831–34*. New York: Leavitt, Lord & Co., 1835.

Webb, James. *Fields of Fire*. Annapolis, Md.: U.S. Naval Institute Press, 2000. Reprint of 1978 edn.

Welles, Sumner. *Naboth's Vineyard: The Dominican Republic, 1844–1924*. 2 vols. Mamaroneck, N.Y.: Paul P. Appel, 1966. Reprint of 1926 edition.

Werstein, Irving. *The Cruise of the Essex: An Incident from the War of 1812*. Philadelphia: Macrae Smith Co., 1969.

West, F. J., Jr. *The Village*. New York: Harper & Row, 1972.

Westmoreland, William. *A Soldier Reports*. Garden City, N.Y.: Doubleday, 1976.

Wheeler, Gerald E. *Prelude to Pearl Harbor: The United States Navy and the Far East, 1921–1931*. Columbia: University of Missouri Press, n.d.

Wheeler, Richard. *In Pirate Waters*. New York: Thomas Y. Crowell, 1969.

Whipple, A. B. C. *To the Shores of Tripoli: The Birth of the U.S. Navy and Marines*. New York: William Morrow and Company, 1991.

———. *Fighting Sail*. Alexandria, Va.: Time Life Books, 1978.

White, John A. *The Siberian Intervention*. Princeton: Princeton University Press, 1950.

Wilcox, Marrion. *Harper's History of the War in the Philippines*. New York: Harper & Brothers, 1900.

Wilkes, Charles. *Autobiography of Rear Admiral Charles Wilkes, U.S. Navy, 1798–1877*. Washington: Naval History Division, Department of the Navy, 1978.

Williams, Robert Hugh. *The Old Corps: A Portrait of the U.S. Marine Corps Between the Wars*. Annapolis, Md.: U.S. Naval Institute Press, 1982.

Williams, Vernon. *Lieutenant Patton and the American Army in the Mexican Punitive Expedition, 1915–1916*. Austin, Texas: Presidial, 1983.

Winik, Jay. *April 1865: The Month That Saved America*. New York: HarperCollins, 2001.

Wirkus, Faustin, and Taney Dudley. *The White King of La Gonave*. Garden City, N.Y.: Doubleday, Doran & Co., 1931.

Wise, Frederic May, and Meigs O. Frost. *A Marine Tells It to You*. New York: J. H. Sears & Co., 1929.

Wohlforth, William C. "The Stability of a Unipolar World." *International Security* 24 (Summer 1999).

Wolfers, Arnold. *Discord and Collaboration: Essays on International Politics*. Baltimore: Johns Hopkins University Press, 1962.

Wolff, Leon. *Little Brown Brother*. New York: Doubleday, 1961.

Wright, Louis B., and Julia H. MacLeod. *The First Americans in North Africa: William Eaton's Struggle for a Vigorous Policy Against the Barbary Pirates, 1799–1805*. New York: Greenwood, 1945.

Yerxa, Donald A. *Admirals and Empire: The United States Navy and the Caribbean, 1898–1945*. Columbia: University of South Carolina Press, 1991.

Yoo, John. "The Continuation of Politics by Other Means: the Original Understanding of War Powers." *California Law Review,* 1996.

Zaffiri, Samuel. *Westmoreland: A Biography of General William C. Westmoreland*. New York: William Morrow, 1994.

Zakaria, Fareed. *From Wealth to Power: The Unusual Origins of America's World Role*. Princeton: Princeton University Press, 1998.

Zha, Qiang. "Beijing and the Vietnam Conflict, 1964–1965: New Chinese Evidence." Unpublished paper, Cold War International History Project Bulletin. Washington: Woodrow Wilson Center for Scholars, n.d.

———. "Beijing and the Vietnam Peace Talks, 1965–1968: New Evidence from Chinese Sources." Working paper, Cold War International History Project. Washington: Woodrow Wilson Center for Scholars, June 1997.

ACKNOWLEDGMENTS

To begin, let me thank all the librarians who made my research possible: the staff of the Naval War College library, Newport, R.I.; Fred Allison and Bob Aquilina at the Marine Corps Historical Center, Washington, D.C.; the staff of the National Archives, both in Washington and College Park, Md., especially archivists Trevor Plante, Mitch Yockelson and Kate Flaherty; the staff of the Manuscript Room, Library of Congress, Washington, D.C; the staff of the Army Military History Institute, Carlisle Barracks, Penn., especially Richard J. Sommers and R.L. Baker; the staff of the Marine Corps Research Center Archives, Quantico, Va., especially Mike Miller; the staff of the Naval Institute and the Naval Academy Museum at the Naval Academy in Annapolis, Md. Above all there was Mrs. Anderson, of my local public library in Larchmont, N.Y., who was indefatigable in tracking down obscure books from distant collections and magically making them materialize in my hands.

A number of people—some close friends, some academic specialists whom I don't even know—gave generously of their time to critique parts of the manuscript. I thank Adam Hoffman, Mark Shulman, Vincent Pollard, Ben Rhodes, Brian Linn, Joseph A. Stout Jr., Jonathan Rauch, Michael O'Hanlon, and Gideon Rose. My greatest debt in this department is to Nicholas X. Rizopoulos and Jay Winik. Nick made detailed and invaluable suggestions for how I could improve the book. He then allowed me to present my findings to the Carnegie Council roundtable on foreign affairs, whose members gave me more excellent feedback. Jay took time off from publicizing his own best-selling history book to spur me on to make a last round of revisions; he then somehow found time to read and critique the entire manuscript. In addition to those named above, this book greatly benefited from conversations I had with a number of people, especially Stephen Jay Rosen, Colonel Gary Anderson, USMC, and Andrew Krepinevich.

I must also thank the Naval War College and Kiron Skinner of the Council on Foreign Relations for inviting me to give presentations about my ideas. I don't know if the audiences benefited from my remarks, but I definitely benefited from their questions. Captain Scott Cubbler, USMC, was kind enough to set up a visit for me to Camp Lejeune to watch Marine combat exercises on October 4, 2000. Les Gelb, president of the Council on Foreign Relations, invited me on a highly educational tour of military bases in May 2001. And the New Atlantic Initiative and the German Marshall Fund took me on a fascinating trip to Greece, Kosovo, and Montenegro in the fall of 1999. This book was enriched by all these experiences.

The Smith Richardson Foundation provided generous funding for my work. I thank especially Nadia Schadlow and Marin Strimecki at the foundation. My agents, Glen Hartley and Lynn Chu, were wise guides through the publishing jungle. Ib Ohlsson drew the excellent maps. I thank Tim Bartlett for acquiring my proposal for Basic Books. After he left Basic, Bill Frucht was a sensitive and supportive editor. His assistant, Vanessa Mobley, ably oversaw the book's production. All the other people at Basic are first-rate too, starting with John Donatich.

Between the appearance of the hardcover and paperback editions of this book I switched jobs. I thank both my new colleagues at the Council on Foreign Relations and my old colleagues at the *Wall Street Journal* for their support and encouragement. At the Council, I am especially grateful to Walter Russell Mead, Mike Peters, Theo Gemelas, and, above all, to Les Gelb, who has been a great boss. At the *Journal*, I thank in particular Paul Gigot, Bob Bartley, Melanie Kirkpatrick, Erich Eichman, and Bill McGurn. And I remember with fondness all of my fellow features staffers over the years—Tunku Varadarajan, Rob Pollock, Kim Strassel, Bret Stephens, James Taranto, Joann Joseph, and Marie Coyle—who made putting out the newspaper such a joy.

Finally I think my wife and best friend, Jeannette K. Boot, who kept the home front going, who read the manuscript and who provided copious conversation, love, and encouragement. And I thank our children, Victoria, Abigail, and William, for being understanding when daddy was locked away in his office working. Well, some of the time anyway.

INDEX